THE COLLECTED PAPERS OF BERTRAND RUSSELL
VOLUME 8

THE COLLECTED PAPERS OF BERTRAND RUSSELL

―――――――――――

The McMaster University Edition

―――――――――――

HONORABLE BERTRAND RUSSELL

LECTURER AND FELLOW OF TRINITY COLLEGE, CAMBRIDGE, SECOND
SON OF THE LATE VISCOUNT AMBERLEY, AND GRANDSON OF THE
FAMOUS LORD RUSSELL, PRIME MINISTER OF ENGLAND 1846-52
AND 1865-66.

BERTRAND RUSSELL

The Philosophy
of Logical Atomism
and Other Essays
1914–19

Edited by
John G. Slater

London
GEORGE ALLEN & UNWIN
Boston   Sydney

George Allen & Unwin (Publishers) Ltd.
40 Museum Street, London WC1A 1LU, U.K.

George Allen & Unwin (Publishers) Ltd.
Park Lane, Hemel Hempstead, Herts HP2 4TE, U.K.

Allen & Unwin Inc.,
9 Winchester Terrace, Winchester, Mass. 01890, U.S.A.

George Allen & Unwin Australia Pty Ltd.
8 Napier Street, North Sydney, NSW 2060, Australia

First published in 1986

Bertrand Russell's unpublished letters, Paper **18** and Appendixes II–III, © McMaster University 1986. Papers **3**, **6–16** and **19** © The Bertrand Russell Estate 1913, 1914, 1915, 1917, 1918, 1919. Papers **1**, **2**, **4** and **5** © George Allen & Unwin Ltd. 1932. Papers **17** and **20** © George Allen & Unwin Ltd. 1956. Appendix I © *New Statesman* 1915. Editorial matter © John G. Slater 1986.

Funds to edit this volume were provided by a major editorial grant from the Social Sciences and Humanities Research Council of Canada and by McMaster University.

British Library Cataloguing in Publication Data

Russell, Bertrand
   The philosophy of logical atomism and other essays: 1914–19.—(The Collected papers of Bertrand Russell; v. 8)
   1. Philosophy
   I. Title   II. Slater, John G.   III. Series
   192   B1649.R91

   ISBN 0–04–920074–7

Library of Congress Cataloging in Publication Data

Russell, Bertrand, 1872–1970.
   The philosophy of logical atomism and other essays, 1914–19.

   (The Collected papers of Bertrand Russell; v. 8)
   "Philosophical books read in prison": p.
   Bibliography: p.
   Includes indexes.
   1. Philosophy—Addresses, essays, lectures.   I. Slater, John G. (John Greer)
   II. Title.   III. Series: Russell, Bertrand, 1872–1970.   Selections.   1983; v. 8.
   B1649.R91   1983   vol. 8   192 s [146′.5]   85–18609
   ISBN 0–04–920074–7

Set in 10 on 12 point V.I.P. Plantin by
The Bertrand Russell Editorial Project, McMaster University
and printed and bound in Great Britain by
William Clowes Limited, Beccles and London

THE COLLECTED PAPERS OF BERTRAND RUSSELL

Contents

Abbreviations

To GIVE THE reader an uncluttered text, abbreviations and symbols have been kept to a minimum. The few necessary to the referencing system are as follows.

The papers printed in the volume are given a boldface number for easy reference. For example, "Mysticism and Logic" is Paper **2**. Angle brackets in the text distinguish rare editorial insertions from Russell's more common square brackets.

Bibliographical references are usually in the form of author, date and page, e.g. "Clark *1975*, 316–17". Consultation of the Bibliographical Index shows that this reference is to pp. 316–17 of Ronald W. Clark, *The Life of Bertrand Russell* (London: Jonathan Cape and Weidenfeld & Nicolson, 1975).

The location of archival documents cited in the edition is the Bertrand Russell Archives at McMaster University ("RA"), unless a different location is given. File numbers of documents in the Russell Archives are provided only when manuscripts of papers printed here are cited or when files are difficult to identify. "RA REC. ACQ." refers to the files of recent acquisitions in the Russell Archives.

Cross-references to annotations are preceded by "A" and followed by page and line numbers (as in "A44: 4").

Cross-references to textual notes are preceded by "T". Further abbreviations are used in the Textual Notes, but they are identified at the beginning of each set of notes.

The numbers and dates of Russell's letters to Lady Ottoline Morrell refer to photocopies in the Bertrand Russell Archives at McMaster. The original letters are at The Harry Ransom Research Center, University of Texas, Austin. The numbering was established while the letters were still in the possession of Lady Ottoline and it has not been revised. When a letter is dated by Russell that date is simply given; but when the date is taken from a postmark, "pmk." signifies the fact, while a date inferred from other evidence is put in square brackets.

Introduction

THE PAPERS PRINTED here are fruits of several projects, some major and some not so major, that Russell undertook during the years from 1912 to 1918. His major concerns were: (1) "the problem of matter", (2) the re-thinking of the philosophy of logical atomism to take account of Wittgenstein's criticisms of it, and (3) the analysis of mind. Of lesser importance were: (4) the exposition of his philosophical method, and (5) the "popular" restatement of his "technical" philosophical positions on certain questions. He also devoted a considerable amount of time to (6) the reviewing of books for both philosophical and popular journals. As a rule, the papers themselves are not the source for our knowledge that he had these projects; that knowledge comes from his private correspondence, especially his letters to Lady Ottoline Morrell. This introduction and many of the headnotes to particular papers draw heavily upon facts to be found only in that extraordinary correspondence.

I. THE PROBLEM OF MATTER

"The problem of matter", or "matter" for short, was Russell's usual way of referring to the problem of providing philosophical foundations for physics. His interest in this problem was first aroused shortly after he had finished work on his Fellowship dissertation for Trinity College, which was published in 1897 as *An Essay on the Foundations of Geometry*. He planned to follow this book with one on the philosophy of physics. "Sixteen years ago now I started gaily on the philosophy of matter," he wrote Lady Ottoline in 1913, "and after a year I found there were a few preliminaries to be settled, which have taken all my time till now. Now I have the necessary groundwork at last. In matters of *work* my life has had very great continuity and unconscious unity" (#695, pmk. 8 Feb.). The "few preliminaries", thus ironically described, consisted in that investigation of the philosophical foundations of mathematics which he and Whitehead had provided in *Principia Mathematica* (1910–13).

After his contribution to the creative work on *Principia* was finished, sometime between 1910 and 1912, he had resumed his investigations into the foundations of physics. In the autumn of 1910 he began teaching at

Trinity College, Cambridge, having accepted the position primarily because it afforded him the opportunity to disseminate the discoveries in logic and the foundations of mathematics which were being published in *Principia*. During his first two years of teaching, in addition to expounding these findings to a small number of pupils, he was kept busy by the daunting task of seeing "the big book" through the press. The start of his third year found him eager to take on another big piece of work. *Principia* laid out, in elaborate detail, the à priori element in mathematics. His new aim was to apply the same sort of analysis to other bodies of our knowledge, especially physics, in order to reveal their à priori components. "The analysis of a piece of actual knowledge into pure sense and pure à priori is often very difficult, but almost always very important: the pure à priori, like the pure metal, is infinitely more potent and beautiful than the ore from which it was extracted" (#616, pmk. 30 Oct. 1912). Two related problems, causality and matter, he cited as being of special interest:

> It is these that I want to get hold of now—I am only quite at the beginning—it is a vast problem of analysis, wanting tools that one has to make oneself before getting to work. It is very hard, to begin with, to make out what science really asserts—for example, what the law of gravitation means. Neither science nor philosophy helps one there—mathematical logic is the only help. And when one thinks one has found out what it asserts, one can't state the result so as to be intelligible to any one who doesn't know mathematical logic. So one's audience must be small!   (*Ibid.*)

Much of his thinking over the next two or three years was concentrated on this problem. He kept Lady Ottoline posted on his progress. By early February 1913 he reported:

> What occupies me now is how to divide my problem, so as to be able to work at separate bits without always remembering the whole. I see I shall have to do as I did with the *Principles of Mathematics*, make successive drafts growing gradually more precise. Complete precision involves such labour and length of detail that one loses sight of the whole unless one has some fairly elaborate sketch. I talk a little to my young men about the philosophy of matter, and always find that my ideas interest them profoundly. Perhaps in time some of them will take it up and do parts of the work—it is too vast for one man's powers.   (#693, pmk. 6 Feb.)

He was searching for a starting-point which would permit him to begin translating some of the propositions of physics into the symbols of mathematical logic, but it would be a while before he discovered this starting-point. Two weeks later he wrote: "I am much less worried about Matter than I was—I see ideas are growing slowly, and at this stage I doubt if they would grow much faster if I could give my whole time to it. Later on, when I have the fundamental ideas, the time will come for long hours, but I haven't reached that stage yet" (#703, pmk. 19 Feb.). Only four days later he had reached the stage during which his ideas required incubation.

> I see my way better and better as regards my work, though I don't think I shall be able to accomplish all I hoped to do—the task is too big, and there are too many preliminaries. But I shall probably be able to do the difficult part of the work, and leave the rest to others. This last week I have read endless silly novels, which is the only way at certain stages of a piece of work. I find anything except novels not enough of a rest. (#707, pmk. 23 Feb.)

Later in the same letter he returned to the subject of his work:

> I want to get on with Matter—that wants first and foremost a fundamental novelty as to the nature of sensation, which I think I am on the track of—that will be the most important single idea involved. Then I must discover the truth about Causality—in the paper ⟨"On the Notion of Cause"⟩ I read the other day, I only showed that all current views are wrong, and I am quite at a loss as to what is right. Then I must reduce both ordinary dynamics and electro-dynamics to neat sets of axioms—this possibly I might get some one else to do for me. If all this were done, I could begin the actual carrying out of the work. But when I think of it all, and all the labour and fatigue and discouragement and wrong ideas that have to be abandoned, my courage quails, and I wish some one else would do it. But no one I know could except Wittgenstein, and he is embarked on a more difficult piece of work. Ten years ago, I could have written a book with the stock of ideas I have already, but now I have a higher standard of exactness. Wittgenstein has persuaded me that the early parts of *Principia Mathematica* are very inexact, but fortunately it is his business to put them right, not mine.

At this point he believed he had found the key to the overall logic of the problem of matter. Correct analyses of the nature of sensation and causality were essential for a start. To meet his standards correct analyses had to be written in purely logical notation. The requirement that dynamics and electro-dynamics be axiomatized before his own work could begin, and the fact that someone else could do that part of the work, shows clearly that he was relying upon his earlier work on the foundations of mathematics as a guide to correct methodology. Peano had axiomatized arithmetic and had shown that only three primitive, or unanalyzed, arithmetical terms—"zero", "number" and "successor"—were required, in addition to purely logical notions. After he had mastered Peano's work, Russell focused on providing definitions of these three terms in purely logical language. With assistance from Frege's published works he and Whitehead had offered such definitions in *Principia*.

By analogy, axiom systems for dynamics and electro-dynamics would be stated in terms of a limited set of primitive dynamic notions; "mass", "force" and "motion" will serve as examples of such terms. Only after such axiom sets were in place would Russell be able to undertake the philosophical work of deducing these axioms from statements about causal relations between sensations—and whatever else turned out to be necessary. When his work was completed, the axioms of dynamics and electro-dynamics would appear as theorems entailed by a set of philosophical axioms which served to ground physics, just as Peano's postulates were all proved as theorems from the set of axioms in *Principia* which provided a foundation for some parts of mathematics.

During the course of writing *Theory of Knowledge* (1984), he reported that he had "got a bright idea as to the difference between sensation and imagination. I am delighted with it, and find it helps with dreams (my old bugbears) and memory" (#777, pmk. 16 May 1913). Although the idea was of immediate use in his epistemological work, he linked it to his thinking about the problem of matter: "It is all really still the same problem as 'Matter' was—the things I am doing now are preliminaries, but I think the question of matter will be easy when the preliminaries are done" (*ibid.*). *Theory of Knowledge*, then, was conceived as being simply another preliminary to his grand enterprise. But a few days later the role of this book was expanded. "A very great part of the problem of Matter will come in at the end of this book. Indeed I think all that is really difficult and fundamental can come in—then some day I can work it out in full mathematical detail" (#784, pmk. 23 May). *Theory of Knowledge*, on this account, would, when completed, stand to his projected book on matter as *The Principles of Mathematics* (1903) stood to *Principia*.

By September, when he was drafting his Lowell Lectures, later published as *Our Knowledge of the External World* (1914), he alluded again to his overriding philosophical concern:

> The problem of matter has grown clearer to me while I was writing. I
> find the order of the lectures is wrong—I will rearrange them when I
> have finished. From what you say, I suppose the third and fourth are
> the most difficult; if so, I had better put them at the end. I think I can

build the whole course round the problem of our knowledge of the external world, and bring in Zeno in that connection, towards the end of the course. It will make the whole much better. (#875, pmk. 23 Sept.)

The problem of matter had emerged as the search for a logical construction out of our "hard" and "soft" data which would have all the properties physicists expect matter to have. Hard data—the prime examples are particular facts of sense and general logical truths—are "those which resist the solvent influence of critical reflection"; soft data—examples are our own specific memories and the testimonials of others—are those which when exposed to criticism "become to our minds more or less doubtful" (*1914*, 70; *1926*, 77–8; *1929*, 75). Again the analogy with his work in the foundations of mathematics is striking, for there, too, the key to success had been the formulation of logical constructions of classes, numbers, etc., with all the properties mathematicians required of the notions themselves. In October he reported having a new idea: "It is odd how the whole perspective of the world changes. In writing my lectures, I got a new idea about matter—the distinction and relations of the three kinds of space in Lecture VII—and it makes me see my way through that problem" (#881, pmk. 1 Oct.). In the published book these new ideas about space are found in Chapter III, "On Our Knowledge of the External World", so it was, presumably, Chapter VII in the first draft. "The Relation of Sense-Data to Physics" (**1**) also contains a discussion of his new spatial ideas. This essay was dictated during the first week of January 1914 and was, he told Lady Ottoline, part of "a task that will last me the rest of my life" (#962, pmk. 10 Jan.). (Four years later, when he was in Brixton Prison, he had come to regard this essay and his Lowell Lectures as constituting his solution to the problem of matter. The letter in which this judgment is recorded is printed in the Headnote to Paper **18**.)

His trip to America was drawing nearer and as the time approached for him to sail he began to resent the interruption: "I do wish I didn't have to go. I *hate* leaving you now, and besides it interrupts my work—my mind is full of ideas, and I could be very fruitful if I had leisure. 'Matter' goes on in my head all the time. I have just lately got hold of a new idea, still vague, but obviously fruitful and very important" (#991, pmk. 21 Feb. 1914). He did not, either here or later in the correspondence, reveal what this new idea was. His fears that he would get no writing done in America proved correct. He returned to England in mid-June expecting to resume his work, but six weeks later the war broke out and completely disrupted his life. His new idea never developed on paper, nor did he try to do original work again until early 1918. And shortly after he resumed his work, as we have seen, he came to believe he had solved the problem of matter before the war began.

From his correspondence it is clear that his aim in working on the problem of matter was to write a big book on the foundations of physics which would be a companion to *Principia Mathematica*. The à priori elements of physics were to be distilled into a set of axioms whose primitive terms would be defined by logical constructions having all the properties physicists attached to the (alleged) denotata of the terms themselves. These logical constructions would be stated in the language of *Principia* supplemented by whatever additions were required to incorporate the subject-matter of physics. In symbolic notation, with a bare minimum of expository prose, and with its theorems ordered by their deductive relationships, the completed book would very likely have borne a strong resemblance to *Principia*. Events conspired to prevent the writing of this projected book. Instead he sketched in prose his central ideas. Although not in the language of *Principia*, *Our Knowledge of the External World*, "The Relation of Sense-Data to Physics" (1), and "The Ultimate Constituents of Matter" (5), record his progress toward realizing his grand plan.

II. HIS RE-THINKING OF LOGICAL ATOMISM

This project, which was forced upon him by the criticisms Wittgenstein made of his *Theory of Knowledge* manuscript in June 1913, was interrupted, firstly, by the preparation of his Lowell Lectures and his trip to America to deliver them and to teach at Harvard, and, secondly, by the outbreak of the First World War, which left him with little taste for philosophical work. Throughout the war years he worried about Wittgenstein's safety and tried to come to terms with Wittgenstein's severe judgment of the worth of his philosophical work. This project, then, is intimately entwined with the bittersweet relationship between these two men. There can be no doubt that Wittgenstein was the single most important influence on Russell's thinking during the years covered by this volume, even if, as we shall see, he in some measure exaggerated its effect on his ambitions.

Russell's face-to-face contact with Wittgenstein had nearly ceased by early 1914. They had met on the eighteenth of October in 1911, when Wittgenstein was twenty-two and Russell thirty-nine. On the advice of his teachers at the University of Manchester, Wittgenstein had come to Cambridge to hear Russell's lectures on logic and the philosophy of mathematics. By the summer of 1912 Russell was beginning to treat him as a peer, trying out his new philosophical ideas on the younger man before committing them to print. And Wittgenstein's criticisms of Russell's lectures led Russell to conclude that the lectures would have to be reworked. "Also talking with Wittgenstein has made me feel that I must alter my lectures and put more into them. Hitherto they have contained chiefly what I have published, but I must put in more general remarks on method, and on what is and what is not possible in philosophy" (#569, pmk. 7 Sept.). Wittgenstein continued as his pupil during 1912–13, and by Christmas Russell was thinking of him as his own replacement at Cambridge.

Thoughts of a replacement arose from his dream of founding a school. As might be expected he told Lady Ottoline about it:

> It has long been one of my dreams to found a great school of mathematically-trained philosophers, but I don't know whether I shall ever get it accomplished. I had hopes of Norton, but he has not the physique. Broad is all right, but has no fundamental originality. Wittgenstein of course is exactly my dream. But I should like to make mathematics the ordinary training for a philosopher—I am sure it ought to be. That would require a tremendous propaganda of the sort that moves educational bodies; and I am afraid vested interests would always be too strong. However, when I am too old for original work I dare say I shall take it up.   (#663, 29 Dec. 1912)

Two months later he mentioned his dream again as a condition he would like to fulfil before he could leave teaching with a clear conscience: "If once I had a school of mathematical-logic established here, with Wittgenstein teaching, and people recognizing that it ought to be learnt, I should have no hesitation in leaving" (#693, pmk. 6 Feb. 1913). Again the key figure is Wittgenstein. Two weeks later he returned to this subject: "I want very much to found a school of mathematical philosophy, because I believe the method is capable of bearing much fruit, beyond what I can ever accomplish" (#707, pmk. 23 Feb.). This is the last time in the correspondence that he mentions this ambition. Like so many others it was to fall a victim to the war.

By the spring of 1913 Russell clearly accepted Wittgenstein as his peer in philosophy, even though he was still technically Russell's pupil. During the course of writing *Theory of Knowledge* he informed Lady Ottoline that "Wittgenstein came to see me last night with a refutation of the theory of judgment which I used to hold. He was right, but I think the correction required is not very serious. I shall have to make up my mind within a week as I shall soon reach judgment" (#782, pmk. 21 May). "The theory of judgment I used to hold" would be that of *The Problems of Philosophy* (1912). In June, Russell permitted Wittgenstein to read his manuscript. The story of the devastating effect of his critique has been ably told by Elizabeth Eames in her Introduction to *Theory of Knowledge*.

When the new academic year opened in October 1913 Wittgenstein arrived to inform Russell that he would not be in residence. "Wittgenstein arrived—he has decided he must be quite alone to work," Russell wrote Lady Ottoline, "so he is going to Norway, giving up Cambridge. I expect he will commit suicide towards the end of the winter, but it can't be helped. He has done *admirable* work" (#882, pmk. 2 Oct.). Russell was at once distressed and relieved by this decision as he explained in a letter to her four days later:

> I am so *very* sorry I wrote a depressing letter—it was quite irrelevant—really my thoughts are not *at all* of a sort to depress you. I think it was Wittgenstein—he wears me out nervously so that I long for nothing but escape from all serious thought and feeling. His decision to go to Norway was a blow and an anxiety, and at the same time he was explaining a number of very difficult logical ideas which I could only just understand by stretching my mind to the utmost. He was certainly the chief cause of my fatigue before. I feel him so terribly important and precarious that I go on making efforts when I should have given up with anybody else. For my own sake (and for yours) it is a godsend his going to Norway. It turns out that he can come back at any time to finish the residence for a degree, and he says he means to come back when he has got something written. He has promised to leave me a written statement of what he has already done before he starts for Norway. The more he talks about it, the more admirable I think it. He is certainly quite supreme. He and Whitehead and I are all in a fruitful vein, so I feel very happy about work. (#886, pmk. 6 Oct.).

Extracting a written statement from Wittgenstein proved more difficult than Russell anticipated. On 19 October he wrote Lucy Donnelly the whole story about Norway.

> Then my Austrian, Wittgenstein, burst in like a whirlwind, just back from Norway, and determined to return there at once, to live in complete solitude until he has solved *all* the problems of logic. I said it would be dark, and he said he hated daylight. I said it would be lonely, and he said he prostituted his mind talking to intelligent people. I said he was mad, and he said God preserve him from sanity. [God certainly will.] Now Wittgenstein, during August and September, had done work on logic, still rather in the rough, but as good, in my opinion, as any work that ever has been done in logic by any one. But his artistic conscience prevents him from writing anything until he has got it perfect, and I am persuaded he will commit suicide in February. What was I to do? He told me his ideas, but they were so subtle that I kept on forgetting them. I begged him to write them out, and he tried, but after much groaning said it was

absolutely impossible. At last I made him talk in the presence of a short-hand writer, and so secured some record of his ideas. This business took up the whole of my time and thought for about a week.

The shorthand writer produced a typescript, now called "Notes on Logic", which Russell translated and edited for use in his courses in Harvard. These notes were to influence Russell's own thinking; his lectures on logical atomism (Paper 17) owe some of their inspiration to Wittgenstein's recorded remarks.

Wittgenstein did indeed go to Norway in late 1913. In February 1914 he wrote Russell breaking off their relationship. "Since I began writing this", he told Lady Ottoline on 17 February, "I have had a letter from Wittgenstein saying he and I are so dissimilar that it is useless to attempt friendship, and he will never write to me or see me again. I dare say his mood will change after a while. I find I don't care on his account, but only for the sake of Logic. And yet I believe I do really care too much to look at it. It is my fault—I have been too sharp with him" (#989). Russell wrote him a conciliatory letter on 23 February, but he was not to see him again before the outbreak of war when Wittgenstein returned to Austria and joined its army. This separation saddened Russell. On 12 November 1914 he wrote Lady Ottoline: "It seems strange that of all the people in the war the one I care for much the most should be Wittgenstein who is an 'enemy'. I feel an absolute conviction that he will not survive—he is too reckless and blind and ill. I can know nothing till the war is over. If he does survive, I think the war will have done him good" (#1148).

Thoughts of Wittgenstein continued to haunt Russell throughout the war. They may have led him to magnify the force of the criticism Wittgenstein had offered of his *Theory of Knowledge* manuscript. It was not until early 1919 that Russell had news of his post-war condition. John Maynard Keynes had written to Wittgenstein and received a reply. Wittgenstein asked that a copy of Russell's *Introduction to Mathematical Philosophy*, which had been published in March of that year, be sent to him. Russell sent a copy which Wittgenstein read and condemned as showing that Russell had learned nothing from his "Notes on Logic".

Russell had a tendency to brood upon Wittgenstein's criticisms of his work. On 4 March 1916 he wrote Lady Ottoline:

Do you remember that at the time when you were seeing Vittoz I wrote a lot of stuff about theory of knowledge, which Wittgenstein criticized with the greatest severity? His criticism, though I don't think you realized it at the time, was an event of first-rate importance in my life, and affected everything I have done since. I saw he was right, and I saw that I could not hope ever again to do fundamental work in philosophy. My impulse was shattered, like a wave dashed to pieces against a breakwater. I became filled with utter despair, and tried to turn to you for consolation. But you were occupied with Vittoz and could not give me time. So I took to casual philandering, and that increased my despair. I *had* to produce lectures for America, but I took a metaphysical subject although I was and am convinced that all fundamental work in philosophy is logical. My reason was that Wittgenstein persuaded me that what wanted doing in logic was too difficult for me. So there was no really vital satisfaction of my philosophical impulse in that work, and philosophy lost its hold on me. That was due to Wittgenstein more than to the war. What the war has done is to give me a new and less difficult ambition, which seems to me quite as good as the old one. My lectures ⟨"Principles of Social Reconstruction"⟩ have persuaded me that there is a possible life and activity in the new ambition. So I want to work quietly, and I feel more at peace as regards work than I have ever done since Wittgenstein's onslaught.   (#1123)

Taken literally this letter flatly contradicts all of those letters of early 1914, some of which are quoted in the Headnote to Paper **1**; in them Russell is brimming with confidence in his ability to do original work.

Although Russell's letters at times offer inconsistent accounts of his resulting inner states, there can be no doubt about Wittgenstein's importance to his philosophical thinking during this period. In the beginning his influence was mainly negative, stopping dead in its tracks an important Russell manuscript. But by early 1914 his effect on Russell's work became positive. Russell studied "Notes on Logic" with great care and spent much time explaining and defending them in his courses at Harvard. This immersion made them part and parcel of his own thinking about logic. Whenever he returned to work on logical questions Wittgenstein's views and criticisms came forcibly back to mind, and gradually Russell came to terms with them. "The Philosophy of Logical Atomism" (**17**) was, he explained in a prefatory note (160: 1–9), a development of what he had learned from Wittgenstein. Not all that influence is to be found in "Notes on Logic", of course, because, as we have seen, nearly all their interactions on logical questions were oral exchanges. The nature of their exchanges presents an historical problem which is unlikely ever to be solved to everyone's satisfaction.

III. THE ANALYSIS OF MIND

When, late in 1917, Russell reluctantly came to the conclusion that his campaign against the war had been fruitless, he decided to return to philosophy full-time. He reviewed the work he had already done and, as we have seen, concluded that he had exhausted what he had to say on the problem of matter in 1914. Since the problem of mind had often surfaced in his pre-war work, it is not surprising to find him advancing it as his next big project. Right from the start he called it "the analysis of mind". He aimed to do for mind what he thought he had done for matter just before the war, which was to provide logical constructions as definitions for its central concepts.

Preliminary study for this new work went back to the days when he was preparing to write *Theory of Knowledge*. Stimulation had come from his reading of William James's *Essays in Radical Empiricism*. "I have been stimulated lately", he wrote Lady Ottoline, "by meditating on James's theory (in a posthumous book) that there is no such thing as 'consciousness' or anything specifically 'mental'. At first I thought it merely a wild paradox, but gradually I have begun to see the sense of it, at any rate so far as to understand how it can be believed" (#703, pmk. 19 Feb. 1913). But he himself did not at that time believe it. Three months later, when he was hard at work producing ten pages of manuscript per day of *Theory of Knowledge*, he told her: "I have finished refuting James's view that there is no such thing as consciousness, and now I have to give my own account of it" (#772, pmk. 11 May). Chapter II of that book is devoted to a detailed refutation of the doctrines of neutral monism, including the theory that consciousness is non-existent. Neutral monism, as Russell understood it, is the doctrine that there is one and only one fundamental stuff, which when organized by one set of causal laws gives mind and by another set yields matter. For James, the neutral stuff was pure experience; for Russell, in the 1920s, the neutral entities were sensations or events.

By the time Russell delivered his lectures on logical atomism in the winter of 1918, he was ready to admit that some of the arguments he had used against neutral monism in 1913 were not valid. But there was still sufficient force left in his criticisms of it to prevent him from accepting its doctrines. He confessed, nevertheless, that they had a strong appeal for him, largely because they exemplified Occam's Razor and so generated pleasant work for mathematical logicians. The work, of course, consisted in fashioning out of "the smallest possible apparatus" (195: 32–3) logical constructions which "look like the entities you used to assume" (195: 38). Because he had not, however, heard an answer to his earlier objection concerning emphatic particulars (195–6), he continued to distance himself from neutral monism. When he wrote "On Propositions: What They Are and How They Mean" (20) in February and March 1919, he was still both admitting the attractiveness of neutral monism and confessing his inability to find it wholly credible: "William James, in his *Essays in Radical Empiricism*, developed the view that the mental and the physical are not distinguished by the stuff of which they are made, but only by their causal laws. This view is very attractive, and I have made great endeavours to believe it" (289: 23–6). During the course of this essay, however, he moved a considerable distance toward overcoming his doubts. When discussing the nature of belief, he rejected the theory he defended in *The Problems of Philosophy*, because he had come around to the view that there was no such thing as the "subject". He stated that he had found his own way to this position reinforced by the arguments of James and the American New Realists. He was not accepting James's own theory of belief, which he criticized in "The Philosophy of Logical Atomism" (194), because he held that the content of a belief is (usually) a proposition; whereas James, according to Russell, held that the object of a belief is a thing. By 1921, in *The Analysis of Mind*, Russell had accepted James's rejection of consciousness, but he was still not prepared to adopt neutral monism in its entirety.

> My own belief—for which the reasons will appear in subsequent lectures—is that James is right in rejecting consciousness as an entity, and that the American realists are partly right, though not wholly, in considering that both mind and matter are composed of a neutral-stuff which, in isolation, is neither mental nor material. I should admit this view as regards sensations: what is heard or seen belongs equally to psychology and to physics. But I should say that images belong only to the mental world, while those occurrences (if any) which do not form part of any "experience" belong only to the physical world.   (*1921*, 25)

He took "neutral" to mean that an entity must be subject to both physical and psychological laws, so that both images and unexperienced events (if there are any) failed to be neutral; the first because they were not subject to physical laws, the second because they were not subject to psychological laws.

In addition to James and to a lesser extent his followers, the American New Realists, Russell was influenced in his work on the analysis of mind by the writings of the behaviourist psychologists, especially John B. Watson. During the four and one-half months he spent as a prisoner in 1918 he read widely in the writings of Watson and several of his followers. (See Appendix III.) In general he found himself in sympathy with their stand against introspection and with their attempt to explain psychological phenomena by appealing only to external observation, but he believed their account of memory and habit to be faulty. The behaviourists denied the existence of those images which Russell took as central in his own account of memory and habit.

Russell spent some of his time in prison—from the first of May until the middle of September, 1919—on preliminary work for the analysis of mind. The surviving working papers are printed here as Paper **18**. Two previously published papers (**19** and **20**) also resulted from this project, the final fruit of which was published in 1921 as *The Analysis of Mind*.

IV. HIS PHILOSOPHICAL METHOD

Often when Russell was thinking about a philosophical problem he was also—perhaps not at exactly the same time—thinking about the nature of his philosophical thinking. A striking instance is to be found in Paper **17**. Very few people, he tells us, prove to be capable of thinking about philosophical matters because they fall victim to the temptation to attribute to the thing they want to think about the properties of the symbol they are using to stand for the thing. This "is especially likely in very abstract studies such as philosophical logic, because the subject-matter that you are supposed to be thinking of is so exceedingly difficult and elusive that any person who has ever tried to think about it knows you do not think about it except perhaps once in six months for half a minute. The rest of the time you think about the symbols, because they are tangible, but the thing you are supposed to be thinking about is fearfully difficult and one does not often manage to think about it. The really good philosopher is the one who does once in six months think about it for a minute. Bad philosophers never do" (166: 11–20). Russell did not claim that he had always resisted this temptation; he only claimed that occasionally he had been able to think about the logical things for which his symbols were the marks. His letters to Lady Ottoline contain many descriptions of the way he did philosophical work. Some account of these passages will assist the reader in understanding the rather formal statement of his method in "On Scientific Method in Philosophy" (**4**).

On 23 September 1911 he described for her the way he wrote. On that day he had written twenty pages of a paper, "On the Relations of Universals and Particulars", for delivery as his presidential address to the Aristotelian Society:

> In spite of experience, I still always feel, with whatever I have to write, as if it were impossible I should get it done, until suddenly I see my way and it all comes out. All the real work is over when I begin writing. But any one would think, beforehand, that I am shamefully idle, as I spend most of my day on anything but work. I do enough sitting over the job to have my mind quite full of it, and then the rest of the time I occupy myself with other things, until I see how to do it. In former times I used to sit over the job all day long, and think my brain had got addled. Writing is a funny business. I

can't imagine Logan's ⟨Logan Pearsall Smith, his brother-in-law⟩ plan of minute re-writing. If the first draft doesn't do, I always find the second has to be done all over again, quite independently. And even in matters of pure style, I do best when I write fastest.   (#191)

In its main points this passage encapsulates his settled view of the way he worked. There is, at the start, a period of active research which was guided by the problem to hand. At this stage the formulation of the problem was probably not as clear as it became later, but it was sufficiently clear to direct his reading. Learning what others had said about the problem was essential, partly because it warned of blind alleys and wrong turnings, and partly because it provided leads which had not yet been fully worked out. When all the likely sources had been explored and thought about, there came a period of incubation during which he did other things and did not consciously think of the problem at all. He made it clear that this stage could not be hurried along: "today I got back to matter—reading mostly, but also a little writing. There is no harm in being rather kept from it at present, because it gives time for the fundamental ideas to grow at their own pace, without the fret that comes of trying to make them come faster than they choose. But when I have got the main lines right, there will come a time when I shall want to work all day at it. I don't seriously doubt that I shall be able to do *something* fairly important, even if I can't do all I should like to do" (#693, pmk. 6 Feb. 1913). The final stage was to write out the product of all this effort when it came flooding into consciousness.

The description given so far does not allude to the real philosophical work that must go on if the problem is to be successfully resolved. This work is thinking, about which he also had something to say. During the period when the nature of matter was his primary concern, he wrote:

This morning I got a good morning's work—I am much less worried about Matter than I was—I see ideas are growing slowly, and at this stage I doubt if they would grow much faster if I could give my whole time to it. Later on, when I have the fundamental ideas, the time will come for long hours, but I haven't reached that stage yet. I am groping my way to a new fundamental idea, which I half see, but not wholly; if I had it clear, the rest of the work would be easy. I find that by some obscure process I have come to understand the problems very much better than I did at the beginning of the term, which is a comfort. And the more I think about it, the more important the subject becomes. I can now picture myself sitting down to write about it—it has grown *solid*. Thinking in philosophy is very queer—it is only at quite a late stage that one finds out what it is that one has been thinking about.   (#703, pmk. 19 Feb.)

He went on to say that his recent stimulation had come from James's theory that there is no such thing as consciousness. Four days later he had reached the incubation stage and was spending his time reading "silly novels" (#707, pmk. 23 Feb.) When that period was completed, ideas would erupt into consciousness and then he felt himself to be "just a very competent machine—the points that turn up as I write I see how to deal with, by a kind of easy instinct—it really means being tremendously strung up, but it feels oddly easy. For years I have been wondering if one could make a relational theory of time, and have not seen how it could be done—yesterday I reached that point, and just made the theory in the course of a few hours. It is odd how one's mental capacity varies" (#781, pmk. 20 May). The machine's energy, as he described it, came from passions and desires, and that energy somehow got directed into the sequences of words that poured from his pen at the rate of ten pages per day. This language is about as clear as any he used to describe the creative process. In one letter he wrote of "the mad fire just below the smooth surface of life" (#886, pmk. 6 Oct.) and in another of a "work-desire" that "instinctively fights against anything else that absorbs energy" (#710, 26 Feb.). Whatever the right name for this drive might be, it is clear from his letters to her that he was dominated by it most of the time.

It was the strength of this desire which led him to concentrate on those philosophical problems which caught his attention, despite the great pain such concentration involved: "work is always an agony, except in the rare moments of success. I had years and years of absolute torture over *Principia Mathematica*, and I must expect the same over this" (*ibid.*). Earlier he had written : "The impulse to this work on Matter is extraordinarily strong, it quite possesses me, and drives me on like the lash of a slave-driver" (#663, 29 Dec. 1912). Still earlier, when that problem was just beginning to surface as his new concern, he gave a graphic account of his philosophical work:

> The impulse to philosophy remains very strong in me—I feel that I really have got a method that gives more precision than there has ever been before, and more power of getting at the skeleton of the world—the framework that things are built on. It is difficult to get people to see it, because philosophers are not trained to precision, but probably I have many years' work ahead of me, so I ought to accomplish a good deal. The work I have done since the big book was finished has some unity that I can't get hold of; if I could, I should probably see how to write a big book. But as yet I don't know what the central theme is. It is an odd blind impulse—I dread the slavery of another big book—it is really frightful—yet I would do *anything* to get hold of the central idea that would make a big book. However, I ought really to be unfettered for another year or so, just thinking at large. (#615 [29 Oct. 1912])

Obviously he found philosophical thinking irresistible despite the travail it brought with it.

He recognized that there were certain dangers inherent in the kind of work he did. "I think the habit of abstract thought tends to produce a certain oppression and timidity that lead to failure. That is exactly what has happened to ⟨G. E.⟩ Moore—also to an elderly logician named ⟨W. E.⟩ Johnson here, who has quite as good an intellect as I have, but has produced almost nothing—from failure of will and energy" (#616, pmk. 30 Oct.). He gallantly attributed his success to her love for him; for all that he had already shown his will and energy in *Principia*.

Demands by his students for guidance in their own philosophical work obliged him to formulate his method, which he later published as "On Scientific Method in Philosophy" (**4**). His reflections on his own original work in logic and the foundations of mathematics led him to compare the method he had employed with the method used by scientists. To his great satisfaction he found many similarities and no important differences between the two methods. Both involved collaboration between people occupied with the same problem; both enjoined a systematic search for facts once a problem was formulated clearly enough to determine which facts were relevant to it; both demanded a survey of the literature to establish whether an hypothesis accounting for the facts had been previously discovered and, of equal importance, to learn of any hypotheses that had been tried and found wanting; both, to have any chance at all for success, required the researcher, by thinking alone, to invent an hypothesis which fit the facts closely enough to warrant further testing; and both, when successful, resulted in an hypothesis which fitted the facts and also passed all further tests to which it was subjected. Such an hypothesis would then be published as the best available solution to the problem. Others interested in the problem would be expected to take it up and test it further, correcting it, or even abandoning it, where necessary. Application of this method by large numbers of researchers would gradually lead to older sciences being advanced and made more complete and to newer ones, like mathematical logic, being established on a firm footing.

The principal difference between philosophy and science lay, he thought, in the kinds of hypotheses each favoured: scientific hypotheses are, in the earlier stages of a science's history, empirical statements, in later stages they include, as components, hypothetical constructs—Rutherford's model of the atom will serve as an example—similar to Russell's logical constructions; philosophical hypotheses are logical statements, having the two essential properties of being à priori and universal, and usually involving logical constructions of the sort we discussed earlier. The scientist arrives at his hypotheses by analytical thinking about physical or biological or psychological facts within the context of known laws; the philosopher uses a similar kind of analytical thinking, supplemented by the techniques of mathematical logic, within the context of known logical truths. With both methods genius, or something akin to it, is required for the formulation of fresh hypotheses. Once an hypothesis is to hand, the testing of it is a fairly routine matter. The exciting and difficult step, for Russell, is the thinking up of new hypotheses. The account of his philosophical work given earlier provides some indication of the way Russell thought such hypotheses emerged.

V. "POPULAR" VERSUS "TECHNICAL" PHILOSOPHY

Several of the papers in this volume were written for the general reader. "Mysticism and Logic" (2) is the prime exhibit in this category, but many of the reviews also qualify for inclusion. Russell called such writings "popular philosophy" and contrasted them with "technical philosophy", a distinction brought to the fore by his relationship with Lady Ottoline. Because she had almost no training in academic philosophy, Russell, who very much wanted to share his work with her, found himself forced to try to give accounts of his various philosophical positions in a vocabulary she could understand. These attempts led him to reflect upon the differences between the two kinds of philosophical writing.

Two other factors also contributed to his interest in popular philosophy. The first was his desire—probably a consequence of his family's expectations of him—not to be merely a philosopher's philosopher, but to enjoy a wide readership. When such a mood was dominant, Lady Ottoline may have been seen as the ideal general reader. This hypothesis has the merit of accounting for the extraordinary way in which so many of his love letters to her seem to be addressed to the world at large. A second factor was his chronic shortage of money beginning around the time he separated from his wife Alys in 1911, although in fairness to Alys it should be noted that no action of hers was the cause of his penury. Writing popular philosophy promised a welcome increase in his income.

The Problems of Philosophy (1912), or his "Shilling Shocker" as he called it in his letters to Lady Ottoline, first raised the distinction. In contracting to write it he had agreed that it should appeal to a wide audience; it was to be aimed at the general public and not at students and teachers of philosophy. One day, when he was reading proofs for the book, he wrote to her:

> I am surprised to find how much of my philosophy comes into the Shilling Shocker—of course in technical writing all sorts of points would have to be more gone into, and there would have to be controversy; but the essentials are all there. It is odd I have no doubt philosophy is worth teaching, but I have grave doubt as to how far it

is worth giving one's life to original work in it. The amount that can be learnt in youth is certainly useful, but I don't know if more is. (#243 [4 Nov. 1912])

Two points of distinction between the two kinds of philosophical writing emerge here. In the first place, popular writing in philosophy is content to let its generalizations stand without a detailed examination of their foundations; technical writing by contrast must go into much greater detail, both of statement and of foundation. In the second place, popular writing avoids controversy as much as possible; positions of other authors must, of course, be criticized, but presumably in such a way as to avoid starting controversy. To a certain extent the second point follows from the first, since controversy is hardly possible unless one gives arguments very close scrutiny. Technical writing, on the other hand, demands that all controversial points be fully debated.

He returned to this distinction in a later letter; the passage is a striking one and well worth quoting in full:

I have an uneasiness about philosophy altogether; what remains for *me* to do in philosophy (I mean in *technical* philosophy) does not seem of first-rate importance. The shilling shocker really seems to be better worth doing. It is all puzzling and obscure. For so many years I have had absolutely no choice as to work that I have got out of the way of wondering what is best to do. I think really the important thing now is to make the ideas I already have intelligible. And I ought to try to get away from pedantry. My feelings have changed about all this; I did think the technical philosophy that remains for me to do very important indeed.

I will try to write out what I think about philosophy; it will help to clear up my own ideas. All the historic problems of philosophy seem to me either insoluble or soluble by methods which are not philosophical, but mathematical or scientific. The last word of philosophy on all of them seems to me to be that à priori any of the alternatives is possible. Thus e.g. as to God: traditional philosophy proved him: I think some forms of God impossible, some possible, none necessary. As to immortality: philosophy can only say it may be true or it may be false; any more definite answer would have to come from psychical research. As to whether nothing exists except mind: philosophy, it seems to me, can only say that all the arguments adduced on either side are fallacious, and that there is absolutely no evidence either way. And I should say the same of optimism and pessimism. Except as a stimulus to the imagination, almost the only use of philosophy, I should say, is to combat errors induced by science and religion. Religion says all things work together for good; philosophy says this belief is groundless. Science leads people to think there is no absolute good and bad, but only evolved beliefs about good and bad, which are useful to gregarious animals in the struggle for existence; philosophy equally says *this* belief is groundless.

All this is rather dismal. But as a stimulus to the imagination I think philosophy *is* important. But this use is not so much for the technical philosopher but rather for the man who wants to see his own special pursuit connected with the cosmos; therefore it is popular rather than technical philosophy that fulfils this need. This is fundamentally why I think it is more useful to write popular than technical philosophy.

There is one great question: Can human beings *know* anything, and if so what and how? This question is really the most essentially philosophical of all questions. But ultimately one has to come down to a sheer assertion that one does know this or that—e.g. one's own existence—and then one can ask why one knows it, and whether anything else fulfils the same conditions. But what is important in this inquiry can, I think, be done quite popularly; the technical refinements add very little except controversy and long words. I was reinforced in this view by finding how much I could say on the question in the shilling shocker.   (#286, 13 Dec. 1911)

A third point of difference is noted here: popular philosophy—both, one assumes, the reading and the writing of it—stimulates the imagination more than does technical philosophy. Perhaps the reason he thought it has this effect on people is that it has sweep and generality and avoids expounding details whose evaluation would demand concentrated intellectual effort.

The writing of popular philosophy appealed, as already mentioned, to another strong desire he had, namely, the desire to influence the thoughts of others. Technical books in philosophy have few readers; popular ones, a large audience. Therefore, since he believed his philosophical innovations to be of great worth, and since he had this propagandistic streak in his character, it was natural for him to think of writing popular accounts of his philosophy. During the course of delivering the lectures published in 1916 as *Principles of Social Reconstruction* (entitled *Why Men Fight* in the U.S.A.), he wrote Lucy Donnelly:

I have given up writing on the war because I have said my say and there is nothing new to say.—My ambitions are more vast and less immediate than my friends' ambitions for me. I don't care for the applause one gets by saying what others are thinking; I want actually to *change* people's thoughts. Power over people's minds is the main personal desire of my life; and this sort of power is not acquired by saying popular things. In philosophy, when I was young, my views were as unpopular and strange as they could be; yet I have had a very great measure of success. Now I have started on a new career, and if I live and keep my faculties, I shall probably be equally success- ful. (10 Feb. 1916)

Power over other people's minds is not ordinarily achieved, one might add, by popular philosophical writing alone; it must be preceded by technical work that some experts (at least) agree is an original contribution to the subject. Popular writing which is informed by such a background stands a good chance of having the sort of influence Russell wanted to have, because the general reader will sense that the writer knows that of which he speaks and could expound and defend that knowledge if challenged.

VI. REVIEWING THE WORKS OF OTHERS

From the start of his career Russell devoted some of his philosophical energies to writing reviews, both signed and unsigned, of the books others, and not only philosophers, had written. Although one does not find him saying so, it seems likely that he regarded reviewing as one of his duties as a member of the philosophical community. (At times, too, it greatly stimu- lated his own thinking; for instance, he learned of Cantor's work when sent Arthur Hannequin's *Essai critique sur l'hypothèse des atomes* for review in 1896. See Grattan-Guinness *1977*, 143–4.) It is certain, however, that he did not regard the writing of reviews as creative or original work. Instead he thought of it as merely a critical task.

The distinction between creative and critical writing is made in a letter to Lady Ottoline written just after he finished writing "The Philosophy of Bergson" in March 1912:

How easy critical work is—one only has to go through a mechanical process and the result emerges. It is really vastly inferior to original work. The difficult thing is imposing form on chaos. In criticism, form is given—it is mind on mind, not mind on outer night. And in criticism one doesn't have to settle what to talk about. (#373, pmk. 8 March)

He was always to find reviewing easy. To write a review required only that he had read the book; the review would be in place in his mind by the time he finished and he would simply have to write it out. The author of the book under review had told him what the problems were and in what order they were to be considered. All Russell had to do was bring his formidable command of logic to bear upon the text. Creative or original work—the imposition of "form on chaos"—demanded much more effort with no guarantee of success. Such work always required novelty of some kind with regard to the substance of the matter under consideration; critical work, in his opinion, seldom, if ever, did. That is why he thought critical work so inferior to original work.

The undertaking of these projects, especially the major ones, indicates that Russell's philosophical ambitions were set very high during these years. The reception of *Principia*, particularly among American philosophers, encouraged these ambitions. "I am more of an authority in America than anywhere else", he wrote Lady Ottoline (#99 [3 June 1911]); he was commenting upon a letter, which he enclosed for her to read, from Ralph Barton Perry, the Chairman of Harvard's Philosophy Department, inviting him to spend a year at Harvard. In his letter Perry remarked that Russell was now "one of our great men!" (17 May 1911).

In a letter he offered his own judgment as to his place in the philosophic pantheon:

How I loved the time after reading the *Times* Review, when I talked to you about my work. I don't often think about my work in that general way. It is rather inspiring. I don't know if it is too conceited, but I do feel myself in a way at home among the great philosophers. Spinoza and Leibniz on my mantlepiece seem like friends, I have conversations with them in which I explain how I am carrying on their work, and I can hardly resist the feeling that they hear and approve—sometimes it is all but a delusion, it grows so strong. It is one of the joys of work. An immense proportion of my work remains to be done. If I didn't think well of my work I should be almost ashamed of offering myself to you—for I don't think much of myself as a human being. (#185 [20 Sept. 1911])

And he reported that Whitehead now had a similar opinion of him.

Whitehead ... has been telling me that my mind has improved very greatly the last two or three years, that in fact it has risen to an altogether higher class. He says I used to have great ingenuity in defending rather narrow and limited points of view, but now I have an altogether broader scope, and that if my present work develops as it promises, it will put me among the few great philosophers. Al-

though this is so agreeable, I think it is true, and it is largely due to
you. Other things have come in—getting away from Alys, and
having the stimulus of Wittgenstein—but really you have been the
chief cause. (#992, pmk. 23 Feb. 1914)

It is of a certain interest that his discussion with Whitehead came several
months after Wittgenstein's attack on his manuscript, which, as we have
seen, Russell later claimed had convinced him that he could never do
original work in logic again. Whitehead's observation, and Russell's agreement with it, do not contain any such reservations. To repeat a conclusion
drawn earlier: the evidence seems to indicate that Russell magnified and
transformed the effect on him of Wittgenstein's criticism, partly, one
suspects, because of the anguish and frustration he felt about the war. But
whatever the reason there is no trace of the supposed effect in his letters of
early 1914; in them his philosophical ambitions know no bounds.

Acknowledgements

THIS VOLUME COULD not have been completed without the generous assistance of the University of Toronto, McMaster University and the Social Sciences and Humanities Research Council of Canada. The Council's award of a Major Editorial Grant, beginning in July 1980, has been of crucial significance for our plan to publish the *Collected Papers*. Without this grant the Russell Editorial Project could neither have obtained the extensive time freed from other duties needed for the editors, nor assembled the staff and equipment to produce this volume and the many volumes that are planned for the future.

Kenneth Blackwell, the archivist of the Bertrand Russell Archives, has rendered invaluable help on all aspects of this volume. His command of Russell's works is without parallel, now that Russell himself is dead. Nicholas Griffin, a fellow editor, also provided a great deal of assistance in setting matters straight in the volume; and both Richard Rempel, another fellow editor, and Margaret Moran, an associate editor, picked up points requiring my attention. My thanks to them all.

Bernd Frohmann compiled both the Bibliographical Index and the General Index and made many valuable suggestions on other aspects of the work. He also secured all of the necessary copyright permissions. John King was responsible for the Textual Notes and for Russell's text generally. He proved to be a meticulous workman whose unfailing good cheer lightened my work. Sheila Turcon put together the Chronology from a myriad of sources. I greatly appreciate the high quality work these three have done for me.

On the research for the volume I have received valuable assistance from Reuben Abel, Robert C. Marsh, Leonard Linsky, Don D. Roberts, and Heinz Wetzel. My assistants on the Project, Bernd Frohmann, Lois Pineau, Eldon Soifer, William Stratton, Jeffrey Verman and Mark Wright, have been of enormous help in tracking down the data reported in the annotations. Jeffrey Verman was especially persistent in continuing where others had abandoned hope, and he was successful more often than not.

It is a pleasure to thank members of the Advisory Editorial Board for their assistance to the Project. John Passmore and Katharine Tait were especially helpful in the production of this volume.

I wish also to express my appreciation to the various persons in administrative positions in the University of Toronto and McMaster University whose attention to their duties made my work much easier.

The production of camera-ready copy for Volume 8 of the *Collected Papers* was supervised by the Production Manager, Diane M. Kerss. Among her staff I should mention the typesetting and paste-up work of Joy Drew and Arlene Hill. Diane Kerss' management has greatly facilitated all technical aspects of producing the actual volume, in accord with the specifications of our publisher George Allen & Unwin Ltd. For their good offices we thank Rayner Unwin, together with Keith Ashfield formerly with that firm. McMaster's Printing Services, managed by Don Henwood, rendered important services in the production of the volume.

For permission to quote from material in her copyright, I wish to thank Mrs. Muriel M. Sinclair for the letters of May Sinclair. Acknowledgement is also made to the following institutions, publishers and journals: The Aristotelian Society (Paper **20**); *The Cambridge Review* (Papers **9** and **10**); The Harry Ransom Humanities Research Center, The University of Texas at Austin for the letters to Lady Ottoline Morrell; *The Journal of Philosophy* (Papers **6** and **16**); *The Monist* (Papers **5** and **17**); Thomas Nelson & Sons and Charles Scribner's Sons (Paper **3**); *New Statesman* (Papers **8, 11, 13** and **14**).

Chronology:
Russell's Life and Writings, 1914–19

FROM 1914 TO 1918 Russell was preoccupied with anti-war work. Some events bearing on the war have been included in this Chronology, but readers should consult Volumes 13 and 14 for a more detailed chronology of his anti-war campaign. The writings listed here also omit nearly all those inspired by the war. In addition, readers interested in Russell's work on the theory of knowledge should consult the Volume 7 Chronology.

	Life	Writings
31 Sept. 1913		**8** written.
10 Oct. 1913	Cambridge term begins. Alternately at Cambridge or at his London flat.	
Oct. 1913	Persuades Wittgenstein to dictate his ideas on logic ("Notes on Logic") before he leaves for Norway.	
Nov. 1913	Begins informal classes in philosophy for science students.	
3 Nov. 1913		**9** written.
27 Nov. 1913		**9** published.
8 Dec. 1913	Cambridge term ends.	
c. 19–c. 30 Dec. 1913	Sees Lady Ottoline Morrell in Rome and travels in Italy.	
c. 2–c. 7 Jan. 1914	At Cambridge.	**1** written.
9–15 Jan. 1914		**2** written.
12–19 Jan. 1914		**3** written.
16 Jan. 1914	Cambridge term begins.	
24 Jan. 1914		Delivers **2** at Queen's College, Cambridge.
31 Jan. 1914		**8** published.
mid to late Feb. 1914		**10** written.

1 Mar. 1914		Delivers **2** to the Cambridge Heretics.
4 Mar. 1914		**10** published.
7–14 Mar. 1914	Sails from Britain to the U.S.A.	
14 Mar.–26 May 1914	Lectures at Harvard on logic and the theory of knowledge.	
16 Mar.–9 Apr. 1914		Delivers the Lowell lectures in Boston.
4 Apr. 1914		Delivers **2** at Greenwich College.
14 Apr. 1914		Delivers **2** at Wellesley College.
20–25 Apr. 1914		Delivers **1** at three eastern American universities.
Apr. 1914		**3** published.
5 May 1914		Lectures on "The World of Physics and the World of Sense" (Chap. 4 of *Our Knowledge of the External World*) at Yale.
26 May–6 June 1914	Lecture tour of the Midwest (Chicago, Madison, Ann Arbor).	
6–14 June 1914	Sails from the U.S.A. to Britain.	
July 1914	Alternately at Cambridge and at his London flat.	**1** and **2** published.
Aug. 1914	War declared. Helps to found the Union of Democratic Control (UDC).	*Our Knowledge of the External World* published.
13 Oct. 1914	Cambridge term begins.	
late Oct.–mid Nov. 1914		**4** written.
18 Nov. 1914		Delivers **4** as the Herbert Spencer lecture at Oxford. It was published in pamphlet form before the end of the year.
11 Dec. 1914	Cambridge term ends.	
25 Dec. 1914	With the Whiteheads in London.	
15 Jan. 1915	Cambridge term begins.	
c.21 Jan.–14 Feb. 1915		**5** written.
31 Jan. 1915	Discusses the concept of matter with H. A. Prichard, at Oxford. Harvard cables inviting him to lecture.	

15 Feb. 1915		Delivers **5** to the Philosophical Society of Manchester.
Feb. 1915	First meets D. H. Lawrence.	
15 Mar. 1915	Cambridge term ends.	
23 Apr. 1915	Cambridge term begins.	
18 May 1915	Awarded Butler Gold Medal by Columbia University.	
28 May 1915	Trinity College, Cambridge renews his five year lectureship commencing 1 Oct. 1915.	
7 June 1915		**6** written.
12 June 1915	Cambridge term ends.	
summer 1915	At Garsington, the Morrells' house near Oxford.	
July 1915		**5** published.
8 July 1915		**6** published.
Oct. 1915	His leave of absence from Cambridge for the Michaelmas and Lent terms begins.	
23–27 Dec. 1915	Spends Christmas at Telegraph House, his brother Frank's house in Sussex.	
5 Jan. 1916	Professor J. H. Woods offers him a lectureship at Harvard.	
18 Jan.–7 Mar. 1916		Delivers series of lectures at the Caxton Hall Westminster published later in the year as *Principles of Social Reconstruction*.
20–30 Mar. 1916	Takes walking trip with Jean Nicod in Sussex.	
early Apr. 1916	Begins to work actively for the No-Conscription Fellowship.	
28 Apr. 1916	Cambridge term begins.	
30 May 1916	Receives summons to appear at the Mansion House.	
5 June 1916	Found guilty of making "statements likely to prejudice the recruiting and discipline of His Majesty's forces". Fined £100 plus £10 costs.	
8 June 1916	Request for passport to travel to Harvard to take up a teaching position denied.	

12 June 1916	Cambridge term ends.	
29 June 1916	Appeal dismissed at the City Quarter Sessions.	
11 July 1916	Trinity College, Cambridge, dismisses him from his lectureship.	
c. 17 July 1916	Decides to sublet his flat and stay with his brother Frank at Gordon Square when in London.	
16 Aug. 1916	Asked to stand for the rectorship of the University of St. Andrew's by C. D. Broad. (He was not elected.)	
1 Sept. 1916	Banned from all prohibited areas by Lt. Col. A. Russell.	
23 Sept. 1916	Begins affair with Lady Constance Malleson (Colette O'Niel).	
16 Oct. 1916		Starts a six-week lecture tour in Manchester on the topic, "The World As It Can Be Made" published in 1917 as *Political Ideals*.
Dec. 1916	Spends Christmas with the Morrells at Garsington.	
late Aug. 1917		**11** written and **12** probably written.
5 Sept. 1917	Writes to P. E. B. Jourdain that his interest in philosophy is reviving.	
8 Sept. 1917		**11** published.
Oct. 1917		**12** published.
30 Oct.–18 Dec. 1917		Delivers series of lectures on mathematical logic (later rewritten as *Introduction to Mathematical Philosophy*) at Dr. Williams' Library.
10 Nov. 1917		**13** published.
25 Dec. 1917	Spends Christmas day with Colette and her family, then goes on to Garsington.	
22 Jan.–12 Mar. 1918		Delivers a series of lectures (**17**) on "The Philosophy of Logical Atomism" at Dr. Williams' Library.

4 Feb. 1918	Receives summons to appear at Bow Street.	
9 Feb. 1918	Found guilty of "having in a printed publication made certain statements likely to prejudice His Majesty's relations with the U.S.A." Sentenced to six months in the Second Division.	
1 May 1918	Appeal dismissed at London Quarter Sessions but sentence reduced to imprisonment in the First Division; enters Brixton prison.	
May 1918		**16** probably written. *Introduction to Mathematical Philosophy* written.
after 1 July 1918		**15** written while still in prison.
latter half of 1918		Most of the papers which make up **18** written.
20 July 1918		**14** published.
31 July 1918		**18h** written.
10 Aug. 1918		**18i** written.
29 Aug. 1918		**19** written.
14 Sept. 1918	Released from prison.	
Oct. 1918		**15** published. Part of **17** published.
20 Dec. 1918–14 Jan. 1919	With Colette and Clifford Allen at Lynton, N. Devon.	
2 Jan. 1919		**7** published.
Jan. 1919		**16** published.
Jan., Apr., July 1919		Remainder of **17** published.
1 Feb. 1919		**19** published.
11 Feb. 1919	Asked by the Socialist Club of the University of Glasgow to stand for the rectorship. (He was not elected.)	
17 Feb. 1919	Begins to share Clifford Allen's flat in Battersea; after a few days moves to Garsington until mid–April.	
c.23 Feb.–4 Mar. 1919		**20** written.
4 Mar. 1919		*Introduction to Mathematical Philosophy* published.

6 May–24 June 1919		Delivers a series of lectures on "The Analysis of Mind" at Dr. Williams' Library.
24 June–29 Sept. 1919	Rents Newlands Farm, Lulworth with J. E. Littlewood.	
11 July 1919		**20** read to a joint session of the Aristotelian Society, the British Psychology Society, and the Mind Association. It was published later in the year.

Part I

Theory of Knowledge and Philosophical Method

1

The Relation of Sense-Data to Physics [1914]

THIS PAPER WAS published in both English and French in *Scientia*, 16 (July 1914): 1–27 and supp. 3–34. The French version, which was prepared by M. Georges Bourgin, was corrected by Russell.

Russell wrote the paper during the first week of 1914. "Since I came back," he wrote Lady Ottoline Morrell on the morning of 8 January, "I have read and analysed innumerable articles, prepared a number of lectures on Theory of Knowledge, made some important discoveries, written a long paper for a New York Philosophical Society—about 12,000 words—and compiled most of a lecture on the philosophy of evolution. This is five days' work" (#960). He went on to say that he dictated part of the paper to a secretary who took it down in shorthand. "I don't think my brain has been more clear, or more willing to do all I ask of it, any time since 1900." During the afternoon of 17 January he reported to her that the secretary had just delivered the typescript. "It is very good! I don't believe I have ever done anything better, at any rate as regards clearness and manner of exposition" (#971). He gave Lucy Donnelly, a professor of English at Bryn Mawr College and his life-long friend and correspondent, a similar account on 20 February: "I am reading a paper to a Philosophical Club in New York.... I wrote it in the first days of the year, just after returning from Rome. It is 11,000 words and took me three days—don't tell them, or they will think it worthless, whereas it is one of the best things I ever did!"

Although Russell wrote the paper for delivery at Columbia University, he read it first, on 20 April 1914, to a group at The Johns Hopkins University. No account of the paper's reception there survives. It was circulated in mimeographed form to the Philosophical Club of Columbia some days before the meeting. Russell then led a discussion of it. "It roused great opposition," he reported to Lady Ottoline on 24 April, the day after the meeting, "as I knew it would. The most effective criticism was from Dewey, who again impressed me very greatly, both as a philosopher and as a lovable man" (#1022). At Princeton, where he read it the next day, to an audience of mathematicians and philosophers, "the mathematicians in a body announced that they agreed with me (it was sense-data and physics), so they rather took the wind out of the sails of the philosophers, who were not much good except a Scotchman named Bowman" (*ibid.*).

In content the paper follows closely the position Russell developed in *Our Knowledge of the External World* (1914). There is one important innovation with regard to terminology: "sensibile" and its plural "sensibilia" are introduced to refer to what were called either "possible sense-data" or "ideal appearances of a thing" in the book. The requirement that space have six dimensions is not explicitly mentioned in the book, but it would seem that his account of the logical construction of a thing (*1914*, 87ff.), which Kenneth Blackwell has persuasively argued (*1973*, 11–13) was added to the book after "The Relation of Sense-data to Physics" was written, would require six dimensions. In *My Philosophical Development* (*1959*, 105) he wrote: "There were several novelties in the theory of our knowledge of the external world which burst upon me on New Year's Day, 1914. The most important of these was the theory that space has six dimensions and not only three." No doubt this is one of the "important discoveries" he referred to in his letter to Lady Ottoline quoted above. *Our Knowledge of the External World* had been written some months earlier; but in revising it for publication he omitted discussion of the dimensionality of space so prominent in the paper. The paper consolidates and refines the position argued for in the book, and it seems likely that such a compact statement of such a complex matter would not have been possible without the previous thought which went into the book.

The paper exists in five forms. There is a holograph manuscript of Part 1, "The Problem Stated" (RA 220.011400). A copy of the mimeographed version distributed to members of the Philosophical Club of Columbia survives, and there are the two published versions of the paper, one in English and one in French. Finally, Russell included the paper in *Mysticism and Logic, and Other Essays* (1918). All versions have been collated and the results reported in the Textual Notes. The copy-text is that of *Mysticism and Logic.*

I. THE PROBLEM STATED

PHYSICS IS SAID to be an empirical science, based upon observation and experiment.

It is supposed to be verifiable, i.e. capable of calculating beforehand results subsequently confirmed by observation and experiment.

What can we learn by observation and experiment?

Nothing, so far as physics is concerned, except immediate data of sense: certain patches of colour, sounds, tastes, smells, etc., with certain spatio-temporal relations.

The supposed contents of the physical world are *primâ facie* very different from these: molecules have no colour, atoms make no noise, electrons have no taste, and corpuscles do not even smell.

If such objects are to be verified, it must be solely through their relation to sense-data: they must have some kind of correlation with sense-data, and must be verifiable through this correlation *alone*.

But how is the correlation itself ascertained? A correlation can only be ascertained empirically by the correlated objects being constantly *found* together. But in our case, only one term of the correlation, namely the sensible term, is ever *found*: the other term seems essentially incapable of being found. Therefore, it would seem, the correlation with objects of sense, by which physics was to be verified, is itself utterly and for ever unverifiable.

There are two ways of avoiding this result.

(1) We may say that we know some principle a priori, without the need of empirical verification, e.g. that our sense-data have *causes* other than themselves, and that something can be known about these causes by inference from their effects. This way has been often adopted by philosophers. It may be necessary to adopt this way to some extent, but in so far as it is adopted physics ceases to be empirical or based upon experiment and observation alone. Therefore this way is to be avoided as much as possible.

(2) We may succeed in actually defining the objects of physics as functions of sense-data. Just in so far as physics leads to expectations, this *must* be possible, since we can only *expect* what can be experienced. And in so far as the physical state of affairs is inferred from sense-data, it must be capable of expression as a function of sense-data. The problem of accomplishing this expression leads to much interesting logico-mathematical work.

In physics as commonly set forth, sense-data appear as functions of physical objects: when such-and-such waves impinge upon the eye, we see such-and-such colours, and so on. But the waves are in fact inferred from the colours, not vice versa. Physics cannot be regarded as validly based upon empirical data until the waves have been expressed as functions of the colours and other sense-data.

Thus if physics is to be verifiable we are faced with the following problem: Physics exhibits sense-data as functions of physical objects, but verification is only possible if physical objects can be exhibited as functions of sense-data. We have therefore to solve the equations giving sense-data in terms of physical objects, so as to make them instead give physical objects in terms of sense-data.

II. CHARACTERISTICS OF SENSE-DATA

When I speak of a "sense-datum", I do not mean the whole of what is given in sense at one time. I mean rather such a part of the whole as might be
10 singled out by attention: particular patches of colour, particular noises, and so on. There is some difficulty in deciding what is to be considered *one* sense-datum: often attention causes divisions to appear where, so far as can be discovered, there were no divisions before. An observed complex fact, such as that this patch of red is to the left of that patch of blue, is also to be regarded as a datum from our present point of view: epistemologically, it does not differ greatly from a simple sense-datum as regards its function in giving knowledge. Its *logical* structure is very different, however, from that of sense: *sense* gives acquaintance with particulars, and is thus a two-term relation in which the object can be *named* but not *asserted*, and is inherently
20 incapable of truth or falsehood, whereas the observation of a complex fact, which may be suitably called perception, is not a two-term relation, but involves the propositional form on the object-side, and gives knowledge of a truth, not mere acquaintance with a particular. This logical difference, important as it is, is not very relevant to our present problem; and it will be convenient to regard data of perception as included among sense-data for the purposes of this paper. It is to be observed that the particulars which are constituents of a datum of perception are always sense-data in the strict sense.

Concerning sense-data, we know that they are there while they are data,
30 and this is the epistemological basis of all our knowledge of external particulars. (The meaning of the word "external" of course raises problems which will concern us later.) We do not know, except by means of more or less precarious inferences, whether the objects which are at one time sense-data continue to exist at times when they are not data. Sense-data at the times when they are data are all that we directly and primitively know of the external world; hence in epistemology the fact that they are *data* is all-important. But the fact that they are all that we directly know gives, of course, no presumption that they are all that there is. If we could construct an impersonal metaphysic, independent of the accidents of our knowledge
40 and ignorance, the privileged position of the actual data would probably disappear, and they would probably appear as a rather haphazard selection

from a mass of objects more or less like them. In saying this, I assume only that it is probable that there are particulars with which we are not acquainted. Thus the special importance of sense-data is in relation to epistemology, not to metaphysics. In this respect, physics is to be reckoned as metaphysics: it is impersonal, and nominally pays no special attention to sense-data. It is only when we ask how physics can be *known* that the importance of sense-data re-emerges.

III. SENSIBILIA

I shall give the name *sensibilia* to those objects which have the same metaphysical and physical status as sense-data, without necessarily being data to any mind. Thus the relation of a *sensibile* to a sense-datum is like that of a man to a husband: a man becomes a husband by entering into the relation of marriage, and similarly a *sensibile* becomes a sense-datum by entering into the relation of acquaintance. It is important to have both terms; for we wish to discuss whether an object which is at one time a sense-datum can still exist at a time when it is not a sense-datum. We cannot ask "Can sense-data exist without being given?" for that is like asking "Can husbands exist without being married?" We must ask "Can *sensibilia* exist without being given?" and also "Can a particular *sensibile* be at one time a sense-datum, and at another not?" Unless we have the word *sensibile* as well as the word "sense-datum", such questions are apt to entangle us in trivial logical puzzles.

It will be seen that all sense-data are *sensibilia*. It is a metaphysical question whether all *sensibilia* are sense-data, and an epistemological question whether there exist means of inferring *sensibilia* which are not data from those that are.

A few preliminary remarks, to be amplified as we proceed, will serve to elucidate the use which I propose to make of *sensibilia*.

I regard sense-data as not mental, and as being, in fact, part of the actual subject-matter of physics. There are arguments, shortly to be examined, for their subjectivity, but these arguments seem to me only to prove *physiological* subjectivity, i.e. causal dependence on the sense-organs, nerves, and brain. The appearance which a thing presents to us is causally dependent upon these, in exactly the same way as it is dependent upon intervening fog or smoke or coloured glass. Both dependences are contained in the statement that the appearance which a piece of matter presents when viewed from a given place is a function not only of the piece of matter, but also of the intervening medium. (The terms used in this statement—"matter", "view from a given place", "appearance", "intervening medium"—will all be defined in the course of the present paper.) We have not the means of ascertaining how things appear from places not surrounded by brain and nerves and sense-organs, because we cannot leave the body; but continuity makes it not unreasonable to suppose that they present *some* appearance at such places. Any such appearance would be included among *sensibilia*. If—*per impossibile*—there were a complete human body with no mind inside it, all those *sensibilia* would exist, in relation to that body, which would be sense-data if there were a mind in the body. What the mind adds to *sensibilia*, in fact, is *merely* awareness: everything else is physical or physiological.

IV. SENSE-DATA ARE PHYSICAL

10 Before discussing this question it will be well to define the sense in which the terms "mental" and "physical" are to be used. The word "physical", in all preliminary discussions, is to be understood as meaning "what is dealt with by physics". Physics, it is plain, tells us something about some of the constituents of the actual world; what these constituents are may be doubtful, but it is they that are to be called physical, whatever their nature may prove to be.

The definition of the term "mental" is more difficult, and can only be satisfactorily given after many difficult controversies have been discussed and decided. For present purposes therefore I must content myself with
20 assuming a dogmatic answer to these controversies. I shall call a particular "mental" when it is aware of something, and I shall call a fact "mental" when it contains a mental particular as a constituent.

It will be seen that the mental and the physical are not necessarily mutually exclusive, although I know of no reason to suppose that they overlap.

The doubt as to the correctness of our definition of the "mental" is of little importance in our present discussion. For what I am concerned to maintain is that sense-data are physical, and this being granted it is a matter of indifference in our present inquiry whether or not they are also mental.
30 Although I do not hold, with Mach and James and the "new realists", that the difference between the mental and the physical is *merely* one of arrangement, yet what I have to say in the present paper is compatible with their doctrine and might have been reached from their standpoint.

In discussions on sense-data, two questions are commonly confused, namely:

(1) Do sensible objects persist when we are not sensible of them? In other words, do *sensibilia* which are data at a certain time sometimes continue to exist at times when they are not data? And (2) are sense-data mental or physical?
40 I propose to assert that sense-data are physical, while yet maintaining that they probably never persist unchanged after ceasing to be data. The view

that they do not persist is often thought, quite erroneously in my opinion, to imply that they are mental; and this has, I believe, been a potent source of confusion in regard to our present problem. If there were, as some have held, a *logical impossibility* in sense-data persisting after ceasing to be data, that certainly would tend to show that they were mental; but if, as I contend, their non-persistence is merely a probable inference from empirically ascertained causal laws, then it carries no such implication with it, and we are quite free to treat them as part of the subject-matter of physics.

Logically a sense-datum is an object, a particular of which the subject is aware. It does not contain the subject as a part, as for example beliefs and volitions do. The existence of the sense-datum is therefore not logically dependent upon that of the subject; for the only way, so far as I know, in which the existence of *A* can be *logically* dependent upon the existence of *B* is when *B* is part of *A*. There is therefore no a priori reason why a particular which is a sense-datum should not persist after it has ceased to be a datum, nor why other similar particulars should not exist without ever being data. The view that sense-data are mental is derived, no doubt, in part from their physiological subjectivity, but in part also from a failure to distinguish between sense-data and "sensations". By a sensation I mean the fact consisting in the subject's awareness of the sense-datum. Thus a sensation is a complex of which the subject is a constituent and which therefore is mental. The sense-datum, on the other hand, stands over against the subject as that external object of which in sensation the subject is aware. It is true that the sense-datum is in many cases in the subject's body, but the subject's body is as distinct from the subject as tables and chairs are, and is in fact merely a part of the material world. So soon, therefore, as sense-data are clearly distinguished from sensations, and as their subjectivity is recognized to be physiological not psychical, the chief obstacles in the way of regarding them as physical are removed.

V. "SENSIBILIA" AND "THINGS"   30

But if "sensibilia" are to be recognized as the ultimate constituents of the physical world, a long and difficult journey is to be performed before we can arrive either at the "thing" of common sense or at the "matter" of physics. The supposed impossibility of combining the different sense-data which are regarded as appearances of the same "thing" to different people has made it seem as though these "sensibilia" must be regarded as mere subjective phantasms. A given table will present to one man a rectangular appearance, while to another it appears to have two acute angles and two obtuse angles; to one man it appears brown, while to another, towards whom it reflects the light, it appears white and shiny. It is said, not wholly without plausibility, that these different shapes and different colours cannot co-exist simultaneously in the same place, and cannot therefore both be constituents of the physical world. This argument I must confess appeared to me until recently to be irrefutable. The contrary opinion has, however, been ably maintained by Dr. T. P. Nunn in an article entitled: "Are Secondary Qualities Independent of Perception?"[1] The supposed impossibility derives its apparent force from the phrase: "*in the same place*", and it is precisely in this phrase that its weakness lies. The conception of space is too often treated in philosophy—even by those who on reflection would not defend such treatment—as though it were as given, simple, and unambiguous as Kant, in his psychological innocence, supposed. It is the unperceived ambiguity of the word "place" which, as we shall shortly see, has caused the difficulties to realists and given an undeserved advantage to their opponents. Two "places" of different kinds are involved in every sense-datum, namely the place *at* which it appears and the place *from* which it appears. These belong to different spaces, although, as we shall see, it is possible, with certain limitations, to establish a correlation between them. What we call the different appearances of the same thing to different observers are each in a space private to the observer concerned. No place in the private world of one observer is identical with a place in the private world of another observer. There is therefore no question of combining the different appearances in the one place; and the fact that they cannot all exist in one place affords accordingly no ground whatever for questioning their physical reality. The "thing" of common sense may in fact be identified with the whole class of its appearances—where, however, we must include among appearances not only those which are actual sense-data, but also those "sensibilia", if any, which, on grounds of continuity and resemblance, are to be regarded as belonging to the same system of appearances, although there happen to be no observers to whom they are data.

An example may make this clearer. Suppose there are a number of people in a room, all seeing, as they say, the same tables and chairs, walls and pictures. No two of these people have exactly the same sense-data, yet there is sufficient similarity among their data to enable them to group together certain of these data as appearances of one "thing" to the several spectators, and others as appearances of another "thing". Besides the appearances which a given thing in the room presents to the actual spectators, there are, we may suppose, other appearances which it would present to other possible spectators. If a man were to sit down between two others, the appearance which the room would present to him would be intermediate between the appearances which it presents to the two others; and although this appearance would not exist as it is without the sense organs, nerves and brain, of the newly arrived spectator, still it is not unnatural to suppose that, from the

---

1 *Proc. Arist. Soc.*, 1909–1910, pp. 191–218.

position which he now occupies, *some* appearance of the room existed before his arrival. This supposition, however, need merely be noticed and not insisted upon.

Since the "thing" cannot, without indefensible partiality, be identified with any single one of its appearances, it came to be thought of as something distinct from all of them and underlying them. But by the principle of Occam's razor, if the class of appearances will fulfil the purposes for the sake of which the thing was invented by the prehistoric metaphysicians to whom common sense is due, economy demands that we should identify the thing with the class of its appearances. It is not necessary to *deny* a substance or substratum underlying these appearances; it is merely expedient to abstain from asserting this unnecessary entity. Our procedure here is precisely analogous to that which has swept away from the philosophy of mathematics the useless menagerie of metaphysical monsters with which it used to be infested.

VI. CONSTRUCTIONS VERSUS INFERENCES

Before proceeding to analyze and explain the ambiguities of the word "place", a few general remarks on method are desirable. The supreme maxim in scientific philosophizing is this:

> *Wherever possible, logical constructions are to be substituted for inferred entities.*

Some examples of the substitution of construction for inference in the realm of mathematical philosophy may serve to elucidate the uses of this maxim. Take first the case of irrationals. In old days, irrationals were inferred as the supposed limits of series of rationals which had no rational limit; but the objection to this procedure was that it left the existence of irrationals merely optative, and for this reason the stricter methods of the present day no longer tolerate such a definition. We now define an irrational number as a certain class of ratios, thus constructing it logically by means of ratios, instead of arriving at it by a doubtful inference from them. Take again the case of cardinal numbers. Two equally numerous collections appear to have something in common: this something is supposed to be their cardinal number. But so long as the cardinal number is inferred from the collections, not constructed in terms of them, its existence must remain in doubt, unless in virtue of a metaphysical postulate *ad hoc*. By defining the cardinal number of a given collection as the class of all equally numerous collections, we avoid the necessity of this metaphysical postulate, and thereby remove a needless element of doubt from the philosophy of arithmetic. A similar method, as I have shown elsewhere, can be applied to classes themselves, which need not be supposed to have any metaphysical reality, but can be regarded as symbolically constructed fictions.

The method by which the construction proceeds is closely analogous in these and all similar cases. Given a set of propositions nominally dealing with the supposed inferred entities, we observe the properties which are required of the supposed entities in order to make these propositions true. By dint of a little logical ingenuity, we then construct some logical function of less hypothetical entities which has the requisite properties. This constructed function we substitute for the supposed inferred entities, and thereby obtain a new and less doubtful interpretation of the body of propo-
10 sitions in question. This method, so fruitful in the philosophy of mathematics, will be found equally applicable in the philosophy of physics, where, I do not doubt, it would have been applied long ago but for the fact that all who have studied this subject hitherto have been completely ignorant of mathematical logic. I myself cannot claim originality in the application of this method to physics, since I owe the suggestion and the stimulus for its application entirely to my friend and collaborator Dr. Whitehead, who is engaged in applying it to the more mathematical portions of the region intermediate between sense-data and the points, instants and particles of physics.
20   A complete application of the method which substitutes constructions for inferences would exhibit matter wholly in terms of sense-data, and even, we may add, of the sense-data of a single person, since the sense-data of others cannot be known without some element of inference. This, however, must remain for the present an ideal, to be approached as nearly as possible, but to be reached, if at all, only after a long preliminary labour of which as yet we can only see the very beginning. The inferences which are unavoidable can, however, be subjected to certain guiding principles. In the first place they should always be made perfectly explicit, and should be formulated in the most general manner possible. In the second place the inferred entities
30 should, whenever this can be done, be similar to those whose existence is given, rather than, like the Kantian *Ding an sich*, something wholly remote from the data which nominally support the inference. The inferred entities which I shall allow myself are of two kinds: (a) the sense-data of other people, in favour of which there is the evidence of testimony, resting ultimately upon the analogical argument in favour of minds other than my own; (b) the "sensibilia" which would appear from places where there happen to be no minds, and which I suppose to be real although they are no one's data. Of these two classes of inferred entities, the first will probably be allowed to pass unchallenged. It would give me the greatest satisfaction to
40 be able to dispense with it, and thus establish physics upon a solipsistic basis; but those—and I fear they are the majority—in whom the human affections are stronger than the desire for logical economy, will, no doubt, not share my desire to render solipsism scientifically satisfactory. The

second class of inferred entities raises much more serious questions. It may be thought monstrous to maintain that a thing can present any appearance at all in a place where no sense organs and nervous structure exist through which it could appear. I do not myself feel the monstrosity; nevertheless I should regard these supposed appearances only in the light of a hypothetical scaffolding, to be used while the edifice of physics is being raised, though possibly capable of being removed as soon as the edifice is completed. These "sensibilia" which are not data to anyone are therefore to be taken rather as an illustrative hypothesis and as an aid in preliminary statement than as a dogmatic part of the philosophy of physics in its final form.   10

VII. PRIVATE SPACE AND THE SPACE OF PERSPECTIVES

We have now to explain the ambiguity in the word "place", and how it comes that two places of different sorts are associated with every sense-datum, namely the place *at* which it is and the place *from* which it is perceived. The theory to be advocated is closely analogous to Leibniz's monadology, from which it differs chiefly in being less smooth and tidy.

The first fact to notice is that, so far as can be discovered, no sensibile is ever a datum to two people at once. The things seen by two different people are often closely similar, so similar that the same *words* can be used to denote them, without which communication with others concerning sensible ob-   20 jects would be impossible. But, in spite of this similarity, it would seem that some difference always arises from difference in the point of view. Thus each person, so far as his sense-data are concerned, lives in a private world. This private world contains its own space, or rather spaces, for it would seem that only experience teaches us to correlate the space of sight with the space of touch and with the various other spaces of other senses. This multiplicity of private spaces, however, though interesting to the psychologist, is of no great importance in regard to our present problem, since a merely solipsistic experience enables us to correlate them into the one private space which embraces all our own sense-data. The place *at*   30 which a sense-datum is, is a place in private space. This place therefore is different from any place in the private space of another percipient. For if we assume, as logical economy demands, that all position is relative, a place is only definable by the things in or around it, and therefore the same place cannot occur in two private worlds which have no common constituent. The question, therefore, of combining what we call different appearances of the same thing in the same place does not arise, and the fact that a given object appears to different spectators to have different shapes and colours affords no argument against the physical reality of all these shapes and colours.

In addition to the private spaces belonging to the private worlds of   40 different percipients, there is, however, another space, in which one whole private world counts as a point, or at least as a spatial unit. This might be described as the space of points of view, since each private world may be regarded as the appearance which the universe presents from a certain point of view. I prefer, however, to speak of it as the space of *perspectives*, in order to obviate the suggestion that a private world is only real when someone views it. And for the same reason, when I wish to speak of a private world without assuming a percipient, I shall call it a "perspective".

We have now to explain how the different perspectives are ordered in one space. This is effected by means of the correlated "sensibilia" which are 10 regarded as the appearances, in different perspectives, of one and the same thing. By moving, and by testimony, we discover that two different perspectives, though they cannot both contain the same "sensibilia", may nevertheless contain very similar ones; and the spatial order of a certain group of "sensibilia" in a private space of one perspective is found to be identical with, or very similar to, the spatial order of the correlated "sensibilia" in the private space of another perspective. In this way one "sensibile" in one perspective is correlated with one "sensibile" in another. Such correlated "sensibilia" will be called "appearances of one thing". In Leibniz's monadology, since each monad mirrored the whole universe, there was 20 in each perspective a "sensibile" which was an appearance of each thing. In our system of perspectives, we make no such assumption of completeness. A given thing will have appearances in some perspectives, but presumably not in certain others. The "thing" being defined as the class of its appearances, if κ is the class of perspectives in which a certain thing θ appears, then θ is a member of the multiplicative class of κ, κ being a class of mutually exclusive classes of "sensibilia". And similarly a perspective is a member of the multiplicative class of the things which appear in it.

The arrangement of perspectives in a space is effected by means of the differences between the appearances of a given thing in the various perspec- 30 tives. Suppose, say, that a certain penny appears in a number of different perspectives; in some it looks larger and in some smaller, in some it looks circular, in others it presents the appearance of an ellipse of varying eccentricity. We may collect together all those perspectives in which the appearance of the penny is circular. These we will place on one straight line, ordering them in a series by the variations in the apparent size of the penny. Those perspectives in which the penny appears as a straight line of a certain thickness will similarly be placed upon a plane (though in this case there will be many different perspectives in which the penny is of the same size; when one arrangement is completed these will form a circle concentric with the 40 penny), and ordered as before by the apparent size of the penny. By such means, all those perspectives in which the penny presents a visual appearance can be arranged in a three-dimensional spatial order. Experience shows that the same spatial order of perspectives would have resulted if, instead of the penny, we had chosen any other thing which appeared in all the perspectives in question, or any other method of utilizing the differences between the appearances of the same things in different perspectives. It is this empirical fact which has made it possible to construct the one all-embracing space of physics.

The space whose construction has just been explained, and whose elements are whole perspectives, will be called "perspective-space".

VIII. THE PLACING OF "THINGS" AND "SENSIBILIA" IN PERSPECTIVE SPACE

The world which we have so far constructed is a world of six dimensions, 10 since it is a three-dimensional series of perspectives, each of which is itself three-dimensional. We have now to explain the correlation between the perspective space and the various private spaces contained within the various perspectives severally. It is by means of this correlation that the one three-dimensional space of physics is constructed; and it is because of the unconscious performance of this correlation that the distinction between perspective space and the percipient's private space has been blurred, with disastrous results for the philosophy of physics. Let us revert to our penny: the perspectives in which the penny appears larger are regarded as being nearer to the penny than those in which it appears smaller, but as far as 20 experience goes the apparent size of the penny will not grow beyond a certain limit, namely, that where (as we say) the penny is so near the eye that if it were any nearer it could not be seen. By touch we may prolong the series until the penny touches the eye, but no further. If we have been travelling along a line of perspectives in the previously defined sense, we may, however, by imagining the penny removed, prolong the line of perspectives by means, say, of another penny; and the same may be done with any other line of perspectives defined by means of the penny. All these lines meet in a certain place, that is, in a certain perspective. This perspective will be defined as "the place where the penny is". 30

It is now evident in what sense two places in constructed physical space are associated with a given "sensibile". There is first the place which is the perspective of which the "sensibile" is a member. This is the place *from* which the "sensibile" appears. Secondly there is the place where the thing is of which the "sensibile" is a member, in other words an appearance; this is the place *at* which the "sensibile" appears. The "sensibile" which is a member of one perspective is correlated with another perspective, namely, that which is the place where the thing is of which the "sensibile" is an appearance. To the psychologist the "place from which" is the more interesting, and the "sensibile" accordingly appears to him subjective and 40 where the percipient is. To the physicist the "place at which" is the more interesting, and the "sensibile" accordingly appears to him physical and external. The causes, limits and partial justification of each of these two apparently incompatible views are evident from the above duplicity of places associated with a given "sensibile".

We have seen that we can assign to a physical thing a place in the perspective space. In this way different parts of our body acquire positions in perspective space, and therefore there is a meaning (whether true or false need not much concern us) in saying that the perspective to which our sense-data belong is inside our head. Since our mind is correlated with the
10 perspective to which our sense-data belong, we may regard this perspective as being the position of our mind in perspective space. If, therefore, this perspective is, in the above defined sense, inside our head, there is a good meaning for the statement that the mind is in the head. We can now say of the various appearances of a given thing that some of them are nearer to the thing than others; those are nearer which belong to perspectives that are nearer to "the place where the thing is". We can thus find a meaning, true or false, for the statement that more is to be learnt about a thing by examining it close to than by viewing it from a distance. We can also find a meaning for the phrase "the things which intervene between the subject and a thing of
20 which an appearance is a datum to him". One reason often alleged for the subjectivity of sense-data is that the appearance of a thing may change when we find it hard to suppose that the thing itself has changed—for example, when the change is due to our shutting our eyes, or to our screwing them up so as to make the thing look double. If the thing is defined as the class of its appearances (which is the definition adopted above), there is of course necessarily *some* change in the thing whenever any one of its appearances changes. Nevertheless there is a very important distinction between two different ways in which the appearances may change. If after looking at a thing I shut my eyes, the appearance of my eyes changes in every perspec-
30 tive in which there is such an appearance, whereas most of the appearances of the thing still remain unchanged. We may say, as a matter of definition, that a thing changes when, however near to the thing an appearance of it may be, there are changes in appearances as near as, or still nearer to, the thing. On the other hand we shall say that the change is in some other thing if all appearances of the thing which are at not more than a certain distance from the thing remain unchanged, while only comparatively distant appear-ances of the thing are altered. From this consideration we are naturally led to the consideration of *matter*, which must be our next topic.

IX. THE DEFINITION OF MATTER

40 We defined the "physical thing" as the class of its appearances, but this can hardly be taken as a definition of matter. We want to be able to express the

fact that the appearance of a thing in a given perspective is causally affected
by the matter between the thing and the perspective. We have found a
meaning for "between a thing and a perspective". But we want matter to be
something other than the whole class of appearances of a thing, in order to
state the influence of matter on appearances.

We commonly assume that the information we get about a thing is more
accurate when the thing is nearer. Far off, we see it is a man; then we see it is
Jones; then we see he is smiling. Complete accuracy would only be attainable as a limit: if the appearances of Jones as we approach him tend towards a
limit, that limit may be taken to be what Jones really is. It is obvious that 10
from the point of view of physics the appearances of a thing close to "count"
more than the appearances far off. We may therefore set up the following
tentative definition:

The *matter* of a given thing is the limit of its appearances as their distance
from the thing diminishes.

It seems probable that there is something in this definition, but it is not
quite satisfactory, because empirically there is no such limit to be obtained
from sense-data. The definition will have to be eked out by constructions
and definitions. But probably it suggests the right direction in which to
look.
                                                                          20
We are now in a position to understand in outline the reverse journey
from matter to sense-data which is performed by physics. The appearance
of a thing in a given perspective is a function of the matter composing the
thing and of the intervening matter. The appearance of a thing is altered by
intervening smoke or mist, by blue spectacles or by alterations in the
sense-organs or nerves of the percipient (which also must be reckoned as
part of the intervening medium). The nearer we approach to the thing, the
less its appearance is affected by the intervening matter. As we travel further
and further from the thing, its appearances diverge more and more from
their initial character; and the causal laws of their divergence are to be stated 30
in terms of the matter which lies between them and the thing. Since the
appearances at very small distances are less affected by causes other than the
thing itself, we come to think that the limit towards which these appearances tend as the distance diminishes is what the thing "really is", as
opposed to what it merely seems to be. This, together with its necessity for
the statement of causal laws, seems to be the source of the entirely erroneous
feeling that matter is more "real" than sense-data.

Consider for example the infinite divisibility of matter. In looking at a
given thing and approaching it, one sense-datum will become several, and
each of these will again divide. Thus *one* appearance may represent *many* 40
things, and to this process there seems no end. Hence in the limit, when we
approach indefinitely near to the thing, there will be an indefinite number of
units of matter corresponding to what, at a finite distance, is only one

appearance. This is how infinite divisibility arises.

The whole causal efficacy of a thing resides in its matter. This is in some sense an empirical fact, but it would be hard to state it precisely, because "causal efficacy" is difficult to define.

What can be known empirically about the matter of a thing is only approximate, because we cannot get to know the appearances of the thing from very small distances, and cannot accurately infer the limit of these appearances. But it *is* inferred *approximately* by means of the appearances we can observe. It then turns out that these appearances can be exhibited by
10 physics as a function of the matter in our immediate neighbourhood; e.g. the visual appearance of a distant object is a function of the light-waves that reach the eyes. This leads to confusions of thought, but offers no real difficulty.

One appearance, of a visible object for example, is not sufficient to determine its other simultaneous appearances, although it goes a certain distance towards determining them. The determination of the hidden structure of a thing, so far as it is possible at all, can only be effected by means of elaborate dynamical inferences.

X. TIME[2]

20 It seems that the one all-embracing time is a construction, like the one all-embracing space. Physics itself has become conscious of this fact through the discussions connected with relativity.

Between two perspectives which both belong to one person's experience, there will be a direct time-relation of before and after. This suggests a way of dividing history in the same sort of way as it is divided by different experiences, but without introducing experience or anything mental: we may define a "biography" as everything that is (directly) earlier or later than, or simultaneous with, a given "sensibile". This will give a series of perspectives, which *might* all form parts of one person's experience, though
30 it is not necessary that all or any of them should actually do so. By this means, the history of the world is divided into a number of mutually exclusive biographies.

We have now to correlate the times in the different biographies. The natural thing would be to say that the appearances of a given (momentary) thing in two different perspectives belonging to different biographies are to be taken as simultaneous; but this is not convenient. Suppose A shouts to B, and B replies as soon as he hears A's shout. Then between A's hearing of his

---

2 On this subject, compare *A Theory of Time and Space*, by Mr. A. A. Robb (Camb. Univ. Press), which first suggested to me the views advocated here, though I have, for present
40 purposes, omitted what is most interesting and novel in his theory. Mr. Robb has given a sketch of his theory in a pamphlet with the same title (Heffer and Sons, Cambridge, 1913).

own shout and his hearing of B's there is an interval; thus if we made A's and B's hearing of the same shout exactly simultaneous with each other, we should have events exactly simultaneous with a given event but not with each other. To obviate this, we assume a "velocity of sound". That is, we assume that the time when B hears A's shout is half-way between the time when A hears his own shout and the time when he hears B's. In this way the correlation is effected.

What has been said about sound applies of course equally to light. The general principle is that the appearances, in different perspectives, which are to be grouped together as constituting what a certain thing is at a certain moment, are not to be all regarded as being at that moment. On the contrary they spread outward from the thing with various velocities according to the nature of the appearances. Since no *direct* means exist of correlating the time in one biography with the time in another, this temporal grouping of the appearances belonging to a given thing at a given moment is in part conventional. Its motive is partly to secure the verification of such maxims as that events which are exactly simultaneous with the same event are exactly simultaneous with one another, partly to secure covenience in the formulation of causal laws.

XI. THE PERSISTENCE OF THINGS AND MATTER

Apart from any of the fluctuating hypotheses of physics, three main problems arise in connecting the world of physics with the world of sense, namely:

1. the construction of a single space;
2. the construction of a single time;
3. the construction of permanent things or matter.

We have already considered the first and second of these problems; it remains to consider the third.

We have seen how correlated appearances in different perspectives are combined to form one "thing" at one moment in the all-embracing time of physics. We have now to consider how appearances at different times are combined as belonging to one "thing", and how we arrive at the persistent "matter" of physics. The assumption of permanent substance, which technically underlies the procedure of physics, cannot of course be regarded as metaphysically legitimate: just as the one thing simultaneously seen by many people is a construction, so the one thing seen at different times by the same or different people must be a construction, being in fact nothing but a certain grouping of certain "sensibilia".

We have seen that the momentary state of a "thing" is an assemblage of "sensibilia", in different perspectives, not all simultaneous in the one constructed time, but spreading out from "the place where the thing is" with velocities depending upon the nature of the "sensibilia". The time *at* which the "thing" is in this state is the lower limit of the times at which these appearances occur. We have now to consider what leads us to speak of another set of appearances as belonging to the same "thing" at a different time.

For this purpose, we may, at least to begin with, confine ourselves within a single biography. If we can always say when two "sensibilia" in a given biography are appearances of one thing, then, since we have seen how to connect "sensibilia" in different biographies as appearances of the same momentary state of a thing, we shall have all that is necessary for the complete construction of the history of a thing.

It is to be observed, to begin with, that the identity of a thing for common sense is not always correlated with the identity of matter for physics. A human body is one persisting thing for common sense, but for physics its matter is constantly changing. We may say, broadly, that the common-sense conception is based upon continuity in appearances at the ordinary distances of sense-data, while the physical conception is based upon the continuity of appearances at very small distances from the thing. It is probable that the common-sense conception is not capable of complete precision. Let us therefore concentrate our attention upon the conception of the persistence of matter in physics.

The first characteristic of two appearances of the same piece of matter at different times is *continuity*. The two appearances must be connected by a series of intermediaries, which, if time and space form compact series, must themselves form a compact series. The colour of the leaves is different in autumn from what it is in summer; but we believe that the change occurs gradually, and that, if the colours are different at two given times, there are intermediate times at which the colours are intermediate between those at the given times.

But there are two considerations that are important as regards continuity.

First, it is largely hypothetical. We do not observe any one thing continuously, and it is merely a hypothesis to assume that, while we are not observing it, it passes through conditions intermediate between those in which it is perceived. During uninterrupted observation, it is true, continuity is nearly verified; but even here, when motions are very rapid, as in the case of explosions, the continuity is not actually capable of direct verification. Thus we can only say that the sense-data are found to *permit* a hypothetical complement of "sensibilia" such as will preserve continuity, and that therefore there *may* be such a complement. Since, however, we have already made such use of hypothetical "sensibilia", we will let this point pass, and admit such "sensibilia" as are required to preserve continuity.

Secondly, continuity is not a sufficient criterion of material identity. It is true that in many cases, such as rocks, mountains, tables, chairs, etc., where the appearances change slowly, continuity is sufficient, but in other cases, such as the parts of an approximately homogeneous fluid, it fails us utterly. We can travel by sensibly continuous gradations from any one drop of the sea at any one time to any other drop at any other time. We infer the motions of sea-water from the effects of the current, but they cannot be inferred from direct sensible observation together with the assumption of continuity.

The characteristic required in addition to continuity is conformity with the laws of dynamics. Starting from what common sense regards as persistent things, and making only such modifications as from time to time seem reasonable, we arrive at assemblages of "sensibilia" which are found to obey certain simple laws, namely those of dynamics. By regarding "sensibilia" at different times as belonging to the same piece of matter, we are able to define *motion*, which presupposes the assumption or construction of something persisting throughout the time of the motion. The motions which are regarded as occurring, during a period in which all the "sensibilia" and the times of their appearance are given, will be different according to the manner in which we combine "sensibilia" at different times as belonging to the same piece of matter. Thus even when the whole history of the world is given in every particular, the question what motions take place is still to a certain extent arbitrary even after the assumption of continuity. Experience shows that it is possible to determine motions in such a way as to satisfy the laws of dynamics, and that this determination, roughly and on the whole, is fairly in agreement with the common-sense opinions about persistent things. This determination, therefore, is adopted, and leads to a criterion by which we can determine, sometimes practically, sometimes only theoretically, whether two appearances at different times are to be regarded as belonging to the same piece of matter. The persistence of all matter throughout all time can, I imagine, be secured by definition.

To recommend this conclusion, we must consider what it is that is proved by the empirical success of physics. What is proved is that its hypotheses, though unverifiable where they go beyond sense-data, are at no point in contradiction with sense-data, but, on the contrary, are ideally such as to render all sense-data calculable when a sufficient collection of "sensibilia" is given. Now physics has found it empirically possible to collect sense-data into series, each series being regarded as belonging to one "thing", and behaving, with regard to the laws of physics, in a way in which series not belonging to one thing would in general not behave. If it is to be unambiguous whether two appearances belong to the same thing or not, there must be only one way of grouping appearances so that the resulting things obey the laws of physics. It would be very difficult to prove that this is the case, but for our present purposes we may let this point pass, and assume that there is only one way. Thus we may lay down the following definition: *Physical things are those series of appearances whose matter obeys the laws of physics.* That such series exist is an empirical fact, which constitutes the verifiability of physics.

XII. ILLUSIONS, HALLUCINATIONS, AND DREAMS

It remains to ask how, in our system, we are to find a place for sense-data which apparently fail to have the usual connection with the world of physics. Such sense-data are of various kinds, requiring somewhat different
10 treatment. But all are of the sort that would be called "unreal", and therefore, before embarking upon the discussion, certain logical remarks must be made upon the conceptions of reality and unreality.

Mr. A. Wolf[3] says:

> The conception of mind as a system of transparent activities is, I think, also untenable because of its failure to account for the very possibility of dreams and hallucinations. It seems impossible to realise how a bare, transparent activity can be directed to what is not there, to apprehend what is not given.

This statement is one which, probably, most people would endorse. But
20 it is open to two objections. First, it is difficult to see how an activity, however un-"transparent", can be directed towards a nothing: a term of a relation cannot be a mere nonentity. Secondly, no reason is given, and I am convinced that none can be given, for the assertion that dream-objects are not "there" and not "given". Let us take the second point first.

(1) The belief that dream-objects are not given comes, I think, from failure to distinguish, as regards waking life, between the sense-datum and the corresponding "thing". In dreams, there is no such corresponding "thing" as the dreamer supposes; if, therefore, the "thing" were given in waking life, as e.g. Meinong maintains,[4] then there would be a difference in
30 respect of givenness between dreams and waking life. But if, as we have maintained, what is given is never the thing, but merely one of the "sensibilia" which compose the thing, then what we apprehend in a dream is just as much given as what we apprehend in waking life.

Exactly the same argument applies as to the dream-objects being "there". They have their position in the private space of the perspective of the dreamer; where they fail is in their correlation with other private spaces and

3 "Natural Realism and Present Tendencies in Philosophy", *Proc. Arist. Soc.*, 1908–1909, p. 165.
4 *Die Erfahrungsgrundlagen unseres Wissens*, p. 28.

therefore with perspective space. But in the only sense in which "there" can be a datum, they are "there" just as truly as any of the sense-data of waking life.

(2) The conception of "illusion" or "unreality", and the correlative conception of "reality", are generally used in a way which embodies profound logical confusions. Words that go in pairs, such as "real" and "unreal", "existent" and "non-existent", "valid" and "invalid", etc., are all derived from the one fundamental pair, "true" and "false". Now "true" and "false" are applicable only—except in derivative significations—to *propositions*. Thus wherever the above pairs can be significantly applied, we must be dealing either with propositions or with such incomplete phrases as only acquire meaning when put into a context which, with them, forms a proposition. Thus such pairs of words can be applied to *descriptions*,[5] but not to proper names: in other words, they have no application whatever to data, but only to entities or non-entities described in terms of data.

Let us illustrate by the terms "existence" and "non-existence". Given any datum x, it is meaningless either to assert or to deny that x "exists". We might be tempted to say: "Of course x exists, for otherwise it could not be a datum." But such a statement is really meaningless, although it is significant and true to say "My present sense-datum exists", and it may also be true that "x is my present sense-datum". The inference from these two propositions to "x exists" is one which seems irresistible to people unaccustomed to logic; yet the apparent proposition inferred is not merely false, but strictly meaningless. To say "My present sense-datum exists" is to say (roughly): "There is an object of which 'my present sense-datum' is a description." But we cannot say: "There is an object of which 'x' is a description", because "x" is (in the case we are supposing) a name, not a description. Dr. Whitehead and I have explained this point fully elsewhere (*loc. cit.*) with the help of symbols, without which it is hard to understand; I shall not therefore here repeat the demonstration of the above propositions, but shall proceed with their application to our present problem.

The fact that "existence" is only applicable to descriptions is concealed by the use of what are grammatically proper names in a way which really transforms them into descriptions. It is, for example, a legitimate question whether Homer existed; but here "Homer" means "the author of the Homeric poems", and is a description. Similarly we may ask whether God exists; but then "God" means "the Supreme Being" or "the *ens realissimum*" or whatever other description we may prefer. If "God" were a proper name, God would have to be a datum; and then no question could arise as to His existence. The distinction between existence and other

---

5 Cf. *Principia Mathematica*, Vol. I, *14, and Introduction, Chap. III. For the definition of existence, cf. *14.02.

predicates, which Kant obscurely felt, is brought to light by the theory of descriptions, and is seen to remove "existence" altogether from the fundamental notions of metaphysics.

What has been said about "existence" applies equally to "reality", which may, in fact, be taken as synonymous with "existence". Concerning the immediate objects in illusions, hallucinations, and dreams, it is meaningless to ask whether they "exist" or are "real". There they are, and that ends the matter. But we may legitimately inquire as to the existence or reality of "things" or other "sensibilia" inferred from such objects. It is the unreality of these "things" and other "sensibilia", together with a failure to notice that they are not data, which has led to the view that the objects of dreams are unreal.

We may now apply these considerations in detail to the stock arguments against realism, though what is to be said will be mainly a repetition of what others have said before.

(1) We have first the variety of normal appearances, supposed to be incompatible. This is the case of the different shapes and colours which a given thing presents to different spectators. Locke's water which seems both hot and cold belongs to this class of cases. Our system of different perspectives fully accounts for these cases, and shows that they afford no argument against realism.

(2) We have cases where the correlation between different senses is unusual. The bent stick in water belongs here. People say it looks bent but is straight: this only means that it is straight to the touch, though bent to sight. There is no "illusion", but only a false inference, if we think that the stick would feel bent to the touch. The stick would look just as bent in a photograph, and, as Mr. Gladstone used to say, "the photograph cannot lie".[6] The case of seeing double also belongs here, though in this case the cause of the unusual correlation is physiological, and would therefore not operate in a photograph. It is a mistake to ask whether the "thing" is duplicated when we see it double. The "thing" is a whole system of "sensibilia", and it is only those visual "sensibilia" which are data to the percipient that are duplicated. The phenomenon has a purely physiological explanation; indeed, in view of our having two eyes, it is in less need of explanation than the single visual sense-datum which we normally obtain from the things on which we focus.

(3) We come now to cases like dreams, which may, at the moment of dreaming, contain nothing to arouse suspicion, but are condemned on the ground of their supposed incompatibility with earlier and later data. Of course it often happens that dream-objects fail to behave in the accustomed

---

6 *Cf.* Edwin B. Holt, "The Place of Illusory Experience in a Realistic World", *The New Realism*, p. 305, both on this point and as regards *seeing double*.

manner: heavy objects fly, solid objects melt, babies turn into pigs or undergo even greater changes. But none of these unusual occurrences *need* happen in a dream, and it is not on account of such occurrences that dream-objects are called "unreal". It is their lack of continuity with the dreamer's past and future that makes him, when he wakes, condemn them; and it is their lack of correlation with other private worlds that makes others condemn them. Omitting the latter ground, our reason for condemning them is that the "things" which we infer from them cannot be combined according to the laws of physics with the "things" inferred from waking sense-data. This might be used to condemn the laws of physics; but it is simpler to use it to condemn the "things" inferred from the data of dreams. Dream-data are no doubt appearances of "things", but not of such "things" as the dreamer supposes. I have no wish to combat psychological theories of dreams, such as those of the psycho-analysts. But there certainly are cases where (whatever psychological causes may contribute) the presence of physical causes also is very evident. For instance, a door banging may produce a dream of a naval engagement, with images of battleships and sea and smoke. The whole dream will be an appearance of the door banging, but owing to the peculiar condition of the body (especially the brain) during sleep, this appearance is not that expected to be produced by a door banging, and thus the dreamer is led to entertain false beliefs. But his sense-data are still physical, and are such as a completed physics would include and calculate.

(4) The last class of illusions are those which cannot be discovered within one person's experience, except through the discovery of discrepancies with the experiences of others. Dreams might conceivably belong to this class, if they were jointed sufficiently neatly into waking life; but the chief instances are recurrent sensory hallucinations of the kind that lead to insanity. What makes the patient, in such cases, become what others call insane is the fact that, within his own experience, there is nothing to show that the hallucinatory sense-data do not have the usual kind of connection with "sensibilia" in other perspectives. Of course he may learn this through testimony, but he probably finds it simpler to suppose that the testimony is untrue and that he is being wilfully deceived. There is, so far as I can see, no theoretical criterion by which the patient can decide, in such a case, between the two equally satisfactory hypotheses of his madness and of his friends' mendacity.

From the above instances it would appear that abnormal sense-data, of the kind which we regard as deceptive, have intrinsically just the same status as any others, but differ as regards their correlations or causal connections with other "sensibilia" and with "things". Since the usual correlations and connections become part of our unreflective expectations, and even seem, except to the psychologist, to form part of our data, it comes to be thought, mistakenly, that in such cases the data are unreal, whereas they are merely the causes of false inferences. The fact that correlations and connections of unusual kinds occur adds to the difficulty of inferring things from sense and of expressing physics in terms of sense-data. But the unusualness would seem to be always physically or physiologically explicable, and therefore raises only a complication, not a philosophical objection.

I conclude, therefore, that no valid objection exists to the view which regards sense-data as part of the actual substance of the physical world, and that, on the other hand, this view is the only one which accounts for the empirical verifiability of physics. In the present paper, I have given only a rough preliminary sketch. In particular, the part played by *time* in the construction of the physical world is, I think, more fundamental than would appear from the above account. I should hope that, with further elaboration, the part played by unperceived "sensibilia" could be indefinitely diminished, probably by invoking the history of a "thing" to eke out the inferences derivable from its momentary appearance.

2

Mysticism and Logic [1914]

THIS PAPER WAS published first in *The Hibbert Journal*, 12 (July 1914): 780–803. Four years later Russell reprinted it, in a slightly revised form, in *Mysticism and Logic, and Other Essays* (1918).

The first mention of this essay is found in a letter to Lady Ottoline Morrell of 9 January 1914:

> I have not got anything actually done today, because I am contemplating a lecture on "Mysticism and Logic". I have to have a popular lecture to give in America, and I feel as if I could do something good on that subject. I know now what I really believe about it—I no longer oscillate with changing moods. If I could do it right, it might be very good. (#961)

"I have nearly finished my lecture on Mysticism and Logic," he reported the very next evening, "but it is not as good as it ought to be. I shall have to alter it" (#962, pmk. 10 Jan.). In a letter whose number (#919) is out of sequence but which must have been written during the evening of 11 January, the only "Sunday evg." which fits the contents of other letters mentioning both this essay and his preface to Poincaré's *Science and Method* (3), he wrote: "I have finished my lecture on 'Mysticism and Logic'. It is not very good—it is mostly made up of scraps from the other lectures—but it will have to do." In an undated letter written "Thursday mg." (which as the next letter to be quoted will show must be 15 January 1914) he wrote that he was re-working the essay. "I am re-writing my paper on mysticism and logic, making it much more what I hoped. I was in too much of a hurry before. It doesn't aim at eloquence, but only at careful exact statement" (#968). He went on to say that she was mistaken in thinking him depressed. He detailed what has been on his mind and concluded: "I think perhaps too I was disappointed about 'Mysticism and Logic', but that too is all right now." That evening the work continued:

> I have all but finished my paper on mysticism and logic. It is very much improved, though still far short of what it ought to be. But I think it is interesting enough to do as a lecture. I will give it you when you come home. (#969, pmk. 15 Jan.)

The next morning he breathed a sigh of relief.

> What has made America such a weight is having to produce a body of work
> by a given date. I haven't the journalist's faculty for turning things out to
> order, and I get worried for fear of not getting any ideas in time. But now all
> that load is off my mind: I finished "mysticism and logic" at midnight last
> night. It is not so good as it ought to be, but it will do. It is sober, careful, and
> balanced, not eloquent.   (#970, pmk. 16 Jan.)

Although he had written "Mysticism and Logic" for his American visit, he read it to
two groups in Cambridge before he sailed. The first occasion was a meeting in
Queens' College, Cambridge, on 24 January. "The Queens' people altered my date
to tonight, so I escaped Miss Jones, and read my paper on mysticism and logic. They
seemed nice people, but not clever—mostly going into the Church" (#975, pmk. 24
Jan.). His relief at escaping E. E. Constance Jones refers to a meeting of the Moral
Sciences Club: "poor Miss Jones (Principal of Girton, inventor of a new law of
thought, motherly, prissy, and utterly stupid) is reading" (#937, undated but 19
Jan.). The second reading took place on 1 March to the Heretics, a Cambridge
society which discussed religious matters (#995, pmk. 26 Feb.). An advertisement
for this meeting was carried in *The Cambridge Magazine* for 28 February.

In the United States he read it at least three times. On Saturday, 4 April, he made a
weekend visit, for which he was paid £8, to two women, Miss Lowndes and Miss
Rees, who kept a school in Connecticut. "I read my paper on Mysticism and Logic to
an assembled crowd of neighbours Saturday night. Greenwich, where they live, is a
weekend place, where Rockefellers and other millionaires have places. All the
people seemed odious" (#1014, 6 April). On 14 April he read it at Wellesley College;
he admired the campus, "but the mental atmosphere struck me as goody-goody"
(#1017, 15 April). He also read it to a gathering in Madison, Wisconsin.

When Russell remarked that this paper "is mostly made up of scraps from the
other lectures" (#919) he was referring to his Lowell Lectures which were published
as *Our Knowledge of the External World* (1914). This essay depends heavily upon that
book; indeed, the section called "Reason and Intuition" appears verbatim in the
book. (The Textual Notes detail this and other overlapping passages.) The tension
between the mystical and the logical is a prominent theme of the book and the
principal theme of this paper. It was a tension Russell felt within himself, and on
which he had often reflected. As early as 13 March 1912 he had written Lady
Ottoline: "Some part of me is left out now whatever I do, intellect one way and
mystic vision the other. They ought *both* to come in" (#386). A remark about the
tension between mysticism and logic is made in passing in his discussion of Plato's
theories in the chapter (9) on universals in *The Problems of Philosophy* (1912). It was,
therefore, a theme of long-standing concern, although the present paper is his first
attempt to deal with it in print.

Russell sent the manuscript to L. P. Jacks, the editor of *The Hibbert Journal*,
shortly after it was finished. Jacks wrote Russell on 31 January 1914 and asked him
to shorten the essay because it was longer than was usual for the magazine. Russell

refused his request. In a letter of 28 April Jacks accepted Russell's refusal: "This is a length we admit only in the case of exceptionally valuable articles—as yours is." Later, Jacks returned the manuscript to Russell who may have given it to Lucy Donnelly. In a letter to her written on The Twentieth Century Limited on his way to Chicago, 26 May 1914, he said: "You can keep the mysticism and logic for ever. I am glad you liked it." The manuscript has not been found among her papers.

Since Russell selected this essay as the title essay for his *Mysticism and Logic, and Other Essays*, and since he saw that book through the press, the 1918 version has been selected as copy-text. It has been read against *The Hibbert Journal* version and the results reported in the Textual Notes.

METAPHYSICS, OR THE attempt to conceive the world as a whole by means of thought, has been developed, from the first, by the union and conflict of two very different human impulses, the one urging men towards mysticism, the other urging them towards science. Some men have achieved greatness through one of these impulses alone, others through the other alone: in Hume, for example, the scientific impulse reigns quite unchecked, while in Blake a strong hostility to science coexists with profound mystic insight. But the greatest men who have been philosophers have felt the need both of science and of mysticism: the attempt to harmonize the two was what made their life, and what always must, for all its arduous uncertainty, make philosophy, to some minds, a greater thing than either science or religion.

Before attempting an explicit characterization of the scientific and the mystical impulses, I will illustrate them by examples from two philosophers whose greatness lies in the very intimate blending which they achieved. The two philosophers I mean are Heraclitus and Plato.

Heraclitus, as every one knows, was a believer in universal flux: time builds and destroys all things. From the few fragments that remain, it is not easy to discover how he arrived at his opinions, but there are some sayings that strongly suggest scientific observation as the source.

"The things that can be seen, heard, and learned", he says, "are what I prize the most." This is the language of the empiricist, to whom observation is the sole guarantee of truth. "The sun is new every day", is another fragment; and this opinion, in spite of its paradoxical character, is obviously inspired by scientific reflection, and no doubt seemed to him to obviate the difficulty of understanding how the sun can work its way underground from west to east during the night. Actual observation must also have suggested to him his central doctrine, that Fire is the one permanent substance, of which all visible things are passing phases. In combustion we see things change utterly, while their flame and heat rise up into the air and vanish.

"This world, which is the same for all," he says, "no one of gods or men has made; but it was ever, is now, and ever shall be, an ever-living Fire, with measures kindling, and measures going out."

"The transformations of Fire are, first of all, sea; and half of the sea is earth, half whirlwind."

This theory, though no longer one which science can accept, is nevertheless scientific in spirit. Science, too, might have inspired the famous saying to which Plato alludes: "You cannot step twice into the same rivers; for fresh waters are ever flowing in upon you." But we find also another statement among the extant fragments: "We step and do not step into the same rivers; we are and are not."

The comparison of this statement, which is mystical, with the one quoted by Plato, which is scientific, shows how intimately the two tendencies are blended in the system of Heraclitus. Mysticism is, in essence, little more than a certain intensity and depth of feeling in regard to what is believed about the universe; and this kind of feeling leads Heraclitus, on the basis of his science, to strangely poignant sayings concerning life and the world, such as:

"Time is a child playing draughts, the kingly power is a child's."

It is poetic imagination, not science, which presents Time as despotic lord of the world, with all the irresponsible frivolity of a child. It is mysticism, too, which leads Heraclitus to assert the identity of opposites: "Good and ill are one", he says; and again: "To God all things are fair and good and right, but men hold some things wrong and some right."

Much of mysticism underlies the ethics of Heraclitus. It is true that a scientific determinism alone might have inspired the statement: "Man's character is his fate"; but only a mystic would have said:

"Every beast is driven to the pasture with blows"; and again:

"It is hard to fight with one's heart's desire. Whatever it wishes to get, it purchases at the cost of soul"; and again:

"Wisdom is one thing. It is to know the thought by which all things are steered through all things."[1]

Examples might be multiplied, but those that have been given are enough to show the character of the man: the facts of science, as they appeared to him, fed the flame in his soul, and in its light he saw into the depths of the world by the reflection of his own dancing swiftly penetrating fire. In such a nature we see the true union of the mystic and the man of science—the highest eminence, as I think, that it is possible to achieve in the world of thought.

In Plato, the same twofold impulse exists, though the mystic impulse is distinctly the stronger of the two, and secures ultimate victory whenever the conflict is sharp. His description of the cave is the classical statement of belief in a knowledge and reality truer and more real than that of the senses:

Imagine a number of men living in an underground cavernous chamber, with an entrance open to the light, extending along the entire length of the cavern, in which they have been confined, from their childhood, with their legs and necks so shackled that they are obliged to sit still and look straight forwards, because their chains render it impossible for them to turn their heads round: and imagine a bright fire burning some way off, above and behind them, and an elevated roadway passing between the fire and the prisoners, with a low wall built along it, like the screens which conjurors put up in

[1] All the above quotations are from Burnet's *Early Greek Philosophy* (2nd ed., 1908), pp. 146–156.

front of their audience, and above which they exhibit their wonders.

I have it, he replied.

Also figure to yourself a number of persons walking behind this wall, and carrying with them statues of men, and images of other animals, wrought in wood and stone and all kinds of materials, together with various other articles, which overtop the wall; and, as you might expect, let some of the passers-by be talking, and others silent.

You are describing a strange scene, and strange prisoners.

They resemble us, I replied.

Now consider what would happen if the course of nature brought them a release from their fetters, and a remedy for their foolishness, in the following manner. Let us suppose that one of them has been released, and compelled suddenly to stand up, and turn his neck round and walk with open eyes towards the light; and let us suppose that he goes through all these actions with pain, and that the dazzling splendour renders him incapable of discerning those objects of which he used formerly to see the shadows. What answer should you expect him to make, if some one were to tell him that in those days he was watching foolish phantoms, but that now he is somewhat nearer to reality, and is turned towards things more real, and sees more correctly; above all, if he were to point out to him the several objects that are passing by, and question him, and compel him to answer what they are? Should you not expect him to be puzzled, and to regard his old visions as truer than the objects now forced upon his notice?

Yes, much truer....

Hence, I suppose, habit will be necessary to enable him to perceive objects in that upper world. At first he will be most successful in distinguishing shadows; then he will discern the reflections of men and other things in water, and afterwards the realities; and after this he will raise his eyes to encounter the light of the moon and stars, finding it less difficult to study the heavenly bodies and the heaven itself by night, than the sun and the sun's light by day.

Doubtless.

Last of all, I imagine, he will be able to observe and contemplate the nature of the sun, not as it *appears* in water or on alien ground, but as it *is* in itself in its own territory.

Of course.

His next step will be to draw the conclusion, that the sun is the author of the seasons and the years, and the guardian of all things in the visible world, and in a manner the cause of all those things which he and his companions used to see.

Obviously, this will be his next step....

Now this imaginary case, my dear Glaucon, you must apply in all
its parts to our former statements, by comparing the region which
the eye reveals, to the prison house, and the light of the fire therein to
the power of the sun: and if, by the upward ascent and the contemplation of the upper world, you understand the mounting of the soul
into the intellectual region, you will hit the tendency of my own
surmises, since you desire to be told what they are; though, indeed,
God only knows whether they are correct. But, be that as it may, the
view which I take of the subject is to the following effect. In the
world of knowledge, the essential Form of Good is the limit of our
enquiries, and can barely be perceived; but, when perceived, we
cannot help concluding that it is in every case the source of all that is
bright and beautiful,—in the visible world giving birth to light and
its master, and in the intellectual world dispensing, immediately and
with full authority, truth and reason;—and that whosoever would
act wisely, either in private or in public, must set this Form of Good
before his eyes.[2]

But in this passage, as throughout most of Plato's teaching, there is an
identification of the good with the truly real, which became embodied in the
philosophical tradition, and is still largely operative in our own day. In thus
allowing a legislative function to the good, Plato produced a divorce between philosophy and science, from which, in my opinion, both have
suffered ever since and are still suffering. The man of science, whatever his
hopes may be, must lay them aside while he studies nature; and the
philosopher, if he is to achieve truth, must do the same. Ethical considerations can only legitimately appear when the truth has been ascertained: they
can and should appear as determining our feeling towards the truth, and our
manner of ordering our lives in view of the truth, but not as themselves
dictating what the truth is to be.

There are passages in Plato—among those which illustrate the scientific
side of his mind—where he seems clearly aware of this. The most noteworthy is the one in which Socrates, as a young man, is explaining the theory of
ideas to Parmenides.

After Socrates has explained that there is an idea of the good, but not of
such things as hair and mud and dirt, Parmenides advises him "not to
despise even the meanest things", and this advice shows the genuine scientific temper. It is with this impartial temper that the mystic's apparent
insight into a higher reality and a hidden good has to be combined if
philosophy is to realize its greatest possibilities. And it is failure in this

2 *Republic*, 514–17, translated by Davies and Vaughan.

respect that has made so much of idealistic philosophy thin, lifeless, and insubstantial. It is only in marriage with the world that our ideals can bear fruit: divorced from it, they remain barren. But marriage with the world is not to be achieved by an ideal which shrinks from fact, or demands in advance that the world shall conform to its desires.

Parmenides himself is the source of a peculiarly interesting strain of mysticism which pervades Plato's thought—the mysticism which may be called "logical" because it is embodied in theories on logic. This form of mysticism, which appears, so far as the West is concerned, to have originated with Parmenides, dominates the reasonings of all the great mystical metaphysicians from his day to that of Hegel and his modern disciples. Reality, he says, is uncreated, indestructible, unchanging, indivisible; it is "immovable in the bonds of mighty chains, without beginning and without end; since coming into being and passing away have been driven afar, and true belief has cast them away". The fundamental principle of his inquiry is stated in a sentence which would not be out of place in Hegel: "Thou canst not know what is not—that is impossible—nor utter it; for it is the same thing that can be thought and that can be." And again: "It needs must be that what can be thought and spoken of is; for it is possible for it to be, and it is not possible for what is nothing to be." The impossibility of change follows from this principle; for what is past can be spoken of, and therefore, by the principle, still is.

Mystical philosophy, in all ages and in all parts of the world, is characterized by certain beliefs which are illustrated by the doctrines we have been considering.

There is, first, the belief in insight as against discursive analytic knowledge: the belief in a way of wisdom, sudden, penetrating, coercive, which is contrasted with the slow and fallible study of outward appearance by a science relying wholly upon the senses. All who are capable of absorption in an inward passion must have experienced at times the strange feeling of unreality in common objects, the loss of contact with daily things, in which the solidity of the outer world is lost, and the soul seems, in utter loneliness, to bring forth, out of its own depths, the mad dance of fantastic phantoms which have hitherto appeared as independently real and living. This is the negative side of the mystic's initiation: the doubt concerning common knowledge, preparing the way for the reception of what seems a higher wisdom. Many men to whom this negative experience is familiar do not pass beyond it, but for the mystic it is merely the gateway to an ampler world.

The mystic insight begins with the sense of a mystery unveiled, of a hidden wisdom now suddenly become certain beyond the possibility of a doubt. The sense of certainty and revelation comes earlier than any definite belief. The definite beliefs at which mystics arrive are the result of reflection upon the inarticulate experience gained in the moment of insight. Often,

beliefs which have no real connection with this moment become subsequently attracted into the central nucleus; thus in addition to the convictions which all mystics share, we find, in many of them, other convictions of
a more local and temporary character, which no doubt become amalgam-
ated with what was essentially mystical in virtue of their subjective certainty. We may ignore such inessential accretions, and confine ourselves to
the beliefs which all mystics share.

The first and most direct outcome of the moment of illumination is belief
in the possibility of a way of knowledge which may be called revelation or
insight or intuition, as contrasted with sense, reason, and analysis, which 10
are regarded as blind guides leading to the morass of illusion. Closely
connected with this belief is the conception of a Reality behind the world of
appearance and utterly different from it. This Reality is regarded with an
admiration often amounting to worship; it is felt to be always and
everywhere close at hand, thinly veiled by the shows of sense, ready, for the
receptive mind, to shine in its glory even through the apparent folly and
wickedness of Man. The poet, the artist, and the lover are seekers after that
glory: the haunting beauty that they pursue is the faint reflection of its sun.
But the mystic lives in the full light of the vision: what others dimly seek he
knows, with a knowledge beside which all other knowledge is ignorance. 20

The second characteristic of mysticism is its belief in unity, and its refusal
to admit opposition or division anywhere. We found Heraclitus saying
"good and ill are one"; and again he says, "the way up and the way down is
one and the same." The same attitude appears in the simultaneous assertion
of contradictory propositions, such as: "We step and do not step into the
same rivers; we are and are not." The assertion of Parmenides, that reality is
one and indivisible, comes from the same impulse towards unity. In Plato,
this impulse is less prominent, being held in check by his theory of ideas;
but it reappears, so far as his logic permits, in the doctrine of the primacy of
the Good. 30

A third mark of almost all mystical metaphysics is the denial of the reality
of Time. This is an outcome of the denial of division; if all is one, the
distinction of past and future must be illusory. We have seen this doctrine
prominent in Parmenides; and among moderns it is fundamental in the
systems of Spinoza and Hegel.

The last of the doctrines of mysticism which we have to consider is its
belief that all evil is mere appearance, an illusion produced by the divisions
and oppositions of the analytic intellect. Mysticism does not maintain that
such things as cruelty, for example, are good, but it denies that they are real:
they belong to that lower world of phantoms from which we are to be 40
liberated by the insight of the vision. Sometimes—for example in Hegel,
and at least verbally in Spinoza—not only evil, but good also, is regarded as
illusory, though nevertheless the emotional attitude towards what is held to

be Reality is such as would naturally be associated with the belief that Reality is good. What is, in all cases, ethically characteristic of mysticism is absence of indignation or protest, acceptance with joy, disbelief in the ultimate truth of the division into two hostile camps, the good and the bad. This attitude is a direct outcome of the nature of the mystical experience: with its sense of unity is associated a feeling of infinite peace. Indeed it may be suspected that the feeling of peace produces, as feelings do in dreams, the whole system of associated beliefs which make up the body of mystic doctrine. But this is a difficult question, and one on which it cannot be hoped that mankind will reach agreement.

Four questions thus arise in considering the truth or falsehood of mysticism, namely:

I.   Are there two ways of knowing, which may be called respectively reason and intuition? And if so, is either to be preferred to the other?

II. Is all plurality and division illusory?

III. Is time unreal?

IV. What kind of reality belongs to good and evil?

On all four of these questions, while fully developed mysticism seems to me mistaken, I yet believe that, by sufficient restraint, there is an element of wisdom to be learned from the mystical way of feeling, which does not seem to be attainable in any other manner. If this is the truth, mysticism is to be commended as an attitude towards life, not as a creed about the world. The metaphysical creed, I shall maintain, is a mistaken outcome of the emotion, although this emotion, as colouring and informing all other thoughts and feelings, is the inspirer of whatever is best in Man. Even the cautious and patient investigation of truth by science, which seems the very antithesis of the mystic's swift certainty, may be fostered and nourished by that very spirit of reverence in which mysticism lives and moves.

I. REASON AND INTUITION[3]

Of the reality or unreality of the mystic's world I know nothing. I have no wish to deny it, nor even to declare that the insight which reveals it is not a genuine insight. What I do wish to maintain—and it is here that the scientific attitude becomes imperative—is that insight, untested and unsupported, is an insufficient guarantee of truth, in spite of the fact that much

3 This section, and also one or two pages in later sections, have been printed in a course of Lowell lectures on *Our Knowledge of the External World*, published by the Open Court Publishing Company. But I have left them here, as this is the context for which they were originally written.

of the most important truth is first suggested by its means. It is common to speak of an opposition between instinct and reason; in the eighteenth century, the opposition was drawn in favour of reason, but under the influence of Rousseau and the romantic movement instinct was given the preference, first by those who rebelled against artificial forms of government and thought, and then, as the purely rationalistic defence of traditional theology became increasingly difficult, by all who felt in science a menace to creeds which they associated with a spiritual outlook on life and the world. Bergson, under the name of "intuition", has raised instinct to the position of sole arbiter of metaphysical truth. But in fact the opposition of instinct and reason is mainly illusory. Instinct, intuition, or insight is what first leads to the beliefs which subsequent reason confirms or confutes; but the confirmation, where it is possible, consists, in the last analysis, of agreement with other beliefs no less instinctive. Reason is a harmonizing, controlling force rather than a creative one. Even in the most purely logical realm, it is insight that first arrives at what is new.

Where instinct and reason do sometimes conflict is in regard to single beliefs, held instinctively, and held with such determination that no degree of inconsistency with other beliefs leads to their abandonment. Instinct, like all human faculties, is liable to error. Those in whom reason is weak are often unwilling to admit this as regards themselves, though all admit it in regard to others. Where instinct is least liable to error is in practical matters as to which right judgment is a help to survival: friendship and hostility in others, for instance, are often felt with extraordinary discrimination through very careful disguises. But even in such matters a wrong impression may be given by reserve or flattery; and in matters less directly practical, such as philosophy deals with, very strong instinctive beliefs are sometimes wholly mistaken, as we may come to know through their perceived inconsistency with other equally strong beliefs. It is such considerations that necessitate the harmonizing mediation of reason, which tests our beliefs by their mutual compatibility, and examines, in doubtful cases, the possible sources of error on the one side and on the other. In this there is no opposition to instinct as a whole, but only to blind reliance upon some one interesting aspect of instinct to the exclusion of other more commonplace but not less trustworthy aspects. It is such one-sidedness, not instinct itself, that reason aims at correcting.

These more or less trite maxims may be illustrated by application to Bergson's advocacy of "intuition" as against "intellect". There are, he says, "two profoundly different ways of knowing a thing. The first implies that we move round the object: the second that we enter into it. The first depends on the point of view at which we are placed and on the symbols by which we express ourselves. The second neither depends on a point of view nor relies on any symbol. The first kind of knowledge may be said to stop at the *relative*; the second, in those cases where it is possible, to attain the *absolute*."[4] The second of these, which is intuition, is, he says, "the kind of *intellectual sympathy* by which one places oneself within an object in order to coincide with what is unique in it and therefore inexpressible" (p. 6). In illustration, he mentions self-knowledge: "there is one reality, at least, which we all seize from within, by intuition and not by simple analysis. It is our own personality in its flowing through time—our self which endures" (p. 8). The rest of Bergson's philosophy consists in reporting, through the imperfect medium of words, the knowledge gained by intuition, and the consequent complete condemnation of all the pretended knowledge derived from science and common sense.

This procedure, since it takes sides in a conflict of instinctive beliefs, stands in need of justification by proving the greater trustworthiness of the beliefs on one side than of those on the other. Bergson attempts this justification in two ways, first by explaining that intellect is a purely practical faculty to secure biological success, secondly by mentioning remarkable feats of instinct in animals and by pointing out characteristics of the world which, though intuition can apprehend them, are baffling to intellect as he interprets it.

Of Bergson's theory that intellect is a purely practical faculty, developed in the struggle for survival, and not a source of true beliefs, we may say, first, that it is only through intellect that we know of the struggle for survival and of the biological ancestry of man: if the intellect is misleading, the whole of this merely inferred history is presumably untrue. If, on the other hand, we agree with him in thinking that evolution took place as Darwin believed, then it is not only intellect, but all our faculties, that have been developed under the stress of practical utility. Intuition is seen at its best where it is directly useful, for example in regard to other people's characters and dispositions. Bergson apparently holds that capacity for this kind of knowledge is less explicable by the struggle for existence than, for example, capacity for pure mathematics. Yet the savage deceived by false friendship is likely to pay for his mistake with his life; whereas even in the most civilized societies men are not put to death for mathematical incompetence. All the most striking of his instances of intuition in animals have a very direct survival value. The fact is, of course, that both intuition and intellect have been developed because they are useful, and that, speaking broadly, they are useful when they give truth and become harmful when they give falsehood. Intellect, in civilized man, like artistic capacity, has occasionally been developed beyond the point where it is useful to the individual; intuition, on the other hand, seems on the whole to diminish as civilization increases. It is greater, as a rule, in children than in adults, in the unedu-

4 *Introduction to Metaphysics*, p. 1.

cated than in the educated. Probably in dogs it exceeds anything to be found in human beings. But those who see in these facts a recommendation of intuition ought to return to running wild in the woods, dyeing themselves with woad and living on hips and haws.

Let us next examine whether intuition possesses any such infallibility as Bergson claims for it. The best instance of it, according to him, is our acquaintance with ourselves; yet self-knowledge is proverbially rare and difficult. Most men, for example, have in their nature meannesses, vanities, and envies of which they are quite unconscious, though even their best friends can perceive them without any difficulty. It is true that intuition has a convincingness which is lacking to intellect: while it is present, it is almost impossible to doubt its truth. But if it should appear, on examination, to be at least as fallible as intellect, its greater subjective certainty becomes a demerit, making it only the more irresistibly deceptive. Apart from self-knowledge, one of the most notable examples of intuition is the knowledge people believe themselves to possess of those with whom they are in love: the wall between different personalities seems to become transparent, and people think they see into another soul as into their own. Yet deception in such cases is constantly practised with success; and even where there is no intentional deception, experience gradually proves, as a rule, that the supposed insight was illusory, and that the slower more groping methods of the intellect are in the long run more reliable.

Bergson maintains that intellect can only deal with things in so far as they resemble what has been experienced in the past, while intuition has the power of apprehending the uniqueness and novelty that always belong to each fresh moment. That there is something unique and new at every moment, is certainly true; it is also true that this cannot be fully expressed by means of intellectual concepts. Only direct acquaintance can give knowledge of what is unique and new. But direct acquaintance of this kind is given fully in sensation, and does not require, so far as I can see, any special faculty of intuition for its apprehension. It is neither intellect nor intuition, but sensation, that supplies new data; but when the data are new in any remarkable manner, intellect is much more capable of dealing with them than intuition would be. The hen with a brood of ducklings no doubt has intuition which seems to place her inside them, and not merely to know them analytically; but when the ducklings take to the water, the whole apparent intuition is seen to be illusory, and the hen is left helpless on the shore. Intuition, in fact, is an aspect and development of instinct, and, like all instinct, is admirable in those customary surroundings which have moulded the habits of the animal in question, but totally incompetent as soon as the surroundings are changed in a way which demands some non-habitual mode of action.

The theoretical understanding of the world, which is the aim of

philosophy, is not a matter of great practical importance to animals, or to savages, or even to most civilized men. It is hardly to be supposed, therefore, that the rapid, rough-and-ready methods of instinct or intuition will find in this field a favourable ground for their application. It is the older kinds of activity, which bring out our kinship with remote generations of animal and semi-human ancestors, that show intuition at its best. In such matters as self-preservation and love, intuition will act sometimes (though not always) with a swiftness and precision which are astonishing to the critical intellect. But philosophy is not one of the pursuits which illustrate
10 our affinity with the past: it is a highly refined, highly civilized pursuit, demanding, for its success, a certain liberation from the life of instinct, and even, at times, a certain aloofness from all mundane hopes and fears. It is not in philosophy, therefore, that we can hope to see intuition at its best. On the contrary, since the true objects of philosophy, and the habits of thought demanded for their apprehension, are strange, unusual, and remote, it is here, more almost than anywhere else, that intellect proves superior to intuition, and that quick unanalyzed convictions are least deserving of uncritical acceptance.

In advocating the scientific restraint and balance, as against the self-
20 assertion of a confident reliance upon intuition, we are only urging, in the sphere of knowledge, that largeness of contemplation, that impersonal disinterestedness, and that freedom from practical preoccupations which have been inculcated by all the great religions of the world. Thus our conclusion, however it may conflict with the explicit beliefs of many mystics, is, in essence, not contrary to the spirit which inspires those beliefs, but rather the outcome of this very spirit as applied in the realm of thought.

II. UNITY AND PLURALITY

One of the most convincing aspects of the mystic illumination is the apparent revelation of the oneness of all things, giving rise to pantheism in
30 religion and to monism in philosophy. An elaborate logic, beginning with Parmenides, and culminating in Hegel and his followers, has been gradually developed, to prove that the universe is one indivisible Whole, and that what seem to be its parts, if considered as substantial and self-existing, are mere illusion. The conception of a Reality quite other than the world of appearance, a reality one, indivisible, and unchanging, was introduced into Western philosophy by Parmenides, not, nominally at least, for mystical or religious reasons, but on the basis of a logical argument as to the impossibility of not-being, and most subsequent metaphysical systems are the outcome of this fundamental idea.
40   The logic used in defence of mysticism seems to me faulty as logic, and open to technical criticisms, which I have explained elsewhere. I shall not

here repeat these criticisms, since they are lengthy and difficult, but shall instead attempt an analysis of the state of mind from which mystical logic has arisen.

Belief in a reality quite different from what appears to the senses arises with irresistible force in certain moods, which are the source of most mysticism, and of most metaphysics. While such a mood is dominant, the need of logic is not felt, and accordingly the more thoroughgoing mystics do not employ logic, but appeal directly to the immediate deliverance of their insight. But such fully developed mysticism is rare in the West. When the intensity of emotional conviction subsides, a man who is in the habit of reasoning will search for logical grounds in favour of the belief which he finds in himself. But since the belief already exists, he will be very hospitable to any ground that suggests itself. The paradoxes apparently proved by his logic are really the paradoxes of mysticism, and are the goal which he feels his logic must reach if it is to be in accordance with insight. The resulting logic has rendered most philosophers incapable of giving any account of the world of science and daily life. If they had been anxious to give such an account, they would probably have discovered the errors of their logic; but most of them were less anxious to understand the world of science and daily life than to convict it of unreality in the interests of a super-sensible "real" world.

It is in this way that logic has been pursued by those of the great philosophers who were mystics. But since they usually took for granted the supposed insight of the mystic emotion, their logical doctrines were presented with a certain dryness, and were believed by their disciples to be quite independent of the sudden illumination from which they sprang. Nevertheless their origin clung to them, and they remained—to borrow a useful word from Mr. Santayana—"malicious" in regard to the world of science and common sense. It is only so that we can account for the complacency with which philosophers have accepted the inconsistency of their doctrines with all the common and scientific facts which seem best established and most worthy of belief.

The logic of mysticism shows, as is natural, the defects which are inherent in anything malicious. The impulse to logic, not felt while the mystic mood is dominant, reasserts itself as the mood fades, but with a desire to retain the vanishing insight, or at least to prove that it *was* insight, and that what seems to contradict it is illusion. The logic which thus arises is not quite disinterested or candid, and is inspired by a certain hatred of the daily world to which it is to be applied. Such an attitude naturally does not tend to the best results. Every one knows that to read an author simply in order to refute him is not the way to understand him; and to read the book of Nature with a conviction that it is all illusion is just as unlikely to lead to understanding. If our logic is to find the common world intelligible, it must not be hostile, but must be inspired by a genuine acceptance such as is not usually to be found among metaphysicians.

III. TIME

The unreality of time is a cardinal doctrine of many metaphysical systems, often nominally based, as already by Parmenides, upon logical arguments, but originally derived, at any rate in the founders of new systems, from the certainty which is born in the moment of mystic insight. As a Persian Sufi poet says:

> Past and future are what veil God from our sight.
> Burn up both of them with fire! How long
> Wilt thou be partitioned by these segments as a reed?[5]

The belief that what is ultimately real must be immutable is a very common one: it gave rise to the metaphysical notion of substance, and finds, even now, a wholly illegitimate satisfaction in such scientific doctrines as the conservation of energy and mass.

It is difficult to disentangle the truth and the error in this view. The arguments for the contention that time is unreal and that the world of sense is illusory must, I think, be regarded as fallacious. Nevertheless there is some sense—easier to feel than to state—in which time is an unimportant and superficial characteristic of reality. Past and future must be acknowledged to be as real as the present, and a certain emancipation from slavery to time is essential to philosophic thought. The importance of time is rather practical than theoretical, rather in relation to our desires than in relation to truth. A truer image of the world, I think, is obtained by picturing things as entering into the stream of time from an eternal world outside, than from a view which regards time as the devouring tyrant of all that is. Both in thought and in feeling, even though time be real, to realize the unimportance of time is the gate of wisdom.

That this is the case may be seen at once by asking ourselves why our feelings towards the past are so different from our feelings towards the future. The reason for this difference is wholly practical: our wishes can affect the future but not the past—the future is to some extent subject to our power, while the past is unalterably fixed. But every future will some day be past; if we see the past truly now, it must, when it was still future, have been just what we now see it to be, and what is now future must be just what we shall see it to be when it has become past. The felt difference of quality between past and future, therefore, is not an intrinsic difference, but only a

---

5 Whinfield's translation of the *Masnavi* (Trübner, 1887), p. 34.

difference in relation to us: to impartial contemplation, it ceases to exist. And impartiality of contemplation is, in the intellectual sphere, that very same virtue of disinterestedness which, in the sphere of action, appears as justice and unselfishness. Whoever wishes to see the world truly, to rise in thought above the tyranny of practical desires, must learn to overcome the difference of attitude towards past and future, and to survey the whole stream of time in one comprehensive vision.

The kind of way in which, as it seems to me, time ought not to enter into our theoretic philosophical thought, may be illustrated by the philosophy which has become associated with the idea of evolution, and which is exemplified by Nietzsche, pragmatism, and Bergson. This philosophy, on the basis of the development which has led from the lowest forms of life up to man, sees in *progress* the fundamental law of the universe, and thus admits the difference between *earlier* and *later* into the very citadel of its contemplative outlook. With its past and future history of the world, conjectural as it is, I do not wish to quarrel. But I think that, in the intoxication of a quick success, much that is required for a true understanding of the universe has been forgotten. Something of Hellenism, something, too, of Oriental resignation, must be combined with its hurrying Western self-assertion before it can emerge from the ardour of youth into the mature wisdom of manhood. In spite of its appeals to science, the true scientific philosophy, I think, is something more arduous and more aloof, appealing to less mundane hopes, and requiring a severer discipline for its successful practice.

Darwin's *Origin of Species* persuaded the world that the difference between different species of animals and plants is not the fixed immutable difference that it appears to be. The doctrine of natural kinds, which had rendered classification easy and definite, which was enshrined in the Aristotelian tradition, and protected by its supposed necessity for orthodox dogma, was suddenly swept away for ever out of the biological world. The difference between man and the lower animals, which to our human conceit appears enormous, was shown to be a gradual achievement, involving intermediate beings who could not with certainty be placed either within or without the human family. The sun and the planets had already been shown by Laplace to be very probably derived from a primitive more or less undifferentiated nebula. Thus the old fixed landmarks became wavering and indistinct, and all sharp outlines were blurred. Things and species lost their boundaries, and none could say where they began or where they ended.

But if human conceit was staggered for a moment by its kinship with the ape, it soon found a way to reassert itself, and that way is the "philosophy" of evolution. A process which led from the amoeba to Man appeared to the philosophers to be obviously a progress—though whether the amoeba would agree with this opinion is not known. Hence the cycle of changes

which science had shown to be the probable history of the past was welcomed as revealing a law of development towards good in the universe—an
evolution or unfolding of an ideal slowly embodying itself in the actual. But
such a view, though it might satisfy Spencer and those whom we may call
Hegelian evolutionists, could not be accepted as adequate by the more
whole-hearted votaries of change. An ideal to which the world continuously
approaches is, to these minds, too dead and static to be inspiring. Not only
the aspiration, but the ideal too, must change and develop with the course of
evolution: there must be no fixed goal, but a continual fashioning of fresh
needs by the impulse which is life and which alone gives unity to the
process.

Life, in this philosophy, is a continuous stream, in which all divisions are
artificial and unreal. Separate things, beginnings and endings, are mere
convenient fictions: there is only smooth unbroken transition. The beliefs of
today may count as true today, if they carry us along the stream; but
tomorrow they will be false, and must be replaced by new beliefs to meet the
new situation. All our thinking consists of convenient fictions, imaginary
congealings of the stream: reality flows on in spite of all our fictions, and
though it can be lived, it cannot be conceived in thought. Somehow,
without explicit statement, the assurance is slipped in that the future,
though we cannot foresee it, will be better than the past or the present: the
reader is like the child which expects a sweet because it has been told to open
its mouth and shut its eyes. Logic, mathematics, physics disappear in this
philosophy, because they are too "static"; what is real is an impulse and
movement towards a goal which, like the rainbow, recedes as we advance,
and makes every place different when we reach it from what it appeared to
be at a distance.

I do not propose to enter upon a technical examination of this philosophy.
I wish only to maintain that the motives and interests which inspire it are so
exclusively practical, and the problems with which it deals are so special,
that it can hardly be regarded as touching any of the questions that, to my
mind, constitute genuine philosophy.

The predominant interest of evolutionism is in the question of human
destiny, or at least of the destiny of Life. It is more interested in morality
and happiness than in knowledge for its own sake. It must be admitted that
the same may be said of many other philosophies, and that a desire for the
kind of knowledge which philosophy can give is very rare. But if philosophy
is to attain truth, it is necessary first and foremost that philosophers should
acquire the disinterested intellectual curiosity which characterizes the
genuine man of science. Knowledge concerning the future—which is the
kind of knowledge that must be sought if we are to know about human
destiny—is possible within certain narrow limits. It is impossible to say how
much the limits may be enlarged with the progress of science. But what is

evident is that any proposition about the future belongs by its subject-matter to some particular science, and is to be ascertained, if at all, by the methods of that science. Philosophy is not a short cut to the same kind of results as those of the other sciences: if it is to be a genuine study, it must have a province of its own, and aim at results which the other sciences can neither prove nor disprove.

Evolutionism, in basing itself upon the notion of *progress*, which is change from the worse to the better, allows the notion of time, as it seems to me, to become its tyrant rather than its servant, and thereby loses that impartiality of contemplation which is the source of all that is best in philosophic thought and feeling. Metaphysicians, as we saw, have frequently denied altogether the reality of time. I do not wish to do this; I wish only to preserve the mental outlook which inspired the denial, the attitude which, in thought, regards the past as having the same reality as the present and the same importance as the future. "In so far", says Spinoza,[6] "as the mind conceives a thing according to the dictate of reason, it will be equally affected whether the idea is that of a future, past, or present thing." It is this "conceiving according to the dictate of reason" that I find lacking in the philosophy which is based on evolution.

IV. GOOD AND EVIL

Mysticism maintains that all evil is illusory, and sometimes maintains the same view as regards good, but more often holds that all Reality is good. Both views are to be found in Heraclitus: "Good and ill are one", he says, but again, "To God all things are fair and good and right, but men hold some things wrong and some right." A similar twofold position is to be found in Spinoza, but he uses the word "perfection" when he means to speak of the good that is not merely human. "By reality and perfection I mean the same thing", he says;[7] but elsewhere we find the definition: "By *good* I shall mean that which we certainly know to be useful to us."[8] Thus perfection belongs to Reality in its own nature, but goodness is relative to ourselves and our needs, and disappears in an impartial survey. Some such distinction, I think, is necessary in order to understand the ethical outlook of mysticism: there is a lower mundane kind of good and evil, which divides the world of appearance into what seem to be conflicting parts; but there is also a higher, mystical kind of good, which belongs to Reality and is not opposed by any correlative kind of evil.

It is difficult to give a logically tenable account of this position without

6 *Ethics*, Bk. IV, Prop. LXII.
7 *Ibid.*, Pt. II, Df. VI.
8 *Ibid.*, Pt. IV, Df. I.

recognizing that good and evil are subjective, that what is good is merely that towards which we have one kind of feeling, and what is evil is merely that towards which we have another kind of feeling. In our active life, where we have to exercise choice, and to prefer this to that of two possible acts, it is necessary to have a distinction of good and evil, or at least of better and worse. But this distinction, like everything pertaining to action, belongs to what mysticism regards as the world of illusion, if only because it is essentially concerned with time. In our contemplative life, where action is not called for, it is possible to be impartial, and to overcome the ethical dualism which action requires. So long as we remain *merely* impartial, we may be content to say that both the good and the evil of action are illusions. But if, as we must do if we have the mystic vision, we find the whole world worthy of love and worship, if we see

> The earth, and every common sight....
> Apparell'd in celestial light,

we shall say that there is a higher good than that of action, and that this higher good belongs to the whole world as it is in reality. In this way the twofold attitude and the apparent vacillation of mysticism are explained and justified.

The possibility of this universal love and joy in all that exists is of supreme importance for the conduct and happiness of life, and gives inestimable value to the mystic emotion, apart from any creeds which may be built upon it. But if we are not to be led into false beliefs, it is necessary to realize exactly *what* the mystic emotion reveals. It reveals a possibility of human nature—a possibility of a nobler, happier, freer life than any that can be otherwise achieved. But it does not reveal anything about the non-human, or about the nature of the universe in general. Good and bad, and even the higher good that mysticism finds everywhere, are the reflections of our own emotions on other things, not part of the substance of things as they are in themselves. And therefore an impartial contemplation, freed from all pre-occupation with Self, will not judge things good or bad, although it is very easily combined with that feeling of universal love which leads the mystic to say that the whole world is good.

The philosophy of evolution, through the notion of progress, is bound up with the ethical dualism of the worse and the better, and is thus shut out, not only from the kind of survey which discards good and evil altogether from its view, but also from the mystical belief in the goodness of everything. In this way the distinction of good and evil, like time, becomes a tyrant in this philosophy, and introduces into thought the restless selectiveness of action. Good and evil, like time, are, it would seem, not general or fundamental in the world of thought, but late and highly specialized members of the intellectual hierarchy.

Although, as we saw, mysticism can be interpreted so as to agree with the view that good and evil are not intellectually fundamental, it must be admitted that here we are no longer in verbal agreement with most of the great philosophers and religious teachers of the past. I believe, however, that the elimination of ethical considerations from philosophy is both scientifically necessary and—though this may seem a paradox—an ethical advance. Both these contentions must be briefly defended.

The hope of satisfaction to our more human desires—the hope of demonstrating that the world has this or that desirable ethical characteristic—is not one which, so far as I can see, a scientific philosophy can do anything whatever to satisfy. The difference between a good world and a bad one is a difference in the particular characteristics of the particular things that exist in these worlds: it is not a sufficiently abstract difference to come within the province of philosophy. Love and hate, for example, are ethical opposites, but to philosophy they are closely analogous attitudes towards objects. The general form and structure of those attitudes towards objects which constitute mental phenomena is a problem for philosophy, but the difference between love and hate is not a difference of form or structure, and therefore belongs rather to the special science of psychology than to philosophy. Thus the ethical interests which have often inspired philosophers must remain in the background: some kind of ethical interest may inspire the whole study, but none must obtrude in the detail or be expected in the special results which are sought.

If this view seems at first sight disappointing, we may remind ourselves that a similar change has been found necessary in all the other sciences. The physicist or chemist is not now required to prove the ethical importance of his ions or atoms; the biologist is not expected to prove the utility of the plants or animals which he dissects. In pre-scientific ages this was not the case. Astronomy, for example, was studied because men believed in astrology: it was thought that the movements of the planets had the most direct and important bearing upon the lives of human beings. Presumably, when this belief decayed and the disinterested study of astronomy began, many who had found astrology absorbingly interesting decided that astronomy had too little human interest to be worthy of study. Physics, as it appears in Plato's *Timaeus* for example, is full of ethical notions: it is an essential part of its purpose to show that the earth is worthy of admiration. The modern physicist, on the contrary, though he has no wish to deny that the earth is admirable, is not concerned, as physicist, with its ethical attributes: he is merely concerned to find out facts, not to consider whether they are good or bad. In psychology, the scientific attitude is even more recent and more difficult than in the physical sciences: it is natural to consider that human nature is either good or bad, and to suppose that the difference between good and bad, so all-important in practice, must be important in theory also. It is only during the last century that an ethically neutral psychology has grown up; and here too, ethical neutrality has been essential to scientific success.

In philosophy, hitherto, ethical neutrality has been seldom sought and hardly ever achieved. Men have remembered their wishes, and have judged philosophies in relation to their wishes. Driven from the particular sciences, the belief that the notions of good and evil must afford a key to the understanding of the world has sought a refuge in philosophy. But even from this last refuge, if philosophy is not to remain a set of pleasing dreams, this belief must be driven forth. It is a commonplace that happiness is not best achieved by those who seek it directly; and it would seem that the same is true of the good. In thought, at any rate, those who forget good and evil and seek only to know the facts are more likely to achieve good than those who view the world through the distorting medium of their own desires.

We are thus brought back to our seeming paradox, that a philosophy which does not seek to impose upon the world its own conceptions of good and evil is not only more likely to achieve truth, but is also the outcome of a higher ethical standpoint than one which, like evolutionism and most traditional systems, is perpetually appraising the universe and seeking to find in it an embodiment of present ideals. In religion, and in every deeply serious view of the world and of human destiny, there is an element of submission, a realization of the limits of human power, which is somewhat lacking in the modern world, with its quick material successes and its insolent belief in the boundless possibilities of progress. "He that loveth his life shall lose it"; and there is danger lest, through a too confident love of life, life itself should lose much of what gives it its highest worth. The submission which religion inculcates in action is essentially the same in spirit as that which science teaches in thought; and the ethical neutrality by which its victories have been achieved is the outcome of that submission.

The good which it concerns us to remember is the good which it lies in our power to create—the good in our own lives and in our attitude towards the world. Insistence on belief in an external realization of the good is a form of self-assertion, which, while it cannot secure the external good which it desires, can seriously impair the inward good which lies within our power, and destroy that reverence towards fact which constitutes both what is valuable in humility and what is fruitful in the scientific temper.

Human beings cannot, of course, wholly transcend human nature; something subjective, if only the interest that determines the direction of our attention, must remain in all our thought. But scientific philosophy comes nearer to objectivity than any other human pursuit, and gives us, therefore, the closest contact and the most intimate relation with the outer world that it is possible to achieve. To the primitive mind, everything is either friendly or hostile; but experience has shown that friendliness and hostility are not the conceptions by which the world is to be understood. Scientific philosophy thus represents, though as yet only in a nascent condition, a higher form of thought than any pre-scientific belief or imagination, and, like every approach to self-transcendence, it brings with it a rich reward in increase of scope and breadth and comprehension. Evolutionism, in spite of its appeals to particular scientific facts, fails to be a truly scientific philosophy because of its slavery to time, its ethical preoccupations, and its predominant interest in our mundane concerns and destiny. A truly scientific philosophy will be more humble, more piecemeal, more 10 arduous, offering less glitter of outward mirage to flatter fallacious hopes, but more indifferent to fate, and more capable of accepting the world without the tyrannous imposition of our human and temporary demands.

3

Preface to Poincaré, *Science and Method* [1914]

THIS PREFACE WAS published with the English translation of *Science et méthode* (1908) by Thomas Nelson and Sons in Great Britain and Charles Scribner's Sons in the United States of America. Neither edition of the book bears a date, but the date of publication is known to be April 1914 because of its listing in *The English Catalogue of Books*. The American edition uses English sheets. Francis Maitland is the translator. His translation was later reissued by both The Science Press, Lancaster, Pennsylvania, in 1946, and Dover Publications, New York, in 1952. Neither publisher reprints Russell's preface, although some copies of the Dover edition have "With a Preface by the Hon. Bertrand Russell, F.R.S." on the title page.

Although the preface is short, its writing caused Russell considerable anguish. He seems to have agreed, sometime during 1913, to write it, with a delivery date set for early 1914. His first mention of it to Lady Ottoline Morrell is in a letter (#925) postmarked 1 December 1913.

> I have been reading Poincaré, the book I have to write a preface to. He is an admirable writer, very witty, very clear, and full of good things. There is an essay ⟨"Mathematical Discovery"⟩ on how discoveries are made in mathematics which would interest you.

The next day he noted that he had "Poincaré to read" (#927).

He did not mention the preface again until letter #919, which, as the headnote to "Mysticism and Logic" (2) makes clear, must have been written on Sunday, 11 January 1914. "I still have the Poincaré preface to do before term begins." The next day he wrote her: "Today I have been working at Poincaré; I must finish him this week" (#963, pmk. 12 Jan. 1914). On the 15th he reported that he has "postponed Poincaré" (#968) and will have "to do him during term". But the very next day he wrote that he "*must* finish Poincaré in the next few days" (#970). On Sunday, the 18th, he returned to the subject of Poincaré:

> I am reading a number of the *Revue de Métaphysique et de Morale*, entirely on Poincaré. He certainly was a wonderful man.... There is no one in science now who is quite as eminent as he was. (#972)

Russell went on to copy out a long passage of tribute from one of the contributors. He also mentioned the commemorative issue in his preface.

In an undated letter (#937), but one that must have been written on the 19th of January (the only "Tuesday evening" that fits with the contents of the other letters), he reported its completion.

> At last I have finished the Poincaré preface—the *very* last moment before the rush of term. It cost me a frightful lot of time and thought for such a short thing. It was a delicate matter, as the book contains a fierce attack on me, which I thought ignorant and unfair, but which nearly destroyed my reputation in France. It doesn't prevent my finding delight in Poincaré and loving him, but I felt it would be affectation to ignore it, and yet difficult to mention it in the right way. I am glad to have got it done.

Later in the same letter he wrote:

> I enclose the Preface. You might give it back to me Monday, but it is not very important as I made a fair copy for the publishers.

The manuscript has not been found among her papers or his. On the 26th of January he reported that he has received payment of £5 for the preface (#977).

Jules Henri Poincaré (1854–1912) made original contributions to many branches of mathematics and science. He also wrote on a wide variety of topics concerned with the methodology of the sciences; his scientific eminence and his agreeable writing style made these works very popular.

Since no manuscript is known, the copy-text is that printed in the first British edition.

H ENRI POINCARÉ WAS, by general agreement, the most eminent scientific man of his generation—more eminent, one is tempted to think, than any man of science now living. From the mere variety of the subjects which he illuminated, there is certainly no one who can appreciate critically the whole of his work. Some conception of his amazing comprehensiveness may be derived from the obituary number of the *Revue de Métaphysique et de Morale* (September 1913), where, in the course of 130 pages, four eminent men—a philosopher, a mathematician, an astronomer, and a physicist—tell in outline the contributions which he made to their several subjects. In all we find the same characteristics—swiftness, comprehensiveness, unexampled lucidity, and the perception of recondite but fertile analogies.

Poincaré's philosophical writings, of which the present volume is a good example, are not those of a professional philosopher: they are the untrammelled reflections of a broad and cultivated mind upon the procedure and the postulates of scientific discovery. The writing of professional philosophers on such subjects has too often the deadness of merely external description; Poincaré's writing, on the contrary, as the reader of this book may see in his account of mathematical invention, has the freshness of actual experience, of vivid, intimate contact with what he is describing. There results a certain richness and resonance in his words: the sound emitted is not hollow, but comes from a great mass of which only the polished surface appears. His wit, his easy mastery, and his artistic love of concealing the labour of thought, may hide from the non-mathematical reader the background of solid knowledge from which his apparent paradoxes emerge: often, behind what may seem a light remark, there lies a whole region of mathematics which he himself has helped to explore.

A philosophy of science is growing increasingly necessary at the present time, for a variety of reasons. Owing to increasing specialization, and to the constantly accelerated accumulation of new facts, the general bearings of scientific systems become more and more lost to view, and the synthesis that depends on coexistence of multifarious knowledge in a single mind becomes increasingly difficult. In order to overcome this difficulty, it is necessary that, from time to time, a specialist capable of detachment from details should set forth the main lines and essential structure of his science as it exists at the moment. But it is not results, which are what mainly interests the man in the street, that are what is essential in a science: what is essential is its method, and it is with method that Poincaré's philosophical writings are concerned.

Another reason which makes a philosophy of science specially useful at the present time is the revolutionary progress, the sweeping away of what had seemed fixed landmarks, which has so far characterized this century, especially in physics. The conception of the "working hypothesis", provisional, approximate, and merely useful, has more and more pushed aside the comfortable eighteenth century conception of "laws of nature". Even the Newtonian dynamics, which for over two hundred years had seemed to embody a definite conquest, must now be regarded as doubtful, and as probably only a first rough sketch of the ways of matter. And thus, in virtue of the very rapidity of our progress, a new theory of knowledge has to be sought, more tentative and more modest than that of more confident but less successful generations. Of this necessity Poincaré was acutely conscious, and it gave to his writings a tone of doubt which was hailed with joy by sceptics and pragmatists. But he was in truth no sceptic: however conscious of the difficulty of attaining knowledge, he never admitted its impossibility. "It is a mistake to believe", he said, "that the love of truth is indistinguishable from the love of certainty"; and again: "To doubt everything or to believe everything are two equally convenient solutions; both dispense with the necessity of reflection." His was the active, eager doubt that inspires a new scrutiny, not the idle doubt that acquiesces contentedly in nescience.

Two opposite and conflicting qualities are required for the successful practice of philosophy—comprehensiveness of outlook, and minute, patient analysis. Both exist in the highest degree in Descartes and Leibniz; but in their day comprehensiveness was less difficult than it is now. Since Leibniz, I do not know of any philosopher who has possessed both: broadly speaking, British philosophers have excelled in analysis, while those of the Continent have excelled in breadth and scope. In this respect, Poincaré is no exception: in philosophy, his mind was intuitive and synthetic; wonderfully skilful, it is true, in analyzing a science until he had extracted its philosophical essence, and in combining this essence with those of other sciences, but not very apt in those further stages of analysis which fall within the domain of philosophy itself. He built wonderful edifices with the philosophic materials that he found ready to hand, but he lacked the patience and the minuteness of attention required for the creation of new materials. For this reason, his philosophy, though brilliant, stimulating, and instructive, is not among those that revolutionize fundamentals, or compel us to remould our imaginative conception of the nature of things. In fundamentals, broadly speaking, he remained faithful to the authority of Kant.

Readers of the following pages will not be surprised to learn that his criticisms of mathematical logic do not appear to me to be among the best parts of his work. He was already an old man when he became aware of the existence of this subject, and he was led, by certain indiscreet advocates, to suppose it in some way opposed to those quick flashes of insight in mathematical discovery which he has so admirably described. No such opposition in fact exists; but the misconception, however regrettable, was in no way surprising.

To be always right is not possible in philosophy; but Poincaré's opinions, right or wrong, are always the expression of a powerful and original mind with a quite unrivalled scientific equipment; a masterly style, great wit, and a profound devotion to the advancement of knowledge. Through these merits, his books supply, better than any others known to me, the growing need for a generally intelligible account of the philosophic outcome of modern science.

4

On Scientific Method in Philosophy [1914]

THIS PAPER WAS first published as a pamphlet in 1914, having previously been delivered as The Herbert Spencer Lecture at Oxford University on 18 November 1914.

The composition of the lecture was not easy for Russell, owing largely to the fact that it was written during the first months of the First World War when he was consumed by his feelings of revulsion toward the war. The history of its composition can be pieced together from his letters to Lady Ottoline Morrell. On 29 October he wrote her, in the course of a letter largely devoted to his views of the war, that "I have to lecture in Oxford, three weeks hence, and the lecture will have to be published. It is terribly hard to think of philosophy" (#1141). On 11 November he reported that he is "back again at my wretched lecture for Oxford" (#1147), taking notes and preparing to dictate it to a secretary. "It worries me, because I can't get interested, or feel that it matters whether I do it well or ill. It will bring me £20, but it will be a miserable pot-boiler" (*ibid*.). The next evening he wrote her that he had had a busy day which included "four hours dictating my Oxford lecture to a short-hand writer". "Dictating", he allowed, "is grand as a way of saving time, but it is very tiring because one has to think so much more quickly than when one writes oneself" (#1148). He planned to continue dictating the next day, but he was depressed about his "wretched Oxford lecture—it *is* a dull lecture" (*ibid*.).

During the evening of 18 November he commented on the reception of the lecture.

> Oxford was beastly and I was glad to be there such a short time—only three hours! Professor Poulson is a stupid old stick-in-the-mud. Gilbert Murray, who was there, was as squashy as a slug, and J. A. Smith was preparing to pontificate as soon as I was gone. Schiller, bounder and cad as he is, was the only person with whom I felt in any degree in sympathy. To my surprise, when I came to read my lecture I thought it was really good, but it was designed to infuriate the Oxford pundits. What I hate is their attempt to make an impressive manner a cloak for complete intellectual atrophy. They were very nice to me personally, and the lecture was a success. (#1149)

He wrote Lucy Donnelly on 14 December a briefer account of the lecture, implying that the passage about progress from the protozoon to the philosopher (62: 27–63: 6) was designed to irritate his hearers.

The tone of the lecture must have led Professor Samuel Alexander to seek an explanation from Russell. Russell replied:

> My H⟨erbert⟩ S⟨pencer⟩ lecture was partly inspired by disgust at the universal outburst of "righteousness" in all nations since the war began. It seems the essence of virtue is persecution, and it has given me a disgust of all ethical notions, which evidently are chiefly useful as an excuse for murder.

His letter is dated 5 February 1915; he was writing Alexander regarding the oral delivery of "The Ultimate Constituents of Matter" (5) at Manchester. In a letter to Ralph Barton Perry on the 21st of February Russell wrote more frankly: "I am sending you herewith a lecture called 'On Scientific Method in Philosophy'—but its *real* title is 'Philosophers and Pigs' (cf. pp. 12, 13) inspired by the bloodthirstiness of professors here and in Germany. I gave it at Oxford, and it produced all the disgust I had hoped." Russell's reference (which is to the pamphlet version) drew Perry's attention to the well-known passage about the Grand Augur and the pigs. (See 62: 32–63: 6).

When Russell, even if only momentarily, described this lecture as a pot-boiler, he was acknowledging its heavy dependence upon *Our Knowledge of the External World* (1914), which he had written over a year earlier. The central methodological points made in the lecture are all to be found in the book, even if they are put into sharper focus in the lecture. His requirement that all philosophical propositions be both general and à priori, and his claim that *"philosophy is the science of the possible"* (65: 29), are two examples of points made explicit in the lecture which are implicit in the book. Most of the examples discussed in the lecture are also to be found in the book, but the discussion of them is, in nearly all cases, fresh.

The lecture exists in two forms: the pamphlet version and the version reprinted in *Mysticism and Logic, and Other Essays* (1918). The latter has been selected as copy-text. The two versions have been collated and the results are reported in the Textual Notes.

WHEN WE TRY to ascertain the motives which have led men to the investigation of philosophical questions, we find that, broadly speaking, they can be divided into two groups, often antagonistic, and leading to very divergent systems. These two groups of motives are, on the one hand, those derived from religion and ethics, and, on the other hand, those derived from science. Plato, Spinoza, and Hegel may be taken as typical of the philosophers whose interests are mainly religious and ethical, while Leibniz, Locke, and Hume may be taken as representatives of the scientific wing. In Aristotle, Descartes, Berkeley, and Kant we find both groups of motives strongly present. 10

Herbert Spencer, in whose honour we are assembled today, would naturally be classed among scientific philosophers: it was mainly from science that he drew his data, his formulation of problems, and his conception of method. But his strong religious sense is obvious in much of his writing, and his ethical preoccupations are what make him value the conception of evolution—that conception in which, as a whole generation has believed, science and morals are to be united in fruitful and indissoluble marriage.

It is my belief that the ethical and religious motives, in spite of the splendidly imaginative systems to which they have given rise, have been on the whole a hindrance to the progress of philosophy, and ought now to be 20 consciously thrust aside by those who wish to discover philosophical truth. Science, originally, was entangled in similar motives, and was thereby hindered in its advances. It is, I maintain, from science, rather than from ethics and religion, that philosophy should draw its inspiration.

But there are two different ways in which a philosophy may seek to base itself upon science. It may emphasize the most general *results* of science, and seek to give even greater generality and unity to these results. Or it may study the *methods* of science, and seek to apply these methods, with the necessary adaptations, to its own peculiar province. Much philosophy inspired by science has gone astray through preoccupation with the *results* 30 momentarily supposed to have been achieved. It is not results, but *methods*, that can be transferred with profit from the sphere of the special sciences to the sphere of philosophy. What I wish to bring to your notice is the possibility and importance of applying to philosophical problems certain broad principles of method which have been found successful in the study of scientific questions.

The opposition between a philosophy guided by scientific method and a philosophy dominated by religious and ethical ideas may be illustrated by two notions which are very prevalent in the works of philosophers, namely the notion of *the universe*, and the notion of *good and evil*. A philosopher is 40 expected to tell us something about the nature of the universe as a whole, and to give grounds for either optimism or pessimism. Both these expectations seem to me mistaken. I believe the conception of "the universe" to be, as its etymology indicates, a mere relic of pre-Copernican astronomy; and I believe the question of optimism and pessimism to be one which the philosopher will regard as outside his scope, except, possibly, to the extent of maintaining that it is insoluble.

In the days before Copernicus, the conception of the "universe" was defensible on scientific grounds: the diurnal revolution of the heavenly bodies bound them together as all parts of one system, of which the earth was the centre. Round this apparent scientific fact, many human desires rallied: the wish to believe Man important in the scheme of things, the theoretical desire for a comprehensive understanding of the Whole, the hope that the course of nature might be guided by some sympathy with our wishes. In this way, an ethically inspired system of metaphysics grew up, whose anthropocentrism was apparently warranted by the geocentrism of astronomy. When Copernicus swept away the astronomical basis of this system of thought, it had grown so familiar, and had associated itself so intimately with men's aspirations, that it survived with scarcely diminished force—survived even Kant's "Copernican revolution", and is still now the unconscious premiss of most metaphysical systems.

The oneness of the world is an almost undiscussed postulate of most metaphysics. "Reality is not merely one and self-consistent, but is a system of reciprocally determinate parts"[1]—such a statement would pass almost unnoticed as a mere truism. Yet I believe that it embodies a failure to effect thoroughly the "Copernican revolution", and that the apparent oneness of the world is merely the oneness of what is seen by a single spectator or apprehended by a single mind. The Critical Philosophy, although it intended to emphasize the subjective element in many apparent characteristics of the world, yet, by regarding the world in itself as unknowable, so concentrated attention upon the subjective representation that its subjectivity was soon forgotten. Having recognized the categories as the work of the mind, it was paralyzed by its own recognition, and abandoned in despair the attempt to undo the work of subjective falsification. In part, no doubt, its despair was well founded, but not, I think, in any absolute or ultimate sense. Still less was it a ground for rejoicing, or for supposing that the nescience to which it ought to have given rise could be legitimately exchanged for a metaphysical dogmatism.

I

As regards our present question, namely, the question of the unity of the world, the right method, as I think, has been indicated by William James.[2]

1 Bosanquet, *Logic*, ii, p. 211.
2 *Some Problems of Philosophy*, p. 124-6.

"Let us now turn our backs upon ineffable or unintelligible ways of accounting for the world's oneness, and inquire whether, instead of being a principle, the 'oneness' affirmed may not merely be a name like 'substance', descriptive of the fact that certain *specific and verifiable connections* are found among the parts of the experiential flux.... We can easily conceive of things that shall have no connection whatever with each other. We may assume them to inhabit different times and spaces, as the dreams of different persons do even now. They may be so unlike and incommensurable, and so inert towards one another, as never to jostle or interfere. Even now there may actually be whole universes so disparate from ours that we who know ours have no means of perceiving that they exist. We conceive their diversity, however; and by that fact the whole lot of them form what is known in logic as 'a universe of discourse.' To form a universe of discourse argues, as this example shows, no further kind of connexion. The importance attached by certain monistic writers to the fact that any chaos may become a universe by being merely named, is to me incomprehensible." We are thus left with two kinds of unity in the experienced world; the one that we may call the epistemological unity, due merely to the fact that my experienced world is what *one* experience selects from the sum total of existence; the other that tentative and partial unity exhibited in the prevalence of scientific laws in those portions of the world which science has hitherto mastered. Now a generalization based upon either of these kinds of unity would be fallacious. That the things which we experience have the common property of being experienced by us is a truism from which obviously nothing of importance can be deducible: it is clearly fallacious to draw from the fact that whatever we experience is experienced the conclusion that therefore everything must be experienced. The generalization of the second kind of unity, namely, that derived from scientific laws, would be equally fallacious, though the fallacy is a trifle less elementary. In order to explain it let us consider for a moment what is called the reign of law. People often speak as though it were a remarkable fact that the physical world is subject to invariable laws. In fact, however, it is not easy to see how such a world could fail to obey general laws. Taking any arbitrary set of points in space, there is a function of the time corresponding to these points, i.e. expressing the motion of a particle which traverses these points: this function may be regarded as a general law to which the behaviour of such a particle is subject. Taking all such functions for all the particles in the universe, there will be theoretically some one formula embracing them all, and this formula may be regarded as the single and supreme law of the spatio-temporal world. Thus what is surprising in physics is not the existence of general laws, but their extreme simplicity. It is not the uniformity of nature that should surprise us, for, by sufficient analytic ingenuity, any conceivable course of nature might be shown to exhibit uniformity. What should surprise us is the fact that the uniformity is simple enough for us to be able to discover it. But it is just this characteristic of simplicity in the laws of nature hitherto discovered which it would be fallacious to generalize, for it is obvious that simplicity has been a part cause of their discovery, and can, therefore, give no ground for the supposition that other undiscovered laws are equally simple.

The fallacies to which these two kinds of unity have given rise suggest a caution as regards all use in philosophy of general *results* that science is supposed to have achieved. In the first place, in generalizing these results beyond past experience, it is necessary to examine very carefully whether there is not some reason making it more probable that these results should hold of all that has been experienced than that they should hold of things universally. The sum total of what is experienced by mankind is a selection from the sum total of what exists, and any general character exhibited by this selection may be due to the manner of selecting rather than to the general character of that from which experience selects. In the second place, the most general results of science are the least certain and the most liable to be upset by subsequent research. In utilizing these results as the basis of a philosophy, we sacrifice the most valuable and remarkable characteristic of scientific method, namely, that, although almost everything in science is found sooner or later to require some correction, yet this correction is almost always such as to leave untouched, or only slightly modified, the greater part of the results which have been deduced from the premiss subsequently discovered to be faulty. The prudent man of science acquires a certain instinct as to the kind of uses which may be made of present scientific beliefs without incurring the danger of complete and utter refutation from the modifications likely to be introduced by subsequent discoveries. Unfortunately the use of scientific generalizations of a sweeping kind as the basis of philosophy is just that kind of use which an instinct of scientific caution would avoid, since, as a rule, it would only lead to true results if the generalization upon which it is based stood in *no* need of correction.

We may illustrate these general considerations by means of two examples, namely, the conservation of energy and the principle of evolution.

(1) Let us begin with the conservation of energy, or, as Herbert Spencer used to call it, the persistence of force. He says:[3]

> Before taking a first step in the rational interpretation of Evolution, it is needful to recognise, not only the facts that Matter is indestructible and Motion continuous, but also the fact that Force persists. An attempt to assign the *causes* of Evolution would manifestly be absurd if that agency to which the metamorphosis in general and in detail is due, could either come into existence or cease to exist. The succes-

3 *First Principles* (1862), Part II, beginning of Chap. viii.

sion of phenomena would in such case be altogether arbitrary, and deductive Science impossible.

This paragraph illustrates the kind of way in which the philosopher is tempted to give an air of absoluteness and necessity to empirical generalizations, of which only the approximate truth in the regions hitherto investigated can be guaranteed by the unaided methods of science. It is very often said that the persistence of something or other is a necessary presupposition of all scientific investigation, and this presupposition is then thought to be exemplified in some quantity which physics declares to be constant. There are here, as it seems to me, three distinct errors. First, the detailed scientific 10 investigation of nature does not *presuppose* any such general laws as its results are found to verify. Apart from particular observations, science need presuppose nothing except the general principles of logic, and these principles are not laws of nature, for they are merely hypothetical, and apply not only to the actual world but to whatever is *possible*. The second error consists in the identification of a constant quantity with a persistent entity. Energy is a certain function of a physical system, but is not a thing or substance persisting throughout the changes of the system. The same is true of mass, in spite of the fact that mass has often been defined as *quantity of matter*. The whole conception, of quantity, involving, as it does, numerical 20 measurement based largely upon conventions, is far more artificial, far more an embodiment of mathematical convenience, than is commonly believed by those who philosophize on physics. Thus even if (which I cannot for a moment admit) the persistence of some entity were among the necessary postulates of science, it would be a sheer error to infer from this the constancy of any physical quantity, or the a priori necessity of any such constancy which may be empirically discovered. In the third place, it has become more and more evident with the progress of physics that large generalizations, such as the conservation of energy or mass, are far from certain and are very likely only approximate. Mass, which used to be 30 regarded as the most indubitable of physical quantities, is now generally believed to vary according to velocity, and to be, in fact, a vector quantity which at a given moment is different in different directions. The detailed conclusions deduced from the supposed constancy of mass for such motions as used to be studied in physics will remain very nearly exact, and therefore over the field of the older investigations very little modification of the older results is required. But as soon as such a principle as the conservation of mass or of energy is erected into a universal a priori law, the slightest failure in absolute exactness is fatal, and the whole philosophic structure raised upon this foundation is necessarily ruined. The prudent philosopher, 40 therefore, though he may with advantage study the methods of physics, will be very chary of basing anything upon what happen at the moment to be the most general results apparently obtained by those methods.

(2) The philosophy of evolution, which was to be our second example, illustrates the same tendency to hasty generalization, and also another sort, namely, the undue preoccupation with ethical notions. There are two kinds of evolutionist philosophy, of which both Hegel and Spencer represent the older and less radical kind, while Pragmatism and Bergson represent the more modern and revolutionary variety. But both these sorts of evolutionism have in common the emphasis on *progress*, that is, upon a continual change from the worse to the better, or from the simpler to the more complex. It would be unfair to attribute to Hegel any scientific motive or foundation, but all the other evolutionists, including Hegel's modern disciples, have derived their impetus very largely from the history of biological development. To a philosophy which derives a law of universal progress from this history there are two objections. First, that this history itself is concerned with a very small selection of facts confined to an infinitesimal fragment of space and time, and even on scientific grounds probably not an average sample of events in the world at large. For we know that decay as well as growth is a normal occurrence in the world. An extra-terrestrial philosopher, who had watched a single youth up to the age of twenty-one and had never come across any other human being, might conclude that it is the nature of human beings to grow continually taller and wiser in an indefinite progress towards perfection; and this generalization would be just as well founded as the generalization which evolutionists base upon the previous history of this planet. Apart, however, from this scientific objection to evolutionism, there is another, derived from the undue admixture of ethical notions in the very idea of progress from which evolutionism derives its charm. Organic life, we are told, has developed gradually from the protozoon to the philosopher, and this development, we are assured, is indubitably an advance. Unfortunately it is the philosopher, not the protozoon, who gives us this assurance, and we can have no security that the impartial outsider would agree with the philosopher's self-complacent assumption. This point has been illustrated by the philosopher Chuang Tzŭ in the following instructive anecdote:

The Grand Augur, in his ceremonial robes, approached the shambles and thus addressed the pigs: "How can you object to die? I shall fatten you for three months. I shall discipline myself for ten days and fast for three. I shall strew fine grass, and place you bodily upon a carved sacrificial dish. Does not this satisfy you?"

Then, speaking from the pigs' point of view, he continued: "It is better, perhaps, after all, to live on bran and escape the shambles...."

"But then," added he, speaking from his own point of view, "to enjoy honour when alive one would readily die on a war-shield or in the headsman's basket."

So he rejected the pigs' point of view and adopted his own point of view. In what sense, then, was he different from the pigs?

I much fear that the evolutionists too often resemble the Grand Augur and the pigs.

The ethical element which has been prominent in many of the most famous systems of philosophy is, in my opinion, one of the most serious obstacles to the victory of scientific method in the investigation of philosophical questions. Human ethical notions, as Chuang Tzŭ perceived, are essentially anthropocentric, and involve, when used in metaphysics, an attempt, however veiled, to legislate for the universe on the basis of the present desires of men. In this way they interfere with that receptivity to fact which is the essence of the scientific attitude towards the world. To regard ethical notions as a key to the understanding of the world is essentially pre-Copernican. It is to make man, with the hopes and ideals which he happens to have at the present moment, the centre of the universe and the interpreter of its supposed aims and purposes. Ethical metaphysics is fundamentally an attempt, however disguised, to give legislative force to our own wishes. This may, of course, be questioned, but I think that it is confirmed by a consideration of the way in which ethical notions arise. Ethics is essentially a product of the gregarious instinct, that is to say, of the instinct to cooperate with those who are to form our own group against those who belong to other groups. Those who belong to our own group are good; those who belong to hostile groups are wicked. The ends which are pursued by our own group are desirable ends, the ends pursued by hostile groups are nefarious. The subjectivity of this situation is not apparent to the gregarious animal, which feels that the general principles of justice are on the side of its own herd. When the animal has arrived at the dignity of the metaphysician, it invents ethics as the embodiment of its belief in the justice of its own herd. So the Grand Augur invokes ethics as the justification of Augurs in their conflicts with pigs. But, it may be said, this view of ethics takes no account of such truly ethical notions as that of self-sacrifice. This, however, would be a mistake. The success of gregarious animals in the struggle for existence depends upon cooperation within the herd, and cooperation requires sacrifice, to some extent, of what would otherwise be the interest of the individual. Hence arises a conflict of desires and instincts, since both self-preservation and the preservation of the herd are biological ends to the individual. Ethics is in origin the art of recommending to others the sacrifices required for cooperation with oneself. Hence, by reflexion, it comes, through the operation of social justice, to recommend sacrifices by oneself, but all ethics, however refined, remains more or less subjective.

Even vegetarians do not hesitate, for example, to save the life of a man in a fever, although in doing so they destroy the lives of many millions of microbes. The view of the world taken by the philosophy derived from ethical notions is thus never impartial and therefore never fully scientific. As compared with science, it fails to achieve the imaginative liberation from self which is necessary to such understanding of the world as man can hope to achieve, and the philosophy which it inspires is always more or less parochial, more or less infected with the prejudices of a time and a place.

I do not deny the importance or value, within its own sphere, of the kind
10 of philosophy which is inspired by ethical notions. The ethical work of Spinoza, for example, appears to me of the very highest significance, but what is valuable in such work is not any metaphysical theory as to the nature of the world to which it may give rise, nor indeed anything which can be proved or disproved by argument. What is valuable is the indication of some new way of feeling towards life and the world, some way of feeling by which our own existence can acquire more of the characteristics which we must deeply desire. The value of such work, however immeasurable it is, belongs with practice and not with theory. Such theoretic importance as it may possess is only in relation to human nature, not in relation to the world at
20 large. The scientific philosophy, therefore, which aims only at understanding the world and not directly at any other improvement of human life, cannot take account of ethical notions without being turned aside from that submission to fact which is the essence of the scientific temper.

II

If the notion of the universe and the notion of good and evil are extruded from scientific philosophy, it may be asked what specific problems remain for the philosopher as opposed to the man of science? It would be difficult to give a precise answer to this question, but certain characteristics may be noted as distinguishing the province of philosophy from that of the special
30 sciences.

In the first place a philosophical proposition must be general. It must not deal specially with things on the surface of the earth, or with the solar system, or with any other portion of space and time. It is this need of generality which has led to the belief that philosophy deals with the universe as a whole. I do not believe that this belief is justified, but I do believe that a philosophical proposition must be applicable to everything that exists or may exist. It might be supposed that this admission would be scarcely distinguishable from the view which I wish to reject. This, however, would be an error, and an important one. The traditional view would make the
40 universe itself the subject of various predicates which could not be applied to any particular thing in the universe, and the ascription of such peculiar

predicates to the universe would be the special business of philosophy. I maintain, on the contrary, that there are no propositions of which the "universe" is the subject; in other words, that there is no such thing as the "universe". What I do maintain is that there are general propositions which may be asserted of each individual thing, such as the propositions of logic. This does not involve that all the things there are form a whole which could be regarded as another thing and be made the subject of predicates. It involves only the assertion that there are properties which belong to each separate thing, not that there are properties belonging to the whole of things collectively. The philosophy which I wish to advocate may be called logical atomism or absolute pluralism, because, while maintaining that there are many things, it denies that there is a whole composed of those things. We shall see, therefore, that philosophical propositions, instead of being concerned with the whole of things collectively, are concerned with all things distributively; and not only must they be concerned with all things, but they must be concerned with such properties of all things as do not depend upon the accidental nature of the things that there happen to be, but are true of any possible world, independently of such facts as can only be discovered by our senses.

This brings us to a second characteristic of philosophical propositions, namely, that they must be a priori. A philosophical proposition must be such as can be neither proved nor disproved by empirical evidence. Too often we find in philosophical books arguments based upon the course of history, or the convolutions of the brain, or the eyes of shell-fish. Special and accidental facts of this kind are irrelevant to philosophy, which must make only such assertions as would be equally true however the actual world were constituted.

We may sum up these two characteristics of philosophical propositions by saying that *philosophy is the science of the possible*. But this statement unexplained is liable to be misleading, since it may be thought that the possible is something other than the general, whereas in fact the two are indistinguishable.

Philosophy, if what has been said is correct, becomes indistinguishable from logic as that word has now come to be used. The study of logic consists, broadly speaking, of two not very sharply distinguished portions. On the one hand it is concerned with those general statements which can be made concerning everything without mentioning any one thing or predicate or relation, such for example as "if x is a member of the class α and every member of α is a member of β, then x is a member of the class β, whatever x, α, and β may be". On the other hand, it is concerned with the analysis and enumeration of logical *forms*, i.e. with the kinds of propositions that may occur, with the various types of facts, and with the classification of the constituents of facts. In this way logic provides an inventory of possibilities, a repertory of abstractly tenable hypotheses.

It might be thought that such a study would be too vague and too general to be of any very great importance, and that, if its problems became at any point sufficiently definite, they would be merged in the problems of some special science. It appears, however, that this is not the case. In some problems, for example, the analysis of space and time, the nature of perception, or the theory of judgment, the discovery of the logical form of the facts involved is the hardest part of the work and the part whose performance has been most lacking hitherto. It is chiefly for want of the right logical 10 hypothesis that such problems have hitherto been treated in such an unsatisfactory manner, and have given rise to those contradictions or antinomies in which the enemies of reason among philosophers have at all times delighted.

By concentrating attention upon the investigation of logical forms, it becomes possible at last for philosophy to deal with its problems piecemeal, and to obtain, as the sciences do, such partial and probably not wholly correct results as subsequent investigation can utilize even while it supplements and improves them. Most philosophies hitherto have been constructed all in one block, in such a way that, if they were not wholly correct, 20 they were wholly incorrect, and could not be used as a basis for further investigations. It is chiefly owing to this fact that philosophy, unlike science, has hitherto been unprogressive, because each original philosopher has had to begin the work again from the beginning, without being able to accept anything definite from the work of his predecessors. A scientific philosophy such as I wish to recommend will be piecemeal and tentative like other sciences; above all, it will be able to invent hypotheses which, even if they are not wholly true, will yet remain fruitful after the necessary corrections have been made. This possibility of successive approximations to the truth is, more than anything else, the source of the triumphs of science, and 30 to transfer this possibility to philosophy is to ensure a progress in method whose importance it would be almost impossible to exaggerate.

The essence of philosophy as thus conceived is analysis, not synthesis. To build up systems of the world, like Heine's German professor who knit together fragments of life and made an intelligible system out of them, is not, I believe, any more feasible than the discovery of the philosopher's stone. What is feasible is the understanding of general forms, and the division of traditional problems into a number of separate and less baffling questions. "Divide and conquer" is the maxim of success here as elsewhere.

Let us illustrate these somewhat general maxims by examining their 40 application to the philosophy of space, for it is only in application that the meaning or importance of a method can be understood. Suppose we are confronted with the problem of space as presented in Kant's Transcendental Aesthetic, and suppose we wish to discover what are the elements of the problem and what hope there is of obtaining a solution of them. It will soon appear that three entirely distinct problems, belonging to different studies, and requiring different methods for their solution, have been confusedly combined in the supposed single problem with which Kant is concerned. There is a problem of logic, a problem of physics, and a problem of theory of knowledge. Of these three, the problem of logic can be solved exactly and perfectly; the problem of physics can probably be solved with as great a degree of certainty and as great an approach to exactness as can be hoped in an empirical region; the problem of theory of knowledge, however, remains very obscure and very difficult to deal with. Let us see how these three 10 problems arise.

(1) The logical problem has arisen through the suggestions of non-Euclidean geometry. Given a body of geometrical propositions, it is not difficult to find a minimum statement of the axioms from which this body of propositions can be deduced. It is also not difficult, by dropping or altering some of these axioms, to obtain a more general or a different geometry, having, from the point of view of pure mathematics, the same logical coherence and the same title to respect as the more familiar Euclidean geometry. The Euclidean geometry itself is true perhaps of actual space (though this is doubtful), but certainly of an infinite number of purely 20 arithmetical systems, each of which, from the point of view of abstract logic, has an equal and indefeasible right to be called a Euclidean space. Thus space as an object of logical or mathematical study loses its uniqueness; not only are there many kinds of spaces, but there are an infinity of examples of each kind, though it is difficult to find any kind of which the space of physics may be an example, and it is impossible to find any kind of which the space of physics is certainly an example. As an illustration of one possible logical system of geometry we may consider all relations of three terms which are analogous in certain formal respects to the relation "between" as it appears to be in actual space. A space is then defined by means of one such 30 three-term relation. The points of the space are all the terms which have this relation to something or other, and their order in the space in question is determined by this relation. The points of one space are necessarily also points of other spaces, since there are necessarily other three-term relations having those same points for their field. The space in fact is not determined by the class of its points, but by the ordering three-term relation. When enough abstract logical properties of such relations have been enumerated to determine the resulting kind of geometry, say, for example, Euclidean geometry, it becomes unnecessary for the pure geometer in his abstract capacity to distinguish between the various relations which have all these 40 properties. He considers the whole class of such relations, not any single one among them. Thus in studying a given kind of geometry the pure mathematician is studying a certain class of relations defined by means of

certain abstract logical properties which take the place of what used to be called axioms. The nature of geometrical *reasoning* therefore is purely deductive and purely logical; if any special epistemological peculiarities are to be found in geometry, it must not be in the reasoning, but in our knowledge concerning the axioms in some given space.

(2) The physical problem of space is both more interesting and more difficult than the logical problem. The physical problem may be stated as follows: to find in the physical world, or to construct from physical materials, a space of one of the kinds enumerated by the logical treatment of geometry. This problem derives its difficulty from the attempt to accommodate to the roughness and vagueness of the real world some system possessing the logical clearness and exactitude of pure mathematics. That this can be done with a certain degree of approximation is fairly evident. If I see three people A, B, and C sitting in a row, I become aware of the fact which may be expressed by saying that B is between A and C rather than that A is between B and C, or C is between A and B. This relation of "between" which is thus perceived to hold has some of the abstract logical properties of those three-term relations which, we saw, give rise to a geometry, but its properties fail to be exact, and are not, as empirically given, amenable to the kind of treatment at which geometry aims. In abstract geometry we deal with points, straight lines, and planes; but the three people A, B, and C whom I see sitting in a row are not exactly points, nor is the row exactly a straight line. Nevertheless physics, which formally assumes a space containing points, straight lines, and planes, is found empirically to give results applicable to the sensible world. It must therefore be possible to find an interpretation of the points, straight lines, and planes of physics in terms of physical data, or at any rate in terms of data together with such hypothetical additions as seem least open to question. Since all data suffer from a lack of mathematical precision through being of a certain size and somewhat vague in outline, it is plain that if such a notion as that of a point is to find any application to empirical material, the point must be neither a datum nor a hypothetical addition to data, but a *construction* by means of data with their hypothetical additions. It is obvious that any hypothetical filling out of data is less dubious and unsatisfactory when the additions are closely analogous to data than when they are of a radically different sort. To assume, for example, that objects which we see continue, after we have turned away our eyes, to be more or less analogous to what they were while we were looking, is a less violent assumption than to assume that such objects are composed of an infinite number of mathematical points. Hence in the physical study of the geometry of physical space, points must not be assumed *ab initio* as they are in the logical treatment of geometry, but must be constructed as systems composed of data and hypothetical analogues of data. We are thus led naturally to define a physical

point as a certain class of those objects which are the ultimate constituents of the physical world. It will be the class of all those objects which, as one would naturally say, *contain* the point. To secure a definition giving this result, without previously assuming that physical objects are composed of points, is an agreeable problem in mathematical logic. The solution of this problem and the perception of its importance are due to my friend Dr. Whitehead. The oddity of regarding a point as a class of physical entities wears off with familiarity, and ought in any case not to be felt by those who maintain, as practically every one does, that points are mathematical fictions. The word "fiction" is used glibly in such connexions by many men who seem not to feel the necessity of explaining how it can come about that a fiction can be so useful in the study of the actual world as the points of mathematical physics have been found to be. By our definition, which regards a point as a class of physical objects, it is explained both how the use of points can lead to important physical results, and how we can nevertheless avoid the assumption that points are themselves entities in the physical world.

Many of the mathematically convenient properties of abstract logical spaces cannot be either known to belong or known not to belong to the space of physics. Such are all the properties connected with continuity. For to know that actual space has these properties would require an infinite exactness of sense-perception. If actual space is continuous, there are nevertheless many possible non-continuous spaces which will be empirically indistinguishable from it; and, conversely, actual space may be non-continuous and yet empirically indistinguishable from a possible continuous space. Continuity, therefore, though obtainable in the a priori region of arithmetic, is not with certainty obtainable in the space or time of the physical world: whether these are continuous or not would seem to be a question not only unanswered but for ever unanswerable. From the point of view of philosophy, however, the discovery that a question is unanswerable is as complete an answer as any that could possibly be obtained. And from the point of view of physics, where no empirical means of distinction can be found, there can be no empirical objection to the mathematically simplest assumption, which is that of continuity.

The subject of the physical theory of space is a very large one, hitherto little explored. It is associated with a similar theory of time, and both have been forced upon the attention of philosophically minded physicists by the discussions which have raged concerning the theory of relativity.

(3) The problem with which Kant is concerned in the Transcendental Aesthetic is primarily the epistemological problem: "How do we come to have knowledge of geometry a priori?" By the distinction between the logical and physical problems of geometry, the bearing and scope of this question are greatly altered. Our knowledge of pure geometry is a priori but

is wholly logical. Our knowledge of physical geometry is synthetic, but is not a priori. Our knowledge of pure geometry is hypothetical, and does not enable us to assert, for example, that the axiom of parallels is true in the physical world. Our knowledge of physical geometry, while it does enable us to assert that this axiom is approximately verified, does not, owing to the inevitable inexactitude of observation, enable us to assert that it is verified *exactly*. Thus, with the separation which we have made between pure geometry and the geometry of physics, the Kantian problem collapses. To the question, "How is synthetic a priori knowledge possible?" we can now
10 reply, at any rate so far as geometry is concerned, "It is not possible", if "synthetic" means "not deducible from logic alone". Our knowledge of geometry, like the rest of our knowledge, is derived partly from logic, partly from sense, and the peculiar position which in Kant's day geometry appeared to occupy is seen now to be a delusion. There are still some philosophers, it is true, who maintain that our knowledge that the axiom of parallels, for example, is true of actual space, is not to be accounted for empirically, but is as Kant maintained derived from an a priori intuition. This position is not logically refutable, but I think it loses all plausibility as soon as we realize how complicated and derivative is the notion of physical
20 space. As we have seen, the application of geometry to the physical world in no way demands that there should really be points and straight lines among physical entities. The principle of economy, therefore, demands that we should abstain from assuming the existence of points and straight lines. As soon, however, as we accept the view that points and straight lines are complicated constructions by means of classes of physical entities, the hypothesis that we have an a priori intuition enabling us to know what happens to straight lines when they are produced indefinitely becomes extremely strained and harsh; nor do I think that such an hypothesis would ever have arisen in the mind of a philosopher who had grasped the nature of
30 physical space. Kant, under the influence of Newton, adopted, though with some vacillation, the hypothesis of absolute space, and this hypothesis, though logically unobjectionable, is removed by Occam's razor, since absolute space is an unnecessary entity in the explanation of the physical world. Although, therefore, we cannot refute the Kantian theory of an a priori intuition, we can remove its grounds one by one through an analysis of the problem. Thus, here as in many other philosophical questions, the analytic method, while not capable of arriving at a demonstrative result, is nevertheless capable of showing that all the positive grounds in favour of a certain theory are fallacious and that a less unnatural theory is capable of
40 accounting for the facts.

Another question by which the capacity of the analytic method can be shown is the question of realism. Both those who advocate and those who combat realism seem to me to be far from clear as to the nature of the

problem which they are discussing. If we ask: "Are our objects of perception *real* and are they *independent* of the percipient?" it must be supposed
that we attach some meaning to the words "real" and "independent", and
yet, if either side in the controversy of realism is asked to define these two
words, their answer is pretty sure to embody confusions such as logical
analysis will reveal.

Let us begin with the word "real". There certainly are objects of perception, and therefore, if the question whether these objects are real is to be a
substantial question, there must be in the world two sorts of objects,
namely, the real and the unreal, and yet the unreal is supposed to be   10
essentially what there is not. The question what properties must belong to
an object in order to make it real is one to which an adequate answer is
seldom if ever forthcoming. There is of course the Hegelian answer, that the
real is the self-consistent and that nothing is self-consistent except the
Whole; but this answer, true or false, is not relevant in our present discussion, which moves on a lower plane and is concerned with the status of
objects of perception among other objects of equal fragmentariness. Objects
of perception are contrasted, in the discussions concerning realism, rather
with psychical states on the one hand and matter on the other hand than
with the all-inclusive whole of things. The question we have therefore to   20
consider is the question as to what can be meant by assigning "reality" to
some but not all of the entities that make up the world. Two elements, I
think, make up what is felt rather than thought when the word "reality" is
used in this sense. A thing is real if it persists at times when it is not
perceived; or again, a thing is real when it is correlated with other things in a
way which experience has led us to expect. It will be seen that reality in
either of these senses is by no means necessary to a thing, and that in fact
there might be a whole world in which nothing was real in either of these
senses. It might turn out that the objects of perception failed of reality in one
or both of these respects, without its being in any way deducible that they   30
are not parts of the external world with which physics deals. Similar
remarks will apply to the word "independent". Most of the associations of
this word are bound up with ideas as to causation which it is not now
possible to maintain. *A* is independent of *B* when *B* is not an indispensable
part of the *cause* of *A*. But when it is recognized that causation is nothing
more than correlation, and that there are correlations of simultaneity as well
as of succession, it becomes evident that there is no uniqueness in a series of
causal antecedents of a given event, but that, at any point where there is a
correlation of simultaneity, we can pass from one line of antecedents to
another in order to obtain a new series of causal antecedents. It will be   40
necessary to specify the causal law according to which the antecedents are to
be considered. I received a letter the other day from a correspondent who
had been puzzled by various philosophical questions. After enumerating

them he says: "These questions led me from Bonn to Strassburg, where I found Professor Simmel." Now, it would be absurd to deny that these questions caused his body to move from Bonn to Strassburg, and yet it must be supposed that a set of purely mechanical antecedents could also be found which would account for this transfer of matter from one place to another. Owing to this plurality of causal series antecedent to a given event, the notion of *the* cause becomes indefinite, and the question of independence becomes correspondingly ambiguous. Thus, instead of asking simply whether *A* is independent of *B*, we ought to ask whether there is a series determined by such and such causal laws leading from *B* to *A*. This point is important in connexion with the particular question of objects of perception. It may be that no objects quite like those which we perceive ever exist unperceived; in this case there will be a causal law according to which objects of perception are not independent of being perceived. But even if this be the case, it may nevertheless also happen that there are purely physical causal laws determining the occurrence of objects which are perceived by means of other objects which perhaps are not perceived. In that case, in regard to such causal laws objects of perception will be independent of being perceived. Thus the question whether objects of perception are independent of being perceived is, as it stands, indeterminate, and the answer will be yes or no according to the method adopted of making it determinate. I believe that this confusion has borne a very large part in prolonging the controversies on this subject, which might well have seemed capable of remaining for ever undecided. The view which I should wish to advocate is that objects of perception do not persist unchanged at times when they are not perceived, although probably objects more or less resembling them do exist at such times; that objects of perception are part, and the only empirically knowable part, of the actual subject-matter of physics, and are themselves properly to be called physical; that purely physical laws exist determining the character and duration of objects of perception without any reference to the fact that they are perceived; and that in the establishment of such laws the propositions of physics do not presuppose any propositions of psychology or even the existence of mind. I do not know whether realists would recognize such a view as realism. All that I should claim for it is, that it avoids difficulties which seem to me to beset both realism and idealism as hitherto advocated, and that it avoids the appeal which they have made to ideas which logical analysis shows to be ambiguous. A further defence and elaboration of the positions which I advocate, but for which time is lacking now, will be found indicated in my book on *Our Knowledge of the External World*. [4]

The adoption of scientific method in philosophy, if I am not mistaken,

4 Open Court Company, 1914.

compels us to abandon the hope of solving many of the more ambitious and humanly interesting problems of traditional philosophy. Some of these it relegates, though with little expectation of a successful solution, to special sciences, others it shows to be such as our capacities are essentially incapable of solving. But there remain a large number of the recognized problems of philosophy in regard to which the method advocated gives all those advantages of division into distinct questions, of tentative, partial, and progressive advance, and of appeal to principles with which, independently of temperament, all competent students must agree. The failure of philosophy hitherto has been due in the main to haste and ambition: patience and modesty, here as in other sciences, will open the road to solid and durable progress.

<h1 style="text-align:center">5</h1>

The Ultimate Constituents of Matter [1915]

THIS PAPER WAS published in *The Monist*, 25 (July 1915): 399–417. As Russell noted, it was delivered first as a lecture to the Philosophical Society of Manchester on 15 February 1915. Russell included it in *Mysticism and Logic* (1918).

Russell had agreed to deliver the paper by 17 October 1914 when he wrote Professor Samuel Alexander confirming the date. He went on to ask: "Are there really people in Manchester interested in philosophy still? I am not. I will do my best, but I am afraid I shall have no *new* ideas. What did I say I would lecture on?" The mood expressed in this letter gripped Russell right up until the time of the lecture. In a letter to Lady Ottoline Morrell written on the 21st of January he complained of all the work he had to do, including "a paper on Matter at Manchester" (#1205). On the 2nd of February he remarked that "the Manchester lecture has to be written out in full" (#1216). He did not mention the paper again until the 14th of February: "I am dreadfully tired, from the effort of doing my paper on Matter in a hurry" (#1223).

He told Alexander on the 5th of February, in a letter detailing his travel plans, that he would "enjoy questions and discussion". He was not disappointed.

> Manchester was a great success. I had a large and enthusiastic audience, and I made the acquaintance of Rutherford, who next to J. J. Thomson is the best physicist in England. But it was very tiring, as I had to go on arguing till midnight, and Alexander (my host) is deaf.   (#1224, pmk. 17 Feb.)

This account was written for Lady Ottoline the day after the lecture.

When Russell arranged the essays in *Mysticism and Logic* he placed this one directly before "The Relation of Sense-Data to Physics" (1). His reason for doing so probably has to do with the fact that, although written after 1, this paper makes no mention of "sensibilia" which are so prominent in 1. Instead he favours "data of sense", "sense-data", "sensible objects", "objects of sense" and "particulars". The language of this essay, then, resembles more closely the language of *Our Knowledge of the External World* (1914) and its derivative, "On Scientific Method in Philosophy" (4), than the language of 1. By placing it before 1 in his book Russell seems to be treating it as a popular introduction to the technical topics in 1.

There is no manuscript, so the *Mysticism and Logic* version, which Russell saw through the press, has been selected as copy-text. The results of collating this version with *The Monist* text are reported in the Textual Notes.

I WISH TO discuss in this article[1] no less a question than the ancient metaphysical query, "What is matter?" The question, "What is matter?" in so far as it concerns philosophy, is, I think, already capable of an answer which in principle will be as complete as an answer can hope to be; that is to say, we can separate the problem into an essentially soluble and an essentially insoluble portion, and we can now see how to solve the essentially soluble portion, at least as regards its main outlines. It is these outlines which I wish to suggest in the present article. My main position, which is realistic, is, I hope and believe, not remote from that of Professor Alexander, by whose writings on this subject I have profited greatly.[2] It is also in close accord with that of Dr. Nunn.[3]

Common sense is accustomed to the division of the world into mind and matter. It is supposed by all who have never studied philosophy that the distinction between mind and matter is perfectly clear and easy, that the two do not at any point overlap, and that only a fool or a philosopher could be in doubt as to whether any given entity is mental or material. This simple faith survives in Descartes and in a somewhat modified form in Spinoza, but with Leibniz it begins to disappear, and from his day to our own almost every philosopher of note has criticized and rejected the dualism of common sense. It is my intention in this article to defend this dualism; but before defending it we must spend a few moments on the reasons which have prompted its rejection.

Our knowledge of the material world is obtained by means of the senses, of sight and touch and so on. At first it is supposed that things are just as they seem, but two opposite sophistications soon destroy this naïve belief. On the one hand the physicists cut up matter into molecules, atoms, corpuscles, and as many more such subdivisions as their future needs may make them postulate, and the units at which they arrive are uncommonly different from the visible, tangible objects of daily life. A unit of matter tends more and more to be something like an electromagnetic field filling all space, though having its greatest intensity in a small region. Matter consisting of such elements is as remote from daily life as any metaphysical theory. It differs from the theories of metaphysicians only in the fact that its practical efficacy proves that it contains some measure of truth and induces business men to invest money on the strength of it; but, in spite of its connection with the money market, it remains a metaphysical theory none the less.

The second kind of sophistication to which the world of common sense has been subjected is derived from the psychologists and physiologists. The physiologists point out that what we see depends upon the eye, that what we

1 An address delivered to the Philosophical Society of Manchester in February, 1915.
2 *Cf.* especially Samuel Alexander, "The Basis of Realism", *British Academy*, Vol. VI.
3 "Are Secondary Qualities Independent of Perception?", *Proc. Arist. Soc.*, 1909-10, pp. 191-218.

hear depends upon the ear, and that all our senses are liable to be affected by anything which affects the brain, like alcohol or hasheesh. Psychologists point out how much of what we think we see is supplied by association or unconscious inference, how much is mental interpretation, and how doubtful is the residuum which can be regarded as crude datum. From these facts it is argued by the psychologists that the notion of a datum passively received by the mind is a delusion, and it is argued by the physiologists that even if a pure datum of sense could be obtained by the analysis of experience, still this datum could not belong, as common sense supposes, to the
10 outer world, since its whole nature is conditioned by our nerves and sense organs, changing as they change in ways which it is thought impossible to connect with any change in the matter supposed to be perceived. This physiologist's argument is exposed to the rejoinder, more specious than solid, that our knowledge of the existence of the sense organs and nerves is obtained by that very process which the physiologist has been engaged in discrediting, since the existence of the nerves and sense organs is only known through the evidence of the senses themselves. This argument may prove that some reinterpretation of the results of physiology is necessary before they can acquire metaphysical validity. But it does not upset the
20 physiological argument in so far as this constitutes merely a *reductio ad absurdum* of naïve realism.

These various lines of argument prove, I think, that some part of the beliefs of common sense must be abandoned. They prove that, if we take these beliefs as a whole, we are forced into conclusions which are in part self-contradictory; but such arguments cannot of themselves decide what portion of our common-sense beliefs is in need of correction. Common sense believes that what we see is physical, outside the mind, and continuing to exist if we shut our eyes or turn them in another direction. I believe that common sense is right in regarding what we see as physical and (in one of
30 several possible senses) outside the mind, but is probably wrong in supposing that it continues to exist when we are no longer looking at it. It seems to me that the whole discussion of matter has been obscured by two errors which support each other. The first of these is the error that what we see, or perceive through any of our other senses, is subjective: the second is the belief that what is physical must be persistent. Whatever physics may regard as the ultimate constituents of matter, it always supposes these constituents to be indestructible. Since the immediate data of sense are not indestructible but in a state of perpetual flux, it is argued that these data themselves cannot be among the ultimate constituents of matter. I believe
40 this to be a sheer mistake. The persistent particles of mathematical physics I regard as logical constructions, symbolic fictions enabling us to express compendiously very complicated assemblages of facts; and, on the other hand, I believe that the actual data in sensation, the immediate objects of

sight or touch or hearing, are extra-mental, purely physical, and among the ultimate constituents of matter.

My meaning in regard to the impermanence of physical entities may perhaps be made clearer by the use of Bergson's favourite illustration of the cinematograph. When I first read Bergson's statement that the mathematician conceives the world after the analogy of a cinematograph, I had never seen a cinematograph, and my first visit to one was determined by the desire to verify Bergson's statement, which I found to be completely true, at least so far as I am concerned. When, in a picture palace, we see a man rolling down hill, or running away from the police, or falling into a river, or doing 10 any of those other things to which men in such places are addicted, we know that there is not really only one man moving, but a succession of films, each with a different momentary man. The illusion of persistence arises only through the approach to continuity in the series of momentary men. Now what I wish to suggest is that in this respect the cinema is a better metaphysician than common sense, physics, or philosophy. The real man too, I believe, however the police may swear to his identity, is really a series of momentary men, each different one from the other, and bound together, not by a numerical identity, but by continuity and certain intrinsic causal laws. And what applies to men applies equally to tables and chairs, the sun, 20 moon and stars. Each of these is to be regarded, not as one single persistent entity, but as a series of entities succeeding each other in time, each lasting for a very brief period, though probably not for a mere mathematical instant. In saying this I am only urging the same kind of division in time as we are accustomed to acknowledge in the case of space. A body which fills a cubic foot will be admitted to consist of many smaller bodies, each occupying only a very tiny volume; similarly a thing which persists for an hour is to be regarded as composed of many things of less duration. A true theory of matter requires a division of things into time-corpuscles as well as into space-corpuscles.   30

The world may be conceived as consisting of a multitude of entities arranged in a certain pattern. The entities which are arranged I shall call "particulars". The arrangement or pattern results from relations among particulars. Classes or series of particulars, collected together on account of some property which makes it convenient to be able to speak of them as wholes, are what I call logical constructions or symbolic fictions. The particulars are to be conceived, not on the analogy of bricks in a building, but rather on the analogy of notes in a symphony. The ultimate constituents of a symphony (apart from relations) are the notes, each of which lasts only for a very short time. We may collect together all the notes played by one 40 instrument: these may be regarded as the analogues of the successive particulars which common sense would regard as successive states of one "thing". But the "thing" ought to be regarded as no more "real" or "substantial" than, for example, the rôle of the trombone. As soon as "things" are conceived in this manner it will be found that the difficulties in the way of regarding immediate objects of sense as physical have largely disappeared.

When people ask, "Is the object of sense mental or physical?" they seldom have any clear idea either what is meant by "mental" or "physical", or what criteria are to be applied for deciding whether a given entity belongs to one class or the other. I do not know how to give a sharp definition of the word "mental", but something may be done by enumerating occurrences
10 which are indubitably mental: believing, doubting, wishing, willing, being pleased or pained, are certainly mental occurrences; so are what we may call experiences, seeing, hearing, smelling, perceiving generally. But it does not follow from this that what is seen, what is heard, what is smelt, what is perceived, must be mental. When I see a flash of lightning, my seeing of it is mental, but what I see, although it is not quite the same as what anybody else sees at the same moment, and although it seems very unlike what the physicist would describe as a flash of lightning, is not mental. I maintain, in fact, that if the physicist could describe truly and fully all that occurs in the physical world when there is a flash of lightning, it would contain as a
20 constituent what I see, and also what is seen by anybody else who would commonly be said to see the same flash. What I mean may perhaps be made plainer by saying that if my body could remain in exactly the same state in which it is, although my mind had ceased to exist, precisely that object which I now see when I see the flash would exist, although of course I should not see it, since my seeing is mental. The principal reasons which have led people to reject this view have, I think, been two: first, that they did not adequately distinguish between my seeing and what I see; secondly, that the causal dependence of what I see upon my body has made people suppose that what I see cannot be "outside" me. The first of these reasons need not
30 detain us, since the confusion only needs to be pointed out in order to be obviated; but the second requires some discussion, since it can only be answered by removing current misconceptions, on the one hand as to the nature of space, and on the other, as to the meaning of causal dependence.

When people ask whether colours, for example, or other secondary qualities are inside or outside the mind, they seem to suppose that their meaning must be clear, and that it ought to be possible to say yes or no without any further discussion of the terms involved. In fact, however, such terms as "inside" or "outside" are very ambiguous. What is meant by asking whether this or that is "in" the mind? The mind is not like a bag or a
40 pie; it does not occupy a certain region in space, or, if (in a sense) it does, what is in that region is presumably part of the brain, which would not be said to be in the mind. When people say that sensible qualities are in the mind, they do not mean "spatially contained in" in the sense in which the

blackbirds were in the pie. We might regard the mind as an assemblage of particulars, namely, what would be called "states of mind", which would belong together in virtue of some specific common quality. The common quality of all states of mind would be the quality designated by the word "mental"; and besides this we should have to suppose that each separate person's states of mind have some common characteristic distinguishing them from the states of mind of other people. Ignoring this latter point, let us ask ourselves whether the quality designated by the word "mental" does, as a matter of observation, actually belong to objects of sense, such as colours or noises. I think any candid person must reply that, however 10 difficult it may be to know what we mean by "mental", it is not difficult to see that colours and noises are not mental in the sense of having that intrinsic peculiarity which belongs to beliefs and wishes and volitions, but not to the physical world. Berkeley advances on this subject a plausible argument[4] which seems to me to rest upon an ambiguity in the word "pain". He argues that the realist supposes the heat which he feels in approaching a fire to be something outside his mind, but that as he approaches nearer and nearer to the fire the sensation of heat passes imperceptibly into pain, and that no one could regard pain as something outside the mind. In reply to this argument, it should be observed in the first place that the heat of which we are 20 immediately aware is not in the fire but in our own body. It is only by inference that the fire is judged to be the cause of the heat which we feel in our body. In the second place (and this is the more important point), when we speak of pain we may mean one of two things: we may mean the object of the sensation or other experience which has the quality of being painful, or we may mean the quality of painfulness itself. When a man says he has a pain in his great toe, what he means is that he has a sensation associated with his great toe and having the quality of painfulness. The sensation itself, like every sensation, consists in experiencing a sensible object, and the experiencing has that quality of painfulness which only mental occurrences 30 can have, but which may belong to thoughts or desires, as well as to sensations. But in common language we speak of the sensible object experienced in a painful sensation as a pain, and it is this way of speaking which causes the confusion upon which the plausibility of Berkeley's argument depends. It would be absurd to attribute the quality of painfulness to anything non-mental, and hence it comes to be thought that what we call a pain in the toe must be mental. In fact, however, it is not the sensible object in such a case which is painful, but the sensation, that is to say, the experience of the sensible object. As the heat which we experience from the fire grows greater, the experience passes gradually from being pleasant to 40 being painful, but neither the pleasure nor the pain is a quality of the object

4 First dialogue between Hylas and Philonous, *Works* (Fraser's edition 1901), I, p. 384.

experienced as opposed to the experience, and it is therefore a fallacy to argue that this object must be mental on the ground that painfulness can only be attributed to what is mental.

If, then, when we say that something is in the mind we mean that it has a certain recognizable intrinsic characteristic such as belongs to thoughts and desires, it must be maintained on grounds of immediate inspection that objects of sense are not in any mind.

A different meaning of "in the mind" is, however, to be inferred from the arguments advanced by those who regard sensible objects as being in the
10 mind. The arguments used are, in the main, such as would prove the causal dependence of objects of sense upon the percipient. Now the notion of causal dependence is very obscure and difficult, much more so in fact than is generally realized by philosophers. I shall return to this point in a moment. For the present, however, accepting the notion of causal dependence without criticism, I wish to urge that the dependence in question is rather upon our bodies than upon our minds. The visual appearance of an object is altered if we shut one eye, or squint, or look previously at something dazzling; but all these are bodily acts, and the alterations which they effect are to be explained by physiology and optics, not by psychology.[5] They are
20 in fact of exactly the same kind as the alterations effected by spectacles or a microscope. They belong therefore to the theory of the physical world, and can have no bearing upon the question whether what we see is causally dependent upon the mind. What they do tend to prove, and what I for my part have no wish to deny, is that what we see is causally dependent upon our body and is not, as crude common sense would suppose, something which would exist equally if our eyes and nerves and brain were absent, any more than the visual appearance presented by an object seen through a microscope would remain if the microscope were removed. So long as it is supposed that the physical world is composed of stable and more or less
30 permanent constituents, the fact that what we see is changed by changes in our body appears to afford reason for regarding what we see as not an ultimate constituent of matter. But if it is recognized that the ultimate constituents of matter are as circumscribed in duration as in spatial extent, the whole of this difficulty vanishes.

There remains, however, another difficulty, connected with space. When we look at the sun we wish to know something about the sun itself, which is ninety-three million miles away; but what we see is dependent upon our eyes, and it is difficult to suppose that our eyes can affect what happens at a distance of ninety-three million miles. Physics tells us that certain elec-
40 tromagnetic waves start from the sun, and reach our eyes after about eight minutes. They there produce disturbances in the rods and cones, thence in

5 This point has been well urged by the American realists.

the optic nerve, thence in the brain. At the end of this purely physical series, by some odd miracle, comes the experience which we call "seeing the sun", and it is such experiences which form the whole and sole reason for our belief in the optic nerve, the rods and cones, the ninety-three million miles, the electromagnetic waves, and the sun itself. It is this curious oppositeness of direction between the order of causation as affirmed by physics, and the order of evidence as revealed by theory of knowledge, that causes the most serious perplexities in regard to the nature of physical reality. Anything that invalidates our seeing, as a source of knowledge concerning physical reality, invalidates also the whole of physics and physiology. And yet, starting from 10 a common-sense acceptance of our seeing, physics has been led step by step to the construction of the causal chain in which our seeing is the last link, and the immediate object which we see cannot be regarded as that initial cause which we believe to be ninety-three million miles away, and which we are inclined to regard as the "real" sun.

I have stated this difficulty as forcibly as I can, because I believe that it can only be answered by a radical analysis and reconstruction of all the conceptions upon whose employment it depends.

Space, time, matter and cause, are the chief of these conceptions. Let us begin with the conception of cause. 20

Causal dependence, as I observed a moment ago, is a conception which it is very dangerous to accept at its face value. There exists a notion that in regard to any event there is something which may be called *the* cause of that event—some one definite occurrence, without which the event would have been impossible and with which it becomes necessary. An event is supposed to be dependent upon its cause in some way in which it is not dependent upon other things. Thus men will urge that the mind is dependent upon the brain, or, with equal plausibility, that the brain is dependent upon the mind. It seems not improbable that if we had sufficient knowledge we could infer the state of a man's mind from the state of his brain, or the state of his 30 brain from the state of his mind. So long as the usual conception of causal dependence is retained, this state of affairs can be used by the materialist to urge that the state of our brain causes our thoughts, and by the idealist to urge that our thoughts cause the state of our brain. Either contention is equally valid or equally invalid. The fact seems to be that there are many correlations of the sort which may be called causal, and that, for example, either a physical or a mental event can be predicted, theoretically, either from a sufficient number of physical antecedents or from a sufficient number of mental antecedents. To speak of *the* cause of an event is therefore misleading. Any set of antecedents from which the event can theoretically 40 be inferred by means of correlations might be called *a* cause of the event. But to speak of *the* cause is to imply a uniqueness which does not exist.

The relevance of this to the experience which we call "seeing the sun" is obvious. The fact that there exists a chain of antecedents which makes our seeing dependent upon the eyes and nerves and brain does not even tend to show that there is not another chain of antecedents in which the eyes and nerves and brain as physical things are ignored. If we are to escape from the dilemma which seemed to arise out of the physiological causation of what we see when we say we see the sun, we must find, at least in theory, a way of stating causal laws for the physical world, in which the units are not material things, such as the eyes and nerves and brain, but momentary particulars of the same sort as our momentary visual object when we look at the sun. The sun itself and the eyes and nerves and brain must be regarded as assemblages of momentary particulars. Instead of supposing, as we naturally do when we start from an uncritical acceptance of the apparent dicta of physics, that *matter* is what is "really real" in the physical world, and that the immediate objects of sense are mere phantasms, we must regard matter as a logical construction, of which the constituents will be just such evanescent particulars as may, when an observer happens to be present, become data of sense to that observer. What physics regards as the sun of eight minutes ago will be a whole assemblage of particulars, existing at different times, spreading out from a centre with the velocity of light, and containing among their number all those visual data which are seen by people who are now looking at the sun. Thus the sun of eight minutes ago is a class of particulars, and what I see when I now look at the sun is one member of this class. The various particulars constituting this class will be correlated with each other by a certain continuity and certain intrinsic laws of variation as we pass outwards from the centre, together with certain modifications correlated extrinsically with other particulars which are not members of this class. It is these extrinsic modifications which represent the sort of facts that, in our former account, appeared as the influence of the eyes and nerves in modifying the appearance of the sun.[6]

The *primâ facie* difficulties in the way of this view are chiefly derived from an unduly conventional theory of space. It might seem at first sight as if we had packed the world much fuller than it could possibly hold. At every place between us and the sun, we said, there is to be a particular which is to be a member of the sun as it was a few minutes ago. There will also, of course, have to be a particular which is a member of any planet or fixed star that may happen to be visible from that place. At the place where I am, there will be particulars which will be members severally of all the "things" I am now said to be perceiving. Thus throughout the world, everywhere, there will be an enormous number of particulars coexisting in the same place. But these troubles result from contenting ourselves too readily with the merely three-

6 *Cf.* T. P. Nunn, "Are Secondary Qualities Independent of Perception?", *Proc. Arist. Soc.*, 1909–1910.

dimensional space to which schoolmasters have accustomed us. The space of the real world is a space of six dimensions, and as soon as we realize this we see that there is plenty of room for all the particulars for which we want to find positions. In order to realize this we have only to return for a moment from the polished space of physics to the rough and untidy space of our immediate sensible experience. The space of one man's sensible objects is a three-dimensional space. It does not appear probable that two men ever both perceive at the same time any one sensible object; when they are said to see the same thing or hear the same noise, there will always be some difference, however slight, between the actual shapes seen or the actual sounds heard. If this is so, and if, as is generally assumed, position in space is purely relative, it follows that the space of one man's objects and the space of another man's objects have no place in common, that they are in fact different spaces, and not merely different parts of one space. I mean by this that such immediate spatial relations as are perceived to hold between the different parts of the sensible space perceived by one man, do not hold between parts of sensible spaces perceived by different men. There are therefore a multitude of three-dimensional spaces in the world: there are all those perceived by observers, and presumably also those which are not perceived, merely because no observer is suitably situated for perceiving them.

But although these spaces do not have to one another the same kind of spatial relations as obtain between the parts of one of them, it is nevertheless possible to arrange these spaces themselves in a three-dimensional order. This is done by means of the correlated particulars which we regard as members (or aspects) of one physical thing. When a number of people are said to see the same object, those who would be said to be near to the object see a particular occupying a larger part of their field of vision than is occupied by the corresponding particular seen by people who would be said to be farther from the thing. By means of such considerations it is possible, in ways which need not now be further specified, to arrange all the different spaces in a three-dimensional series. Since each of the spaces is itself three-dimensional, the whole world of particulars is thus arranged in a six-dimensional space, that is to say, six coordinates will be required to assign completely the position of any given particular, namely, three to assign its position in its own space and three more to assign the position of its space among the other spaces.

There are two ways of classifying particulars: we may take together all those that belong to a given "perspective", or all those that are, as common sense would say, different "aspects" of the same "thing". For example, if I am (as is said) seeing the sun, what I see belongs to two assemblages: (1) the assemblage of all my present objects of sense, which is what I call a "perspective"; (2) the assemblage of all the different particulars which would be called aspects of the sun of eight minutes ago—this assemblage is what I define as *being* the sun of eight minutes ago. Thus "perspectives" and "things" are merely two different ways of classifying particulars. It is to be observed that there is no a priori necessity for particulars to be susceptible of this double classification. There may be what might be called "wild" particulars, not having the usual relations by which the classification is effected; perhaps dreams and hallucinations are composed of particulars which are "wild" in this sense.

The exact definition of what is meant by a perspective is not quite easy. So long as we confine ourselves to visible objects or to objects of touch we might define the perspective of a given particular as "all particulars which have a simple (direct) spatial relation to the given particular". Between two patches of colour which I see now, there is a direct spatial relation which I equally see. But between patches of colour seen by different men there is only an indirect constructed spatial relation by means of the placing of "things" in physical space (which is the same as the space composed of perspectives). Those particulars which have direct spatial relations to a given particular will belong to the same perspective. But if, for example, the sounds which I hear are to belong to the same perspective with the patches of colour which I see, there must be particulars which have no direct spatial relation and yet belong to the same perspective. We cannot define a perspective as all the data of one percipient at one time, because we wish to allow the possibility of perspectives which are not perceived by any one. There will be need, therefore, in defining a perspective, of some principle derived neither from psychology nor from space.

Such a principle may be obtained from the consideration of *time*. The one all-embracing time, like the one all-embracing space, is a construction; there is no *direct* time-relation between particulars belonging to my perspective and particulars belonging to another man's. On the other hand, any two particulars of which I am aware are either simultaneous or successive, and their simultaneity or successiveness is sometimes itself a datum to me. We may therefore define the perspective to which a given particular belongs as "all particulars simultaneous with the given particular", where "simultaneous" is to be understood as a direct simple relation, not the derivative constructed relation of physics. It may be observed that the introduction of "local time" suggested by the principle of relativity has effected, for purely scientific reasons, much the same multiplication of times as we have just been advocating.

The sum-total of all the particulars that are (directly) either simultaneous with or before or after a given particular may be defined as the "biography" to which that particular belongs. It will be observed that, just as a perspective need not be actually perceived by any one, so a biography need not be actually lived by any one. Those biographies that are lived by no one are called "official".

The definition of a "thing" is effected by means of continuity and of correlations which have a certain differential independence of other "things". That is to say, given a particular in one perspective, there will usually in a neighbouring perspective be a very similar particular, differing from the given particular, to the first order of small quantities, according to a law involving only the difference of position of the two perspectives in perspective space, and not any of the other "things" in the universe. It is this continuity and differential independence in the law of change as we pass from one perspective to another that defines the class of particulars which is to be called "one thing".

Broadly speaking, we may say that the physicist finds it convenient to classify particulars into "things", while the psychologist finds it convenient to classify them into "perspectives" and "biographies", since one perspective *may* constitute the momentary data of one percipient, and one biography *may* constitute the whole of the data of one percipient throughout his life.

We may now sum up our discussion. Our object has been to discover as far as possible the nature of the ultimate constituents of the physical world. When I speak of the "physical world", I mean, to begin with, the world dealt with by physics. It is obvious that physics is an empirical science, giving us a certain amount of knowledge and based upon evidence obtained through the senses. But partly through the development of physics itself, partly through arguments derived from physiology, psychology or metaphysics, it has come to be thought that the immediate data of sense could not themselves form part of the ultimate constituents of the physical world, but were in some sense "mental", "in the mind", or "subjective". The grounds for this view, in so far as they depend upon physics, can only be adequately dealt with by rather elaborate constructions depending upon symbolic logic, showing that out of such materials as are provided by the senses it is possible to construct classes and series having the properties which physics assigns to matter. Since this argument is difficult and technical, I have not embarked upon it in this article. But in so far as the view that sense-data are "mental" rests upon physiology, psychology, or metaphysics, I have tried to show that it rests upon confusions and prejudices—prejudices in favour of permanence in the ultimate constituents of matter, and confusions derived from unduly simple notions as to space, from the causal correlation of sense-data with sense-organs, and from failure to distinguish between sense-data and sensations. If what we have said on these subjects is valid, the existence of sense-data is logically independent of the existence of mind, and is causally dependent upon the *body* of the percipient rather than upon his mind. The causal dependence upon the body of the percipient, we found, is a more complicated matter than it appears to be, and, like all causal dependence, is apt to give rise to erroneous beliefs through misconceptions as to the nature of causal correlation. If we have been right in our contentions, sense-data are merely those among the ultimate constituents of the physical world, of which we happen to be immediately aware; they themselves are purely physical, and all that is mental in connection with them is our awareness of them, which is irrelevant to their nature and to their place in physics.

Unduly simple notions as to space have been a great stumbling-block to realists. When two men look at the same table, it is supposed that what the one sees and what the other sees are in the same place. Since the shape and colour are not quite the same for the two men, this raises a difficulty, hastily solved, or rather covered up, by declaring what each sees to be purely "subjective"—though it would puzzle those who use this glib word to say what they mean by it. The truth seems to be that space—and time also—is much more complicated than it would appear to be from the finished structure of physics, and that the one all-embracing three-dimensional space is a logical construction, obtained by means of correlations from a crude space of six dimensions. The particulars occupying this six-dimensional space, classified in one way, form "things", from which with certain further manipulations we can obtain what physics can regard as matter; classified in another way, they form "perspectives" and "biographies", which may, if a suitable percipient happens to exist, form respectively the sense-data of a momentary or of a total experience. It is only when physical "things" have been dissected into series of classes of particulars, as we have done, that the conflict between the point of view of physics and the point of view of psychology can be overcome. This conflict, if what has been said is not mistaken, flows from different methods of classification, and vanishes as soon as its source is discovered.

In favour of the theory which I have briefly outlined, I do not claim that it is *certainly* true. Apart from the likelihood of mistakes, much of it is avowedly hypothetical. What I do claim for the theory is that it *may* be true, and that this is more than can be said for any other theory except the closely analogous theory of Leibniz. The difficulties besetting realism, the confusions obstructing any philosophical account of physics, the dilemma resulting from discrediting sense-data, which yet remain the sole source of our knowledge of the outer world—all these are avoided by the theory which I advocate. This does not prove the theory to be true, since probably many other theories might be invented which would have the same merits. But it does prove that the theory has a better chance of being true than any of its present competitors, and it suggests that what can be known with certainty is likely to be discoverable by taking our theory as a starting-point, and gradually freeing it from all such assumptions as seem irrelevant, unnecessary, or unfounded. On these grounds, I recommend it to attention as a hypothesis and a basis for further work, though not as itself a finished or adequate solution of the problem with which it deals.

6

Letter on Sense-Data [1915]

THIS LETTER WAS published in *The Journal of Philosophy, Psychology, and Scientific Methods*, 12 (8 July 1915): 391–2.

As a reading of Appendix 1 will make clear, the misinterpretation of his position which Russell was concerned to correct arose from a published report in the *Athenaeum* of a meeting of the Aristotelian Society held on 12 April 1915 at which C. D. Broad read a paper entitled "Phenomenalism". Someone in attendance wrote a summary of both the paper and Russell's discussion of it. In his paper Broad wrote that Russell, in *Our Knowledge of the External World* (1914), advocated phenomenalism as "the ideal which he sets before himself" (*1915*, 227). His evidence for this claim was Russell's remark that ideally he would like to construct matter in terms of the sense-data of one person. (See **1**, 12: 20–7.) Broad explicitly denied that Russell was actually a phenomenalist. On that point, then, the *Athenaeum* report was incorrect in its summary. Although he does not mention it by name, Broad must also have used "The Relation of Sense-Data to Physics" (**1**) in preparing his paper, because he discussed the role of "sensibilia" in Russell's theory, and, as was noted in the headnote to Paper **1**, Russell did not use the words "sensibile" and "sensibilia" in his book.

There is no manuscript, so the *Journal* version is the copy-text.

IN A QUOTATION from the *Athenaeum* printed in this Journal,[1] I am represented as having said, "there may be perspectives where there are no minds; but we can not know anything of what sort of perspectives they may be, for the sense-datum is mental." I did not see the *Athenaeum*, and do not remember what I said, but it can not have been what I am reported as having said, for I hold strongly that the sense-datum is *not* mental—indeed my whole philosophy of physics rests upon the view that the sense-datum is purely physical. The fact of being a datum is mental, but a particular which is a datum is not logically dependent upon being a datum. A particular which is a datum does, however, appear to be causally dependent upon sense-organs and nerves and brain. Since we carry those about with us, we can not discover what sensibilia, if any, belong to perspectives from places where there is no brain. And since a particular of which we are aware is a sense-datum, we can not be aware of particulars which are not sense-data, and can, therefore, have no empirical evidence as to their nature. This is merely the "egocentric predicament"; it is a tautology, not a "great truth". It is for this reason, and not because "sense-data are mental", that we can not know the nature of those perspectives (if any) which belong to places where there are no minds.

I do not know what is the definition of "mental". In order to obtain a definition, I should first inquire what would necessarily be removed from the world if it were what one would naturally call a world without mind. I see no reason why colours or noises should be removed, but facts which involve such relations as perceiving, remembering, desiring, enjoying, believing would necessarily be removed. This suggests that no *particulars* of which we have experience are to be called "mental", but that certain *facts*, involving certain *relations*, constitute what is essentially mental in the world of our experience. (I use the word "fact" to designate that which makes a proposition true or false; it includes, I think, everything in the world except what is simple.) The term "mental", therefore, will be applicable to all facts involving such relations as those enumerated above. This is not yet a definition, since obviously these relations all have some common characteristic, and it must be this characteristic which will yield the proper definition of the term "mental". But I do not know what this characteristic is.—Very truly yours,

B. RUSSELL.

Trinity College, Cambridge,
June 7, 1915.

---

[1] Volume XII, page 308.

7

Note on C. D. Broad's
Article in the July *Mind* [1919]

THIS NOTE WAS published in *Mind*, n.s. 28 (Jan. 1919): 124.

The paper by C. D. Broad to which this note refers is a highly technical essay in symbolic logic whose title, "A General Notation for the Logic of Relations", very aptly summarizes its contents.

On 11 July 1918 the following message was sent to Broad by way of Russell's brother, Frank:

> Lord Russell is desired by Mr. Bertrand Russell to convey the following message to Mr. Broad:—"I have read him in this month's *Mind* with much pleasure and approval, but I don't altogether like shrieks upside-down. Tell him he should get into communication with Whitehead as to notation."

Russell was at this time in prison and limited in the number of letters he was permitted to send. (For Broad's use of exclamation points, or "shrieks", upside-down, see page 299 of his article.)

Russell was concerned in this note to give Whitehead the credit due him for his contribution to *Principia Mathematica*. Other writings in which Russell detailed Whitehead's contributions to that book are "Whitehead and Principia Mathematica" in *Mind*, n.s. 57 (April 1948): 137–8 and *My Philosophical Development* (1959, 74–5).

No manuscript of this note survives, therefore the copy-text is that printed in *Mind*.

MR. BROAD'S VERY interesting article in the July *Mind* on "A General Notation for the Logic of Relations" attributes to me (for what reason I cannot guess) a number of notations employed in *Principia Mathematica*. As far as my memory serves me, all these were invented by Dr. Whitehead, who, in fact, is responsible for most of the notation in that work. My original notation, before he came to my assistance, may be found in Peano's *Revue de Mathématiques*, Vols. vii and viii.

Part II

Reviews

8

Competitive Logic [1914]

THIS REVIEW WAS published unsigned in *The Nation*, 14 (31 Jan. 1914): 771–2. It is known to be Russell's because on 29 September 1913 he wrote Lady Ottoline Morrell:

> I have got an international book on logic to review for the *Nation*, consisting of articles by two Germans, two Italians, a Frenchman, an American, and a Russian. My vanity at first predisposed me in its favour, as I found from the index that Kant was the only philosopher more referred to than myself, while Aristotle and Hegel tied with me and the rest were nowhere! But alas on reading it I find it very bad; they (the authors) are the recognized authorities. (#879)

He wrote her again the next day: "I have all but finished the book on logic I was reading—it is totally worthless" (#880). On the following day he had completed his work on it: "I wrote the review of the cooperative logic—you will see it in the *Nation* in due course" (#881). It is not known why his review was not published until late January.

The book was originally published in German in 1912. According to the Preface by the editor of the English translation, Henry Jones, it was to be followed by a number of volumes dealing with other branches of philosophy. Probably because of the outbreak of war, no further volumes were published in any language.

No manuscript of the review survives, so the copy-text is the printed version in *The Nation*.

Encyclopaedia of the Philosophical Sciences. Volume I. *Logic.* By Arnold Ruge, Wilhelm Windelband, Josiah Royce, Louis Couturat, Benedetto Croce, Federigo Enriques and Nicolaj Losskij. Translated by B. Ethel Meyer. London: Macmillan, 1913. Pp. x, 269.

THIS WORK, IN spite of its title, is not an encyclopaedia in any recognized sense. It does not consist of alphabetically arranged articles on various topics, like the ordinary modern general encyclopaedias, nor of a progressive account of a whole science mapped out by an editor among many contributors, such, for instance, as the German ency-
10 clopaedia of mathematics; nor, again, like *the* encyclopaedia, of a collection of articles largely by one man, and all designed to exhibit and reinforce a certain outlook and general tendency. All these forms of encyclopaedia would be almost impossible for philosophy in its present state. But it may well be doubted whether the subject is as yet suitable for encyclopaedic treatment in any form; and the present volume does not allay this doubt. Each of the contributors—with the exception of Arnold Ruge, who merely contributes an editorial introduction, intended to be neutral and uncontroversial, yet full of disputable statements—treats, more or less, of the whole of logic as he conceives it, in a manner necessarily brief, and therefore
20 dogmatic, dry, and unconvincing. Each, one feels, is very conscious of the terrible views being advocated by the others, and is therefore tempted to force the note, in hopes of persuading the reader of the superior attractiveness of his own wares. This, however, does not apply to Windelband, whose amiable, ambling article sets forth a somewhat watered Hegelianism in apparent complete ignorance of all work since Sigwart.

"According to the Critical Method," he says, "through which alone there is assigned to philosophy a problem and province of inquiry of its own, clearly marked off against all other sciences, philosophical thought is everywhere directed towards the task of inquiring into those activities of
30 human reason by means of which, in the course of history, the entire structure of civilization has grown up. The object of such an inquiry is to discover how far general postulates of reason, which are independent of the specific conditions of humanity, ... have attained to consciousness and effective value."

He proceeds to speak about the "mental nature common to all men"; but how this has been ascertained, or how logic so defined can fail to be a branch of psychology, he, like the whole critical tradition, entirely fails to explain.

The same point of view, essentially, is taken up by Benedetto Croce, who, however, has become conscious, through his compatriot Peano, of the
40 existence of newer and more exact methods in logic. He has not studied these methods, but knows them to be pernicious, and speaks of them as Royal Academicians speak of Post-Impressionism, pouring scorn on "mod-

ern logicians, bitten, as most of them are, with intellectualism". Philosophy, he says, truly enough, is in essence the *amor Dei intellectualis*; but, unfortunately, his own contribution shows more of *odium hominis* than of *amor Dei*.

Professor Royce, in whom a great enthusiasm for the newer mathematical logic co-exists with a certain loyalty to the idealist tradition, begins by explaining why logic can no longer be regarded as "norms for correct thinking", but rather as a science of "forms" which belong to objects, and have no more essential relation to thought than the subject-matter of other non-psychological sciences. Logic, he says, "is the General Science of Order". In some very general sense of "order" this may be true. But he proceeds to explain the technical mathematical meaning of "order", and suggests, though he does not state explicitly, that order in this or some closely analogous sense is the special subject-matter of logic. Order in this sense, however, is merely one among many ideas analyzed by mathematical logic, and its importance is by no means so fundamental or so general as that of certain more abstract ideas which emerge in the course of the analysis. In the middle of his account of the newer logical ideas, the idealist tradition incongruously reappears in a supposed "postulate of individuality", which is said to be a "fundamental demand of the rational will", though no reason is shown why the universe should grant this demand rather than (say) a demand that we should all have £10,000 a year.

The next article is by M. Louis Couturat, who has in the past done admirable work on logic, particularly in publishing and interpreting the logical manuscripts of Leibniz. In recent years, however, he has devoted himself almost entirely to advocacy of Ido, a modification of Esperanto; his contribution, accordingly, shows signs of haste and lack of fresh thought. Moreover, in his eagerness to recommend "logistic" (i.e. mathematical logic), he has been led to minimize its difficulties, giving smooth and specious solutions which conceal one of its chief philosophical merits— namely, the eliciting of new, puzzling, but not insoluble, problems, the answers to which give hopes of a more scientific metaphysic than any that has hitherto been possible. Occasionally, in his article, one feels the intrusion of a misleading party spirit. For example, a certain kind of definition, called "definition by abstraction", which is of great importance in modern logic, is dismissed, after a very cursory criticism, with the remark that it "has contributed no little to spread first among mathematicians and then among philosophers the kind of nominalism which exaggerates the part played by the conventional and arbitrary, and indirectly favors those sceptical tendencies fashionable today under the name of *pragmatism*".

Professor Enriques contributes an article on "the problems of logic", which is, more or less, positivist in tendency. It shows a great desire to avoid metaphysics, to make everything clear and definite and formal. But it partly ignores and partly rejects the best efforts of modern formalists, and, from fear of metaphysics, it presents a set of doctrines far simpler and easier to understand than the real world appears to be. Moreover, his statements are so compressed that it may be doubted whether they would convey any meaning to a reader not already familiar with the topics discussed.

Professor Nicolaj Losskij contributes an article on "the transformation of the concept of consciousness in modern epistemology and its bearing on logic". What he says on theory of knowledge is good, consisting, in the main, of grounds for rejecting the view that what is immediately known to us must be psychical or subjective; but when he comes to logic, his choice of problems and the form of his discussion become somewhat antiquated.

The translation is good on the whole, though it is to be regretted that (as stated in the preface) the two Italian articles were not translated directly, but from the German versions. Occasionally, there is evidence of lack of familiarity with the technical vocabulary. Several of M. Couturat's terms, for example, are translations or adaptations of English technical terms, and ought to have been translated back into the originals. Also the word "Schluss" is always translated by "conclusion", whereas it often ought to be either "inference" or "syllogism".

The authors are the recognized authorities in their several countries, and the failure of the book seems not so much due to any fault which the contributors could have avoided as to the impossibility of an authoritative compilation on a subject in a state of revolution. The book, in fact, resembles a compendium on the British Constitution composed during the Civil War, with an introduction by King Charles and an epilogue by Oliver Cromwell.

9

Review of Ruge *et al.*,
Encyclopaedia of the Philosophical Sciences [1913]

THIS REVIEW WAS published in *The Cambridge Review*, 35 (27 Nov. 1913): 161.

Although it was published before his longer review (**8**) in *The Nation*, this review was written later. "Since dinner", he wrote Lady Ottoline Morrell on 3 November 1913, "I have written another review of the cooperative logic I reviewed for the *Nation*. I am very fit, and up to any amount of work" (#904).

The copy-text is the magazine version, the only one that survives.

Encyclopaedia of the Philosophical Sciences. Volume I. *Logic*. By Arnold Ruge, Wilhelm Windelband, Josiah Royce, Louis Couturat, Benedetto Croce, Federigo Enriques and Nicolaj Losskij. Translated by B. Ethel Meyer. London: Macmillan, 1913. Pp. x, 269.

I N THIS WORK, six eminent authorities each treat the whole of logic in some sixty pages, while Arnold Ruge contributes an introduction which is intended, I believe, to be uncontroversial. I find in it, however, such statements as the following: "There always lurks in the notion of Philosophy the idea of an unceasing striving towards a unity which in its totality and timelessness can never be grasped and reduced to a fixed formula by finite minds"; and again: "As every system of Philosophy must begin with the doctrine of thought, the *Encyclopaedia of the Philosophical Sciences* begins with the doctrine of thought-forms, namely, with Logic." Of the above two statements, the first seems to me meaningless, and the second false; thus even with the best will in the world it is impossible to make a non-controversial statement in philosophy. The subsequent writers make no such attempt, but fight for the reader like advertisements in Piccadilly Circus. Windelband offers Hegel in a mild form, Croce offers him virulent—philosophy, he says, is the very same study as history. Royce and Couturat offer accounts of modern mathematical logic, but Royce's account leads up to idealism and Couturat's to the international language—the new love to whom one feels him panting to return from the logic which he loved in his younger days. Enriques is sketchy and formalist, with a background of positivism; Losskij, on "the transformation of the concept of consciousness in modern epistemology and its bearing on logic", is excellent so long as he confines himself to theory of knowledge, but ignorant of modern work in logic.

The book as a whole seems to me a mistake. Philosophy is not yet in a position where an encyclopaedia is possible, except perhaps in the form of quotations from important writers on subjects arranged alphabetically. Even then, it would be matter of controversy which writers were important and which quotations gave their real opinions. On the whole, it would seem that until something is known in philosophy it is useless to make encyclopaedias of mutually destructive assertions such as are found in the present volume.

10

Mr. Balfour's Natural Theology [1914]

THIS PAPER WAS published in *The Cambridge Review*, 35 (4 March 1914): 338–9. As Russell noted, his review of the lectures was based upon a reading of newspaper accounts. The lectures were published in 1915 under the title *Theism and Humanism*.

The first mention of this review in his letters to Lady Ottoline Morrell came on 17 February 1914: "I am reading Balfour's Gifford lectures—rhetorical dishonest sentimental twaddle. The quality of his mind is more disgusting to me than anybody else's in the world" (#989). Four days later he mentioned that he had "Balfour's lectures to read" (#991). By the 24th his review was partly written: "I have been writing on Balfour—not finished yet. It is incredible balderdash. There is something about every word of his writing that fills me with loathing. I suppose he is not utterly and totally vile, but I feel as if he were" (#993). Two days later he reported: "This morning I finished writing on Balfour" (#995).

Arthur James Balfour (1848–1930), after 1922 the first Earl of Balfour, spent nearly all his working life as a Member of Parliament, rising to be Prime Minister from 1902–05. He was trained in philosophy, principally by Henry Sidgwick, who was also one of Russell's teachers, at Trinity College, Cambridge. During his political career he pursued his interest in philosophy, publishing two widely-read books, *A Defence of Philosophic Doubt* (1879) and *Foundations of Belief* (1895). It was often said of him that the politicians thought he must be a good philosopher, the philosophers that he must be a good politician. His second series of Gifford Lectures, which were to have been delivered in 1915, were postponed until 1922–23 on account of the First World War in which Balfour played an active part; they were published as *Theism and Thought, a Study in Familiar Beliefs* in 1923. Chapter 4 of this book is devoted to a criticism of Russell's philosophical method as it is stated in *Our Knowledge of the External World* (1914).

In 1918, after he was sentenced to six months' imprisonment in the second division, Russell appealed to Balfour, through intermediaries, to use his influence with the government to have the sentence served in the first division. "For anybody not in the first division," Russell wrote in the second volume of his *Autobiography*, "especially for a person accustomed to reading and writing, prison is a severe and terrible punishment; but for me, thanks to Arthur Balfour, this was not so. I owe him gratitude for his intervention although I was bitterly opposed to all his policies" (*1968*, 30).

There is no manuscript, so the copy-text is the version printed in *The Cambridge Review*.

Mr. Balfour's Gifford Lectures are as yet only available in newspaper reports, which are of course compressed and not always quite accurate. It is therefore only possible to consider the broad lines of his argument, remembering that apparent lacunae may be due to omissions in the reports.

Mr. Balfour's purpose is no less than to establish the existence of God—not of a pantheistic God, or of an Absolute, or of a mere remote First Cause, but of a "social God", of whom it would be true, though inadequate, to say that He takes sides. The argument, as was to be expected, proceeds from the consideration of values, aesthetic, moral, and intellectual, none of which, we are told, could be what we believe them to be if theism were untrue.

Aesthetic values are considered first. Our aesthetic emotions, Mr. Balfour contends, are not to be explained by natural selection. But, he says, when we look at a picture, for example, a large part of our enjoyment is due to the knowledge that it has been made by an artist—I suppose because we feel what a wonderful man he must have been. Similarly our enjoyment of the beauties of nature depends upon believing them to be due to a Divine Artist, and would be immeasurably lessened by a real conviction that they were due to chance or to anything except design.

Apart from the question whether, in fact, enjoyment of a work of art depends upon belief in an artist, or whether enjoyment of scenery is diminished by atheism, the above argument fails through not showing why a view which diminishes aesthetic enjoyment should be false. Until this link is supplied—and there is no reason to suppose that it can be supplied—what is said by Mr. Balfour remains wholly irrelevant.

Ethical beliefs are next considered, and it is maintained that, but for theism, the higher forms of altruism would be indefensible. The ground for this view is the usual one throughout these lectures, namely, that natural selection is inadequate as an explanation. Mr. Balfour assumes the exhaustiveness of the alternative: "Natural Selection or God". Everything in human life, he seems to think, must be causally explicable by one or other of these two hypotheses. This view was not surprising in 1860, when Huxley and Bishop Wilberforce waged their historic fight; but it is surprising in these days, when the biologists have almost forgotten that there ever was such a phrase as "natural selection". It would be a mistake, however, to attempt a refutation of Mr. Balfour on the basis of present scientific fashion; the true answer is that causal antecedents are irrelevant to the truth of beliefs. But before developing this answer, let us consider the criticism of science, which is the best part of these lectures.

Science, says Mr. Balfour, rests throughout upon certain beliefs which are not self-evident, not logically inevitable, not derivable from experience, and yet such as no one is willing to abandon. Such are: our belief in the external world, our belief in the regularity of nature, in induction, in atomism, in the conservation of mass or energy. We are not asked to abandon these beliefs: we are only asked to realize the absence of scientific reasons in their favour. In regard to the external world, for example, Mr. Balfour points out the elaborate causal chain which, according to science, intervenes between an object and what common sense regards as an immediate perception of that object. This consideration is not new, but the difficulties which it raises are none the less real. The lectures would have served a useful purpose if such difficulties had been employed to stimulate thought, rather than to discourage any attempt at intellectual sobriety. But Mr. Balfour never aims at promoting thought: he aims rather at showing that it is so painful and laborious as to be better evaded by means of theatrical heroic solutions.

The immediate purpose of Mr. Balfour's criticism of science is to show that it rests on beliefs which, unless theism is assumed, must appear baseless and unwarrantable. The instances given in support of this thesis are well chosen, and a complete answer would fill volumes. It would consist in showing that, of the beliefs which he mentions, some are unnecessary, some are mere methodological precepts, some (as Poincaré used to contend) are definitions in disguise, while the residue are not so unreasonable as they seem. To accomplish this work, however, requires patience and goodwill: it is impossible if every momentary obstacle is to be taken as insuperable in order to declare the bankruptcy of science.

But let us, for the present, admit what Mr. Balfour says as regards the scientific groundlessness of the beliefs upon which daily life and science itself must build, and let us examine the consequences which he deduces. His argument, he says, rests upon the contrast between the *causes* and the *reasons* of our beliefs. We can all see that beliefs, like other phenomena, have causes, and that the chain of causation can be traced backward indefinitely. But the causes of a belief are very seldom reasons for its truth, so long as we remain among scientifically attainable causes; and yet, in spite of the scepticism which should result from this conflict, we are none of us, in fact, prepared to abandon our beliefs.

The nerve of his whole contention, he says, is that the value of a belief is affected by its origin, and must suffer unless some adequate source can be found in the causal series. And since it is impossible to imagine how matter could have made will and reason, it seems more reasonable to suppose that will and reason made matter. This is the whole of Mr. Balfour's deduction of God from science. What occurs beyond this in the six lectures devoted to stating the deduction is only required in order to create an atmosphere.

There are two arguments in the above, but the second, that matter could not have produced will and reason, is only used more or less incidentally, and may be ignored, since it will be met by what is to be said in criticism of the first. Let us analyze the first and see what assumptions it involves.

The value of a belief, we are told, is affected by its origin. No grounds are given for *this* belief, and the value of its origin may be doubted. When it is said that the value of a belief is affected by its origin, what would seem to be meant is that there is some correlation between its truth and the ethical excellence of its cause. Now this can certainly not be maintained if we take a more or less proximate cause. If I believe that Jones hates me, my belief is true if it is caused by Jones actually hating me, and is false if it is caused by his dissembling his love for a good purpose. Thus my belief is true if its cause is bad, and false if its cause is good. We must, therefore, in order to
10 give any plausibility to Mr. Balfour's dogma, take the "origin" of a belief to be some remote First Cause, for if there were not a beginning to the causal chain there would be no cause that could properly be called the "origin" of our belief. On an ordinary scientific view, all our beliefs, true and false alike, are due to a chain of causes taking us back to the nebula or to some other purely material world, where there are no ethical values at all. If Mr. Balfour's dogma is true, this must be impossible: there must, if we go back far enough, be virtuous causes of our present true beliefs and wicked causes of our false ones. He does not draw the latter conclusion, because Satan is out of fashion; but since some beliefs are certainly false, it is impossible to
20 justify the one conclusion without the other, or to uphold his dogma unless both conclusions are accepted.

What Mr. Balfour means, however, is perhaps something rather different from this. We might perhaps expand his argument as follows: The beliefs of men have proximate causes which are physical and unintelligent, and no more apt (so far as physics can show) to produce true beliefs than to produce false ones. Nevertheless, even after we have realized this fact, we continue to entertain, as before, those very beliefs which, by the laws of chance, ought to be just as likely to be false as to be true. Unless some general reason can be found why our beliefs should be true, it is irrational to continue to
30 hold them; but we cannot really believe that it is irrational, and no hypothesis will make it rational except God. This, I think, is Mr. Balfour's line of argument: he holds that the physical causes of our beliefs are divinely pre-arranged in such a way as to produce true beliefs rather than false ones.

Apart from minor objections, there are two which seem to me fatal to such an argument as the above. The first is that it assumes more knowledge than it has any right to assume; the second is that it attempts to elicit a positive conclusion from our ignorance.

First, as regards the too great assumption of knowledge: Mr. Balfour assumes that the chain of physical and psychophysical causation is quite
40 beyond question, and that not even the wildest sceptic could throw doubt upon it. He assumes also that the electrons of the physicist are what really exists in the physical world, rather than the patches of colour, etc., which are what we immediately perceive. It may be held that the electron is merely

a logical construction summing up the laws of change in such things as patches of colour; and it must be held that traditional common-sense notions of cause (which are assumed unquestioningly by Mr. Balfour) are a belated survival of savage animism and fetish-worship. It would take too long to explain these two points, but the second especially is important: broadly speaking, whenever the word "cause" is mentioned, either in daily life or in philosophy, it must be regarded as indicating the "pathetic fallacy", as an illegitimate endowing of material things with desire or purpose. And it will be observed that in physics (as treated by the best exponents) the word "cause" does not occur.

The second point against Mr. Balfour's argument is that it attempts to elicit a positive conclusion from our ignorance. Our beliefs, he says, have causes, among which *we do not know* any which should predispose us towards truth rather than falsehood; nevertheless, he maintains, our beliefs are in fact true, and this can *only* be accounted for by a God who has pre-ordained their causes. Mr. Balfour neglects the fact that many of our beliefs are false, and that his hypothesis seems ill-designed to explain this fact. But even if we were to admit that more than half of our beliefs are true, i.e. more are true than pure chance would lead us to expect, still in a matter about which (apart from any criticism of the notion of "cause") we know so little as the causes of belief, it is extraordinarily rash to argue that there can be *no* natural causes predisposing to truth. Mr. Balfour's contention is exactly parallel to the habit of explaining every surprising phenomenon by witchcraft: it assumes that our knowledge of the natural causes of belief is so complete as to enable us to say with certainty that none of them give any bias in favour of truth. But such an assumption has only to be stated in order to be seen to be groundless.

The scientific procedure in regard to the problems raised by Mr. Balfour will be quite different from his. In the first place, it will not forget error, or invent a hypothesis which makes error impossible. In the second place, it will endeavour, by induction and analysis, to discover the circumstances under which what is subsequently acknowledged as error arises, and it will, if it can, find classes of beliefs in regard to which error appears to be rare or non-existent. In some such way, it may gradually find more or less trustworthy criteria of truth and error in various kinds of cases, and arrive in the end at a natural history of true belief. In all this, of course, universal scepticism is being rejected, just as Mr. Balfour rejects it. But the resulting problem is treated piecemeal, patiently, by the usual scientific methods, not hastily, as an unanalyzed whole, and with the assumption that every tenable hypothesis must have already occurred to our minds. The habit of dogmatic haste, of failure to break up large problems whose parts require separate treatment, of willingness to acquiesce contentedly in the first hypothesis that suggests itself, is what has chiefly prevented philosophy from becoming scientific or yielding solid knowledge. The fundamental defect of Mr. Balfour's lectures, it seems to me, is that, in spite of their allusions to science, they are designed to discourage the scientific habit in philosophy; and this criticism would remain valid even if it should be found hereafter that every single one of his theses is in fact true.

11

Idealism on the Defensive [1917]

THIS REVIEW OF May Sinclair's *Defence of Idealism* (1917) was published in *The Nation*, 21 (8 Sept. 1917): 588, 590. It was written after 20 August because on that day Russell wrote Sinclair that her "really valuable book" had arrived in the same post as a request from *The Nation* for a review of it, and he, mistakenly, had assumed the copy had been sent by the journal. He was, he reported, about half-way through it, and was pleased that she had given so much space and attention to the new realism. "It will not be possible in the *Nation* to reply to your arguments against it, but if it will not bore you, I will send you an answer when I have finished the book." On the same day he wrote Lady Constance Malleson: "I am reading May Sinclair's *Defence of Idealism* for review—it is not very bad." On 1 September Sinclair wrote to thank him for "All those long typed notes!" His notes have not survived, but it is apparent from her attempt to reply to them that the points he made in them were similar to those he advanced in his published review.

On 21 September she wrote him again, this time to reply at greater length to some of his points of criticism. For her mistake of quoting *The Principles of Mathematics* and calling it *Principia Mathematica* she was greatly embarrassed, explaining that she had taken notes from a copy borrowed from a library and abbreviated the title to *Prin. Math.* which later she misinterpreted. Russell replied on 26 September succinctly setting out certain misunderstandings in her letter and thanking her for "the friendliness with which you have listened to my, perhaps somewhat impertinent, criticisms".

May Amelia St. Clair Sinclair (1863–1946) is best known as a novelist, although she had a life-long interest in philosophy. Russell, when annotating letters for possible inclusion in his *Autobiography*, wrote on one of hers that "She wrote novels and philosophy alternately" (14 Nov. 1907). Her very first publications were essays in philosophy. She wrote only two books on philosophical questions, the one reviewed here and *The New Idealism* (1922) which Russell reviewed for *The Nation & the Athenaeum*, 31 (5 Aug. 1922): 625–6.

Her book is not in Russell's library. He may have sold it to C. K. Ogden, for on 23 June 1922 he wrote Ogden offering to sell a book (or books) by May Sinclair if Ogden, who was a secondhand bookseller on the side, could sell them.

No manuscript of the review survives, so the copy-text is that of *The Nation*.

A Defence of Idealism: Some Questions and Conclusions. By May Sinclair. London: Macmillan, 1917. Pp. xxii, 396.

I T IS EVIDENTLY much easier to write philosophy than to write a novel, for certainly no novel by a philosopher of repute could hope to be half as readable as Miss Sinclair's book of philosophy. In certain parts of the book, her novelist's training has perhaps been of use to her; for example, in connection with Samuel Butler on the one hand and the New Mysticism on the other. There are also some charming passages about Professor Thorndike and his cat. It appears that this "heartless intellectual" kept the
10 poor beast in a cage with a saucer of milk just outside, to be reached only through a door requiring a good deal of intelligence to get open. The clumsy movements of the cat, the accidental success, and the subsequent knowledge are dealt with sympathetically by Miss Sinclair.

Miss Sinclair's ultimate allegiance is chiefly to Hegel, but, on many matters concerning the relation of soul and body, she follows Mr. McDougall. She deals critically with every form of psychophysical parallelism, and decides in favour of interaction between mind and matter. "Shut up a puppy by himself in your study when he is teething, or let loose a speculative builder over a square mile of virgin wood and field, and observe
20 the change their psychic processes will effect in the order and integrity of material objects." She does not, as much as one could wish, go into the question as to whether there is any difference, and if so what, between mind and matter. Idealists say all matter is really mind; Materialists say all mind is really matter; American Realists say mind and matter are the same thing, but neither mental nor material. Idealists and Materialists alike take very little trouble to define mind and matter. Since they agree that the two are really the same, it is difficult to see wherein they disagree. As a matter of fact, they differ chiefly in what they take as the standard of the familiar. To Dr. Johnson and the Materialists, the most familiar reality is the stone that
30 one kicks with one's foot; to Idealists, who spend most of their lives in chairs so comfortable as not to obtrude themselves upon consciousness, the most familiar reality is what they call "thought". Both commit the common error of supposing that the familiar must be the prototype of metaphysical reality. Men of science have come to know that the most instructive phenomena are rare and complicated products of laboratory conditions. They, too, at one time took the familiar as synonymous with the real. They supposed the world to consist of billiard balls, perpetually hitting each other. For the men of science these naïve days have passed, but for the philosophers they still persist.
40 Miss Sinclair's method of reaching her conclusions is largely that which has been consecrated by the usage of metaphysicians. You first arrive at a theory of the world which is agreeable, both because it is easy to imagine,

and because it fulfils your hopes while thwarting those of your enemies. You then establish your metaphysic by refuting all arguments designed to prove that some other metaphysic *must* be true.

In all these repects the New Realism has aimed at inculcating a greater restraint. It is the natural tendency of the human mind to draw stronger conclusions from facts than the facts themselves warrant. The New Realism has tried to invent a logical method by which the legitimate conclusions and no more can be extracted from any body of data. This modest and scientific spirit on the constructive side has perhaps been concealed from readers by a certain arrogance on the critical side, for the New Realism holds that, though there are an infinite number of metaphysical theories which may be true and comparatively few which must be false, it so happens that all the ambitious systems with the exception of that of Leibniz, belong to those few that are demonstrably false. The issue may be taken as an issue between Monism and Pluralism; but, if so, we must distinguish two stages in the question, one logical and the other based upon observation. The advocate of unity maintains, on the ground of a certain logic, that there must be an ultimate oneness in the world, and that its apparent multiplicity must be illusory. He then sets to work to deal as best he can with the empirically given world of "appearance", which has somehow to be drilled into this unity. Pluralism maintains, on the other hand, that there is nothing in logic to show whether the world is ultimately one or many; that, as far as logic is concerned, there might be no world at all, or a world consisting of one thing, or a world consisting of any finite or infinite number of things. It maintains that the issue between these different possibilities must rest solely upon observation, not upon abstract reason. The only use which it makes of logic in this discussion, is to show that logic cannot decide the question, and that the idealistic logic, which professes to decide it, is erroneous. Miss Sinclair is an advocate of unity, in the sense in which it has been advocated by the Idealists; but she concedes that, in view of the attacks of the New Realism, a certain restatement of the Idealistic position and an abandonment of some part of its contentions have become necessary.

Readers of *The Nation* will be surprised to learn from her that "It is dangerous to differ from Mr. Bertrand Russell." They may have supposed that it was more dangerous to agree with him. But she is speaking of the realm of Reason, where truth is decided by argument, not by Defence of the Realm Regulations. "Atomistic Realism", she says, "gives no support to the 'Belief in the Beyond,' and very little encouragement, if any, to the 'Hope of the Hereafter,' and in this world there is an enormous number of people (probably the majority of the human race) whose instincts and feelings are passionately opposed to any theory which would deprive them of the Belief in the Beyond and of the Hope of the Hereafter."

Atomistic Realism does not supply any argument against the Beyond and

the Hereafter. It does not profess to have shown them to be non-existent. The only thing that it does is to dissect certain arguments professing to demonstrate them. It professes to show that these arguments are invalid, but it does not claim to have shown that the conclusion is false. In regard to the conclusion, it adopts the position of absolute nescience. It does not deny that other minds may have other sources of knowledge. It regards it as a pure accident that we remember the past rather than the future. It will concede that possibly in Mars people remember the future but not the past, and that in that planet advocates of free will, while admitting that the future
10 is, of course, now irrevocable, nevertheless hold that the past can be modified by judicious choice. It would be perfectly willing to concede, if empirical evidence were forthcoming, that there are people in this world who have the same kind of immediate knowledge concerning the future that memory gives us concerning the past. All such questions it regards as empirical. The only thing that it sets its face against is a priori arguments professing to demonstrate the Beyond and the Hereafter on abstract grounds. It may, however, well be doubted whether the instincts and feelings concerned with the Beyond and the Hereafter are anything like so passionate or so widespread as their advocates pretend. Interest in religious
20 questions seems in most times and places to have been confined to a small minority; usually the interest which others professed was not genuinely religious, but partisan and controversial. Modern experience shows that it is easy for interest in religion to die out almost completely among large sections of civilized populations. Religion has been kept alive partly by the financial and political interests associated with it, partly by the need of consolation for the appalling suffering which mankind have brought upon themselves by their own folly. If the world were not very bad, no one would believe it ultimately wholly good, and if mankind ever came to realize the ideals of peace and freedom, which many of them profess to cherish, it is
30 probable that religion would die out for want of the sustenance which it finds in human despair.

   Miss Sinclair's criticism of the New Realism shows as great an appreciation of its importance as any of its friends could desire, but she suffers somewhat, as she herself confesses, from ignorance of mathematical logic, as a result of which a good deal of its thought is inaccessible to her and a good deal of its writing is unknown to her. For example, there is no evidence that she is acquainted with *Principia Mathematica*. (The work which she alludes to under this title is *The Principles of Mathematics*, an earlier work which leaves unsolved a number of problems with which the later work professes
40 to deal satisfactorily.) Where she touches on the theory of infinite number, in which, like other idealists, she professes to find contradictions, she does not seem to realize that she is dealing with a definite branch of mathematics, having precisely that degree of truth and certainty (whatever that may be)

that belongs to the multiplication table. There is always a tendency for those who only know the popular explanations of a technical subject to interpret its statements so as to have an untechnical and not merely a technical interest. For example, Miss Sinclair says, "The law of conservation of energy is nothing if not a confession that, as far as the physical world goes, incorrigible multiplicity and difference do not obtain." No one who understood the conservation of energy on its technical side would make such a statement as this. One feels that if Miss Sinclair thoroughly understood what the conservation of energy really does mean, she would think it totally uninteresting and would wonder why so much fuss has been made about it. In some of her attempts to interpret the arithmetic of infinite numbers, there is a similar tendency to read into technical statements an untechnical interest which they do not possess. For example, having learnt that an infinite number is not increased by the addition of a finite number, she says, "that is to say, finite and infinite are not affected by each other's vagaries. They neither negate nor limit, nor do they define each other." This is not the kind of statement that would be made by anyone who understood the mathematical theory of infinity. Some arithmetical operations with finite numbers leave infinite numbers unaffected, and others do not. To say of two numbers "that they neither negate nor limit, nor do they define each other", is to say something which to a mind accustomed to mathematical precision appears as mere words without meaning. Any two different numbers negate each other in the sense that a collection which has the one number does not have the other. As to what can be meant by saying that two numbers define each other, I confess I am completely at a loss; still less is it possible for two numbers to limit each other, since a limit has to be the limit of a series, not of a single term. And the smallest of the infinite numbers *is* the limit of the whole series of finite numbers. The theory of infinite numbers, like every other branch of mathematics, has to be learnt laboriously, and does not lend itself to hasty generalization or to vague rhetorical phrases. The definite contradictions which Miss Sinclair professes to find in the New Realism are bound up with her failure to understand the theory of the infinite, with one exception, which depends upon the question-begging assumption that there can be no relatedness unless it is of the kind postulated by Idealistic logic.

There is one other serious misunderstanding of the New Realism in Miss Sinclair's book. She assumes that in looking, for example, at a table the New Realism assumes that the "real" table is that which appears to a normal eye. "Appearances presented to the normal human eye", she says, "will not rank as appearances but as real objects normally perceived, and all variations from the normal will be attributed to flaws in the mechanism of perception. This question of the standard is crucial for the New Realism." This is a complete misapprehension. It is of the essence of the New Realism to be equally hospitable to all "appearances", to treat them all as indisputable and wholly real. What appears in dreams and hallucinations or to the most abnormal eye imaginable has for the New Realism precisely the same reality as what appears to the normal eye in waking life. The things which common sense calls unreal or illusory are not so; they are only peculiar in the character of their correlations with other things, so that when we do not realize that these correlations are peculiar, they give rise to false inferences. Thus a mirage would be called an illusion, but not a reflection in a looking-glass, unless we fail to realize that it is a reflection. Both the mirage and the reflection are for the New Realism parts of ultimate physical reality. By a somewhat elaborate argument it undertakes to show that all the usual objections to such a view are capable of refutation. What the New Realism claims to be real, is not physical objects, such as tables and chairs, or atoms and electrons, but the very kind of thing that is given immediately in sensation, and this is exactly as real in the case of an hallucination as in any other case.

In spite of the criticisms we have mentioned, Miss Sinclair's book is extremely interesting and full of good things. The account of Butler at the beginning and the account of the New Mysticism at the end are both admirable. The book is singularly free from the arrogance which is customary in the writings of almost all professional philosophers, and it is certainly successful in what appears to be its main object, namely, in bringing before an untechnical public the kind of discussions and the kind of issues with which current philosophy is concerned, in such a manner as to make it clear that these issues have a genuine human interest for people to whom the technical language of philosophy is repellent, if not unintelligible. Even if Miss Sinclair's conclusions should ultimately prove untenable, it is probable that they will share this fate with the conclusions of all other philosophers, both living and dead.

12

Metaphysics [1917]

THIS REVIEW WAS published anonymously in *The English Review*, 25 (Oct. 1917): 381–4. In addition to the internal evidence, which seems overwhelming, there is the fact that Sinclair was informed by someone that Russell was the reviewer, since she wrote him on 10 October to thank him "for another generous (and merciful) review". She promised not to write on philosophy again until she had "considered all the points where your criticism bears hardest; and to this end I am sending for the 'Principia Mathematica' (not the 'Principles of Mathematics.')" Russell had repeated his point of her need to learn mathematical logic if she was to become an effective critic of the new realism. Russell's pocket diary for 1917–18 has "Lunch May Sinclair?" as an entry for Tuesday, 30 October 1917. There is no evidence in the Russell Archives to prove that the meeting took place.

Since no manuscript survives, the copy-text is that of *The English Review*.

A Defence of Idealism: Some Questions and Conclusions. By May Sinclair.
London: Macmillan, 1917. Pp. xxii, 396.

MISS SINCLAIR HAS written a very readable and interesting book,
more readable by far than many more professional treatises. The
amateur in philosophy has a distinct function, not as the inventor
of new systems or new arguments, but as the interpreter of systems to a
public which is not likely to read the technical works of professionals, and
also as showing to professionals how their work appears to those whose
human interests are not destroyed by familiarity with the controversies of
the Schools. This function Miss Sinclair's book admirably performs.

Her own attitude to philosophy is, broadly speaking, Hegelian, though
she protests against an undue emphasis upon Hegel's logic at the expense of
the rest of his system. With some originality she begins her book by an
account of Samuel Butler's views on heredity, which, as she amusingly
shows, reduced to a form of ancestor worship, the very last form of religion
that would have been voluntarily adopted by the author of *The Way of All
Flesh*. She advances through Bergson, Mr. McDougall, and the Pragmatists
to the New Realism, and thence by a somewhat sudden transition to the
New Mysticism, chiefly exemplified by Sir Rabindranath Tagore.

I do not think that Miss Sinclair always wholly understands the position
of those whom she criticizes—as, indeed, who does? In speaking of William
James's distinction between the Tender-minded and the Tough-minded,
she says: "Observe how Pragmatism appropriates all the robust and heroic
virtues, and will not leave its opponent one of them. Think of the sheer
terrorism of the performance. Could you wonder if, covered with that
six-shooter, Professor James's audience plumped for Pragmatism before it
had heard a single argument? Each member of it must have registered an
inward vow: 'Tough-minded? *I'll* be *that!*'" As a matter of fact, William
James was attempting a reconciliation of the Tender-minded and the
Tough-minded. He did not regard his own philosophy as belonging wholly
to either variety. Certainly the image of a six-shooter is very far removed
from the large sympathy which characterized him, no less when he was
poking kindly fun than when he was praising. He enumerates six characteristics of the Tender-minded: Rationalistic, intellectualistic, idealistic,
optimistic, religious, free-willist. The last three of these adjectives apply to
his own system; it is only the first three that he rejects.

Miss Sinclair is concerned throughout to defend the claims of unity
against the pluralistic assaults of Pragmatists and Realists; the latter in
particular occupy many pages of her book. "Certain vulnerable forms of
Idealism", she says, "are things of the past, and the new Atomistic Realism
is a thing of the future, at any rate of the immediate future. But we know of
Old Realisms that died and decayed, and were buried, and of New Idealisms

that died and rose again." She is no doubt right in assuming that Monism and Idealism are perennial in philosophy; ever since serious philosophy began there have been a certain number of Schools adapted to different types of mind. It is not likely that any of these Schools will quite die out so long as interest in philosophy survives.

It is curious how different a controversy looks from different sides. To the New Realists it appears that they are fighting an uphill battle against tremendous odds. To Miss Sinclair, on the contrary, their battalions appear so formidable that it requires great courage to stand firm against their advance. "I feel", she says, "that any reputation I may have is already so imperilled by my devout adhesion to the Absolute, that I simply cannot afford to be suspected of tenderness or even toleration for the professors of the occult." She expresses astonishment that the New Realists should regard Idealism as now a fashionable philosophy. Yet, by any statistical test, it is so. The majority of professors of philosophy in Great Britain are certainly Idealists, and probably the majority of philosophical teachers of all grades. Any young man intending to make his living by teaching philosophy, if he believed with the Pragmatists that "the truth is what pays", would certainly adopt Idealism as his creed. If the Idealists have not made so much noise as Pragmatists or Realists, it is only because they have felt themselves in a secure position.

Miss Sinclair believes that the ultimate reality is Spirit. "To the unity and the reality we are looking for, we can give no name but Spirit. This leaves a wide margin for the Unknown." It certainly does, since no one quite knows what is meant by Spirit. If Miss Sinclair knows, she keeps the knowledge to herself. She says: "Raise either psychic energy or physical energy to their highest pitch of intensity, and you get Spirit." I confess I cannot understand what this means. Does it mean that if an express train were to go really fast it would acquire a soul?—for that certainly is what it *seems* to say.

A quarter of the whole book is occupied with an account and criticism of the New Realism. It is, of course, impossible to achieve a complete absence of bias in regard to a system which one has oneself advocated, but it does not seem to me that the criticisms advanced in this book are very formidable. Miss Sinclair herself confesses, with admirable candour, that mathematical logic is for her a difficult and unfamiliar country. She is unacquainted with it on its technical side, and is therefore sometimes mistaken as to what it asserts. In some respects she concedes more than it would claim. For example, she states that the New Realism has succeeded in refuting Subjective Idealism, which I for my part do not profess to be able to do. It is of the essence of the new philosophy that it regards many questions as insoluble, and considers that many philosophical controversies have arisen solely because philosophers would not realize that no sufficient evidence for a positive opinion existed.

Miss Sinclair professes to discover a number of specific contradictions in the Atomistic Logic upon which the New Realism is based. I do not think that these will appear very convincing to anyone acquainted with modern mathematical logic, but it is impossible in the space of a review to indicate either their nature or a reply to them.

There is a tendency throughout the book to hold that one may believe a philosophy if it is pleasant and cannot be shown to be false. Even if all Miss Sinclair's arguments were valid, she would hardly have done more than refute certain objections to Idealism, without advancing any positive argu-

10 ments to prove that it must be accepted. It is a very difficult thing to prove that a philosophy is false, though it is generally not a difficult thing to prove that the arguments by which it is supported are invalid, as well as the arguments by which it is attacked. When we have proved that there is no conclusive argument against it, we have done nothing to show that it is true so long as there are many other views which are equally irrefutable. But such criticisms are equally applicable to almost all philosophical writing. Miss Sinclair deserves praise for having placed the argument for Idealism upon a new footing, and for having freed it from much that is irrelevant and indefensible, and she is so free from philosophical arrogance that perhaps

20 this is as much as she would claim to have achieved.

13

A Metaphysical Defence of the Soul [1917]

THIS REVIEW WAS published in *The Nation*, 22 (10 Nov. 1917): 210, 212. It is not signed, but it is known to be by Russell because, in addition to the internal evidence which is very strong, Russell, in a letter to his brother from prison (16 May 1918) in which he gave instructions regarding the sorts of books he wanted to have brought him, remarked: "Have already read and reviewed Laird on Himself." From his pocket diary for 1917–18 we know that he was paid for a number of reviews by *The Nation*; the payment of £2.2.0 in December is almost certainly the payment for this review.

John Laird (1887–1946) had been Russell's most promising pupil in 1910–11, but his promise, in Russell's opinion, did not survive his first teaching position.

> I am afraid most people grow less interesting when they get settled in life. Broad and Laird are both duller than when they were here. Laird came last night and we had a long argument on ethics—he was very muddle-headed, in the way that comes of no longer having any passion for clear thinking; intellectual laziness is coming on him. I told him he was muddled and he was a little vexed. He has been a whole year teaching, instead of learning. Broad will be a good teacher, for people who already have a great enthusiasm for philosophy, but for others he will be deadly. Laird will be deadly for everybody. They were the best people in philosophy in their respective years. (#505)

This report, in a letter to Lady Ottoline Morrell, is undated, but it was written during 1912. The tenor of Russell's review provides evidence that in 1917 he still regarded Laird as lacking a "passion for clear thinking", especially when he pointed out that "Mr. Laird's logic is not very clear" (117: 42).

Laird had a long career in philosophy, with appointments in the University of St. Andrews, Dalhousie University, Queen's University in Belfast, and, finally, the University of Aberdeen where he was Regius Professor of Moral Philosophy for twenty-two years. Of his eighteen books Russell reviewed only one more, *Recent Philosophy* (1936). That review appeared in *The Listener* (1936), supp. iii.

There is no surviving manuscript, so the copy-text is that printed in *The Nation*.

Problems of the Self. An essay based on the Shaw Lectures given in the University of Edinburgh, March 1914. By John Laird. London: Macmillan, 1917. Pp. xiii, 375.

THE AIM OF this book, as we are told in the preface, "is to show why there must be a soul, and in what sense precisely this soul should be understood". The question whether or not there is such a thing as the soul is one which has acquired a perhaps undeserved importance in the popular mind through its supposed connection with the problem of immortality. It was held that human beings have souls, though animals have none; but it was not supposed by plain men that animals were mere unconscious automata, as Descartes taught. The soul was conceived as something implied not by the kind of consciousness and life that belongs to animals, but rather by moral responsibility and the knowledge of good and evil: it was essentially the subject of rewards or punishments after death. Since Darwin, metaphysicians have widened the franchise; the benefits which they wish to confer on Man have to be extended, at least in some degree, to the higher animals, if not to everything that has life. Accordingly those who now defend the soul no longer regard it as specifically human. Moreover, Mr. Laird will disappoint some readers by confessing that the soul, as he understands it, affords no guarantee of immortality, though it leaves open the possibility of survival after death.

Mr. Laird's attitude towards philosophical problems is, on the whole, a conservative one. There is much discussion of the views of the great philosophers, including some who (like Fichte, for example), though always appearing in the list of eminent names, are seldom honoured nowadays by any further mention. One feels that the author's bias is towards what is safe and traditional; he has little sympathy for iconoclastic theories. For example, the theory of the American realists, following William James, to the effect that there is no difference between the mental and the physical except as two ways of arranging the same material, is only very briefly discussed in connection with James's essay, "Does Consciousness Exist?" No one who has studied this theory in its developments, and has seriously attempted to refute it, can regard Mr. Laird's discussion as even approximately adequate; yet it is obvious that such a theory must be solidly refuted before the existence of the soul can be regarded as established. Nevertheless, within its limitations, the present volume is a careful and lucid discussion of an important topic. The author's meaning is generally made quite clear, though he does not always defend his contentions adequately against objections which are likely to occur to readers who disagree with him.

Mr. Laird's appeal throughout is professedly to purely empirical data. From such data, in spite of cases of multiple personality and kindred phenomena, he deduces the unity and continuity of the self, and attempts to demonstrate that the soul is a "substance". The word "substance" is somewhat *démodé*, and it requires courage to lay emphasis on it; but in spite of a good deal of discussion the meaning assigned to it in this book is not made as clear as could be wished. One traditional definition, according to which a substance is an "ultimate subject"—i.e. something which can only occur in a proposition as its subject, never as adjective or verb—is rejected as inadequate, since it is held that, though all substances are ultimate subjects, some ultimate subjects are universals, and therefore not substances. This appears to be a logical error, but a very pardonable one, since the question what terms can be ultimate subjects is difficult, and existing 10 philosophical literature throws little light upon it. Mr. Laird's view appears to be that the unity and continuity of one man's life make the system of his experiences combine into one single thing, the soul. Here also, in supposing that a system of many things can be one thing, he will have against him a body of logical opinion which, whether true or false, must be refuted before his conclusion can be regarded as safe from criticism.

Personal identity is partly a plain fact, partly a theory. It is clear beyond dispute that one man's experiences belong together in a unity in a way which separates them from the experiences of other men, however similar in quality they may be to those other experiences. The plain man is convinced 20 that the unity of his experiences is due to the fact that they all belong to *him*, and that *he* is a persistent entity, the same today as he was yesterday. He rejects unhesitatingly such theories as those of Hume or James (if he ever hears of them), according to which there is no single unitary self, but only a succession of thoughts and feelings and volitions bound together in various ways. But this unreflecting belief does not long survive a process of critical scrutiny, unless it can obtain the support of what look like arguments. It may be doubted whether there would be the same eagerness to find arguments if the pragmatic unimportance of the question were realized. The interconnection of one man's experiences is an important fact, but whether 30 this is brought about by direct relations between the experiences or by their being all related to one more or less persistent thing—the Ego—is a question of which the importance is purely metaphysical. The question would only have practical importance if it were held that every substance must be indestructible—a view which was maintained by Descartes and his followers, but which is rightly rejected by Mr. Laird. From an empirical standpoint such as his, it can make no difference to our expectations whether we accept or reject the unitary Ego, since the series of our experiences will be the same on either hypothesis.

The question as to what can be inferred concerning the nature of the Ego 40 from our empirical knowledge of its experiences, turns, as do all similar questions, upon logic. Mr. Laird's logic is not very clear. On the one hand, he rejects the monistic logic of Hegel and those who descend from him, and

he denies that "relations necessarily make a difference to the intrinsic character of the terms related" (p. 228), which is the central doctrine of this school. On the other hand, his Ego, though a substance, seems to be conceived, not as a simple thing, whose experiences are its adjectives, but as the system of which its experiences are parts. To regard such a system as one thing seems to belong to the Hegelian logic which has been rejected. Mr. Laird very properly rejects, in successive chapters, the views which regard feeling alone, or will alone, or knowledge alone, as constituting the essence of the Self. But when he has so widened the Self as to embrace all that
10 happens to it, and when he has rejected the notion of a metaphysical subject *behind* phenomena, it is difficult to see how a man's soul differs from the series of his experiences. Such difference as there is would seem to rest upon a somewhat inadequate logic. But the adequacy of a logic may be tested by the paucity of the conclusions that it allows: the better our logic, the less it will permit us to infer. This is a gloomy conclusion for the metaphysician, but to that vast majority who abominate metaphysics it can bring nothing but comfort.

14

Pure Reason at Königsberg [1918]

THIS REVIEW WAS published in *The Nation*, 23 (20 July 1918): 426, 428, while Russell was in prison. Its publication brought him a certain fame among his fellow prisoners.

> Quite half the inmates of the prison read my review of Kant in the *Nation* and had some sensible critical opinion about it. This is what the criminal classes are in reality. The other half are mostly debtors and bigamists, and a sprinkling of men who have got drunk and committed some folly.

This report is found in a letter to Lady Ottoline Morrell written on 11 September 1918 from Brixton Prison.

Norman Duncan Smith (1872–1958), after 1910 Norman Kemp Smith, a Scottish philosopher, was almost an exact contemporary of Russell, having been born thirteen days before him. At the time he wrote the book under review he held a Professorship in Philosophy in Princeton University. He occupied this position from 1906 to 1919 when he resigned to accept appointment as Professor of Logic and Metaphysics in the University of Edinburgh, a post he held until his retirement in 1945. In addition to his work in the philosophy of Kant—he published what has become the standard English translation of *The Critique of Pure Reason* in 1929—he also published important studies of Descartes and Hume.

There is no manuscript, so the copy-text is that of *The Nation*.

A Commentary to Kant's "Critique of Pure Reason". By Norman Kemp Smith. London: Macmillan, 1918. Pp. xi, 615.

KANT PASSES HABITUALLY for the greatest of modern philosophers, except among the diminishing number who regard him as second to Hegel. The present reviewer belongs to a minority who do not place Kant on such an eminence: he would rank Descartes, Leibniz, and Hume above him, and would regard the whole movement brought about by the Critical Philosophy as a mistaken one, from which speculation must return if real progress is to be made. But however Kant's purely intellectual merits may be decided, there can be no disputing the charm of character displayed in his writing—a charm derived from perfect sincerity, intense earnestness, and the utmost effort of thought at every moment. He is always puzzled, always genuinely seeking, never glib or perfunctory. As he appears in the *Critique of Pure Reason*, he presents the spectacle of a struggle between early habits of mind and recent doubts, both very tenacious, causing together an inward confusion and tension which compelled him to burrow more and more into deep and difficult thoughts until, in the resulting darkness, he could no longer see that no real reconciliation had been effected. He believed that Hume had awakened him from his dogmatic slumbers, but, in fact, Hume only produced that partial awakening which shows itself in nightmare.

Kant's philosophy cannot be understood unless we take account of his intense conservatism, and of the naive simplicity that characterized him in his unprofessional moments. The religion and morality which he had been taught in infancy were sacred to him; the morality was the most certain thing in the world, the religion needed at most a slight adjustment. The Leibniz–Wolffian philosophy, which he had learnt in youth, was not indeed so sacred as what he had learnt in infancy; he did succeed in throwing it off to a great extent. But the difficulty he had in throwing it off is shown in the "Transcendental Dialectic", where he represents it as the natural and all but inevitable belief of the human race. The turgid quality and the apparent profundity of his thought are due to the instinctive resistance which he offered to Hume's scepticism; too conservative to accept the sceptical position, he was too honest to reject it, except for reasons so complicated and confused that he could not see them to be fallacious. Such, at least, his philosophy appears to a sceptic.

Professor Norman Smith's work is admirably done. He is an affectionate but not undiscriminating admirer of Kant's work, a very careful student, not only of Kant, but of his predecessors.[1] His *Studies in the Cartesian*

1 With the possible exception of Leibniz, whom he interprets somewhat too traditionally; there is no evidence of acquaintance with Couturat's *La Logique de Leibniz*, which threw a flood of new light on to the dark places of his system.

Philosophy would have predisposed us in his favour, but the present volume more than justifies our expectations. Kant's inconsistencies are recognized, and the various stages of his thought are exposed to view. One is almost reminded of the higher criticism of the Pentateuch:

> The publication of Kant's *Reflexionen* and *Lose Blätter*, and the devoted labours of Benno Erdmann, Vaihinger, Adickes, Reicke, and others, have, indeed, placed the issue upon an entirely new plane. It can now be proved that the *Critique* is not a unitary work, and that in the five months in which, as Kant tells us, it was "brought to completion" (*zu Stande gebracht*), it was not actually written, but was pieced together by the combination of manuscripts written at various dates throughout the period 1772–1780. (P. xx)

The *Critique*, we are told, "was more or less mechanically constructed through the piecing together of older manuscript.... Kant, it would almost seem, objected to nothing so much as the sacrifice of an argument once consecrated by committal to paper.... Thus the 'Subjective and Objective Deductions' of the first edition can be broken up, as we shall find, into at least four distinct layers, which, like geological strata, remain to the bewilderment of the reader" (p. xxi). The contradictory character which Professor Norman Smith recognizes in Kant's work is attributable to this manner of composition, but also, as he justly observes, to "Kant's supreme merit as a philosophical thinker ... his open-minded recognition of the complexity of his problems". A candid philosopher should acknowledge that he is not very likely to have arrived at ultimate truth, but, in view of the incurable tendency to discipleship in human nature, he will be thought to have done so unless he makes his failure very evident. The duty of making this evident was one which Kant's candour led him to perform better than most other philosophers.

Professor Norman Smith considers that the Transcendental Aesthetic represents an early and rather crude stage of the thought that is embodied in the *Critique*. "The most flagrant example", he says, "of Kant's failure to live up to his own critical principles is to be found in his doctrine of pure intuition. It represents a position which he adopted in the precritical period." This doctrine, because it comes at the beginning of the book, represents Kant to most people as much as, for the same reason, the windmills episode represents Don Quixote; but the grounds assigned by the author are weighty, and it is difficult to see how to refute them. The latest and best of the various doctrines embodied in the *Critique*, according to Professor Smith, is chiefly to be found in the "Transcendental Analytic". He distinguishes, in Kant, an earlier subjectivist view and a later phenomenalist view. All disciples of Kant nowadays try, in varying degrees, to acquit him of the charge of subjectivism. Professor Smith is too careful and honest to do so wholly, but he regards all the subjectivist passages as early. The present reviewer, as a hostile critic of Kant, is unable to see anything in his "phenomenalist" doctrines except subjectivism which has become shame-faced and muddle-headed. The problem of knowledge for Kant, in his finished doctrine, we are told, "is no longer how consciousness, individually conditioned, can lead us beyond its own bounds, but what a consciousness, which is at once consciousness of objects and also consciousness of a self, must imply for its possibility" (p. 274). But as we have to employ our own mental apparatus in discussing this problem, it would seem that a genuine criticism of knowledge is impossible: criticism must be from within, and cannot therefore yield any but subjective confirmation, though it might conceivably lead to refutation, if internal inconsistency were revealed. But it is impossible to justify this position within the compass of a review.

However this may be, Professor Smith as a critic is full of wisdom. His wisdom is illustrated in such passages as:

> What is most fundamental in Kant's thinking is frequently that of which he was himself least definitely aware. Like other thinkers, he was most apt to discuss what he himself was inclined to question and feel doubt over. The sources of his insight as well as the causes of his failure often lay beyond the purview of his explicitly developed tenets; and only under the stimulus of criticism was he constrained and enabled to bring them within the circle of reasoned conviction. (P. 292)

Professor Smith's book is a much-needed addition to British Kant-literature. We have been too much at the mercy of Hegelianizing commentators, who are concerned, not to find out what Kant thought, but only to show that if he had thought a little more he would have become Hegel. And it is good to have a book in English which makes such judicious use of the careful investigators mentioned above. It is with a strange heartache that one looks back to the days when the Königsberg philosopher lived a life of pure reason; in our time the life of reason is more difficult and more painful. But the thought of lives such as his has by no means lost its value on that account.

15

Review of Broad,
Perception, Physics, and Reality [1918]

THIS REVIEW WAS published in *Mind*, n.s. 27 (Oct. 1918): 492–8.

In a letter of 1 July 1918 to his brother Frank from Brixton Prison, Russell wrote in answer to a query in Frank's (lost) letter: "Will do review for Stout." This cryptic message must refer to this review, because G. F. Stout was then the editor of *Mind* and there are no other reviews by Russell in that journal during the succeeding three years. He did not mention the review again in his surviving prison letters, but he did write it there, since he listed it as "written in prison" in "Philosophical Books Read in Prison" which is printed as Appendix III.

The book had been published in 1914, an earlier version of it having been submitted, in 1911, as Broad's Fellowship dissertation. Russell read it then as one of the examiners. In an undated letter to Lady Ottoline Morrell, but one which was written during September 1911, he had this to say about the dissertation:

> I have finished my first reading of Broad: solid and sound and dull. He never makes either a mistake or an important discovery. His worst offences are his jokes, which have a kind of terrible flatness, like soda-water after the fizz has gone out of it. (#184)

Two days later he reported: "I have finished re-reading Broad, and written a report on him.... I am glad to be done with Broad—he is dull" (#185). Early in October he wrote her that of the candidates' three-hour essay papers Broad's was "much the best" (#206). Broad was elected a Fellow.

In 1912 Broad visited Russell in Cambridge, which led to this report to Lady Ottoline:

> As he ⟨Cobden-Sanderson⟩ left Broad appeared—I had recognized the bedmaker's description "a bald gentleman not middle-aged"—he teaches at St. Andrews now. I found myself disliking him—he is in some way ignoble. But he is *very* much abler than any of my present pupils except Wittgenstein. He is much the most *reliable* pupil I have had—practically certain to do a good deal of useful but not brilliant work. (#384, pmk. 15 March)

On the 16th of July 1914 Russell wrote her that "Broad has published a book—his fellowship thesis, almost unaltered. He seems to me to be stagnating; he is as good as he was but no better" (#1053). Russell's review shows that four years later he still held the same opinions about Broad. Indeed there is no evidence that he ever changed them.

Charlie Dunbar Broad (1887–1970), after several years at St. Andrews, was elected in 1920 to the professorship in the University of Bristol. Three years later he resigned to become a Fellow of Trinity College, Cambridge. In 1933 he was elected Knightsbridge Professor of Moral Philosophy in Cambridge, which post he held until his retirement. He published ten books during his lifetime. Of them Russell reviewed two more: *Scientific Thought* (1923) for the *Mathematical Gazette* (1923); and *The Mind and its Place in Nature* (1925) for *The Nation & the Athenaeum* (1925), and for *Mind* (1926).

The copy-text is that printed in *Mind*.

Perception, Physics, and Reality; an Enquiry into the Information that Physical Science can Supply about the Real. By C. D. Broad. Cambridge: University Press, 1914. Pp. xii, 388.

THIS BOOK HAS a peculiar and unusual quality, in virtue of which it serves a purpose analogous to that which examiners are supposed to serve in education. It does not advance any fundamental novelties of its own, but it appraises, with extraordinary justice and impartiality and discrimination, the arguments that have been advanced by others on the topics with which it deals. Mr. G. E. Moore's "Refutation of Idealism" is awarded an Alpha-minus (*cf.* p. 177n.); the rest of us receive such betas and gammas as we deserve, except Locke, who I think may be said to be ploughed.

Locke is the chief victim in the first chapter, "on the arguments against naïf realism independent of the causal theory of perception". There is a long discussion of Locke's two hands in luke-warm water, ending, apparently, with the conclusion that whatever *prima facie* case this experiment may seem to establish against realism can be avoided through the assumption that hands are warmed by being put in cold water and cooled by being put in hot water, or through various other less plausible assumptions.

Mr. Broad's general attitude is that of one who wishes to defend realism, but finds the task difficult. As he proceeds, the arguments against realism grow more and more formidable. At the end, he is left with only a certain degree of probability in favour of a view which is only a pale shadow of the robust realism of common sense. Accepting from Mr. Moore the importance of distinguishing between a perception and its immediate object, the problem for Mr. Broad is as to the relation of this immediate object to the "real" in the physical world. His definition of "real" is to be gathered from the following passage: "Whatever else may or may not exist, it is quite certain that what we perceive exists and has the qualities that it is perceived to have. The worst that can be said of it is that it is not also *real*, i.e. that it does not exist when it is not the object of someone's perception" (p. 3). That is to say, the "real" is what does not exist only when it is perceived. Much might be said in criticism of this definition, but it is at any rate clear and definite. He formulates two questions immediately after giving this definition, namely (a) do objects of perception themselves continue to exist at times when they are not perceived? and (b) do things exist which are not perceived but are inferrible from perceived objects and have some relation to these objects such as could be called "correspondence" with them? In the main, the first chapter rejects (rightly as I think) such arguments against realism as are familiar from Locke and Berkeley. But the different visual appearances of a given thing from different places lead to the conclusion that touch is a sounder source of knowledge as to shape than sight. This conclusion is adhered to throughout the rest of the book. The ellipses of various eccentricities which are seen from various places in looking at a circle cannot, Mr. Broad thinks, be *all* real, not because such a view would be logically impossible, but because it would be so terribly complicated (p. 41).

I think that we have here the first effect of an undiscussed dogma which is embedded in Mr. Broad's conception of "reality". What makes Mr. Broad call unperceived objects "real" is not the mere fact of their being unperceived, but the supposed fact that they persist. He seems, in fact, to work
10 with the notion of substance,[1] with the belief that the physical world must consist of permanent entities with changing relations. I think the contrary view, that permanence is constructed, and is that of a temporal series of successive existents, makes the relation of the object of perception to physical reality much simpler. We can then hold that, although we do not perceive everything, all that we do perceive is "real" in the only sense in which anything is "real". All the visual ellipses "corresponding" to the one tactual circle are "real" while we see them, and nothing that exists (so far as our evidence goes) persists for very long. This view is not more complicated than the view that denies "reality" to the visual ellipses. For on Mr. Broad's
20 view they exist, and must have their place in an inventory of the world; but on his view there is something else of a different kind, more "real" than they are, whereas on the view that I should advocate there is nothing more "real", though there may be many things which we do not perceive.

There is a very good discussion (p. 45ff.) of the reasons which make it impossible to know that such words as "red" and "green" have the same meaning to two different people, but possible to know that such words as "agreement" and "difference" have the same meaning. The point is very important, and I do not know of any author who has made it so well.

The second chapter is "On causation; and on the arguments that have
30 been used against causal laws". It begins by stating that it will assume the validity of arguments from probability, and of induction as a means of establishing probability. There is in the early part of the chapter a certain amount of discussion of somewhat familiar themes, such as whether a cause is a thing or an event, and whether a cause is to be interpreted in terms of activity or of regularity. Naturally the regularity view is adopted. Equally naturally, it is decided that transeunt causality is quite as possible as immanent causality (p. 105). The discussion on "causal laws and time" (p. 106ff.) is to my mind unsatisfactory because it seems to assume the continuity (or at least the compactness) of change, not merely as applied to the
40 world as a whole, but also as applied to small portions of the world. If, as I

---

1 This notion is rejected on page 103, and is certainly not *intended* to be assumed anywhere. But I think it is "real", i.e. exists when Mr. Broad does not perceive it.

believe, whatever exists persists for a finite time (however small), the truth must be more like the modern physical theory of *quanta*. Continuity, like permanence and everything else that is mathematically convenient, will be a matter of logical construction. This, if it be the case, compels a somewhat new discussion of such questions as the temporal contiguity of cause and effect. Something like this view is discussed on page 114, but in connection with what I should regard as an unduly conventional theory of time and space.

It is often thought that, when an effect is complex, its cause must be equally complex. A sound, for example, has the characteristics of pitch, loudness, and quality. Must the cause of the sound which we hear have three corresponding characteristics? Mr. Broad shows that there is no ground for thinking so (p. 139). The point is important from its bearing on the possibility of mechanical explanation in general.

The conclusion of Chapter ii had better be given in Mr. Broad's own words, as it would be difficult to state it either more briefly or more clearly:

That every event has a cause means on our theory that to every true proposition asserting the occurrence of an event at any given time there is a number of true propositions asserting the occurrence of other events at different (and perhaps, to be in accord with tradition, we should add earlier) times such that relative to this set the probability of the event's occurrence is 1. This proposition does not seem to me self-evident, nor do I know of any means of proving it. At the same time it obviously cannot be disproved and it is advantageous to assume it as a methodological postulate. (P. 161)

I can find no criticism to make of this statement, given the author's apology as regards probability (p. x). I feel less convinced as regards what we are told (p. 114) is an a priori truth, namely, "the law that a system that has been quiescent for a finite time can only be set in motion by a causal process transeunt to itself"; but in view of the fact that no instance of a quiescent system is known, the question is perhaps not of great importance.

Chapter iii, "On phenomenalism", discusses the views of Mach, defended, not by Mach's arguments, but by those much better ones which Mr. Broad would advance if the views were his. Phenomenalism is defined as the theory which "holds, not merely that the objects of all our perceptions exist only when they are perceived, but also that there are no permanent real things with laws of their own that cause these perceptions and in some measure resemble their objects" (p. 164). It is pointed out (p. 165) that this theory is incompatible with the causal theory of perception, according to which our sense-organs are part causes of our perceptions. For if phenomenalism is true we have no eye except when some one sees it, and therefore what we see when we are not under observation cannot be caused by the structure of the eye. This is a perfectly irrefutable argument. It does not provide any ground against phenomenalism, but if phenomenalism were otherwise acceptable it would afford a ground against the causal theory. It does not *prove* that it is impossible to deduce phenomenalism from the causal theory, since there is no fallacy in using a false premiss for the purpose of proving its own falsehood. The one thing it does prove is that phenomenalism and the causal theory cannot both be true; and this is important, since those who believe either generally believe the other, and the two together (though both cannot be true) are far more plausible than either separately, though either separately may be true.

This chapter does not seem to me very satisfactory. "I think it is perfectly clear", says Mr. Broad, "that an absolutely pure phenomenalism that wishes to explain and anticipate our perceptions can be ruled out of court. We will suppose that it is allowed to assume present perceptions and those that it can remember. It is quite clear that with these alone there are no causal laws possible that will account for the perceptions we may expect to have anything like as well as the assumptions which science makes will do" (p. 168). This certainly *seems* true; but is it? I am troubled by an argument which needs to be tested by practice, but which meanwhile I will advance with due hesitation. My problem is: How can we ever obtain any evidence for a causal law except through perception? And, that being so, must not the unperceived elements in such a law be definable as functions of the perceived elements? And, in that case, do these functions serve any vital purpose except *as* functions of perceived elements, and is there any reason to suppose that they represent independent reals? It seems to me that a world sparsely dotted with perceived elements can be "filled out" in the same kind of way in which a descriptive space is filled out until it becomes projective. The elements added will be functions of the elements given, just as are the "ideal" points, lines, and planes that are added to a descriptive space in constructing a projective space from it. The assumption that the ideal elements "exist" is, it seems to me, theoretically otiose, and merely convenient as affording resting-places for our feeble logical imagination. I grant at once that undiluted phenomenalism cannot yield as well-filled a science of physics as we are accustomed to, but I contend that what would have to be omitted represents mere prejudice or guess-work, for which there is no shred of empirical evidence. If all this is true, it does not, of course, prove that phenomenalism is true, but only that it cannot be shown to be untrue, and that it is the most economical of all the theories that may be true. The prudent philosopher, it seems to me, will no longer aim at finding one certainly true complete theory in any subject: he will be more likely to find that an infinite number of theories are compatible with all the data, and he will assert only the common part (if any) of all these theories. In the problem with which we are concerned at present, this common part, I suggest, is what is *positively* asserted by phenomenalism. I do not say this is certainly the case; I merely think it may be, and Mr. Broad has not shown that it is not.

Chapter iv, a very long chapter, is on "The causal theory of perception". This theory, to begin with, is described as "the view which is certainly held vaguely by educated common-sense that our perceptions have causes and that some relation is to be found between the nature of these causes and the reality of the objects perceived" (p. 187). He suggests (*ibid.*) that this theory *may* be a will o' the wisp, but he certainly does not succeed in proving that it is. He distinguishes it from the "instrumental" theory, according to which our sense-organs under suitable circumstances are instruments for perceiving reality, while under other circumstances they lead us to illusion. This theory, after considerable argument, is criticized, mainly on the following ground:

> Grant that there is illusion whether small or great and you must grant that the complex mechanism involved in perception can produce two entirely different results. Entirely different in one sense and yet on the other hand unfortunately very much alike. It is the combination of their extreme likeness and their utter difference that threatens to wreck the instrumental theory, and with it, the science of physics as ordinarily understood. When we perceive reality, if we ever do so, the effect of the whole process in the reality, the organ, the brain, and the mind is to establish a relation between the mind and the reality that we perceive. When we perceive appearance, the effect of much the same process in the organs and the brain is to produce, not a relation to something already existing, but a whole of object + relation to mind. Now two effects could hardly be more unlike than this. Yet on the other hand there is an immense likeness between them. (Pp. 239–40)

This leads up to the question: "Can you really believe that practically the same mechanism can produce such utterly different results?" Nevertheless Mr. Broad does not *entirely* accept the conclusion to which the argument points. He adheres to the view that in touch, at least, we become acquainted with primary qualities which resemble those of their causes—not, oddly enough, their immediate causes, but others far enough back to be also causes of the visual appearances of the "same" things. The scientific theory of the causation of our perceptions, he points out, "assumes that the remote causes of our perceptions resemble their objects not only in the general way that both have primary qualities, but also in the much more particular one that there is a general resemblance between the shape of the appearance and the shape of the remote cause" (p. 245). The queerness of such an assumption is fully recognized, but nevertheless, with limitations, it is allowed to be reasonable as regards tactual shapes (see p. 262). The final statement is as follows:

> Our conclusion, then, is that it is most probable that there is a real counterpart corresponding point for point to what is perceived in most (perhaps in all) the tactual perceptions that we have of figure, though doubtless more differentiated than the tactual objects themselves; and that events in this reality are the causes of our visual perceptions, according to laws which science, stating its position in terms of perceptible primaries, is able to discover.   (P. 265)

For my part, I cannot believe that a conclusion of this sort can represent the truth of the matter in its simplest form. The whole theory seems to me unduly ingenious and complicated in its developments, too much *ad hoc*, and too destitute of a large simple structure. It reminds me of the successive epicycles by which the Ptolemaic astronomy was emended before it gave way to Copernicus. Whatever the truth may be about perception and reality, I feel convinced that, as in Copernican astronomy, the difficulty of discovering it lies in a difficulty of imagination at the beginning, not in subleties at late stages of the development. Mr. Broad's book produces upon me the impression of listening to a long cross-examination of a plausible witness by a highly-skilled barrister, Mr. Broad himself fulfilling both roles. At first the witness's story seems quite straightforward. Gradually little points are elicited, none of them fatal, but each requiring a more or less unplausible addition to the original evidence. At the end, though the story has not been actually refuted, we are left with an uneasy feeling that it is wrong from beginning to end. My own firm conviction is that all the conceptions traditionally employed—reality, perception, cause, matter, space, time, mind—need such radical overhauling that theories stated in terms of them can hardly be judged at all until they have been translated into new language and vitally transformed by the translation. But so long as the traditional conceptions remain unchanged, I do not see what better discussion is possible than that to be found in Mr. Broad's book.

The last chapter, on "The laws of mechanics", is less important than its predecessors. The author is entirely justified in his criticisms of the present reviewer's arguments in favour of absolute motion, which is neither logically necessary nor logically impossible, but on grounds of economy should not be employed in stating the laws of mechanics. The subject of Newtonian dynamics is hackneyed, and it is difficult to say anything very new or very interesting within the framework of the traditional conceptions. We could wish that Mr. Broad had given a more important position to the principle of relativity, instead of relegating it to an appendix. Moreover, even concerning Newtonian dynamics, there are things to be said which we should have wished to find. Take, for example, the first law of motion. It may be a definition of equal times, or of all sorts of things. For my part, I should regard it as a definition (or a way of reaching a definition) of the "same" thing at different times. This cannot be obtained from continuity alone, as may be seen by considering a sensibly homogeneous fluid. But this topic is too large for the end of a review.

Mr. Broad's book preserves a uniform level of very high excellence. There is not one foolish word in it; everything is clear, definite, and well reasoned. But one could wish that he would apply his immense abilities to the invention of genuinely new theories, rather than to the fitting together of an extraordinarily ingenious mosaic of bits of old theories. His book is exceedingly useful as showing the best that can be done in that way; but I do not believe it is the most useful book he is capable of writing.

16

Professor Dewey's
Essays in Experimental Logic [1919]

THIS REVIEW WAS published in *The Journal of Philosophy, Psychology, and Scientific Methods*, 16 (2 Jan. 1919): 5–26. It is reprinted in *Dewey and His Critics* (1977), 231–52 edited by Sidney Morgenbesser.

Wendell T. Bush, one of the editors of the journal, wrote Russell late in 1916 inviting him to review Dewey's book. Russell replied on the 14th of December:

> Your letter of November 23 has been forwarded to me from Oxford, though I never had any connection with that University. I should like to write something on Dewey's logic if I could find the time, but I am much occupied at present and I cannot be sure. I do not possess Dewey's *Essays in Experimental Logic* and books are difficult to get here at present. Would you be so kind as to send me a copy? How soon do you want the article, in case I am able to do it?

There is nothing more on this review until he is a prisoner. Russell entered prison early in May 1918. In a message to Wildon Carr, dated 10 June 1918, he wrote:

> Have written about 10,000 words on Dewey, by request, for (American) *Journal of Philosophy, Psychology* etc. Will get it typed and sent to you. Could you get it sent to U.S. There is some fuss with the censorship to be gone through.

The letter in which this message is found was written to Russell's brother and sister-in-law. It is not clear just when Russell sent his manuscript off for typing, but it must have been about this date, because in a letter to his brother dated 24 June he wrote: "Please tell Miss Kyle to send the *Dewey* manuscript and typescript to Carr *as soon as possible*." Miss Kyle's bill for typing an original and two carbons exists; it records that they were typed on 1 July 1918. The existing correspondence does not contain any evidence to account for the six-month delay in publication.

A letter to Lady Constance Malleson of 4 September indicates that he had checked the typescript by that date: "In the typescript I gave you for Miss Wrinch, I should like you to read the last sentence, and pages 26–30 ⟨147: 35–148: 43⟩. The rest is too technical to amuse you." Presumably Miss Wrinch was to send it to the editor of the *Journal*.

Russell had met John Dewey (1859–1952) during his visit to the United States in the spring of 1914. Their first meeting was recorded on 22 March, the day after it took place, in a letter to Lady Ottoline Morrell.

> Dewey (the third pragmatist, with James and Schiller) has been here. I met him at lunch yesterday and then had a walk with him. To my surprise I liked him very much. He has a large slow-moving mind, very empirical and candid, with something of the impassivity and impartiality of a natural force. He and Perry and I had a long argument about "I"—Dewey saw a point I was making but Perry didn't—he is a good man but not a very clever one, as the country gentleman said of Dizzy.   (#1008)

He met Dewey again when he read Paper **1** at Columbia where Dewey again impressed him favourably. In a letter of 29 April, in a string of complaints about America, he wrote: "With the exception of Dewey and Simon Flexner, I have met hardly a soul who had any quality, and neither of them is in the least civilized" (#1025).

He was, then, quite favourably disposed toward Dewey when he wrote this review. Later when he met Dewey in China he changed his mind:

> The Deweys, who are here, and who got in trouble in America during the war for their liberalism, are as bad as anybody—American imperialists, hating England as ⟨Leo⟩ Maxse used to hate Germany, and unwilling to face any unpleasant facts. In 1914, I liked Dewey better than any other academic American; now I can't stand him.   (#1583, 21 Feb. 1921)

Russell's opinion of Dewey was negative for the rest of his life, despite the many kindnesses Dewey paid him at the time of Russell's dismissal from The College of the City of New York in 1940.

The typescript from which the printer set type survives (RA REC. ACQ. 411). It has been selected as copy-text. The results of collating it with the printed version are reported in the Textual Notes.

Essays in Experimental Logic. By John Dewey. Chicago: University of Chicago Press, 1916. Pp. vii, 444.

IN READING THIS collection of Essays, I have been conscious of a much greater measure of agreement than the author would consider justifiable on my part. In particular, in passages dealing with my own views, I have often found that the only thing I disagreed with was the opinion that what was said constituted a criticism of me. There seems to me quite clearly to be, in Professor Dewey's outlook, a misunderstanding of some, at least, of the "analytic realists". I shall try, in what follows, chiefly to remove this
10 misunderstanding. Philosophical writing, as a rule, is to my mind far too eristic. There are various classes of difficulties to be dealt with in philosophy, each fairly easy to solve if it stood alone. Each philosopher invents a solution applicable to his own problems, and refuses to recognize those of others. He sees that the theories of others do not solve his problems, but he refuses to see that his theories do not solve the problems of others. I do not wish to offer merely another example of this kind of blindness, since I consider that it constitutes a most serious obstacle to the progress of philosophy. In return, I would beg Professor Dewey to believe that certain questions which interest me cannot be solved unless his doctrines are
20 supplemented by theories brought from a region into which, as yet, he has not thought it necessary to penetrate.

A misunderstanding, as between him and those who hold views more akin to mine, is likely to arise through different use of terms. What he calls "logic" does not seem to me to be part of logic at all; I should call it part of psychology. He takes the view—for which there is much better authority than for mine—that logic is concerned with thought. The ways in which we become possessed of what we call "knowledge" are, for him, questions of "logic". His book is said to consist of studies in experimental "logic". Now in the sense in which I use the word, there is hardly any "logic" in the book
30 except the suggestion that judgments of practice yield a special form—a suggestion which belongs to logic in my sense, though I do not accept it as a valid one. A great deal of his criticism of my views on the external world rests, I think, upon this difference of terminology. He insists that what I call data are logical, not psychological, data, and in his sense of these words I entirely agree. I never intended them to be regarded as data which would be psychological in his sense. The subject which I call "logic" is one which apparently does not seem to Professor Dewey a very important one. No doubt he feels that I attach too little importance to matters which he regards as vital. This differing estimate of relative importance is, I think, the main
40 source of differences between him and me. I hope that, if both recognize this, the differences may come to be greatly diminished. It is in this hope, and not in a spirit of controversy, that the following pages are written.

I. LOGICAL AND PSYCHOLOGICAL DATA

I will try first of all to set forth what I conceive to be the most important features, from my point of view, in Professor Dewey's doctrine as regards data. To a great extent I am in agreement with his doctrine; but I shall leave the critical consideration of it until I have endeavoured to state it. Let us begin with some quotations.

(1). "That fruitful thinking—thought that terminates in valid knowledge—goes on in terms of the distinction of facts and judgment, and that valid knowledge is precisely genuine correspondence or agreement, *of some sort*, of fact and judgment, is the common and undeniable assumption." (P. 231)

(2). "A functional logic ... has never for a moment denied the prima facie working distinction between 'ideas,' 'thoughts,' 'meanings,' and 'facts,' 'existences,' 'the environment,' nor the necessity of a control of meaning by facts." (P. 236)

(3). "The position taken in the essays is frankly realistic in acknowledging that certain brute existences, detected or laid bare by thinking but in no way constituted out of thought or any mental process, set every problem for reflection and hence serve to test its otherwise merely speculative results." (P. 35)

(4). *Perceptions* are not themselves cases of knowledge, but they are the source of all our knowledge of the world: "They are the sole ultimate data, the sole media, of inference to all natural objects and processes. While we do not, in any intelligible or verifiable sense, know *them*, we know all things that we do know *with* or *by* them. They furnish the only ultimate evidence of the existence and nature of the objects which we infer, and they are the sole ultimate checks and tests of the inferences. Because of this characteristic use of perceptions, the perceptions themselves acquire, by 'second intention,' a knowledge status. They *become* objects of minute, accurate, and experimental scrutiny." (Pp. 259–260)

(5). But this cognitive function of perceptions is derivative. It is a "superstition" that "sensations-perceptions are cases of knowledge.... Let them [the realists] try the experiment of conceiving perceptions as pure natural events, not as cases of awareness or apprehension, and they will be surprised to see how little they miss." (P. 262)

(6). "To find out *what is* given is an inquiry which taxes reflection to the uttermost. Every important advance in scientific method means better agencies, more skilled technique for simply detaching and describing what is barely there, or given." (P. 152)

(7). "According to Mr. James, for example, the original datum is large but confused, and specific sensible qualities represent the result of discriminations. In this case, the elementary data, instead of being primitive empirical data, are the last terms, the limits, of the discriminations we have been able to make." (Pp. 298–9)

These quotations may serve for the moment to illustrate Professor Dewey's doctrine as regards data.

The first three raise no point of controversy as between him and me. The sixth and seventh, though I believe he would regard them as affording an argument against some of my views, certainly do not say anything that I disagree with, except in so far as there is an ambiguity in the second sentence of the seventh: "primitive empirical data" may mean primitive in time, or primitive in logic. The logical articulation of a man's knowledge changes as his knowledge increases; at every stage, there will be parts of his knowledge that are logically more primitive and parts that are logically less so. What, at an advanced stage of knowledge, is primitive in logic, may be very far from primitive in time. The last terms in our discriminations are very likely to become *logically* primitive in our knowledge very soon after we have reached them. But if Professor Dewey means "primitive in time", there is no matter of disagreement between us so far.

The different senses in which things may be "data" need to be considered somewhat more fully, if misunderstandings are to be removed. When I speak of "data", more particularly of "hard data", I am not thinking of those objects which constitute data to children or monkeys: I am thinking of the objects which seem data to a trained scientific observer. It is quite consciously and deliberately, not by mistake, that I am thinking of the trained observer. The kind of "datum" I have in mind is the kind which constitutes the outcome of an experiment, say in physics. We have reason to expect *this* or *that*; *this* happens. Then *this* is what I call a datum. The fact that *this* has happened is a premiss in the reasoning of the man of science; it is not deduced, but simply observed. The state of mind that I am imagining in investigating the problem of the physical world is not a naive state of mind, but one of Cartesian doubt.

The confusion between the two kinds of primitiveness[1] is not always easy

---

[1] When Professor Dewey speaks (p. 406) of "Russell's trusting confidence in 'atomic' propositions as psychological primitives", he is imagining that I mean one sort of primitiveness when in fact I mean another. I mean what would be a premiss to a careful man of science, not what is a premiss to a baby or a gorilla.

to avoid. In those whose knowledge has not reached a high level of logical articulation, there will be comparatively little that is logically derivative. The habit of reasoning and inferring and binding together different pieces of knowledge into a single logical system increases the proportion of logically derivative knowledge, and the deductive weight that has to be supported by what remains logically primitive. One thing that makes the problem exceedingly confusing is that even what we are calling the *logical* articulation of a man's knowledge is still a question of psychology, in part at least. If a man believes two propositions p and q, and if p implies q though he has never noticed this fact, then p and q are separate pieces of his knowledge, though not separate in abstract logic. The logical articulation of a man's knowledge is subject to restrictions imposed by logic, since we shall not regard one part of his knowledge as logically derivative in relation to another unless it is logically inferrible, as well as psychologically inferred by him; but although logic thus enters in as controlling the possible articulations of a man's knowledge, logic alone cannot determine them, and his individual psychology is required in addition in order to fix the actual logical order among his beliefs.

We have thus three different problems, one of pure psychology, one of mixed psychology and logic, and one of pure logic. We may illustrate the three problems by means of the science of physics.

(1) The problem of pure psychology is this: How do we, as a matter of history, come by the beliefs we have about material objects? What earlier beliefs preceded those which we now entertain, either in the individual or in the race? What vaguer state than "belief" precedes the growth of even the earliest beliefs? And what vaguer objects than those presented to a trained observation are to be found in a less sophisticated experience? All these are questions of psychology. They are questions which I, for my part, have not attempted to discuss. Nothing that I have said on the problem of the external world is intended to be applicable to them.

(2) The problem of mixed psychology and logic is this: How do we, ordinary persons with a working knowledge of physics, organize our physical beliefs from a logical point of view? What, if we are challenged, and an attempt is made to make us doubt the truth of physics, shall we fall back upon as giving a basis for our belief which we are not prepared to abandon? Take, say, the facts out of which modern physics grew: Galileo's observations on falling bodies. We have in Galileo's work a mixture of argument, inference, mathematics, with something else which is not argued or inferred, but observed. For him, this something else constituted part of what was logically primitive. To those who are troubled by scepticism, the discovery of what is logically primitive in their own beliefs (or half-beliefs) appears important as a possible help in deciding as to their truth or falsehood. We will call the primitive in this sense the "epistemological primitive". It is the

primitive in this sense that I mean when I speak of "data". I agree entirely with Professor Dewey when he says (p. 428): "To make sure that a given fact *is* just and such a shade of red is, one may say, a final triumph of scientific method"; but when he goes on to say: "To turn around and treat it as something naturally or psychologically given is a monstrous superstition", we shall no longer agree if we are speaking of "data" in the sense of "epistemological primitives" rather than temporal primitives.

(3) In addition to these, there is, or may be, a third kind of primitive, namely, the *pure* logical primitive. This, when it can be defined, can only be defined by logical simplicity or deductive power. A deductive system is preferable when its premisses are few and simple than when they are many and complicated, but this seems to be mainly an aesthetic question. There is, however, something beyond this in logical simplicity. The law of gravitation, for example, implies Kepler's three laws, and much besides; in this sense, as a premiss, it is logically preferable to them. Although, often, in a deductive system, there will be a certain element of arbitrariness in the choice of premisses, yet the arbitrariness is restricted: there will be, usually, a fairly small collection of propositions from among which it is clear that the logical premisses should be chosen. And the more advanced the logical organization of the system, the more restricted will be the choice of premisses. But this sense of "primitive" does not enter into inquiries of which the purpose is to find out whether the grounds for believing some body of scientific propositions are sufficient. In such inquiries, it is the second sense of "primitive", the epistemological sense, that is important. The pure psychological and the pure logical are alike irrelevant. And it is in the second sense that I speak of "data" in discussing the problem of the external world. As an example of the search for the logical primitive in physics, we may take Hertz's *Prinzipien der Mechanik*. In this book the author is not concerned to persuade us that physics is true, but to find the best way of stating premisses from which physics (supposed known) can be deduced.

There is a problem as regards the comparative merit of the differing psychological data at various levels. The common-sense view is that greater discrimination and more analytic observation yield more knowledge. It is supposed that we know more about an object which we have inspected closely, with attention to parts and differentiation, than about an object of which we have only what is called a "general impression". The successes of science, whose observation of facts is highly analytic, have confirmed the view that observation of this sort yields the most information. But as against this common-sense view we have a sort of artificially archaistic view, which opposes analysis, believes in a faculty of "intuition" possessed by peasant women, dogs, and ichneumon wasps, loves savage religions, and maintains that the progress of intellect has driven wisdom away from almost all men except the few immovable philosophers among whom intellect has not progressed. Those who adopt this artificially archaistic view believe that the large confused data spoken of by James (in the seventh of our above quotations) have more capacity for revealing truth than is to be found in scientific observations. I do not think that Professor Dewey belongs to those who take this view. Accordingly he does not regard the vaguer data as giving more knowledge than those that are more analysed. But there are aspects of his theories which might mistakenly suggest that he took this view.

I do not wish, at the moment, to consider Professor Dewey's views so much as to consider the problem in itself. The problem concerned is what we may call the problem of "vagueness". It may be illustrated by what occurs while we watch a man walking towards us on a long straight road. At first we see only a vague dot; we cannot tell whether it is moving; we only guess that it is a human being because it seems about the right size. Gradually it passes through various grades of growing distinctness: we recognize it as so-and-so, and at last we see what sort of expression he has on his face, and whether he looks well or ill. In this case, it is clear that the more analysed apprehension enables us to know more. We can more or less infer what a man would look like a long way off when we see him near at hand; but the converse inference is much more circumscribed. Now although, in the case of the man approaching along a road, our attention remains throughout equally analytic in character, and the changes that occur are due merely to the fact that the object comes nearer, yet I think that there is a close analogy between the quick changes in this case and the slow changes in the case of increasing powers of analytic attention. In these changes also, I think, what happens is that more differentiations exist in the new datum, and that the new datum allows more inferences than the old one. At the same time, as in the case of the man approaching, what (to save trouble) we may call the same physical object gradually comes to occupy a larger portion of the field of attention, so that, although more is known about an object which remains within the field of attention, there are fewer such objects at any one time. A man who is reading sees differences on the printed page which are probably more minute than any that a dog ever sees, but while he is seeing them he may miss other things which the dog would never miss, for instance a person speaking to him. There seems no reason to reject the common-sense view that, through trained attention, we acquire more knowledge about the things we attend to, but become more restricted as regards the area of attention.

Following the analogy of the man on the road, whom I will now suppose seen simultaneously by a number of people at different distances, I suggest that it is possible, theoretically at least, to distinguish elements, in the perceptions of all these people, which are correlated and may be called perceptions "of" the one man. For the moment I do not wish to go into the meaning of this "of"; it is enough that these elements are correlated in the

way that leads to their being said to be "of" one object. It is not necessary that the element which is a perception of the man in question should be consciously isolated and attended to by the person who has it: it is enough that it occurs, regardless of whether anybody knows that it does. (But of course the hypothesis that it sometimes occurs without anybody's knowing is based upon what *is* known.) Now among the correlated occurrences which we call perceptions of the one man, some allow more inference as to the others and some less. Those that allow less we will define as "vaguer"; those that allow more, as "less vague". Those that are less vague are more
10 differentiated: they consist of more parts. In a very vague perception of the man, he is an undifferentiated dot. In a still vaguer perception, the whole man may be absorbed into the smallest discriminated element: we may see a distant regiment as a speck, without being able to distinguish its component men. In all this, I am accepting common sense. It may be necessary to abandon common sense on some points, but in all that concerns vagueness what I wish to maintain is in the closest agreement with common sense.

We may lay down the following common-sense propositions. (1) All that we learn through the senses is more or less vague. (2) What we learn by careful analytic attention of the scientific kind is less vague than what we
20 learn by casual untrained attention; what we learn by seeing things close at hand is less vague than what we learn by seeing them at a distance. (3) Even the vaguest perception has *some* value for purposes of inference, but the vaguer it is the smaller becomes its value for inference. From these characteristics we may advance to those implied in the above definition of vagueness. The inferences drawn from what we perceive (or the expectations aroused) are motived by habitual correlations.[2] And the correlations of this sort (e.g. those between what are called appearances of a given object at different distances) are many-one correlations: many different appearances near-to will all correspond to the same appearance further off. Wherever we
30 have a many-one correlation, the "one" can be inferred from any of the "many", but not vice versa; we have the "one" determined by any of the "many" but not any of the "many" by the "one". It seems to me that the vague data of unanalytic attention are just as "true" as the more precise data of trained observation, but allow fewer inferences. We might illustrate the matter by an analogy. If you are told that a man is descended from Adam, that gives you the vaguest possible information as to his ancestry; if you are told that he is descended from William the Conqueror, that is still pretty vague; but as the generations grow later, the information that a man is descended from so-and-so becomes more and more significant. The reason
40 is that the relation of son to father is many-one: when you are told that B is a

2 These inferences are not logically cogent, and are sometimes mistaken, but that is a point that need not concern us at this moment.

son of A, and Z is descended from B, you can infer that Z is descended from A; but when you are told that Z is descended from A, you cannot infer that he is descended from B, because he may be descended from one of A's other children. So it is with correlated perceptions: the vaguer correspond to the earlier generations and the more precise to the later. But of course in the case of perceptions there is possible continuity instead of the discreteness of generations.

I claim for the above view of the relation between psychologically primitive data and the precise data of science various merits which, as I shall try to show, do not seem to be possessed by Professor Dewey's theory.   10

(a) The transition, as we have been explaining it, is a continuous one, and is one not having a terminus in either direction. No perception can be so precise as to be incapable of greater precision—unless, indeed, we were to accept, in regard to all physical things, the theory of *quanta*, and hold that all physical quantities are discrete, in which case there would be a theoretical limit of complete exactitude, though of course far below the threshold of our perceptions. And at the other end of the scale, no perception can be so vague as to be incapable of greater vagueness, unless, indeed, the world appeared always just the same whatever the environment might be. Perhaps absence of life might consist in this absolute vagueness; but where there is life, even   20 so low in the scale as the amoeba, an environment which contains food will seem different from one which does not (to judge by behaviour), and will therefore be perceived with less than the maximum of vagueness.

(b) Another advantage of our definition and theory is that it allows *some* inferential value to even very vague data. It does not have to say: The precise observation of the scientist gives truth, and the vague feeling of the infant gives error. Still less does it have to say the opposite. Assuming a common-sense world, and leaving aside all doubts as to causality, induction, etc., our perceptions always give tolerable ground for *some* expectation or inference; but though the vaguer perceptions may give inferences which (in some   30 sense) cover a wider field, the more precise perceptions allow more inferences within the field they cover. That is to say, suppose what is originally one vague object of attention A (a crowd, say) is correlated with what are later ten more precise objects of attention (ten men, say), then regarding any one of these ten (Z, say) the system of its correlates can be better known when Z is perceived than it could when only A was perceived.

(c). Connected with this is one of the great merits of our theory, namely, that it does not involve an Unknowable, either at the beginning or at the end, because the differences involved are differences of degree, and it is not necessary to assume the existence of an unattainable limit in either direc-   40 tion. There will doubtless be degrees that are *unknown*, but that is a different matter from having to declare them *unknowable*. Any one of them might become known at any moment. The case is analogous to that of a large finite integer which no one has ever happened to think of: any one *might* think of it at any moment. In like manner any degree of vagueness or exactitude might be attained, and there is no need to suppose that there is such a thing as an absolute exactitude, which would be unattainable.

There are, not unconnected with our last point, certain other questions which, to my mind, raise difficulties as to Professor Dewey's instrumentalism. It would seem to follow from what he says that, although we can know that there are crude data, yet we can never know any particular crude datum, because objects of *knowledge* have to be objects of a certain kind, and crude data are not of this kind. Now I do not say that such a view is impossible, but I do say that it is difficult, and that, before it can be accepted, something must be done to show that the difficulties are not insurmountable. This brings us, however, to a general discussion of what Professor Dewey calls "instrumentalism".[3]

II. INSTRUMENTALISM

The theory which Professor Dewey calls instrumentalism is a form of pragmatism, but (as appears by the twelfth essay, on "What Pragmatism Means by Practical") it is a pragmatism which is not intended to be used for the support of ancient superstitions or for bolstering up common prejudices. Some quotations, again, will serve to state the position which he advocates.

(1) "If we exclude acting upon the idea, no conceivable amount or kind of intellectualistic procedure can confirm or confute an idea, or throw any light upon its validity." (P. 240)

(2) "Instrumentalism means a behaviorist theory of thinking and knowing. It means that knowing is literally something which we do; that analysis is ultimately physical and active; that meanings in their logical quality are standpoints, attitudes, and methods of behaving towards facts, and that active experimentation is essential to verification." (Pp. 331–2)

(3) "The thesis of the essays is that thinking is instrumental to a control of the environment, a control effected through acts which would not be undertaken without the prior resolution of a complex situation

3 I leave on one side, for the present, the question raised in the fourth and fifth of the quotations with which we began this section, namely, the question whether sensations and perceptions are cases of knowledge. I do not myself believe that this question is of great importance to the issue between him and me. I shall return to this topic briefly at a later stage.

into assured elements and an accompanying projection of possibilities —without, that is to say, thinking. Such an instrumentalism seems to analytic realism but a variant of idealism. For it asserts that processes of reflective inquiry play a part in shaping the objects—namely, terms and propositions—which constitute the bodies of scientific knowledge. Now it must not only be admitted but proclaimed that the doctrine of the essays holds that intelligence is not an otiose affair, nor yet a mere preliminary to a spectator-like apprehension of terms and propositions. In so far as it is idealistic to hold that objects of knowledge *in their capacity of distinctive objects of knowledge* are determined by intelligence, it is idealistic." (P. 30)

(4) "Again, the question may be asked: Since instrumentalism admits that the table is really 'there,' why make such a fuss about whether it is there as a means or as an object of knowledge? ... Respect for knowledge and its object is the ground for insisting upon the distinction. The object of knowledge is, so to speak, a more dignified, a more complete, sufficient, and self-sufficing thing than any datum can be. To transfer the traits of the object as known to the datum of reaching it, is a material, not a merely verbal, affair." (Pp. 44–5)

The view of Professor Dewey, if I understand him rightly, might be re-stated roughly as follows: The essence of knowledge is *inference* (p. 259), which consists in passing from objects present to others not now present. In order that this may be possible, one of the essentials is that the material originally given should be so shaped as to become an available tool for inference. After this shaping, it becomes what *science* calls a datum; it is then something different from what was there before. The essence of a belief is the behaviour which exemplifies it (which *is* it, one is tempted to say); this behaviour is such as is intended to achieve a certain end, and the belief is shown in the behaviour adopted for that purpose. The belief is called *true* when the behaviour which exemplifies it achieves its end, and false when it does not—omitting refinements due to cooperation of different beliefs. Knowledge is like a railway journey: it is a humanly constructed means of moving from place to place, and its matter, like the rails, is as much a human product as the rest of it, though dependent upon a crude ore which, in its unmanufactured state, would be as useless to intellectual locomotion as iron ore to locomotion by train.

There is a great deal that is attractive in this theory. I am not prepared dogmatically to deny its truth, at any rate in great part. But there are some problems which it *seems* to be unable to deal with.

First and foremost, we have the problem of the crude datum. The crude datum, in Professor Dewey's view—the "large but confused" original datum of William James—is something which lies outside knowledge. This has to do with the other thesis, exemplified in the fourth and fifth quotations of our previous section, that sensations and perceptions are not cases of knowledge, but inference alone is a case of knowledge. This, further, has to do with the practical bias—the view that knowledge must be treated as a means to something else. It is true, I think, that as a help in practical life the sort of knowledge we need is the sort that embodies or suggests inference.

10 We want to know what will help or hinder, which is always a question of inference in a behaviourist sense. And here, further, if we are to take behaviourism seriously, we must contend, for example, that a man or animal who eats something believes (unless he is tired of life) that it is nourishing food, however little he may reflect—for he has adopted the behaviour appropriate to that belief, and belief must not depend for its existence upon anything except behaviour. Thus in every case of eating there will be a case of inference. But the sort of knowledge that would be called "contemplation" has to be abandoned on this view.

Let us develop the point of view which is suggested, rather than fully

20 stated, by Professor Dewey. It might with advantage, I think, be brought into connection with the thesis which the "neutral monists" have taken over from William James, that there is no such thing as "consciousness", and that what are called the mental and the physical are composed of the same material. It is not difficult to make sensation and perception fit into this view, by means of the thesis, urged in some of the above quotations, that they are not cases of knowledge at all. It is more difficult to fit in judgment and inference. But judgment is practically denied by Professor Dewey, as something distinct from inference; and inference is interpreted on be- haviouristic lines. Interpreting him, we might say: "Inference is behaviour

30 caused by an object A and appropriate if A is succeeded or accompanied by B." I do not say that this definition would be accepted: it is schematic, and artificially simplified, but it may serve to exemplify the theory we are examining. We thus arrive at some such picture as the following: Man, an animal struggling for self-preservation in a difficult environment, has learnt to behave towards objects as "signs"—a practice which exists also among other animals, but in less developed forms. An object which is not in itself either useful or harmful may come to be a "sign" of something useful or harmful which is frequently found in its neighbourhood, that is to say, it may come to promote behaviour appropriate to that of which it is a sign,

40 rather than to itself. Such behaviour may be said to embody inference, or the "knowledge" that the object in question is a sign of the inferred object. Objects which are useful as signs acquire a special interest, and it is an essential part of the business of science to perfect the manufacture of such

objects out of the material presented in nature. Such, it seems to me, is Professor Dewey's theory in outline.

I do not wish to maintain that this theory is false; I wish only to suggest that the reasons for thinking it true are far from adequate.

The first criticism that naturally occurs to any one who has endeavoured to ascertain the truth about causality is, that the theory is amazingly light-hearted in its assumption of knowledge as to causality.[4] The writings of Hume, I know, are inconvenient. There are two recognized methods of dealing with what he has to say on Cause: one is to maintain that Kant answered him, the other is to preserve silence on the matter. I do not know which of these is the more inadequate. The second is the one adopted by Professor Dewey (in common with other pragmatists). His conception of signs and inference, his whole notion of knowledge as instrumental, depends throughout upon acceptance of the ordinary common-sense view of causation. I do not wish to be misunderstood in this criticism. I am willing to believe that there may be a great measure of truth in the common-sense view of causation, and I am incapable of saying or writing much without assuming it, at least verbally. The point is not that this view must be false, but that, for instrumentalism, it must be *known* to be true. We must actually know particular causal laws. Our beliefs will be beliefs in causal laws, and we must know what effects are caused by our beliefs, since this is the test of their value as instruments. The very conception of an "instrument" is unintelligible otherwise. For those who are troubled by Hume's arguments, this bland ignoring of them is a difficulty, suggesting, at least, that a good deal of re-statement and further analysis is necessary before instrumentalism can take its place among articulate possible philosophies.

The second criticism which occurs to me is closely allied to the first. It is, that Professor Dewey ignores all fundamental scepticism. To those who are troubled by the question: "Is knowledge possible at all?", he has nothing to say. Probably such a question would appear to him otiose; he would argue (no doubt justly) that to a *fundamental* scepticism there can be no answer except a practical one. Nevertheless, a theory of knowledge should have more to say on the matter than he has to say. There are different levels of scepticism; there are popular prejudices which are easily dissolved by a little reflection, there are beliefs which we can just succeed in feeling to be doubtful by prolonged destructive analysis (such as the law of causation for example), and there are beliefs which it is practically impossible to doubt for more than a moment, such as the elementary propositions of arithmetic. But the beliefs which are epistemologically primitive in Professor Dewey's system will have to involve propositions which even the most hardened

4 "The term 'pragmatic' means only the rule of referring all thinking, all reflective consider-ations, to *consequences* for final meaning and test" (p. 330). "Consequences" is a causal word.

anti-sceptic could be made to doubt without much trouble. For, if the truth of a belief is proved by its being a good instrument, we have to know what effects the belief has, what effects other beliefs would have had, and which are better. This sort of knowledge is surely about as doubtful as any that would ever be called knowledge. We also assume to begin with, in Professor Dewey's system, the whole of what is involved in the biological position of man: the environment, the struggle for existence, and so on. Thus our theory of knowledge begins only after we have assumed as much as amounts practically to a complete metaphysic.

10   This might be admitted, since Professor Dewey considers that "theory of knowledge", as a subject, is a mistake. I suppose he would say, what I should agree to in a certain fundamental sense, that knowledge must be accepted as a fact, and cannot be proved from outside. I find, however, both in this respect and as regards data, an insufficient realization of the importance of degrees and continuous transitions. The passage from crude data to the most refined data of science must be continuous, with truth at every stage, but *more* truth in the later stages. So there is a gradation of truths; and similarly there is a gradation of beliefs, a continuous passage from what we feel to be very uncertain up to what we cannot doubt, with some degree of
20   belief at each stage, but more at the later stages. And theory of knowledge exists as a subject which endeavours to organize our beliefs according to the degree of conviction, and to attach as many as possible to those that have a high degree of conviction. If it be asked: "Is a belief of which I feel strong conviction more likely to be true than one of which I feel a good deal of doubt?" we can only answer that, *ex hypothesi*, we *think* it more likely to be true. And there is no miracle by which we can jump outside the circle of what we *think* to be true into the region of what *is* true whether we think so or not.

    Professor Dewey, in an admirable passage, points out the effect of bias in
30   forming the theories of philosophers. He says:

   It is an old story that philosophers, in common with theologians and social theorists, are as sure that personal habits and interests shape their opponents' doctrines as they are that their own beliefs are "absolutely" universal and objective in quality. Hence arises that dishonesty, that insincerity characteristic of philosophic discussion.... Now the moment the complicity of the personal factor in our philosophic valuations is recognized, is recognized fully, frankly, and generally, that moment a new era in philosophy will begin.... So long as we ignore this factor, its deeds will be largely evil, not
40   because *it* is evil, but because, flourishing in the dark, it is without responsibility and without check. The only way to control it is by recognizing it.   (Pp. 326-7)

These are very wise words. In spite of the risk, I propose to take the advice, and set down, as far as I can, the personal motives which make me like or dislike different aspects of behaviourism and instrumentalism, i.e. motives which would make me *wish* them to be true or false.

I have a strong bias in favour of the view, urged by James and most American realists, that the mental and the physical are merely different arrangements of the same stuff, because this (like every other application of Occam's razor) gives opportunities for those logical constructions in which I take pleasure. I tried (in my *External World*) to show how the particulars that (in my view) make up the stuff of the world are capable of a two-fold classification, one as physical things, the other as biographies or monads, or parts of monads. Such logical constructions I find enjoyable. Desire for enjoyment of this sort is a creative bias in my philosophy—i.e. what Kant (less self-consciously) would call a regulative idea of reason. The same bias makes me like behaviourism, since it would enable me to define a belief as a certain series of acts. An act inspired by two beliefs would be a member of the two series which would be the respective beliefs. In this definition I find, further, a good-natured malicious pleasure in thinking that even the theories conceived by those who hate mathematical logic can be taken over and stated in such terms as will make them repulsive to their own parents. I recognize that this is a shameful motive, but it does not cease to operate on that account. All these motives combine to make me like behaviourism and neutral monism, and to search for reasons in their favour.

My bias as regards instrumentalism and pragmatism is quite different. Often (though not in Professor Dewey) pragmatism is connected with what I regard as theological superstition, and with the habit of accepting beliefs because they are pleasant. Some ascetic instinct makes me desire that a portion, at least, of my beliefs should be of the nature of a hair shirt; and, as is natural to an ascetic, I incline to condemn the will-to-believers as voluptuaries. But these feelings are not roused in me by the pragmatism which is advocated in this book: on the contrary, the very genuine scientific temper in the book appeals to me. Nevertheless there is a profound instinct in me which is repelled by instrumentalism: the instinct of contemplation, and of escape from one's own personality.

Professor Dewey has nothing but contempt for the conception of knowledge as contemplation. He is full of that democratic philanthropy which makes him impatient of what seems to him a form of selfish idleness. He speaks of

> that other great rupture of continuity which analytic realism would maintain: that between the world and the knower as something outside of it, engaged in an otiose contemplative survey of it. I can understand the social conditions which generated this conception of

an aloof knower. I can see how it protected the growth of responsible inquiry which takes effect in change of the environment, by cultivating a sense of the innocuousness of knowing, and thus lulling to sleep the animosity of those who, being in control, had no desire to permit reflection which had practical import.   (P. 72–3)

and so on, and so on.

Will the present amusing inappropriateness of these remarks to the case of one at least among analytic realists suggest to Professor Dewey that perhaps he has somewhat misunderstood the ideal of contemplation? It is not essential to this ideal that contemplation should remain without effect on action. But those to whom contemplative knowledge appears a valuable ideal find in the practice of it the same kind of thing that some have found in religion: they find something that, besides being valuable on its own account, seems capable of purifying and elevating practice, making its aims larger and more generous, its disappointments less crushing, and its triumphs less intoxicating. In order to have these effects, contemplation must be for its own sake, not for the sake of the effects: for it is the very contrast between action and pure contemplation that gives rise to the effects. William James in his *Psychology* urges (if I remember right) that when a man has been enjoying music he should show how he has benefited by being kind to his aunt; but the man who could not appreciate music apart from its effect on conduct would never be enough stirred by it to have his conduct improved, and would be just as unkind to his aunt after a concert as at other times. The habit of making everything subservient to practice is one which takes the colour out of life, and removes most of the incentives to practice of a really noble kind.

Escape from one's own personality is something which has been desired by the mystics of all ages, and in one way or another by all in whom ardent imagination has been a dominant force. It is, of course, a matter of degree: complete escape is impossible, but some degree of escape is possible, and knowledge is one of the gateways into the world of freedom. Instrumentalism does its best to shut this gateway. The world which it allows us to know is man-made, like the scenery on the Underground: there are bricks and platforms and trains and lights and advertisements, but the sun and stars, the rain and the dew and the sea, are no longer there—sometimes we seem to catch a glimpse of them, but that is a mistake, we only see a picture made by some human being as an advertisement. It is a safe and comfortable world: we know how the trains will move, since we laid down the rails for them. If you find it a little dull, you are suffering from the "genteel tradition", you belong to an "upper" class given to a detached and parasitic life (p. 72). I have now expressed my bias as regards the view that we are not free to know anything but what our own hands have fashioned.

III. THE EXTERNAL WORLD AS A PROBLEM

I come now to the defence of certain views of my own against the criticisms of Professor Dewey, especially as contained in the eleventh essay, on "The Existence of the World as a Logical Problem".

A great deal of what is said in this essay depends upon the misunderstanding as to the sense in which I use "data", which we have already discussed. For example, on p. 290ff., I am criticized for taking as "really known" (when we observe a table from different points of view) a set of facts which are complicated, involving series and logical correlations. Now such criticism all rests upon the supposition that what is "really known" is intended to be something which is believed at an earlier time than what is (if possible) to be proved by its means. This is not how I conceive the problem. I find myself, when I begin reflecting on the external world, full of hitherto unquestioned assumptions, for many of which I quickly realize that I have as yet no adequate reason. The question then arises: what sort of reason could I hope to discover? What, apart from argument and inference, shall I find surviving a critical scrutiny? And what inferences will then be possible? I give the name "data" or rather "hard data" to all that survives the most severe critical scrutiny of which I am capable, excluding what, *after the scrutiny*, is only arrived at by argument and inference. There is always much argument and inference in reaching the epistemological premises of any part of our knowledge, but when we have completed the logical articulation of our knowledge the arguments by which we reached the premises fall away.

The chief thing that I wish to make clear is that, in discussing the world as a logical problem, I am dealing in a scientific spirit with a genuine scientific question, in fact a question of physics. Professor Dewey, almost wilfully as it seems, refuses to perceive the question I am discussing, and points out the irrelevance of what I say to all sorts of other questions. It is perfectly clear that, starting from a common-sense basis, what a physicist believes himself to know is based partly upon observation and partly upon inference. It is also clear that what we *think* we observe is usually much more than what, after closer attention and more analysis, we find we really did observe— because habitual inferences become unintentionally mixed up with what was actually observed. Thus the conception of a "datum" becomes, as it were, a limiting conception of what we may call scientific common sense. The more skilled an observer has become, the more what he thinks he has observed will approximate to what I should call a "datum". In all this, we are proceeding along ordinary scientific lines. And the utility of such analytic data for inference is fully recognized by Professor Dewey. But he is continually misled by the recurrent belief that I must be speaking about beliefs that are early in time, either in the history of the individual or in that of the race. However, I have said enough already on this aspect of the question.

A phrase about "our own" data leads to the question: "Who are the 'we', and what does 'own' mean?" (p. 282n.). The answer to this is that it is quite unnecessary to have any idea what these terms mean. The problem with which I am concerned is this: Enumerate particulars in the world and facts about the world as long as you can; reject what you feel to be doubtful; eliminate what you see to be inferred. There then remains a residuum, which we may call "data". The outsider may define this residuum as "your" data—but to you they are not *defined* in their totality, they are merely enumerated: they are a certain collection of particulars and facts, and they are the total store from which, at the moment, you can draw your knowledge of the world. Then the question arises: what inferences are justified by this store of particulars and facts? This is a perfectly genuine problem. It is no use to find fault with me on the ground that my problem is not some other, which is more interesting to Professor Dewey, and which I am supposed to be intending to attack in a muddle-headed way. And it is no use to shut one's eyes to my problem on the ground that it may be inconvenient. Every philosophy has been invented to solve some one problem, and is incapable of dealing with many others; hence every philosophy is compelled to be blind to all problems except its own. It is time that philosophers learnt more toleration of each other's problems.

Some of Professor Dewey's criticisms are so easily answered that I feel he must have found my views extraordinarily distasteful or he would never have made objections with so little cogency. Take, e.g., the contention that it is a mistake to call colour "visual" or sound "auditory" until we know that they are connected with eye and ear respectively. The answer is, that, quite apart from physiology, objects which (as we say) are "seen" have a common quality which enables us to distinguish them from objects "heard". We do not need to experiment by shutting the eyes and stopping the ears in order to find out whether the sense-datum of the moment is "visual" or "auditory": we know this by its intrinsic quality. When I speak of "visual sense-data", I mean colours and shapes, and it is not the least necessary to know that it is through the eye that I become acquainted with them. Another very feeble argument is the objection (p. 285n.) to my calling certain things "self-evident" on the ground that a thing cannot offer evidence for itself. This is not what is meant by "self-evident". What is meant is "known otherwise than by inference". Professor Dewey's contention almost suggests a quibble à la Plato to prove that no man can be self-taught, because we can only teach what we know and learn what we do not know, and therefore it is impossible that teacher and learner should be one and the same. But this is not the type of argument that Professor Dewey would wish to be caught using.

Another source of confusion in Professor Dewey's arguments is that he is apparently unaware of the distinction that I draw between the universal "red" and particulars which are instances of it.[5] I dare say this distinction may be mistaken, but it is in any case an essential part of my theory, and I cannot be refuted by arguments which ignore it. This applies particularly to the paragraph on p. 288 beginning, "If anything is an eternal essence, it is surely such a thing as color taken by itself, as by definition it must be taken in the statement of the question by Mr. Russell. Anything more simple, timeless, and absolute than a red can hardly be thought of." And at the end of the same paragraph another even larger question is raised, namely that of the temporal position of a simple particular. In the case which I am suppos- ing, we are told, "we are dealing in the case of the colored surface with an ultimate, simple datum. It can have no implications beyond itself, no concealed dependencies. How then can its existence, even if its perception be but momentary, raise a question of 'other times' at all?" (p. 289). One might retort simply by a *tu quoque*: tell us, one might say, what is your way of reaching other times? One might reply that it is of the very essence of my theory that the datum is usually *not* simple—that it is a fact, and facts are not simple (statements both noted by Professor Dewey, but supposed to con- stitute an inconsistency). One might point out that Professor Dewey, repeatedly, shows that he has failed to take account of the analysis of the time-order suggested both in Chapter IV of the book he is discussing and in the *Monist* for 1915—an analysis which, right or wrong, demands discus- sion in this connection. But the chief thing to point out is that, in the problem in question, we are up against the very question of causality and knowledge of the future, which, so far as I can discover, Professor Dewey has never faced.

After a description of the kind of world which I accept as datum, the Essay proceeds (p. 292): "How this differs from the external world of common sense I am totally unable to see. It may not be a very big external world, but having begged a small external world, I do not see why one should be too squeamish about extending it over the edges." Now there are several points to be made in reply to this criticism: (1) as to what I mean by an "external" world; (2) in what sense the world I start from is "begged"; and (3) how this world that I start from differs from that of common sense.

(1) The word "external" is perhaps an unfortunate one to have chosen, and the word "inferred" would have been better. Professor Dewey does not admit that we can be said to "know" what I call sense-data; according to him they simply occur. But this point, though he makes much of it, seems to me to make very little difference as regards our present question. He admits (pp. 259–60) that perceptions are the source of our knowledge of the world,

---

5 See "On the Relations of Universals and Particulars", *Proc. Arist. Soc.*, 1911–1912.

and that is enough for my purposes. I am quite willing to concede, for the sake of argument, that perceptions are not cases of cognition; indeed my desire to accept neutral monism if possible gives me a bias in that direction. I see objections which I think he has not shown how to meet, but I am not at all sure that they cannot be met. However that may be, Professor Dewey and I are at one in regarding perceptions as affording data, i.e. as giving the basis for our knowledge of the world. This is enough for the present; the question of the cognitive status of perceptions need not concern us.

Now it is a plain fact that what I see and hear has some relation to my knowledge which is not possessed by information obtained through historical or geographical reading. This is admitted, implicitly, by Professor Dewey in the passage just referred to. The words used for describing the difference are immaterial. When the difference is first noticed, it is vague and blurred, as is usually the case with newly cognized differences. Reflection tends to show that, as the difference comes to be drawn with more skill, less and less appears on the same side as what is seen and heard, and more and more appears on the same side as what we learn through reading. Nevertheless, if I am not mistaken, even the most rigid scrutiny will leave, on the same side with what is seen or heard, certain things remembered (with the fact that they are past), various observed relations (in part rather complicated), and some à priori knowledge—whether all of it logical or not, I do not know.

All this group of particulars and facts constitute what I call "data". They make up the world which I am intending to contrast with the "external" world. I do not wish spatial notions to obtrude: the world that I call "external" is so called only in this sense that it lies outside the group of data—"outside" in the logical sense. The problem that I wish to discuss is: "Can we make any valid inferences from data to non-data in the empirical world?" In the mathematical world we know that we can. Starting with a few numbers, we can infer other numbers *ad lib*. In the physical world, science and common sense believe that similar inferences are possible. Are they justified? If so, why? If we cannot at present decide the question, can we see any way by which it *might* be decided? These problems are genuine, and no useful purpose is served by trying to evade them.

(2) To say that I have "begged" a small external world is to miss the point. I have accepted it as datum, because that is the sort of world that, speaking empirically, seems to me, rightly or wrongly, to be given. Professor Dewey does not argue that this is not the case; he merely contends that it is not the world that is "given" in a different sense, i.e., as I understand, given to babies, which is irrelevant. The "given" world that I am speaking of is that which is "given" to the most educated person to be found in the matter of physical observation and the distinguishing of observation from inference. If I have wrongly described the "given" world (in this sense), I

am ready to amend the description. It makes very little difference to my problem what is the *detail* of the description of the given world. If Professor Dewey will offer me an alternative (provided he will remember that it is not the *historical* primitive that I want), I make little doubt that the bulk of my argument will be able to adapt itself with little alteration. I have not "begged" my small external world any more than Columbus begged the West Indies; I have merely chronicled what I observe. I cannot prove that it is there except by pointing to it, any more than Columbus could. But if others do not see what I point to, that does not prove that *I* do not observe it. There is no reason why what one person can observe should be also open to   10
the observation of another. Nevertheless, to chronicle what one observes is not the same thing as to "beg" a world.

(3) As to how my initial world of data differs from the world of common sense, there are various ways: (a) by extrusion of the notion of *substance*, since I do not consider a physical thing, such as a table, to be a datum at all, and I do consider that it is a series of classes of particulars, not a single particular. (I am not speaking of the fact that the table has physical parts: what I say would be equally true of an atom or electron, according to the theory.) (b) Among *data* we can only include the existence of a particular during the time when it is a datum: its existence or non-existence before and   20
after that time, if knowable at all, can only be known by inference. The things that Professor Dewey says on this subject (pp. 286–290) are only explicable to me by supposing that, when I speak of "inference to other times", he thinks that I mean inference to the existence of other times, whereas I mean inference to the existence-of-something-described at a time when something else is known to be existing. E.g. I look out of the window and see, as we say, a tree; I look back to my book and see print. Can I know whether what I saw when I looked out of the window, or anything in any way correlated with it, exists while I am looking at my book? My world of data does not include anything which gives an answer to this, whether   30
affirmative or negative; an answer will not be possible unless there are valid inferences from particulars at certain times to (described) particulars at certain other times. (c) In particular, my world of data does not include anything of other people except their outward show. In these and other ways it is very fragmentary as compared with the world of common sense.

Professor Dewey takes advantage (e.g. p. 295) of occasions when, for the sake of brevity, I have adopted the language of common sense. To avoid this altogether would hardly be possible without adopting the language of mathematical logic. But there are hardly a dozen philosophers living who will take the trouble to read anything written in that language. And so long   40
as one uses language they will condescend to read, one is condemned to the vaguenesses, inaccuracies and ambiguities which keep philosophy alive.

There is much that, if space permitted, I should have wished to say on the

subject of *time*. Meanwhile, I will conclude with the hope that the reader will perceive the reality of the problem which concerns me. There is a passage in the Essay we have been considering which seems to show why Professor Dewey and I have such difficulty in understanding one another. He says (p. 299): "No one can deny that inference from one thing to another is itself an empirical event, and that just as soon as such inference occurs, even in the simplest form of anticipation and prevision, a world exists like in kind to that of the adult." Certainly no one denies that inference is an empirical event. What is being examined is not its *occurrence*, but its *validity*. The
10 above passage seems to suggest that if I infer a world, there is a world. Yet I am not the Creator. Not all my inferences and expectations could prevent the world from coming to an end to-night, if so it were to happen. I trace in the above quotation, as in much of what pragmatists write, that instinctive belief in the omnipotence of Man and the creative power of his beliefs which is perhaps natural in a young, growing, and prosperous country, where men's problems have been simpler than in Europe and usually soluble by energy alone. Dr. Schiller says that the external world was first discovered by a low marine animal whom he calls "Grumps", who swallowed a bit of rock that disagreed with him, and argued that he would not have given
20 himself such a pain, and therefore there must be an external world. One is tempted to think that, at the time when Professor Dewey wrote, many people in the newer countries had not yet made the disagreeable experience which Grumps made. Meanwhile, whatever accusations pragmatists may bring, I shall continue to protest that it was not I who made the world.

Part III

The Philosophy of Logical Atomism

Contents

17

The Philosophy of Logical Atomism [1918]

THESE LECTURES WERE published in *The Monist*, 28 (Oct. 1918): 495–527; 29 (Jan., April, July 1919): 32–63, 190–222, 345–80. Russell lectured from a syllabus, which is now lost, and at times, as his remarks at the beginning of some of the lectures make clear, fell seriously behind its schedule. In a letter to Stanley Unwin of 23 March 1919 he gave an account of their genesis:

> With regard to the *Monist* articles you have been misinformed. They are verbatim reports, taken at the time by a short-hand writer, of lectures which I delivered in Jan.–March of last year. They were sent to America before I went to prison, and though I believe I kept a duplicate, I have not seen them since.

It appears from this that Russell read the transcript before it went off, but, if he did, he did not attempt to remove its informality. These papers are our best example of Russell's lecturing style in philosophy.

By 1917 Russell's financial position was straitened. He had divested himself of most of his inheritance for the duration of the war, and he had lost his income from Trinity College, Cambridge, with his dismissal from his lectureship on 11 July 1916. He was obliged to live on the earnings his writing brought in, but in that year they proved insufficient. To improve his income he proposed to H. Wildon Carr and others that he give two sets of logic lectures, one in the autumn of 1917 and one the following winter, for which sponsors would be sought and an admission fee collected. Carr undertook to raise money from sponsors, to sell tickets, and to organize and advertise the lectures. The goal for each set of eight lectures appears to have been £45, of which Russell was to receive £40. For the fall lectures, which were on mathematical logic, £50 was raised from guarantors and £10 from the sale of tickets. The syllabus for this set of lectures is lost, but they probably covered much of the same ground as his *Introduction to Mathematical Philosophy* (1919) which he wrote while a prisoner. In a message to Wildon Carr from prison, 21 May 1918, he wrote that the book follows the "lines of lectures *before* Xmas". Carr was much less successful in finding sponsors for Russell's winter series; he wrote Russell on 21 November 1917 asking whether Russell was willing to deliver the winter course for a fee of £25. It is not clear that Russell was paid even that much, for his pocket diary for 1917–18 records £50 for the fall series but only £10 for those delivered in the winter.

Both sets of lectures were delivered on Tuesday evenings in a hired room in Dr. Williams' Library in Gordon Square in London. The first course began on 30 October 1917 and finished on 18 December; the second started on 22 January 1918 and ended on 12 March. When one considers that Russell was summoned to court on 4 February, tried and convicted on 9 February, and sentenced the same day to six months imprisonment, the detached tone of the lectures shows that, for an hour or so each week, he was able to forget his worries. Due to appeals he did not enter prison until the first of May.

To increase his financial reward for the second set of lectures Russell offered them to P. E. B. Jourdain, the European editor of *The Monist*, who had paid Russell well for his earlier contributions. Jourdain accepted the lectures and promised to pay Russell for them. The two men had had a long and fruitful relationship which is fully reported by Ivor Grattan-Guinness in his *Dear Russell–Dear Jourdain* (1977). In 1918 their friendship soured because of a disagreement over an issue in mathematical logic. When Russell's *Introduction to Mathematical Philosophy* was published in March 1919 Jourdain wrote Stanley Unwin charging Russell (who had not yet been paid by *The Monist*) with infringement of copyright: the content of the book, he claimed, was the same as that of the lectures then appearing in *The Monist* as "The Philosophy of Logical Atomism". Russell assured Unwin on 23 March that the charge was false, and any reader of both titles will be obliged to agree with Russell. "The lectures", he wrote, "deal with matters more philosophical and less mathematical than the matters dealt with in the book." By this time Jourdain was seriously ill and still very angry with Russell over his "proof". He continued to put off Russell's demands for payment until his death on 1 October 1919. Russell was finally paid in December 1919.

The unpleasantness associated with their publication in *The Monist* may be the reason Russell did not republish these lectures in book form. It did occur to him that they would make a book, for he wrote his brother from prison on 16 May 1918 that *The Analysis of Mind* (1921), when it was published, would require a supplementary book on logic "on the lines of the lectures I gave after Xmas: without such a supplement it would be scarcely intelligible". And it appears that he toyed with the idea of reworking these lectures into a book while he was imprisoned, for on 21 May he sent a message to Carr through his brother Frank that when *Introduction to Mathematical Philosophy* was finished he would "then work over lectures *after* Xmas (which I have, thanks)". The work he proposed had nothing to do with preparing them for publication in *The Monist* because on the same day he sent a message to Jourdain, this time by way of Gladys Rinder: "Is he going to print two of my logic lectures in July and two each subsequent quarter? I hope so. And can he guess how much money I shall get from him for them *during the present year*?" This query makes sense only on the assumption that Jourdain already had transcripts of the lectures ready for printing. No other mention of these lectures is to be found in his surviving prison letters.

For students of his philosophy these lectures occupy a special place in his *oeuvre* despite the fact that for many years they were not very accessible. In the late 1940s the Philosophy Club of the University of Minnesota decided to raise money for speakers by reproducing the lectures for sale to students of that and other institutions. Roger C. Buck and Robert G. Turnbull, then the Club's officers, wrote Russell for his permission. "He replied very graciously expressing some surprise at the interest displayed in the lectures and giving permission for us to produce 500 copies" (Turnbull to the editor, 5 Sept. 1984). Although none of the correspondence with Russell survives, Buck and Turnbull feel sure that the corrections they made in the text had Russell's approval. The lectures were typed onto mimeograph stencils, not once, but twice, and the stapled copies were provided with a printed cardboard cover.

In 1956 Robert Charles Marsh, with Russell's approval, reprinted the lectures in a collection of Russell's papers entitled *Logic and Knowledge: Essays, 1901–1950*. Russell supplied a prefatory note for the book, but, with the exception of responding to Marsh's queries, had no hand in its editing. After Russell's death David Pears edited the lectures for paperback publication by Fontana (Russell *1972*); he also wrote a lengthy introduction to them.

The publication history shows that their first publication in *The Monist* is the only one for which Russell may have read proofs. He often did read proofs for that journal, but in this case there is no evidence that he did. Since it is known that he did not read proofs for either the Marsh or the Minnesota versions but did approve some alterations, *The Monist* version has been selected as copy-text and has been collated with the other two, the results of which are reported in the Textual Notes.

(The following articles are the first two lectures of a course of eight lectures delivered in London in the first months of 1918, and are very largely concerned with explaining certain ideas which I learnt from my friend and former pupil Ludwig Wittgenstein. I have had no opportunity of knowing his views since August, 1914, and I do not even know whether he is alive or dead. He has therefore no responsibility for what is said in these lectures beyond that of having originally supplied many of the theories contained in them. The six other lectures will appear in the three following numbers of *The Monist*.—B. R.)

THIS COURSE OF lectures which I am now beginning I have called the Philosophy of Logical Atomism. Perhaps I had better begin by saying a word or two as to what I understand by that title. The kind of philosophy that I wish to advocate, which I call Logical Atomism, is one which has forced itself upon me in the course of thinking about the philosophy of mathematics, although I should find it hard to say exactly how far there is a definite logical connection between the two. The things I am going to say in these lectures are mainly my own personal opinions and I do not claim that they are more than that.

20   As I have attempted to prove in *The Principles of Mathematics*, when we analyze mathematics we bring it all back to logic. It all comes back to logic in the strictest and most formal sense. In the present lectures, I shall try to set forth in a sort of outline, rather briefly and rather unsatisfactorily, a kind of logical doctrine which seems to me to result from the philosophy of mathematics—not exactly logically, but as what emerges as one reflects: a certain kind of logical doctrine, and on the basis of this a certain kind of metaphysic. The logic which I shall advocate is atomistic, as opposed to the monistic logic of the people who more or less follow Hegel. When I say that my logic is atomistic, I mean that I share the common-sense belief that there 30 are many separate things; I do not regard the apparent multiplicity of the world as consisting merely in phases and unreal divisions of a single indivisible Reality. It results from that that a considerable part of what one would have to do to justify the sort of philosophy I wish to advocate would consist in justifying the process of analysis. One is often told that the process of analysis is falsification, that when you analyze any given concrete whole you falsify it and that the results of analysis are not true. I do not think that is a right view. I do not mean to say, of course, and nobody would maintain, that when you have analyzed you keep everything that you had before you analyzed. If you did, you would never attain anything in analyzing. I do not 40 propose to meet the views that I disagree with by controversy, by arguing against those views, but rather by positively setting forth what I believe to

be the truth about the matter, and endeavouring all the way through to
make the views that I advocate result inevitably from absolutely undeniable
data. When I talk of "undeniable data" that is not to be regarded as
synonymous with "true data", because "undeniable" is a psychological
term and "true" is not. When I say that something is "undeniable", I mean
that it is not the sort of thing that anybody is going to deny; it does not follow
from that that it is true, though it does follow that we shall all think it
true—and that is as near to truth as we seem able to get. When you are
considering any sort of theory of knowledge, you are more or less tied to a
certain unavoidable subjectivity, because you are not concerned simply 10
with the question what is true of the world, but "What can I know of the
world?" You always have to start any kind of argument from something
which appears to you to be true; if it appears to you to be true, there is no
more to be done. You cannot go outside yourself and consider abstractly
whether the things that appear to you to be true are true; you may do this in a
particular case, where one of your beliefs is changed in consequence of
others among your beliefs.

The reason that I call my doctrine *logical* atomism is because the atoms
that I wish to arrive at as the sort of last residue in analysis are logical atoms
and not physical atoms. Some of them will be what I call "particulars"— 20
such things as little patches of colour or sounds, momentary things—and
some of them will be predicates or relations and so on. The point is that the
atom I wish to arrive at is the atom of logical analysis, not the atom of
physical analysis.

It is a rather curious fact in philosophy that the data which are undeniable
to start with are always rather vague and ambiguous. You can, for instance,
say: "There are a number of people in this room at this moment." That is
obviously in some sense undeniable. But when you come to try and define
what this room is, and what it is for a person to be in a room, and how you are
going to distinguish one person from another, and so forth, you find that 30
what you have said is most fearfully vague and that you really do not know
what you meant. That is a rather singular fact, that everything you are really
sure of, right off is something that you do not know the meaning of, and the
moment you get a precise statement you will not be sure whether it is true or
false, at least right off. The process of sound philosophizing, to my mind,
consists mainly in passing from those obvious, vague, ambiguous things,
that we feel quite sure of, to something precise, clear, definite, which by
reflection and analysis we find is involved in the vague thing that we started
from, and is, so to speak, the real truth of which that vague thing is a sort of
shadow. I should like, if time were longer and if I knew more than I do, to 40
spend a whole lecture on the conception of vagueness. I think vagueness is
very much more important in the theory of knowledge that you would judge
it to be from the writings of most people. Everything is vague to a degree you

do not realize till you have tried to make it precise, and everything precise is so remote from everything that we normally think, that you cannot for a moment suppose that is what we really mean when we say what we think.

When you pass from the vague to the precise by the method of analysis and reflection that I am speaking of, you always run a certain risk of error. If I start with the statement that there are so and so many people in this room, and then set to work to make that statement precise, I shall run a great many risks and it will be extremely likely that any precise statement I make will be something not true at all. So you cannot very easily or simply get from these vague undeniable things to precise things which are going to retain the undeniability of the starting-point. The precise propositions that you arrive at may be *logically* premisses to the system that you build up upon the basis of them, but they are not premisses for the theory of knowledge. It is important to realize the difference between that from which your knowledge is, in fact, derived, and that from which, if you already had complete knowledge, you would deduce it. Those are quite different things. The sort of premiss that a logician will take for a science will not be the sort of thing which is first known or easiest known: it will be a proposition having great deductive power, great cogency and exactitude, quite a different thing from the actual premiss that your knowledge started from. When you are talking of the premiss for theory of knowledge, you are not talking of anything objective, but of something that will vary from man to man, because the premisses of one man's theory of knowledge will not be the same as those of another man's. There is a great tendency among a very large school to suppose that when you are trying to philosophize about what you know, you ought to carry back your premisses further and further into the region of the inexact and vague, beyond the point where you yourself are, right back to the child or monkey, and that anything whatsoever that *you* seem to know—but that the psychologist recognizes as being the product of previous thought and analysis and reflection on your part—cannot really be taken as a premiss in your own knowledge. That, I say, is a theory which is very widely held and which is used against that kind of analytic outlook which I wish to urge. It seems to me that when your object is, not simply to study the history or development of mind, but to ascertain the nature of the world, you do not want to go any further back than you are already yourself. You do not want to go back to the vagueness of the child or monkey, because you will find that quite sufficient difficulty is raised by your own vagueness. But there one is confronted by one of those difficulties that occur constantly in philosophy, where you have two ultimate prejudices conflicting and where argument ceases. There is the type of mind which considers that what is called primitive experience must be a better guide to wisdom than the experience of reflective persons, and there is the type of mind which takes exactly the opposite view. On that point I cannot see any argument whatsoever. It is quite clear that a highly educated person sees, hears, feels, does everything in a very different way from a young child or animal, and that this whole manner of experiencing the world and of thinking about the world is very much more analytic than that of a more primitive experience. The things we have got to take as premises in any kind of work of analysis are the things which appear to *us* undeniable—to us here and now, as we are—and I think on the whole that the sort of method adopted by Descartes is right: that you should set to work to doubt things and retain only what you cannot doubt because of its clearness and distinctness, not because you are sure not to be induced into error, for there does not exist a method which will safeguard you against the possibility of error. The wish for perfect security is one of those snares we are always falling into, and is just as untenable in the realm of knowledge as in everything else. Nevertheless, granting all this, I still think that Descartes's method is on the whole a sound one for the starting-point.

I propose, therefore, always to begin any argument that I have to make by appealing to data which will be quite ludicrously obvious. Any philosophical skill that is required will consist in the selection of those which are capable of yielding a good deal of reflection and analysis, and in the reflection and analysis themselves.

What I have said so far is by way of introduction.

The first truism to which I wish to draw your attention—and I hope you will agree with me that these things that I call truisms are so obvious that it is almost laughable to mention them—is that the world contains facts, which are what they are whatever we may choose to think about them, and that there are also beliefs, which have reference to facts, and by reference to facts are either true or false. I will try first of all to give you a preliminary explanation of what I mean by a "fact". When I speak of a fact—I do not propose to attempt an exact definition, but an explanation, so that you will know what I am talking about—I mean the kind of thing that makes a proposition true or false. If I say "It is raining", what I say is true in a certain condition of weather and is false in other conditions of weather. The condition of weather that makes my statement true (or false as the case may be), is what I should call a "fact". If I say "Socrates is dead", my statement will be true owing to a certain physiological occurrence which happened in Athens long ago. If I say, "Gravitation varies inversely as the square of the distance", my statement is rendered true by astronomical fact. If I say, "Two and two are four", it is arithmetical fact that makes my statement true. On the other hand, if I say "Socrates is alive", or "Gravitation varies directly as the distance", or "Two and two are five", the very same facts which made my previous statements true show that these new statements are false.

I want you to realize that when I speak of a fact I do not mean a particular existing thing, such as Socrates or the rain or the sun. Socrates himself does not render any statement true or false. You might be inclined to suppose that all by himself he would give truth to the statement "Socrates existed", but as a matter of fact that is a mistake. It is due to a confusion which I shall try to explain in the sixth lecture of this course, when I come to deal with the notion of existence. Socrates[1] himself, or any particular thing just by itself, does not make any proposition true or false. "Socrates is dead" and "Socrates is alive" are both of them statements about Socrates. One is true and the other false. What I call a fact is the sort of thing that is expressed by a whole sentence, not by a single name like "Socrates". When a single word does come to express a fact, like "fire" or "wolf", it is always due to an unexpressed context, and the full expression of a fact will always involve a sentence. We express a fact, for example, when we say that a certain thing has a certain property, or that it has a certain relation to another thing; but the thing which has the property or the relation is not what I call a "fact".

It is important to observe that facts belong to the objective world. They are not created by our thoughts or beliefs except in special cases. That is one of the sort of things which I should set up as an obvious truism, but, of course, one is aware, the moment one has read any philosophy at all, how very much there is to be said before such a statement as that can become the kind of position that you want. The first thing I want to emphasize is that the outer world—the world, so to speak, which knowledge is aiming at knowing—is not completely described by a lot of "particulars", but that you must also take account of these things that I call facts, which are the sort of things that you express by a sentence, and that these, just as much as particular chairs and tables, are part of the real world. Except in psychology, most of our statements are not intended merely to express our condition of mind, though that is often all that they succeed in doing. They are intended to express facts, which (except when they are psychological facts) will be about the outer world. There are such facts involved, equally when we speak truly and when we speak falsely. When we speak falsely it is an objective fact that makes what we say false, and it is an objective fact which makes what we say true when we speak truly.

There are a great many different kinds of facts, and we shall be concerned in later lectures with a certain amount of classification of facts. I will just point out a few kinds of facts to begin with, so that you may not imagine that facts are all very much alike. There are particular facts, such as "This is white"; then there are general facts, such as "All men are mortal." Of course, the distinction between particular and general facts is one of the most important. There again it would be a very great mistake to suppose

---

1 I am here for the moment treating Socrates as a "particular". But we shall see shortly that this view requires modification.

that you could describe the world completely by means of particular facts alone. Suppose that you had succeeded in chronicling every single particular fact throughout the universe, and that there did not exist a single particular fact of any sort anywhere that you had not chronicled, you still would not have got a complete description of the universe unless you also added: "These that I have chronicled are all the particular facts there are." So you cannot hope to describe the world completely without having general facts as well as particular facts. Another distinction, which is perhaps a little more difficult to make, is between positive facts and negative facts, such as "Socrates was alive"—a positive fact—and "Socrates is not alive"—you might say a negative fact.[2] But the distinction is difficult to make precise. Then there are facts concerning particular things or particular qualities or relations, and, apart from them, the completely general facts of the sort that you have in logic, where there is no mention of any constituent whatever of the actual world, no mention of any particular thing or particular quality or particular relation, indeed strictly you may say no mention of anything. That is one of the characteristics of logical propositions, that they mention nothing. Such a proposition is: "If one class is part of another, a term which is a member of the one is also a member of the other." All those words that come in the statement of a pure logical proposition are words really belonging to syntax. They are words merely expressing form or connection, not mentioning any particular constituent of the proposition in which they occur. This is, of course, a thing that wants to be proved; I am not laying it down as self-evident. Then there are facts about the properties of single things; and facts about the relations between two things, three things, and so on; and any number of different classifications of some of the facts in the world, which are important for different purposes.

It is obvious that there is not a dualism of true and false facts; there are only just facts. It would be a mistake, of course, to say that all facts are true. That would be a mistake because true and false are correlatives, and you would only say of a thing that it was true if it was the sort of thing that *might* be false. A fact cannot be either true or false. That brings us on to the question of statements or propositions or judgments, all those things that do have the duality of truth and falsehood. For the purposes of logic, though not, I think, for the purposes of theory of knowledge, it is natural to concentrate upon the proposition as the thing which is going to be our typical vehicle on the duality of truth and falsehood. A proposition, one may say, is a sentence in the indicative, a sentence asserting something, not questioning or commanding or wishing. It may also be a sentence of that sort preceded by the word "that". For example, "That Socrates is alive", "That two and two are four", "That two and two are five", anything of that sort will be a proposition.

---

2 Negative facts are further discussed in a later lecture.

A proposition is just a symbol. It is a complex symbol in the sense that it has parts which are also symbols: a symbol may be defined as complex when it has parts that are symbols. In a sentence containing several words, the several words are each symbols, and the sentence composing them is therefore a complex symbol in that sense. There is a good deal of importance to philosophy in the theory of symbolism, a good deal more than at one time I thought. I think the importance is almost entirely negative, i.e. the importance lies in the fact that unless you are fairly self-conscious about symbols, unless you are fairly aware of the relation of the symbol to what it symbolizes, you will find yourself attributing to the thing properties which only belong to the symbol. That, of course, is especially likely in very abstract studies such as philosophical logic, because the subject-matter that you are supposed to be thinking of is so exceedingly difficult and elusive that any person who has ever tried to think about it knows you do not think about it except perhaps once in six months for half a minute. The rest of the time you think about the symbols, because they are tangible, but the thing you are supposed to be thinking about is fearfully difficult and one does not often manage to think about it. The really good philosopher is the one who does once in six months think about it for a minute. Bad philosophers never do. That is why the theory of symbolism has a certain importance, because otherwise you are so certain to mistake the properties of the symbolism for the properties of the thing. It has other interesting sides to it too. There are different kinds of symbols, different kinds of relation between symbol and what is symbolized, and very important fallacies arise from not realizing this. The sort of contradictions about which I shall be speaking in connection with types in a later lecture all arise from mistakes in symbolism, from putting one sort of symbol in the place where another sort of symbol ought to be. Some of the notions that have been thought absolutely fundamental in philosophy have arisen, I believe, entirely through mistakes as to symbolism—e.g. the notion of existence, or, if you like, reality. Those two words stand for a great deal that has been discussed in philosophy. There has been the theory about every proposition being really a description of reality as a whole and so on, and altogether these notions of reality and existence have played a very prominent part in philosophy. Now my own belief is that as they have occurred in philosophy, they have been entirely the outcome of a muddle about symbolism, and that when you have cleared up that muddle, you find that practically everything that has been said about existence is sheer and simple mistake, and that is all you can say about it. I shall go into that in a later lecture, but it is an example of the way in which symbolism is important.

Perhaps I ought to say a word or two about what I am understanding by symbolism, because I think some people think you only mean mathematical symbols when you talk about symbolism. I am using it in a sense to include all language of every sort and kind, so that every word is a symbol, and every sentence, and so forth. When I speak of a symbol I simply mean something that "means" something else, and as to what I mean by "meaning" I am not prepared to tell you. I will in the course of time enumerate a strictly infinite number of different things that "meaning" may mean, but I shall not consider that I have exhausted the discussion by doing that. I think that the notion of meaning is always more or less psychological, and that it is not possible to get a pure logical theory of meaning, nor therefore of symbolism. I think that it is of the very essence of the explanation of what you mean by a symbol to take account of such things as knowing, of cognitive relations, and probably also of association. At any rate I am pretty clear that the theory of symbolism and the use of symbolism is not a thing that can be explained in pure logic without taking account of the various cognitive relations that you may have to things.

As to what one means by "meaning", I will give a few illustrations. For instance, the word "Socrates", you will say, means a certain man; the word "mortal" means a certain quality; and the sentence "Socrates is mortal" means a certain fact. But these three sorts of meaning are entirely distinct, and you will get into the most hopeless contradictions if you think the word "meaning" has the same meaning in each of these three cases. It is very important not to suppose that there is just one thing which is meant by "meaning", and that therefore there is just one sort of relation of the symbol to what is symbolized. A name would be a proper symbol to use for a person; a sentence (or a proposition) is the proper symbol for a fact.

A belief or a statement has duality of truth and falsehood, which the fact does not have. A belief or a statement always involves a proposition. You say that a man believes that so and so is the case. A man believes that Socrates is dead. What he believes is a proposition on the face of it, and for formal purposes it is convenient to take the proposition as the essential thing having the duality of truth and falsehood. It is very important to realize such things, for instance, as that propositions are not names for facts. It is quite obvious as soon as it is pointed out to you, but as a matter of fact I never had realized it until it was pointed out to me by a former pupil of mine, Wittgenstein. It is perfectly evident as soon as you think of it, that a proposition is not a name for a fact, from the mere circumstance that there are *two* propositions corresponding to each fact. Suppose it is a fact that Socrates is dead. You have two propositions: "Socrates is dead" and "Socrates is not dead." And those two propositions corresponding to the same fact, there is one fact in the world which makes one true and one false. That is not accidental, and illustrates how the relation of proposition to fact is a totally different one from the relation of name to the thing named. For each fact there are two propositions, one true and one false, and there is nothing in the nature of the symbol to show us which is the true one and which is the false one. If there

were, you could ascertain the truth about the world by examining propositions without looking round you.

There are two different relations, as you see, that a proposition may have
to a fact: the one the relation that you may call being true to the fact, and the
other being false to the fact. Both are equally essentially logical relations
which may subsist between the two, whereas in the case of a name, there is
only one relation that it can have to what it names. A name can just name a
particular, or, if it does not, it is not a name at all, it is a noise. It cannot be a
name without having just that one particular relation of naming a certain
10 thing, whereas a proposition does not cease to be a proposition if it is false. It
has these two ways, of being true and being false, which together correspond to the property of being a name. Just as a word may be a name or be
not a name but just a meaningless noise, so a phrase which is apparently a
proposition may be either true or false, or may be meaningless, but the true
and false belong together as against the meaningless. That shows, of course,
that the formal logical characteristics of propositions are quite different
from those of names, and that the relations they have to facts are quite
different, and therefore propositions are not names for facts. You must not
run away with the idea that you can name facts in any other way; you cannot.
20 You cannot name them at all. You cannot properly name a fact. The only
thing you can do is to assert it, or deny it, or desire it, or will it, or wish it, or
question it, but all those are things involving the whole proposition. You
can never put the sort of thing that makes a proposition to be true or false in
the position of a logical subject. You can only have it there as something to
be asserted or denied or something of that sort, but not something to be
named.

DISCUSSION

Q.: Do you take your starting-point "That there are many things" as a
postulate which is to be carried along all through, or has to be proved
30 afterward?

Mr. Russell: No, neither the one nor the other. I do not take it as a postulate
that "There are many things." I should take it that, in so far as it can be
proved, the proof is empirical, and that the disproofs that have been offered
are a priori. The empirical person would naturally say, there are many
things. The monistic philosopher attempts to show that there are not. I
should propose to refute his a priori arguments. I do not consider there is
any *logical* necessity for there to be many things, nor for there not to be
many things.

Q.: I mean in making a start, whether you start with the empirical or the a
40 priori philosophy, do you make your statement just at the beginning and
come back to prove it, or do you never come back to the proof of it?

Mr. Russell: No, you never come back. It is like the acorn to the oak. You never get back to the acorn in the oak. I should like a statement which would be rough and vague and have that sort of obviousness that belongs to things of which you never know what they mean, but I should never get back to that statement. I should say, here is a thing. We seem somehow convinced that there is truth buried in this thing somewhere. We will look at it inside and out until we have extracted something and can say, now that is true. It will not really be the same as the thing we started from because it will be so much more analytic and precise.

Q.: Does it not look as though you could name a fact by a date?

Mr. Russell: You can apparently name facts, but I do not think you can really: you would always find that if you set out the whole thing fully, it was not so. Suppose you say "The death of Socrates". You might say, that is a name for the fact that Socrates died. But it obviously is not. You can see that the moment you take account of truth and falsehood. Supposing he had not died, the phrase would still be just as significant although there could not be then anything you could name. But supposing he had never lived, the sound "Socrates" would not be a name at all. You can see it in another way. You can say "The death of Socrates is a fiction." Suppose you had read in the paper that the Kaiser had been assassinated, and it turned out to be not true. You could then say, "The death of the Kaiser is a fiction." It is clear that there is no such thing in the world as a fiction, and yet that statement is a perfectly sound statement. From this it follows that "The death of the Kaiser" is not a name.

II. PARTICULARS, PREDICATES, AND RELATIONS

I propose to begin today the analysis of facts and propositions, for in a way the chief thesis that I have to maintain is the legitimacy of analysis, because if one goes into what I call Logical Atomism that means that one does believe the world can be analyzed into a number of separate things with relations and so forth, and that the sort of arguments that many philosophers use against analysis are not justifiable.

In a philosophy of logical atomism one might suppose that the first thing to do would be to discover the kinds of atoms out of which logical structures are composed. But I do not think that is quite the first thing; it is one of the early things, but not quite the first. There are two other questions that one has to consider, and one of these at least is prior. You have to consider:

1. Are the things that look like logically complex entities really complex?
2. Are they really entities?

The second question we can put off; in fact, I shall not deal with it fully until my last lecture. The first question, whether they are really complex, is one that you have to consider at the start. Neither of these questions is, as it stands, a very precise question. I do not pretend to start with precise questions. I do not think you can start with anything precise. You have to achieve such precision as you can, as you go along. Each of these two questions, however, is *capable* of a precise meaning, and each is really important.

There is another question which comes still earlier, namely: what shall we take as *primâ facie* examples of logically complex entities? That really is the first question of all to start with. What sort of things shall we regard as *primâ facie* complex?

Of course, all the ordinary objects of daily life are apparently complex entities: such things as tables and chairs, loaves and fishes, persons and principalities and powers—they are all on the face of it complex entities. All the kinds of things to which we habitually give proper names are on the face of them complex entities: Socrates, Piccadilly, Rumania, *Twelfth Night* or anything you like to think of, to which you give a proper name, they are all apparently complex entities. They seem to be complex systems bound together into some kind of a unity, that sort of a unity that leads to the bestowal of a single appellation. I think it is the contemplation of this sort of apparent unity which has very largely led to the philosophy of monism, and to the suggestion that the universe as a whole is a single complex entity more or less in the sense in which these things are that I have been talking about.

For my part, I do not believe in complex entities of this kind, and it is not such things as these that I am going to take as the *primâ facie* examples of complex entities. My reasons will appear more and more plainly as I go on. I cannot give them all today, but I can more or less explain what I mean in a preliminary way. Suppose, for example, that you were to analyze what appears to be a fact about Piccadilly. Suppose you made any statement about Piccadilly, such as: "Piccadilly is a pleasant street." If you analyze a statement of that sort correctly, I believe you will find that the fact corresponding to your statement does not contain any constituent corresponding to the word "Piccadilly". The word "Piccadilly" will form part of many significant propositions, but the facts corresponding to these propositions do not contain any single constituent, whether simple or complex, corresponding to the word "Piccadilly". That is to say, if you take language as a guide in your analysis of the fact expressed, you will be led astray in a statement of that sort. The reasons for that I shall give at length in Lecture VI, and partly also in Lecture VII, but I could say in a preliminary way certain things that would make you understand what I mean. "Piccadilly", on the face of it, is the name for a certain portion of the earth's surface, and I suppose, if you wanted to define it, you would have to define it as a series of classes of material entities, namely those which, at varying times, occupy that portion of the earth's surface. So that you would find that the logical status of Piccadilly is bound up with the logical status of series and classes, and if you are going to hold Piccadilly as real, you must hold that series of classes are real, and whatever sort of metaphysical status you assign to them, you must assign to it. As you know, I believe that series and classes are of the nature of logical fictions: therefore that thesis, if it can be maintained, will dissolve Piccadilly into a fiction. Exactly similar remarks will apply to other instances: Rumania, *Twelfth Night*, and Socrates. Socrates, perhaps, raises some special questions, because the question what constitutes a person has special difficulties in it. But, for the sake of argument, one might identify Socrates with the series of his experiences. He would be really a series of classes, because one has many experiences simultaneously. Therefore he comes to be very like Piccadilly.

Considerations of that sort seem to take us away from such *primâ facie* complex entities as we started with to others as being more stubborn and more deserving of analytic attention, namely facts. I explained last time what I meant by a fact, namely, that sort of thing that makes a proposition true or false, the sort of thing which is the case when your statement is true and is not the case when your statement is false. Facts are, as I said last time, plainly something you have to take account of if you are going to give a complete account of the world. You cannot do that by merely enumerating the particular things that are in it: you must also mention the relations of these things, and their properties, and so forth, all of which are facts, so that facts certainly belong to an account of the objective world, and facts do seem much more clearly complex and much more not capable of being explained away than things like Socrates and Rumania. However you may explain away the meaning of the word "Socrates", you will still be left with the truth that the proposition "Socrates is mortal" expresses a fact. You may not know exactly what Socrates means, but it is quite clear that "Socrates is mortal" does express a fact. There is clearly some valid meaning in saying that the fact expressed by "Socrates is mortal" is *complex*. The things in the world have various properties, and stand in various relations to each other. That they have these properties and relations are *facts*, and the things and their qualities or relations are quite clearly in some sense or other components of the facts that have those qualities or relations. The analysis of apparently complex *things* such as we started with can be reduced by various means, to the analysis of facts which are apparently about those things. Therefore it is with the analysis of *facts* that one's consideration of the problem of complexity must begin, not by the analysis of apparently complex things.

The complexity of a fact is evidenced, to begin with, by the circumstance that the proposition which asserts a fact consists of several words, each of which may occur in other contexts. Of course, sometimes you get a proposition expressed by a single word, but if it is expressed fully it is bound to contain several words. The proposition "Socrates is mortal" may be replaced by "Plato is mortal" or by "Socrates is human"; in the first case we alter the subject, in the second the predicate. It is clear that all the propositions in which the word "Socrates" occurs have something in common, and again all the propositions in which the word "mortal" occurs have something in common, something which they do not have in common with all propositions, but only with those which are about Socrates or mortality. It is clear, I think, that the facts corresponding to propositions in which the word "Socrates" occurs have something in common corresponding to the common word "Socrates" which occurs in the propositions, so that you have that sense of complexity to begin with, that in a fact you can get something which it may have in common with other facts, just as you may have "Socrates is human" and "Socrates is mortal", both of them facts, and both having to do with Socrates, although Socrates does not constitute the whole of either of these facts. It is quite clear that in that sense there is a possibility of cutting up a fact into component parts, of which one component may be altered without altering the others, and one component may occur in certain other facts though not in all other facts. I want to make it clear, to begin with, that there is a sense in which facts can be analyzed. I am not concerned with all the difficulties of any analysis, but only with meeting the *primâ facie* objections of philosophers who think you really cannot analyze at all.

I am trying as far as possible again this time, as I did last time, to start with perfectly plain truisms. My desire and wish is that the things I start with should be so obvious that you wonder why I spend my time stating them. That is what I aim at, because the point of philosophy is to start with something so simple as not to seem worth stating, and to end with something so paradoxical that no one will believe it.

One *primâ facie* mark of complexity in propositions is the fact that they are expressed by several words. I come now to another point, which applies primarily to propositions and thence derivatively to facts. You can understand a proposition when you understand the words of which it is composed even though you never heard the proposition before. That seems a very humble property, but it is a property which marks it as complex and distinguishes it from words whose meaning is simple. When you know the vocabulary, grammar, and syntax of a language, you can understand a proposition in that language even though you never saw it before. In reading a newspaper, for example, you become aware of a number of statements which are new to you, and they are intelligible to you immediately, in spite of the fact that they are new, because you understand the words of which they are composed. This characteristic, that you can understand a proposition through the understanding of its component words, is absent from the component words when those words express something simple. Take the word "red", for example, and suppose—as one always has to do—that "red" stands for a particular shade of colour. You will pardon that assumption, but one never can get on otherwise. You cannot understand the meaning of the word "red" except through seeing red things. There is no other way in which it can be done. It is no use to learn languages, or to look up dictionaries. None of these things will help you to understand the meaning of the word "red". In that way it is quite different from the meaning of a proposition. Of course, you can give a definition of the word "red", and here it is very important to distinguish between a definition and 10 an analysis. All analysis is only possible in regard to what is complex, and it always depends, in the last analysis, upon direct acquaintance with the objects which are the meanings of certain simple symbols. It is hardly necessary to observe that one does not define a thing but a symbol. (A "simple" symbol is a symbol whose parts are not symbols.) A simple symbol is quite a different thing from a simple thing. Those objects which it is impossible to symbolize otherwise than by simple symbols may be called "simple", while those which can be symbolized by a combination of symbols may be called "complex". This is, of course, a preliminary definition, and perhaps somewhat circular, but that does not much matter at this stage. 20

I have said that "red" could not be understood except by seeing red things. You might object to that on the ground that you can define red, for example, as "the colour with the greatest wave-length". That, you might say, is a definition of "red" and a person could understand that definition even if he had seen nothing red, provided he understood the physical theory of colour. But that does not really constitute the meaning of the word "red" in the very slightest. If you take such a proposition as "This is red" and substitute for it "This has the colour with the greatest wave-length", you have a different proposition altogether. You can see that at once, because a person who knows nothing of the physical theory of colour can understand 30 the proposition "This is red", and can know that it is true, but cannot know that "This has the colour which has the greatest wave-length." Conversely, you might have a hypothetical person who could not see red, but who understood the physical theory of colour and could apprehend the proposition "This has the colour with the greatest wave-length", but who would not be able to understand the proposition "This is red", as understood by the normal uneducated person. Therefore it is clear that if you define "red" as "The colour with the greatest wave-length" you are not giving the actual meaning of the word at all; you are simply giving a true description, which is quite a different thing, and the propositions which result are different 40 propositions from those in which the word "red" occurs. In that sense the word "red" cannot be defined, though in the sense in which a correct description constitutes a definition it can be defined. In the sense of analysis you cannot define "red". That is how it is that dictionaries are able to get on, because a dictionary professes to define all words in the language by means of words in the language, and therefore it is clear that a dictionary must be guilty of a vicious circle somewhere, but it manages it by means of correct descriptions.

I have made it clear, then, in what sense I should say that the word "red" is a simple symbol and the phrase "This is red" a complex symbol. The word "red" can only be understood through acquaintance with the object, whereas the phrase "Roses are red" can be understood if you know what "red" is and what "roses" are, without ever having heard the phrase before. That is a clear mark of what is complex. It is the mark of a complex symbol, and also the mark of the object symbolized by the complex symbol. That is to say, propositions are complex symbols, and the facts they stand for are complex.

The whole question of the meaning of words is very full of complexities and ambiguities in ordinary language. When one person uses a word, he does not mean by it the same thing as another person means by it. I have often heard it said that that is a misfortune. That is a mistake. It would be absolutely fatal if people meant the same things by their words. It would make all intercourse impossible, and language the most hopeless and useless thing imaginable, because the meaning you attach to your words must depend on the nature of the objects you are acquainted with, and since different people are acquainted with different objects, they would not be able to talk to each other unless they attached quite different meanings to their words. We should have to talk only about logic—a not wholly undesirable result. Take, for example, the word "Piccadilly". We, who are acquainted with Piccadilly, attach quite a different meaning to that word from any which could be attached to it by a person who had never been in London; and, supposing that you travel in foreign parts and expatiate on Piccadilly, you will convey to your hearers entirely different propositions from those in your mind. They will know Piccadilly as an important street in London; they may know a lot about it, but they will not know just the things one knows when one is walking along it. If you were to insist on language which was unambiguous, you would be unable to tell people at home what you had seen in foreign parts. It would be altogether incredibly inconvenient to have an unambiguous language, and therefore mercifully we have not got one.

Analysis is not the same thing as definition. You can define a term by means of a correct description, but that does not constitute an analysis. It is analysis, not definition, that we are concerned with at the present moment, so I will come back to the question of analysis.

We may lay down the following provisional definitions:

That the components of a proposition are the symbols we must
understand in order to understand the proposition;

That the components of the fact which makes a proposition true or
false, as the case may be, are the *meanings* of the symbols which we
must understand in order to understand the proposition.

That is not absolutely correct, but it will enable you to understand my
meaning. One reason why it fails of correctness is that it does not apply to
words which, like "or" and "not", are parts of propositions without corresponding to any part of the corresponding facts. This is a topic for Lecture
III.   10

I call these definitions *preliminary* because they start from the complexity
of the proposition, which they define psychologically, and proceed to the
complexity of the fact, whereas it is quite clear that in an orderly, proper
procedure it is the complexity of the fact that you would start from. It is also
clear that the complexity of the fact cannot be something merely
psychological. If in astronomical fact the earth moves round the sun, that is
genuinely complex. It is not that you think it complex, it is a sort of genuine
objective complexity, and therefore one ought in a proper, orderly procedure to start from the complexity of the world and arrive at the complexity
of the proposition. The only reason for going the other way round is that in   20
all abstract matters symbols are easier to grasp. I doubt, however, whether
complexity, in that fundamental objective sense in which one starts from
complexity of a fact, is definable at all. You cannot analyze what you mean
by complexity in that sense. You must just apprehend it—at least so I am
inclined to think. There is nothing one could say about it, beyond giving
criteria such as I have been giving. Therefore, when you cannot get a real
proper analysis of a thing, it is generally best to talk round it without
professing that you have given an exact definition.

It might be suggested that complexity is essentially to do with symbols, or
that it is essentially psychological. I do not think it would be possible   30
seriously to maintain either of these views, but they are the sort of views that
will occur to one, the sort of thing that one would try, to see whether it
would work. I do not think they will do at all. When we come to the
principles of symbolism which I shall deal with in Lecture VII, I shall try to
persuade you that in a logically correct symbolism there will always be a
certain fundamental identity of structure between a fact and the symbol for
it; and that the complexity of the symbol corresponds very closely with the
complexity of the facts symbolized by it. Also, as I said before, it is quite
directly evident to inspection that the fact, for example, that two things
stand in a certain relation to one another—e.g. that this is to the left of   40
that—is itself objectively complex, and not merely that the apprehension of
it is complex. The fact that two things stand in a certain relation to each

other, or any statement of that sort, has a complexity all of its own. I shall therefore in future assume that there is an objective complexity in the world, and that it is mirrored by the complexity of propositions.

A moment ago I was speaking about the great advantages that we derive from the logical imperfections of language, from the fact that our words are all ambiguous. I propose now to consider what sort of language a logically perfect language would be. In a logically perfect language the words in a proposition would correspond one by one with the components of the corresponding fact, with the exception of such words as "or", "not", "if", "then", which have a different function. In a logically perfect language, there will be one word and no more for every simple object, and everything that is not simple will be expressed by a combination of words, by a combination derived, of course, from the words for the simple things that enter in, one word for each simple component. A language of that sort will be completely analytic, and will show at a glance the logical structure of the facts asserted or denied. The language which is set forth in *Principia Mathematica* is intended to be a language of that sort. It is a language which has only syntax and no vocabulary whatsoever. Barring the omission of a vocabulary I maintain that it is quite a nice language. It aims at being that sort of a language that, if you add a vocabulary, would be a logically perfect language. Actual languages are not logically perfect in this sense, and they cannot possibly be, if they are to serve the purposes of daily life. A logically perfect language, if it could be constructed, would not only be intolerably prolix, but, as regards its vocabulary, would be very largely private to one speaker. That is to say, all the names that it would use would be private to that speaker and could not enter into the language of another speaker. It could not use proper names for Socrates or Piccadilly or Rumania for the reasons which I went into earlier in the lecture. Altogether you would find that it would be a very inconvenient language indeed. That is one reason why logic is so very backward as a science, because the needs of logic are so extraordinarily different from the needs of daily life. One wants a language in both, and unfortunately it is logic that has to give way, not daily life. I shall, however, assume that we have constructed a logically perfect language, and that we are going on state occasions to use it, and I will now come back to the question which I intended to start with, namely, the analysis of facts.

The simplest imaginable facts are those which consist in the possession of a quality by some particular thing. Such facts, say, as "This is white." They have to be taken in a very sophisticated sense. I do not want you to think about the piece of chalk I am holding, but of what you see when you look at the chalk. If one says, "This is white" it will do for about as simple a fact as you can get hold of. The next simplest would be those in which you have a relation between two facts, such as: "This is to the left of that." Next you come to those where you have a triadic relation between three particulars. (An instance which Royce gives is "*A* gives *B* to *C*.") So you get relations which require as their minimum three terms, those we call triadic relations; and those which require four terms, which we call tetradic, and so on. There you have a whole infinite hierarchy of facts—facts in which you have a thing and a quality, two things and a relation, three things and a relation, four things and a relation, and so on. That whole hierarchy constitutes what I call *atomic* facts, and they are the simplest sort of fact. You can distinguish among them some simpler than others, because the ones containing a quality are simpler than those in which you have, say, a pentadic relation, and so on. The whole lot of them, taken together, are as facts go very simple, and are what I call atomic facts. The propositions expressing them are what I call atomic propositions.

In every atomic fact there is one component which is naturally expressed by a verb (or, in the case of quality, it may be expressed by a predicate, by an adjective). This one component is a quality or dyadic or triadic or tetradic ... relation. It would be very convenient, for purposes of talking about these matters, to call a quality a "monadic relation" and I shall do so; it saves a great deal of circumlocution.

In that case you can say that all atomic propositions assert relations of varying orders. Atomic facts contain, besides the relation, the terms of the relation—one term if it is a monadic relation, two if it is dyadic, and so on. These "terms" which come into atomic facts I define as "particulars".

Particulars = terms of relations in atomic facts.   *Definition*

That is the definition of particulars, and I want to emphasize it because the definition of a particular is something purely logical. The question whether this or that is a particular, is a question to be decided in terms of that logical definition. In order to understand the definition it is not necessary to know beforehand "This is a particular" or "That is a particular." It remains to be investigated what particulars you can find in the world, if any. The whole question of what particulars you actually find in the real world is a purely empirical one which does not interest the logician as such. The logician as such never gives instances, because it is one of the tests of a logical proposition that you need not know anything whatsoever about the real world in order to understand it.

Passing from atomic facts to atomic propositions, the word expressing a monadic relation or quality is called a "predicate", and the word expressing a relation of any higher order would generally be a verb, sometimes a single verb, sometimes a whole phrase. At any rate the verb gives the essential nerve, as it were, of the relation. The other words that occur in the atomic propositions, the words that are not the predicate or verb, may be called the subjects of the proposition. There will be one subject in a monadic proposition, two in a dyadic one, and so on. The subjects in a proposition will be the words expressing the terms of the relation which is expressed by the proposition.

The only kind of word that is theoretically capable of standing for a particular is a *proper name*, and the whole matter of proper names is rather curious.

Proper Names = words for particulars.   *Definition*

I have put that down although, as far as common language goes, it is
10 obviously false. It is true that if you try to think how you are to talk about particulars, you will see that you cannot ever talk about a particular particular except by means of a proper name. You cannot use general words except by way of description. How are you to express in words an atomic proposition? An atomic proposition is one which does mention actual particulars, not merely describe them but actually name them, and you can only name them by means of names. You can see at once for yourself, therefore, that every other part of speech except proper names is obviously quite incapable of standing for a particular. Yet it does seem a little odd if, having made a dot on the blackboard, I call it "John". You would be
20 surprised, and yet how are you to know otherwise what it is that I am speaking of. If I say, "The dot that is on the right-hand side is white" that is a proposition. If I say "This is white" that is quite a different proposition. "This" will do very well while we are all here and can see it, but if I wanted to talk about it tomorrow it would be convenient to have christened it and called it "John". There is no other way in which you can mention it. You cannot really mention *it* itself except by means of a name.

What pass for names in language, like "Socrates", "Plato", and so forth, were originally intended to fulfil this function of standing for particulars, and we do accept, in ordinary daily life, as particulars all sorts of things that
30 really are not so. The names that we commonly use, like "Socrates", are really abbreviations for descriptions; not only that, but what they describe are not particulars but complicated systems of classes or series. A name, in the narrow logical sense of a word whose meaning is a particular, can only be applied to a particular with which the speaker is acquainted, because you cannot name anything you are not acquainted with. You remember, when Adam named the beasts, they came before him one by one, and he became acquainted with them and named them. We are not acquainted with Socrates, and therefore cannot name him. When we use the word "Socrates", we are really using a description. Our thought may be rendered by some
40 such phrase as, "The Master of Plato", or "The philosopher who drank the hemlock", or "The person whom logicians assert to be mortal", but we

certainly do not use the name as a name in the proper sense of the word.

That makes it very difficult to get any instance of a name at all in the proper strict logical sense of the word. The only words one does use as names in the logical sense are words like "this" or "that". One can use "this" as a name to stand for a particular with which one is acquainted at the moment. We say "This is white." If you agree that "This is white", meaning the "this" that you see, you are using "this" as a proper name. But if you try to apprehend the proposition that I am expressing when I say "This is white", you cannot do it. If you mean this piece of chalk as a physical object, then you are not using a proper name. It is only when you use "this" quite strictly, to stand for an actual object of sense, that it is really a proper name. And in that it has a very odd property for a proper name, namely that it seldom means the same thing two moments running and does not mean the same thing to the speaker and to the hearer. It is an *ambiguous* proper name, but it is really a proper name all the same, and it is almost the only thing I can think of that is used properly and logically in the sense that I was talking of for a proper name. The importance of proper names, in the sense of which I am talking, is in the sense of logic, not of daily life. You can see why it is that in the logical language set forth in *Principia Mathematica* there are not any names, because there we are not interested in particular particulars but only in general particulars, if I may be allowed such a phrase.

Particulars have this peculiarity, among the sort of objects that you have to take account of in an inventory of the world, that each of them stands entirely alone and is completely self-subsistent. It has that sort of self-subsistence that used to belong to substance, except that it usually only persists through a very short time, so far as our experience goes. That is to say, each particular that there is in the world does not in any way logically depend upon any other particular. Each one might happen to be the whole universe; it is a merely empirical fact that this is not the case. There is no reason why you should not have a universe consisting of one particular and nothing else. That is a peculiarity of particulars. In the same way, in order to understand a name for a particular, the only thing necessary is to be acquainted with that particular. When you are acquainted with that particular, you have a full, adequate, and complete understanding of the name, and no further information is required. No further information as to the facts that are true of that particular would enable you to have a fuller understanding of the meaning of the name.

DISCUSSION

Mr. Carr: You think there are simple facts that are not complex. Are complexes all composed of simples? Are not the simples that go into complexes themselves complex?

Mr. Russell: No facts are simple. As to your second question, that is, of course, a question that might be argued—whether when a thing is complex it is necessary that it should in analysis have constituents that are simple. I think it is perfectly possible to suppose that complex things are capable of analysis *ad infinitum*, and that you never reach the simple. I do not think it is true, but it is a thing that one might argue, certainly. I do myself think that complexes—I do not like to talk of complexes—but that facts are composed of simples, but I admit that that is a difficult argument, and it might be that analysis could go on forever.

10 *Mr. Carr*: You do not mean that in calling the thing complex, you have asserted that there really are simples?

Mr. Russell: No, I do not think that is *necessarily* implied.

Mr. Neville: I do not feel clear that the proposition "This is white" is in any case a simpler proposition than the proposition "This and that have the same colour."

Mr. Russell: That is one of the things I have not had time for. It may be the same as the proposition "This and that have the same colour." It may be that white is defined as the colour of "this", or rather that the proposition "This is white" means "This is identical in colour with that", the colour of

20 "that" being, so to speak, the definition of white. That may be, but there is no special reason to think that it is.

Mr. Neville: Are there any monadic relations which would be better examples?

Mr. Russell: I think not. It is perfectly obvious a priori that you can get rid of all monadic relations by that trick. One of the things I was going to say if I had had time was that you can get rid of dyadic and reduce to triadic, and so on. But there is no particular reason to suppose that that is the way the world begins, that it begins with relations of order *n* instead of relations of order 1. You cannot reduce them downward, but you can reduce them upward.

30 *Q.*: If the proper name of a thing, a "this", varies from instant to instant, how is it possible to make any argument?

Mr. Russell: You can keep "this" going for about a minute or two. I made that dot and talked about it for some little time. I mean it varies often. If you argue quickly, you can get some little way before it is finished. I think things last for a finite time, a matter of some seconds or minutes or whatever it may happen to be.

Q.: You do not think that air is acting on that and changing it?

Mr. Russell: It does not matter about that if it does not alter its appearance enough for you to have a different sense-datum.

III. ATOMIC AND MOLECULAR PROPOSITIONS

I did not quite finish last time the syllabus that I intended for Lecture II, so I must first do that.

I had been speaking at the end of my last lecture on the subject of the self-subsistence of particulars, how each particular has its being independently of any other and does not depend upon anything else for the logical possibility of its existence. I compared particulars with the old conception of substance, that is to say, they have the quality of self-subsistence that used to belong to substance, but not the quality of persistence through time. A particular, as a rule, is apt to last for a very short time indeed, not an instant but a very short time. In that respect particulars differ from the old substances but in their logical position they do not. There is, as you know, a logical theory which is quite opposed to that view, a logical theory according to which, if you really understood any one thing, you would understand everything. I think that rests upon a certain confusion of ideas. When you have acquaintance with a particular, you understand that particular itself quite fully, independently of the fact that there are a great many propositions about it that you do not know, but propositions concerning the particular are not necessary to be known in order that you may know what the particular itself is. It is rather the other way round. In order to understand a proposition in which the name of a particular occurs, you must already be acquainted with that particular. The acquaintance with the simpler is presupposed in the understanding of the more complex, but the logic that I should wish to combat maintains that in order thoroughly to know any one thing, you must know all its relations and all its qualities, all the propositions in fact in which that thing is mentioned; and you deduce of course from that that the world is an interdependent whole. It is on a basis of that sort that the logic of monism develops. Generally one supports this theory by talking about the "nature" of a thing, assuming that a thing has something which you call its "nature" which is generally elaborately confounded and distinguished from the thing, so that you can get a comfortable see-saw which enables you to deduce whichever results suit the moment. The "nature" of the thing would come to mean all the true propositions in which the thing is mentioned. Of course it is clear that since everything has relations to everything else, you cannot know all the facts of which a thing is a constituent without having some knowledge of everything in the universe. When you realize that what one calls "knowing a particular" merely means acquaintance with that particular and is presupposed in the understanding of any proposition in which that particular is mentioned, I think you also realize that you cannot take the view that the understanding of the name of the particular presupposes knowledge of all the propositions concerning that particular.

I should like to say about understanding, that that phrase is often used mistakenly. People speak of "understanding the universe" and so on. But, of course, the only thing you can really understand (in the strict sense of the word) is a symbol, and to understand a symbol is to know what it stands for.

I pass on from particulars to predicates and relations and what we mean by understanding the words that we use for predicates and relations. A very great deal of what I am saying in this course of lectures consists of ideas which I derived from my friend Wittgenstein. But I have had no opportunity of knowing how far his ideas have changed since August 1914, nor whether he is alive or dead, so I cannot make any one but myself responsible for them.

Understanding a predicate is quite a different thing from understanding a name. By a predicate, as you know, I mean the word that is used to designate a quality such as red, white, square, round, and the understanding of a word like that involves a different kind of act of mind from that which is involved in understanding a name. To understand a name you must be acquainted with the particular of which it is a name, and you must know that it is the name of that particular. You do not, that is to say, have any suggestion of the form of a proposition, whereas in understanding a predicate you do. To understand "red", for instance, is to understand what is meant by saying that a thing is red. You have to bring in the form of a proposition. You do not have to know, concerning any particular "this", that "This is red" but you have to know what is the meaning of saying that anything is red. You have to understand what one would call "being red". The importance of that is in connection with the theory of types, which I shall come to later on. It is in the fact that a predicate can never occur except as a predicate. When it seems to occur as a subject, the phrase wants amplifying and explaining, unless, of course, you are talking about the word itself. You may say "'Red' is a predicate", but then you must have "red" in inverted commas because you are talking about the word "red". When you understand "red" it means that you understand propositions of the form that "x is red". So that the understanding of a predicate is something a little more complicated than the understanding of a name, just because of that. Exactly the same applies to relations, and in fact all those things that are not particulars. Take, e.g., "before" in "x is before y": you understand "before" when you understand what that would mean if x and y were given. I do not mean you know whether it is true, but you understand the proposition. Here again the same thing applies. A relation can never occur except as a relation, never as a subject. You will always have to put in hypothetical terms, if not real ones, such as "If I say that x is before y, I assert a relation between x and y." It is in this way that you will have to expand such a statement as "'Before' is a relation" in order to get its meaning.

The different sorts of words, in fact, have different sorts of uses and must be kept always to the right use and not to the wrong use, and it is fallacies arising from putting symbols to wrong uses that lead to the contradictions concerned with types.

There is just one more point before I leave the subjects I meant to have dealt with last time, and that is a point which came up in discussion at the conclusion of the last lecture, namely, that if you like you can get a formal reduction of (say) monadic relations to dyadic, or of dyadic to triadic, or of all the relations below a certain order to all above that order, but the converse reduction is not possible. Suppose one takes, for example, "red". One says, "This is red", "That is red", and so forth. Now, if any one is of opinion that there is reason to try to get on without subject-predicate propositions, all that is necessary is to take some standard red thing and have a relation which one might call "colour-likeness", sameness of colour, which would be a direct relation, not consisting in having a certain colour. You can then define the things which are red, as all the things that have colour-likeness to this standard thing. That is practically the treatment that Berkeley and Hume recommended, except that they did not recognize that they were reducing qualities to relations, but thought they were getting rid of "abstract ideas" altogether. You can perfectly well do in that way a formal reduction of predicates to relations. There is no objection to that either empirically or logically. If you think it is worth while you can proceed in exactly the same way with dyadic relations, which you can reduce to triadic. Royce used to have a great affection for that process. For some reason he always liked triadic relations better than dyadic ones; he illustrated his preference in his contributions to mathematical logic and the principles of geometry.

All that is possible. I do not myself see any particular point in doing it as soon as you have realized that it is possible. I see no particular reason to suppose that the simplest relations that occur in the world are (say) of order *n*, but there is no a priori reason against it. The converse reduction, on the other hand, is quite impossible except in certain special cases where the relation has some special properties. For example, dyadic relations can be reduced to sameness of predicate when they are symmetrical and transitive. Thus, e.g., the relation of colour-likeness will have the property that if *A* has exact colour-likeness with *B* and *B* with *C*, then *A* has exact colour-likeness with *C*; and if *A* has it with *B*, *B* has it with *A*. But the case is otherwise with asymmetrical relations.

Take for example "*A* is greater than *B*." It is obvious that "*A* is greater than *B*" does not consist in *A* and *B* having a common predicate, for if it did it would require that *B* should also be greater than *A*. It is also obvious that it does not consist merely in their having different predicates, because if *A* has a different predicate from *B*, *B* has a different predicate from *A*, so that in either case, whether of sameness or difference of predicate, you get a symmetrical relation. For instance, if A is of a different colour from B, B is of a different colour from A. Therefore when you get symmetrical relations, you have relations which it is formally possible to reduce to either sameness of predicate or difference of predicate, but when you come to asymmetrical relations there is no such possibility. This impossibility of reducing dyadic relations to sameness or difference of predicate is a matter of a good deal of importance in connection with traditional philosophy, because a great deal of traditional philosophy depends upon the assumption that every proposition really is of the subject-predicate form, and that is certainly not the case.

10 That theory dominates a great part of traditional metaphysics and the old idea of substance and a good deal of the theory of the Absolute, so that that sort of logical outlook which had its imagination dominated by the theory that you could always express a proposition in a subject-predicate form has had a very great deal of influence upon traditional metaphysics.

That is the end of what I ought to have said last time, and I come on now to the proper topic of today's lecture, that is *molecular* propositions. I call them molecular propositions because they contain other propositions which you may call their atoms, and by molecular propositions I mean propositions having such words as "or", "if", "and", and so forth. If I say, "Either

20 today is Tuesday, or we have all made a mistake in being here", that is the sort of proposition that I mean that is molecular. Or if I say, "If it rains, I shall bring my umbrella", that again is a molecular proposition because it contains the two parts "It rains" and "I shall bring my umbrella." If I say, "It did rain and I did bring my umbrella", that again is a molecular proposition. Or if I say, "The supposition of its raining is incompatible with the supposition of my not bringing my umbrella", that again is a molecular proposition. There are various propositions of that sort, which you can complicate *ad infinitum*. They are built up out of propositions related by such words as "or", "if", "and", and so on. You remember that I defined an

30 atomic proposition as one which contains a single verb. Now there are two different lines of complication in proceeding from these to more complex propositions. There is the line that I have just been talking about, where you proceed to molecular propositions, and there is another line which I shall come to in a later lecture, where you have not two related propositions, but one proposition containing two or more verbs. Examples are got from believing, wishing, and so forth. "I believe Socrates is mortal." You have there two verbs, "believe" and "is". Or "I wish I were immortal." Anything like that where you have a wish or a belief or a doubt involves two verbs. A lot of psychological attitudes involve two verbs, not, as it were, crystallized

40 out, but two verbs within one unitary proposition. But I am talking today about molecular propositions, and you will understand that you can make propositions with "or" and "and" and so forth, where the constituent propositions are not atomic, but for the moment we can confine ourselves to

the case where the constituent propositions are atomic. When you take an atomic proposition, or one of these propositions like "believing", when you take any proposition of that sort, there is just one fact which is pointed to by the proposition, pointed to either truly or falsely. The essence of a proposition is that it can correspond in two ways with a fact, in what one may call the true way or the false way. You might illustrate it in a picture like this:

True: $\overrightarrow{\text{Prop.}}$ Fact

False: Fact $\overrightarrow{\text{Prop.}}$

Supposing you have the proposition "Socrates is mortal", either there would be the fact that Socrates is mortal or there would be the fact that Socrates is not mortal. In the one case it corresponds in a way that makes the proposition true, in the other case in a way that makes the proposition false. That is one way in which a proposition differs from a name.

There are, of course, two propositions corresponding to every fact, one true and one false. There are no false facts, so you cannot get one fact for every proposition but only for every pair of propositions. All that applies to atomic propositions. But when you take such a proposition as "*p* or *q*", "Socrates is mortal or Socrates is living still", there you will have two different facts involved in the truth or the falsehood of your proposition "*p* or *q*". There will be the fact that corresponds to *p* and there will be the fact that corresponds to *q*, and both of those facts are relevant in discovering the truth or falsehood of "*p* or *q*". I do not suppose there is in the world a single disjunctive fact corresponding to "*p* or *q*". It does not look plausible that in the actual objective world there are facts going about which you could describe as "*p* or *q*", but I would not lay too much stress on what strikes one as plausible: it is not a thing you can rely on altogether. For the present I do not think any difficulties will arise from the supposition that the truth or falsehood of this proposition "*p* or *q*" does not depend upon a single objective fact which is disjunctive but depends on the two facts one of which corresponds to *p* and the other *q*: *p* will have a fact corresponding to it and *q* will have a fact corresponding to it. That is to say, the truth or falsehood of this proposition "*p* or *q*" depends upon two facts and not upon one, as *p* does and as *q* does. Generally speaking, as regards these things that you make up out of two propositions, the whole of what is necessary in order to know their meaning is to know under what circumstances they are true, given the truth or falsehood of *p* and the truth or falsehood of *q*. That is perfectly obvious. You have as a schema,

for "*p* or *q*", using "TT" for "*p* and *q* both true"
          "TF" for "*p* true and *q* false", etc.,

TT TF FT FF
 T   T   T   F

where the bottom line states the truth or the falsehood of "p or q". You must not look about the real world for an object which you can call "or", and say, "Now, look at this. This is 'or'." There is no such thing, and if you try to analyze "p or q" in that way you will get into trouble. But the meaning of disjunction will be entirely explained by the above schema.

I call these things truth-functions of propositions, when the truth or falsehood of the molecular proposition depends only on the truth or false-
10 hood of the propositions that enter into it. The same applies to "p and q" and "if p then q" and "p is incompatible with q." When I say "p is incompatible with q" I simply mean to say that they are not both true. I do not mean any more. Those sort of things are called truth-functions, and these molecular propositions that we are dealing with today are instances of truth-functions. If p is a proposition, the statement that "I believe p" does not depend for its truth or falsehood, simply upon the truth or falsehood of p, since I believe some but not all true propositions and some but not all false propositions.

I just want to give you a little talk about the way these truth-functions are
20 built up. You can build up all these different sorts of truth-functions out of one source, namely "p is incompatible with q", meaning by that that they are not both true, that one at least of them is false.

We will denote "p is incompatible with q" by p/q.

Take for instance p/p, i.e. "p is incompatible with itself." In that case clearly p will be false, so that you can take "p/p" as meaning "p is false", i.e. $p/p = $ not p. The meaning of molecular propositions is entirely determined by their truth-schema and there is nothing more in it than that, so that when you have got two things of the same truth-schema you can identify them.

Suppose you want "if p then q", that simply means that you cannot have p
30 without having q, so that p is incompatible with the falsehood of q. Thus,

$$\text{"If } p \text{ then } q\text{"} = p/(q/q).$$

When you have that, it follows of course at once that if p is true, q is true, because you cannot have p true and q false.

Suppose you want "p or q", that means that the falsehood of p is incompatible with the falsehood of q. If p is false, q is not false, and vice versa. That will be

$$(p/p)/(q/q).$$

Suppose you want "p and q are both true". That will mean that p is not incompatible with q. When p and q are both true, it is not the case that at least one of them is false. Thus,

$$\text{``}p \text{ and } q \text{ are both true''} = (p/q)/(p/q).$$

The whole of the logic of deduction is concerned simply with complications and developments of this idea. This idea of incompatibility was first shown to be sufficient for the purpose by Mr. Sheffer, and there was a good deal of work done subsequently by M. Nicod. It is a good deal simpler when it is done this way than when it is done in the way of *Principia Mathematica*, where there are two primitive ideas to start with, namely "or" and "not". Here you can get on with only a single premiss for deduction. I will not develop this subject further because it takes you right into mathematical logic.

I do not see any reason to suppose that there is a complexity in the facts corresponding to these molecular propositions, because, as I was saying, the correspondence of a molecular proposition with facts is of a different sort from the correspondence of an atomic proposition with a fact. There is one special point that has to be gone into in connection with this, that is the question: Are there negative facts? Are there such facts as you might call the fact that "Socrates is not alive"? I have assumed in all that I have said hitherto that there are negative facts, that for example if you say "Socrates is alive", there is corresponding to that proposition in the real world the fact that Socrates is not alive. One has a certain repugnance to negative facts, the same sort of feeling that makes you wish not to have a fact "p or q" going about the world. You have a feeling that there are only positive facts, and that negative propositions have somehow or other got to be expressions of positive facts. When I was lecturing on this subject at Harvard I argued that there were negative facts, and it nearly produced a riot: the class would not hear of there being negative facts at all. I am still inclined to think that there are. However, one of the men to whom I was lecturing at Harvard, Mr. Demos, subsequently wrote an article in *Mind* to explain why there are no negative facts. It is in *Mind* for April 1917. I think he makes as good a case as can be made for the view that there are no negative facts. It is a difficult question. I really only ask that you should not dogmatize. I do not say positively that there are, but there may be.

There are certain things you can notice about negative propositions. Mr. Demos points out, first of all, that a negative proposition is not in any way dependent on a cognitive subject for its definition. To this I agree. Suppose you say, when I say "Socrates is not alive", I am merely expressing disbelief in the proposition that Socrates is alive. You have got to find something or other in the real world to make this disbelief true, and the only question is what. That is his first point.

His second is that a negative proposition must not be taken at its face value. You cannot, he says, regard the statement "Socrates is not alive" as being an expression of a fact in the same sort of direct way in which "Socrates is human" would be an expression of a fact. His argument for that is solely that he cannot believe that there are negative facts in the world. He maintains that there cannot be in the real world such facts as "Socrates is not alive", taken, i.e., as simple facts, and that therefore you have got to find some explanation of negative propositions, some interpretation, and that they cannot be just as simple as positive propositions. I shall come back to that point, but on this I do not feel inclined to agree.

His third point I do not entirely agree with: that when the word "not" occurs, it cannot be taken as a qualification of the predicate. For instance, if you say that "This is not red", you might attempt to say that "not-red" is a predicate, but that of course won't do; in the first place because a great many propositions are not expressions of predicates; in the second place because the word "not" applies to the whole proposition. The proper expression would be "not: this is red"; the "not" applies to the whole proposition "this is red", and of course in many cases you can see that quite clearly. If you take a case I took in discussing descriptions: "The present king of France is not bald", then, if you take "not-bald" as a predicate, that would have to be judged false on the ground that there is not a present king of France. But it is clear that the proposition "The present king of France is bald" is a false proposition, and therefore the negative of that will have to be a true proposition, and that could not be the case if you take "not-bald" as a predicate, so that in all cases where "not" comes in, the "not" has to be taken to apply to the whole proposition. "Not-p" is the proper formula.

We have come now to the question, how are we really to interpret "not-p", and the suggestion offered by Mr. Demos is that when we assert "not-p" we are really asserting that there is some proposition q which is true and is incompatible with p ("an opposite of p" is his phrase, but I think the meaning is the same). That is his suggested definition:

"not-p" means "There is a proposition q which is true and is incompatible with p."

As, e.g., if I say "This chalk is not red", I shall be meaning to assert that there is some proposition, which in this case would be the proposition "This chalk is white", which is inconsistent with the proposition "It is red", and that you use these general negative forms because you do not happen to know what the actual proposition is that is true and is incompatible with p. Or, of course, you may possibly know what the actual proposition is, but you may be more interested in the fact that p is false than you are in the particular example which makes it false. As, for instance, you might be anxious to prove that some one is a liar, and you might be very much interested in the falsehood of some proposition which he had asserted. You might also be more interested in the general proposition than in the particular case, so that if some one had asserted that that chalk was red, you might be more interested in the fact that it was not red than in the fact that it was white.

I find it very difficult to believe that theory of falsehood. You will observe that in the first place there is this objection, that it makes incompatibility fundamental and an objective fact, which is not so very much simpler than allowing negative facts. You have got to have here "That p is incompatible with q" in order to reduce "not" to incompatibility, because this has got to be the corresponding fact. It is perfectly clear, whatever may be the interpretation of "not", that there is *some* interpretation which will give you a fact. If I say "There is not a hippopotamus in this room", it is quite clear there is some way of interpreting that statement according to which there is a corresponding fact, and the fact cannot be merely that every part of this room is filled up with something that is not a hippopotamus. You would come back to the necessity for some kind or other of fact of the sort that we have been trying to avoid. We have been trying to avoid both negative facts and molecular facts, and all that this succeeds in doing is to substitute molecular facts for negative facts, and I do not consider that that is very successful as a means of avoiding paradox, especially when you consider this, that even if incompatibility is to be taken as a sort of fundamental expression of fact, incompatibility is not between facts but between propositions. If I say "p is incompatible with q", one at least of p and q has got to be false. It is clear that no two *facts* are incompatible. The incompatibility holds between the propositions, between the p and the q, and therefore if you are going to take incompatibility as a fundamental fact, you have got, in explaining negatives, to take as your fundamental fact something involving propositions as opposed to facts. It is quite clear that propositions are not what you might call "real". If you were making an inventory of the world, propositions would not come in. Facts would, beliefs, wishes, wills would, but propositions would not. They do not have being independently, so that this incompatibility of propositions taken as an ultimate fact of the real world will want a great deal of treatment, a lot of dressing up before it will do. Therefore as a simplification to avoid negative facts, I do not think it really is very successful. I think you will find that it is simpler to take negative facts as facts, to assume that "Socrates is not alive" is really an objective fact in the same sense in which "Socrates is human" is a fact. This theory of Mr. Demos's that I have been setting forth here is a development of the one one hits upon at once when one tries to get round negative facts, but for the reasons that I have given, I do not think it really answers to take things that way, and I think you will find that it is better to take negative facts as ultimate. Otherwise you will find it so difficult to say what it is that

corresponds to a proposition. When, e.g., you have a false positive proposition, say "Socrates is alive", it is false because of a fact in the real world. A thing cannot be false except because of a fact, so that you find it extremely difficult to say what exactly happens when you make a positive assertion that is false, unless you are going to admit negative facts. I think all those questions are difficult and there are arguments always to be adduced both ways, but on the whole I do incline to believe that there are negative facts and that there are not disjunctive facts. But the denial of disjunctive facts leads to certain difficulties which we shall have to consider in connection
10 with general propositions in a later lecture.

DISCUSSION

Q.: Do you consider that the proposition "Socrates is dead" is a positive or a negative fact?

Mr. Russell: It is partly a negative fact. To say that a person is dead is complicated. It is two statements rolled into one: "Socrates was alive" and "Socrates is not alive."

Q.: Does putting the "not" into it give it a formal character of negative and vice versa?

Mr. Russell: No, I think you must go into the meaning of words.

20 *Q.*: I should have thought there was a great difference between saying that "Socrates is alive" and saying that "Socrates is not a living man." I think it is possible to have what one might call a negative existence and that things exist of which we cannot take cognizance. Socrates undoubtedly did live but he is no longer in the condition of living as a man.

Mr. Russell: I was not going into the question of existence after death but simply taking words in their every-day signification.

Q.: What is precisely your test as to whether you have got a positive or negative proposition before you?

Mr. Russell: There is no formal test.

30 *Q.*: If you had a formal test, would it not follow that you would know whether there were negative facts or not?

Mr. Russell: No, I think not. In the perfect logical language that I sketched in theory, it would always be obvious at once whether a proposition was positive or negative. But it would not bear upon how you are going to interpret negative propositions.

Q.: Would the existence of negative facts ever be anything more than a mere definition?

Mr. Russell: Yes, I think it would. It seems to me that the business of metaphysics is to describe the world, and it is in my opinion a real definite
40 question whether in a complete description of the world you would have to mention negative facts or not.

Q.: How do you define a negative fact?
Mr. Russell: You could not give a general definition if it is right that negativeness is an ultimate.

IV. PROPOSITIONS AND FACTS WITH MORE THAN ONE VERB;
BELIEFS, ETC.

You will remember that after speaking about atomic propositions I pointed out two more complicated forms of propositions which arise immediately on proceeding further than that: the first, which I call molecular propositions, which I dealt with last time, involving such words as "or", "and", "if", and the second involving two or more verbs such as believing, wishing, willing, and so forth. In the case of molecular propositions it was not clear that we had to deal with any new form of fact, but only with a new form of proposition, i.e. if you have a disjunctive proposition such as "*p* or *q*" it does not seem very plausible to say that there is in the world a disjunctive fact corresponding to "*p* or *q*" but merely that there is a fact corresponding to *p* and a fact corresponding to *q*, and the disjunctive proposition derives its truth or falsehood from those two separate facts. Therefore in that case one was dealing only with a new form of proposition and not with a new form of fact. Today we have to deal with a new form of fact.

I think one might describe philosophical logic, the philosophical portion of logic which is the portion that I am concerned with in these lectures since Christmas [1917], as an inventory, or if you like a more humble word, a "Zoo" containing all the different forms that facts may have. I should prefer to say "forms of facts"rather than "forms of propositions". To apply that to the case of molecular propositions which I dealt with last time, if one were pursuing this analysis of the forms of facts, it would be *belief in* a molecular proposition that one would deal with rather than the molecular proposition itself. In accordance with the sort of realistic bias that I should put into all study of metaphysics, I should always wish to be engaged in the investigation of some actual fact or set of facts, and it seems to me that that is so in logic just as much as it is in zoology. In logic you are concerned with the forms of facts, with getting hold of the different sorts of facts, different *logical* sorts of facts, that there are in the world. Now I want to point out today that the facts that occur when one believes or wishes or wills have a different logical form from the atomic facts containing a single verb which I dealt with in my second lecture. (There are, of course, a good many forms that facts may have, a strictly infinite number, and I do not wish you to suppose that I pretend to deal with all of them.) Suppose you take any actual occurrence of a belief. I want you to understand that I am not talking about beliefs in the sort of way in which judgment is spoken of in theory of knowledge, in which you would say there is *the* judgment that two and two are four. I am talking of the actual occurrence of a belief in a particular person's mind at a particular moment, and discussing what sort of a fact that is. If I say "What day of the week is this?" and you say "Tuesday", there occurs in your mind at that moment the belief that this is Tuesday. The thing I want to deal with today is the question, What is the form of the fact which occurs when a person has a belief? Of course you see that the sort of obvious first notion that one would naturally arrive at would be that a belief is a relation to the proposition. "I believe the proposition p." "I believe that today is Tuesday." "I believe that two and two are four." Something like that. It seems on the face of it as if you had there a relation of the believing subject to a proposition. That view won't do for various reasons which I shall go into. But you have therefore got to have a theory of belief which is not exactly that. Take any sort of proposition, say "I believe Socrates is mortal." Suppose that that belief does actually occur. The statement that it occurs is a statement of fact. You have there two verbs. You may have more than two verbs, you may have any number greater than one. I may believe that Jones is of opinion that Socrates is mortal. There you have more than two verbs. You may have any number, but you cannot have less than two. You will perceive that it is not only the proposition that has the two verbs, but also the fact, which is expressed by the proposition, has two constituents corresponding to verbs. I shall call those constituents verbs for the sake of shortness, as it is very difficult to find any word to describe all those objects which one denotes by verbs. Of course, that is strictly using the word "verb" in two different senses, but I do not think it can lead to any confusion if you understand that it is being so used. This fact (the belief) is one fact. It is not like what you had in molecular propositions where you had (say) "p or q". It is just one single fact that you have a belief. That is obvious from the fact that you can believe a falsehood. It is obvious from the fact of false belief that you cannot cut off one part: you cannot have

I believe/Socrates is mortal.

There are certain questions that arise about such facts, and the first that arises is, Are they undeniable facts or can you reduce them in some way to relations of other facts? Is it really necessary to suppose that there are irreducible facts, of which that sort of thing is a verbal expression? On that question until fairly lately I should certainly not have supposed that any doubt could arise. It had not really seemed to me until fairly lately that that was a debatable point. I still believe that there are facts of that form, but I see that it is a substantial question that needs to be discussed.

1. *Are beliefs, etc., irreducible facts?*

"Etc." covers understanding a proposition; it covers desiring, willing, any other attitude of that sort that you may think of that involves a proposition. It seems natural to say one believes a proposition and unnatural to say one desires a proposition, but as a matter of fact that is only a prejudice. What you believe and what you desire are of exactly the same nature. You may desire to get some sugar tomorrow and of course you may possibly believe that you will. I am not sure that the logical form is the same in the case of will. I am inclined to think that the case of will is more analogous to that of perception, in going direct to facts, and excluding the possibility of falsehood. In any case desire and belief are of exactly the same form logically.

Pragmatists and some of the American realists, the school whom one calls neutral monists, deny altogether that there is such a phenomenon as belief in the sense I am dealing with. They do not deny it in words, they do not use the same sort of language that I am using, and that makes it difficult to compare their views with the views I am speaking about. One has really to translate what they say into language more or less analogous to ours before one can make out where the points of contact or difference are. If you take the works of James in his *Essays in Radical Empiricism* or Dewey in his *Essays in Experimental Logic* you will find that they are denying altogether that there is such a phenomenon as belief in the sense I am talking of. They use the word "believe" but they mean something different. You come to the view called "behaviourism", according to which you mean, if you say a person believes a thing, that he behaves in a certain fashion; and that hangs together with James's pragmatism. James and Dewey would say: when I believe a proposition, that *means* that I act in a certain fashion, that my behaviour has certain characteristics, and my belief is a true one if the behaviour leads to the desired result and is a false one if it does not. That, if it is true, makes their pragmatism a perfectly rational account of truth and falsehood, if you do accept their view that belief as an isolated phenomenon does not occur. That is therefore the first thing one has to consider. It would take me too far from logic to consider that subject as it deserves to be considered, because it is a subject belonging to psychology, and it is only relevant to logic in this one way that it raises a doubt whether there are any facts having the logical form that I am speaking of. In the question of this logical form that involves two or more verbs you have a curious interlacing of logic with empirical studies, and of course that may occur elsewhere, in this way, that an empirical study gives you an example of a thing having a certain logical form, and you cannot really be sure that there are things having a given logical form except by finding an example, and the finding of an example is itself empirical. Therefore in that way empirical facts are relevant to logic at certain points. I think theoretically one might know that there were those forms without knowing any instance of them, but practically, situated as we are, that does not seem to occur. Practically, unless you can find an example of the form you won't know that there is that form. If I cannot find an example containing two or more verbs, you will not have reason to believe in the theory that such a form occurs.

When you read the works of people like James and Dewey on the subject of belief, one thing that strikes you at once is that the sort of thing they are thinking of as the object of belief is quite different from the sort of thing I am thinking of. They think of it always as a thing. They think you believe in
10 God or Homer: you believe in an object. That is the picture they have in their minds. It is common enough, in common parlance, to talk that way, and they would say, the first crude approximation that they would suggest would be that you believe truly when there is such an object and that you believe falsely when there is not. I do not mean they would say that exactly, but that would be the crude view from which they would start. They do not seem to have grasped the fact that the objective side in belief is better expressed by a proposition than by a single word, and that, I think, has a great deal to do with their whole outlook on the matter of what belief consists of. The object of belief in their view is generally, not relations
20 between things, or things having qualities, or what not, but just single things which may or may not exist. That view seems to me radically and absolutely mistaken. In the first place there are a great many judgments you cannot possibly fit into that scheme, and in the second place it cannot possibly give any explanation to false beliefs, because when you believe that a thing exists and it does not exist, the thing is not there, it is nothing, and it cannot be the right analysis of a false belief to regard it as a relation to what is really nothing. This is an objection to supposing that belief consists simply in relation to the object. It is obvious that if you say "I believe in Homer" and there was no such person as Homer, your belief cannot be a relation to
30 Homer, since there is no "Homer". Every fact that occurs in the world must be composed entirely of constituents that there are, and not of constituents that there are not. Therefore when you say "I believe in Homer" it cannot be the right analysis of the thing to put it like that. What the right analysis is I shall come on to in the theory of descriptions. I come back now to the theory of behaviourism which I spoke of a moment ago. Suppose, e.g., that you are said to believe that there is a train at 10.25. This means, we are told, that you start for the station at a certain time. When you reach the station you see it is 10.24 and you run. That behaviour constitutes your belief that there is a train at that time. If you catch your train by running, your belief
40 was true. If the train went at 10.23, you miss it, and your belief was false. That is the sort of thing that they would say constitutes belief. There is not a single state of mind which consists in contemplating this eternal verity, that the train starts at 10.25. They would apply that even to the most abstract

things. I do not myself feel that that view of things is tenable. It is a difficult one to refute because it goes very deep and one has the feeling that perhaps, if one thought it out long enough and became sufficiently aware of all its implications, one might find after all that it was a feasible view; but yet I do not *feel* it feasible. It hangs together, of course, with the theory of neutral monism, with the theory that the material constituting the mental is the same as the material constituting the physical, just like the Post Office directory which gives you people arranged geographically and alphabetically. This whole theory hangs together with that. I do not mean necessarily that all the people that profess the one profess the other, but that the two do essentially belong together. If you are going to take that view, you have to explain away belief and desire, because things of that sort do seem to be mental phenomena. They do seem rather far removed from the sort of thing that happens in the physical world. Therefore people will set to work to explain away such things as belief, and reduce them to bodily behaviour; and your belief in a certain proposition will consist in the behaviour of your body. In the crudest terms that is what that view amounts to. It does enable you to get on very well without mind. Truth and falsehood in that case consist in the relation of your bodily behaviour to a certain fact, the sort of distant fact which is the purpose of your behaviour, as it were, and when your behaviour is satisfactory in regard to that fact your belief is true, and when your behaviour is unsatisfactory in regard to that fact your belief is false. The logical essence, in that view, will be a relation between two facts having the same sort of form as a causal relation, i.e. on the one hand there will be your bodily behaviour which is one fact, and on the other hand the fact that the train starts at such and such a time, which is another fact, and out of a relation of those two the whole phenomenon is constituted. The thing you will get will be logically of the same form as you have in cause, where you have "This fact causes that fact." It is quite a different logical form from the facts containing two verbs that I am talking of today.

I have naturally a bias in favour of the theory of neutral monism because it exemplifies Occam's razor. I always wish to get on in philosophy with the smallest possible apparatus, partly because it diminishes the risk of error, because it is not necessary to deny the entities you do not assert, and therefore you run less risk of error the fewer entities you assume. The other reason—perhaps a somewhat frivolous one—is that every diminution in the number of entities increases the amount of work for mathematical logic to do in building up things that look like the entities you used to assume. Therefore the whole theory of neutral monism is pleasing to me, but I do find so far very great difficulty in believing it. You will find a discussion of the whole question in some articles I wrote in *The Monist*, especially in July 1914, and in the two previous numbers also. I should really want to rewrite them rather because I think some of the arguments I used against neutral

monism are not valid. I place most reliance on the argument about "emphatic particulars", "this", "I", all that class of words, that pick out certain particulars from the universe by their relation to oneself, and I think by the fact that they, or particulars related to them, are present to you at the moment of speaking. "This", of course, is what I call an "emphatic particular". It is simply a proper name for the present object of attention, a proper name, meaning nothing. It is ambiguous, because, of course, the object of attention is always changing from moment to moment and from person to person. I think it is extremely difficult, if you get rid of conscious-
10 ness altogether, to explain what you mean by such a word as "this", what it is that makes the absence of impartiality. You would say that in a purely physical world there would be a complete impartiality. All parts of time and all regions of space would seem equally emphatic. But what really happens is that we pick out certain facts, past and future and all that sort of thing; they all radiate out from "this", and I have not myself seen how one can deal with the notion of "this" on the basis of neutral monism. I do not lay that down dogmatically, only I do not see how it can be done. I shall assume for the rest of this lecture that there are such facts as beliefs and wishes and so forth. It would take me really the whole of my course to go into the question
20 fully. Thus we come back to more purely logical questions from this excursion into psychology, for which I apologize.

2. *What is the status of p in "I believe p"?*

You cannot say that you believe *facts*, because your beliefs are sometimes wrong. You can say that you *perceive* facts, because perceiving is not liable to error. Wherever it is facts alone that are involved, error is impossible. Therefore you cannot say you believe facts. You have to say that you believe propositions. The awkwardness of that is that obviously propositions are nothing. Therefore that cannot be the true account of the matter. When I say "Obviously propositions are nothing" it is not perhaps quite obvious.
30 Time was when I thought there were propositions, but it does not seem to me very plausible to say that in addition to facts there are also these curious shadowy things going about such as "That today is Wednesday" when in fact it is Tuesday. I cannot believe they go about the real world. It is more than one can manage to believe, and I do think no person with a vivid sense of reality can imagine it. One of the difficulties of the study of logic is that it is an exceedingly abstract study dealing with the most abstract things imaginable, and yet you cannot pursue it properly unless you have a vivid instinct as to what is real. You must have that instinct rather well developed in logic. I think otherwise you will get into fantastic things. I think Meinong
40 is rather deficient in just that instinct for reality. Meinong maintains that there is such an object as the round square only it does not exist, and it does not even subsist, but nevertheless there is such an object, and when you say

"The round square is a fiction", he takes it that there is an object "the round square" and there is a predicate "fiction". No one with a sense of reality would so analyze that proposition. He would see that the proposition wants analyzing in such a way that you won't have to regard the round square as a constituent of that proposition. To suppose that in the actual world of nature there is a whole set of false propositions going about is to my mind monstrous. I cannot bring myself to suppose it. I cannot believe that they are there in the sense in which facts are there. There seems to me something about the fact that "Today is Tuesday" ⟨which puts it⟩ on a different level of reality from the supposition "That today is Wednesday". When I speak of the proposition "That today is Wednesday" I do not mean the occurrence in future of a state of mind in which you think it is Wednesday, but I am talking about the theory that there is something quite logical, something not involving mind in any way; and such a thing as that I do not think you can take a false proposition to be. I think a false proposition must, wherever it occurs, be subject to analysis, be taken to pieces, pulled to bits, and shown to be simply separate pieces of one fact in which the false proposition has been analyzed away. I say that simply on the ground of what I should call an instinct of reality. I ought to say a word or two about "reality". It is a vague word, and most of its uses are improper. When I talk about reality as I am now doing, I can explain best what I mean by saying that I mean everything you would have to mention in a complete description of the world; that will convey to you what I mean. Now I do not think that false propositions would have to be mentioned in a complete description of the world. False beliefs would, of course, false suppositions would, and desires for what does not come to pass, but not false propositions all alone, and therefore when you, as one says, believe a false proposition, that cannot be an accurate account of what occurs. It is not accurate to say "I believe the proposition p" and regard the occurrence as a twofold relation between me and p. The logical form is just the same whether you believe a false or a true proposition. Therefore in all cases you are not to regard belief as a two-term relation between yourself and a proposition, and you have to analyze up the proposition and treat your belief differently. Therefore the belief does not really contain a proposition as a constituent but only contains the constituents of the proposition as constituents. You cannot say when you believe, "What is it that you believe?" There is no answer to that question, i.e. there is not a single thing that you are believing. "I believe that today is Tuesday." You must not suppose that "That today is Tuesday" is a single object which I am believing. That would be an error. That is not the right way to analyze the occurrence, although that analysis is linguistically convenient, and one may keep it provided one knows that it is not the truth.

3. *How shall we describe the logical form of a belief?*

I want to try to get an account of the way that a belief is made up. That is not an easy question at all. You cannot make what I should call a map-in-space of a belief. You can make a map of an atomic fact but not of a belief, for the simple reason that space-relations always are of the atomic sort or complications of the atomic sort. I will try to illustrate what I mean. The point is in connection with there being two verbs in the judgment and with the fact that both verbs have got to occur as verbs, because if a thing is a verb it cannot occur otherwise than as a verb. Suppose I take "*A* believes that *B*
10 loves *C*." "Othello believes that Desdemona loves Cassio." There you have a false belief. You have this odd state of affairs that the verb "loves" occurs in that proposition and seems to occur as relating Desdemona to Cassio whereas in fact it does not do so, but yet it does occur as a verb, it does occur in the sort of way that a verb should do. I mean that when *A* believes that *B* loves *C*, you have to have a verb in the place where "loves" occurs. You cannot put a substantive in its place. Therefore it is clear that the subordinate verb (i.e. the verb other than believing) is functioning as a verb, and seems to be relating two terms, but as a matter of fact does not when a judgment happens to be false. That is what constitutes the puzzle about the
20 nature of belief. You will notice that wherever one gets to really close quarters with the theory of error one has the puzzle of how to deal with error without assuming the existence of the non-existent. I mean that every theory of error sooner or later wrecks itself by assuming the existence of the non-existent. As when I say "Desdemona loves Cassio", it seems as if you have a non-existent love between Desdemona and Cassio, but that is just as wrong as a non-existent unicorn. So you have to explain the whole theory of judgment in some other way. I come now to this question of a map. Suppose you try such a map as this:

OTHELLO

|

30   believes

↓

DESDEMONA —————→ CASSIO
            loves

This question of making a map is not so strange as you might suppose because it is part of the whole theory of symbolism. It is important to realize where and how a symbolism of that sort would be wrong: where and how it is wrong is that in the symbol you have this relationship relating these two things and in the fact it doesn't really relate them. You cannot get in space any occurrence which is logically of the same form as belief. When I say "logically of the same form" I mean that one can be obtained from the other by replacing the constituents of the one by the new terms. If I say "Des-
40 demona loves Cassio" that is of the same form as "*A* is to the right of *B*."

Those are of the same form, and I say that nothing that occurs in space is of the same form as belief. I have got on here to a new sort of thing, a new beast for our Zoo, not another member of our former species but a new species. The discovery of this fact is due to Mr. Wittgenstein.

There is a great deal that is odd about belief from a logical point of view. One of the things that are odd is that you can believe propositions of all sorts of forms. I can believe that "This is white" and that "Two and two are four." They are quite different forms, yet one can believe both. The actual occurrence can hardly be of exactly the same logical form in those two cases because of the great difference in the forms of the propositions believed. Therefore it would seem that belief cannot strictly be logically one in all different cases but must be distinguished according to the nature of the proposition that you believe. If you have "I believe p" and "I believe q" those two facts, if p and q are not of the same logical form, are not of the same logical form in the sense I was speaking of a moment ago, that is in the sense that from "I believe p" you can derive "I believe q" by replacing the constituents of one by the constituents of the other. That means that belief itself cannot be treated as being a proper sort of single term. Belief will really have to have different logical forms according to the nature of what is believed. So that the apparent sameness of believing in different cases is more or less illusory.

There are really two main things that one wants to notice in this matter that I am treating of just now. The first is the impossibility of treating the proposition believed as an independent entity, entering as a unit into the occurrence of the belief, and the other is the impossibility of putting the subordinate verb on a level with its terms as an object term in the belief. That is a point in which I think that the theory of judgment which I set forth once in print some years ago was a little unduly simple, because I did then treat the object verb as if one could put it as just an object like the terms, as if one could put "loves" on a level with Desdemona and Cassio as a term for the relation "believe". That is why I have been laying such an emphasis in this lecture today on the fact that there are two verbs at least. I hope you will forgive the fact that so much of what I say today is tentative and consists of pointing out difficulties. The subject is not very easy and it has not been much dealt with or discussed. Practically nobody has until quite lately begun to consider the problem of the nature of belief with anything like a proper logical apparatus and therefore one has very little to help one in any discussion and so one has to be content on many points at present with pointing out difficulties rather than laying down quite clear solutions.

4. *The question of nomenclature.*

What sort of name shall we give to verbs like "believe" and "wish" and so forth? I should be inclined to call them "propositional verbs". This is merely a suggested name for convenience, because they are verbs which have the *form* of relating an object to a proposition. As I have been explaining, that is not what they really do, but it is convenient to call them propositional verbs. Of course you might call them "attitudes", but I should not like that because it is a psychological term, and although all the instances in our experience are psychological, there is no reason to suppose that all the verbs I am talking of are psychological. There is never any reason to suppose that sort of thing. One should always remember Spinoza's infinite attributes of Deity. It is quite likely that there are in the world the analogues of his infinite attributes. We have no acquaintance with them, but there is no reason to suppose that the mental and the physical exhaust the whole universe, so one can never say that all the instances of any logical sort of thing are of such and such a nature which is not a logical nature: you do not know enough about the world for that. Therefore I should not suggest that all the verbs that have the form exemplified by believing and willing are psychological. I can only say all I know are.

I notice that in my syllabus I said I was going to deal with truth and falsehood today, but there is not much to say about them specifically as they are coming in all the time. The thing one first thinks of as true or false is a proposition, and a proposition is nothing. But a belief is true or false in the same way as a proposition is, so that you do have facts in the world that are true or false. I said a while back that there was no distinction of true and false among facts, but as regards that special class of facts that we call "beliefs", there is, in that sense that a belief which occurs may be true or false, though it is equally a fact in either case. One *might* call wishes false in the same sense when one wishes something that does not happen. The truth or falsehood depends upon the proposition that enters in. I am inclined to think that perception, as opposed to belief, does go straight to the fact and not through the proposition. When you perceive the fact you do not, of course, have error coming in, because the moment it is a fact that is your object error is excluded. I think that verification in the last resort would always reduce itself to the perception of facts. Therefore the logical form of perception will be different from the logical form of believing, just because of that circumstance that it is a *fact* that comes in. That raises also a number of logical difficulties which I do not propose to go into, but I think you can see for yourself that perceiving would also involve two verbs just as believing does. I am inclined to think that volition differs from desire logically, in a way strictly analogous to that in which perception differs from belief. But it would take us too far from logic to discuss this view.

V. GENERAL PROPOSITIONS AND EXISTENCE

I am going to speak today about general propositions and existence. The two subjects really belong together; they are the same topic, although it might not have seemed so at the first glance. The propositions and facts that I have been talking about hitherto have all been such as involved only perfectly definite particulars, or relations, or qualities, or things of that sort, never involved the sort of indefinite things one alludes to by such words as "all", "some", "a", "any", and it is propositions and facts of that sort that I am coming on to today.

Really all the propositions of the sort that I mean to talk of today collect themselves into two groups—the first that are about "all", and the second that are about "some". These two sorts belong together; they are each other's negations. If you say, for instance, "All men are mortal", that is the negative of "Some men are not mortal." In regard to general propositions, the distinction of affirmative and negative is arbitrary. Whether you are going to regard the propositions about "all" as the affirmative ones and the propositions about "some" as the negative ones, or vice versa, is purely a matter of taste. For example, if I say "I met no one as I came along", that, on the face of it, you would think is a negative proposition. Of course, that is really a proposition about "all", i.e. "All men are among those whom I did not meet." If, on the other hand, I say "I met a man as I came along", that would strike you as affirmative, whereas it is the negative of "All men are among those I did not meet as I came along." If you consider such propositions as "All men are mortal" and "Some men are not mortal", you might say it was more natural to take the general propositions as the affirmative and the existence-propositions as the negative, but, simply because it is quite arbitrary which one is to choose, it is better to forget these words and to speak only of general propositions and propositions asserting existence. All general propositions deny the existence of something or other. If you say "All men are mortal", that denies the existence of an immortal man, and so on.

I want to say emphatically that general propositions are to be interpreted as not involving existence. When I say, for instance, "All Greeks are men", I do not want you to suppose that that implies that there are Greeks. It is to be considered emphatically as not implying that. That would have to be added as a separate proposition. If you want to interpret it in that sense, you will have to add the further statement "and there are Greeks". That is for purposes of practical convenience. If you include the fact that there are Greeks, you are rolling two propositions into one, and it causes unnecessary confusion in your logic, because the sorts of propositions that you want are those that do assert the existence of something and general propositions which do not assert existence. If it happened that there were no Greeks,

both the proposition that "All Greeks are men" and the proposition that "No Greeks are men" would be true. The proposition "No Greeks are men" is, of course, the proposition "All Greeks are not-men." Both propositions will be true simultaneously if it happens that there are no Greeks. All statements about all the members of a class that has no members are true, because the contradictory of any general statement does assert existence and is therefore false in this case. This notion, of course, of general propositions not involving existence is one which is not in the traditional doctrine of the syllogism. In the traditional doctrine of the syllogism, it was assumed that
10 when you have such a statement as "All Greeks are men", that implies that there are Greeks, and this produced fallacies. For instance, "All chimeras are animals, and all chimeras breathe flame, therefore some animals breathe flame." This is a syllogism in Darapti, but that mood of the syllogism is fallacious, as this instance shows. That was a point, by the way, which had a certain historical interest, because it impeded Leibniz in his attempts to construct a mathematical logic. He was always engaged in trying to construct such a mathematical logic as we have now, or rather such a one as Boole constructed, and he was always failing because of his respect for Aristotle. Whenever he invented a really good system, as he did several
20 times, it always brought out that such moods as Darapti are fallacious. If you say "All A is B and all A is C, therefore some B is C"—if you say this you incur a fallacy, but he could not bring himself to believe that it was fallacious, so he began again. That shows you that you should not have too much respect for distinguished men.[3]

Now when you come to ask what really is asserted in a general proposition, such as "All Greeks are men" for instance, you find that what is asserted is the truth of all values of what I call a propositional function. A *propositional function* is simply *any expression containing an undetermined constituent, or several undetermined constituents, and becoming a proposition as*
30 *soon as the undetermined constituents are determined*. If I say "x is a man" or "n is a number", that is a propositional function; so is any formula of algebra, say $(x+y)(x-y) = x^2-y^2$. A propositional function is nothing, but, like most of the things one wants to talk about in logic, it does not lose its importance through that fact. The only thing really that you can do with a propositional function is to assert either that it is always true, or that it is sometimes true, or that it is never true. If you take:

"If x is a man, x is mortal",

that is always true (just as much when x is not a man as when x is a man); if you take:
40   "x is a man",

3 *Cf.* Couturat, *La Logique de Leibniz.*

that is sometimes true; if you take:

"x is a unicorn",

that is never true.

One may call a propositional function

> *necessary*, when it is always true;
> *possible*, when it is sometimes true;
> *impossible*, when it is never true.

Much false philosophy has arisen out of confusing propositional functions and propositions. There is a great deal in ordinary traditional philosophy which consists simply in attributing to propositions the predi- 10 cates which only apply to propositional functions, and, still worse, sometimes in attributing to individuals predicates which merely apply to propositional functions. This case of *necessary*, *possible*, *impossible*, is a case in point. In all traditional philosophy there comes a heading of "modality", which discusses *necessary*, *possible*, and *impossible* as properties of propositions, whereas in fact they are properties of propositional functions. Propositions are only true or false.

If you take "x is x", that is a propositional function which is true whatever "x" may be, i.e. a necessary propositional function. If you take "x is a man", that is a possible one. If you take "x is a unicorn", that is an 20 impossible one.

Propositions can only be true or false, but propositional functions have these three possibilities. It is important, I think, to realize that the whole doctrine of modality only applies to propositional functions, not to propositions.

Propositional functions are involved in ordinary language in a great many cases where one does not usually realize them. In such a statement as "I met a man", you can understand my statement perfectly well without knowing whom I met, and the actual person is not a constituent of the proposition. You are really asserting there that a certain propositional function is some- 30 times true, namely the propositional function "I met x and x is human." There is at least one value of x for which that is true, and that therefore is a possible propositional function. Whenever you get such words as "a", "some", "all", "every", it is always a mark of the presence of a propositional function, so that these things are not, so to speak, remote or recondite: they are obvious and familiar.

A propositional function comes in again in such a statement as "Socrates is mortal", because "to be mortal" means "to die at some time or other". You mean there is a time at which Socrates dies, and that again involves a propositional function, namely, that "t is a time, and Socrates dies at t" is 40

possible. If you say "Socrates is immortal", that also will involve a propositional function. That means that "If t is any time whatever, Socrates is alive
at time t", if we take immortality as involving existence throughout the
whole of the past as well as throughout the whole of the future. But if we
take immortality as only involving existence throughout the whole of the
future, the interpretation of "Socrates is immortal" becomes more complex, viz., "There is a time t, such that if t' is any time later than t, Socrates
is alive at t'." Thus when you come to write out properly what one means by
a great many ordinary statements, it turns out a little complicated. "Soc-
10 rates is mortal" and "Socrates is immortal" are not each other's contradic-
tories, because they both imply that Socrates exists in time, otherwise he
would not be either mortal or immortal. One says, "There is a time at which
he dies", and the other says, "Whatever time you take, he is alive at that
time", whereas the contradictory of "Socrates is mortal" would be true if
there is not a time at which he lives.

An undetermined constituent in a propositional function is called a
variable.

Existence. When you take any propositional function and assert of it that
it is possible, that it is sometimes true, that gives you the fundamental
20 meaning of "existence". You may express it by saying that there is at least
one value of x for which that propositional function is true. Take "x is a
man", there is at least one value of x for which this is true. That is what one
means by saying that "There are men", or that "Men exist." Existence is
essentially a property of a propositional function. It means that that propositional function is true in at least one instance. If you say "There are
unicorns", that will mean that "There is an x, such that x is a unicorn."
That is written in phrasing which is unduly approximated to ordinary
language, but the proper way to put it would be "(x is a unicorn) is
possible." We have got to have some idea that we do not define, and one
30 takes the idea of "always true", or of "sometimes true", as one's undefined
idea in this matter, and then you can define the other one as the negative of
that. In some ways it is better to take them both as undefined, for reasons
which I shall not go into at present. It will be out of this notion of *sometimes*,
which is the same as the notion of *possible*, that we get the notion of
existence. To say that unicorns exist is simply to say that "(x is a unicorn) is
possible".

It is perfectly clear that when you say "Unicorns exist", you are not saying
anything that would apply to any unicorns there might happen to be,
because as a matter of fact there are not any, and therefore if what you say
40 had any application to the actual individuals, it could not possibly be
significant unless it were true. You can consider the proposition "Unicorns
exist" and can see that it is false. It is not nonsense. Of course, if the
proposition went through the general conception of the unicorn to the

individual, it could not be even significant unless there were unicorns. Therefore when you say "Unicorns exist", you are not saying anything about any individual things, and the same applies when you say "Men exist." If you say that "Men exist, and Socrates is a man, therefore Socrates exists", that is exactly the same sort of fallacy as it would be if you said "Men are numerous, Socrates is a man, therefore Socrates is numerous", because existence is a predicate of a propositional function, or derivatively of a class. When you say of a propositional function that it is numerous, you will mean that there are several values of x that will satisfy it, that there are more than one; or, if you like to take "numerous" in a larger sense, more than ten, more than twenty, or whatever number you think fitting. If x, y, and z all satisfy a propositional function, you may say that that propositional function is numerous, but x, y, and z severally are not numerous. Exactly the same applies to existence, that is to say that the actual things that there are in the world do not exist, or, at least, that is putting it too strongly, because that is utter nonsense. To say that they do not exist is strictly nonsense, but to say that they do exist is also strictly nonsense.

It is of propositional functions that you can assert or deny existence. You must not run away with the idea that this entails consequences that it does not entail. If I say "The things that there are in the world exist", that is a perfectly correct statement, because I am there saying something about a certain class of things; I say it in the same sense in which I say "Men exist." But I must not go on to "This is a thing in the world, and therefore this exists." It is there the fallacy comes in, and it is simply, as you see, a fallacy of transferring to the individual that satisfies a propositional function a predicate which only applies to a propositional function. You can see this in various ways. For instance, you sometimes know the truth of an existence-proposition without knowing any instance of it. You know that there are people in Timbuctoo, but I doubt if any of you could give me an instance of one. Therefore you clearly can know existence-propositions without knowing any individual that makes them true. Existence-propositions do not say anything about the actual individual but only about the class or function.

It is exceedingly difficult to make this point clear as long as one adheres to ordinary language, because ordinary language is rooted in a certain feeling about logic, a certain feeling that our primeval ancestors had, and as long as you keep to ordinary language you find it very difficult to get away from the bias which is imposed upon you by language. When I say, e.g., "There is an x such that x is a man", that is not the sort of phrase one would like to use. "There is an x" is meaningless. What is "an x" anyhow? There is not such a thing. The only way you can really state it correctly is by inventing a new language *ad hoc*, and making the statement apply straight off to "x is a man", as when one says "(x is a man) is possible", or invent a special symbol for the statement that "*x* is a man" is sometimes true.

I have dwelt on this point because it really is of very fundamental importance. I shall come back to existence in my next lecture: existence as it applies to descriptions, which is a slightly more complicated case than I am discussing here. I think an almost unbelievable amount of false philosophy has arisen through not realizing what "existence" means.

As I was saying a moment ago, a propositional function in itself is nothing: it is merely a schema. Therefore in the inventory of the world, which is what I am trying to get at, one comes to the question, What is there really in the world that corresponds with these things? Of course, it is clear that we have general *propositions*, in the same sense in which we have atomic propositions. For the moment I will include existence-propositions with general propositions. We have such propositions as "All men are mortal" and "Some men are Greeks." But you have not only such *propositions*; you have also such *facts*, and that, of course, is where you get back to the inventory of the world: that, in addition to particular facts, which I have been talking about in previous lectures, there are also general facts and existence-facts, that is to say, there are not merely *propositions* of that sort but also *facts* of that sort. That is rather an important point to realize. You cannot ever arrive at a general fact by inference from particular facts, however numerous. The old plan of complete induction, which used to occur in books, which was always supposed to be quite safe and easy as opposed to ordinary induction, that plan of complete induction, unless it is accompanied by at least one general proposition, will not yield you the result that you want. Suppose, for example, that you wish to prove in that way that "All men are mortal", you are supposed to proceed by complete induction, and say "*A* is a man that is mortal", "*B* is a man that is mortal", "*C* is a man that is mortal", and so on until you finish. You will not be able, in that way, to arrive at the proposition "All men are mortal" unless you know when you have finished. That is to say that, in order to arrive by this road at the general proposition "All men are mortal", you must already have the general proposition "All men are among those I have enumerated." You never can arrive at a general proposition by inference from particular propositions alone. You will always have to have at least one general proposition in your premisses. That illustrates, I think, various points. One, which is epistemological, is that if there is, as there seems to be, knowledge of general propositions, then there must be *primitive* knowledge of general propositions (I mean by that, knowledge of general propositions which is not obtained by inference), because if you can never infer a general proposition except from premisses of which one at least is general, it is clear that you can never have knowledge of such propositions by inference unless there is knowledge of some general propositions which is not by inference. I think that the sort of way such knowledge—or rather the belief that we have such knowledge—comes into ordinary life is probably very odd. I mean to say that we do habitually assume general propositions which are exceedingly doubtful; as, for instance, one might, if one were counting up the people in this room, assume that one could see all of them, which is a general proposition, and very doubtful as there may be people under the tables. But, apart from that sort of thing, you do have in any empirical verification of general propositions some kind of assumption that amounts to this, that what you do not see is not there. Of course, you would not put it so strongly as that, but you would assume that, with certain limitations and certain qualifications, if a thing does not appear to your senses, it is not there. That is a general proposition, and it is only through such propositions that you arrive at the ordinary empirical results that one obtains in ordinary ways. If you take a census of the country, for instance, you assume that the people you do not see are not there, provided you search properly and carefully, otherwise your census might be wrong. It is some assumption of that sort which would underlie what seems purely empirical. You could not prove empirically that what you do not perceive is not there, because an empirical proof would consist in perceiving, and by hypothesis you do not perceive it, so that any proposition of that sort, if it is accepted, has to be accepted on its own evidence. I only take that as an illustration. There are many other illustrations one could take of the sort of propositions that are commonly assumed, many of them with very little justification.

I come now to a question which concerns logic more nearly, namely, the reasons for supposing that there are general facts as well as general propositions. When we were discussing molecular propositions I threw doubt upon the supposition that there are molecular facts, but I do not think one can doubt that there are general facts. It is perfectly clear, I think, that when you have enumerated all the atomic facts in the world, it is a further fact about the world that those are all the atomic facts there are about the world, and that is just as much an objective fact about the world as any of them are. It is clear, I think, that you must admit general facts as distinct from and over and above particular facts. The same thing applies to "All men are mortal." When you have taken all the particular men that there are, and found each one of them severally to be mortal, it is definitely a new fact that all men are mortal; how new a fact, appears from what I said a moment ago, that it could not be inferred from the mortality of the several men that there are in the world. Of course, it is not so difficult to admit what I might call existence-facts—such facts as "There are men", "There are sheep", and so on. Those, I think, you will readily admit as separate and distinct facts over and above the atomic facts I spoke of before. Those facts have got to come into the inventory of the world, and in that way propositional functions come in as involved in the study of general facts. I do not profess to know what the right analysis of general facts is. It is an exceedingly difficult question, and one which I should very much like to see studied. I am sure that, although the convenient technical treatment is by means of propositional functions, that is not the whole of the right analysis. Beyond that I cannot go.

There is one point about whether there are molecular facts. I think I mentioned, when I was saying that I did not think there were disjunctive facts, that a certain difficulty does arise in regard to general facts. Take "All men are mortal." That means:

> " 'x is a man' implies
> 'x is a mortal' whatever
> x may be."

You can see at once that it is a hypothetical proposition. It does not imply that there are any men, nor who are men, and who are not; it simply says that if you have anything which is a man, that thing is mortal. As Mr. Bradley has pointed out in the second chapter of his *Principles of Logic*, "Trespassers will be prosecuted" may be true even if no one trespasses, since it means merely that, *if* any one trespasses, he will be prosecuted. It comes down to this that

> " 'x is a man' implies 'x is a mortal'
> is always true,"

is a fact. It is perhaps a little difficult to see how that can be true if one is going to say that " 'Socrates is a man' implies 'Socrates is a mortal' " is not itself a fact, which is what I suggested when I was discussing disjunctive facts. I do not feel sure that you could not get round that difficulty. I only suggest it as a point which should be considered when one is denying that there are molecular facts, since, if it cannot be got round, we shall have to admit molecular facts.

Now I want to come to the subject of *completely general* propositions and propositional functions. By those I mean propositions and propositional functions that contain only variables and nothing else at all. This covers the whole of logic. Every logical proposition consists wholly and solely of variables, though it is not true that every proposition consisting wholly and solely of variables is logical. You can consider stages of generalizations as, e.g.,

> "Socrates loves Plato"
> "x loves Plato"
> "x loves y"
> "x R y".

There you have been going through a process of successive generalization.

When you have got to xRy, you have got a schema consisting only of variables, containing no constants at all, the pure schema of dual relations, and it is clear that any proposition which expresses a dual relation can be derived from xRy by assigning values to x and R and y. So that that is, as you might say, the pure form of all those propositions. I mean by the form of a proposition that which you get when for every single one of its constituents you substitute a variable. If you want a different definition of the form of a proposition, you might be inclined to define it as the class of all those propositions that you can obtain from a given one by substituting other constituents for one or more of the constitutents the proposition contains. E.g., in "Socrates loves Plato", you can substitute somebody else for Socrates, somebody else for Plato, and some other verb for "loves". In that way there are a certain number of propositions which you can derive from the proposition "Socrates loves Plato", by replacing the constituents of that proposition by other constituents, so that you have there a certain class of propositions, and those propositions all have a certain form, and one can, if one likes, say that the form they all have is the class consisting of all of them. That is rather a provisional definition, because as a matter of fact, the idea of form is more fundamental than the idea of class. I should not suggest that as a really good definition, but it will do provisionally to explain the sort of thing one means by the form of a proposition. The form of a proposition is that which is in common between any two propositions of which the one can be obtained from the other by substituting other constituents for the original ones. When you have got down to those formulas that contain only variables, like xRy, you are on the way to the sort of thing that you can assert in logic.

To give an illustration, you know what I mean by the domain of a relation: I mean all the terms that have that relation to something. Suppose I say: "xRy implies that x belongs to the domain of R", that would be a proposition of logic and is one that contains only variables. You might think it contains such words as "belong" and "domain", but that is an error. It is only the habit of using ordinary language that makes those words appear. They are not really there. That is a proposition of pure logic. It does not mention any particular thing at all. This is to be understood as being asserted whatever x and R and y may be. All the statements of logic are of that sort.

It is not a very easy thing to see what are the constituents of a logical proposition. When one takes "Socrates loves Plato", "Socrates" is a constituent, "loves" is a constituent, and "Plato" is a constituent. Then you turn "Socrates" into x, "loves" into R, and "Plato" into y. x and R and y are nothing, and they are not constituents, so it seems as though all the propositions of logic were entirely devoid of constituents. I do not think that can quite be true. But then the only other thing you can seem to say is that the *form* is a constituent, that propositions of a certain form are always true: that *may* be the right analysis, though I very much doubt whether it is.

There is, however, just this to observe, viz., that the form of a proposition is never a constituent of that proposition itself. If you assert that "Socrates loves Plato", the form of that proposition is the form of the dual relation, but this is not a constituent of the proposition. If it were you would have to have that constituent related to the other constituents. You will make the form much too substantial if you think of it as really one of the things that have that form, so that the form of a proposition is certainly not a constituent of the proposition itself. Nevertheless it may possibly be a constituent of general statements about propositions that have that form, so I think it is *possible that* logical propositions might be interpreted as being about forms.

I can only say, in conclusion, as regards the constituents of logical propositions, that it is a problem which is rather new. There has not been much opportunity to consider it. I do not think any literature exists at all which deals with it in any way whatever, and it is an interesting problem.

I just want now to give you a few illustrations of propositions which can be expressed in the language of pure variables but are not propositions of logic. Among the propositions that are propositions of logic are included all the propositions of pure mathematics, all of which cannot only be expressed in logical terms but can also be deduced from the premises of logic, and therefore they are logical propositions. Apart from them there are many that can be expressed in logical terms, but cannot be proved from logic, and are certainly not propositions that form part of logic. Suppose you take such a proposition as: "There is at least one thing in the world." That is a proposition that you can express in logical terms. It will mean, if you like, that the propositional function "$x = x$" is a possible one. That is a proposition, therefore, that you can express in logical terms; but you cannot know from logic whether it is true or false. So far as you do know it, you know it empirically, because there might happen not to be a universe, and then it would not be true. It is merely an accident, so to speak, that there is a universe. The proposition that there are exactly 30,000 things in the world can also be expressed in purely logical terms, and is certainly not a proposition of logic but an empirical proposition (true or false), because a world containing more than 30,000 things and a world containing fewer than 30,000 things are both possible, so that if it happens that there are exactly 30,000 things, that is what one might call an accident and is not a proposition of logic. There are again two propositions that one is used to in mathematical logic, namely, the multiplicative axiom and the axiom of infinity. These also can be expressed in logical terms, but cannot be proved or disproved by logic. In regard to the axiom of infinity, the impossibility of logical proof or disproof may be taken as certain, but in the case of the multiplicative axiom, it is perhaps still open to some degree to doubt.

Everything that is a proposition of logic has got to be in some sense or other like a tautology. It has got to be something that has some peculiar quality, which I do not know how to define, that belongs to logical propositions and not to others. Examples of typical logical propositions are:

"If p implies q and q implies r, then p implies r."
"If all a's are b's and all b's are c's, then all a's are c's."
"If all a's are b's, and x is an a, then x is a b."

Those are propositions of logic. They have a certain peculiar quality which marks them out from other propositions and enables us to know them a priori. But what exactly that characteristic is, I am not able to tell you. Although it is a necessary characteristic of logical propositions that they should consist solely of variables, i.e. that they should assert the universal truth, or the sometimes-truth, of a propositional function consisting wholly of variables—although that is a necessary characteristic, it is not a sufficient one.

I am sorry that I have had to leave so many problems unsolved. I always have to make this apology, but the world really is rather puzzling and I cannot help it.

DISCUSSION

Q.: Is there any word you would substitute for "existence" which would give existence to individuals? Are you applying the word "existence" to two ideas, or do you deny that there are two ideas?
Mr. Russell: No, there is not an idea that will apply to individuals. As regards the actual things there are in the world, there is nothing at all you can say about them that in any way corresponds to this notion of existence. It is a sheer mistake to say that there is anything analogous to existence that you can say about them. You get into confusion through language, because it is a perfectly correct thing to say "All the things in the world exist", and it is so easy to pass from this to "This exists because it is a thing in the world." There is no sort of point in a predicate which could not conceivably be false. I mean, it is perfectly clear that, if there were such a thing as this existence of individuals that we talk of, it would be absolutely impossible for it not to apply, and that is the characteristic of a mistake.

VI. DESCRIPTIONS AND INCOMPLETE SYMBOLS

I am proposing to deal this time with the subject of descriptions, and what I call "incomplete symbols", and the existence of described individuals. You will remember that last time I dealt with the existence of *kinds* of things, what you mean by saying "There are men" or "There are Greeks" or phrases of that sort, where you have an existence which may be plural. I am going to deal today with an existence which is asserted to be singular, such as "The man with the iron mask existed" or some phrase of that sort, where you have some object described by the phrase "The so-and-so" in the singular, and I want to discuss the analysis of propositions in which phrases of that kind occur.

There are, of course, a great many propositions very familiar in metaphysics which are of that sort: "I exist" or "God exists" or "Homer existed", and other such statements are always occurring in metaphysical discussions, and are, I think, treated in ordinary metaphysics in a way which embodies a simple logical mistake that we shall be concerned with today, the same sort of mistake that I spoke of last week in connection with the existence of kinds of things. One way of examining a proposition of that sort is to ask yourself what would happen if it were false. If you take such a proposition as "Romulus existed", probably most of us think that Romulus did not exist. It is obviously a perfectly significant statement, whether true or false, to say that Romulus existed. If Romulus himself entered into our statement, it would be plain that the statement that he did not exist would be nonsense, because you cannot have a constituent of a proposition which is nothing at all. Every constituent has got to be there as one of the things in the world, and therefore if Romulus himself entered into the propositions that he existed or that he did not exist, both these propositions could not only not be true, but could not be even significant, unless he existed. That is obviously not the case, and the first conclusion one draws is that, although it *looks* as if Romulus were a constituent of that proposition, that is really a mistake. Romulus does not occur in the proposition "Romulus did not exist."

Suppose you try to make out what you do mean by that proposition. You can take, say, all the things that Livy has to say about Romulus, all the properties he ascribes to him, including the only one probably that most of us remember, namely, the fact that he was called "Romulus". You can put all this together, and make a propositional function saying "x has such-and-such properties", the properties being those you find enumerated in Livy. There you have a propositional function, and when you say that Romulus did not exist you are simply saying that that propositional function is never true, that it is impossible in the sense I was explaining last time, i.e. that there is no value of x that makes it true. That reduces the non-existence of Romulus to the sort of non-existence I spoke of last time, where we had the non-existence of unicorns. But it is not a *complete* account of this kind of existence or non-existence, because there is one other way in which a described individual can fail to exist, and that is where the description applies to more than one person. You cannot, e.g., speak of "*The* inhabitant of London", not because there are none, but because there are so many.

You see, therefore, that this proposition "Romulus existed" or "Romulus did not exist" does introduce a propositional function, because the name "Romulus" is not really a name but a sort of truncated description. It stands for a person who did such-and-such things, who killed Remus, and founded Rome, and so on. It is short for that description; if you like, it is short for "the person who was called 'Romulus'". If it were really a name, the question of existence could not arise, because a name has got to name something or it is not a name, and if there is no such person as Romulus there cannot be a name for that person who is not there, so that this single word "Romulus" is really a sort of truncated or telescoped description, and if you think of it as a name you will get into logical errors. When you realize that it is a description, you realize therefore that any proposition about Romulus really introduces the propositional function embodying the description, as (say) "x was called 'Romulus'." That introduces you at once to a propositional function, and when you say "Romulus did not exist", you mean that this propositional function is not true for one value of x.

There are two sorts of descriptions, what one may call "ambiguous descriptions", when we speak of "a so-and-so", and what one may call "definite descriptions", when we speak of "the so-and-so" (in the singular). Instances are:

Ambiguous: A man, a dog, a pig, a Cabinet Minister.
Definite: The man with the iron mask.
                  The last person who came into this room.
                  The only Englishman who ever occupied the Papal See.
                  The number of the inhabitants of London.
                  The sum of 43 and 34.

(It is not necessary for a description that it should describe an individual: it may describe a predicate or a relation or anything else.)

It is phrases of that sort, definite descriptions, that I want to talk about today. I do not want to talk about ambiguous descriptions, as what there was to say about them was said last time.

I want you to realize that the question whether a phrase is a definite description turns only upon its form, not upon the question whether there is a definite individual so described. For instance, I should call "The inhabitant of London" a definite description, although it does not in fact describe any definite individual.

The first thing to realize about a definite description is that it is not a name. We will take "The author of *Waverley*". That is a definite description, and it is easy to see that it is not a name. A name is a simple symbol (i.e. a symbol which does not have any parts that are symbols), a simple symbol

used to designate a certain particular or by extension an object which is not a particular but is treated for the moment as if it were, or is falsely believed to be a particular, such as a person. This sort of phrase, "The author of *Waverley*", is not a name because it is a complex symbol. It contains parts which *are* symbols. It contains four words, and the meanings of those four words are already fixed and they have fixed the meaning of "The author of *Waverley*" in the only sense in which that phrase does have any meaning. In that sense, its meaning is already determinate, i.e. there is nothing arbitrary or conventional about the meaning of that whole phrase, when the meanings
10 of "the", "author", "of", and "*Waverley*" have already been fixed. In that respect, it differs from "Scott", because when you have fixed the meaning of all the other words in the language, you have done nothing toward fixing the meaning of the name "Scott". That is to say, if you understand the English language, you would understand the meaning of the phrase "The author of *Waverley*" if you had never heard it before, whereas you would not understand the meaning of "Scott" if you had never heard the word before because to know the meaning of a name is to know who it is applied to.

You sometimes find people speaking as if descriptive phrases were names, and you will find it suggested, e.g., that such a proposition as "Scott
20 is the author of *Waverley*" really asserts that "Scott" and "the author of *Waverley*" are two names for the same person. That is an entire delusion; first of all, because "the author of *Waverley*" is not a name, and, secondly, because, as you can perfectly well see, if that were what is meant, the proposition would be one like "Scott is Sir Walter", and would not depend upon any fact except that the person in question was so called, because a name is what a man is called. As a matter of fact, Scott was the author of *Waverley* at a time when no one called him so, when no one knew whether he was or not, and the fact that he was the author was a physical fact, the fact that he sat down and wrote it with his own hand, which does not have
30 anything to do with what he was called. It is in no way arbitrary. You cannot settle by any choice of nomenclature whether he is or is not to be the author of *Waverley*, because in actual fact he chose to write it and you cannot help yourself. That illustrates how "the author of *Waverley*" is quite a different thing from a name. You can prove this point very clearly by formal arguments. In "Scott is the author of *Waverley*" the "is", of course, expresses identity, i.e. the entity whose name is Scott is identical with the author of *Waverley*. But, when I say "Scott is mortal" this "is" is the "is" of predication, which is quite different from the "is" of identity. It is a mistake to interpret "Scott is mortal" as meaning "Scott is identical with one among
40 mortals", because (among other reasons) you will not be able to say what "mortals" are except by means of the propositional function "x is mortal", which brings back the "is" of predication. You cannot reduce the "is" of predication to the other "is". But the "is" in "Scott is the author of

Waverley" is the "is" of identity and not of predication.[4]

If you were to try to substitute for "the author of *Waverley*" in that proposition any name whatever, say "*c*", so that the proposition becomes "Scott is *c*", then if "*c*" is a name for anybody who is not Scott, that proposition would become false, while if, on the other hand, "*c*" is a name for Scott, then the proposition will become simply a tautology. It is at once obvious that if "*c*" were "Scott" itself, "Scott is Scott" is just a tautology. But if you take any other name which is just a name for Scott, then if the name is being used *as* a name and not as a description, the proposition will still be a tautology. For the name itself is merely a means of pointing to the thing, and does not occur in what you are asserting, so that if one thing has two names, you make exactly the same assertion whichever of the two names you use, provided they are really names and not truncated descriptions.

So there are only two alternatives. If "*c*" is a name, the proposition "Scott is *c*" is either false or tautologous. But the proposition "Scott is the author of *Waverley*" is neither, and therefore is not the same as any proposition of the form "Scott is *c*", where "*c*" is a name. That is another way of illustrating the fact that a description is quite a different thing from a name.

I should like to make clear what I was saying just now, that if you substitute another name in place of "Scott" which is also a name of the same individual, say, "Scott is Sir Walter", then "Scott" and "Sir Walter" are being used as names and not as descriptions, your proposition is strictly a tautology. If one asserts "Scott is Sir Walter", the way one would mean it would be that one was using the names as descriptions. One would mean that the person called "Scott" is the person called "Sir Walter", and "the person called 'Scott'" is a description, and so is "the person called 'Sir Walter'". So that would not be a tautology. It would mean that the person called "Scott" is identical with the person called "Sir Walter". But if you are using both as names, the matter is quite different. You must observe that the name does not occur in that which you assert when you use the name. The name is merely that which is a means of expressing what it is you are trying to assert, and when I say "Scott wrote *Waverley*", the name "Scott" does not occur in the thing I am asserting. The thing I am asserting is about the person, not about the name. So if I say "Scott is Sir Walter", using these two names *as* names, neither "Scott" nor "Sir Walter" occurs in what I am asserting, but only the person who has these names, and thus what I am asserting is a pure tautology.

It is rather important to realize this about the two different uses of names or of any other symbols: the one when you are talking about the symbol and the other when you are using it *as* a symbol, as a means of talking about

4 The confusion of these two meanings of "is" is essential to the Hegelian conception of identity-in-difference.

something else. Normally, if you talk about your dinner, you are not talking about the word "dinner" but about what you are going to eat, and that is a different thing altogether. The ordinary use of words is as a means of getting through to things, and when you are using words in that way the statement "Scott is Sir Walter" is a pure tautology, exactly on the same level as "Scott is Scott."

That brings me back to the point that when you take "Scott is the author of *Waverley*" and you substitute for "the author of *Waverley*" a name in the place of a description, you get necessarily either a tautology or a
10 falsehood—a tautology if you substitute "Scott" or some other name for the same person, and a falsehood if you substitute anything else. But the proposition itself is neither a tautology nor a falsehood, and that shows you that the proposition "Scott is the author of *Waverley*" is a different proposition from any that can be obtained if you substitute a name in the place of "the author of *Waverley*". That conclusion is equally true of any other proposition in which the phrase "the author of *Waverley*" occurs. If you take any proposition in which that phrase occurs and substitute for that phrase a proper name, whether that name be "Scott" or any other, you will get a different proposition. Generally speaking, if the name that you sub-
20 stitute is "Scott", your proposition, if it was true before will remain true, and if it was false before will remain false. But it is a *different* proposition. It is not *always* true that it will remain true or false, as may be seen by the example: "George IV wished to know if Scott was the author of *Waverley*." It is not true that George IV wished to know if Scott was Scott. So it is even the case that the truth or the falsehood of a proposition is sometimes changed when you substitute a name of an object for a description of the same object. But in any case it is always a different proposition when you substitute a name for a description.

Identity is a rather puzzling thing at first sight. When you say "Scott is the
30 author of *Waverley*", you are half-tempted to think there are two people, one of whom is Scott and the other the author of *Waverley*, and they happen to be the same. That is obviously absurd, but that is the sort of way one is always tempted to deal with identity.

When I say "Scott is the author of *Waverley*" and that "is" expresses identity, the reason that identity can be asserted there truly and without tautology is just the fact that the one is a name and the other a description. Or they might both be descriptions. If I say "The author of *Waverley* is the author of *Marmion*", that, of course, asserts identity between two descriptions.
40   Now the next point that I want to make clear is that when a description (when I say "description" I mean, for the future, a *definite* description) occurs in a proposition, there is no constituent of that proposition corresponding to that description as a whole. In the true analysis of the proposi-

tion, the description is broken up and disappears. That is to say, when I say "Scott is the author of *Waverley*" it is a wrong analysis of that to suppose that you have there three constituents, "Scott", "is", and "the author of *Waverley*". That, of course, is the sort of way you might think of analyzing. You might admit that "the author of *Waverley*" was complex and could be further cut up, but you might think the proposition could be split into those three bits to begin with. That is an entire mistake. "The author of *Waverley*" is not a constituent of the proposition at all. There is no constituent really there corresponding to the descriptive phrase. I will try to prove that to you now.

The first and most obvious reason is that you can have significant propositions denying the existence of "the so-and-so". "The unicorn does not exist." "The greatest finite number does not exist." Propositions of that sort are perfectly significant, are perfectly sober, true, decent propositions, and that could not possibly be the case if the unicorn were a constituent of the proposition, because plainly it could not be a constituent as long as there were not any unicorns. Because the constituents of propositions, of course, are the same as the constituents of the corresponding facts, and since it is a fact that the unicorn does not exist, it is perfectly clear that the unicorn is not a constituent of that fact, because if there were any fact of which the unicorn was a constituent, there would be a unicorn, and it would not be true that it did not exist. That applies in this case of descriptions particularly. Now since it is possible for "the so-and-so" not to exist and yet for propositions in which "the so-and-so" occurs to be significant and even true, we must try to see what is meant by saying that the so-and-so does exist.

The occurrence of tense in verbs is an exceedingly annoying vulgarity due to our preoccupation with practical affairs. It would be much more agreeable if they had no tense, as I believe is the case in Chinese, but I do not know Chinese. You ought to be able to say "Socrates exists in the past", "Socrates exists in the present" or "Socrates exists in the future", or simply "Socrates exists", without any implication of tense, but language does not allow that, unfortunately. Nevertheless, I am going to use language in this tenseless way: when I say "The so-and-so exists", I am not going to mean that it exists in the present or in the past or in the future, but simply that it exists, without implying anything involving tense.

"The author of *Waverley* exists": there are two things required for that. First of all, what is "the author of *Waverley*"? It is the person who wrote *Waverley*, i.e. we are coming now to this, that you have a propositional function involved, viz., "x.writes *Waverley*", and the author of *Waverley* is the person who writes *Waverley*, and in order that the person who writes *Waverley* may exist, it is necessary that this propositional function should have two properties:

1. It must be true for *at least* one *x*.
2. It must be true for *at most* one *x*.

If nobody had ever written *Waverley* the author could not exist, and if two people had written it, *the* author could not exist. So that you want these two properties, the one that it is true for at least one *x*, and the other that it is true for at most one *x*, both of which are required for existence.

The property of being true for at least one *x* is the one we dealt with last time: what I expressed by saying that the propositional function is *possible*. Then we come on to the second condition, that it is true for at most one *x*,
10 and that you can express in this way: "If *x* and *y* wrote *Waverley*, then *x* is identical with *y*, whatever *x* and *y* may be." That says that at most one wrote it. It does not say that anybody wrote *Waverley* at all, because if nobody had written it, that statement would still be true. It only says that at most one person wrote it.

The first of these conditions for existence fails in the case of the unicorn, and the second in the case of the inhabitant of London.

We can put these two conditions together and get a portmanteau expression including the meaning of both. You can reduce them both down to this, that: "('*x* wrote *Waverley*' is equivalent to '*x* is *c*' whatever *x* may be) is
20 possible in respect of *c*." That is as simple, I think, as you can make the statement.

You see that means to say that there is some entity *c*, we may not know what it is, which is such that when *x* is *c*, it is true that *x* wrote *Waverley*, and when *x* is not *c*, it is not true that *x* wrote *Waverley*, which amounts to saying that *c* is the only person who wrote *Waverley*; and I say there is a value of *c* which makes that true. So that this whole expression, which is a propositional function about *c*, is *possible* in respect of *c* (in the sense explained last time).

That is what I mean when I say that the author of *Waverley* exists. When I
30 say "the author of *Waverley* exists", I mean that there is an entity *c* such that "*x* wrote *Waverley*" is true when *x* is *c*, and is false when *x* is not *c*. "The author of *Waverley*" as a constituent has quite disappeared there, so that when I say "The author of *Waverley* exists" I am not saying anything about the author of *Waverley*. You have instead this elaborate to-do with propositional functions, and "the author of *Waverley*" has disappeared. That is why it is possible to say significantly "The author of *Waverley* did not exist." It would not be possible if "the author of *Waverley*" were a constituent of propositions in whose verbal expression this descriptive phrase occurs.

The fact that you can discuss the proposition "God exists" is a proof that
40 "God", as used in that proposition, is a description and not a name. If "God" were a name, no question as to existence could arise.

I have now defined what I mean by saying that a thing described exists. I have still to explain what I mean by saying that a thing described has a certain property. Supposing you want to say "The author of *Waverley* was human", that will be represented thus: "('*x* wrote *Waverley*' is equivalent to '*x* is *c*' whatever *x* may be, and *c* is human) is possible with respect to *c*."

You will observe that what we gave before as the meaning of "The author of *Waverley* exists" is part of this proposition. It is part of any proposition in which "the author of *Waverley*" has what I call a "primary occurrence". When I speak of a "primary occurrence" I mean that you are not having a proposition about the author of *Waverley* occurring as a part of some larger proposition, such as "I believe that the author of *Waverley* was human" or "I believe that the author of *Waverley* exists." When it is a primary occurrence, i.e. when the proposition concerning it is not just part of a larger proposition, the phrase which we defined as the meaning of "The author of *Waverley* exists" will be part of that proposition. If I say the author of *Waverley* was human, or a poet, or a Scotsman, or whatever I say about the author of *Waverley* in the way of a primary occurrence, always this statement of his existence is part of the proposition. In that sense all these propositions that I make about the author of *Waverley* imply that the author of *Waverley* exists. So that any statement in which a description has a primary occurrence implies that the object described exists. If I say "The present King of France is bald", that implies that the present King of France exists. If I say, "The present King of France has a fine head of hair", that also implies that the present King of France exists. Therefore unless you understand how a proposition containing a description is to be denied, you will come to the conclusion that it is not true either that the present King of France is bald or that he is not bald, because if you were to enumerate all the things that are bald you would not find him there, and if you were to enumerate all the things that are not bald, you would not find him there either. The only suggestion I have found for dealing with that on conventional lines is to suppose that he wears a wig. You can only avoid the hypothesis that he wears a wig by observing that the denial of the proposition "The present King of France is bald" will not be "The present King of France is not bald", if you mean by that "There is such a person as the King of France and that person is not bald." The reason for this is that when you state that the present King of France is bald you say "There is a *c* such that *c* is now King of France and *c* is bald" and the denial is not "There is a *c* such that *c* is now King of France and *c* is not bald." It is more complicated. It is: "Either there is not a *c* such that *c* is now King of France, or, if there is such a *c*, then *c* is not bald." Therefore you see that, if you want to deny the proposition "The present King of France is bald", you can do it by denying that he exists, instead of by denying that he is bald. In order to deny this statement that the present King of France is bald, which is a statement consisting of two parts, you can proceed by denying either part. You can deny the one part, which would lead you to suppose that the present King of France exists but is not bald, or the other part, which will lead you to the denial that the present King of France exists; and either of those two denials will lead you to the falsehood of the proposition "The present King of France is bald." When you say "Scott is human" there is no possibility of a double denial. The only way you can deny "Scott is human" is by saying "Scott is not human." But where a descriptive phrase occurs, you do have the double possibility of denial.

It is of the utmost importance to realize that "the so-and-so" does not
10 occur in the analysis of propositions in whose verbal expression it occurs, that when I say "The author of *Waverley* is human", "the author of *Waverley*" is not the subject of that proposition, in the sort of way that Scott would be if I said "Scott is human", using "Scott" as a name. I cannot emphasize sufficiently how important this point is, and how much error you get into metaphysics if you do not realize that when I say "The author of *Waverley* is human" that is not a proposition of the same form as "Scott is human." It does not contain a constituent "the author of *Waverley*". The importance of that is very great for many reasons, and one of them is this question of existence. As I pointed out to you last time, there is a vast
20 amount of philosophy that rests upon the notion that existence is, so to speak, a property that you can attribute to things, and that the things that exist have the property of existence and the things that do not exist do not. That is rubbish, whether you take kinds of things, or individual things described. When I say, e.g., "Homer existed", I am meaning by "Homer" some description, say "the author of the Homeric poems", and I am asserting that those poems were written by one man, which is a very doubtful proposition; but if you could get hold of the actual person who did actually write those poems (supposing there was such a person), to say of him that he existed would be uttering nonsense, not a falsehood but non-
30 sense, because it is only of persons described that it can be significantly said that they exist. Last time I pointed out the fallacy in saying "Men exist, Socrates is a man, therefore Socrates exists." When I say "Homer exists, this is Homer, therefore this exists", that is a fallacy of the same sort. It is an entire mistake to argue: "This is the author of the Homeric poems and the author of the Homeric poems exists, therefore this exists." It is only where a propositional function comes in that existence may be significantly asserted. You can assert "The so-and-so exists", meaning that there is just one *c* which has those properties, but when you get hold of a *c* that has them, you cannot say of this *c* that it exists, because that is nonsense: it is not false, but
40 it has no meaning at all.

So the individuals that there are in the world do not exist, or rather it is nonsense to say that they exist and nonsense to say that they do not exist. It is not a thing you can say when you have named them, but only when you have described them. When you say "Homer exists", you mean "Homer" is a description which applies to something. A description when it is fully stated is always of the form "the so-and-so".

The sort of things that are like these descriptions in that they occur in words in a proposition, but are not in actual fact constituents of the proposition rightly analyzed, things of that sort I call "incomplete symbols". There are a great many sorts of incomplete symbols in logic, and they are sources of a great deal of confusion and false philosophy, because people get misled by grammar. You think that the proposition "Scott is mortal" and the proposition "The author of *Waverley* is mortal" are of the same form. You think that they are both simple propositions attributing a predicate to a subject. That is an entire delusion: one of them is (or rather might be) and one of them is not. These things, like "the author of *Waverley*", which I call incomplete symbols, are things that have absolutely no meaning whatsoever in isolation but merely acquire a meaning in a context. "Scott" taken as a name has a meaning all by itself. It stands for a certain person, and there it is. But "the author of *Waverley*" is not a name, and does not all by itself mean anything at all, because when it is rightly used in propositions, those propositions do not contain any constituent corresponding to it.

There are a great many other sorts of incomplete symbols besides descriptions. These are classes, which I shall speak of next time, and relations taken in extension, and so on. Such aggregations of symbols are really the same thing as what I call "logical fictions", and they embrace practically all the familiar objects of daily life: tables, chairs, Piccadilly, Socrates, and so on. Most of them are either classes, or series, or series of classes. In any case they are all incomplete symbols, i.e. they are aggregations that only have a meaning in use and do not have any meaning in themselves.

It is important, if you want to understand the analysis of the world, or the analysis of facts, or if you want to have any idea what there really is in the world, to realize how much of what there is in phraseology is of the nature of incomplete symbols. You can see that very easily in the case of "the author of *Waverley*" because "the author of *Waverley*" does not stand simply for Scott, nor for anything else. If it stood for Scott, "Scott is the author of *Waverley*" would be the same proposition as "Scott is Scott", which it is not, since George IV wished to know the truth of the one and did not wish to know the truth of the other. If "the author of *Waverley*" stood for anything other than Scott, "Scott is the author of *Waverley*" would be false, which it is not. Hence you have to conclude that "the author of *Waverley*" does not, in isolation, really stand for anything at all; and that is the characteristic of incomplete symbols.

VII. THE THEORY OF TYPES AND SYMBOLISM: CLASSES

Before I begin today the main subject of my lecture, I should like to make a few remarks in explanation and amplification of what I have said about existence in my previous two lectures. This is chiefly on account of a letter I have received from a member of the class, raising many points which, I think, were present in other minds too.

The first point I wish to clear up is this: I did not mean to say that when one says a thing exists, one means the same as when one says it is possible. What I meant was, that the fundamental logical idea, the primitive idea, out of which both those are derived is the same. That is not quite the same thing as to say that the statement that a thing exists is the same as the statement that it is possible, which I do not hold. I used the word "possible" in perhaps a somewhat strange sense, because I wanted some word for a fundamental logical idea for which no word exists in ordinary language, and therefore if one is to try to express in ordinary language the idea in question, one has to take some word and make it convey the sense that I was giving to the word "possible", which is by no means the only sense that it has but is a sense that was convenient for my purpose. We say of a propositional function that it is possible, where there are cases in which it is true. That is not exactly the same thing as what one ordinarily means, for instance, when one says that it is possible it may rain tomorrow. But what I contend is, that the ordinary uses of the word "possible" are derived from this notion by a process. E.g., normally when you say of a proposition that it is possible, you mean something like this: first of all it is implied that you do not know whether it is true or false, and I think it is implied; secondly, that it is one of a class of propositions, some of which are known to be true. When I say, e.g., "It is possible that it may rain tomorrow"—"It will rain tomorrow" is one of the class of propositions "It rains at time t", where t is different times. We mean partly that we do not know whether it will rain or whether it will not, but also that we do know that that is the sort of proposition that is quite apt to be true, that it is a value of a propositional function of which we know some value to be true. Many of the ordinary uses of "possible" come under that head, I think you will find. That is to say, that if you say of a proposition that it is possible, what you have is this: "There is in this proposition some constituent, which, if you turn it into a variable, will give you a propositional function that is sometimes true." You ought not therefore to say of a proposition simply that it is possible, but rather that it is possible in respect of such-and-such a constituent. That would be a more full expression.

When I say, for instance, that "Lions exist", I do not mean the same as if I said that lions were possible; because when you say "Lions exist", that means that the propositional function "x is a lion" is a possible one in the sense that there are lions, while when you say "Lions are possible" that is a different sort of statement altogether, not meaning that a casual individual animal may be a lion, but rather that a *sort* of animal may be the *sort* that we call "lions". If you say "Unicorns are possible", e.g., you would mean that you do not know any reason why there should not be unicorns, which is quite a different proposition from "Unicorns exist." As to what you would mean by saying that unicorns are possible, it would always come down to the same thing as "It is possible it may rain tomorrow." You would mean, the proposition "There are unicorns" is one of a certain set of propositions some of which are known to be true, and that the description of the unicorn does not contain in it anything that *shows* there could not be such beasts.   10

When I say a propositional function is possible, meaning there are cases in which it is true, I am consciously using the word "possible" in an unusual sense, because I want a single word for my fundamental idea, and cannot find any word in ordinary language that expresses what I mean.

Secondly, it is suggested that when one says a thing exists, it means that it is in time, or in time and space, at any rate in time. That is a very common suggestion, but I do not think that really there is much to be said for that use of the words; in the first place, because if that were all you meant, there would be no need for a separate word. In the second place, because after all in the sense, whatever that sense may be, in which the things are said to exist   20 that one ordinarily regards as existing, one may very well wish to discuss the question whether there are things that exist without being in time. Orthodox metaphysics hold that whatever is really real is not in time, that to be in time is to be more or less unreal, and that what really exists is not in time at all. And orthodox theology holds that God is not in time. I see no reason why you should frame your definition of existence in such a way as to preclude that notion of existence. I am inclined to think that there are things that are not in time, and I should be sorry to use the word existence in that sense when you have already the phrase "being in time" which quite sufficiently expresses what you mean.   30

Another objection to that definition is, that it does not in the least fit the sort of use of "existence" which was underlying my discussion, which is the common one in mathematics. When you take existence-theorems, for instance, as when you say "An even prime exists", you do not mean that the number two is in time but that you can find a number of which you can say "This is even and prime." One does ordinarily in mathematics speak of propositions of that sort as existence-theorems, i.e. you establish that there is an object of such-and-such a sort, that object being, of course, in mathematics a logical object, not a particular, not a thing like a lion or a unicorn, but an object like a function or a number, something which plainly   40 does not have the property of being in time at all, and it is that sort of sense of existence-theorems that is relevant in discussing the meaning of existence as I was doing in the last two lectures. I do, of course, hold that that sense of existence can be carried on to cover the more ordinary uses of existence, and does in fact give the key to what is underlying those ordinary uses, as when one says that "Homer existed" or "Romulus did not exist", or whatever we may say of that kind.

I come now to a third suggestion about existence, which is also a not uncommon one, that of a given particular "this" you can say "This exists" in the sense that it is not a phantom or an image or a universal. Now I think that use of existence involves confusions which it is exceedingly important to get out of one's mind, really rather dangerous mistakes. In the first place, we must separate phantoms and images from universals; they are on a different level. Phantoms and images do undoubtedly exist in that sense, whatever it is, in which ordinary objects exist. I mean, if you shut your eyes and imagine some visual scene, the images that are before your mind while you are imagining are undoubtedly there. They are images, something is happening, and what is happening is that the images are before your mind, and these images are just as much part of the world as tables and chairs and anything else. They are perfectly decent objects, and you only call them unreal (if you call them so), or treat them as non-existent, because they do not have the usual sort of relations to other objects. If you shut your eyes and imagine a visual scene and you stretch out your hand to touch what is imaged, you won't get a tactile sensation, or even necessarily a tactile image. You will not get the usual correlation of sight and touch. If you imagine a heavy oak table, you can remove it without any muscular effort, which is not the case with oak tables that you actually see. The general correlations of your images are quite different from the correlations of what one chooses to call "real" objects. But that is not to say images are unreal. It is only to say they are not part of physics. Of course, I know that this belief in the physical world has established a sort of reign of terror. You have got to treat with disrespect whatever does not fit into the physical world. But that is really very unfair to the things that do not fit in. They are just as much there as the things that do. The physical world is a sort of governing aristocracy, which has somehow managed to cause everything else to be treated with disrespect. That sort of attitude is unworthy of a philosopher. We should treat with exactly equal respect the things that do not fit in with the physical world, and images are among them.

"Phantoms", I suppose, are intended to differ from "images" by being of the nature of hallucinations, things that are not merely imagined but that go with belief. They again are perfectly real; the only odd thing about them is their correlations. Macbeth sees a dagger. If he tried to touch it, he would not get any tactile sensation, but that does not imply that he was not *seeing* a dagger, it only implies that he was not *touching* it. It does not in any way imply that the visual sensation was not there. It only means to say that the sort of correlation between sight and touch that we are used to is the normal rule but not a universal one. In order to pretend that it is universal, we say that a thing is unreal when it does not fit in. You say "Any man who is a man will do such-and-such a thing." You then find a man who will not, and you say, he is not a man. That is just the same sort of thing as with these daggers that you cannot touch.

I have explained elsewhere the sense in which phantoms are unreal.[5] When you see a "real" man, the immediate object that you see is one of a whole system of particulars, all of which belong together and make up collectively the various "appearances" of the man to himself and others. On the other hand, when you see a phantom of a man, that is an isolated particular, not fitting into a system as does a particular which one calls an appearance of the "real" man. The phantom is in itself just as much part of the world as the normal sense-datum, but it lacks the usual correlation and therefore gives rise to false inferences and becomes deceptive.

As to universals, when I say of a particular that it exists, I certainly do not mean the same thing as if I were to say that it is not a universal. The statement concerning any particular that it is not a universal is quite strictly nonsense—not false, but strictly and exactly nonsense. You never can place a particular in the sort of place where a universal ought to be, and vice versa. If I say "a is not b", or if I say "a is b", that implies that a and b are of the same logical type. When I say of a universal that it exists, I should be meaning it in a different sense from that in which one says that particulars exist. E.g., you might say "Colours exist in the spectrum between blue and yellow." That would be a perfectly respectable statement, the colours being taken as universals. You mean simply that the propositional function "x is a colour between blue and yellow" is one which is capable of truth. But the x which occurs there is not a particular, it is a universal. So that you arrive at the fact that the ultimate important notion involved in existence is the notion that I developed in the lecture before last, the notion of a propositional function being sometimes true, or being, in other words, possible. The distinction between what some people would call real existence, and existence in people's imagination or in my subjective activity, that distinction, as we have just seen, is entirely one of correlation. I mean that anything which appears to you, you will be mistakenly inclined to say has some more glorified form of existence if it is associated with those other things I was talking of in the way that the appearance of Socrates to you would be associated with his appearance to other people. You would say he was only in your imagination if there were not those other correlated appearances that you would naturally expect. But that does not mean that the appearance to you is not exactly as much a part of the world as if there were other

---

5 See *Our Knowledge of the External World*, Chap. III. Also Section XII of "Sense-Data and Physics" in *Mysticism and Logic*. ⟨See Paper **1**.⟩

correlated appearances. It will be exactly as much a part of the real world, only it will fail to have the correlations that you expect. That applies to the question of sensation and imagination. Things imagined do not have the same sort of correlations as things sensated. If you care to see more about this question, I wrote a discussion in *The Monist* for January, 1915, and if any of you are interested, you will find the discussion there.

I come now to the proper subject of my lecture, but shall have to deal with it rather hastily. It was to explain the theory of types and the definition of classes. Now first of all, as I suppose most of you are aware, if you proceed
10 carelessly with formal logic, you can very easily get into contradictions. Many of them have been known for a long time, some even since the time of the Greeks, but it is only fairly recently that it has been discovered that they bear upon mathematics, and that the ordinary mathematician is liable to fall into them when he approaches the realms of logic, unless he is very cautious. Unfortunately the mathematical ones are more difficult to expound, and the ones easy to expound strike one as mere puzzles or tricks.

You can start with the question whether or not there is a greatest cardinal number. Every class of things that you can choose to mention has some cardinal number. That follows very easily from the definition of cardinal
20 numbers as classes of similar classes, and you would be inclined to suppose that the class of all things there are in the world would have about as many members as a class could be reasonably expected to have. The plain man would suppose you could not get a larger class than the class of all the things there are in the world. On the other hand, it is very easy to prove that if you take selections of some of the members of a class, making those selections in every conceivable way that you can, the number of different selections that you can make is greater than the original number of terms. That is easy to see with small numbers. Suppose you have a class with just three numbers, a, b, c. The first selection that you can make is the selection
30 of no terms. The next of a alone, b alone, c alone. Then bc, ca, ab, abc, which makes in all 8 (i.e. 2^3) selections. Generally speaking, if you have n terms, you can make 2^n selections. It is very easy to prove that 2^n is always greater than n, whether n happens to be finite or not. So you find that the total number of things in the world is not so great as the number of classes that can be made up out of those things. I am asking you to take all these propositions for granted, because there is not time to go into the proofs, but they are all in Cantor's work. Therefore you will find that the total number of things in the world is by no means the greatest number. On the contrary, there is a hierarchy of numbers greater than that. That, on the face of it,
40 seems to land you in a contradiction. You have, in fact, a perfectly precise arithmetical proof that there are *fewer* things in heaven or earth than are dreamt of in *our* philosophy. That shows how philosophy advances.

You are met with the necessity, therefore, of distinguishing between classes and particulars. You are met with the necessity of saying that a class consisting of two particulars is not itself in turn a fresh particular, and that has to be expanded in all sorts of ways; i.e. you will have to say that in the sense in which there are particulars, in that sense it is not true to say there are classes. The sense in which there are classes is a different one from the sense in which there are particulars, because if the senses of the two were exactly the same, a world in which there are three particulars and therefore eight classes, would be a world in which there are at least eleven things. As the Chinese philosopher pointed out long ago, a dun cow and a bay horse makes three things: separately they are each one, and taken together they are another, and therefore three.

I pass now to the contradiction about classes that are not members of themselves. You would say generally that you would not expect a class to be a member of itself. For instance, if you take the class of all the teaspoons in the world, that is not in itself a teaspoon. Or if you take all the human beings in the world, the whole class of them is not in turn a human being. Normally you would say you cannot expect a whole class of things to be itself a member of that class. But there are apparent exceptions. If you take, e.g., all the things in the world that are not teaspoons and make up a class of them, that class obviously (you would say) will not be a teaspoon. And so generally with negative classes. And not only with negative classes, either, for if you think for a moment that classes are things in the same sense in which things are things, you will then have to say that the class consisting of all the things in the world is itself a thing in the world, and that therefore this class is a member of itself. Certainly you would have thought that it was clear that the class consisting of all the classes in the world is itself a class. That I think most people would feel inclined to suppose, and therefore you would get there a case of a class which is a member of itself. If there is any sense in asking whether a class is a member of itself or not, then certainly in all the cases of the ordinary classes of everyday life you find that a class is not a member of itself. Accordingly, that being so, you could go on to make up the class of all those classes that are not members of themselves, and you can ask yourself, when you have done that, is that class a member of itself or is it not?

Let us first suppose that it is a member of itself. In that case it is one of those classes that are not members of themselves, i.e. it is not a member of itself. Let us then suppose that it is not a member of itself. In that case it is not one of those classes that are not members of themselves, i.e. it is one of those classes that are members of themselves, i.e. it is a member of itself. Hence either hypothesis, that it is or that it is not a member of itself, leads to its contradiction. If it is a member of itself, it is not, and if it is not, it is.

That contradiction is extremely interesting. You can modify its form; some forms of modification are valid and some are not. I once had a form suggested to me which was not valid, namely the question whether the barber shaves himself or not. You can define the barber as "one who shaves all those, and those only, who do not shave themselves". The question is, does the barber shave himself? In this form the contradiction is not very difficult to solve. But in our previous form I think it is clear that you can only get around it by observing that the whole question whether a class is or is not a member of itself is nonsense, i.e. that no class either is or is not a member of itself, and that it is not even true to say that, because the whole form of words is just a noise without meaning. That has to do with the fact that classes, as I shall be coming on to show, are incomplete symbols in the same sense in which the descriptions are that I was talking of last time; you are talking nonsense when you ask yourself whether a class is or is not a member of itself, because in any full statement of what is meant by a proposition which seems to be about a class, you will find that the class is not mentioned at all and that there is nothing about a class in that statement. It is absolutely necessary, if a statement about a class is to be significant and not pure nonsense, that it should be capable of being translated into a form in which it does not mention the class at all. This sort of statement, "Such-and-such a class is or is not a member of itself", will not be capable of that kind of translation. It is analogous to what I was saying about descriptions: the symbol for a class is an incomplete symbol; it does not really stand for part of the propositions in which symbolically it occurs, but in the right analysis of those propositions that symbol has been broken up and disappeared.

There is one other of these contradictions that I may as well mention, the most ancient, the saying of Epimenides that "All Cretans are liars." Epimenides was a man who slept for sixty years without stopping, and I believe that it was at the end of that nap that he made the remark that all Cretans were liars. It can be put more simply in the form: if a man makes the statement "I am lying", is he lying or not? If he is, that is what he said he was doing, so he is speaking the truth and not lying. If, on the other hand, he is not lying, then plainly he is speaking the truth in saying that he is lying, and therefore he is lying, since he says truly that that is what he is doing. It is an ancient puzzle, and nobody treated that sort of thing as anything but a joke until it was found that it had to do with such important and practical problems as whether there is a greatest cardinal or ordinal number. Then at last these contradictions were treated seriously. The man who says "I am lying" is really asserting "There is a proposition which I am asserting and which is false." That is presumably what you mean by lying. In order to get out the contradiction you have to take that whole assertion of his as one of the propositions to which his assertion applies; i.e. when he says "There is a proposition which I am asserting and which is false", the word "proposition" has to be interpreted as to include among propositions his statement to the effect that he is asserting a false proposition. Therefore you have to suppose that you have a certain totality, viz., that of propositions, but that that totality contains members which can only be defined in terms of itself. Because when you say "There is a proposition which I am asserting and which is false", that is a statement whose meaning can only be got by reference to the totality of propositions. You are not saying which among all the propositions there are in the world it is that you are asserting and that is false. Therefore it presupposes that the totality of propositions is spread out before you and that some one, though you do not say which, is being asserted falsely. It is quite clear that you get into a vicious circle if you first suppose that this totality of propositions is spread out before you, so that you can without picking any definite one say "Some one out of this totality is being asserted falsely", and that yet, when you have gone on to say "Some one out of this totality is being asserted falsely", that assertion is itself one of the totality you were to pick out from. That is exactly the situation you have in the paradox of the liar. You are supposed to be given first of all a set of propositions, and you assert that some one of these is being asserted falsely, then that assertion itself turns out to be one of the set, so that it is obviously fallacious to suppose the set already there in its entirety. If you are going to say anything about "all propositions", you will have to define propositions, first of all, in some such way as to exclude those that refer to all the propositions of the sort already defined. It follows that the word "proposition", in the sense in which we ordinarily try to use it, is a meaningless one, and that we have got to divide propositions up into sets and can make statements about all propositions in a given set, but those propositions will not themselves be members of the set. For instance, I may say "All atomic propositions are either true or false", but that itself will not be an atomic proposition. If you try to say "All propositions are either true or false", without qualification, you are uttering nonsense, because if it were not nonsense it would have to be itself a proposition and one of those included in its own scope, and therefore the law of excluded middle as enunciated just now is a meaningless noise. You have to cut propositions up into different types, and you can start with atomic propositions or, if you like, you can start with those propositions that do not refer to sets of propositions at all. Then you will take next those that refer to sets of propositions of that sort that you had first. Those that refer to sets of propositions of the first type, you may call the second type, and so on.

If you apply that to the person who says "I am lying", you will find that the contradiction has disappeared, because he will have to say what type of liar he is. If he says "I am asserting a false proposition of the first type", as a matter of fact that statement, since it refers to the totality of propositions of the first type, is of the second type. Hence it is not true that he is asserting a false proposition of the first type, and he remains a liar. Similarly, if he said he was asserting a false proposition of the 30,000th type, that would be a statement of the 30,001st type, so he would still be a liar. And the counter-argument to prove that he was also not a liar has collapsed.

You can lay it down that a totality of any sort cannot be a member of itself. That applies to what we are saying about classes. For instance, the totality of classes in the world cannot be a class in the same sense in which they are. So we shall have to distinguish a hierarchy of classes. We will start with the classes that are composed entirely of particulars: that will be the first type of classes. Then we will go on to classes whose members are classes of the first type: that will be the second type. Then we will go on to classes whose members are classes of the second type: that will be the third type, and so on. Never is it possible for a class of one type either to be or not to be identical with a class of another type. That applies to the question I was discussing a moment ago, as to how many things there are in the world. Supposing there are three particulars in the world. There are then, as I was explaining, 8 classes of particulars. There will be 2^8 (i.e. 256) classes of classes of particulars, and 2^{256} classes of classes of classes of particulars, and so on. You do not get any contradiction arising out of that, and when you ask yourself the question: "Is there, or is there not a greatest cardinal number?" the answer depends entirely upon whether you are confining yourself within some one type, or whether you are not. Within any given type there is a greatest cardinal number, namely, the number of objects of that type, but you will always be able to get a larger number by going up to the next type. Therefore, there is no number so great but what you can get a greater number in a sufficiently high type. There you have the two sides of the argument: the one side when the type is given, the other side when the type is not given.

I have been talking, for brevity's sake, as if there really were all these different sorts of things. Of course, that is nonsense. There are particulars, but when one comes on to classes, and classes of classes, and classes of classes of classes, one is talking of logical fictions. When I say there are no such things, that again is not correct. It is not significant to say "There are such things" in the same sense of the words "there are" in which you can say "There are particulars." If I say "There are particulars" and "There are classes", the two phrases "there are" will have to have different meanings in those two propositions, and if they have suitable different meanings, both propositions may be true. If, on the other hand, the words "there are" are used in the same sense in both, then one at least of those statements must be nonsense, not false but nonsense. The question then arises, what is the sense in which one can say "There are classes", or in other words, what do you mean by a statement in which a class appears to come in? First of all, what are the sort of things you would like to say about classes? They are just the same as the sort of things you want to say about propositional functions. You want to say of a propositional function that it is sometimes true. That is the same thing as saying of a class that it has members. You want to say that it is true for exactly 100 values of the variables. That is the same as saying of a class that it has a hundred members. All the things you want to say about classes are the same as the things you want to say about propositional functions excepting for accidental and irrelevant linguistic forms, with, however, a certain proviso which must now be explained.

Take, e.g., two propositional functions such as "x is a man", "x is a featherless biped." Those two are formally equivalent, i.e. when one is true so is the other, and vice versa. Some of the things that you can say about a propositional function will not necessarily remain true if you substitute another formally equivalent propositional function in its place. For instance, the propositional function "x is a man" is one which has to do with the concept of humanity. That will not be true of "x is a featherless biped." Or if you say, "So-and-so asserts that such-and-such is a man" the propositional function "x is a man" comes in there, but "x is a featherless biped" does not. There are a certain number of things which you can say about a propositional function which would be not true if you substitute another formally equivalent propositional function. On the other hand, any statement about a propositional function which will remain true or remain false, as the case may be, when you substitute for it another formally equivalent propositional function, may be regarded as being about the class which is associated with the propositional function. I want you to take the words *may be regarded* strictly. I am using them instead of *is*, because *is* would be untrue. "Extensional" statements about functions are those that remain true when you substitute any other formally equivalent function, and these are the ones that may be regarded as being about the class. If you have any statement about a function which is not extensional, you can always derive from it a somewhat similar statement which is extensional, viz., there is a function formally equivalent to the one in question about which the statement in question is true. This statement, which is manufactured out of the one you started with, will be extensional. It will always be equally true or equally false of any two formally equivalent functions, and this derived extensional statement may be regarded as being the corresponding statement about the associated class. So, when I say that "The class of men has so-and-so many members", that is to say "There are so-and-so many men in the world", that will be derived from the statement that "x is human" is satisfied by so-and-so many values of x, and in order to get it into the extensional form, one will put it in this way, that "There is a function formally equivalent to 'x is human', which is true for so-and-so many values of x." That I should define as what I mean by saying "The class of men has so-and-so many members." In that way you find that all the formal properties that you desire of classes, all their formal uses in mathematics, can be obtained without supposing for a moment that there are such things as classes, without supposing, that is to say, that a proposition in which symbolically a class occurs, does in fact contain a constituent corresponding to that symbol, and when rightly analyzed that symbol will disappear, in the same sort of way as descriptions disappear when the propositions are rightly analyzed in which they occur.

There are certain difficulties in the more usual view of classes, in addition to those we have already mentioned, that are solved by our theory. One of these concerns the null-class, i.e. the class consisting of no members, which is difficult to deal with on a purely extensional basis. Another is concerned
10 with unit-classes. With the ordinary view of classes you would say that a class that has only one member was the same as that one member. That will land you in terrible difficulties, because in that case that one member is a member of that class, namely, itself. Take, e.g., the class of "Lecture audiences in Gordon Square".[6] That is obviously a class of classes, and probably it is a class that has only one member, and that one member itself (so far) has more than one member. Therefore if you were to identify the class of lecture audiences in Gordon Square with the only lecture audience that there is in Gordon Square, you would have to say both that it has one member and that it has twenty members, and you will be landed in con-
20 tradictions, because this audience has more than one member, but the class of audiences in Gordon Square has only one member. Generally speaking, if you have any collection of many objects forming a class, you can make a class of which that class is the only member, and the class of which that class is the only member will have only one member, though this only member will have many members. This is one reason why you must distinguish a unit-class from its only member. Another is that, if you do not, you will find that the class is a member of itself, which is objectionable, as we saw earlier in this lecture. I have omitted a subtlety connected with the fact that two formally equivalent functions may be of different types. For the way of
30 treating this point, see *Principia Mathematica*, *20, and Introduction, Chapter III.

I have not said quite all that I ought to have said on this subject. I meant to have gone a little more into the theory of types. The theory of types is really a theory of symbols, not of things. In a proper logical language it would be perfectly obvious. The trouble that there is arises from our inveterate habit of trying to name what cannot be named. If we had a proper logical language, we should not be tempted to do that. Strictly speaking, only particulars can be named. In that sense in which there are particulars, you cannot say either truly or falsely that there is anything else. The word "there
40 is" is a word having "systematic ambiguity", i.e. having a strictly infinite number of different meanings which it is important to distinguish.

6 [These lectures were given in Gordon Square, London.—Ed⟨itor of *The Monist*⟩.]

DISCUSSION

Q.: Could you lump all those classes, and classes of classes, and so on, together?

Mr. Russell: All are fictions, but they are different fictions in each case. When you say "There are classes of particulars", the statement "there are" wants expanding and explaining away, and when you have put down what you really do mean, or ought to mean, you will find that it is something quite different from what you thought. That process of expanding and writing down fully what you mean, will be different if you go on to "There are classes of classes of particulars." There are infinite numbers of meanings to "there are". The first only is fundamental, so far as the hierarchy of classes is concerned.

Q.: I was wondering whether it was rather analogous to spaces, where the first three dimensions are actual, and the higher ones are merely symbolic. I see there is a difference, there are higher dimensions, but you can lump those together.

Mr. Russell: There is only one fundamental one, which is the first one, the one about particulars, but when you have gone to classes, you have travelled already just as much away from what there is as if you have gone to classes of classes. There are no classes really in the physical world. The particulars are there, but not classes. If you say "There is a universe" that meaning of "there is" will be quite different from the meaning in which you say "There is a particular", which means that "the propositional function 'x is a particular' is sometimes true".

All those statements are about symbols. They are never about the things themselves, and they have to do with "types". This is really important and I ought not to have forgotten to say it, that the relation of the symbol to what it means is different in different types. I am not now talking about this hierarchy of classes and so on, but the relation of a predicate to what it means is different from the relation of a name to what it means. There is not one single concept of "meaning" as one ordinarily thinks there is, so that you can say in a uniform sense "All symbols have meaning", but there are infinite numbers of different ways of meaning, i.e. different sorts of relation of the symbol to the symbolized, which are absolutely distinct. The relation, e.g., of a proposition to a fact, is quite different from the relation of a name to a particular, as you can see from the fact that there are two propositions always related to one given fact, and that is not so with names. That shows you that the relation that the proposition has to the fact is quite different from the relation of a name to a particular. You must not suppose that there is, over and above that, another way in which you could get at facts by naming them. You can always only get at the thing you are aiming at by the proper sort of symbol, which approaches it in the appropriate way. That is the real philosophical truth that is at the bottom of all this theory of types.

VIII. EXCURSUS INTO METAPHYSICS: WHAT THERE IS

I come now to the last lecture of this course, and I propose briefly to point to a few of the morals that are to be gathered from what has gone before, in the way of suggesting the bearing of the doctrines that I have been advocating upon various problems of metaphysics. I have dwelt hitherto upon what one may call philosophical grammar, and I am afraid I have had to take you through a good many very dry and dusty regions in the course of that investigation, but I think the importance of philosophical grammar is very
10 much greater than it is generally thought to be. I think that practically all traditional metaphysics is filled with mistakes due to bad grammar, and that almost all the traditional problems of metaphysics and traditional results— supposed results—of metaphysics are due to a failure to make the kind of distinctions in what we may call philosophical grammar with which we have been concerned in these previous lectures.

Take, as a very simple example, the philosophy of arithmetic. If you think that 1, 2, 3, and 4, and the rest of the numbers, are in any sense entities, if you think that there are objects, having those names, in the realm of being, you have at once a very considerable apparatus for your
20 metaphysics to deal with, and you have offered to you a certain kind of analysis of arithmetical propositions. When you say, e.g., that 2 and 2 are 4, you suppose in that case that you are making a proposition of which the number 2 and the number 4 are constituents, and that has all sorts of consequences, all sorts of bearings upon your general metaphysical outlook. If there has been any truth in the doctrines that we have been considering, all numbers are what I call logical fictions. Numbers are classes of classes, and classes are logical fictions, so that numbers are, as it were, fictions at two removes, fictions of fictions. Therefore you do not have, as part of the ultimate constituents of your world, these queer entities that you are
30 inclined to call numbers. The same applies in many other directions.

One purpose that has run through all that I have said, has been the justification of analysis, i.e. the justification of logical atomism, of the view that you can get down in theory, if not in practice, to ultimate simples, out of which the world is built, and that those simples have a kind of reality not belonging to anything else. Simples, as I tried to explain, are of an infinite number of sorts. There are particulars and qualities and relations of various orders, a whole hierarchy of different sorts of simples, but all of them, if we were right, have in their various ways some kind of reality that does not belong to anything else. The only other sort of object you come across in the
40 world is what we call *facts*, and facts are the sort of things that are asserted or

denied by propositions, and are not properly entities at all in the same sense in which their constituents are. That is shown in the fact that you cannot name them. You can only deny, or assert, or consider them, but you cannot name them because they are not there to be named, although in another sense it is true that you cannot know the world unless you know the facts that make up the truths of the world; but the knowing of facts is a different sort of thing from the knowing of simples.

Another purpose which runs through all that I have been saying is the purpose embodied in the maxim called Occam's Razor. That maxim comes in, in practice, in this way: take some science, say physics. You have there a given body of doctrine, a set of propositions expressed in symbols—I am including words among symbols—and you think that you have reason to believe that on the whole those propositions, rightly interpreted, are fairly true, but you do not know what is the actual meaning of the symbols that you are using. The meaning they have *in use* would have to be explained in some pragmatic way: they have a certain kind of practical or emotional significance to you which is a datum, but the logical significance is not a datum, but a thing to be sought, and you go through, if you are analyzing a science like physics, these propositions with a view to finding out what is the smallest empirical apparatus—or the smallest apparatus, not necessarily wholly empirical—out of which you can build up these propositions. What is the smallest number of simple undefined things at the start, and the smallest number of undemonstrated premisses, out of which you can define the things that need to be defined and prove the things that need to be proved? That problem, in any case that you like to take, is by no means a simple one, but on the contrary an extremely difficult one. It is one which requires a very great amount of logical technique; and the sort of thing that I have been talking about in these lectures is the preliminaries and first steps in that logical technique. You cannot possibly get at the solution of such a problem as I am talking about if you go at it in a straightforward fashion with just the ordinary acumen that one accumulates in the course of reading or in the study of traditional philosophy. You do need this apparatus of symbolical logic that I have been talking about. (The description of the subject as symbolical logic is an inadequate one. I should like to describe it simply as logic, on the ground that nothing else really is logic, but that would sound so arrogant that I hesitate to do so.)

Let us consider further the example of physics for a moment. You find, if you read the works of physicists, that they reduce matter down to certain elements—atoms, ions, corpuscles, or what not. But in any case the sort of thing that you are aiming at in the physical analysis of matter is to get down to very little bits of matter that still are just like matter in the fact that they persist through time, and that they travel about in space. They have in fact all the ordinary everyday properties of physical matter, not the matter that one has in ordinary life—they do not taste or smell or appear to the naked eye—but they have the properties that you very soon get to when you travel toward physics from ordinary life. Things of that sort, I say, are not the ultimate constituents of matter in any metaphysical sense. Those things are all of them, as I think a very little reflection shows, logical fictions in the sense that I was speaking of. At least, when I say they are, I speak somewhat too dogmatically. It is possible that there may be all these things that the physicist talks about in actual reality, but it is impossible that we should ever have any reason whatsoever for supposing that there are. That is the situation that you arrive at generally in such analyses. You find that a certain thing which has been set up as a metaphysical entity can either be assumed dogmatically to be real, and then you will have no possible argument either for its reality or against its reality; or, instead of doing that, you can construct a logical fiction having the same formal properties, or rather having formally analogous formal properties to those of the supposed metaphysical entity and itself composed of empirically given things, and that logical fiction can be substituted for your supposed metaphysical entity and will fulfil all the scientific purposes that anybody can desire. With atoms and the rest it is so, with all the metaphysical entities whether of science or of metaphysics. By metaphysical entities I mean those things which are supposed to be part of the ultimate constituents of the world, but not to be the kind of thing that is ever empirically given—I do not say merely not being itself empirically given, but not being the *kind* of thing that is empirically given. In the case of matter, you can start from what is empirically given, what one sees and hears and smells and so forth, all the ordinary data of sense, or you can start with some definite ordinary object, say this desk, and you can ask yourselves, "What do I mean by saying that this desk that I am looking at now is the same as the one I was looking at a week ago?" The first simple ordinary answer would be that it *is* the same desk, it is actually identical, there is a perfect identity of substance, or whatever you like to call it. But when that apparently simple answer is suggested, it is important to observe that you cannot have an empirical reason for such a view as that, and if you hold it, you hold it simply because you like it and for no other reason whatever. All that you really know is such facts as that what you see now, when you look at the desk, bears a very close similarity to what you saw a week ago when you looked at it. Rather more than that one fact of similarity I admit you know, or you may know. You might have paid some one to watch the desk continuously throughout the week, and might then have discovered that it was presenting appearances of the same sort all through that period, assuming that the light was kept on all through the night. In that way you could have established continuity. You have not in fact done so. You do not in fact know that that desk has gone on looking the same all the time, but we will assume that. Now the essential point is this: What is the empirical reason that makes you call a number of appearances, appearances of the same desk? What makes you say on successive occasions, I am seeing the same desk? The first thing to notice is this, that it does not matter what is the answer, so long as you have realized that the answer consists in something empirical and not in a recognized metaphysical identity of substance. There is something given in experience which makes you call it the same desk, and having once grasped that fact, you can go on and say, it is that something (whatever it is) that makes you call it the same desk which shall be *defined* as *constituting* it the same desk, and there shall be no assumption of a metaphysical substance which is identical throughout. It is a little easier to the untrained mind to conceive of an identity than it is to conceive of a system of correlated particulars, hung one to another by relations of similarity and continuous change and so on. That idea is apparently more complicated, but that is what is empirically given in the real world, and substance, in the sense of something which is continuously identical in the same desk, is not given to you. Therefore in all cases where you seem to have a continuous entity persisting through changes, what you have to do is to ask yourself what makes you consider the successive appearances as belonging to one thing. When you have found out what makes you take the view that they belong to the same thing, you will then see that that which has made you say so, is all that is *certainly* there in the way of unity. Anything that there may be over and above that, I shall recognize as something I cannot know. What I can know is that there are a certain series of appearances linked together, and the series of those appearances I shall define as being a desk. In that way the desk is reduced to being a logical fiction, because a series is a logical fiction. In that way all the ordinary objects of daily life are extruded from the world of what there is, and in their place as what there is you find a number of passing particulars of the kind that one is immediately conscious of in sense. I want to make clear that I am not *denying* the existence of anything; I am only refusing to affirm it. I refuse to affirm the existence of anything for which there is no evidence, but I equally refuse to deny the existence of anything against which there is no evidence. Therefore I neither affirm nor deny it, but merely say, that is not in the realm of the knowable and is certainly not a part of physics; and physics, if it is to be interpreted, must be interpreted in terms of the sort of thing that can be empirical. If your atom is going to serve purposes in physics, as it undoubtedly does, your atom has got to turn out to be a construction, and your atom will in fact turn out to be a series of classes of particulars. The same process which one applies to physics, one will also apply elsewhere. The application to physics I explained briefly in my book on the *External World*, Chapters III and IV (Open Court Publishing Co., 1914).

I have talked so far about the unreality of the things we think real. I want

to speak with equal emphasis about the reality of things we think unreal, such as phantoms and hallucinations. Phantoms and hallucinations, considered in themselves, are, as I explained in the preceding lectures, on exactly the same level as ordinary sense-data. They differ from ordinary sense-data only in the fact that they do not have the usual correlations with other things. In themselves they have the same reality as ordinary sense-data. They have the most complete and absolute and perfect reality that anything can have. They are part of the ultimate constituents of the world, just as the fleeting sense-data are. Speaking of the fleeting sense-data, I think it is very
10 important to remove out of one's instincts any disposition to believe that the real is the permanent. There has been a metaphysical prejudice always that if a thing is really real, it has to last either forever or for a fairly decent length of time. That is to my mind an entire mistake. The things that are really real last a very short time. Again I am not denying that there *may* be things that last forever, or for thousands of years; I only say that those are not within our experience, and that the real things that we know by experience last for a very short time, one tenth or half a second, or whatever it may be. Phantoms and hallucinations are among those, among the ultimate constituents of the world. The things that we call real, like tables and chairs, are systems, series
20 of classes of particulars, and the particulars are the real things, the particulars being sense-data when they happen to be given to you. A table or chair will be a series of classes of particulars, and therefore a logical fiction. Those particulars will be on the same level of reality as a hallucination or a phantom. I ought to explain in what sense a chair is a series of classes. A chair presents at each moment a number of different appearances. All the appearances that it is presenting at a given moment make up a certain class. All those sets of appearances vary from time to time. If I take a chair and smash it, it will present a whole set of different appearances from what it did before, and without going as far as that, it will always be changing as the
30 light changes, and so on. So you get a series in time of different sets of appearances, and that is what I mean by saying that a chair is a series of classes. That explanation is too crude, but I leave out the niceties, as that is not the actual topic I am dealing with. Now each single particular which is part of this whole system is linked up with the others in the system. Supposing, e.g., I take as my particular the appearance which that chair is presenting to me at this moment. That is linked up first of all with the appearance which the same chair is presenting to any one of you at the same moment, and with the appearance which it is going to present to me at later moments. There you get at once two journeys that you can take away from
40 that particular, and that particular will be correlated in certain definite ways with the other particulars which also belong to that chair. That is what you mean by saying—or what you ought to mean by saying—that what I see before me is a real thing as opposed to a phantom. It means that it has a

whole set of correlations of different kinds. It means that that particular, which is the appearance of the chair to me at this moment, is not isolated but is connected in a certain well-known familiar fashion with others, in the sort of way that makes it answer one's expectations. And so, when you go and buy a chair, you buy not only the appearance which it presents to you at that moment, but also those other appearances that it is going to present when it gets home. If it were a phantom chair, it would not present any appearances when it got home, and would not be the sort of thing you would want to buy. The sort one calls real is one of a whole correlated system, whereas the sort you call hallucinations are not. The respectable particulars in the world are all of them linked up with other particulars in respectable, conventional ways. Then sometimes you get a wild particular, like a merely visual chair that you cannot sit on, and say it is a phantom, a hallucination, you exhaust all the vocabulary of abuse upon it. That is what one means by calling it unreal, because "unreal" applied in that way is a term of abuse and never would be applied to a thing that *was* unreal because you would not be so angry with it.

I will pass on to some other illustrations. Take a person. What is it that makes you say, when you meet your friend Jones, "Why, this is Jones"? It is clearly not the persistence of a metaphysical entity inside Jones somewhere, because even if there be such an entity, it certainly is not what you see when you see Jones coming along the street; it certainly is something that you are not acquainted with, not an empirical datum. Therefore plainly there is something in the empirical appearances which he presents to you, some-thing in their relations one to another, which enables you to collect all these together and say, "These are what I call the appearances of one person", and that something that makes you collect them together is not the persistence of a metaphysical subject, because that, whether there be such a persistent subject or not, is certainly not a datum, and that which makes you say "Why, it is Jones" is a datum. Therefore Jones is not constituted as he is known by a sort of pin-point ego that is underlying his appearances, and you have got to find some correlations among the appearances which are of the sort that make you put all those appearances together and say, they are the appearances of one person. Those are different when it is other people and when it is yourself. When it is yourself, you have more to go by. You have not only what you look like, you have also your thoughts and memories and all your organic sensations, so that you have a much richer material and are therefore much less likely to be mistaken as to your own identity than as to some one else's. It happens, of course, that there are mistakes even as to one's own identity, in cases of multiple personality and so forth, but as a rule you will know that it is you because you have more to go by than other people have, and you would know it is you, not by a consciousness of the ego at all but by all sorts of things, by memory, by the way you feel and the way you look and a host of things. But all those are empirical data, and those enable you to say that the person to whom something happened yesterday was yourself. So you can collect a whole set of experiences into one string as all belonging to you, and similarly other people's experiences can be collected together as all belonging to them by relations that actually are observable and without assuming the existence of the persistent ego. It does not matter in the least to what we are concerned with, what exactly is the given empirical relation between two experiences that makes us say, "These are two experiences of the same person." It does not matter precisely what that relation is, because the logical formula for the construction of the person is the same whatever that relation may be, and because the mere fact that you can know that two experiences belong to the same person proves that there is such an empirical relation to be ascertained by analysis. Let us call the relation R. We shall say that when two experiences have to each other the relation R, then they are said to be experiences of the same person. That is a definition of what I mean by "experiences of the same person". We proceed here just in the same way as when we are defining numbers. We first define what is meant by saying that two classes "have the same number", and then define what a number is. The person who has a given experience x will be the class of all those experiences which are "experiences of the same person" as the one who experiences x. You can say that two events are co-personal when there is between them a certain relation R, namely that relation which makes us say that they are experiences of the same person. You can define the person who has a certain experience as being those experiences that are co-personal with that experience, and it will be better perhaps to take them as a series than as a class, because you want to know which is the beginning of a man's life and which is the end. Therefore we shall say that a person is a certain series of experiences. We shall not deny that there may be a metaphysical ego. We shall merely say that it is a question that does not concern us in any way, because it is a matter about which we know nothing and can know nothing, and therefore it obviously cannot be a thing that comes into science in any way. What we know is this string of experiences that makes up a person, and that is put together by means of certain empirically given relations, such, e.g., as memory.

I will take another illustration, a kind of problem that our method is useful in helping to deal with. You all know the American theory of neutral monism, which derives really from William James and is also suggested in the work of Mach, but in a rather less developed form. The theory of neutral monism maintains that the distinction between the mental and the physical is entirely an affair of arrangement, that the actual material arranged is exactly the same in the case of the mental as it is in the case of the physical, but they differ merely in the fact that when you take a thing as belonging in the same context with certain other things, it will belong to psychology, while when you take it in a certain other context with other things, it will belong to physics, and the difference is as to what you consider to be its context, just the same sort of difference as there is between arranging the people in London alphabetically or geographically. So, according to William James, the actual material of the world can be arranged in two different ways, one of which gives you physics and the other psychology. It is just like rows or columns: in an arrangement of rows and columns, you can take an item as either a member of a certain row or a member of a certain column; the item is the same in the two cases, but its context is different.

If you will allow me a little undue simplicity I can go on to say rather more about neutral monism, but you must understand that I am talking more simply than I ought to do because there is not time to put in all the shadings and qualifications. I was talking a moment ago about the appearances that a chair presents. If we take any one of these chairs, we can all look at it, and it presents a different appearance to each of us. Taken all together, taking all the different appearances that that chair is presenting to all of us at this moment, you get something that belongs to physics. So that, if one takes sense-data and arranges together all those sense-data that appear to different people at a given moment and are such as we should ordinarily say are appearances of the same physical object, then that class of sense-data will give you something that belongs to physics, namely, the chair at this moment. On the other hand, if instead of taking all the appearances that that chair presents to all of us at this moment, I take all the appearances that the different chairs in this room present to me at this moment, I get quite another group of particulars. All the different appearances that different chairs present to me now will give you something belonging to psychology, because that will give you my experiences at the present moment. Broadly speaking, according to what one may take as an expansion of William James, that should be the definition of the difference between physics and psychology.

We commonly assume that there is a phenomenon which we call seeing the chair, but what I call my seeing the chair according to neutral monism is merely the existence of a certain particular, namely the particular which is the sense-datum of that chair at that moment. And I and the chair are both logical fictions, both being in fact a series of classes of particulars, of which one will be that particular which we call my seeing the chair. That actual appearance that the chair is presenting to me now is a member of me and a member of the chair, I and the chair being logical fictions. That will be at any rate a view that you can consider if you are engaged in vindicating neutral monism. There is no simple entity that you can point to and say: this entity is physical and not mental. According to William James and neutral monists that will not be the case with any simple entity that you may take. Any such entity will be a member of physical series and a member of mental

series. Now I want to say that if you wish to test such a theory as that of neutral monism, if you wish to discover whether it is true or false, you cannot hope to get any distance with your problem unless you have at your fingers' end the theory of logic that I have been talking of. You never can tell otherwise what can be done with a given material, whether you can concoct out of a given material the sort of logical fictions that will have the properties you want in psychology and in physics. That sort of thing is by no means easy to decide. You can only decide it if you really have a very considerable technical facility in these matters. Having said that, I ought to proceed to
10 tell you that I have discovered whether neutral monism is true or not, because otherwise you may not believe that logic is any use in the matter. But I do not profess to know whether it is true or not. I feel more and more inclined to think that it may be true. I feel more and more that the difficulties that occur in regard to it are all of the sort that may be solved by ingenuity. But nevertheless there *are* a number of difficulties; there are a number of problems, some of which I have spoken about in the course of these lectures. One is the question of belief and the other sorts of facts involving two verbs. If there are such facts as this, that, I think, may make neutral monism rather difficult, but as I was pointing out, there is the theory
20 that one calls behaviourism, which belongs logically with neutral monism, and that theory would altogether dispense with those facts containing two verbs, and would therefore dispose of that argument against neutral monism. There is, on the other hand, the argument from emphatic particulars, such as "this" and "now" and "here" and such words as that, which are not very easy to reconcile, to my mind, with the view which does not distinguish between a particular and experiencing that particular. But the argument about emphatic particulars is so delicate and so subtle that I cannot feel quite sure whether it is a valid one or not, and I think the longer one pursues philosophy, the more conscious one becomes how extremely
30 often one has been taken in by fallacies, and the less willing one is to be quite sure that an argument is valid if there is anything about it that is at all subtle or elusive, at all difficult to grasp. That makes me a little cautious and doubtful about all these arguments, and therefore although I am quite sure that the question of the truth or falsehood of neutral monism is not to be solved except by these means, yet I do not profess to know whether neutral monism is true or is not. I am not without hopes of finding out in the course of time, but I do not profess to know yet.

As I said earlier in this lecture, one thing that our technique does, is to give us a means of constructing a given body of symbolic propositions with
40 the minimum of apparatus, and every diminution in apparatus diminishes the risk of error. Suppose, e.g., that you have constructed your physics with a certain number of entities and a certain number of premisses; suppose you discover that by a little ingenuity you can dispense with half of those entities

and half of those premises, you clearly have diminished the risk of error, because if you had before 10 entities and 10 premises, then the 5 you have now would be all right, but it is not true conversely that if the 5 you have now are all right, the 10 must have been. Therefore you diminish the risk of error with every diminution of entities and premises. When I spoke about the desk and said I was not going to assume the existence of a persistent substance underlying its appearances, it is an example of the case in point. You have anyhow the successive appearances, and if you can get on without assuming the metaphysical and constant desk, you have a smaller risk of error than you had before. You would not necessarily have a smaller risk of error if you were tied down to *denying* the metaphysical desk. That is the advantage of Occam's Razor, that it diminishes your risk of error. Considered in that way you may say that the whole of our problem belongs rather to science than to philosophy. I think perhaps that is true, but I believe the only difference between science and philosophy is, that science is what you more or less know and philosophy is what you do not know. Philosophy is that part of science which at present people choose to have opinions about, but which they have no knowledge about. Therefore every advance in knowledge robs philosophy of some problems which formerly it had, and if there is any truth, if there is any value in the kind of procedure of mathematical logic, it will follow that a number of problems which had belonged to philosophy will have ceased to belong to philosophy and will belong to science. And of course the moment they become soluble, they become to a large class of philosophical minds uninteresting, because to many of the people who like philosophy, the charm of it consists in the speculative freedom, in the fact that you can play with hypotheses. You can think out this or that which *may* be true, which is a very valuable exercise until you discover what *is* true; but when you discover what is true the whole fruitful play of fancy in that region is curtailed, and you will abandon that region and pass on. Just as there are families in America who from the time of the Pilgrim Fathers onward had always migrated westward, toward the backwoods, because they did not like civilized life, so the philosopher has an adventurous disposition and likes to dwell in the region where there are still uncertainties. It is true that the transferring of a region from philosophy into science will make it distasteful to a very important and useful type of mind. I think that is true of a good deal of the applications of mathematical logic in the directions that I have been indicating. It makes it dry, precise, methodical, and in that way robs it of a certain quality that it had when you could play with it more freely. I do not feel that it is my place to apologize for that, because if it is true, it is true. If it is not true, of course, I do owe you an apology; but if it is, it is not my fault, and therefore I do not feel I owe any apology for any sort of dryness or dullness in the world. I would say this too, that for those who have any taste for mathematics, for those who like symbolic constructions, that sort of world is a very delightful one, and if you do not find it otherwise attractive, all that is necessary to do is to acquire a taste for mathematics, and then you will have a very agreeable world, and with that conclusion I will bring this course of lectures to an end.

Part IV
Towards the Analysis of Mind

18

Manuscript Notes [1918]

THESE SHORT PAPERS, which are published here for the first time, were almost certainly written in 1918. During the early months of 1918 when he was faced with the prospect of a term in prison for his anti-war campaign Russell drew up a plan of philosophical work he proposed to undertake "if circumstances permit". That plan is printed in Appendix II. The larger work of which this detailed plan is but a part was a book to be called *The Analysis of Mind*, which, he wrote his brother from prison on 16 May, "if successful should be another big and important piece of work". He did, of course, write this book and publish it in 1921.

His friends, who were trying to get his prison sentence set aside on appeal or, failing that, to have him serve it in the first division where he could work at philosophy, required a statement of his intentions. Russell, who had decided in late 1917 to abandon his protest against the war, found it easy to outline the direction in which his philosophical inquiries were moving. He saw himself applying to mind the same method he had applied to matter in 1913 and the first months of 1914. He would simply be resuming the work which the war had interrupted. In a letter to Lady Ottoline Morrell dated 25 July [1918] from prison he made the connection explicitly:

> Do you remember how I used to think and talk about Matter, first at Churn and then at the Beetle and Wedge? I am in the same stage now as regards Mind. But it is a bigger job. Matter I got done just before the war. Mind will probably take about five years. It is delicious having a big new problem to play with—and it is heavenly to find I am still capable of new ideas. They are the supreme ecstasy—but oh how rare—I have had perhaps one hour of it in my life. The rest, effort or retrospect.

The work he had done at Churn and the Beetle and Wedge was intensive study of the works of others and concentrated thought aimed at sorting out the logic of the problem of matter.

His work on mind required a similar study of the latest and best theories the psychologists had to offer. It is hardly surprising that he found the behaviourists most congenial, for they too had a fondness for Occam's Razor. He did read some Freud, but he seems not to have found him as useful in his thinking as were the behaviourists. It would be a mistake to conclude that Russell adopted the behaviourists' position. He did not, largely because he found their account of images in striking contrast to his own experience. His analysis of mind would have to provide a place for images, whereas John B. Watson, the founder of behaviourism, denied images altogether. But this was not Russell's only criticism of behaviourism. "No behaviourist so far as I can discover", he wrote Carr on 21 May 1918, "tackles any of the difficult parts of his problem. If any of them have written intelligently on analysis of *belief*, I wish to read them."

After one unsuccessful and one successful appeal, Russell was made a first division prisoner, and he worked at his outline in a way to make his supporters proud. He read widely in current psychological literature: Appendix III lists the books and articles he read in Brixton Prison. He also began to write short pieces as ideas came to him. In a note printed in Appendix III he reports that he wrote "a large number of notes on the principles of symbolism" which were smuggled out by obliging visitors. We have no way of knowing how many of these notes were lost. Nine that survive are printed here. Others probably found their way into "On Propositions" (**20**) and *The Analysis of Mind*, for Russell was a very efficient recycler of manuscripts.

He found it difficult to do original work in prison, but not through any loss of ambition. He wrote Lady Ottoline from prison that "Ambition is oddly revived in me, I suppose because my health is better. I feel only on the threshold of the work I want to do—vast schemes I have. My technical philosophical schemes you know" (1 Aug. 1918). The difficulty lay in the monotony and repressive character of prison life. "I read enormously and write a good deal," he wrote Gladys Rinder on 21 May, "but it would be impossible to do really good work here because one dare not get excited." "Excitement", he wrote Lady Ottoline in an undated letter from prison, "brings ideas to the point of expression." He could write up work he had already done, turning his lecture series of the fall of 1917 into *Introduction to Mathematical Philosophy* (1919), which, in a message from prison to T. S. Eliot, he described as "a text-book of the *Principia*"; and he could write reviews of the books of others; but the conditions were not right for sustained original writing. "I have hit on big important new ideas in philosophy, but they will take a long time to bring to fruition, and I shan't manage it in here. Being here damps one, like putting a mute on a violin. One loses vividness and force: if one kept them, the lack of liberty would be unbearable." This theme, from a letter of 14 July to Lady Ottoline, runs through his prison letters. No wonder then that the manuscripts bearing on his new work are so short and scrappy.

His work reached a peak during the first half of July. In a letter to Frank Russell, dated 1 July, he included a message for Whitehead:

> I find seeing Whitehead an immense stimulus, please tell him. I have been thinking a great deal about matters he and I discussed, and there seems to me a lot of interesting work to be done on Facts, Judgments, and propositions. I

had given up Logic years ago in despair of finding out anything more about it but now I begin to see hope. Approaching the old questions from a radically new point of view, as I have been doing lately, makes new ideas possible.

A week later, in his next letter to Frank dated 8 July, he had more developments to report:

Tell her ⟨Gladys Rinder⟩ and my other philosophical friends that "Facts, Judgments, and Propositions" opens out—it was for its sake that I wanted to study behaviourism, because the first problem is to have a tenable theory of judgment. I see my way to a really big piece of work, and incidentally to a definition of "logic", hitherto lacking. All the psychology that I have been reading and meaning to read was for the sake of logic; but I have reached a point in logic where I need theories of (a) judgment (b) symbolism, both of which are psychological problems.

No later reports from prison are quite so optimistic as this one.
  By the 1st of August he had concluded that he had done all in prison he could do.

When I came here, I had reached a creative mood, in which I was no longer haunted by horrors to the verge of madness. The quiet, the reading and thinking, the absence of excitement, have done me a world of good. Earlier, I could hardly have stood it, but now it is fruitful. However I have had enough of it. I have had time to think out everything I can think out in here and now I need the stimulus of talk. I want to discuss philosophy in order to get on with my new notions.

Again it was Lady Ottoline to whom he confided. Talk had always been an important aspect of his philosophical work; it helped him hit upon the best vocabulary for his purposes. "I like words to cut like a scimitar, clean deep cuts, further each time than you would think such an apparently easy blow could penetrate." This sentence came later in the same letter; it was his gloss on what it means to be "sharp and clear, *net*", the aim he had set for himself. The original work he was producing in prison did not measure up to this standard. He had proof of this to report to her on 14 August. Some of his writings had been read by Dorothy Wrinch and Raphael Demos, two former pupils. "From what she writes and Demos says I see they don't understand the new ideas I am at. It is no wonder as my ideas are still rather vague. I *know* they are *very* important and novel, but I can't get expression for them yet." He was priming himself for his release from prison when unfettered discussion—or more likely, at first at least, monologue—would again be possible. The pressure to discuss his new ideas, "which have come simply because they were due, like cuckoos in April" (4 Sept.), continued to build. On the 30th of August he wrote Lady Ottoline of his plans upon release: "All kinds of delights float before my mind—above all talk, *talk*, TALK." Less than three weeks later he was free to indulge himself.

The copy-texts are the manuscripts.

NOTES SPECIFIC TO THE MANUSCRIPTS

18a. Because it records Russell's first espousal of neutral monism, the doctrine that there is one and only one primal stuff and mind and matter differ merely in their organization of it, it must have been written after he gave his lectures on "The Philosophy of Logical Atomism" (**17**). In those lectures he said that "the whole theory of neutral monism is pleasing to me, but I do find so far very great difficulty in believing it" (195: 39–40). By the time he finished "On Propositions: What They Are, and How They Mean" (**20**) on 4 March 1919 he had completed his move to neutral monism. Thus this paper was probably written in 1918.

Russell used this paper in the composition of *The Analysis of Mind*. The passages shared by the two works are recorded in the annotations.

18b. The conclusion he reaches, that behaviourism cannot provide a complete analysis of knowledge, is also the one he reaches in *The Analysis of Mind (1921*, 157), and largely for the same reasons. No passages from the paper appear *verbatim* in the book; the examples of the dog and bird are used, but in expanded form (*ibid.*, 27–8). Russell wrote "[Impt MS]" at the top of the first folio.

18c. This paper appears to be his first attempt to draft what he thought about introspection, the polished result of which was published in "On Propositions" (**20**) and in *The Analysis of Mind*, Lecture 6. In that lecture he offers a long critique of the first article by Knight Dunlap from which he quotes toward the end of **18c**. He then passes on to a discussion of "whether introspection is a source of knowledge" (*1921*, 117), but he offers a different definition there. See the annotations for an account of parallel passages in *The Analysis of Mind*.

18d. These notes were used in the writing of *The Analysis of Mind*. Documentation for this claim is provided in the annotations.

18e. Strictly speaking the title is ambiguous, since "subject" may refer back to "judgment", in which case judgment itself is what is discarded; or "subject" may be taken in its other sense in which it is opposed to "object", and this seems to be Russell's intention. Evidence for this comes in his remark that "the pin-point subject is discarded" (265: 6–7).

18f. In the annotations the results of comparing this paper with corresponding parts of *The Analysis of Mind* are reported in detail.

18g. From internal evidence it is clear that this paper could not have been written before June 1918. The evidence consists in the argument it develops against a behaviouristic view of names. Russell did not begin studying behaviourism until the spring of 1918. In a letter to Gilbert Murray, dated 9 April 1918, H. Wildon Carr wrote that Russell's "friends are collecting all the recent literature on 'Behaviourism' which is the subject he appears to have chosen for study in prison".

The vocabulary which is developed in this paper differs from the one used in *The Analysis of Mind*, although it is not inconsistent with that used in the book. This paper cannot, therefore, with confidence be called a working paper for the book, except to the extent, as already mentioned, that it explores the limits of behaviourism, which is also one of the principal aims of his book.

The ontology adopted in this paper is that of "The Philosophy of Logical Atomism" (**17**) and the first section of "On Propositions" (**20**), both of which take facts as the ultimate constituents of the world. The theory of symbolism outlined is also to be found more fully developed in Lecture 1 of Paper **17**.

18h. Russell dated the manuscript "July 31:18", a day he was in prison. The content of the paper fits his prison plan of research into the philosophy of mind, but the positions he takes on the same questions in *The Analysis of Mind* are less formal, perhaps because the book was originally delivered as a series of lectures open to the public. The sort of purely formal theory which is developed at the end of this paper is not very suitable for oral delivery. See the annotations for a comparison of these texts.

18i. Russell dated the manuscript "Aug. 10.18", a day he was in prison. It is clearly a working paper for *The Analysis of Mind*, although when he wrote it he had not yet developed his distinction between image-propositions and word-propositions which is so prominent in the book. (See "On Propositions" [20] for Russell's first statement of this distinction.) His acceptance of images and image-propositions is probably the reason that there is so little discussion in *The Analysis of Mind* of the physiological alternative outlined in **18i**.

18a On Sensations and Ideas [1918]

THE ORTHODOX VIEW of presentations was, until fairly recently, that they could be analysed into three elements: act, content, and object. Meinong's theory of knowledge, for example, is built on this theory. As against this tripartite analysis, however, there is a tendency for idealists to drop the object and for realists to drop the content. I myself have believed, for many years now, that presentations consist of act and object, with a relation of awareness. But William James and Professor Dewey, as well as the great majority of American realists, reject wholly the relational
10 view of presentations: what has hitherto been the object remains alone, and ought no longer to be called by the name "object", since this term suggests a relation to a subject. It has gradually come to seem to me possible that this view may be the correct one. The question is of almost boundless importance, since the whole problem of the relation of mind and matter turns upon it. If there is only, in presentations, what used to be the "object", then, so far at least as cognition is concerned, it may be possible to adopt William James's view that there is nothing specifically mental except certain kinds of causal relations between entities which, with other causal relations, occur equally in physics. If, on the other hand, presentations involve an ultimate
20 relation of awareness, then this relation will be "mental" in a sense more fundamental than any that radical empiricism would allow. It would be easy to find passages in James suggesting that awareness or acquaintance is an ultimate relation in this sense, but it would be a mistake to lay stress on them, and if we did we should misinterpret him. He stands for the view that presentations are not in themselves facts of relation, and it is this view which I now propose to advocate, more or less tentatively.

The following quotation from Brentano may serve to illustrate the theory I wish to combat:

> Every psychical phenomenon is characterized by what the scholas-
30 tics of the Middle Ages called the intentional (also the mental) inexistence of an object, and what we, although with not quite unambiguous expressions, would call relation to a content, direction towards an object (which is not here to be understood as a reality), or immanent objectivity. Each contains something in itself as an object, though not each in the same way. In presentation something is presented, in judgment something is acknowledged or rejected, in love something is loved, in hatred hated, in desire desired, and so on.
> This intentional inexistence is exclusively peculiar to psychical phenomena. No physical phenomenon shows anything similar. And

so we can define psychical phenomena by saying that they are phenomena which intentionally contain an object in themselves.[1]

The essential point here is the dictum: "We may define psychical phenomena by saying that they are phenomena which intentionally contain an object." The kind of argument which formerly made me consider that this must be true, at least in the sphere of cognition, is exceedingly simple. I see, let us suppose, a patch of red. The patch of red is not psychical, but physical; my seeing of it is not physical, but psychical. Therefore my seeing the patch is something other than the patch itself. This argument, to me historically, was directed against idealism: the emphatic part of it was the assertion that the patch of red is physical, not psychical. I shall not at present recapitulate the grounds in favour of the view that the patch of red is physical; I shall merely state that I see no reason to modify them. It does not follow that the red is not also psychical, unless we first assume that the physical and the psychical cannot overlap, which I do not any longer propose to assume. If I am asked for definitions, my answer is simplicity itself: The physical is what is dealt with in physics, and the psychical is what is dealt with in psychology. I do not say that these are final definitions, but I do say that they are the definitions with which our discussions ought to *begin*. William James maintains that the physical and the psychical are merely different arrangements of the same material. If that is so, my seeing of a patch of red cannot consist of an irreducible relation of "awareness" between me (or an "act") and the patch of red. We shall require some theory of sensation which shall be different from Brentano's. What, then, are we to say as regards the relation of the red to my seeing of it?

Can we maintain, quite simply, that my seeing of a patch of red is identical with the patch of red itself? This view is advocated by Professor Dewey. Perceptions, he says, are not *per se* cases of knowledge, but simply natural events with no more knowledge status than (say) a shower.[2] "Let them [the realists] try the experiment of conceiving perceptions as pure natural events, not cases of awareness or apprehension, and they will be surprised to see how little they miss" (*ibid.*, p. 262). I think Professor Dewey is right in this last statement, except in supposing that the realists will be "surprised". Many of them already hold the view which he is advocating, and others are very sympathetic to it. But it will be necessary to reduce everything cognitive to "pure natural events", if "neutral monism" is to be proved tenable. In this paper, I do not propose to consider anything

1 *Psychologie vom empirischen Standpunkte* (1874), pp. 115–16.
2 *Studies in Experimental Logic*, p. 253.

beyond what I have been in the habit of calling "sense-data". I have hitherto supposed that there was a relational occurrence, called "sensation", consisting in awareness of sense-data. I now propose to accept Professor Dewey's invitation, and attempt to dispense with this relational occurrence. If this can be done successfully, the first step will have been taken towards abolishing the dualism of mind and matter.

A few preliminary words, though not logically necessary, may be useful as indicating the general bias in what is to follow. When the dualism of mind and matter is swept away, it is more or less optional whether we say we have reduced everything to matter or everything to mind. American Realists, notably E. B. Holt, reduce everything to "neutral" entities, neither material nor mental, and may therefore be called "neutral monists". I should reduce the stuff of the world to particulars such as occur in seeing, hearing, etc. That is, I should maintain that, apart from qualities and relations, the particulars known to exist all have temporal relations, brief duration, and the sort of causal relations that make them amenable to physics. These particulars do not have the properties belonging to what is called "matter", for matter persists through time, and is spatially divisible to a much greater extent than the sort of particulars that I am speaking of. But a piece of "matter" can be defined as a suitable series of classes of such particulars. Thus our view, to this extent, approximates to materialism. I should say that its bias or flavour is materialistic. The ultimate problem, of which we are considering only one small preliminary portion, is this: Can such terms as "judgment", "pleasure and pain", "knowledge and error", "desire and aversion", be defined by means of suitable systems of particulars of the above kind, in a way analogous ⟨to⟩ that in which "matter" can be defined by means of them? So far as I have been able to discover, those who answer this question in the affirmative avoid all the most difficult problems, while those who answer it in the negative fail to produce any of the most telling arguments. In this paper I propose to imitate both groups in both respects. The most difficult problems seem to me to be those concerning (1) judgment, (2) desire, and (3) "emphatic particulars", i.e. such terms as *I, now, here, this*. Each of these three problems needs independent treatment. But for present purposes I shall confine myself narrowly to the question of awareness of particulars.

It is clear that there is some kind of event which really occurs and may be called "awareness". We say we are aware of a person coming into the room or speaking to us, for example. The question is as to the analysis of such events. If we say we see or hear the person in question, that obviously is not quite what happens. We see a shape, or a series of shapes; we hear a noise, or a series of noises. Let us take, for the sake of definiteness, the case of hearing a noise. Common sense takes the view that the noise is one event, and hearing it is another; it might have occurred when there was no one to hear it. The view advocated by Professor Dewey and those who agree with him maintains that there is only a single event, which may be called indifferently a noise or hearing a noise. The difference—so James would urge—lies only in the suggested context. The noise, considered as an event in physics, has those causal connections that belong with the theory of air-waves; the hearing of the noise, considered as an event in psychology, has quite other causal connections, emotions, cognitions, etc. The distinction between the mental and the physical, in this view, lies entirely in the fact that one particular may occur in two quite different sorts of causal correlations. To say that I am "aware" of a particular will mean, on this view, that it has effects according to the causal laws that belong to psychology, in addition to whatever physical effects it may have. There may be events of which the near effects are all according to physical laws: such events will be wholly material. There may be others of which the near effects are wholly according to psychological laws; these will be wholly mental. Those events which have effects according to both sorts of laws will be both material and mental. This is an outline of the thesis. Is there any fatal objection to this thesis?

There are those who will maintain that they can discern introspectively an event consisting in awareness of a noise, and that they can be certain by inspection that this event is not identical with the mere noise. I do not know how to argue questions of immediate inspection. I am always conscious that others may be able to perceive many things which I cannot perceive. In the present instance, I formerly believed that my own inspection showed me the distinction between a noise and my hearing of a noise, and I am now convinced that it shows me no such thing, and never did. One has to trust inspection for some things, but the less the better; above all, one should trust it only for very broad things. It seems to me now, looking back upon my former belief that I could distinguish a noise from the hearing of it, that the whole belief was based on theory and bias, as indeed philosophical beliefs almost always are. I was anxious to rescue the physical world from the clutches of idealism, and I thought it undeniable that there is an exclusively mental event called "hearing the noise". Therefore I made the noise itself as distinct as possible from the hearing of it, in order that the noise might be physical. My bias remains: I still wish to rescue the physical world from the idealist. But if I could rescue the so-called "mental" world from him too! Then the reason for making a gulf between the mental and the physical would disappear.

Having set this example of candour, I invite those who disagree to imitate it and set forth the bias which determines their own views.

18b Behaviourism and Knowledge [1918]

WHAT ARE THE objections to dealing with knowledge on behaviourist lines? I don't think behaviourism is incapable of inventing a theory that would do formally, but it won't deal with images, which are data.

Observe an animal in circumstances when we should say it "knows" something. Cases of action in relation to a present stimulus are of no account. All these can be explained as mere causation—e.g. when a dog comes when he is called. Similarly as regards instinct: a bird builds a nest because it wants to, not because it knows there will be eggs. More difficult are cases where the stimulus is absent, e.g. where a dog looks for its master. But this may be taken as analogous to looking for food, merely an impulse to certain movements such as the onlooker sees to be appropriate to the result. We may say:

An animal is said to "know" that A is a means to B, when, desiring B, it performs the act A; and "desire" here is defined behaviouristically.

But that seems the most that can be done towards knowledge on behaviourist lines.

Is this adequate for human knowledge?

A great deal of the practical "knowledge" of daily life could be brought under the behaviourist definition. E.g. we "know" that fire burns when we avoid touching it; in fact, nothing that can be strictly called "knowing" is involved, but only a direct causal action of the fire on our muscles—or on muscles via nerves and brain.

From a behaviourist point of view, the most notable fact about knowing is the means it affords of giving causal efficacy to what is absent. I think of a *faux pas* I committed years ago, and the thought makes me draw in my breath and blush. Watson would contend that in such a case actual words occur, and no other form of knowledge; and he would argue that the words have a causal efficacy similar to that of the event they represent. I do not think there is any à priori refutation of this view, which would account for the phenomena that an outsider could observe. But the refutation is purely empirical: images seem just as certain empirically as anything else.

Images are doubtless *connected* with theoretically observable events in the nervous system, but the correlation can only be discovered by introspective knowledge that the images are occurring. They are, however, just as scientifically observable as anything else, because different people, on the whole, agree about them. And sense-data, too, are in strictness private.

Thus the behaviourist view, though useful for suggestions, has absolutely no theoretical warrant.

If we are to go a long way towards behaviourism, it must not be from any theoretical acceptance of its position. Let us see what the reasons are.

1. Introspection is difficult and uncertain; many things which it is supposed to reveal are probably fictions. Cf. psycho-analysis.

2. The evolutionary continuity of men and animals makes it imperative to find explanations of mental phenomena which are not too unlike what we may suppose to occur in animals.

3. Mere external observation of animals leads the unscientific observer to say that they "desire" or "know" various things. This shows that desire and knowledge can be *exemplified* in behaviour; therefore simplicity suggests that they might be *defined* by behaviour; i.e. the sort of behaviour which makes us say that an animal desires some end may be defined as *being* desire for that end.

4. In human beings, behaviour often leads the observer to assume desires of which the subject is unaware. Psycho-analysis gives a wide extension to this method, and seems to show that it gives the causally important sense of desire. But the same arguments may be adduced in favour of unconscious "knowledge".

Nevertheless, memory, abstract knowledge, etc., as introspective data, seem to show that not all knowledge is practical, and that therefore we cannot define knowledge behaviouristically. We ought also to consider, from this point of view, impractical wishes, i.e. such as suggest no activity directed towards their realization. These also seem a difficulty for behaviourism.

I do not think we can define painfulness as the property of stimulating movement. No doubt usually this definition applies, but when we do not know what movement to perform, the painfulness is increased—e.g. in bodily pain for which we know no remedy. This looks as if *desire* must be admitted as fundamental; then a state of affairs is *painful* (by definition) when we desire that it should be changed. In this case, desire, like belief, will be a sensation referring to a proposition. *Aversion* will be more primitive than desire, since it can be directed towards what is present in sensation, whereas desire requires images. Aversion corresponds to sense-perception, and desire to memory. In memory we believe the prototype of an image did exist, in desire we hope it will.

18c Introspection as a Source of Knowledge [1918]

THE FIRST PROBLEM is the definition of introspection, which is by no means simple.

Negatively, perception of noises, colours, smells, etc. is not said to be by introspection, though it *may* be by introspection that we know we perceive them.

Positively, knowledge of thoughts and feelings *is **said*** to be by Introspection.

How about a stomach-ache? Is this known by introspection? It is certainly known by awareness of one's inside. But a stomach-ache is regarded as a physical phenomenon and would not be said to be known by introspection, though its unpleasantness might be.

Privacy is commonly regarded as a mark of what is known by Introspection. But if so Robinson Crusoe knew his island by Introspection till Friday appeared. In fact, all sensible objects are more or less private—the stomach-ache only rather more so. Thus privacy won't do as the mark of Introspection, though it is what makes behaviourists hate it.

I think one must define Introspection as follows:

(a) it includes nothing got by inference
(b) it includes no sensations or knowledge of them
(c) positively, it consists of knowledge, not obtained by inference, of anything that is not a sensation.

Some questions remain as to the definition. Can we include knowledge by way of belief under the head of Introspection? We now recognize no knowledge except beliefs. Therefore we must include beliefs if anything. Thus if we know of the existence of anything except sensations, and if some of this knowledge is immediate, then there is introspection.

But this definition is still inadequate. If we knew of God immediately, or of universals, this would not be introspection. It must be constituents of ourselves that we know if we are to call our knowledge introspective.

Thus we define:

Introspection consists of non-inferential beliefs concerning the existence of constituents of ourselves other than sensations.

This requires definitions of (a) sensations (b) ourselves. The definition of *sensation* is not easy. If we have already defined *physical* and *psychological* causal laws, we can define sensations as particulars which obey both kinds of laws. Assume that this definition is adequate.

We have next to define a *mind*. Given a particular which obeys psychological laws, any other particular connected with it by exclusively psychological laws belongs to the same mind. Can we say conversely that any other particular belonging to the same mind must be connected with this particular by exclusively psychological laws? I think so. Links of memory are bound to exist. Where they fail wholly, we have multiple personality.

We may therefore define:

Introspection consists of non-inferential beliefs concerning the existence of particulars connected with the beliefs in question by exclusively psychological causal laws. Df.

We have to ask whether (a) there are such beliefs, (b) there is any reason to suppose any of them true.

We may simplify our question without material alteration by the definition:

Psychological Perception consists of non-inferential beliefs in particulars obeying only psychological causal laws. Df.

This would include perception of other people's minds if such a thing occurred, but that doesn't matter. We now ask: (a) Is there psychological perception? (b) If so, does it yield knowledge or only false belief?

Having reached this point, we come on to *images*. It is better to define introspection as concerned with particulars *not obeying physical laws*; or thus:

Non-Physical Perception consists of non-inferential beliefs in particulars not obeying physical causal laws. Df.

This definition suffices for our questions, and for introducing the discussion of images—including dreams.

Consider the distinction of physical and psychological laws.

A. There are private and semi-public sensations. Those of sight and hearing are the most public; smell somewhat less so; touch still less; visceral sensations hardly at all. The question turns on the degree and frequency of similarity of sensations in neighbours at the same time. If we hear a clap of thunder when no one else does, we think we are mad; if we feel a stomach-ache when no one else does, we are in no way surprised.

B. On the face of it, *publicity*, not sensation, is the characteristic of what is material. The stomach-ache is *mine*, the thunder is not. But what is mine includes what belongs to the body, and it is here that the stomach-ache belongs. Perhaps the reason for this is *localization*: the stomach-ache has a position near the surface of the stomach, and this surface is visible and palpable. It is not altogether easy to see what is meant by this, but it has some readily recognizable meaning. Whatever is localized is naturally regarded as material. Clearly images are not localized—at any rate visual and auditory images are not. Images of sensations localized in the body tend to be themselves localized in the same part of the body—e.g. of words, in the tongue and throat.

C. In the case of private sensations, their images are less obviously distinct from them than in the case of public ones. The image of pronouncing a word, e.g., may consist of small sensations in tongue and throat, since such sensations are private. But visual images and auditory ones cannot be so treated, since the physical event to which they would point if they were sensations is not taking place.

D. The following seems the best course:

   1. Construct the public world.

2. Consider those sensations which, though not public, are localized in public space.

3. Consider images, etc., which are not localized at all.

It is quite clear that what anti-introspectionists object to is the fact that the phenomena cannot be verified by another observer, i.e. the fact of their *privacy*. This is a matter of degree. Their attitude seems inconsistent with e.g. Dewey's ignoring of scepticism.

The really important phenomena are images of such sensations as are not localized in the body, i.e. especially sight and sound. It is these that are
10 difficult because (a) they are not localized and (b) they are not public. We may take (a) and (b) together as *defining* a purely mental existent.

Knight Dunlap, *Psychological Review*, 1912, pp. 404–413, "The Case Against Introspection", says it is certain there is knowing, but it is never known. "I am never aware of an awareness" (p. 410). Introspection, he says, is confounded with awareness of our bodies.

Ibid. "The Nature of Perceived Relations", *ibid.*, pp. 415–446, "I have pointed out in a previous paper [*supra*] that 'introspection', divested of its mythological suggestion of the observing of consciousness, is really the observation of bodily sensations (sensibles) and feelings (feelables)" (p.
20 427n.).

John B. Watson, *ibid.*, 1913, "Psychology as the Behaviorist Views It", says (p. 174n.): "I should throw out imagery altogether and attempt to show that practically all natural thought goes on in terms of sensori-motor processes in the larynx (but not in terms of imageless thought)."

Eliott Park Frost, *ibid.*, 1914, pp. 204–211, "Cannot Psychology Dispense with Consciousness?" develops a physiological theory of consciousness: α and β–arcs.

Knight Dunlap, 1916, pp. 49–70, "Thought-Content and Feeling", repeats contentions of previous articles and adds (p. 59) that images are
30 muscular contractions.

From above it is clear that Knight Dunlap, at least, regards awareness of bodily sensations as *not* introspection. Take such an instance as this: You are sitting alone in a room, you shut your eyes and visualize a friend sitting in a chair which in fact is empty. You can't locate the visual image in the chair without contradicting physics; but since the image is visual, you cannot locate it in your body. Hence you cannot locate it at all, if you regard it as belonging to the physical world. Thus it seems the physical world does not include all that we are aware of.

18d Three Notes on Memory [1918]

IMPERATIVE TO GET rid of "Subject".
Involves abandonment of distinction between sense-data and sensation.
Involves different theory of imagination and memory.

Tends to make the actual object in memory (e.g.) more remote from present mental occurrence than on old theory.

Memory is a good problem to concentrate on.

(1) No doubt that there *is* knowledge of the past.
(2) Images enter into this knowledge but do not *wholly* constitute it. 10
(3) Truth of memory *cannot* be wholly *practical*.
(4) Distinction between knowing and its object is peculiarly glaring in this case.
(5) "Feeling of recognition" must be analysed.
(6) Is there any form of memory which is infallible like perception?
(7) Immediate and remote memory.
(8) Correspondence theory of truth is on strong ground as regards memory.

II. PROBLEMS OF MEMORY

Two questions must be distinguished:

(1) What is the present mental occurrence in remembering? 20
(2) What is the relation to the past object remembered?

The psychologist as such need only concern himself with (1). It is the epistemologist who must consider (2).

There is a theoretical difficulty: if the past object is not being now experienced, how is the relation of the image to it to be known? But if it is now being experienced, must we not conclude that it still exists? It will be best to examine (1) as carefully as possible before considering this problem.

(1). When I remember (say) my breakfast this morning, I have in mind certainly images, but also the feeling that these images have what we may call "meaning", i.e. in some sense they point to the actual breakfast, and are 30 a means of knowing it. I may be conscious that they are inadequate or redundant: I may know that there are elements that they omit and elements that they add. I can know much more about the breakfast than the images alone would seem capable of conveying.

We must carefully distinguish Bergson's two kinds of memory, i.e. (a) true memory (b) a verbal or other habit. I "remember" the multiplication table in the sense that I can repeat it. I also remember occasions while I was learning it. Only the second of those is true memory. The distinction between the two is clear in theory but not always easy in practice, since what has been true memory becomes of the other sort by repetition.

It is important to understand what constitutes that knowledge of the past which enables us to control memory-images.

Memory-images are probably intrinsically indistinguishable from images of imagination. What makes the difference is that memory-images *mean*, i.e. point to something else. Can this be explained merely as a "feeling of 10 familiarity"? If so, an accurate memory-image might feel more familiar than a less accurate one. This might account for our feeling that an image is partly wrong. But the "feeling of familiarity" seems hardly adequate to the phenomena—e.g. to the accurate placing of a memory among past events. It belongs most noticeably to those vague floating memories about which judgments can hardly be made. And it is hard to resist the view that there is an "imageless" knowledge involved in memory, and that the images used are a more or less irrelevant accompaniment of it, like language. This raises the question whether "ideas", as opposed to "impressions", are something other than images. It looks as if very difficult problems would arise 20 whichever view we take.

III. UNTITLED

Hume (*Treatise*, III, 5) says the only difference between memory and imagination consists in the superior liveliness of the former.

But he goes on to say (G. and G., p. 387) "an idea of the imagination may acquire such force and vivacity, as to pass for an idea of the memory, and counterfeit its effects on the belief and judgment". This shows that he has also an epistemological criterion, otherwise the imagination in such a case would *be* memory.

In memory, the "subject" is represented by images, the "object" by the 30 past event. Having extruded "acquaintance" as an ultimate relation, we shall now say that, in memory, the image is accompanied by a judgment that there was a past object resembling it. In this way the image acquires "meaning". It is a symbol, much as a word is a symbol, though in the case of the word the relation to the object is not that of resemblance.

In sensation, the object merely exists.

In perception, what is sensed leads to a judgment that correlated objects exist *now*—e.g. when from visual data tactile qualities are inferred.

In memory, the image leads to a judgment that something else existed formerly.

40   In imagination, there are no judgments of this sort.

Thus the problems of theory of knowledge are reduced to the problem of *judgment*.

18e Views as to Judgment, Discarding the Subject [1918]

JUDGMENT MAY be either

(a) a definite occurrence, or
(b) a relation of two or more occurrences, or
(c) a characteristic of a number of occurrences, e.g. a causal law.

Of these views, (a) is orthodox intellectualist, (c) is James–Dewey pragmatist. The view (b) is not advocated so far as I know. It *might* be held in some such form as that emotions or volitions are *called* judgments when considered in relation to relevant facts. But it does not seem a plausible view, and may be dropped.

We are left, then, with (a) and (c).

(a). *A judgment as a definite occurrence.* What will a judgment consist of? "Ideas", i.e. images, inter-related; perhaps also some sense-data? But this view is very difficult.

(α). To begin with, we want to judge that objects have relations, and no relations among ideas will give this. As Bradley says, "my idea of the earth goes round my idea of the sun" is not what we want; we want "my idea of the-earth-going-round-the-sun".

(β). Judgment of the most explicit sort seems to be connected by a continuous gradation with the vaguest belief. And belief does not seem to involve *necessarily* any complexity of ideas. A single idea, felt in a certain way, and operative in a certain way, may be a belief, namely what we call the belief that such-and-such a thing "exists", when we try to make the belief explicit and analysed.

This suggests that, if a belief is an occurrence, it is rather to be regarded as composed of *one* idea (possibly complex) with a certain associated feeling and efficacy.

In this case, the logical content of the judgment, when made explicit, would be: "The object of this idea exists." At any rate, that would be one fundamental kind of judgment. But what really occurs is *an idea, a feeling, and a causal efficacy.* Of these three, the third, which pragmatism considers essential, seems to be not so, but to be sometimes absent. Its relevance is chiefly for distinguishing between true and false judgments. [But as we shall see directly, *consciousness* of causal connection *is* sometimes essential.]

Can belief consist of an idea and a feeling?

What, if so, is meant by an "idea"? It will be what occurs when (as we used to say) one "considers" a proposition. It is not essential to an idea to be simple. I have e.g. an idea of a merry-go-round, though a merry-go-round is probably not one of the ultimate constituents of the universe. Now it is suggested that this idea passes into a belief by the mere addition of a feeling.

10 To such a view, however, there are logical objections. I may have two ideas simultaneously, of which I believe one but not the other. If belief consisted in idea plus feeling, merely, I should be believing both if either. The feeling must have *reference* to the idea, it must be a feeling *about* the idea. And this seems to bring us back to judgment in the old sense.

There are various examples of feelings *about* ideas, e.g. *feeling of familiarity*. Recognition cannot consist merely in a sense-datum plus a feeling of familiarity; for, if it did, and I had simultaneously two sense-data and a sense of familiarity, it would be impossible that one of the sense-data should be familiar and the other not. Thus the feeling of familiarity is "the
20 familiarity of *this*", or "this is familiar". Such a "feeling" leaves us with the problem of judgment still on our hands.

It would seem, therefore, that the attempt to reduce judgment to feelings and images is illusory.

But this argument may be turned round, and used to prove that *belief is a definite occurrence*. For the "feeling of familiarity" e.g. is certainly an occurrence, and we have just seen that it is a belief, not a *mere* feeling, i.e. the occurrence is: "This is familiar."

Doubtless there is such a thing as a *detached* feeling of familiarity, where we do not know what gives the feeling. But in such a case we naturally seek
30 out the source of the feeling, and when we have found it we say "oh yes, it was *that* that gave me the feeling"—e.g. when one smells peat-smoke after an interval. We seem to experience, in such a case, (1) the feeling (2) the smell (3) the fact that the smell "causes" the feeling.

There seems to be an experience which one would naturally describe as one of causal connection. This arises most forcibly, perhaps, in volition; but the case of familiarity seems to be an instance of it. We seem to know that so-and-so is the *cause* of our feeling of familiarity; it is this knowledge that essentially constitutes recognition. "Cause", in such judgments, must not have quite the sense it has in physics. Doubtless confusion of the two senses
40 is the source of much in philosophy.

From what has been said, it would seem to follow that *belief* (or judgment) must be accepted as an actual occurrence, not reduced to a causal law or any other complication.

If this is correct, the work of analysing belief is all before us. So far as I know, nothing that has been written throws much light on it.

Recognition seems a good form of belief to take as starting-point in our analysis, because it is very simple and primitive.

One of the chief difficulties in analysing belief is to avoid using the word "consciousness". This word cannot be used as an ultimate when the pinpoint subject is discarded. Yet, somehow, it expresses what we mean. In recognition, e.g., it is not enough that an object should cause a feeling of familiarity; we must be "conscious" that this is so; but what is meant by "conscious" it is by no means easy to see.   10

If this problem were solved, belief would no longer present serious difficulties.

18f Belief and Judgment [1918]

B ELIEF, CONSIDERED PSYCHOLOGICALLY, would seem to be a feeling, having reference to whatever is believed; just as e.g. familiarity is a feeling having reference to what is familiar. Belief, like familiarity, may sometimes be detached from reference: thus James speaks of "The nitrous oxide intoxication, in which a man's very soul will sweat with Conviction, and he be all the while unable to tell what he is convinced of at all" (II, p. 284). Also there seems no reason why belief, when it *is* 20 attached, should not attach to particulars: it is not essential to it that its object should be something expressed in propositional form. Thus we may believe in sense-data e.g.

But as soon as belief is referred to an object, and indeed as soon as *any* feeling is referred to an object, we have *propositional thought*. "This is believed", "this is familiar", are *judgments*.

The problems of *judgment* are twofold:

(1) Those belonging to *belief*,
(2) Those belonging to "propositional occurrences".

It is the second class that are the more interesting. "Propositional occur- 30 rences" include judgment (i.e. believing a *proposition*), desire, doubt, etc. They are involved in all cases in which a feeling has "reference" to something else.

It would seem probable that belief is psychologically simpler than doubt, and volition than hesitation.

Take (say) familiarity. A feeling of familiarity arises, owing to the fact that an object *O* is presented, with which I (i.e. my body) am familiar. But what I feel is "this is familiar" or "the familiarity of this". A problem arises as to (a) the familiarity of this in fact (b) the belief that this is familiar. This kind of discussion does not take us one step nearer to a theory of judgment; it throws no light on the belief as opposed to the fact.

Propositional thought remains stubborn and irreducible, hard to treat on behaviourist lines or on any others.

18g   Three Subjects [1918]

THREE SUBJECTS ARE confusedly combined in what we call logic:

(1) Ontology: what there is. *Facts.*
(2) Theory of true judgments. *Judgments.*
(3) Theory of Symbolism. *Propositions.*

10   I will begin with the third, and take *propositions* as symbols. A *proposition expresses* a thought and *asserts or denies* a fact. We will call the thought its *meaning* and the fact its *objective.* A true proposition asserts its objective, a false one denies it.

But this is only roughly speaking so.

"Today is Tuesday or Wednesday." There is not *in rerum natura* such a day as "Tuesday or Wednesday". Our proposition has two objectives, "Today is Tuesday" and "Today is Wednesday." It does not assert either. In the subject of ontology there will be no disjunctions. Ontology will deal with objectives (in that part of it which corresponds to propositions). There
20   are more true judgments than objectives. "*p* or *q*" is a judgment over and above *p*, and *q*, but does not give rise to a new objective.

Broadly: Every symbol *expresses* something "mental" [whatever that may mean] and *denotes* something "objective" [whatever that may mean]. We need different symbols in cases where the objective part is the same but only the "mental" part is different.

The study of the objective part, of what symbols "denote", is what I call *ontology.*

The study of the "mental" part, of what symbols "express", is theory of knowledge.

30   The theory of symbolism is a distinct topic, logically subsequent to the above two.

Just as we can see without studying the eye unless the eye is diseased, so we can use symbols without studying the theory of symbolism, unless our symbols are diseased. The theory of types is an attempt to cure a disease to which symbols are liable.

Theory of true judgments most nearly gives what is in fact being studied in what we call "logic".

Ontology will consist of such propositions as are indispensable for a complete description of the world. "*p or q*" will not occur in it. "*p*" will if true and atomic; "*q*" will if true and atomic; but not "*p or q*". Thus there is not complete correspondence between the two subjects.

"$(x).\phi x \supset \psi x$" is quite likely to be wanted in ontology. But "$\phi a \supset \psi a$" can only occur in the theory of true judgments. "If Socrates is a man, Socrates is mortal" is not a "fact of nature".

Propositions of the form "$(x).\phi x$" must occur in ontology. After enumerating all particular facts, we should want to say "And these are *all* there are". 10

Theory of Symbolism.

1. *Names.* We generally think of *one* entity, the symbol, pointing to *one* entity, its denotation. Thus "Socrates" points to Socrates. But "Socrates" is a new particular whenever it occurs—"*one*" symbol is a class of particulars. And Socrates is a new particular whenever *he* occurs. Thus the relation of symbol to symbolized is that of a class to a class or to a system of some sort. If we use the "same" word twice, there will be differences both in the word and in what it points to, considered as particulars. It is only by collecting particulars into classes that we arrive at one symbol or one symbolized. In 20 this collecting into classes there is inference, usually causal more or less. There are a number of objects in the world which are all instances of the letter "A". Some (those badly written) are doubtful instances.

What makes a symbol symbolize?

As far as names go, the behaviourist view is logically adequate: there is a causal correlation of particulars of one class (Socrates) with particulars of another class (the sound "Socrates"). When a baby has just learnt to say "Dada", this pretty well describes the observable phenomena. Anything further is hypothesis. Thus a symbol is a class of noises or shapes, all closely similar, which are caused by particulars of another class or system, which is 30 said to be what the symbol "means".

18h Propositions [1918]

A PROPOSITION, AS a symbol, is neutral as between believing, doubting, wishing, etc. The object of my physiological doctrine of symbolism would be to construct, if possible, a theory linking the speaking or writing of a proposition (as a physical occurrence) directly with the *fact*, without any "mental" intermediary. It will be noted that propositions have only two relations to facts, truth and falsehood; and to this it makes no difference whether they are used in beliefs or wishes or etc. The

essence of the proposition considered as a symbol is its duality of possible relation to fact. The constituent simple symbols have each only one possible relation to what they mean. The problem for symbolism is: "Why does this duality belong to a complex symbol though not to the constituent symbols?" I did not think this could be answered except in one of two ways: (a) by allowing as ultimate one or more "mental" dualisms, such as pleasant-unpleasant, desired-feared, true-false (of beliefs); (b) by finding some physiological dualism, such as equilibrium-motion. In any case, dualism is the heart of the problem, from a formal point of view; but perhaps a purely
10 formal dualism can be constructed to meet the case (see p. 269).

It must not be *assumed* that believing, wishing, etc. are irreducible phenomena. If this is assumed, it is very hard to avoid the pin-point Subject, which ought to be avoided if possible. This problem, of getting rid of the pin-point Subject, is a vital one in this topic.

Propositions are not to be defined as symbols for judgments—except when one is confining oneself to theory of knowledge. They are to be defined as "complex symbols having to *facts* one or other of two relations, truth and falsehood"—*fact* being indefinable. We do not judge *facts*; we judge the constituents of facts diffusedly; this results from the existence of false
20 beliefs. The same thing results from vain wishes, as regards desire.

One vital point in the theory is that a proposition *is* a fact. This is why it can *express* a fact.

Judgments must not, at any rate at the outset of our inquiries, be given any pre-eminence over wishes, etc. It is, however, fairly clear that, as a matter of *form*, if any *one* propositional mental attitude is accepted as an indefinable, the others can be defined in terms of it. Thus it *may* turn out that one of these propositional attitudes is more fundamental than the others, though so far I see no reason for thinking so. *If* it is so, I should expect *desire* to be fundamental. But all this requires psychological investi-
30 gation, from two ends: (1) as a matter of empirical fact, what occurs when we desire, etc.? (2) As a matter of formal possibility, what sort of occurrence *can* a propositional attitude be? (I mean by a "propositional attitude" any one of those whose expression involves propositions—desiring, believing, doubting, etc.)

The formal problem of the relation of proposition to fact may be treated (up to a certain point) independently of the question of propositional attitudes, and without asking whether the proposition is to be judged or desired or etc. Propositions are true or false, quite independently of judgment, *provided* that, independently of judgment, we can explain what they
40 express and what is meant by their "meaning". But this cannot be an ultimate way of dealing with the problem. For any ultimate explanation, propositional attitudes must be considered, though possibly they may be explicable in physical terms.

⟨In what follows⟩ the purely formal problem is considered, independently of propositional attitudes.

"xRy", "$x \div Ry$": these two symbols are each of them a *fact*. Each consists in a certain relation between "x" and "y", the first, that "R" stands between them, the second that "$\div R$" stands between them. If x has the relation R to y, there is correspondence between this fact and the fact "xRy"; i.e. if x is replaced by "x", y by "y", and R by "R", xRy becomes "xRy". This suggests a way in which a complex symbol may be "true"; it may result from the fact symbolized by mere substitution. This won't do for *negative* facts. The fact that "R" does not appear between "x" and "y" would be a very inconvenient symbol for the fact that x and y do not have the relation R, because it is so hard to distinguish from the facts that "S", "T", etc. do not appear between "x" and "y". Hence we invent "$\div R$" for this purpose. The lack of parallelism between symbol and symbolized as regards "$x \div Ry$" is a potent source of confusion in the theory of negation.

Perhaps the fundamental dualism is that between facts of the same form except for one being positive and one negative: e.g. suppose xRy and $\sim(zRw)$ are both facts. A proposition asserting xRy will be a fact of the same form: "Brutus killed Caesar" establishes a relation between the word "Brutus" and the word "Caesar". But "$z \div Rw$" is itself a positive fact, not of the same form as the fact it symbolizes; negative facts are unsuitable as symbols. Thus the symbols for negative facts are themselves positive facts, but of a certain sort, i.e. (roughly) such as contain the word "not". It would seem that falsehood lies in the wrong relation of the facts which are propositions to the facts which they "mean". And the possibility of *two* relations results formally from the duality of positive and negative facts. This idea needs developing, but certainly seems promising.

18i Thoughts on Language, Leading to
Language of Thought [1918]

THEORY OF SYMBOLISM. Three Branches:

(1) Formal (2) Physiological (3) Psychological.

(1) Considers formal characteristics of correspondence between symbol and symbolized. E.g. relation of names to things, how it comes that a complex symbol (proposition) can have *two* relations (true–false) to what it stands for, etc.

(2) Considers speech and writing as bodily acts, and inquires what relation (if any) they can have to their "meaning" without bringing in "mind". Seems clear that such a theory could be complete. We could have an

automaton that would make appropriate remarks.

(3) Considers "thought", and words etc. as "expressions" of thought. If (2) were sufficiently satisfactory, (3) might become superfluous.

Not all language is gregarious. A door will squeak when it wants its hinges oiled. This is not as a warning signal to other doors.

Linguistics, Psychology and Logic all required for theory of symbolism. We require an analysis of the conception of *meaning*.

Names of Persons. There is a causal correlation between Jones and "Jones", i.e. (as a first approximation) when I see Jones, I say "Jones". But we want
10 to understand "Jones" as cause, not only as effect. When, without seeing Jones, I hear the name "Jones", it causes what we call the "idea" of Jones. What is this? Images, mainly. To know the meaning of "Jones" is to have images of Jones evoked by the noise "Jones". This reduces the question to that of images, which is a distinct question. In all this, there is no need for the association to be "conscious"; the meaning of "Jones" is known if it is associated with appropriate impressions and images, even if we have not *noticed* the association.

Positive and Negative Atomic Facts and Propositions. Composed of three constituents (two terms and relation). There are two kinds of facts, viz. xRy and
20 $\sim (xRy)$. What is a *fact*, a *constituent of a fact*, and the *form of a fact*, I take as indefinables. I say that there are two forms of dual-relation fact, viz. xRy and $\sim (xRy)$. (The same applies to other sorts of facts.) I say further that the symbols by which we express *both* these forms of facts are themselves facts of the form xRy. "Smith hates Jones" and "Smith does not hate Jones" are both of them facts consisting in a relation between "Smith" and "Jones" —in the first case, that the word "hates" comes between them, in the second, that the words "does not hate" come between them. (It is *just possible* that the fact that symbols for facts are always *positive*, even when the facts symbolized are *negative*, may have something to do with the solution of
30 the contradictions, though at the moment I don't see how.)

[*N.B.* Analogous to this is that all apparent-variable facts are symbolized by facts of the form "$(\exists x).\phi x$". A fact of the form "$(x).\phi x$" would be too cumbrous as a symbol.]

A single word is a class of similar noises. A proposition is a class of series of noises, each noise being a member of a word. Each member of a proposition (i.e. each occasion when the proposition is enunciated) is a fact.

Return to "Smith hates Jones". There are two possible relations of this to the fact which determines its truth or falsehood: Smith may have or not have that relation to Jones which is the meaning of the word "*hates*". This is the formal basis of the possibility of using sentences to symbolize facts: the sentences *are* facts, whose form is the same as or opposite to that of the facts they are to symbolize. Hence truth and falsehood.

Observe that "hates" has meaning in quite a different way from "Smith" and "Jones". "Smith" and "Jones" are to call up *images*. But "hates", by itself, is to call up nothing. When it occurs with other words, so as to create a *fact*, its business is to call up a *belief* (whatever that may be). The word "hates" by itself is strictly devoid of meaning. The purpose of the word "hates" is merely to produce a certain relation between "Smith" and "Jones", so that there may be a fact about "Smith" and "Jones" to corres- 10 pond with the fact about Smith and Jones.

[This view, however, leaves us in the dark as to what is in common among various instances of hatred: Smith hates Jones, and Brown hates Robinson. These are instances of the *same* relation. What does this mean? It was this question that originally led me to assimilate relations to their terms, unduly, as I now think; nevertheless, the question must be remembered.]

It is difficult to say much more on the purely *formal* theory of proposi- tions. What is wanted next is a doctrine of *beliefs* or *judgments*, so as to define the "meaning" of a proposition. [A doctrine of (say) wishes would do equally well.] 20

Articulation of Problem. In considering the central problem of the "Analysis of Mind", we find that everything that is most stubbornly "mental" comes under the head of "propositional occurrences", i.e. occurrences which one would naturally express in such forms as "*A* believes that so-and-so" or "*A* desires that so-and-so" and so on. This makes it vital to the analysis of mind to have a theory of propositions. In dealing with propositions we have to consider (1) what a proposition is (2) its subjective meaning and (3) its objective meaning. As to (1), the matter is not difficult. It is a series of words. As to (3) the matter is not difficult: the objective meaning is the fact which makes the proposition true or false. It is as to (2) that the difficult 30 problems arise. In considering (2) we may ignore (3); the subjective mean- ing is quite independent of truth or falsehood. When I speak of "subjective meaning", I do not *necessarily* assume anything beyond the body. The subjective meaning may *be* a series of bodily acts. As a first approximation, it is whatever constitutes *belief* (but what it is that constitutes belief is not clear). But this is not quite correct, since we can *consider* a proposition or desire it or etc. But it must not be *assumed* as indubitable that when we believe a proposition and when we desire it, the proposition occurs in the same way in the two occurrences. One way of occurring *might* be simpler and more fundamental. 40

19

On "Bad Passions" [1919]

THIS PAPER WAS published in *The Cambridge Magazine*, 8 (1 Feb. 1919): 359. It is signed "O.B.E." but it is known to be by Russell because his letter, dated 21 January 1919, to C. K. Ogden, then the magazine's editor, survives. This letter has been published in facsimile in *Russell*, n.s. 1 (Summer 1981): 57.

> I enclose a little paper on rage, on the chance that you may care to print it in the *Magazine*. You may print it anonymously, or "By a retired diplomatist", or with my name or any other—Snooks Minor e.g. If you don't want it, I should be very grateful if you would return it.
>
> You can omit the allusion to castration if you so desire.

Ogden did not delete the allusion to castration. Russell's suggestion of "Snooks Minor" recalls his threat in 1911 to take the title "Lord Snooks" if he were created a peer in Asquith's plan to pack the House of Lords with Liberals.

A manuscript, entitled "Morality and Oppressive Impulses", exists (RA 220.011910). It bears the partly-obliterated date "Aug. 29.18", a day Russell was in Brixton Prison. The manuscript is nearly that of the published form except that the quotations from G. Stanley Hall's article have not been integrated into Russell's text. In addition the manuscript has one quotation from Hall which is not used in the published version. The result of collating the manuscript and the published version, which has been selected as copy-text, is reported in the Textual Notes.

ONE OF THE most difficult problems before the moralist and the constructive sociologist is the treatment of impulses recognized as undesirable, such as anger, cruelty, envy, etc. These may be classed together as impulses which essentially (not only accidentally) involve the thwarting of the desires and impulses of others. Such oppressive impulses are often so deep and instinctive that a life in which they are simply thwarted will be felt to be as unsatisfying as (say) a life of celibacy. Moreover, they are liable, if thwarted, to break out with a violence all the greater owing to repression.

Professor Stanley Hall has written an article on "The Freudian Methods Applied to Anger" (*American Journal of Psychology*, 1915), some extracts from which may serve to illustrate the nature of the problem.

"Some temperaments", he says, "seem to crave, if not need, outbreaks of it (rage) at certain intervals, like a certain well-poised lady, so sweet-tempered that every one imposed on her, till one day, at the age of 23, she had her first ebullition of temper, and went about to her college mates telling them plainly what she thought of them. She went home rested and happy, full of the peace that passeth understanding. Otto Heinze, and by implication Pfister, think nations that have too long or too assiduously cultivated peace must inevitably, sooner or later, relapse to the barbarisms of war, to vent their instincts for combat."

It is pointed out that anger is an incentive to a great deal of good work. "Richardson has collected 882 cases of mild anger, ... and finds ... that very much of the impulsion that makes us work and strive, attack and solve problems has an element of anger at its root." Thus what used to be called "bad passions" are by no means *wholly* evil in their effects. Nevertheless, society would gain if the good effects could be secured otherwise.

There are, broadly, three ways of dealing with impulses recognized by society as undesirable: (1) Rewards and punishments; (2) Sublimation, and the provision of harmless outlets; (3) Physiological treatment leading to the weakening or destruction of the impulses in question.

(1). Rewards and punishments include the whole of ordinary social morality, since people desire the good opinion of their neighbours and dread their bad opinion. This method is certainly necessary to some extent. Nine street boys out of ten would, if they dared, seize the hats of elderly gentlemen and run off with them; what restrains them is fear of punishment. Acts which, as it is, most people never even think of, would become common. Benvenuto Cellini murdered a man in the afternoon during his "constitutional", and came home to his work as if nothing had happened. However little we may think so, it is owing to the criminal law that we do not do likewise. Punishment forms habits which become automatic, as every one knows in training domestic animals. Therefore it has its uses. But it is a very superficial method. It only destroys certain manifestations of impulses, not the impulses themselves. Being unable to murder a man, we shall slander him or cause him to be dismissed from his employment or injure him in whatever way is safe. This is an improvement, but far from ideal. Moreover society can hardly be sufficiently subtle in its rules for rewarding and punishing: those in whom bad impulses are strong will find some way of being rewarded for harmful actions.

(2). Sublimation and the provision of harmless outlets have always been a great part of the business of religion and education. Religion itself is mainly a sublimation of various impulses. The belief in God and a future life are sublimations of fear; mysticism is primarily a sublimation of sex; hell is a sublimation of hate. Some Persian poet, I am told, relates how when he was tormented by love he took to reading the mystics, and all his earthly love faded away. This is a case of completely successful sublimation, where the impulse passes with all its strength and vitality into quite a new direction, prompting quite different acts from those which it prompted before. Similarly in Stanley Hall's article quoted above, there are cases in which rage has passed into ambition and hard work, in the first instance in order to become superior to the person who was the cause of the rage. This would not be a true case of sublimation until the ambition had actually replaced the rage, so that it no longer needed its original stimulus. Intellectual effort may be a sublimation of rage, a tigerish fury can be expended on abstract thought, when, but for this outlet it would have to vent itself on human beings. Beethoven's furies with his cook are notorious, but they would have been far worse if he had not also had his symphonies to punish.

Peaceful competition, in games, business, politics, etc., affords some outlet of a comparatively harmless kind for the fighting impulse; so do Alpine climbing, exploration, etc., for the few who have the opportunity for such occupations.

Sublimation, when successful, is very valuable. Probably almost all that is best in human achievement owes something to it. But it has very grave dangers. It tends to insincerity and weakness; when applied thoroughly it produces the type which is called "lady-like". If it is only partially accomplished in feeling, while no outlet in action is allowed to the crude impulse, the result is lack of vitality, day-dreaming, insufficient grip of reality, and elaborate self-deception to hide the crude impulse which lurks in the depths. If sublimation is to be compatible with mental health and strength, it needs, as a rule, to be supplemented by *some* indulgence of the crude impulse. It is probable that Beethoven's music would have suffered if he had had no cook upon whom to vent the unsublimated parts of his anger. It is at this point that real practical perplexity comes in. If a man's vigour and vitality depend upon oppressive actions, what is to be done? There is no doubt that, at present, such cases are frequent. The world as it is affords so many tolerated outlets for oppressive impulses that the problem is not acute now, but in a world with more humane institutions it would become pressing. If Beethoven could have been turned into a quiet well-behaved person, the loss to music would have outweighed the gain to his cook. If a man's energies are, in the main, employed in very useful channels, it is not worth while to destroy them by preventing him from being slightly oppressive. But the general rule will be to diminish oppression as much as possible.

(3). The impulsive life can be utterly transformed by physiological means. The most familiar instance is castration; but by stimulating or retarding the action of various glands, it would seem that character may be altogether changed. Such books as Cannon's *Bodily Changes in Pain,* 10 *Hunger, Fear and Rage* suggest immense possibilities in this direction. It is very probable that the ultimate solution of all moral problems is to be sought in facts of this kind. The education authority will decide what form of character is most virtuous, and the medical officers will produce this type of character. One of its distinguishing features will be, of course, respect for public bodies and acquiescence in the *status quo.* Therefore at that point human progress will cease.

20

On Propositions:
What They Are and How They Mean [1919]

THIS PAPER WAS published in *Aristotelian Society Supplementary Volume*, 2 (1919): 1–43. Russell read it to a joint session of the Aristotelian Society, the British Psychological Society, and the Mind Association in London on 11 July 1919. G. E. Moore was in the Chair and the audience was a large one. Robert C. Marsh included it in his collection of Russell's papers entitled *Logic and Knowledge: Essays, 1901– 1950* (1956).

The idea from which this paper grew came to Russell in prison. On 17 June 1918, in a letter to Gladys Rinder, he wrote:

> I keep on reading and thinking about behaviourism. If Wildon Carr is willing, I should like to write an Aristotelian paper on "Is introspection a source of knowledge?" There is a great deal to be done. The behaviourists do not tackle any of the difficult questions; yet there is something in them, though I do not think they are right. They deny images altogether: they say images are small movements of tongue and throat silently pronouncing words. This is obviously rot. But I like them for throwing down a challenge and for not being conventional. James's attack on "consciousness", the study of animal behaviour, and Freud, all naturally belong together. They have got hold of *some* important truth, but I don't know what, and certainly they don't.

As shall be evident shortly, Carr accepted Russell's offer. The proposed paper is not mentioned again in the surviving prison letters.

Russell wrote it between 23 February and 4 March 1919 at Garsington Manor, Lady Ottoline Morrell's country house. On the 23rd of February he wrote Lady Constance Malleson from the London flat he was sharing with Clifford Allen that "There is a terrible lot of psychology and discomfort in the flat at present", caused in part by Allen's ill health and in part by Allen's relationships with women. Russell advised her that he was going to Garsington, "as life here at present is unendurable for anybody of the male sex". "My work prospers", he went on, "every time I sit down to it, it goes better than I expect." Some of this work was preliminary to his writing this paper. He had resumed work on it three weeks earlier: "I have been working at Introspection," he wrote Lady Constance on 6 February, "on which I have to write a paper for the Aristotelian in a few months. No one will understand a word I say." Although the finished paper does not have "Introspection" in its title, as one might expect from this remark and his prison letter, it does play a central role in his argument.

Russell wrote Lady Constance twice on 4 March. In his evening letter he reports on his work:

> Since I have been here I have written a very long paper for the Aristotelian on "Propositions, what they are and how they mean". There is very good stuff in it, but I am not satisfied with it, and shall probably re-write it. I have also written an article for the *Dial* on "Democracy and Direct Action". I have read two books on Language, and am looking out for others. The book I wrote in prison was published today, and I got five copies.

Introduction to Mathematical Philosophy (1919) was the book he wrote in prison. There is no evidence that Russell did rewrite this paper, but the four months intervening before its oral delivery left plenty of time for him to do so. Wartime journalism had turned him into a very efficient writing machine.

Most of the paper found its way into *The Analysis of Mind* (1921); the Textual Notes show in detail where to find verbatim passages from the paper in the book. Part I of the paper summarizes the position he took on facts in Paper 17. The other parts reflect the intensive study of psychological literature he undertook in prison. It is, then, the first important fruit of his prison project.

No manuscript survives, so the copy-text is the *Aristotelian Society* version.

A PROPOSITION MAY be defined as: *What we believe when we believe truly or falsely*. This definition is so framed as to avoid the assumption that, whenever we believe, our belief is true or false. In order to arrive, from the definition, at an account of what a proposition is, we must decide what belief is, what is the sort of thing that can be believed, and what constitutes truth or falsehood in a belief. I take it as evident that the truth or falsehood of a belief depends upon a *fact* to which the belief "refers". Therefore it is well to begin our inquiry by examining the nature of facts.[1]

I. STRUCTURE OF FACTS

10 I mean by a "fact" anything complex. If the world contains no simples, then whatever it contains is a fact; if it contains any simples, then facts are whatever it contains except simples. When it is raining, that is a fact; when the sun is shining, that is a fact. The distance from London to Edinburgh is a fact. That all men die is probably a fact. That the planets move round the sun approximately in ellipses is a fact. In speaking of these as facts, I am not alluding to the phrases in which we assert them, or to our frame of mind while we make the assertions, but to those features in the constitution of the world which make our assertions true (if they are true) or false (if they are false).

20 To say that facts are complex is the same thing as to say that they have *constituents*. That Socrates was Greek, that he married Xantippe, that he died of drinking the hemlock, are facts that all have something in common, namely, that they are "about" Socrates, who is accordingly said to be a constituent of each of them.

Every constituent of a fact has a *position* (or several positions) in the fact. For example, "Socrates loves Plato" and "Plato loves Socrates" have the same constituents, but are different facts, because the constituents do not have the same positions in the two facts. "Socrates loves Socrates" (if it is a fact) contains Socrates in two positions. "Two and two are four" contains 30 *two* in two positions. "$2+2 = 2^2$" contains 2 in four positions.

Two facts are said to have the same "form" when they differ only as regards their constituents. In this case, we may suppose the one to result from the other by *substitution* of different constituents. For example, "Napoleon hates Wellington" results from "Socrates loves Plato" by substituting Napoleon for Socrates, Wellington for Plato, and *hates* for *loves*. It

---

1 In what follows, the first section, on the structure of facts, contains nothing essentially novel, and is only included for the convenience of the reader. I have defended its doctrines elsewhere, and have therefore here set them down dogmatically. On the other hand, later sections contain views which I have not hitherto advocated, resulting chiefly from an 40 attempt to define what constitutes "meaning" and to dispense with the "subject" except as a logical construction.

is obvious that some, but not all, facts can be thus derived from "Socrates loves Plato." Thus some facts have the same form as this, and some have not. We can represent the form of a fact by the use of variables: thus "xRy" may be used to represent the form of the fact that Socrates loves Plato. But the use of such expressions, as well as of ordinary language, is liable to lead to mistakes unless care is taken to avoid them.

There are an infinite number of forms of facts. It will conduce to simplicity to confine ourselves, for the moment, to facts having only three constituents, namely, two terms and a dual (or dyadic) relation. In a fact which has three constituents, two can be distinguished from the third by the circumstance that, if these two are interchanged, we still have a fact, or, at worst, we obtain a fact by taking the contradictory of what results from the interchange, whereas the third constituent (the relation) cannot ever be interchanged with either of the others. Thus if there is such a fact as "Socrates loves Plato", there is either "Plato loves Socrates" or "Plato does not love Socrates", but neither Socrates nor Plato can replace *loves*. (For purposes of illustration, I am for the moment neglecting the fact that Socrates and Plato are themselves complex.) The essentially non-interchangeable constituent of a fact containing three constituents is called a *dual* (or dyadic) *relation*; the other two constituents are called the *terms* of that relation in that fact. The terms of dual relations are called *particulars*.[2]

Facts containing three constituents are not all of the same form. There are two forms that they may have, which are each other's opposites. "Socrates loves Plato" and "Napoleon does not love Wellington" are facts which have opposite forms. We will call the form of "Socrates loves Plato" *positive*, and the form of "Napoleon does not love Wellington" *negative*. So long as we confine ourselves to atomic facts, i.e. to such as contain only one verb and neither generality nor its denial, the distinction between positive and negative facts is easily made. In more complicated cases there are still two kinds of facts, though it is less clear which is positive and which negative.

Thus the forms of facts divide into pairs, such that, given appropriate constituents, there is always a fact of one of the two correlated forms but not of the other. Given any two particulars of a dual relation, say x and y and R, there will be either a fact "xRy", or a fact "not-xRy". Let us suppose, for the sake of illustration, that x has the relation R to y, and z does not have the relation S to w. Each of these facts contains only three constituents, a relation and two terms; but the two facts do not have the same form. In the one, R relates x and y; in the other, S does not relate z and w. It must not be

---

2 The above discussion might be replaced by that of subject-predicate facts or of facts containing triadic, tetradic, ... relations. But it is possible to doubt whether there are subject-predicate facts, and the others are more complicated than those containing three constituents. Hence these are best for purposes of illustration.

supposed that the negative fact contains a constituent corresponding to the word "not". It contains no more constituents than a positive fact of the correlative positive form. The difference between the two forms is ultimate and irreducible. We will call this characteristic of a form its *quality*. Thus facts, and forms of facts, have two opposite qualities, positive and negative.

There is implanted in the human breast an almost unquenchable desire to find some way of avoiding the admission that negative facts are as ultimate as those that are positive. The "infinite negative" has been endlessly abused and interpreted. Usually it is said that, when we deny something, we are really asserting something else which is incompatible with what we deny. If we say "roses are not blue", we mean "roses are white or red or yellow". But such a view will not bear a moment's scrutiny. It is only plausible when the positive quality by which our denial is supposed to be replaced is incapable of existing together with the quality denied. "The table is square" may be denied by "the table is round", but not by "the table is wooden". The only reason we can deny "the table is square" by "the table is round" is that what is round is *not* square. And this has to be a *fact*, though just as negative as the fact that this table is not square. Thus it is plain that incompatibility cannot exist without negative facts.

There might be an attempt to substitute for a negative fact the mere absence of a fact. If A loves B, it may be said, that is a good substantial fact; while if A does not love B, that merely expresses the absence of a fact composed of A and loving and B, and by no means involves the actual existence of a negative fact. But the absence of a fact is itself a negative fact; it is the fact that there is *not* such a fact as A loving B. Thus, we cannot escape from negative facts in this way.

Of the many attempts that have been made to dispense with negative facts, the best known to me is that of Mr. Demos.[3] His view is as follows: There is among propositions an ultimate relation of *opposition*; this relation is indefinable, but has the characteristic that when two propositions are opposites they cannot both be true, though they may both be false. Thus "John is in" and "John is gone to Semipalatinsk" are opposites. When we deny a proposition, what we are really doing is to assert: "Some opposite of this proposition is true." The difficulty of this theory is to state the very important fact that two opposites cannot both be true. "The relation of opposition", says Mr. Demos, "is such that, if p opposes q, p and q are not both true (at least one of them is false). This must not be taken as a definition, for it makes use of the notion 'not' which, I said, is equivalent to the notion 'opposite'. In fact, opposition seems epistemologically to be a primitive notion" (p. 191). Now if we take Mr. Demos's statement that "p

3 "A Discussion of a Certain Type of Negative Proposition", *Mind*, n.s., No. 102 (April 1917), pp. 188–196.

and q are not both true" and apply his definition to it, it becomes "an opposite of 'p and q are both true' is true". But this does not yield what we want. Suppose some obstinate person were to say: "I believe p, and I believe q, and I also believe that an opposite of 'p and q are both true' is true." What could Mr. Demos reply to such a person? He would presumably reply: "Don't you see that that is impossible? It cannot be the case that p and q are both true, and also that an opposite of 'p and q are both true' is true." But an opponent would retort by asking him to state his negation in his own language, in which case all that Mr. Demos could say would be: "Let us give the name P to the proposition 'p and q are both true.' Then the proposition that you assert and that I deny is 'P is true, and also some opposite of P is true.' Calling this proposition Q, and applying my definition of negation, what I am asserting is that some opposite of Q is true." This also the obstinate person would admit. He would go on for ever admitting opposites, but refusing to make any denials. To such an attitude, so far as I can see, there would be no reply except to change the subject. It is, in fact, necessary to admit that two opposites cannot both be true, and not to regard this as a statement to which the suggested definition of negation is to be applied. And the reason is that we must be able to say that a proposition is not true without having to refer to any other proposition.

The above discussion has prematurely introduced propositions, in order to follow Mr. Demos's argument. We shall see later, when we have defined propositions, that all propositions *are* positive facts, even when they assert negative facts. This is, I believe, the source of our unwillingness to admit negative facts as ultimate. The subject of negative facts might be argued at great length, but as I wish to reach the proper topic of my paper, I will say no more about it, and will merely observe that a not dissimilar set of considerations shows the necessity of admitting *general* facts, i.e. facts about all or some of a collection.

II. MEANING OF IMAGES AND WORDS

The questions which arise concerning propositions are so many and various that it is not easy to know where to begin. One very important question is as to whether propositions are what I call "incomplete symbols" or not. Another question is as to whether the word "proposition" can stand for anything except a form of words. A third question is as to the manner in which a proposition refers to the fact that makes it true or false. I am not suggesting that these are the only important questions, but they are, at any rate, questions which any theory of propositions should be able to answer.

Let us begin with the most tangible thing: the proposition as a form of words. Take again "Socrates loves Plato." This is a complex symbol, composed of three symbols, namely "Socrates" and "loves" and "Plato". Whatever may be the meaning of the complex symbol, it is clear that it depends upon the meanings of the separate words. Thus before we can hope to understand the meaning of a proposition as a form of words, we must understand what constitutes the meaning of single words.

Logicians, so far as I know, have done very little towards explaining the nature of the relation called "meaning", nor are they to blame in this, since the problem is essentially one for psychology. But before we tackle the question of the meaning of a word, there is one important observation to be made as to what a word *is*.

If we confine ourselves to spoken words in one language, a word is a class of closely similar noises produced by breath combined with movements of the throat and tongue and lips. This is not a *definition* of "words", since some noises are meaningless, and meaning is part of the definition of "words". It is important, however, to realize at the outset that what we call one word is not a single entity, but a class of entities: there are instances of the word "dog" just as there are instances of dogs. And when we hear a noise, we may be doubtful whether it is the word "dog" badly pronounced or not: the noises that are instances of a word shade off into other noises by continuous gradations, just as dogs themselves may shade off into wolves according to the evolutionary hypothesis. And, of course, exactly the same remarks apply to written words.

It is obvious to begin with that, if we take some such word as "Socrates" or "dog", the meaning of the word consists in some relation to an object or set of objects. The first question to be asked is: Can the relation called "meaning" be a direct relation between the word as a physical occurrence and the object itself, or must the relation pass through a "mental" intermediary, which could be called the "idea" of the object?

If we take the view that no "mental" intermediary is required, we shall have to regard the "meaning" of a word as consisting in what James would call "processes of leading". That is to say, the causes and effects of the occurrence of a word will be connected, in some way to be further defined, with the object which is its meaning. To take an unusually crude instance: You see John, and you say, "Hullo, John"—this gives the *cause* of the word; you call "John", and John appears at the door—this gives the *effect* of the word. Thus, in this case, John is both cause and effect of the word "John". When we say of a dog that he "knows" his name, it is only such causal correlations that are indubitable: we cannot be sure that there is any "mental" occurrence in the dog when we call him and he comes. Is it possible that all use and understanding of language consists merely in the fact that certain events cause it, and it, in turn, causes certain events?

This view of language has been advocated, more or less tentatively, by Professor Watson in his book on *Behavior*.[4] The behaviourist view, as I

4 *Behavior: An Introduction to Comparative Psychology* (New York, 1914), by John B. Watson, Professor of Psychology in the Johns Hopkins University. See especially pp. 321–334.

understand it, maintains that "mental" phenomena, though they may exist, are not amenable to scientific treatment, because each of them can only be observed by one observer—in fact, it is highly doubtful whether even one observer can be aware of anything not reducible to some bodily occurrence. Behaviourism is not a metaphysic, but a principle of method. Since language is an observable phenomenon, and since language has a property which we call "meaning", it is essential to behaviourism to give an account of "meaning" which introduces nothing known only through introspection. Professor Watson recognizes this obligation and sets to work to fulfil it. Nor is it to be lightly *assumed* that he cannot do so, though I incline to the belief 10 that a theory of language which takes no account of images is incomplete in a vital point. But let us first see what is to be said in favour of the behaviourist theory of language.

Professor Watson denies altogether the occurrence of images, which he replaces by faint kinaesthetic sensations, especially those belonging to the pronunciation of words *sotto voce*. He defines "implicit behaviour" as "involving only the speech mechanisms (or the larger musculature in a minimal way; e.g., bodily attitudes or sets)" (p. 19). He adds: "It is implied in these words that there exists, or ought to exist, a method of observing implicit behavior. There is none at present. The larynx and tongue, we 20 believe, are the loci of most of the phenomena" (p. 20). He repeats these views in greater detail in a later chapter. The way in which the intelligent use of words is learnt is thus set forth:

The stimulus (object) to which the child often responds, a box, e.g., by movements such as opening and closing and putting objects into it, may serve to illustrate our argument. The nurse, observing that the child reacts with his hands, feet, etc., to the box, begins to say *"box"* when the child is handed the box, *"open box"* when the child opens it, *"close box"* when he closes it, and *"put doll in box"* when that act is executed. This is repeated over and over again. In 30 the process of time it comes about that without any other stimulus than that of the box which originally called out only the bodily habits, he begins to say *"box"* when he sees it, *"open box"* when he opens it, etc. The visible box now becomes a stimulus capable of releasing either the bodily habits or the word-habit, i.e., development has brought about two things: (1) a series of functional connections among arcs which run from visual receptor to muscles of throat, and (2) a series of already earlier connected arcs which run from the same receptor to the bodily muscles.... The object meets the child's vision. He runs to it and tries to reach it and says *"box"*. 40 ... Finally the word is uttered without the movement of going towards the box being executed.... Habits are formed of going to the box when the arms are full of toys. The child has been taught to deposit them there. When his arms are laden with toys and no box is there, the word-habit arises and he calls *"box"*; it is handed to him and he opens it and deposits the toys therein. This roughly marks what we would call the genesis of a true language habit.   (Pp. 329–330)

A few pages earlier, he says: "We say nothing of reasoning since we do not admit this as a genuine type of human behavior except as a special form of language habit" (p. 319).

The questions raised by the above theory of language are of great importance, since the possibility of what may be called a materialistic psychology turns on them. If a person talks and writes intelligently, he gives us as much evidence as we can ever hope to have of his possessing a mind. If his intelligent speech and writing can be explained on Professor Watson's lines, there seems to remain nothing he can do to persuade us that he is not merely physical.

There is, I think, a valid objection to the behaviouristic view of language on the basis of fact and an invalid one of theory. The objection of fact is that the denial of images appears empirically indefensible. The objection of theory (which, in spite of its apparent force, I do not believe to be unanswerable) is that it is difficult, on the basis of the above quotations, to account for the occurrence of the word when the object is merely desired, not actually present. Let us take these in succession.

(1) *Existence of Images.* Professor Watson, one must conclude, does not possess the faculty of visualizing, and is unwilling to believe that others do. Kinaesthetic images can be explained away, as being really small sensations of the same kind as those that would belong to actual movements. Inner speech, in particular, in so far as it is not accompanied by auditory images, may, I think, really consist of such small sensations, and be accompanied by small movements of the tongue or throat such as behaviourism requires. Tactile images might possibly be similarly explained. But visual and auditory images cannot be so explained, because, if taken as sensations, they actually contradict the laws of physics. The chair opposite to you is empty; you shut your eyes and visualize your friend as sitting in it. This is an event in you, not in the outer world. It *may* be a *physiological* event, but even so it must be radically distinguished from a visual sensation, since it affords no part of the data upon which our knowledge of the physical world outside our own body is built. If you try to persuade an ordinary uneducated person that she cannot call up a visual picture of a friend sitting in a chair, but can only use words describing what such an occurrence would be like, she will conclude that you are mad. (This statement is based upon experiment.) I see no reason whatever to reject the conclusion originally suggested by Galton's investigations, namely, that the habit of abstract pursuits makes learned

men much inferior to the average in the power of visualizing, and much more exclusively occupied with words in their "thinking". When Professor Watson says: "I should throw out imagery altogether and attempt to show that practically all natural thought goes on in terms of sensori-motor processes in the larynx (but not in terms of imageless thought)" (*Psychological Review*, 1913, p. 174n.), he is, it seems to me, mistaking a personal peculiarity for a universal human characteristic.

The rejection of images by behaviourists is, of course, part of their rejection of introspection as a source of knowledge. It will be well, therefore, to consider for a moment the grounds in favour of this rejection. 10

The arguments of those who oppose introspection as a scientific method seem to me to rest upon two quite distinct grounds, of which one is much more explicit in their writings than the other. The ground which is the more explicit is that data obtained by introspection are private and only verifiable by one observer, and cannot therefore have that degree of public certainty which science demands. The other, less explicit, ground is that physical science has constructed a spatio-temporal cosmos obeying certain laws, and it is irritating to have to admit that there are things in the world which do not obey these laws. It is worth while to observe that the definition of introspection is different according as we take the one or the other of these grounds of 20 objection.

If privacy is the main objection to introspective data, we shall have to include among such data all bodily sensations. A tooth-ache, for example, is essentially private. The dentist may see that your tooth is in a condition in which it is likely to ache, but he does not feel your ache, and only knows what you mean by an ache through his own experience of similar occurrences. The correlation of cavities with tooth-aches has been established by a number of observations, each of which was private, in exactly the sense which is considered objectionable. And yet one would not call a person introspective because he was conscious of tooth-ache, and it is not very 30 difficult to find a place for tooth-ache in the physical world. I shall not insist upon the fact that, in the last analysis, all our sensations are private, and the public world of physics is built on similarities, not on identities. But it is worth while to insist upon the privacy of the sensations which gives us knowledge of our own body over and above the knowledge we have of other bodies. This is important, because no one regards as scientifically negligible the knowledge of our own body which is obtained through these private data.

This brings us to the second ground of objection to introspection, namely, that its data do not obey the laws of physics. This, though less emphasized, 40 is, I think, the objection which is really felt the more strongly of the two. And this objection leads to a definition of introspection which is much more in harmony with usage than that which results from making privacy the essential characteristic of its data. For example, Knight Dunlap, a vigorous opponent of introspection, contends that images are really muscular contractions,[5] and evidently regards our awareness of muscular contractions as not coming under the head of introspection. I think it will be found that the essential characteristic of introspective data is concerned with *localization*: either they are not localized at all, or they are localized in a place already physically occupied by something which would be inconsistent with them if they were regarded as part of the physical world. In either case, introspective data have to be regarded as not obeying the laws of physics, and this is, I think, the fundamental reason why an attempt is made to reject them.

The question of the publicity of data and the question of their physical status are not wholly unconnected. We may distinguish a gradually diminishing degree of publicity in various data. Those of sight and hearing are the most public; smell somewhat less so; touch still less; visceral sensations hardly at all. The question turns on the degree and frequency of similarity of sensations in neighbours at the same time. If we hear a clap of thunder when no one else does, we think we are mad; if we feel a stomach-ache when no one else does, we are in no way surprised. We say, therefore, that the stomach-ache is *mine*, while the thunder is not. But what is mine includes what belongs to the body, and it is here that the stomach-ache belongs. The stomach-ache is *localized*: it has a position near the surface of the stomach, which is visible and palpable. (How the localization is effected need not concern us in this connexion.) Now, when we consider the localization of images, we find a difference according to the nature of the images. Images of private sensations can be localized where the private sensations would be, without causing any gross or obvious violation of physical laws. Images of words in the mouth can be located in the mouth. For this reason, there is no *primâ facie* objection to regarding them, as Watson does, as small sensations: this view may or may not be true, but it is not capable of being rejected without more ado. In regard to all private sensations, the distinction between image and sensation is not sharp and definite. But visual and auditory images are in quite a different position, since the physical event to which they would point if they were sensations is not taking place.

Thus the crucial phenomena as regards introspection are images of public sensations, i.e. especially visual and auditory images. On grounds of observation, in spite of Watson, it seems impossible to deny that such images occur. But they are not public, and, if taken as sensations, contradict the

5 *Psychological Review*, 1916, "Thought-Content and Feeling", p. 59. See also his articles in an earlier volume of the same review, "The Case against Introspection", 1912, pp. 404–413, and "The Nature of Perceived Relations", *ibid.*, pp. 415–446. In this last article he states "that 'introspection,' divested of its mythological suggestion of the observing of consciousness, is really the observation of bodily sensations (sensibles) and feelings (feelables)" (p. 427n.).

laws of physics. Reverting to the case of visualizing a friend in a chair which, in fact, is empty, you cannot locate the image in the body because it is visual, nor (as a physical phenomenon) in the chair, because the chair, as a physical object, is empty. Thus it seems that the physical world does not include all that we are aware of, and that introspection must be admitted as a source of knowledge distinct from sensation.

I do not, of course, mean to suggest that visual and auditory images are our only non-physical data. I have taken them as affording the strongest case for the argument; but when they are admitted, there is no longer any reason to reject other images.   10

Our criticism of fact, as against Watson, has led us to the conclusion that it is impossible to escape the admission of images as something radically distinct from sensations, particularly as being not amenable to the laws of physics. It remains to consider a possible criticism of theory, namely, that it is difficult, on his view, to account for the occurrence of a word when an absent object is desired. I do not think this criticism valid, but I think the considerations which it suggests are important.

(2) *Words in the Absence of their Objects.* In the account given by Watson of the child learning to use the word "box", attention is almost wholly concentrated on the way the word comes to occur in the presence of the box. 20 There is only a brief reference to the use of the word when the object is absent but desired: "Habits are formed of going to the box when the arms are full of toys. The child has been taught to deposit them there. When his arms are laden with toys and no box is there, the word-habit arises and he calls '*box*.'" The difficulty—I think not insuperable—which arises in regard to this account is that there seems no adequate stimulus for the word-habit in the circumstances supposed. We are assuming that the habit has been formed of saying "box" when the box is present; but how can such a habit lead to the use of the same word when the box is absent? The believer in images will say that, in the absence of the box, an image of it will occur in 30 the child, and this image will have the same associations as the box has, including the association with the word "box". In this way the use of the word is accounted for; but in Watson's account it remains mysterious. Let us see what this objection amounts to.

The phenomenon called "thinking", however it may be analysed, has certain characteristics which cannot be denied. One of the most obvious of these is that it enables us to act with reference to absent objects, and not only with reference to those that are sensibly present. The tendency of the behaviourist school is to subordinate cognition to action, and to regard action as physically explicable. Now I do not wish to deny that much action, 40 perhaps most, is physically explicable, but nevertheless it seems impossible to account for *all* action without taking account of "ideas", i.e. images of absent objects. If this view is rejected, it will be necessary to explain away all desire. Desire is not dealt with by Watson:[6] it and kindred words are absent from the index to his book. In the absence of such a phenomenon as desire, it is difficult to see what is happening when the child with his arms full of toys says "box". One would naturally say that an image of the box occurs, combined with the feeling we call "desire", and that the image is associated with the word just as the object would be, because the image resembles the object. But Watson requires that the arms full of toys should cause the word "box" without any intermediary. And it is not at first sight obvious how this is to be brought about.

10   To this objection there seem two possible replies: one, that the occurrence of the image on the usual theory is just as mysterious as the occurrence of the word on Watson's theory; the other, that the passage from full arms to the word "box" is a telescoped process, derived from the habit of the transition from full arms to the box and thence to the word "box". The objection to the second of these replies seems to be that the transition to the word "box" in the absence of the box *feels* quite unlike the transition to the word through the actual box: in the latter there is satisfaction, in the former dissatisfaction. Telescoped processes give similar feelings to complete processes; in so far as they differ, they give more satisfaction as involving less

20 effort. The word "box" is not the terminus of the child's efforts, but a stage towards their success. It seems difficult, therefore, to assimilate the occurrence of a word in desire to a telescoped process. The retort to the first reply, namely, that the occurrence of the image is as mysterious as the occurrence of the word, is that, if images are admitted, we can admit psychological causal laws which are different from those of the physical world, whereas on Watson's view we shall have to admit physiological laws which are different from those of physics. In the physical world, if A often causes B, and B often causes C, it does not happen that, in those cases where A fails to cause B, it nevertheless causes C by a telescoped process. I go often to a certain

30 restaurant (A), eat there (B), and find my hunger satisfied (C). But, however often this has happened, if, on a certain occasion, the restaurant is closed, so that B fails, I cannot arrive at C. If I could, economy in wartime would be easier than it is. Now, the process Watson assumes is strictly analogous to this. In his theory we have a frequent transition from arms-full (A) to the box (B) and thence to the word "box" (C). Then one day the transition from A to B fails, but nevertheless the transition from A to C takes place. This demands other causal laws than those of physics—at least *primâ facie*. If images are admitted, it is easy to see that the laws of their occurrence and effects are different from those of physics, and therefore the

40 above difficulty does not exist in regard to them; but if they are denied, a

6 The only discussion of desire by Watson, as far as I know, is in connection with psychoanalysis in his article, "The Psychology of Wish Fulfilment", *Scientific Monthly*, November, 1916.

difference of causal laws is required within the realm of matter.

This argument, however, is by no means conclusive. The behaviour of living matter is obviously in some respects different from that of dead matter, but this does not prove that the difference is ultimate. Gases and solids behave differently, yet both obey ultimate physical laws. The chief peculiarities in the behaviour of animals are those due to habit and association, all of which, I believe, may be summarized in the one law: "When A and B have often existed in close temporal contiguity, either tends to cause the other." This law will only apply to occurrences within the body of a single animal. But I think it suffices to account for telescoped processes, and for the use of words in the absence of their objects. Thus in Watson's instance, the child has frequently experienced the sequence: arms-full, box, the word "box". Thus arms-full and the word "box" have frequently existed in close temporal contiguity, and hence arms-full can come to cause the word "box". They cannot cause the box itself, because this is governed by physical laws independent of the child's body; but they can cause the word. (The above law, however, may be explained on orthodox physical lines by the properties of nervous tissue, and does not demand a *fundamental* distinction between physiology and physics.) If, therefore, images were not empirically undeniable, I should not consider them theoretically necessary in order to account for the occurrence of words in the absence of their objects.

William James, in his *Essays in Radical Empiricism*, developed the view that the mental and the physical are not distinguished by the stuff of which they are made, but only by their causal laws. This view is very attractive, and I have made great endeavours to believe it. I think James is right in making the distinction between the causal laws the essential thing. There do seem to be psychological and physical causal laws which are distinct from each other.[7] We may define psychology as the study of the one sort of laws, and physics as the study of the other. But when we come to consider the stuff of the two sciences, it would seem that there are some particulars which obey only physical laws (namely, unperceived material things), some which obey only psychological laws (namely, images, at least), and some which obey both (namely, sensations). Thus sensations will be both physical and mental, while images will be purely mental. The use of words actually pronounced or written is part of the physical world, but in so far as words obtain their meaning through images, it is impossible to deal adequately with words without introducing psychology and taking account of data obtained by introspection. If this conclusion is valid, the behaviourist theory of language is inadequate, in spite of the fact that it suggests much

7 I do not pretend to know whether the distinction is ultimate and irreducible. I say only that it is to be accepted practically in the present condition of science.

that is true and important.

I shall henceforth assume the existence of images, and shall proceed, on this assumption, to define the "meaning" of words and images.

In considering the meaning of either a word or an image, we have to distinguish

(1) The causes of the word or image,
(2) Its effects,
(3) What is the relation that constitutes meaning.

It is fairly clear that "meaning" is a relation involving causal laws, but it
10 involves also something else which is less easy to define.

The meaning of words differs, as a rule, from that of images by depending upon association, not upon similarity.

To "think" of the meaning of a word is to call up images of what it means. Normally, grown-up people speaking their own language use words without thinking of their meaning. A person "understands" a word when (a) suitable circumstances make him use it, (b) the hearing of it causes suitable behaviour in him. We may call these two active and passive understanding respectively. Dogs often have passive understanding of some words, but not active understanding.

20   It is not necessary to "understanding" a word that a person should "know what it means", in the sense of being able to say "this word means so-and-so." A word has a meaning, more or less vague; but the meaning is only to be discovered by observing its use: the use comes first, and the meaning is distilled out of it. The relation of a word to its meaning is, in fact, of the nature of a causal law, and there is no more reason why a person using a word correctly should be conscious of its meaning than there is for a planet which is moving correctly to be conscious of Kepler's laws.

To illustrate what is meant by "understanding" words and sentences, let us suppose that you are walking in London with an absent-minded friend.
30 You say "look out, there's a motor coming." He will glance round and jump aside without the need of any "mental" intermediary. There need be no "ideas", but only a stiffening of the muscles, followed quickly by action. He "understands" the words, because he does the right thing. Such "understanding" may be regarded as belonging to the nerves and brain, being habits which they have acquired while the language was being learnt. Thus understanding in this sense may be reduced to mere physiological causal laws.

If you say the same thing to a Frenchman with a slight knowledge of English, he will go through some inner speech which may be represented by
40 "Que dit-il? Ah oui, une automobile." After this, the rest follows as with the Englishman. Watson would contend that the inner speech must be actually

incipiently pronounced; we should argue that it might be merely imagined. But this point need not detain us at present.

If you say the same thing to a child who does not yet know the word "motor", but does know the other words you are using, you produce a feeling of anxiety and doubt: you will have to point and say "there, that's a motor." After that, the child will roughly understand the word "motor", though he may include trains and steam-rollers. If this is the first time the child has heard the word "motor", he may, for a long time, continue to recall this scene when he hears the word.

So far we have found four ways of understanding words: 10

(1) On suitable occasions you use the word properly.
(2) When you hear it, you act appropriately.
(3) You associate the word with another word (say in a different language) which has the appropriate effect on behaviour.
(4) When the word is being first learnt, you associate it with an object, which is what it "means"; thus the word acquires some of the same causal efficacy as the object. The word "motor!" can make you leap aside, just as the motor can, but it cannot break your bones.

So far, everything can be accounted for by behaviour. But so far we have only considered what may be called the "demonstrative" use of language to   20 point out a feature in the present environment; we have not considered what we may call its "narrative" use, of which we may take as an instance the telling of some remembered event.

Let us take again the case of the child hearing the word "motor" for the first time. On some later occasion, we will suppose, the child remembers the incident and relates it to someone else. In this case, both the active and passive understanding of words is different from what it is when words are used demonstratively. The child is not seeing a motor, but only remembering one; the hearer does not look round in expectation of seeing a motor coming, but "understands" that a motor came at some earlier time. The   30 whole of this occurrence is much more difficult to account for on behaviourist lines—indeed, it does not call for any particular behaviour. It is clear that, in so far as the child is genuinely remembering, he has a picture of the past occurrence, and his words are chosen so as to describe the picture; and in so far as the hearer is genuinely apprehending what is said, the hearer is acquiring a picture more or less like that of the child. It is true that this process may be telescoped through the operation of the word-habit. The child may not genuinely remember the incident, but only have the habit of the appropriate words, as in the case of a poem which we know by heart though we cannot remember learning it. And the hearer also may only pay   40 attention to the words, and not call up any corresponding picture. But it is nevertheless the possibility of a memory-image in the child and an imagination-image in the hearer that makes the essence of the "meaning" of the words. In so far as this is absent, the words are mere counters, capable of meaning, but not at the moment possessing it. We may say that, while words used demonstratively describe and are intended to cause sensations, the same words used in narrative describe and are intended to cause images.

We have thus two other ways in which words can mean (perhaps not fundamentally distinct), namely, the way of memory and the way of imagination. That is to say:

10 (5) Words may be used to describe or recall a memory-image: to describe it when it already exists, or to recall it where the words exist as a habit and are known to be descriptive of some past experience.

(6) Words may be used to describe or create an imagination-image: to describe it, for example, in the case of a poet or novelist, or to create it in the ordinary case of giving information—though in the latter case, it is intended that the imagination-image, when created, shall be accompanied by belief that something of the sort has occurred.

These two ways of using words may be spoken of together as the use of words in "thinking". This way of using words, since it depends upon 20 images, cannot be fully dealt with on behaviourist lines. And this is really the most essential function of words: that, primarily through their connexion with images, they bring us into touch with what is remote in time or space. When they operate without the medium of images, this seems to be a telescoped process. Thus the problem of the meaning of words is reduced to the problem of the meaning of images.

The "meaning" of images is the simplest kind of meaning, because images resemble what they mean, whereas words, as a rule, do not. Images are said to be "copies" of sensations. It is true that this assumption is liable to sceptical criticism, but I shall assume it to be true. It appears to 30 common sense to be verified by such experiences as, e.g., recalling a familiar room, and then going into the room and finding it as it was remembered. If our memory was wrong, we must suppose that the room and our image of it have undergone similar changes, which does not seem a plausible hypothesis. Thus for practical purposes we are justified in assuming that, in this case, our image resembled what the room was when we previously saw it. We may then say that our image "means" the room.

The question what a given image "means" is partly within the control of our will. The image of a printed word may mean, not the word, but what the word means. The image of a triangle may mean one particular triangle, or 40 triangles in general. In thinking of dogs in general, we may use a vague image of a dog, which means the species, not any individual. Similarly in recalling a friend's face we usually do not recall any one special occasion when we have seen it, but a compromise image of many occasions.

While some images mean particulars and others mean universals (in early stages of thought meaning is too vague to be either definitely particular or definitely universal), all images *are* particulars, but what they mean depends upon the nature of their causal efficacy. An image means a universal if its effects depend only upon its prototype being an instance of that universal. Thus, if I call up an image of a dog with a view to a general statement about dogs, I only *use* those characteristics of my image which it shares with all images of dogs. We can, to some extent, use or ignore the particular features of an image as we choose. In using *words*, we always ignore all that is peculiar to the instance of the word, except in elocution and calligraphy. Two instances of the word "dog" are more alike than two dogs; this is one reason why words help in dealing with universals.

If we accept Hume's principle that simple ideas are derived from impressions, we shall hold that at any rate the simple sensible qualities that enter into an image are "copies" of sensible qualities that have been given in sensation. Complex images are often, but not always, copies of complex sensations; their constituents, if Hume is right, are always copies of something given in sensation. That of which an image is a copy is called its "prototype"; and this, or its parts, by Hume's principle, is always an indispensable part of the cause either of the image, or of its constituents (in the case of a complex imagination-image).

The effects of an image tend to resemble those of its prototype, or to produce desire or aversion for it. This is one link between an image and its meaning. The thought of a drink has effects on a thirsty man which are similar to those of a sight of the foaming glass. This similarity belongs also to words, primarily, no doubt, through their power of calling up images, but afterwards directly.

The way in which an image resembles its prototype is peculiar. Images as a class have (with rare exceptions) characteristic differences from sensations as a class, but individual images, subject to these differences, resemble individual sensations. Images, however, are of various degrees of vagueness, and the vaguer they are the more different objects can be accepted as their prototypes. The nearest approach that I can make to a definition of the relation of image and prototype is this: If an object O is the prototype (or a prototype, in the case of vagueness) of an image, then, in the presence of O, we can recognize it as what we had an image "of". We may then say that O is the "meaning" (or a meaning, in the case of vagueness) of the image. But, as we saw, meaning is to some extent subject to the will: a "generic" image, for example, is simply one intended to be generic.

III. PROPOSITIONS AND BELIEF

In regard to belief, there are three elements to be considered, namely: (1) the content which is believed, (2) the relation of the content to its "objective", i.e. to the fact which makes it true or false, (3) the element which *is* belief, as opposed to consideration of the same content, or doubt concerning it, or desire for it, etc. The second of these questions I propose to postpone until the next section; for the present, therefore, we are not concerned with the question what makes a belief true or false, though it is important to remember that the property of being true or false is what specially charac-
10 terizes beliefs. The other two questions we will consider in this section.

(1) *The Content of a Belief.* The view to be taken on this question depends, to some extent, upon the view we take of "ideas" or "presentations". We have here a great variety of theories urged by different authors. Many analytic psychologists—Meinong, for example—distinguish three elements in a presentation, namely, the act (or subject), the content, and the object. Realists such as Dr. Moore and myself have been in the habit of rejecting the content, while retaining the act and the object. American realists, on the other hand, have rejected both the act and the content, and have kept only the object; while idealists, in effect if not in words, have
20 rejected the object and kept the content.

Is there any way of deciding amid this bewildering variety of hypotheses?

I have to confess that the theory which analyses a presentation into act and object no longer satisfies me. The act, or subject, is schematically convenient, but not empirically discoverable. It seems to serve the same sort of purpose as is served by points and instants, by numbers and particles and the rest of the apparatus of mathematics. All these things have to be *constructed*, not postulated: they are not of the stuff of the world, but assemblages which it is convenient to be able to designate as if they were single things. The same seems to be true of the subject, and I am at a loss to
30 discover any actual phenomenon which could be called an "act" and could be regarded as a constituent of a presentation. The logical analogies which have led me to this conclusion have been reinforced by the arguments of James and the American realists. It seems to me imperative, therefore, to construct a theory of presentation and belief which makes no use of the "subject", or of an "act" as a constituent of a presentation. Not that it is certain that there is no such thing as a "subject", any more than it is certain that there are no points and instants. Such things *may* exist, but we have no reason to suppose that they do, and therefore our theories ought to avoid assuming either that they exist or that they do not exist. The *practical* effect
40 of this is the same as if we assumed that they did not exist, but the theoretical attitude is different.

The first effect of the rejection of the subject is to render necessary a less relational theory of mental occurrences. Brentano's view, for example, that mental phenomena are characterized by "objective reference", cannot be accepted in its obvious sense. A sensation in particular can no longer be regarded as a relation of a subject to a sense-datum; accordingly the distinction between sensation and sense-datum lapses, and it becomes impossible to regard a sensation as in any sense cognitive. *Per contra*, a sensation becomes equally part of the subject-matter of physics and of psychology: it is simultaneously part of the mind of the person who "has" the sensation, and part of the body which is "perceived" by means of the sensation.[8] This topic demands amplification, but not here, since it is not very relevant to our present theme.

Apart from sensations, "presentations" appear, as a matter of observation, to be composed of images. Images, in accordance with what has just been said, are not to be regarded as relational in their own nature; nevertheless, at least in the case of memory-images, they are felt to point beyond themselves to something which they "mean". We have already dealt with the meaning of images as far as was possible without introducing belief; but it is clear that, when we remember by means of images, the images are accompanied by a belief, a belief which may be expressed (though with undue explicitness) by saying that they are felt to be copies of something that existed previously. And, without memory, images could hardly acquire meaning. Thus the analysis of belief is essential even to a full account of the meaning of words and images—for the meaning of words, we found, depends on that of images, which in turn depends on memory, which is itself a form of belief.

We have thus, so far, two sorts of mental "stuff", namely, (a) sensations, which are also physical, and (b) images, which are purely mental. Sensations do not "mean", but images often do, through the medium of belief.

The theory of belief which I formerly advocated, namely, that it consisted in a multiple relation of the subject to the objects constituting the "objective", i.e. the fact that makes the belief true or false, is rendered impossible by the rejection of the subject. The constituents of the belief cannot, when the subject is rejected, be the same as the constituents of its "objective". This has both advantages and disadvantages. The disadvantages are those resulting from the gulf between the content and the objective, which seem to make it doubtful in what sense we can be said to "know" the objective.[9] The advantages are those derived from the rehabilitation of the content, making it possible to admit propositions as actual complex occurrences, and

---

8 Assuming the theory of bodies developed in my *Knowledge of the External World*.

9 An important part of "knowing" will consist in the fact that, by means of "ideas", we are able to act in a way which is appropriate to an absent object, and are not dependent upon the stimulus of present sensation. I have not developed this order of ideas in the present paper, but I do not wish to minimize its importance.

doing away with the difficulty of answering the question: what do we believe when we believe falsely? The theory I wish to advocate, however, is not to be recommended by these advantages, or rejected on account of these disadvantages: it is presented for acceptance on the ground that it accords with what can be empirically observed, and that it rejects everything mythological or merely schematic. Whether it is epistemologically convenient or inconvenient is a question which has no bearing upon its truth or falsehood, and which I do not propose to consider further.

Are sensations and images, suitably related, a sufficient stuff out of which to compose beliefs? I think they are. But this question has to be asked twice over, once as regards the content, i.e. what is believed, and then again as regards the believing. For the present, we are concerned with the content.

That what is believed must always be the sort of thing which we express by a proposition, is a view which I am not concerned either to assert or to deny. It may be that a single simple image may be believed. For our purposes, however, the important beliefs, even if they be not the only ones, are those which, if rendered into explicit words, take the form of a proposition, i.e. that A is B, or that x has the relation R to y, or that all men are mortal, or that something like *this* existed before, or any other such sentence. But the psychological classification of the contents of beliefs is very different from the logical classification, and at present it is psychological questions that concern us. Psychologically, some of the simplest beliefs that occur seem to be among memories and expectations. When you recall some recent event, you are believing something. When you go to a familiar place, you may be expecting to find things much as usual: you may have an image of your host saying how-do-you-do, and you may believe that this will happen. In such cases, the belief is probably not put into words, but if it were, it would take the form of a proposition.

For the present I shall define a "proposition" as *the content of a belief*, except when, if ever, the content is simple. But since we have not yet defined "belief", this definition cannot be regarded as yet as a very valuable one.

The content of a belief *may* consist only of words, but if it does, this is a telescoped process. The primary phenomenon of belief consists of belief in images, of which, perhaps, memory is the most elementary example. But, it may be urged, a memory-belief does not consist *only* of the memory-image, together with bare believing: it is clear that the images may be the same for a memory and an expectation, which are nevertheless different beliefs. I incline to the view that the difference, in this case, is not in the content of what is believed, but in the believing; "believing" seems to be a generic term, covering different kinds of occurrences, of which memory and expectation are two. If this is so, difference of tense, in its psychologically earliest form, is no part of what is believed, but only of the way of believing it; the putting of the tense into the content is a result of later reflection. We may accordingly continue to regard images as giving the whole content of what is believed, when this is not expressed in words.

I shall distinguish a proposition expressed in words as a "word-proposition", and one consisting of images as an "image-proposition". As a general rule, a word-proposition "means" an image-proposition; this is the case with false propositions as well as with true ones, since image-propositions are as capable of falsehood as word-propositions.[10] I shall not speak of the fact which makes a proposition true or false as its "meaning", because this usage would be confusing in the case of falsehood. I shall speak of the relation of the proposition to the fact which makes it true or false as its "objective reference", or simply its "reference". But this will not occupy us till the next section.

The correspondence of word-propositions and image-propositions is, as a rule, by no means exact or simple. A form of words, unless artificially constructed, usually expresses not only the content of a proposition, but also what may be called a "propositional attitude"—memory, expectation, desire, etc. These attitudes do not form part of the proposition, i.e. of the content of what is believed when we believe, or desired when we desire.

Let us illustrate the content of a belief by an example. Suppose I am believing, but not in words, that "it will rain". What is happening? (1) Images, say, of the visual appearance of rain, the feeling of wetness, the patter of drops, interrelated, roughly, as the sensations would be if it were raining, i.e. there is a complex *fact composed of images*, having a structure analogous to that of the objective fact which would make the belief true. (2) There is *expectation*, i.e. that form of belief which refers to the future; we shall examine this shortly. (3) There is a relation between (1) and (2), making us say that (1) is "what is expected". This relation also demands investigation.

The most important thing about a proposition is that, whether it consists of images or of words, it is, whenever it occurs, an actual fact, having a certain analogy of structure—to be further investigated—with the fact which makes it true or false. A word-proposition, apart from niceties, "means" the corresponding image-proposition, and an image-proposition has an objective reference dependent upon the meanings of its constituent images.

(2) *Believing*. We come now to the question what actually constitutes believing, as opposed to the question of the content believed.

"Everyone", says William James, "knows the difference between imagining a thing and believing in its existence, between supposing a proposi-

---

10 There are, however, limitations of parallelism due to the fact that words often express also what belongs to the nature of the believing, as well as what belongs to the content. We have just had an instance of this in the case of tense; another will be considered later as regards negation.

tion and acquiescing in its truth.... *In its inner nature, belief, or the sense of reality, is a sort of feeling more allied to the emotions than to anything else.*"[11]

In the main, this view seems inevitable. When we believe a proposition, we have a certain feeling which is related to the content of the proposition in the way described as "believing that proposition". But I think various different feelings are collected together under the one word "belief", and that there is not any one feeling which pre-eminently *is* belief.

Before we can begin the analysis of belief, however, it is necessary to consider a theory which, whether explicitly advocated or not, seems implicit in pragmatism, and capable, if true, of affording a strong argument in favour of that philosophy. According to this theory—for which I cannot make any author responsible—there is no single occurrence which can be described as "believing a proposition", but belief simply consists in causal efficacy. Some ideas move us to action, others do not; those that do so move us are said to be "believed". A behaviourist who denies images will have to go even further, and deny image-propositions altogether. For him, I suppose, a belief will be, like a force in physics, an imagined fictitious cause of a series of actions. An animal, desiring A (in whatever may be the behaviouristic sense of "desire"), proceeds to try to realize B; we then say that the animal "believes" that B is a means to A. This is merely a way of collecting together a certain set of acts; it does not represent any single occurrence in the animal. But this view, whatever may be said in its favour where animals are concerned, is condemned as regards human beings by the admission of images. These being admitted, it becomes impossible to deny that image-propositions occur in people, and it is clear that belief has specially to do with propositions, given that propositions occur. And, this being admitted, we cannot make the differentia between a proposition believed and a proposition merely considered consist *only* in the presence or absence of causal efficacy. If we adhere to the maxim "same cause, same effect", we must hold that, if a proposition believed has different effects from those of the same proposition merely considered, there must be some *intrinsic* difference between believing and considering. The fact that believing moves us as considering does not, is evidence of some intrinsic difference between the two phenomena, even when the proposition concerned is the same in both cases.[12] This objection seems fatal to the causal-efficacy view as above stated, though I think some things that are true are *suggested* by the view.

It seems to me that there are various feelings that may attach to a proposition, any one of which constitutes belief. Of these I would instance

11 *Psychology*, Vol. II, Chap. XXI, p. 283. James's italics.

12 *Cf.* Brentano, *Psychologie vom empirischen Standpunkte* (Leipzig, 1874), p. 268 (criticizing Bain, *The Emotions and the Will*).

memory, expectation, and bare non-temporal assent. Whether there are others, I do not know. Memory requires for its truth that the objective of the proposition should be in the past, expectation that it should be in the future, while bare assent does not necessitate any special time-relation of the belief to the objective. Possibly disjunctions and implications may involve other kinds of belief-feelings. The chief importance of these different feelings, from our point of view, lies in the difficulty they create in translating the phenomena of belief into words. Tense puts the time-relation, apparently, into the content of what is believed, whereas, if the above theory is correct, tense is primarily embodied in the nature of the belief-feeling. However this may be, we can simplify our discussion by confining ourselves to bare assent, since it is undoubtedly possible to assent to a proposition concerning the past or the future, as opposed to remembering or expecting it.

When a belief, not expressed in words, is occurring in a person, and is constituted by the feeling of assent, what is actually happening, if we are right, is as follows: (a) we have a proposition, consisting of inter-related images, and possibly partly of sensations; (b) we have the feeling of assent; (c) we have a relation, actually subsisting, between the feeling of assent and the proposition, such as is expressed by saying that that is the proposition assented to. For other forms of belief, we have only to substitute other feelings in place of assent.

It might be urged, as against the above theory, that belief is not a positive phenomenon, though doubt and disbelief are so. It might be contended that what we call belief involves only the existence of the appropriate images, which will have the effects that are characteristic of belief unless some other simultaneous force operates against them. It is possible to develop a be-haviouristic logic, starting with the definition that two propositions are logically incompatible when they prompt bodily movements which are physically incompatible. E.g., if one were a fish, one could not at the same time believe the two propositions "this worm is good to eat" and "this worm is on a hook". For beliefs (in this view) would be embodied in behaviour: the one belief, in eating the worm; the other, in avoiding it—always assuming (as behaviourists invariably do) that the fish in question is not tired of life. Without going so far as this, we might nevertheless agree with the passage which James (*loc. cit.*, p. 288) quotes (inaccurately) from Spinoza:

Let us conceive a boy imagining to himself a horse, and taking note of nothing else. As this imagination involves the existence of the horse, *and the boy has no perception which annuls its existence* [James's italics], he will necessarily contemplate the horse as present, nor will he be able to doubt of its existence, however little certain of it he may be. I deny that a man in so far as he imagines [*percipit*] affirms nothing. For what is it to imagine a winged horse but to affirm that the horse [that horse, namely] has wings? For if the mind had nothing before it but the winged horse it would contemplate the same as present, would have no cause to doubt of its existence, nor any power of dissenting from its existence, unless the imagination of the winged horse were joined to an idea which contradicted [*tollit*] its existence.   (*Ethics*, II, 49, Scholium)

To this doctrine James entirely assents, adding in italics:

Any object which remains uncontradicted is ipso facto believed and posited as absolute reality.

10   Now if this view is correct, it would seem to follow (though James does not draw this inference) that there is no need of any specific feeling of belief, and that the mere existence of images yields all that is required. The state of mind in which we merely consider a proposition, without believing or disbelieving it, will then appear as a sophisticated product, the result of some rival force adding to the image-proposition a positive feeling which may be called suspense or non-belief—a feeling which may be compared to that of a man about to run a race, waiting for the signal. Such a man, though not moving, is in a very different condition from that of a man quietly at rest. And so the man who is considering a proposition without believing it
20   will be in a state of tension, restraining the natural tendency to act upon the proposition which he would display if nothing interfered. In this view, belief primarily consists merely in the existence of the appropriate images without any counteracting forces.

What most recommends the above view, to my mind, is the way in which it accords with mental development. Doubt, suspense of judgment, and disbelief all seem later and more complex than a wholly unreflecting assent. Belief as a positive phenomenon, if it exists, seems to be a product of doubt, a decision after debate, an acceptance, not merely of *this*, but of *this-rather-than-that*. It is not difficult to suppose that a dog has images (possibly
30   olfactory) of his absent master, or of the rabbit that he dreams of hunting. But it is very difficult to suppose that he can entertain mere imagination-images to which no assent is given. (When we speak of "assent" we mean for the moment merely that influence upon action which might naturally be expected to accompany belief.) The influence of hallucinatory images also fits well with this theory. Such images, it would seem, often become gradually more and more vivid, until at last they exclude the contrary images which would prevent them from influencing action.

I think it may be conceded that a mere image, without the addition of any positive feeling that could be called "belief", is apt to have a certain dynamic
40   power, and in this sense an uncombated image has the force of a belief. But

although this may be true, it does not account for any but the simplest phenomena in the region of belief. It will not, for example, explain either memory or expectation, in both of which, though they differ widely in their effects on action, the image is a sign, something pointing beyond itself to a different event. Nor can it explain the beliefs which do not issue in any proximate action, such as those of mathematics. I conclude, therefore, that there are belief-feelings of the same order as those of doubt or desire or disbelief, although phenomena closely analogous to those of belief can be produced by mere uncontradicted images.

Instances like that of the boy imagining a winged horse are liable to 10 produce a certain confusion. The image of the winged horse of course exists, and if the boy took this to be real, he would not be in error. But images accompanied by belief are normally taken as signs: the belief is not in the image, but in something else that is indicated (or, in logical language "described") by the image. This is especially obvious in such a case as memory. When we remember an event by means of present images, we are not believing in the present existence of the images, but in the past existence of something resembling them. It is almost impossible to translate what is occurring into words without great distortion. The view which I am advocating is that, in such a case, we have a specific feeling, called remember- 20 ing, which has a certain relation to the memory-image. The memory-image constitutes the image-proposition, but the translation of our belief into words is "something like this *was*", not "something like this *is*", as it would be an assent not of the nature of memory or expectation. And even this translation is hardly accurate, for words point not only to images, but beyond images to what these mean. Therefore, when we use a word as if it meant the image, we need an unnatural duplication of words in order to reach what the image stands for. This produces the appearance of unexpected complication, leading to an undue lack of plausibility. But the whole question of adapting language to psychology, after all the ages during which 30 it has been adapted to bad logic, is so difficult that I can hardly do more than indicate some of its problems.

IV. TRUTH AND FALSEHOOD

We come now to the question which we left on one side at the beginning of our third section, namely: What is the relation of the content of a belief to its "objective", i.e. to the fact which makes it true or false?

In an earlier paper before the Aristotelian Society,[13] in criticism of Mr. Joachim, I have given my reasons for holding that truth consists in corre-

13 "On the Nature of Truth", *Proc. Arist. Soc.*, 1907. Reprinted, with some alterations, in
   Philosophical Essays, under the title, "The Monistic Theory of Truth".   40

spondence rather than in internal consistency. I do not propose to repeat those arguments at present, but shall assume, without more ado, that the truth or falsehood of a belief depends upon its relation to a fact other than itself. This fact I call its "objective". In so doing, I am not following exactly the same usage as Meinong, who holds that there are false objectives as well as true ones, and who, therefore, does not identify his objectives with the facts that make propositions true or false. I cannot call the fact the "meaning" of the proposition, since that is confusing when the proposition is false: if on a fine day I say "it is raining", we cannot say that the meaning of my statement is the fact that the sun is shining. Nor can I use the word "denotation", since that assimilates propositions too much to names and descriptions. But I shall say that a proposition "refers to" its objective. Thus, when we are concerned with image-propositions, "referring to" takes the place of "meaning". Word-propositions, on the other hand, while also "referring to" objectives, may, in simple cases, be legitimately spoken of as "meaning" image-propositions.

According to the theory of propositions suggested in the previous section, it would be a mistake to regard truth and falsehood as relations of the "ideal" to the "real". Propositions are facts in exactly the same sense in which their objectives are facts. The relation of a proposition to its objective is not a relation of something imagined to something actual: it is a relation between two equally solid and equally actual facts. One of these, the proposition, is composed of images, with a possible admixture of sensations; the other may be composed of anything.

Whether an image which is too simple to be called a proposition can be in any sense true or false, is a question which I shall not discuss. It is propositions, and *their* truth and falsehood, that I am concerned with; whether there is any other truth or falsehood may be left an open question.

There are two different questions in regard to truth and falsehood, of which one may be called formal, the other material. The formal question concerns the relations between the form of a proposition and the form of its objective in the respective cases of truth and falsehood; the material question, which has been specially emphasized by pragmatists, concerns the nature of the effects of true and false beliefs respectively. In so far as people wish to believe truly (which I am told is sometimes the case), it is because true beliefs are supposed to be, as a rule, a better means to the realization of desires than false ones. Unless the material question is remembered, the schematic treatment of the formal question may appear very barren and scholastic. Nevertheless, it is to the formal question that I propose to address myself.

The simplest possible schema of correspondence between proposition and objective is afforded by such cases as visual memory-images. I call up a picture of a room that I know, and in my picture the window is to the left of the fire. I give to this picture that sort of belief which we call "memory". When the room was present to sense, the window was, in fact, to the left of the fire. In this case, I have a complex image, which we may analyze, for our purposes, into (a) the image of the window, (b) the image of the fire, (c) the relation that (a) is to the left of (b). The objective consists of the window and the fire with the very same relation between them. In such a case, the objective of a proposition consists of the meanings of its constituent images related (or not related, as the case may be) by the same relation as that which holds between the constituent images in the proposition. When the objective is that the same relation holds, the proposition is true; when the objective is that the same relation does not hold, the proposition is false. According to what was said about negative facts in Section I, there is always one or other of these two possible objectives, and the proposition is therefore always either true or false.

But such idyllic simplicity of correspondence is rare. It is already absent in the word-propositions which mean such simple visual image-propositions. In the phrase "*A* is to the left of *B*", even if we treat "is-to-the-left-of" as one word, we have a fact consisting of *three* terms with a *triadic* relation, not two terms with a dyadic relation. The linguistic symbol for a relation is not itself a relation, but a term as solid as the other words of the sentence. Language might have been so constructed that this should not have been always the case: a few specially important relations might have been symbolized by relations between words. For instance, "*AB*" might have meant "*A* is to the left of *B*." It might have been the practice that pronouncing *A* on a high note and *B* on a low note meant that *A* was *B*'s social superior. But the practical possibilities of this method of symbolizing relations are obviously very limited, and in actual language relations are symbolized by words (verbs and prepositions chiefly) or parts of words (inflections).[14] Hence the linguistic statement of a fact is a more complex fact than that which it asserts, and the correspondence of a word-proposition with its objective is never so simple as the simplest correspondence in the case of image-propositions.

Again, the case of negative facts and negative propositions is full of complexities. Propositions, whether of images or words, are always themselves *positive* facts. In the case of word-propositions, there are different positive facts (phrases), of which one is true when the objective is positive, the other when it is negative: the phrases "*A* loves *B*" and "*A* does not love *B*" are both themselves positive facts. We cannot symbolize the assertion that *A* does not love *B* by merely having the words "*A*" and "*B*" without

---

14 This is not wholly true of very primitive languages. But they are so vague and ambiguous that often they cannot be said to have any way of expressing one relation rather than a number of others that might equally be meant by the phrase which is used.

the word "loves" between them, since we cannot practically distinguish the fact that the word "loves" does not occur between them from the fact that, e.g., the word "hates" does not occur between them. Words and phrases, being intended for communication, have to be sensible; and sensible facts are always positive. Thus there is no identity between the distinction of positive and negative facts and the distinction of positive and negative word-propositions: the latter are themselves both positive facts, though differing by the absence or presence of the word "not".

10   In the case of image-propositions, there is again a lack of parallelism with negative facts, but of a different kind. Not only are image-propositions always positive, but there are not even two kinds of positive image-propositions as there are of word-propositions. There is no "not" in an image-proposition; the "not" belongs to the feeling, not to the content of the proposition. An image-proposition may be believed or disbelieved; these are different feelings towards the same content, not the same feeling towards different contents. There is no way of visualizing "A-not-to-the-left-of-B". When we attempt it, we find ourselves visualizing "A-to-the-right-of-B" or something of the sort. This is one strong reason for the reluctance to admit negative facts.

20   We have thus, as regards the opposition of positive and negative, the following different sorts of duality:

(1) Positive and negative facts.
(2) Image-propositions, which may be believed or disbelieved but do not allow any duality of content corresponding to positive and negative facts.
(3) Word-propositions, which are always positive facts, but are of two kinds, one verified by a positive objective, the other by a negative objective.

Thus the simpler kinds of parallelism between proposition and fact are 30 only to be looked for in the case of positive facts and propositions. Where the fact is negative, the correspondence necessarily becomes more complicated. It is partly the failure to realize the lack of parallelism between negative facts and negative word-propositions that has made a correct theory of negative facts so difficult either to discover or to believe.

Let us now return to positive facts and beliefs in image-propositions. In the case of spatial relations, we found that it is possible for the relation of the constituent images to be the same as the relation of the constituents of the objective. In my visualizing of A to the left of B, my image of A is to the left of my image of B. Does this identity of relation, as between the image-40 proposition and its objective, ever occur except in the case of spatial relations?

The case which it is natural to consider next is that of temporal relations. Suppose I believe that *A* precedes *B*. Can this belief have for its content an image of *A* preceding an image of *B*? At first sight, most people would unhesitatingly reject such an hypothesis. We have been told so often that an idea of succession is not a succession of ideas, that we almost automatically regard the apprehension of a sequence as something in which the earlier and later parts of the sequence must be simultaneously presented. It seems rash to challenge a view so generally regarded as unquestionable, and yet I cannot resist grave doubts as to its truth. Of course it is a fact that we often have successive images without the belief that their prototypes have the same time-order. But that proves nothing, since in any case belief is something which has to be added to an image-proposition. Is it certain that we cannot have an image of *A* followed by an image of *B*, and proceed to *believe* this sequence? And cannot this *be* the belief that *A* precedes *B*? I see no reason why this should not be the case. When, for example, I imagine a person speaking a sentence, or when, for that matter, I actually hear him speak it, there does not seem, as a question of empirical fact, to be any moment at which the whole sentence is present to imagination or sense, and yet, in whatever may be the usual meaning of the phrase, I can "apprehend the sentence as a whole". I hear the words in order, but never the whole sentence at once; yet I apprehend the sentence as a whole, in the sense that it produces upon me the intended effect, whatever that may be. You come to me and say: "Your roof has fallen in, and the rain is pouring down into the rooms, ruining all your furniture." I understand what you say, since I express consternation, ring up the landlord, write to the insurance company, and order a van to remove my belongings. Yet it by no means follows that the whole sentence was imaginatively present to me at any one moment. My belief in your statement is a causal unit, and it is therefore supposed to be a unitary occurrence. But in mental affairs the causal unit may well be several events at different times. This is part of Bergson's point about repetition; it is also suggested by the law of habit. It may well turn out to be one of the fundamental differences between physics and psychology. Thus, there seems no good reason why, when we believe in a succession, there should be any one moment within which the whole content of the belief is existing. The belief in a succession may quite well be itself a succession. If so, temporal relations, like spatial ones, allow the simplest type of correspondence, in which the relation in the image-proposition is identical with that in the objective. But I only wish to suggest this view as a possible one: I do not feel prepared to say with any conviction that it is in fact true.

The correspondence of proposition and fact grows increasingly complicated as we pass to more complicated types of propositions: existence-propositions, general propositions, disjunctive and hypothetical propositions, and so on. The subject is important, and capable, I believe, of throwing much new light on logic; but I shall not pursue it here.

The general nature of the formal correspondence which makes truth or falsehood can be seen from the simplest case: the case of a dyadic relation which is the same in the fact and in the image-proposition. You have an image of A which is to the left of your image of B: this occurrence is an image-proposition. If A is to the left of B, the proposition is true; if A is not to the left of B, it is false. The *phrase* "A is to the left of B" means the image-proposition, and is true when this is true, false when this is false; on the other hand, the phrase "A is not to the left of B" is true when the
10 image-proposition is false, and false when it is true. Thus for this simplest case we have obtained a formal definition of truth and falsehood, both for image-propositions and for word-propositions. It is easy to see that the same *kind* of definition can be extended to more complicated cases.

It will be observed that truth and falsehood, in their formal sense, are primarily properties of propositions rather than of beliefs. Derivatively, we call a belief true when it is belief in a true proposition, and a disbelief true when it is disbelief in a false proposition; but it is to propositions that the *primary* formal meanings of "truth" and "falsehood" apply.

But when we come to what gives importance to truth and falsehood, as
20 opposed to what constitutes their formal definition, it is beliefs, not propositions, that are important. Beliefs influence action, and the effects of true beliefs, I am told, are more agreeable than those of false beliefs. The attempt to *define* truth in this way seems to me a mistake. But so long as we confine ourselves to the formal definition of truth, it is difficult to see why any one should take an interest in it. It is therefore important to remember the connexion of beliefs with action. But I do not think either that the pleasant effects of a belief are alone a sufficient verification of it, or that verification can be used to *define* truth. There are true propositions, for example, about past matters of fact, which cannot be verified. The formal
30 definition of truth by correspondence of a proposition with its objective seems the only one which is theoretically adequate. The further inquiry whether, if our definition of truth is correct, there is anything that can be known, is one that I cannot now undertake; but if the result of such an inquiry should prove adverse, I should not regard that as affording any theoretical objection to the proposed definition.

Appendixes

Appendix 1

C. D. Broad's Paper on Phenomenalism [1915]

THIS REPORT WAS published in *The Athenaeum*, 24 April 1915, p. 385.

At this time *The Athenaeum* published a regular column entitled "Societies" in which the proceedings of the Aristotelian Society were usually reported. No author was named for these pieces, but the quality of the reports makes it likely that some member of the Society supplied them to *The Athenaeum*.

This Appendix is relevant to Paper **6**.

1. *The Athenaeum*, no. 4,565 (24 April 1915): 385.

ARISTOTELIAN. — *April* 12.—Dr. A. Wolf in the chair.—Mr. C. D. Broad read a paper on "Phenomenalism."

Phenomenalism is a philosophical theory which claims to be able to dispense with physical objects. Ordinary common sense distinguishes between mental acts and their objects, but it wants to hold that the objects we perceive with our senses are geometrical parts and qualities of physical objects. The immediate objects, however, by which we judge physical objects to exist are sense-data. The difficulty is to see how we can pass from the existence, qualities, and relations of a certain group of sense-data to assert the existence, qualities, and relations of some determinate physical object of which we can never be directly aware. The phenomenalist proposes to substitute for physical objects classes of which sense-data are particular individuals. The theory has been specially put forward by Mr. Bertrand Russell to avoid the assumption involved in the common view. He has argued on the principle of Ockham's razor, that entities are not to be multiplied without necessity. It is doubtful, however, whether Mr. Russell's theory does not involve an even larger assumption and multiplication of entities than does common sense. The ordinary man believes that sense-data only exist in connexion with living minds and bodies, and he does not assume sensibilia of which no one is aware. But Mr. Russell's theory assumes sensibilia of which no one can be aware, for there are supposed to be perspectives where there are no minds. The claim put forward for it is that only by such a theory can physical laws be verified, for these start from observations on our sense-data, and must ultimately be verified by such observations.

After submitting the theory to a long criticism, and illustrating its working in particular cases, the writer held that, even though it might be impossible to offer a conclusive argument against phenomenalism, it could, at least, be shown (*a*) that phenomenalists had never grasped how much alteration their theory demands in our most ordinary beliefs about a great many other things than physical objects, and (*b*) that it is most unlikely we should have discovered and verified many of the common laws of physics, or had any motive to look for them, unless we had habitually analyzed phenomena and directly verifiable laws into the consilience of more general physical laws.

Mr. Bertrand Russell, replying in the discussion, said that "phenomenalism" was not the term he himself used to denote his theory. His own view was not dogmatic phenomenalism; he had suggested merely a preliminary method. There are two different problems: (1) How much of ordinary physics can be stated in phenomenalistic terms? and (2) If physics cannot be stated in such terms, what conceivable principles can be discovered by which we may find ground for belief in them? The second problem cannot be tackled until the first is solved. The difference between sense-data and physical objects is that the former are not transcendent, and do not last through time; while the essence of the latter is that they persist through a fairly long time.

In reply to a question, Mr. Russell said that sense-data had some duration. They were not purely points, but lasted through an appreciable part of the specious present.

With regard to his own theory, it was only intended to be rough and preliminary, not to be put forth as a finished thing. He had no definite result. His aim was to see how much could be done with the smallest amount of material; and if the material be inadequate, to find out where it is inadequate.

With regard to the criticism that he assumed sensibilia of which no one is or can be aware, he maintained that there may be perspectives where there are no minds; but we cannot know anything of what sort of perspective they may be, for the sense-datum is mental. It was only another way of stating that things having exactly the same status as sense-data could exist without being data. He had nothing particular to say about sensibilia, and wanted to get physics stated without assuming them, whereas physical objects are ordinarily presented as the essence of what physics is about. His real interest was the method.

Appendix II

Bertrand Russell's Notes on the New Work
Which He Intends to Undertake [1918]

RUSSELL FORMULATED THE plan printed here during the first months of 1918 when he faced a term in prison. The short manuscripts in Paper **18** are early attempts to get his new ideas on paper.

The proposal, without its title, survives in manuscript (RA 210.006570). There is also a typescript with the title; it shows changes in Russell's hand. The most noteworthy of these is a change of the title of the proposed work from "Words, Thoughts and Things" to "Things, Words, and Thoughts" and the addition of the bracketed material after the original titles of the various parts. He also added "only" to the note about William James at the end of Part II (314: 16).

On the verso of the last leaf he wrote beneath the title "Words, Thoughts and Things" "[To be given to Wildon Carr, and shown to any one whom it may interest.]" In the same place he wrote: "*Carr* per Miss Rinder, Thursday". Gladys Rinder worked in the offices of the No-Conscription Fellowship. According to Russell, her job was "chiefly concerned with details in the treatment of pacifist prisoners" (*1968*, 88); in this capacity she performed many chores for Russell both before and after he entered prison. Delivery of this plan to Wildon Carr appears to have been one of them.

ii. Bertrand Russell's Notes on the New Work Which He Intends to Undertake

IF CIRCUMSTANCES PERMIT, the following is the work upon which I shall be engaged in the immediate future:

Plan for a work on "Things, Words, and Thoughts", being the section dealing with cognition in a large projected work, *Analysis of Mind*.

Part I. *Facts.*　　　Part II. *Meaning.*　　　Part III. *Judgment.*

Part I. FACTS. [Things]
1. Particulars.
2. Qualities and Relations.
3. Atomic Facts (a) Positive; (b) Negative.
4. General Facts (a) Existence; (b) Universal.
   Query: General Disjunctive Facts?
5. Controversial Questions: (a) Externality of Relations; (b) Nature of Analysis: forms of facts; (c) Possible reduction in numbers of forms of facts.

Part II. MEANING. [Words]
A. *General Account of the nature of meaning.*
   1. Meaning belongs to bodily acts when (a) they are caused by a certain stimulus; (b) they arouse an "image" of the stimulus, or something in some way connected with the stimulus. (A discussion of "images" is necessary at this point.) The essence of a *symbol* is that it is, by association, a causal link between an object and what might be called the "idea" of the object. Its "meaning" is "understood" when the association in question exists: there need not be any reflection or conscious apprehension.
   2. Meaning not *purely* conventional. Conventionality of language a development, like that of hieroglyphics. Essential point is causal connection with object as cause and "idea" as effect.
   3. Meaning largely, not wholly, *social*, consisting in effect on hearer.
   4. Roughly speaking, symbols have an objective and a subjective meaning; approximately, the former is their cause, the latter their effect.
B. *Words.*
   1. *Names.* A name is a class of similar noises causally associated with a class of similar particulars which form what are called appearances of one "person" or "thing".
   2. *Verbs* (and predicates). How they involve the propositional form. Sense in which they have meaning in isolation and sense in which they have not.
   3. *Emphatic Particulars.* I, this, here, now, etc. Nearest approach in language to names for particulars.

C. *Propositions.*

　1. *Positive Atomic Propositions.* These *are* facts, of the same form as the facts that make them true if they are true—or, more exactly, they are classes of facts (e.g. in the symbol "xRy", the function of "R" is to create a relation between "x" and "y"). Their truth or falsehood may be defined *formally* by this sameness of form or its absence.

　2. *Negative Atomic Propositions.* These *are positive* facts, not negative ones.

　3. *Existence Propositions.* These are existence-facts. "$(\exists x).\phi x$" and "$(\exists y).\phi y$" are the same proposition: all that counts is that *there is* a letter where "x" or "y" occurs.

　4. *Universal Propositions.* These also are existence-facts; thus they correspond to 2, and 3 to 1 (above).

　5. *Molecular Propositions.* Different nature of their "meaning". No disjunctive *facts.* Are there molecular facts of other kinds?

D. *Can Meaning be explained without introducing anything mental?*

Here will be examined William James on "consciousness", neutral monism, and behaviourism. None of these, so far, have attacked the difficult parts of their problem, of which a discussion will only become possible after the foregoing theory of symbols.

Part III. JUDGMENT. [Thoughts]

[What is to be said here must depend upon what will have been said in Part II.]

　A. *Images and Ideas.*

　B. *Propositional Occurrences in General*: Beliefs, Wishes, Doubts, Questions, etc.

　C. *Belief*: can it consist, as behaviourists contend or suggest, in bodily acts, particularly propositions asserted, or must it involve something specifically "mental"?

Pragmatist view: A given desire will cause different series of acts on different occasions: the differences in the different series of acts may be *defined* as differing beliefs. (Some such view, obscurely and confusedly, seemed to exist in James.) A belief on this view is a causal law of acts. General question whether cognition can be defined in terms of desire and bodily acts. A fairly complete survey of supposed "mental" existents is necessary at this point.

The "subject" as anything but a construction must be avoided.

The theory of judgment to be ultimately adopted has to suit two main sets of facts: (a) the dualism of true and false; (b) the existence of the other "propositional occurrences" noted under B (above).

Appendix III

Philosophical Books Read in Prison [1918]

THIS APPENDIX PRINTS in edited form Russell's list of the books and articles he read as a prisoner. The manuscript (RA 210.006573) is photographically reproduced in its entirety (pp. 316–25) to allow the reader to study it in its unedited form. It will be seen that nearly all of his prison reading bears upon his plan of work which is printed as Appendix II. We have not printed his notes on his reading; our reason for omitting them is that his Archives contain other sets of notes which he made on his prison reading. There are, for example, notes on Ribot's *Evolution of General Ideas* (RA 210.006587); notes on J. R. Angell's *Psychology* (RA 210.006575); and a "Bibliography" (RA 210.006572) which lists several of the items on the list reproduced here.

The reader will also notice that Russell includes a list of pieces "Written in Prison". They are:

"Introduction to Mathematical Philosophy", a book of 70,000 words, now in the hands of Messrs Allen & Unwin.

A critical examination of Prof. Dewey's Philosophy, about 10,000 words, sent to the Journal of Philosophy, Psychology, and Scientific Method.

A review of Norman Kemp Smith's "Commentary on Kant's Critique of Pure Reason" (published in "The Nation").

A review of C. D. Broad's "Perception, Physics, and Reality", for "Mind".

A large number of notes on the principles of symbolism.

Philosophical Books read in prison May 1918 ff

Norman Smith Commentary on Kant's P. R. Macmillan 1918

Walter B Cannon Bodily Changes in Pain, Hunger, Fear & Rage, N.Y. 1916

Margaret Washburn, The Animal Mind, N.Y. 1908

Edwin Holt, The Concept of Consciousness, Allen & Unwin, 1914.

In Psychological Review, Sp. '17.

John B Watson, "The Acknowledged formulation of the scope of behaviour psychology"

A. P. Weiss, "Relation between functional & behaviour psychology"

Dewey Essays in Experimental Logic, Univ. of Chicago, 1916

A. A. Cock Ontological Argument for existence of God. (Arist. Soc. Proc.)

Watson Behaviour: An Introduction to Comparative Psychology. N.Y. 1914.

J. R. Angell Psychology, 4th ed., Constable, 1911

Pillsbury Psychology of Reasoning, Appleton, 1910

Judd Psychology, Ysler Unwin, 1908

Husserl Logische Untersuchungen Vol. I, 2nd ed. Halle 1913

Broad Perception, Physics, & Reality. Camb. 1914

v. Bechterev Objektive Psychologie, Leipzig u Berlin, 1913. (Portions)

E. B. Titchener Experimental Psychology of the Thought-Processes, N.Y., Macmillan, 1909.

W. Wundt Elements of Folk Psychology, Authorized Translation by E. L. Schaub Ph. D. Allen & Un. 1916

Ribot Evolution of General Ideas. Open Ct. Co. 1899

Written in Prison.

"Introduction to Mathematical Philosophy", a book of 70,000 words, now in
    the hands of Messrs Allen & Unwin.

A critical examination of Prof. Dewey's Philosophy, about 10,000 words, sent
    to the Journal of Philosophy, Psychology, & Scientific Method.

A review of Norman Kemp Smith's "Commentary on Kant's Critique of
    Pure Reason" (published in "the Nation").

A review of C. D. Broad's "Perception, Physics, & Reality", for "Mind".

A large number of notes on the principles of symbolism.

Read in Prison (continued).

American Journal of Psychology:

1910, Sigmund Freud, The origin & development of psycho-analysis.

Carl G. Jung, The association method.

1912, May D. Chapin & M.F. Washburn, A study of the images representing the concept "meaning".

Raymond Dodge, The Theory & limitations of introspection.

E.B. Titchener, The Psychology of the new Britannica.

Prolegomena to a study of introspection.

The schema of introspection

Description vs. statement of meaning

G. Stanley Hall, Why Kant is passing. [p.425: " To conclude, Kantianism is one of the antique cumbersome systems of regarding the world that belong only to the museums of the history of philosophy. It is not a scheme for our time & to install its antiquated gearing in eager & youthful minds greatly reduces their efficiency for the world's work today."]

Archiv für die gesammte Psychologie

Vol. IV (1905). Henry J. Watt, Experimentelle Beiträge zu einer Theorie des Denkens, pp. 289–436

Vol. VIII (1906). August Messer, Experimentell-psychologische Untersuchungen über das Denken, pp. 1–224.

Vol. IX (1907). Karl Bühler, Über Gedanken, pp. 297–365.

Read in Prison (continued).

Articles in "Psychological Review":

1911. W. B. Pillsbury, The place of movement in consciousness.

  G. M. Stratton, The psychology of change: How is the perception of movement related to that of succession.

James R. Angell, Imageless thought.

1912. A. E. Davies, Professor Titchener's Theory of Memory & Imagination.

  E. B. Titchener, Memory & Imagination: a re-statement.

  Knight Dunlap, The Case against Introspection.

  Knight Dunlap, The Nature of perceived Relations.

  Robert Macdougall, Mind as Middle Term.

1913. Rudolf Pintner, Inner Speech during silent reading.

  John B. Watson, Psychology as the Behaviourist views it.

  James R. Angell, Behavior as a category of psychology.

  Anna Wyczoikowska, Theoretical & Experimental Studies in the Mechanism of Speech.

1914. B. H. Bode, Psychology as a science of behavior.

  Knight Dunlap, The Self & the Ego.

  Elliot Park Frost, Can't Psychology dispense with consciousness?

1915. R. S. Woodworth, A revision of imageless thought.

  Knight Dunlap, Color Theory & Realism.

1916. Knight Dunlap, Thought Content & Feeling.

  Herbert Sidney Langfeld, Concerning the Image.

  James R. Angell, A reconsideration of James's Theory of emotion in the light of recent criticisms.

  H. C. McComas, Extravagances in the motor theories of consciousness.

Read in Prison (continued).

Archiv für die gesamte Psychologie   Vol. IX, 1907.

Karl Bühler, Über Gedanken, pp. 297 – 365.

p. 305. "Wir stellen uns also die allgemeine Frage: Was erleben wir, wenn wir denken? Dann versuchen wir uns gar nicht erst an eine vorläufige Bestimmung des Begriffes Denken sondern wählen für die Analyse nur solche Vorgänge, die jedermann als ~~auch~~ Denkvorgänge bezeichnen wird".

p. 316. Most imp't D in Denken is "Bewusstheit dass ....", wh. I call Gedanke.
      Th. must be built out of Vorstellung, or Gedanke [V. = sinnliche V.]

p. 317. In fact, it is Gedanken that are essential to th.

p. 319-20. Th. doesn't need language.

p. 321 "Ja ich behaupte vielmehr, dass prinzipiell jeder Gegenstand vollständig
      ohne Anschauungshilfen bestimmt gedacht (gemeint) werden kann.
      Jede individuelle Nuance der blauen Farbe auf dem Bild, das in
      meinem Zimmer hängt, kann ich mit voller Bestimmtheit
      unanschaulich denken, wenn es nur möglich ist, dass mir der Gegenstand
      auf andere Weise gegeben wird als durch das Mittel der Empfindungen.
      Wie das möglich ist, werden wir später sehen".

p. 325. Gedanken can't be reduced to other psychic occurrences.

p. 334 ff. Regelbewusstsein. p. 342. "Unsere Gedanken bestehen zum grossen
      Teil aus bewussten Regeln".

Ib. Vol. IV, 1905. Henry J. Watt. Experimentelle Beiträge zu einer Theorie des Denkens, pp. 289–436.

Ib. Vol. VIII, 1906. August Messer. Experimentell-Psychologische Untersuchungen über das Denken, pp. 1–224.

p. 83. My 9 words learnt by contiguity assoc".

Psychological Review, 1911.

W. B. Pillsbury, The place of movement in consciousness, pp. 83-99

[Allows it a large place, but not the whole.]

G. M. Stratton, The Psychology of Change: How is the Perception of movement related to that of succession, pp. 262-293.

An interesting & important article. By new experiments, shows that motions not easier to detect than discrete successions. Concludes that j. of motion are species of j. of succession, presupposing j. of succession as the simpler. J of motion more complex & more easily performed; j. of succession simpler. (p. 290). Should call both motion & succession perceptions, not (strictly) either sensations or judgements.

James R. Angell. Imageless Thought. (Contentious rejection.)

Psychological Review, 1912.

A.E. Davies Professor Titchener's Theory of Memory & Imagination.
E.B.
Titchener Memory & Imagination : A re-statement.

Knight Dunlap. The Case against Introspection, pp. 404 - 413

Discusses chiefly James & Stout : former thinks introspection reveals knowing; latter, knowledge. View of latter now common view.

"The Objections to Stout's views are not of the same order as the objections to the theory of James, although just as profound. There can be no denial of the existence of the thing (knowing) which is alleged to be known or observed in this sort of 'introspection'. The allegation that the knowing is observed is that which may be denied. Knowing there certainly is; known, the knowing certainly is not" (p. 410).

"I am never aware of an awareness" (ib)

"It may sound paradoxical to say that one cannot observe the process (or relation) of observation, & yet may be certain that there is such a process; but there is really no inconsistency in the saying. How do I know that there is awareness? By being aware of something. There is no meaning in the term 'awareness' which is not expressed in the statement 'I am aware of a colour (or what not)'" (p.411)

Introspection confounded with awareness of our bodies.

76. The Nature of Perceived Relations, pp 415 - 446.

"I have pointed out in a previous paper [supra] that 'introspection' divested of its mythological suggestion of observing consciousness, is really the observation of bodily sensations (sensibles) & feeling (feelables)". p. 427n.

Robert Macdougall (N.Y. Univ.) Mind as Middle Term, pp. 386 - 403.

Psych. Review, 1912. Knight Dunlap (continued):

p. 431. [Tells how Brown (1812) defines predicables by relns of similarity.]

p. 445. "You can no more prove that the difference between red & green is perceived by any one, than you can prove that green is perceived. These things are fundamental postulates, justifiable only by observation". [How can we "observe" that the difference between red & green is perceived if there is no such thing as introspection?]

1913. Rudolf Pintner, Inner Speech during silent reading, pp. 129–153.

John B. Watson. Psychology as the Behaviorist views it. pp. 158–177

p. 161. "One can assume either the presence or the absence of consciousness anywhere in the phylogenetic scale without affecting the problems of behavior by one jot or tittle; & without influencing in any way the mode of experimental attack upon them".

p. 167. "The psychology which I should attempt to build up would take as a starting point, first, the observable fact that organisms, man & animal alike, do adjust themselves to their environment by means of hereditary & habit equipments." [Adjusting?]

p. 171. [The behaviorist] "nowhere thinks of the animal's response [to colored light] in terms of his own experiences of colours & greys".

p. 174n. "I should throw out imagery altogether & attempt to show that practically all natural thought goes on in terms of sensori-motor processes in the larynx (but not in terms of imageless thought).

p. 175. "I have virtually denied that this realm of psychics is open to experimental investigation. I don't wish to go further into the problem at present because it leads inevitably over into metaphysics".

James R. Angell, Behavior as a category of psychology. pp. 255–270

Anna Wyczoikowska. Theoretical & Experimental Studies in the Mechanism of Speech.
     [? including pronunciation of one's own name?]

Psychological Review, 1914

B. H. Bode, Psychology as a science of behavior. pp. 46–61.

Knight Dunlap The Self & the Ego, pp 62–9.

[Maintains almost exactly the theories of my short articles of 1914–5.]

Eliott Park Frost Cannot Psychology dispense with consciousness? pp. 204–211

Develops a physiological Df of "awareness": whenever stimulus elicits a response. Take any simple sensori-motor path, call it an Alpha-arc. When a further arc, aroused by the alpha-arc rather than by peripheral stimulus, is set in function, let us denote it as a Beta-arc." "We speak of the beta-arc as becoming aware of an alpha-arc, in precisely the same sense that we spoke a moment ago of the alpha-arc as aware of the external stimulus, & for the same reason: it responds to stimulation, characteristically" (p. 207).

1915 R. S. Woodworth A revision of imageless thought, pp. 1–27.

Knight Dunlap Color Theory & Realism, pp 95–103.

1916 " Thought Content & Feeling, pp. 49–70.

p. 52. Objections to introspection: (1) Psych^n fallacy: obj. altered by introspection.

(2) To avoid this, say introsp^n is of past exp^ce only: then (a) will be like other memory, not quite accurate, (b) impossible: "not in th. cs. not t^d in perception." I contend that awareness of awareness never occurs.

p. 56n. A perception is physiologically conditioned, but not the object or sensa-datum. The sort of introspection allowed by Dunlap is bodily sensations, e.g. muscular. Images are muscular contractions (p. 55).

Herbert Sidney Langfeld Concerning the image, pp. 180–189.

James R. Angell. A reconsideration of James's theory of emotion in the light of recent criticisms.

H. C. McComas Extravagances in the motor theories of consciousness. [Strong physiological arguments against Watson.]

7

Wundt *Elements of Folk Psychology*, translated by E. L. Schaub Ph D.,
  Allen + Unwin, 1516.
                                                    + points that spoken
pp. 59 ff. Gesture-Language, esp. of deaf + dumb. p. 65, Order of words fixed in such language.
      in Sudan languages.
pp 69-70. No inflections — only root words. No tenses, or dist⁻ of verbs + nouns.

III. Philosophical Books Read in Prison

Angell, James Rowland. *Psychology: An Introductory Study of the Structure and Function of Human Consciousness*. 4th ed. New York: H. Holt, 1908. [Russell cites an unidentified version published by Constable, 1911.]

—— "Imageless Thought". *The Psychological Review*, 18 (1911): 295–323.

—— "Behavior as a Category of Psychology". *The Psychological Review*, 20 (1913): 255–70.

—— "A Reconsideration of James's Theory of Emotion in the Light of Recent Criticisms". *The Psychological Review*, 23 (1916): 251–61.

Bechterew, W. von. *Objective Psychologie, oder Psychoreflexologie, die Lehre von den Assoziationsreflexen*. Translated from the Russian. Leipzig and Berlin: B. G. Teubner, 1913.

Bode, B. H. "Psychology as a Science of Behavior". *The Psychological Review*, 21 (1914): 46–61.

Bühler, Karl. "Tatsachen und Probleme zu einer Psychologie der Denkvorgänge. I. Über Gedanken". *Archiv für die gesamte Psychologie*, 9 (1907): 297–365.

Cannon, Walter B. *Bodily Changes in Pain, Hunger, Fear and Rage: An Account of Recent Researches into the Function of Emotional Excitement*. New York and London: D. Appleton, 1916.

Chapin, Mary W., and M. F. Washburn. "A Study of the Images Representing the Concept 'Meaning'". *The American Journal of Psychology*, 23 (1912): 109–14.

Cock, Albert A. "The Ontological Argument for the Existence of God". *Proceedings of the Aristotelian Society*, n.s. 18 (1918): 363–84.

Davies, Arthur Ernest. "Professor Titchener's Theory of Memory and Imagination". *The Psychological Review*, 19 (1912): 147–57.

Dodge, Raymond. "The Theory and Limitations of Introspection". *The American Journal of Psychology*, 23 (1912): 214–29.

Dunlap, Knight. "The Case against Introspection". *The Psychological Review*, 19 (1912): 404–13.

—— "The Nature of Perceived Relations". *The Psychological Review*, 19 (1912): 415–46.

—— "The Self and the Ego". *The Psychological Review*, 20 (1913): 62–9.

—— "Color Theory and Realism". *The Psychological Review*, 22 (1915): 99–103.

—— "Thought-Content and Feeling". *The Psychological Review*, 23 (1916): 49–70.

Freud, Sigmund. "The Origin and Development of Psychoanalysis". *The American Journal of Psychology*, 21 (1910): 181–218.

Frost, Eliott Park. "Cannot Psychology Dispense with Consciousness?" *The Psychological Review*, 21 (1914): 204–11.

Hall, G. Stanley. "Why Kant is Passing". *The American Journal of Psychology*, 23 (1912): 370–426.

Holt, Edwin B. *The Concept of Consciousness*. London: George Allen, 1914.

Husserl, Edmund. *Logische Untersuchungen*. Vol. 1. 2nd ed. Halle: Max Niemeyer, 1913.

Judd, Charles Hubbard. *Psychology: General Introduction*. New York: Charles Scribner's Sons, 1907. [Russell cites an unidentified version published by Fischer Unwin, 1908.]

Jung, Carl G. "The Association Method". *The American Journal of Psychology*, 21 (1910): 219–69.

Langfield, Herbert Sidney. "Concerning the Image". *The Psychological Review*, 23 (1916): 180–9.

MacDougall, Robert. "Mind as Middle Term". *The Psychological Review*, 19 (1912): 386–403.

McComas, H. C. "Extravagances in the Motor Theories of Consciousness". *The Psychological Review*, 23 (1916): 397–406.

Messer, August. "Experimentell-psychologische Untersuchungen über das Denken". *Archiv für die gesamte Psychologie*, 8 (1906): 1–224.

Pillsbury, W. B. *The Psychology of Reasoning*. New York and London: D. Appleton, 1910.

—— "The Place of Movement in Consciousness". *The Psychological Review*, 18 (1911): 83–99.

Pintner, Rudolf. "Inner Speech during Silent Reading". *The Psychological Review*, 20 (1913): 129–53.

Ribot, Th. *The Evolution of General Ideas*. Translated by Francis A. Welby. Chicago: Open Court, 1899.

Smith, Norman Kemp. *A Commentary to Kant's "Critique of Pure Reason"*. London: Macmillan, 1918.

Stratton, G. M. "The Psychology of Change: How Is the Perception of Movement Related to that of Succession?" *The Psychological Review*, 18 (1911): 262–93.

Titchener, Edward Bradford. *Lectures on the Experimental Psychology of the Thought-Processes*. New York: Macmillan, 1909.

—— "The Psychology of the New *Britannica*". *The American Journal of Psychology*, 23 (1912): 37–58.

—— "Description vs. Statement of Meaning". *The American Journal of Psychology*, 23 (1912): 165–82.

—— "Prolegomena to a Study of Introspection". *The American Journal of Psychology*, 23 (1912): 427–48.

—— "The Schema of Introspection". *The American Journal of Psychology*, 23 (1912): 485–508.

—— "Memory and Imagination: A Restatement". *The Psychological Review*, 19 (1912): 158–63.

Washburn, Margaret Floy. *The Animal Mind: A Text-Book of Comparative Psychology*. New York: Macmillan, 1908.

Watson, John B. "Psychology as the Behaviorist Views It". *The Psychological Review*, 20 (1913): 158–77.

—— "An Attempted Formulation of the Scope of Behavior Psychology". *The Psychological Review*, 24 (1917): 329–52.

Watt, Henry J. "Experimentelle Beiträge zu einer Theorie des Denkens". *Archiv für die gesamte Psychologie*, 4 (1905): 289–436.

Weiss, A. P. "Relation between Functional and Behavior Psychology". *The Psychological Review*, 24 (1917): 353–68.

Woodworth, R. S. "A Revision of Imageless Thought". *The Psychological Review*, 22 (1915): 1–27.

Wundt, Wilhelm. *Elements of Folk Psychology: Outlines of a Psychological History of the Development of Mankind*. Translated by Edward Leroy Schaub. London: George Allen & Unwin; New York: Macmillan, 1916.

Wyczoikowska, Anna. "Theoretical and Experimental Studies in the Mechanism of Speech". *The Psychological Review*, 20 (1913): 448–58.

Appendix IV

Duddington's Letter on Existence [1918]

THIS LETTER, WHICH is dated 26 February 1918 from 13 Carlton Terrace, Child's Hill, N.W.2, was written immediately after Russell's sixth lecture of "The Philosophy of Logical Atomism" (**17**). The lecture was delivered on the evening of that day. At the beginning of his seventh lecture (222: 4–226: 6) Russell gives an extended reply to the questions raised in this letter. He takes up all her points, usually in her own words.

The letter was written by Nathalie A. Duddington, a young woman who was a member of the Aristotelian Society. She wrote Russell on other occasions. From her translation of Lossky's *The Intuitive Basis of Knowledge* (1919), one learns that she was Russian. It is also apparent from the letter reproduced here that she was an attentive auditor of his lectures and was trained in technical philosophy. Her mention of Lossky toward the end of her letter does not reveal that she knew him and corresponded with him, but her next set of letters to Russell firmly establishes these facts. Lossky, of whose work Russell had a mixed opinion (see 96: 5–10), was starving in Russia in 1921 when Mrs. Duddington next wrote Russell. Russell sent her £5 to buy food for him and his family.

It was not until over thirty years later that she wrote Russell again. On 9 December 1954 she proposed what in effect became the Einstein–Russell manifesto of 1955. The men in the Kremlin, she thought, would pay attention to a statement signed by eminent scientists.

She offered to translate such a statement into Russian and to secure other translations. Russell declined the offer, because he thought the Russian leaders would pay attention only to the views of scientists who were communists or at least fellow-travellers. But less than two months later he was preparing a statement almost exactly like her proposal. The date of her letter makes it likely that she planted the idea with him.

Her last letter to him was written on September 1961 to tell him how much she admired him for going to prison for his views, even though she did not share his belief in civil disobedience. By going to prison she thought he would acquire credibility with Khrushchev, for he would no longer be able to dismiss Russell as "a supporter of 'imperialist warmongers'!" Her letters reveal that she regarded herself as something of an expert on the minds of the Russians.

iv. Duddington's Letter on Existence

13 Carlton Terrace
Child's Hill, N.W. 2
Feb. 26.1918.

DEAR MR. RUSSELL,—Your lectures are so extremely interesting and leave one with so helpless a sense of being entangled in a fascinating net of ideas which one does not want to believe, that I am sure you will forgive me for trying to find if there is a way out of the meshes and for writing to ask you, in the first place, if you really do mean things which shock one's metaphysical instincts so profoundly!

1) Are you saying that we *ought* to mean by the term "exists" the same thing as by the terms "is possible", or that *as a matter of fact* the two expressions are identical in meaning? If the first, there is of course nothing further to be said, but if the second, then surely you are contradicting the ordinary use of language for obviously for the "plain man" the expressions "lions exist" or "there *are* lions" are not equivalent to the expression "lions are possible". And if one were pressed to define what one means by existence in this connection, I think the answer would be that by saying "a thing exists" we mean that it is in space or time—or both—and is a constituent part of a causally interconnected system and so on.

2) If you admit for a moment—just for the sake of argument!—that the term "existence" does bear this limited significance, then surely there would be meaning in predicating existence of a "this" (using the term "this" to designate whatever my attention was for the moment directed upon)—for the existential judgment would then assert or deny—that the "this" is a thing in the external world, or a mind or anything else that falls under the narrow meaning of the term existence—and not a phantom or an image or a universal. That is, the existential judgment would simply determine the *kind* of reality which belongs to the "this". It is not nonsense to suppose this, is it? Or do you think that the "this" can have one kind of reality only?

It would be awfully good of you if after the next lecture you would say a few words more about your definition of existence, and I would be so grateful.

I wonder if you would care to look at this bit of Lossky's book, for he there deals with this very question. It is of course difficult to get at a man's view from a fragment like that but you know Lossky's general view and I thought perhaps this might interest you. Do not trouble to return the proof to me. I am—Yours sincerely,

NATHALIE A. DUDDINGTON.

Annotation

1 The Relation of Sense-Data to Physics

8: 30 **Mach and James and the "new realists"** In Pt. 1, Chap. 2 of *Theory of Knowledge* (*1984*) Russell cites these sources: Ernst Mach, *Contributions to the Analysis of Sensations* (1897); William James, *Essays in Radical Empiricism* (1912); esp. Chaps. 1 and 2; Edwin B. Holt *et al.*, *The New Realism* (1912); Ralph Barton Perry, *Present Philosophical Tendencies* (1912); esp. Chaps. 12 and 13.

10: 4 **Dr. T. P. Nunn** Sir Thomas Percy Nunn (1870–1944), Professor of Education in the University of London, 1913–36. In his earlier years he was a leading defender of realism, and an active member of the Aristotelian Society, serving as its President in 1923–24. He was knighted in 1930.

10: 9–10 **as Kant ... supposed** See his *Critique of Pure Reason* (1781), A23–31 = B37–46.

11: 7 **Occam's razor** In *Theory of Knowledge* (*1984*, 21) Russell writes: "Occam's razor, '*entia non multiplicanda praeter necessitatem*', which I should regard as the supreme methodological maxim in philosophizing". And in *Our Knowledge of the External World* (*1914*, 107; *1926*, 112; *1929*, 113) he states it as "Entities are not to be multiplied without necessity" and calls it "the maxim which inspires all scientific philosophizing".

12: 16 **Dr. Whitehead** Russell refers here to Vol. 4 of *Principia Mathematica* (1910–13) which Alfred North Whitehead (1861–1947) was to write alone. Russell makes a more sweeping acknowledgement in the Preface to *Our Knowledge of the External World* (*1914*, vi). Yet, Whitehead was displeased and later refused to send Russell his working papers on Vol. 4. See Clark *1975*, 316–7.

14: 25 **the multiplicative class** This class plays an important role in Russell and Whitehead's theory of selections, on which in turn their theory of multiplication in *Principia Mathematica* depends. It may be defined by means of the multiplicative axiom which asserts that given any class κ of mutually exclusive non-null classes, there is at least one class, a selected class of κ, formed of one member from each of these classes. The class of all such selected classes of κ is the multiplicative class of κ. Russell and Whitehead's multiplicative axiom is equivalent to Zermelo's axiom of choice and to the proposition that every class can be well-ordered. See Whitehead and Russell *1910*, I: 478ff. More accessible accounts are to be found in Russell's *Introduction to Mathematical Philosophy* (*1919*, 117–30) and *My Philosophical Development* (*1959*, 91–3).

18:38 **Mr. A. A. Robb** Alfred Arthur Robb (1873–1936). One "interesting and novel" aspect of his theory is "that the theory of space is really a part of the theory of time" (Robb *1914*, 369). Russell also discusses Robb's theories in *The ABC of Relativity* (*1925*, 62ff.). Russell, in a letter to Lady Ottoline, provides a striking description of him. "Yesterday I had a visit from a man named Robb—a wild Irishman, who wrote a book called *A theory of time and space*, not yet published, which I read for the University Press and thought highly of. It comes out of reflections on physics, but all the physicists think him mad, and he has never had any success of any sort or kind. I think my praise was the first he ever had. He is a man of about 35. He was terribly shy and nervous, and was not made any happier by ⟨J. E.⟩ Littlewood's treading on his hat. I put a reference to his unpublished book in my paper on Sense-Data and Physics; it was this that led me to write to him and so to his coming. I sketched his theory to Littlewood, who agreed that it seemed admirable. Physicists are the wrong *milieu* for him—they have no philosophy and no care for logic—one might as well expect people in the French Revolution to have a passion for balanced and judicious statement. People who fail to get appreciation through being in the wrong surroundings are pathetic. Robb is full of bad ideas as well as good ones—he might easily spend his life pursuing a will-of-the-wisp. He is fat and absurd to look at" (#974, pmk. 22 Jan. 1914).

20:24–7 **The first characteristic ...** *continuity* **... a compact series.** Russell uses "compact" where contemporary usage favours "dense". Compactness alone does not yield continuity; for the reasons it does not see Russell *1919*, 100–2.

22:13 **Mr. A. Wolf** Abraham Wolf (1876–1948), spent his career teaching philosophy in the University of London; he wrote on logic, scientific method, the history of science, and the philosophies of Spinoza and Nietzsche.

22:29 **as e.g. Meinong maintains** Alexius Meinong (1853–1920). The sentence to which Russell refers is this: "Aber niemand wird ohne besonderen Grund an eine derartige Enthaltsamkeit glauben; und ein Blick auf das, was wir täglich erleben, belehrt uns darüber, dass wir tatsächlich allemal die Dinge wahrnehmen und die Eigenschaften nur an ihnen." ("But without some particular reason no one will believe in such restraint and a glance at what we daily experience teaches us that in fact we perceive things and their properties in them.")

24:1 **which Kant obscurely felt** See *The Critique of Pure Reason*, A598–603 = B626–31.

24:18 **Locke's water** See *An Essay Concerning Human Understanding*, Bk. 2, Chap. 8, §21.

2 Mysticism and Logic

30:6 **Hume** Russell's remark is a commonplace about David Hume (1711–1776). See the final paragraph of *An Enquiry concerning Human Understanding* (1748) for a famous statement of his positivism.

30:7 **Blake** William Blake (1757–1827), English poet, engraver, painter and mystic. According to Northrop Frye, Blake's religious and philosophical concepts "seem to have been derived mainly from a negative reaction to the British empirical tradition of thought" (*1967*, 319).

30: 16 **Heraclitus and Plato** In letters to Lady Ottoline Russell described the effect on him of reading these two great philosophers. "I have been reading all the known fragments of Heraclitus, which are wonderful." After quoting several of his sayings, Russell continued: "He is only known from a few scattered quotations—some mere nonsense—and no one knows what he thought or believed—strange, the genius and fire and agony of it all gone, gone, and only a few swift lightning flashes remembered. We live and suffer, and the grave swallows us up—but while courage is left the rest matters nothing—I believe that is all the wisdom there is" (#820, 30 June 1913). Two and one half months later he wrote of Plato: "Yes, Plato is *wonderful*. But he is not intimate to me—I haven't enough urbanity for him. And I have begun to feel just a hint of the mediaeval prison-house in his authoritativeness and insistence on ethics as against science. Burnet's books made me feel this more. But of course really he is about as great as any man who ever lived" (#870, pmk. 16 Sept. 1913).

30: 21–2 **"The things ... the most."** Burnet *1908*, 147.

30: 23 **"The sun ... day"** Burnet *1908*, 149.

30: 31–3 **"This world ... going out."** Burnet *1908*, 148.

30: 34–5 **"The transformations ... whirlwind."** Burnet *1908*, 148.

30: 38–9 **"You cannot ... upon you."** Burnet *1908*, 150.

30: 40–1 **"We step ... are not."** Burnet *1908*, 153.

31: 6 **"Time ... child's."** Burnet *1908*, 153.

31: 9–10 **"Good ... one"** Burnet *1908*, 151.

31: 10–11 **"To God ... right."** Burnet *1908*, 151.

31: 13–14 **"Man's ... fate"** Burnet *1908*, 155.

31: 15 **"Every ... blows"** Burnet *1908*, 151.

31: 16–17 **"It is hard ... soul"** Burnet *1908*, 154.

31: 18–19 **"Wisdom ... things."** Burnet *1908*, 148.

31: 31–33: 18 **Imagine ... eyes.** See *Republic*, 514–17.

33: 36–7 **"not to despise ... things"** Russell here quotes the Jowett (1871) translation adding "to" for grammatical reasons. Russell's library has the second edition (1875). See Plato's *Parmenides*, 130.

34: 11 **Hegel and his modern disciples** Russell probably intends this reference to include F. H. Bradley (1846–1924), Bernard Bosanquet (1848–1923), and J. McT. E. McTaggart (1866–1925), who were among the more prominent of the British neo-Hegelians.

34: 13–15 **"immovable ... away"** Burnet *1908*, 200.

34: 16–18 **"Thou ... can be."** Burnet *1908*, 198.

34: 18–20 **"It needs ... to be."** Burnet *1908*, 198.

35: 23–4 **"the way up ... same."** Burnet *1908*, 152.

35: 41 **in Hegel** See Hegel *1931*, 776ff. for a statement of this view.

35: 42 **at least verbally in Spinoza** In the preface to Pt. 4 of his *Ethics* (1677) Benedict Spinoza (1632–1677) writes: "As for the terms good and bad, they indicate nothing positive in things considered in themselves, nor are they anything else than modes of thought, or notions, which we form from the comparison of things mutually. For one and the same thing can at the same time be good, bad, and indifferent" (*1910*, 143).

37: 9 **Bergson ... has raised instinct** Henri Louis Bergson (1859–1941), French philosopher much influenced by the theory of evolution. See his *1903*, 3–4; *1912*, 7–9.

39: 23 **Bergson maintains** See his *1903*, 3–4 and 26; *1912*, 7–9 and 66–7.

40: 41 **which I have explained elsewhere** See Russell *1914*, esp. Lecture 6, "The Problem of Infinity Considered Historically". See also his attack on the doctrine of internal relations in "The Monistic Theory of Truth" (*1910*, 160–9).

41: 27–8 **a useful word from Mr. Santayana—"malicious"** George Santayana (1863–1952) accuses transcendental philosophers of being in the grip of a "malicious psychology" inherited from their predecessors, by which he means that transcendentalists criticize science, not to understand and purify it, but rather to provide a ground for rescuing traditional metaphysics and theology from imminent collapse (see *1906*, 309ff.; *1936*, 5: 223ff.).

43: 34 **Laplace** Pierre Simon de Laplace (1749–1827), eminent French physicist and mathematician, advanced the hypothesis that the sun and its planets originated out of a rotating nebula of gases. Immanuel Kant had advanced a similar hypothesis in 1755, forty years before Laplace.

44: 4 **Spencer** Herbert Spencer (1820–1903) devoted his life to developing a philosophy of evolutionism; he was an evolutionist even before Darwin, whose book he welcomed and whose principles he immediately applied to the development of societies and cultures. He was mainly responsible for popularizing "the survival of the fittest" doctrine, and was one of the principal proponents of Social Darwinism.

44: 5 **Hegelian evolutionists** Russell probably refers to such writers as Samuel Alexander (1859–1938) whose *Moral Order and Progress* appeared in 1889 and David G. Ritchie (1853–1903) whose *Darwin and Hegel* was published in 1893, but he may have in mind any of Hegel's followers who espoused the view that the Absolute was gradually realizing Itself through time.

46: 14–15 **The earth ... celestial light** From "Ode: Intimations of Immortality from Recollections of Early Childhood" by William Wordsworth (1770–1850). The ellipsis marks the omission of one line, namely, "To me did seem".

48: 25–6 **"He that loveth ... it"** John 12: 25.

3 Preface to Poincaré, *Science and Method*

52: 8 **four eminent men** They are Léon Brunschvicg, Jacques Hadamard, A. Lebeuf and Paul Langevin.

52: 13 **Poincaré's philosophical writings** These were published in four volumes: *La Science et l'hypothèse* (1901), *La Valeur de la science* (1904), *Science et méthode* (1908), and *Dernières Pensées* (1913). All four have been translated into English.

53: 12–13 **"It is a mistake ... certainty"** From *Savants et écrivains* (*1910*, vii): "Il
ne faut pas croire que l'amour de la vérité se confonde avec celui de la certitude." No
date of publication is given in the book, but Schmid's *Une Philosophie de savant:
Henri Poincaré & la logique mathématique* (1978) gives 1910 as the year of publication.
53: 13–15 **"To doubt ... reflection."** Russell quotes from pages xxii of William
John Greenstreet's 1905 translation of Poincaré's *1902*. The original reads: "Douter
de tout ou tout croire, ce sont deux solutions également commodes, qui l'une et
l'autre nous dispensent de réfléchir" (2).
53: 35–6 **his criticisms of mathematical logic** Russell refers here to Chaps. 3–5 of
Pt. 2 of his book. Originally published as journal articles in 1905 and 1906, they drew
from Russell a reply entitled "Les paradoxes de la logique" (1906). For a full
discussion of this and other exchanges between Russell and Poincaré see Schmid
1978.
53: 38 **certain indiscreet advocates** Unidentified.

4 On Scientific Method in Philosophy

57: 11 **Herbert Spencer** The lecture was in honour of Spencer (1820–1903). See
A44: 4.
58: 17 **Kant's "Copernican revolution"** See *The Critique of Pure Reason* (1781),
"Preface to the Second Edition", esp., Bxvi–xxiv.
58: 20–1 **"Reality ... parts"** Bernard Bosanquet's full sentence reads: "The principle of Excluded Middle, then, ultimately affirms that Reality is not merely one and
self-consistent, but is a system of reciprocally determinate parts."
58: 25 **The Critical Philosophy** The customary name for the Kantian philosophy.
59: 1–16 **"Let us ... incomprehensible."** The ellipsis marks this omission: "This
brings us back to our pragmatic rule: Suppose there is a oneness in things, what may
it be known-as? What differences to you and me will it make? Our question thus
turns upside down, and sets us on a much more promising inquiry."
60: 33–4 **Herbert Spencer ... says** Russell quotes from the first edition (*1862*,
251), the only edition in which this exact paragraph appears.
62: 6 **Bergson** Bergson defended the conception of "creative evolution". For Russell's criticism of his philosophy, see "The Philosophy of Bergson" (1912).
62: 11–12 **Hegel's modern disciples** See A34: 11.
62: 33 **Chuang Tzŭ** A Chinese philosopher and mystic who lived during the fourth
and third centuries before Christ. A selection of his writings, which are based on the
doctrines of Lao Tzŭ, have been translated, with interspersed notes and commen-
taries, by Herbert A. Giles. Russell quotes from this book (Chuang Tzŭ *1889*, 236).
65: 10–11 **logical atomism or absolute pluralism** Russell had been using the name
"logical atomism" for his position since his Paris lectures of 1911. For an extended
account of what he means by "logical atomism" see **17**, 160ff.
66: 33 **like Heine's German professor** Russell refers to stanza 60 of "The Return
Home" by Heinrich Heine (1797–1856): "Life and the world are too fragmentary—

/ The bits to our German Professor I'll carry. / He puts together life's map so neatly, / In a system quite clear he makes all things combine; / With rags from his nightcap and dressing-gown featly / He stops the gaps in the world's design" (Heine *1907*, 174).

69: 6–7 **due to my friend Dr. Whitehead** See A12: 16. Whitehead's solution consisted in the application of his "method of extensive abstraction". See his *1919*, Pt. 3, for a full account of it.

70: 13–14 **peculiar position which in Kant's day geometry appeared to occupy** In *The Analysis of Matter* (*1927*, 174) Russell writes that Kant "was misled by the common opinion of his time, to the effect that geometry, though a branch of pure mathematics, gave information about actual space".

5 The Ultimate Constituents of Matter

75: 9–10 **Professor Alexander** Samuel Alexander (1859–1938), Professor of Philosophy in the University of Manchester from 1893 until his retirement in 1923, is best known for *Space, Time, and Deity* (1920).

75: 11 **Dr. Nunn** See A10: 4.

76: 21 **naïve realism** The view of the external world supposedly held by the man in the street "that things are just as they seem" (75: 24–5).

76: 41 **logical constructions, symbolic fictions** See below (85: 25–30) for Russell's explanation of what he means by these terms. See also 234ff.

77: 4–5 **Bergson's favourite illustration of the cinematograph** Bergson makes extensive use of the cinematograph to illustrate his points in *L'Evolution créatrice* (1907). "Modern, like ancient, science proceeds according to the cinematographical method" (*1911*, 347).

80: 42 **This point ... American realists.** See, for example, "The Place of Illusory Experience in a Realistic World" by Edwin B. Holt in *The New Realism* (1912). For the other contributors to this cöoperative book, see A106: 24.

81: 27–31 **Thus men will urge ... mind.** For a later discussion of this point see Russell's *The Analysis of Matter* (1927), Chap. 37.

83: 2 **a space of six dimensions** For a more detailed account of this concept, see 15: 10ff.

84: 33–5 **"simultaneous" ... "local time" ... relativity** The reader who is unacquainted with these notions is referred to Russell's discussion of them in *The ABC of Relativity* (1925), Chaps. 4 and 5. There Russell calls "local time" "proper time".

86: 30–1 **the closely analogous theory of Leibniz** Russell refers here to Leibniz's theory of monads. For a full discussion of this theory see his *A Critical Exposition of the Philosophy of Leibniz* (1900), esp. Chaps. 6 through 13. See also *My Philosophical Development* (1959, 24ff.) where Russell explicitly compares his own philosophical position to that of Leibniz.

6 Letter on Sense-Data

88: 3 **a quotation from the *Athenaeum*** For the text of this report, see Appendix 1.

88: 4–6 **"there may be perspectives ... mental."** In this quotation the *Athenaeum* has the second "perspectives" in the singular.

88: 18 **the "egocentric predicament"** Ralph Barton Perry, who named this predicament and attributed its discovery to Bishop Berkeley, claimed that it "is one of the most important original discoveries that philosophy has made". He offers a number of statements of the predicament. This one is typical: "one cannot conceive things to exist apart from consciousness, because to conceive is *ipso facto* to bring within consciousness" (Perry *1912*, 129).

7 Note on Broad

90: 2–3 **attributes to me ... a number of notations** The defined notations in question are the following from *Principia Mathematica*: *38.01–*38.03 (287: 17, 20, 25, 33) where Broad substitutes "$\S$" for "$\female$"; *37.01 (293: 5, 294: 29, 297: 11); *30.01 (294: 29); *32.01 (294: 29); *33.01 (294: 29); *31.02 (294: 29); *32.02 (295: 22); *51.01 (302: 30). (The numbers in parentheses are the page:line numbers in Broad's article where the notation in question is discussed.) Also involved is the notation "xRy" (295: 17) which does not have a definition in *Principia* but is used in *30–*38 whenever a propositional function of a dyadic relational form is required.

90: 6–7 **My original notation ... and viii.** Russell refers here to "Sur la Logique des relations avec des applications à la theorie des séries" (1901), republished as "The Logic of Relations" in his *1956*, and "Théorie générale des séries bien-ordonnées" (1902).

8 Competitive Logic

94: 9–10 **the German encyclopaedia of mathematics** Russell undoubtedly refers to *Encyklopädie der mathematischen Wissenschaft mit Einschluss ihrer Anwendung* (1898–1904). Its publication was commissioned by the Academies of Science of Göttingen, Leipzig, Munich, and Vienna.

94: 10–11 **the encyclopaedia ... one man** The most famous of this type is Hegel's *Encyclopaedia of the Philosophical Sciences*, the first edition of which was published in 1817.

94: 16 **Arnold Ruge** Born in 1881, he published his last work in 1940. He was, in the 1930s, a professor in Technische Hochschule in Karlsruhe.

94: 23 **Windelband** Wilhelm Windelband (1848–1915), a professor of philosophy in various Swiss and German universities, is now best known for his *History of Philosophy*, which was translated into English by James H. Tufts in 1893.

94: 25 **Sigwart** Christoph von Sigwart (1830–1904), a German logician whose *Logik*, which first appeared in 1873 and had a number of subsequent editions, was widely used as a textbook in Germany. It was translated into English in 1895 and influenced such British idealist logicians as Bosanquet. Russell thought highly of it during his own idealistic period.

94: 26–34 **"According ... value."** Ruge *1913*, 9. The ellipsis marks the omission of "and which find their justification entirely in themselves". Russell inserted the comma after "humanity".

94: 35 **"mental nature common to all men"** Ruge *1913*, 10.

94: 38 **Benedetto Croce** (1866–1952), Italian philosopher and politician, best known for his work in aesthetics.

94: 39 **Peano** Giuseppe Peano (1858–1932), Italian logician and mathematician, famous for his axiom system for arithmetic. Russell met him in Paris in 1900 at an international congress. Peano's works proved of great value in Russell's own work on logic.

94: 42 **Royal Academicians speak of Post-Impressionism** Russell almost certainly refers to the famous exhibit, "Manet and the Post-Impressionists" mounted by Roger Fry at the Grafton Galleries in November 1910. For an entertaining account of the public's reaction to this exhibit see *Roger Fry: A Biography* (*1940*, 152–7) by Virginia Woolf.

94: 42–95: 1 **"modern ... intellectualism"** Ruge *1913*, 208.

95: 5 **Professor Royce** Josiah Royce (1855–1916), an American idealistic philosopher who developed an interest in symbolic logic late in life. He had visited Russell at Cambridge in 1912 and was in correspondence with him.

95: 7–8 **"norms for correct thinking"** Ruge *1913*, 69.

95: 8 **a science of "forms"** See Ruge *1913*, 69.

95: 10–11 **"is the General Science of Order"** Ruge *1913*, 69.

95: 13 **suggests, though he does not state explicitly** See Ruge *1913*, 78.

95: 19–20 **"postulate ... will"** Ruge *1913*, 126–7.

95: 23 **Louis Couturat** (1868–1914), French philosopher whose book on the logic of Leibniz (1901) arrived at conclusions similar to those reached by Russell in *A Critical Exposition of the Philosophy of Leibniz* (1900). Russell praised Couturat's book highly. Couturat returned the favour by promoting Russell's early writings in France. Their extensive correspondence has been preserved.

95: 24–5 **the logical manuscripts of Leibniz** See Couturat *1903*.

95: 28 **"logistic"** See Ruge *1913*, 137, where Couturat proposes "Logistic" as the best name for logic.

95: 35 **"definition by abstraction"** Ruge *1913*, 178–9.

95: 37–40 **"has ... *pragmatism*"** Ruge *1913*, 179.

95: 41 **Professor Enriques** Federigo Enriques (1871–1946), Italian philosopher and logician best known for his work on the history of logic.

96: 6 **Nicolaj Losskij** (1870–1965), Russian philosopher, from 1916 to 1922 professor of philosophy in the University of St. Petersburg, who was forced to emigrate in 1922 because of the religious character of his views. He settled in Prague.

96: 12–13 **as stated in the preface** See Ruge *1913*, vii.

9 Review of Ruge *et al.*

98: 8–11 **"There ... minds"** Ruge *1913*, 2.

98: 11–13 **"As every ... Logic."** Ruge *1913*, 5.

98: 19 **philosophy, he says, is the very same study as history** See Ruge *1913*, 211.

98: 20–1 **Royce's account leads up to idealism** Royce (121) calls his position "Absolute Pragmatism" but it does have idealistic features. See also A95: 5.

98: 21 **and Couturat's to the international language** Section 6 of his essay culminates (198) in such a recommendation. See also A95: 23. Couturat was a devotee of Ido.

10 Mr. Balfour's Natural Theology

100: 1 **Mr. Balfour's Gifford Lectures** These were delivered in the University of Glasgow from 12 January to 6 February 1914. They were published as *Theism and Humanism* (1915).

100: 1–2 **in newspaper reports** It is not known which newspaper accounts Russell read. Those in *The Times* for 13 January through 7 February have been examined; they contain very few of the quotations Russell cites. For this reason, and also because the lectures are available in book form, all annotations refer to the book.

100: 6 **Mr. Balfour's purpose** See Balfour *1915*, 17–22. There Balfour writes of the "sort of Deity He is whose existence I wish to establish" (19). He does not use the phrase "social God" (nor do *The Times* reports) but the attributes of his God fit it: "I mean a God whom men can love, a God to whom men can pray, who takes sides, who has purposes and preferences, whose attributes, howsoever conceived, leave unimpaired the possibility of a personal relation between Himself and those whom He has created" (21).

100: 9–11 **The argument ... proceeds ... untrue.** See Balfour *1915*, Lecture 2, for an outline of the argument developed in the book. The last two pages (50–1) make the point Russell is criticizing.

100: 12 **Aesthetic values ... first.** See Balfour *1915*, Lecture 3.

100: 12–13 **Our aesthetic emotions ... selection.** See Balfour *1915*, 58–63.

100: 14–15 **our enjoyment ... artist** See Balfour *1915*, 66–7.

100: 16–19 **Similarly our enjoyment ... design.** See Balfour *1915*, 77–81.

100: 26–7 **Ethical beliefs ... indefensible.** Lecture 4 develops the argument Russell summarizes; for Balfour's conclusion see his *1915*, 126–9.

100: 29 **Mr. Balfour assumes** Balfour frequently appeals to this premiss. Here is an early statement of it: "if the only alternative to Naturalism is Theism, as from the common-sense standpoint it certainly is" (*1915*, 18).

100: 32–3 **Huxley and Bishop Wilberforce ... fight** This celebrated debate between Thomas Henry Huxley (1825–1895) and Samuel Wilberforce (1805–1873) occurred *impromptu* at a meeting of the British Association held in Oxford on 30 June 1860. For a lively account of their exchange see *Lord Bishop, the Life of Samuel*

Wilberforce (1970) by S. Meacham, pp. 215–17.

100: 34–5 **the biologists ... selection"** In a footnote (*1915*, 259–60) in his book Balfour acknowledges the truth of this observation and offers a defence of his continued use of "selection". See also his footnote at p. 36.

100: 38–9 **the criticism of science** See Balfour *1915*, Lectures 5–9.

100: 42–3 **our belief ... world** See Balfour *1915*, Lecture 6.

100: 43 **our belief ... nature** See Balfour *1915*, Lecture 8.

100: 43 **in induction** See Balfour *1915*, Lecture 8.

100: 43–101: 1 **in atomism** See Balfour *1915*, Lecture 9, Pt. 2.

101: 1 **in the conservation ... energy** See Balfour *1915*, Lecture 9, Pt. 2.

101: 3–4 **Mr. Balfour points out** See Balfour *1915*, Lecture 6, Pt. 4.

101: 18 **as Poincaré used to contend** See Poincaré *1902*, 66, or the English translations *1905*, 39, and *1905a*, 50.

101: 26–7 **His argument ... beliefs.** See Balfour *1915*, 46–51.

101: 33–5 **The nerve ... series.** See Balfour *1915*. Balfour makes this point in a number of places; in Lecture 10 (249–50) he writes "that if we would maintain the value of our highest beliefs and emotions, we must find for them a congruous origin". He calls this "the root principle" of his lectures. See also p. 44.

101: 40 **the second** See Balfour *1915*, 41–3.

103: 2–3 **traditional common-sense notions of cause** Russell makes a sustained attack on such notions in "On the Notion of Cause", in his *1910*.

103: 12–13 **Our beliefs, he says, have causes** See Balfour *1915*, 135–6.

103: 13–14 **among which ... falsehood** See Balfour *1915*, Lecture 9, Pt. 3, where he argues that "the course of scientific discovery ... cannot be wholly due to reasoning and experience" but requires "a Power that makes for truth" (241).

103: 14–16 **nevertheless, he maintains, ... causes** "I rest the belief in God on a belief in science" (*1915*, 253); and: "He is Himself the condition of scientific knowledge. If He be excluded from the causal series which produces beliefs, the cognitive series which justifies them is corrupted at the root" (274).

103: 16 **Mr. Balfour neglects the fact** Balfour does briefly acknowledge false beliefs (*1915*, 49–50), but makes nothing of them.

103: 37 **just as Mr. Balfour rejects it** See Balfour *1915*, 136–7.

11 Idealism on the Defensive

106: 7 **Samuel Butler** Chap. 1 of her book offers a critique of Butler's pan-psychism, as presented in his *1878*, *1879*, *1880*, *1887* and *1909*. Butler (1835–1902) was both a novelist and a defender against Darwin of quasi-Lamarkian views.

106: 7 **New Mysticism** Chap. 7 discusses the New Mysticism, her name (*1917*, 307; *1917a*, 274) for the blending into one of Eastern and Western mysticism, or "Pantheism absorbing Christian Humanism". In her opinion the writings of Sir Rabindranath Tagore (1861–1941) exhibit it at its best.

106: 8–9 **Professor Thorndike and his cat** The reference is to Edward Lee Thorndike (1874–1949), American psychologist. See Sinclair *1917*, 107–17; *1917a*, 95–104.

106: 15–16 **she follows Mr. McDougall** William McDougall (1871–1938), English psychologist who spent the latter part of his career in the United States. Her Chap. 3 draws heavily upon his *Body and Mind* (1911).

106: 17–21 **"Shut up a puppy ... objects."** Sinclair *1917*, 119; *1917a*, 106–7.

106: 24 **American Realists** The six philosophers who contributed to *The New Realism* (1912). They are: E. B. Holt, W. T. Marvin, W. P. Montague, R. B. Perry, W. B. Pitkin, and E. G. Spaulding.

107: 4 **the New Realism** Under this name Sinclair includes Russell, Alfred North Whitehead and Samuel Alexander, as well as the American Realists. She does not mention G. E. Moore.

107: 33–4 **"It is dangerous ... Russell."** Sinclair *1917*, xiv; *1917a*, xi.

107: 36–7 **Defence of the Realm Regulations** Parliament passed this act in August 1914 giving the government sweeping emergency powers for the duration of the war. It is the act under which Russell was convicted and fined in 1916.

107: 37–42 **"Atomistic Realism ... Hereafter."** Sinclair *1917*, xiv–xv; *1917a*, xii. Russell runs on two of her sentences and drops an initial "Now". "Atomistic Realism" is her name for Russell's version of realism; "atomistic" is taken from "atomistic logic", her name for symbolic logic.

108: 34 **as she herself confesses** See Sinclair *1917*, xvi; *1917a*, xiv.

108: 37–8 **The work which she alludes to** Russell understates his point here; she quotes from *The Principles of Mathematics* (1903) several times (e.g., *1917*, 179; *1917a*, 154: *1917*, 186–7; *1917a*, 162–3: *1917*, 210; *1917a*, 184), each time naming *Principia Mathematica* (1910–13) as her source.

108: 40 **she touches on the theory of infinite number** See Sinclair *1917*, 189–92; *1917a*, 165–7: *1917*, 254–6, *1917a*, 226–8.

109: 4–6 **"The law of conservation of energy ... obtain."** Sinclair *1917*, 329; *1917a*, 292.

109: 15–16 **"that is to say ... define each other."** Sinclair *1917*, 190; *1917a*, 165.

109: 30–1 **The definite contradictions which Miss Sinclair professes to find** At *1917*, 256; *1917a*, 228 she lists six "contradictions", a seventh and eighth at *1917*, 262–3; *1917a*, 234, and at *1917*, 265; *1917a*, 236 she gives the grand total of nine, which presumably includes Bradley's alleged contradiction regarding external relations which Russell says depends "upon a question-begging assumption". Sinclair discusses Bradley's supposed contradiction at *1917*, 232; *1917a*, 205.

109: 38–41 **"Appearances ... Realism."** Sinclair *1917*, 193; *1917a*, 168. Russell begins quoting in the middle of her sentence, dropping "But suppose that the New Realism accepts as the standard lens the lens of the normal human eye", and he continues by including the first sentence of her next paragraph, the whole of which is in parentheses.

12 Metaphysics

112: 12 **she protests against** See Sinclair *1917*, 228–30; *1917a*, 201–3.

112: 14 **Samuel Butler's views** See A106: 7.

112: 14–15 **she amusingly shows** See Sinclair *1917*, 27; *1917a*, 23–4.

112: 17 **Bergson** See A37: 9. Her Chap. 2 discusses his views.

112: 17 **McDougall** See A106: 15–16.

112: 17 **the Pragmatists** Her Chap. 5, "Pragmatism and Humanism", is almost exclusively devoted to F. C. S. Schiller's version of humanism, although William James is also mentioned.

112: 18 **New Realism** See A107: 4.

112: 19–18 **New Mysticism** See A106: 7.

112: 23–8 **"Observe how Pragmatism ... *that!*"** Sinclair *1917*, xi; *1917a*, ix. James makes this distinction in Lecture 1 of *Pragmatism, a New Name for Some Old Ways of Thinking: Popular Lectures on Philosophy* (1907).

112: 39–113: 1 **"Certain vulnerable forms of Idealism ... again."** Sinclair *1917*, vii; *1917a*, v.

113: 10–13 **"I feel ... occult."** Sinclair *1917*, 296; *1917a*, 263.

113: 13 **She expresses astonishment** See Sinclair *1917*, vii; *1917a*, v.

113: 22–4 **"To the unity ... Unknown."** Sinclair *1917*, 144; *1917a*, 126.

113: 26–7 **"Raise either psychic energy ... Spirit."** Sinclair *1917*, 159; *1917a*, 138.

113: 30 **A quarter of the whole book** See Sinclair *1917*, 173–268; *1917a*, 151–239.

113: 34 **Miss Sinclair herself confesses** See Sinclair *1917*, xvi; *1917a*, xiv.

113: 38–9 **she states that ... Subjective Idealism** See Sinclair *1917*, 240; *1917a*, 213.

114: 1 **Miss Sinclair professes to discover ... contradictions** See A109: 30–1.

13 A Metaphysical Defence of the Soul

116: 4–6 **"is to show ... understood"** Laird *1917*, v.

116: 11 **as Descartes taught** Descartes defends this position in many places; see, e.g., his *Discourse* (1637, Pt. 5) and his letter to Reneri for Pollot, April 1638, in his *1970*, 53–4.

116: 19 **Mr. Laird will disappoint** See Laird *1917*, 367–70.

116: 24 **Fichte** Johann Gottlieb Fichte (1762–1814), German idealist who was greatly influenced by Kant's moral philosophy. See Laird *1917*, 165–74.

116: 28 **the theory of the American realists** See Laird *1917*, 77–80. The only author Laird mentions by name is William James.

116: 42–117: 1 **he deduces ... and attempts to demonstrate** Here Russell summarizes Laird's Chaps. 9–11; the attempt to demonstrate is found in Chap. 13.

117: 4–6 **One traditional definition ... is rejected** See Laird *1917*, 339–41.

117: 11–12 **Mr. Laird's view appears to be** See Laird *1917*, 358–67.

117: 14–15 **a body of logical opinion** Russell refers here to his own work with regard to classes considered as one and as many. See Russell *1903*, §70ff., for the distinction.

117: 23 **such theories as those of Hume or James** Laird does mention Hume's theory (*1917*, 9) but he does not discuss it; James's theory is briefly discussed at pp. 77–80.

117: 35–6 **a view ... Descartes and his followers** See Descartes *1641a*: "Nor indeed is there any argument or example calculated to convince us that any substance can perish" (*1911–12*, 2: 47). Russell in his *1900* (216) quotes Leibniz on this point.

117: 36 **but which is rightly rejected by Mr. Laird** See Laird *1917*, 305–11.

117: 43 **he rejects the monistic logic of Hegel** See Laird *1917*, 223–8.

118: 6–9 **Mr. Laird very properly rejects ... Self.** See Laird *1917*, Chaps. 4, 5 and 8.

14 Pure Reason at Königsberg

120: 19–20 **He believed ... slumbers** See the Preface to Kant's *Prolegomena to Any Future Metaphysics* (1783).

120: 27 **Leibniz–Wolffian philosophy** Primarily rationalist and anti-empiricist, this philosophy, developed by Christian Wolff (1679-1754) from an essentially Leibnizian position, dominated Germany when Kant was growing up.

120: 29–31 **the difficulty ... race** See Smith *1918*, 481–3, where he observes that Kant formulated the antinomies "in terms of the dogmatic rationalism of the Leibnizian position" (481).

120: 41 **Couturat** See A95: 23.

121: 2 **Kant's inconsistencies are recognized** "What is much more serious, is that Kant flatly contradicts himself in almost every chapter" (Smith *1918*, xx).

121: 21–3 **"Kant's supreme ... problems."** Smith *1918*, xxii. The ellipsis marks the omission of ", especially as shown in the first *Critique*, — namely,".

121: 31–4 **"The most ... period."** Smith *1918*, 40.

121: 40–1 **He distinguishes ... view.** See Smith *1918*, 270–84.

122: 2–3 **he regards all ... early** See Smith *1918*, 274.

122: 27–8 **Hegelianizing commentators** The most prominent of these are Edward Caird, who wrote *A Critical Account of the Philosophy of Kant* (1877) and *The Critical Philosophy of Immanuel Kant* (1889), and James Hutchison Stirling, who wrote *Textbook to Kant* (1881).

15 Review of Broad

125: 9 **Mr. G. E. Moore's "Refutation of Idealism"** This article first appeared in *Mind* (1903).

125: 13–14 **"on the arguments ... perception"** This is the title of Chap. 1.

125: 14–15 **There is a long ... water** See Broad *1914*, 10–13.

125: 22–4 **At the end ... sense.** See Broad *1914*, 352–3.

125: 24–5 **Accepting ... object** Referring to "Refutation of Idealism" Broad writes: "The great service of that article is to insist on the truism that when you perceive you perceive something, and that what you do perceive cannot be the same as the perception of it" (*1914*, 5).

125: 28–31 **"Whatever ... perception"** Russell quotes part of a sentence, omitting "This is that" at the start and ", not that it does not exist at all." at the end.

125: 34 **He formulates two questions** See Broad *1914*, 5–6.

126: 30–2 **It begins ... probability.** See Broad *1914*, 72.

126: 33–4 **whether a cause ... event** See Broad *1914*, 74–7.

126: 34–5 **whether a cause ... regularity** See Broad *1914*, 77–91.

126: 36–7 **transeunt causality is quite as possible as immanent causality** Broad makes the point in this way: "A causal law is immanent to a given system S when all the data that are required by it are to be found within S at various times and all the states that can be inferred are states of parts of S. But S may be a system with many different parts. Then relatively to the same causal law that law will be transeunt with respect to any part of S that we like to choose, because to infer its states we shall have to consider the states of other parts of S" (Broad *1914*, 104–5). From this he draws the conclusion that both are possible.

126: 39 **the compactness) of change** Contemporary usage prefers "the denseness) of change". See A20: 24–7.

127: 26–7 **the author's apology as regards probability** Broad says there that he does not "feel competent" to discuss the meaning and nature of probability.

127: 28–30 **"the law ... itself"** This is from page 161 with Russell substituting "motion" for "change".

127: 32–4 **the views of Mach ... if the views were his** Broad notes that Ernst Mach (1838–1916) is a phenomenalist, but does not examine his arguments for phenomenalism, because all of them, he contends, involve the mistake Moore (see A125: 24–5) has exposed (*1914*, 163n.).

129: 31–2 **"Can ... results?"** Broad *1914*, 240.

130: 35–6 **his criticisms ... motion** See Broad *1914*, 279–86, 296–9. Broad cites Russell *1903*, 491–3, as his source of Russell's arguments in favour of absolute motion.

131: 1 **an appendix** "Note on the Measurement of the Velocity of Light and on the Theory of Relativity", Broad *1914*, 354–88.

16 Professor Dewey's *Essays in Experimental Logic*

134: 9 **"analytic realists"** Dewey includes within this group Russell and the American New Realists (see A106: 24).

134: 25 **He takes the view** See Dewey *1916*, 78, where he writes that "logical theory" is "a generic account of our thinking behavior".

134: 30 **the suggestion ... form** See Dewey *1916*, 336.

134: 33–4 **He insists ... data** See Dewey *1916*, 292.

136: 26–7 **When I speak of "data"** See Russell *1914*, 65ff.; *1926*, 72ff.; *1929*, 70ff.

136: 27 **"hard data"** See Russell *1914*, 70ff.; *1926*, 77ff.; *1929*, 75ff.

138: 28 **Hertz's *Prinzipien der Mechanik*** Heinrich Hertz (1857–1894) was a German physicist and philosopher of science. His book, which was published in 1894, is a study of classical physics with the aim of reducing its assumptions to the bare minimum and eliminating, as far as possible, all non-empirical assumptions. He takes "time", "space", and "mass", as his primitive terms, and defines "force" and "energy" in terms of them. See the English translation of his book, *1899*, 26–41.

138: 39 **a sort of artificially archaistic view** Russell refers here to Bergson's philosophy. For a more extended account see §1 of Paper 2, 36–40.

139: 2 **large confused data spoken of by James** See James *1890*, 2: 1–9.

140: 30 **a many-one correlation** "A relation is said to be 'one-one' when, if x has the relation in question to y, no other term x' has the same relation to y, and x does not have the same relation to any term y' other than y. When only the first of these two conditions is fulfilled, the relation is called 'one-many'; when only the second is fulfilled, it is called 'many-one'" (Russell *1919*, 15).

141: 38 **an Unknowable** Russell alludes to the philosophy of Herbert Spencer who made this notion central in Pt. 1, Chap. 4 of *First Principles* (1862).

143: 14 **knowledge? ... Respect** The ellipsis marks the omission of: "Is not the distinction mere hair-splitting unless it is a way of smuggling in a quasi-idealistic dependence upon thought? The reply will, I hope, clinch the significance of the distinction, whether or no it makes it acceptable."

143: 23 **The essence ... (p. 259)** There Dewey writes: "With relation to the unquestionable case of Knowledge, the logical or inferential case ...". There is a short manuscript, "Analysis of Mind" (RA 210.006582), which bears on this point:

"*The* fundamental problem for me is *knowledge*.

As regards *data*, I think we can manage with the view that they merely exist, and that being 'known' or 'experienced' consists in their having relations (probably causal at bottom) to other data, of the sort that make both sets of data belong to one 'experience' or 'biography.' These are not the difficulty; particularly as they do not involve error.

The difficulty begins with *judgment* or *belief*. Dewey holds that *inference* is of the essence of the problem. This is only true in the sense that the beliefs that cause trouble (and may be erroneous) are generally *inferred* beliefs. I think Dewey holds that *all* beliefs are inferred. But for us this is irrelevant. *Belief* raises the problem.

We must analyze **belief**."

144: 21 **"neutral monists"** See A8: 30.

144: 22 **no such thing as "consciousness"** James advanced this thesis in "Does Consciousness Exist?" (1904).

144: 27 **judgment is practically denied by Professor Dewey** See Dewey *1916*, Chap. 14, esp. 392–6 and 400–1.

145: 28 **Professor Dewey ignores all fundamental scepticism.** A search of the indexes of *The Early* and *The Middle Works of John Dewey* through 1918 confirms Russell's statement.

146: 10–11 **Professor Dewey considers ... mistake** Russell refers here to Chap. 10, "Epistemological Realism: the Alleged Ubiquity of the Knowledge Relation", which Dewey opens by writing of "the alleged discipline of epistemology" (264).

147: 5–7 **the view, urged by James ... stuff** This is the central doctrine of neutral monism. See A144: 21.

147: 8 **Occam's razor** See A11: 7.

147: 9–12 **I tried ... monads.** See Russell *1914*, Lecture 3, and Papers 1 and 5, esp. 83: 37–84: 7 of Paper 5 and the surrounding discussion.

148: 20 **William James in his *Psychology*** See James *1890*, 1: 125–6; *1981*, 1: 129–30.

150: 25–7 **Take, e.g., the contention ... respectively.** See Dewey *1916*, 283–4.

150: 35 **the objection (p. 285n.)** This note extends to p. 286.

150: 38–9 **a quibble à la Plato** Russell refers to Meno's paradox, sometimes called the paradox of analysis (*Meno*, 80d–80e).

151: 16–19 **the very essence ... inconsistency)** See Dewey *1916*, 285.

151: 22 **the *Monist* for 1915** Russell refers to "On the Experience of Time" which appeared in the April 1915 *Monist*.

151: 36–40 **Professor Dewey does not admit ... world** Perceptions "are the sole ultimate data, the sole media, of inference to all natural objects and processes. While we do not, in any intelligible or verifiable sense, know *them*, we know all things that we do know *with* or *by* them."

152: 39–40 **"given" in a different sense ... irrelevant** Dewey criticizes Russell for favouring a given which is a "*logical* primitive" instead of "a psychological, or historical, primitive" (292).

154: 17–20 **Dr. Schiller says ... world.** A search of all likely sources in which F. C. S. Schiller (1864–1937) might have made this remark did not turn it up. Reuben Abel who quotes (116–17) this passage in his 1955 book on Schiller reports in a letter (2 Oct. 1982) to the editor of this volume that he has not found any reference to Grumps in Schiller's writings. Schiller may, of course, have made the remark in conversation.

17 The Philosophy of Logical Atomism

160: 4 **Ludwig Wittgenstein** See the Introduction for an account of Russell's relationship with Wittgenstein during these years.

160: 28 **people who more or less follow Hegel** Russell almost certainly has F. H. Bradley and Bernard Bosanquet in mind.

160: 34 **One is often told** Russell refers to Hegel and his followers; see, e.g., Bradley *1883*, 95, where he writes: "It is a very common and most ruinous superstition to suppose that analysis is no alteration, and that, whenever we distinguish, we have at once to do with divisible existence." He goes on to call the method of analysis "this cardinal principle of error and delusion".

161: 41 **the conception of vagueness** Russell did return to this concept. See his *1923*.

162: 24 **a very large school** Russell probably refers to John Dewey and his followers. See 163, where he levels a similar charge at Dewey.

163: 7 **the sort of method adopted by Descartes** See his *Meditations* (1641), esp., the first and second.

164: 34 **in later lectures** See Lecture ɪɪ, Lecture ɪɪɪ: 187–90, and Lecture ɪᴠ.

164: 41 **we shall see shortly** See 178: 27–179: 1.

165: 43 **in a later lecture** See 187–90.

166: 6–7 **at one time I thought** Russell refers to his position in *The Principles of Mathematics* (1903); see esp. Chap. 4 where he does attribute "to the thing properties which only belong to the symbol".

166: 26 **in a later lecture** See 226: 7–232: 41.

166: 32–3 **the theory … reality as a whole** Again it is Hegel and his followers to whom Russell refers. See, e.g., Bradley *1883*, 50 and *1914*, 253ff., and Bosanquet *1888*, 78; *1911*, 73.

166: 39 **in a later lecture** See Lecture ᴠɪ.

167: 33 **was pointed out to me by … Wittgenstein** This point is included in the notes Wittgenstein dictated at Russell's urging. See Wittgenstein *1961*, 97. See also Russell *1984*, 148, where Russell makes his first (partial) concession to this view.

168: 35 **The monistic philosopher** See 170: 20–3 where Russell makes it clear that he is referring to the Hegelian school.

169: 29 **many philosophers** See Aɪ60: 34.

170: 1 **my last lecture** See 235–43, where Russell answers that they are all logical fictions.

170: 39 **partly also in Lecture ᴠɪɪ** See 228–32.

171: 5–6 **I believe that series … are … fictions** See Whitehead and Russell, *1910–13*, ɪ: 50; *1925–27*, ɪ: 71–2.

176: 25 **all the names … would be private** See 179: 2–21.

177: 2 **An instance which Royce gives** See Ruge *et al. 1913*, 97; Royce *1951*, 340.

179: 39 **Mr. Carr** Herbert Wildon Carr (1857–1931), the organizer of these lectures and the long-time Secretary of the Aristotelian Society.

180: 13 **Mr. Neville** Eric Harold Neville (1889–1961), Professor of Mathematics in the University of Reading from 1919 to 1954, had been a student of Russell's in Cambridge. Russell made this note on a letter from Neville: "The writer of the above letter is a very brilliant mathematician, but, chiefly owing to his pacifism, his academic career has always been unsatisfactory."

181: 12–15 **a logical theory … you would understand everything** The theory of the Hegelian school that there is, ultimately, one and only one subject (see Aɪ66: 32–3). A poetic example is provided by Tennyson: "Flower in the crannied wall, / I pluck you out of the crannies, / I hold you there, root and all, in my hand, /

Little flower—but *if* I could understand / What you are, root and all, and all in all, / I should know what God and man is." "Flower in the Crannied Wall" (*1974*, 274).

182: 25 **the theory of types** See 226ff.

182: 28–30 **You may say ... "red".** Russell is making the distinction between two levels of language which he was to generalize into a hierarchy in his Introduction to Wittgenstein's *Tractatus Logico-Philosophicus* (*1922*, 23).

183: 2–3 **the contradictions concerned with types** See 226–9.

183: 16–17 **the treatment that Berkeley and Hume recommended** See Berkeley *1710*, Introduction, §8, and Hume *1739–40*, Bk. 1, §7.

183: 23 **Royce** Russell refers to Royce's 1905 article, "The Relation of the Principles of Logic to the Foundations of Geometry". See esp. Royce *1951*, 406ff.

184: 8–9 **traditional philosophy ... subject-predicate form** See Russell *1900*, §10 for another discussion of this point.

184: 34 **a later lecture** See Lecture IV.

185: 38–186: 3 **for "*p or q*" ... "*p or q*"** This is as close as Russell comes in his writings to giving what are now called "truth-tables". J. Lukasiewicz, E. L. Post, and Wittgenstein all published in 1920–21 writings in which truth-tables are made explicit.

187: 4–5 **first shown ... sufficient ... by Mr. Sheffer** Henry Maurice Sheffer (1883–1964) taught logic at Harvard from 1917 until his retirement. Russell refers to his "A Set of Five Independent Postulates for Boolean Algebras, with Application to Logical Constants" (1913).

187: 6 **work done subsequently by M. Nicod** Jean G. P. Nicod (1893–1924) was a pupil of Russell's in Cambridge. In "A Reduction in the Number of Primitive Propositions of Logic" (1916) Nicod, using what is now called the Sheffer stroke, reduces to one the number of axioms required for the propositional calculus. (*Principia Mathematica* used five axioms.) Russell discusses the work of both Sheffer and Nicod in the Introduction to the second edition of *Principia Mathematica* (*1925–27*, I: xiii–xix).

187: 28–9 **Mr. Demos ... *Mind*** Raphael Demos (1892–1968) spent his entire career teaching philosophy at Harvard. Russell's reference is to "A Discussion of a Certain Type of Negative Propositions" (1917). Russell played a role in getting this article published. See his letter to G. F. Stout, then the editor of *Mind*, 7 June 1917 (RA 710.056654).

187: 34–5 **Mr. Demos points out** See Demos *1917*, 188.

187: 41 **His second** See Demos *1917*, 189.

188: 10 **His third point** See Demos *1917*, 189ff.

188: 18 **a case I took** See "On Denoting" (1905).

188: 27 **suggestion offered by Mr. Demos** See Demos *1917*, 190–1.

190: 10 **a later lecture** See Lecture V.

191: 21–2 **these lectures since Christmas [1917]** See Headnote.

193: 13–14 **Pragmatists ... neutral monists** Russell names James and Dewey as the pragmatists; the American realists who are also neutral monists include E. B.

Holt and R. B. Perry. See A8: 30.

194: 6–9 James and Dewey ... thing. See, e.g., James *1912*, 57, where he is discussing the knower–known relationship as it applies to "knowledge of sensible realities" and where he writes that the known is "an object meant or known". See also Dewey *1905* which opens with "Beliefs look both ways, toward persons and toward things."

194: 34 I shall come on to in the theory of descriptions See Lecture VI.

195: 32 Occam's razor See A11: 7.

195: 41 some articles I wrote in *The Monist* Russell refers to "On the Nature of Acquaintance" (1914). They are the first three chapters of Pt. 1 of his *Theory of Knowledge* (1984).

196: 1–2 "emphatic particulars" Russell does not provide an analysis of the meaning of these words in *The Analysis of Mind* (1921), but he gives one in Chap. 7 of *An Inquiry into Meaning and Truth* (1940) where he rechristens them "egocentric particulars". See also 242: 23ff.

196: 30 Time was when I thought there were propositions See his *1903*, 449, where he writes: "*Being* is that which belongs to every conceivable term, to every possible object of thought—in short to everything that can possibly occur in any proposition, true or false, and to all such propositions themselves." He abandoned this view in 1907; see Pt. 3 of "On the Nature of Truth".

196: 40–1 Meinong maintains ... the round square For a thorough discussion of this and other Russellian references to Alexius Meinong (1853–1920), see Griffin *1977*.

199: 4 The discovery ... Mr. Wittgenstein. For a full discussion of this puzzling comment, see Blackwell *1981*, esp. 21ff.

199: 27–8 the theory of judgment ... in print Russell published this theory in Chap. 7 of *Philosophical Essays* (1910), in the Introduction (45ff.) to *Principia Mathematica*, I (1910), and in Chap. 12 of *The Problems of Philosophy* (1912).

200: 8–9 Spinoza's infinite attributes of Deity "God (Deus) I understand to be a being absolutely infinite, that is, a substance consisting of infinite attributes, each of which expresses eternal and infinite essence." Definition 6 of Pt. 1 of *Ethics* (*1910*, I). In Pt. 2 Spinoza proves (Props. I and II) that we know only two divine attributes, namely, thought and extension.

200: 17 my syllabus Attempts to locate this syllabus have proved unsuccessful.

202: 7–9 This notion ... syllogism. See A184: 8–9. Here Russell emphasizes that part of the traditional doctrine which assumed that universal categorical propositions enjoyed existential import.

202: 13 Darapti A mnemonic for a syllogism of the form: All *A* is *B*, All *A* is *C*, Therefore, Some *B* is *C*, which, because universal propositions were assumed to have existential import, is regarded as valid by defenders of the traditional doctrine. In modern logic, which denies the assumption, Darapti is invalid.

202: 23 mood of the syllogism In the theory of the syllogism every syllogism in each of the four figures is described by a three-letter code, e.g. AAI (**Darapti**), which records the forms of the propositions comprising the major premiss, the minor premiss, and the conclusion, in that order. Each code, of which there are 256, identifies a mood of the syllogism. Only 24 of these are valid in the traditional theory of the syllogism.

202: 15 **impeded Leibniz** See Chap. 8, "Le Calcul Logique" of Louis Couturat's *1901* for a full account of Leibniz's many attempts at logical systems. He does not discuss an attempt by Leibniz which was abandoned because Darapti proved invalid, but he does (326–34) outline one which Leibniz appears to have abandoned because it showed AOO in the third figure valid whereas the traditional theory (rightly) held it to be invalid. Robert Sleigh (*1982*, 222–3) points out that Leibniz made a mistake in the numerical values he assigned the terms; Sleigh makes another assignment and AOO in the third figure is shown invalid.

202: 17–18 **a mathematical logic ... such ... as Boole constructed** George Boole (1815–1864), British mathematician and logician. See his *1847* and *1854* which develop what is now called Boolean algebra.

203: 14 **In all traditional philosophy ... "modality"** Russell must be referring to pre-Kantian traditional philosophy, because Kant (*1783*, A70=B95) in his threefold division under "Modality" (see Smith *1918*, 193–4) departs from the tradition Russell summarizes.

208: 13–14 **As Mr. Bradley ... Logic** See Bradley *1883*, 87–90.

210: 39 **the multiplicative axiom** See A14: 25.

210: 39–40 **the axiom of infinity** This axiom is introduced in the system of *Principia Mathematica* at *120.03. It asserts that for every inductive cardinal number there exists a class with that number of members. For a more accessible account see Russell *1919*, Chap. 13.

214: 26–7 **Scott was the author of Waverley** Sir Walter Scott (1771–1832) began publishing the Waverley novels anonymously in 1814, subsequent volumes were published as being "by the author of *Waverley*".

215: 41–2 **the Hegelian conception of identity-in-difference** For one place where Hegel discusses this concept, see Hegel *1874*, 183ff.; *1892*, 212ff. See also F. H. Bradley's discussion in his *1883*, 161; *1922*, 174.

221: 6–7 **"incomplete symbols"** The fullest account of this notion is to be found in Chap. 3 of the Introduction to *Principia Mathematica*, I (1910) which opens with this definition: "By an 'incomplete' symbol we mean a symbol which is not supposed to have any meaning in isolation, but is only defined in certain contexts."

221: 23 **"logical fictions"** See 234ff. where Russell offers a long account of certain logical fictions. A logical fiction is a logical construction which has all the properties of the (alleged) thing for which it is a replacement. See also 295: 26–41.

222: 4–5 **a letter I have received** This letter was written by Nathalie A. Duddington. It is printed as Appendix IV.

223: 22–3 **Orthodox metaphysics hold** Russell refers to the metaphysical tradition stemming from Plato; Aquinas, Descartes, Spinoza, Kant and Hegel are prominent in it.

225: 28–9 **the notion ... developed ... last** See 202–5.

226: 5 **a discussion in** *The Monist* "Sensation and Imagination" (1915).

226: 37 **in Cantor's work** For an accessible account of this work see P. E. B. Jourdain's long introduction to his translation of two of Cantor's papers (Cantor *1915*). For a full account see Dauben *1979*.

226: 40–2 **a perfectly precise proof ...** *our* **philosophy** See Russell *1969*, plate facing p. 97, for his witty proof in reply to Ronald Searle's little poem reminding Russell that Heaven is more densely populated than his philosophy allows.

227: 9 **the Chinese philosopher** See Chaung Tzŭ *1889*, 452. See also A62: 33.

227: 42 **That contradiction** This is Russell's paradox, first published by him in *The Principles of Mathematics* (1903), Chap. 10.

228: 25 **the saying of Epimenides** It does not seem possible to trace the source of this attribution. St. Paul in his *Epistle to Titus* (1: 12–13), which is an early source for this paradox, does not name the Cretan.

232: 30 *Principia Mathematica*, **p. 20** The shorthand writer mistook Russell's "Number 20" for "Page 20"; it should be *20, and esp. *20.111 and *20.112. See also Chap. 3 of the Introduction (*1910–13*, 78ff.; *1925–27*, 74ff.).

233: 21 **"There is a universe"** The context makes it plain that Russell is treating "universe" as a class-word. By contrast see what he writes in Paper **4**, 57: 43–58: 18.

238: 3 **as I explained ... lectures** See 224: 5–226: 6.

239: 12 **wild particular** A particular that is not a member of another biography, taking "biography" widely enough to encompass things and people.

240: 3–6 **So you can collect ... ego.** Russell is offering an informal account of "biography".

240: 36–8 **the American theory ... Mach** See A8: 30.

242: 19–20 **as I was pointing out ... behaviourism** See 193.

18 Manuscript Notes

252: 4 **Meinong's theory of knowledge** Russell in his *1921*, 16 cites Meinong's *1899*, 185–8, as his source for this. In the second edition of *Über Annahmen* (*1910*, 85; *1983*, 291) Meinong remarks in a footnote that Russell in his 1904 articles has misunderstood him. See Russell *1904* for a full discussion of Meinong's views.

252: 6–8 **I myself have believed ... awareness.** Russell adopted this view in "Knowledge by Acquaintance and Knowledge by Description" which he read to the Aristotelian Society on 6 March 1911. As early as 1905, in the final paragraph of "On Denoting", he had sketched the position. It is fully developed in *The Problems of Philosophy* (1912), Chap. 5.

252: 8–10 **William James and Professor Dewey ... presentations** For James see his *1904*; for Dewey see Chaps. 9 and 10 of his *1916*; for the American realists, see Holt *et al.* *1912*, esp., R. B. Perry's essay.

252: 27 **quotation from Brentano** Russell used the same quotation in *The Analysis of Mind* (*1921*, 14–15); his translation is reproduced here. The original passage reads: "Jedes psychische Phänomen ist durch das charakterisirt, was die Scholastiker des Mittelalters die intentionale (auch wohl mentale). Inexistenz eines Gegenstandes genannt haben, und was wir, obwohl mit nicht ganz unzweideutigen Ausdrücken, die Beziehung auf einen Inhalt, die Richtung auf ein Object (worunter hier nicht eine Realität zu verstehen ist), oder die immanente Gegenständlichkeit nennen würden. Jedes enthält etwas als Object in sich, obwohl nicht jedes in gleicher Weise. In der Vorstellung ist etwas vorgestellt, in dem Urtheile ist etwas anerkannt oder verworfen, in der Liebe geliebt, in dem Hasse gehasst, in dem Begehren begehrt u.s.w.). Diese intentionale Inexistenz ist den psychischen Phänomenen ausschliesslich eigenthümlich. Kein physisches Phänomen zeigt etwas Aehnliches. Und somit können wir die psychischen Phänomene definiren, indem wir sagen, sie seien solche Phänomene, welche intentional einen Gegenstand in sich enthalten" (Brentano *1874*, 115-16).

253: 9-10 **This argument ... idealism** See Russell *1912*, 60-71.

253: 11-13 **I shall not ... physical** For his reasons see Paper 1, Sec. IV.

253: 28-35 **Perceptions ... sympathetic to it** See Russell *1921*, 143: 15-24, for a revised edition of this passage.

254: 11-12 **E. B. Holt ... "neutral monists"** In his *1921*, 25 Russell quotes Holt *1914*, 52 on this point.

254: 32 **"emphatic particulars"** See A196: 1-2.

255: 20-2 **There are those ... noise.** G. E. Moore defended this view in "The Refutation of Idealism" (1903).

255: 25-7 **I formerly believed ... did** Compare Russell *1921*, 15: 20-2.

256: 28-30 **Watson would contend ... they represent.** John B. Watson (1878–1958), American psychologist and founder of behaviourism, held that language habits were sufficient to explain the sort of experience Russell reports having. For a relevant passage from Watson see A283: 14. For another account of this point by Russell see his *1921*, 26-7.

258: 28 **definitions of (a) sensations (b) ourselves** Russell attempts these in an unpublished manuscript called "Sensations" (1921).

259: 24-7 *publicity*, **not sensation ... belongs** Compare Russell *1921*, 118-9.

259: 27 **the reason ... is** *localization* Compare Russell *1921*, 120-1.

260: 4 **anti-introspectionists** Russell means the behaviourists.

260: 7 **Dewey's ignoring of scepticism** See A145: 28.

260: 14 **"I am ... awareness"** Russell cites this in *1921*, 115.

260: 16-20 **"I have pointed ... (p. 427n.)."** Russell cites this in *1921*, 120n.

260: 28-30 **Dunlap ... repeats ... contractions** Russell discusses this claim in *1921*, 120.

260: 32-8 **Take such an instance ... of.** Russell uses this argument twice in *1921*: 120-1, 153.

261: 3 **Imperative to get rid of "Subject".** See Russell *1921*, 141-2.

261: 4 **Involves abandonment ... sensation.** See Russell *1921*, 141-2.

261: 5 **Involves different theory ... memory.** See Russell *1921*, 163-4 and 176.

261: 6–7 **Tends to make ... memory (e.g.) more remote ... theory.** See Russell *1921*, 164.

261: 9 **No doubt ... past.** See Russell *1921*, 164–5.

261: 10 **Images ... it.** See Russell *1921*, 176.

261: 11 **Truth ...** *practical*. See Russell *1921*, 165.

261: 12–13 **Distinction ... case.** See Russell *1921*, 172–5.

261: 14 **"Feeling ... analysed.** See Russell *1921*, 168–72.

261: 15 **(6) Is there ... perception?** This question is not taken up in Russell *1921*.

261: 16 **Immediate ... memory.** See Russell *1921*, 174–5, where immediate memory is contrasted with true memory.

261: 17 **Correspondence ... memory.** See Russell *1921*, 165–6.

261: 19–21 **Two questions ... remembered?** See Russell *1921*, 173, where these questions are raised in very slightly modified form.

261: 29–30 **what we may call "meaning"** See Russell *1921*, 179ff.

261: 35 **Bergson's two kinds of memory** Russell (*1921*, 166) gives the second chapter of *Matière et mémoire* (1896) as his source.

262: 7–9 **Memory-images ... else.** See Russell *1921*, 176.

262: 9–10 **"feeling of familiarity"** For a fuller discussion of this feeling see Russell *1921*, 161–3 and 168–72.

262: 24 **G. and G.** This refers to the edition of Hume's *A Treatise of Human Nature* Russell was using; it was edited by T. H. Green and T. H. Grose and published in two volumes in London and New York, 1890.

262: 35 **In sensation ... exists.** See Russell *1921*, 142.

262: 36–7 **In perception ... inferred.** Compare Russell *1921*, 131ff.

262: 38–9 **In memory ... formerly.** See Russell *1921*, 176.

262: 40 **In imagination ... sort.** See Russell *1921*, 176.

263: 8 **orthodox intellectualist** In his *1921*, 247–50 Russell criticizes this theory and quotes (248) William James as one who, in his *Principles of Psychology* (1890), espoused it: "*Any object which remains uncontradicted is ipso facto believed and posited as absolute reality*" (*1890*, 2: 289; *1981*, 2: 918).

263: 8–9 **James–Dewey pragmatist** Russell seems to refer to the pragmatists' principle linking judgment to action. James, in his first statement of pragmatism, "Philosophical Conceptions and Practical Results" (1898), writes: "Beliefs, in short, are really rules for action; and the whole function of thinking is but one step in the production of habits of action" (*1920*, 411; *1978*, 123).

263: 18–20 **As Bradley says ... round-the-sun"** Russell misattributes this; he should have cited Bosanquet's *Logic* (*1888*, 1: 81; *1911*, 1: 76): "In other words, the subject must be outside the judgment in order that the content of the judgment may be predicated of it. If not, we fall back into 'my idea of the earth goes round my idea of the sun,' and this, as we have seen, is never the meaning of 'The earth goes round the sun.' What we want is 'The real world has in it as a fact what I mean by earth-going-round-sun.'" The quotation has not been found in Bradley's pre-1888 writings.

263: 33–264: 1 **the third, which pragmatism considers essential** In his *1921* Russell writes: "The first theory to be examined is the view that the differentia of belief consists in its causal efficacy. I do not wish to make any author responsible for this theory" (244). See also *299*: 11ff.

264: 10–13 **To such a view ... a feeling *about* the idea.** See Russell *1921*, 250–1.

264: 15–16 *feeling of familiarity* See Russell *1921*, 161–3 and 168–72.

264: 24–7 **But this argument ... "This is familiar."** See Russell *1921*, 168–9 and 233–4.

264: 28 **Doubtless there is ... a *detached* feeling of familiarity** See Russell *1921*, 168–9.

264: 34–8 **There seems to be an experience ... recognition.** See Russell *1921*, 171–2.

265: 3–4 *Recognition* ... **primitive** See Russell *1921*, 169–72 for a fuller discussion of recognition.

265: 17–20 **thus James speaks ... (II, p. 284).** In *The Principles of Psychology* (1890), James does not capitalize "Conviction". Russell uses this same passage in his *1921*, 252.

265: 20–3 **Also there seems no reason why belief ... in sense-data** Russell rejects this possibility in his *1921*: "It is impossible for a belief to consist of sensations alone, except when, as in the case of words, the sensations have associations which make them signs possessed of meaning. The reason is that objective reference is of the essence of belief, and objective reference is derived from meaning" (238).

265: 24–6 **But as soon as belief ...*judgments*.** See Russell *1921*, 168, 170, 176, 236 and 237.

265: 30–3 **"Propositional occurrences" ... a feeling has "reference" to something else.** See Russell *1921*, 243–4.

265: 36–9 **Take (say) familiarity.... familiar.** See Russell *1921*, 161–3 and 168–72.

266: 10–11 **A *proposition expresses ... denies* a fact.** Compare Russell *1921*, 241: "A proposition is a series of words (or sometimes a single word) expressing the kind of thing that can be asserted or denied.... Not any series of words is a proposition, but only such series of words as have 'meaning,' or, in our phraseology, 'objective reference.'" He then goes on to "extend the term 'proposition' so as to cover the image-contents of beliefs consisting of images."

266: 34–5 **The theory of types ... liable.** See 166: 41–167: 14 for an extended account of this point.

266: 36–267: 1 *Theory of true judgments* ... **what we call "logic".** Compare his *1921*, 241–2: "In logic we are concerned with propositions rather than beliefs, since logic is not interested in what people do in fact believe, but only in the conditions which determine the truth or falsehood of possible beliefs."

268: 18 *fact* **being indefinable** The basicness which Russell attributes to "fact" here agrees with the position he accords facts in **18g**, 266–7.

268: 21 **a proposition *is* a fact** Compare Russell *1921*, 276: "Word-propositions, like image-propositions, are always positive facts."

269: 1 **the purely formal problem** For another "purely formal definition of truth and falsehood" see his *1921*, 273–8.

269: 3 "$x \doteq Ry$" This notation is taken from *Principia Mathematica* (1910), Vol. I, *23.04, where "$\doteq R$" is defined as "$\hat{x}\hat{y}\{\sim(xRy)\}$". In words: it is the class of all those pairs whose members are not related by R.

269: 36–8 **Considers speech ... complete.** See 18h, 267: 33–7.

270: 8 *Names of Persons.* See Russell *1921*, 192–4.

270: 18–20 **Composed of three constituents ... $\sim(xRy)$.** See Paper 17, 185–97. Compare also **18h**, 269: 3–15 where Russell offers a different notation for these sorts of facts.

270: 20–1 **What is a *fact* ... indefinables.** See 18h, 268: 18 where Russell writes that "fact" is indefinable.

270: 34 **A single word is a class of similar noises.** See Russell *1921*, 189: "A single word, accordingly, is by no means simple: it is a class of similar series of movements (confining ourselves still to the spoken word)." He goes on to note that this is not a definition of "word", because the definition of "word" must involve "meaning".

270: 34–5 **A proposition ... word.** See A266: 10–11.

271: 27 **its subjective meaning** See Russell *1921*, 235–41 and 272–3.

19 On "Bad Passions"

273: 10 **Professor Stanley Hall** Granville Stanley Hall (1844–1924), American psychologist and the first President of Clark University, serving in that office from 1888 to 1920.

273: 13–21 **"Some ... combat."** P. 440. Russell substitutes "every one" for "every-body", and adds commas after "day", "twenty-three", "temper", and "war".

273: 23–5 **"Richardson ... root."** P. 443. The first ellipsis marks the omission of "introspected by graduate students of psychology"; the second "not only over-determination, anger fetishes and occasionally anger in dreams with patent and latent aspects and about all the Freudian mechanism, but what is more important, finds".

273: 38 **Benvenuto Cellini murdered a man** Cellini (1500–1571), Italian gold smith and sculptor, is also famous for his *Autobiography*. Russell's account of the murder is not accurate. Cellini reports two murders, the first of his brother's murderer, the second of a Milanese jeweler who had picked a quarrel with him; in neither case did he return "home to his work as if nothing had happened." See Cellini *1908*, 102, 142. Cellini also believed he had killed one man during a battle in which he was employed as a soldier, but again his report does not support Russell's story. See Cellini *1908*, 66.

274: 11 **Some Persian poet** Unidentified.

274: 16 **in Stanley Hall's article ... there are cases** See pp. 441–2.

275: 10–11 **Cannon's ... *Rage*** Walter Bradford Cannon (1871–1945) was Professor of Physiology in Harvard University from 1906 to 1942. His book was published in 1915. Russell has a longer discussion of Cannon's position in *1921*, 281–3.

20 On Propositions: What They Are and How They Mean

278: 37–8 **I have defended its doctrines elsewhere** See Paper **17**.

280: 8–9 **"infinite negative" ... interpreted** Russell is referring to the Hegelian school. See *1874*, 149; *1892*, 174: "This Infinity is the wrong or negative infinity: it is only a negation of a finite: but the finite rises again, and is never got rid of and absorbed." See also Bradley *1883*, 116–9; *1922*, 120–3, and Bosanquet *1888*, 297ff.; *1911*, 281ff., for a discussion of the same concept, although neither uses the expression "negative infinite".

280: 28 **that of Mr. Demos** Raphael Demos (1892–1968). See Paper **17**, 187ff. for a fuller discussion of Demos's paper.

280: 35–40 **"The relation ... primitive notion"** Russell has added a comma between "that" and "if".

281: 22 **We shall see later** See below 303: 33ff.

281: 33 **"incomplete symbols"** See A221: 6–7.

282: 28–9 **James would call "processes of leading"** See James *1907*, 218; *1975*, 104: "Our account of truth is an account of truths in the plural, of processes of leading, realized *in rebus*, and having only this quality in common, that they *pay*. They pay by guiding us into or towards some part of a system that dips at numerous points into sense-percepts, which we may copy mentally or not, but with which at any rate we are now in the kind of commerce vaguely designated as verification."

283: 14 **Professor Watson denies altogether the occurrence of images** See Watson *1914*, 324: "we denied the necessity of assuming imagery (1) because there is no way of accounting for it on neuro-physiological grounds without doing violence to our conception of brain physiology, (2) for the reason that there is no objective evidence to show that it exists, (3) for the reason that we can substitute for what it is supposed to do a mechanism which is exactly in line with what we have found to exist everywhere else, viz., an enormously developed system of language habits."

283: 18–21 **"It is implied ... phenomena"** Russell set "or ought to exist" off with commas; they are not in Watson.

283: 22 **in a later chapter** See Watson *1914*, Chap. 10.

283: 24–284: 5 **The stimulus ... habit** The first ellipsis marks this omission: "When the box is presented now, which set of arcs will function? Evidently either (1) or (2) or both simultaneously. It is at this time that the influence of the environment upon shaping the language habits comes again clearly to the front." The second: "The box happens to have been put beyond his reach. The nurse, seeing the child's efforts to reach it and hearing the word "*box*," hands it to the child. This situation being repeated day in and day out, not only with this object but with hundreds of others, brings it about that the arcs running from receptor to throat muscles offer the least resistance so far as concerns the neural impulses aroused by the box (frequency, p. 262)." And the third: "There has been a substitution (mechanical process) of a language habit for a bodily habit. One other step and the process is complete. We found in our studies on the maze that every *cul de sac* represented what we might call a simple unit habit. These simple habits when perfected arise serially. When learning is complete we can put the animal down anywhere in the maze, and after a few trial movements the remaining part of the journey is executed without a break. Something similar of course occurs in all complete systems of bodily habit and in language habits as well."

284: 23–4 **Professor Watson ... does not possess** Watson (*1914*, 18) seems to admit this of himself.

284: 41–2 **Galton's investigations** Sir Francis Galton (1822–1911), English scientist who founded the science of eugenics. In his *1883* Galton writes: "scientific men, as a class, have feeble powers of visual representation ... an over ready perception of sharp mental pictures is antagonistic to the acquirements of habits of highly generalized and abstract thought, especially when the steps of reasoning are carried on by words as symbols, and that if the faculty of seeing the pictures was ever possessed by men who think hard, it is very apt to be lost by disuse" (60–1).

285: 3–5 **"I should throw ... thought)"** Watson has "imageless thought" in quotation marks. His article is entitled "Psychology as the Behaviorist Views It".

286: 1 **Knight Dunlap** See A260: 10.

286: 28 **as Watson does** See above (283: 24ff.) for the quotation from Watson.

286: 38 *Psychological Review*, 1916 Russell read some of these articles in prison; see Appendix III.

289: 23 **William James ... developed the view** This is the view Russell calls "neutral monism" at other places in this volume. James states his thesis in his *1912*; *1976*, 4.

290: 41 **Watson would contend** See above 283: 9ff.

293: 15 **Hume's principle** See Hume *1739–40*, Bk. 1, Pt. 1, §1, or Hume *1748*, §2, for a statement of this principle.

294: 14 **Meinong, for example** See A252: 4.

294: 16–17 **Moore and myself ... rejecting** G. E. Moore (1873–1958), see his "Refutation of Idealism" (1903), reprinted in his *1922*, esp. 21–4. Russell rejects "content" in his *1912*, 65–7.

294: 17–18 **American realists ... have rejected** Russell makes it clear below (294: 32–4) that it is the neutral monism of some American realists to which he alludes here.

295: 1 **Brentano's view** Franz Brentano (1838–1917), German philosopher and psychologist. "The intentional inexistence is characteristic exclusively of mental phenomena. No physical phenomenon exhibits anything like it. We can, therefore, define mental phenomena by saying that they are those phenomena which contain an object intentionally within themselves" (*1973*, 89).

295: 29 **The theory of belief which I formerly advocated** See Russell *1912*, Chap. 12.

295: 39 **the theory of bodies in my ... *World*** See Russell *1914*, 89; *1926*, 96–7; *1929*, 94. A thing is a logical construction out of what we customarily call its aspects.

298: 41 *Cf.* **Brentano ... p. 268** See Brentano *1973*, 202–3.

299: 35 **James ... quotes (inaccurately)** James does not note his added emphasis, nor does he indicate an omission in the middle of the passage. A check of the published translations of Spinoza's *Ethics* to 1890 suggests that James made his own translation of the passage, as was Russell in correcting it as indicated in square brackets.

301: 37–8 **criticism of Mr. Joachim** Harold H. Joachim (1868–1938), British philosopher who defended the coherence theory of truth in his *The Nature of Truth* (1906).

302: 5 **Meinong, who holds** See A196: 40–1.

302: 18–19 **it would be a mistake ... "ideal" ... "real"** Russell alludes to Meinong's view. See his *1904*, 353–4; *1973*, 58–9, for one place where he makes this distinction.

305: 30–1 **Bergson's point about repetition** The beneficial effects of repetition for learning are praised by Bergson in *Matière et mémoire* (1896); see the English translation *1911a*, 137–8.

Textual Notes

Textual Principles and Methods

THE COLLECTED PAPERS OF BERTRAND RUSSELL is a critical edition of Russell's writings, which seeks to present his texts in a form we believe, on the basis of the available evidence, that he would have approved. This is not necessarily the same as his "final intentions", since he may simply have had "different" intentions for his work at different times, and it may not be the case that the final version is the one which ought to be printed in an edition such as this. In effect, the "accidental" features of the text (i.e. spelling, punctuation, word-division, etc.) will normally be drawn from manuscript or from an early edition, while variants in "substantive" readings (i.e. the words themselves and their order) will be individually evaluated. Since most publishers introduce changes in accidentals as part of their "house-styling", the accidentals of a published text seldom exactly reproduce those of the author's manuscript. However, changes in substantives rarely occur without an author's knowledge and approval.

Classical textual theory postulates that the copy-text be chosen on the basis of the superiority of its accidentals (that is, accidentals that are closest to the author's), while all substantive variation must be assessed to determine its origin and status. Following standard practice for critical editions, we emend the copy-text by incorporating in it substantive variants from other witnesses which we believe to be authoritative. It is evident that the most authoritative text for the substantives often does not have the best accidentals. A version of a text that an author is known to have closely scrutinized is a better source for accidentals than some other version which did not enjoy such scrutiny, even though the latter might well contain a number of substantive variants that should be adopted. *The term "copy-text", as it is used in this edition, designates the source of the accidentals.* Textual variants are recorded in the Textual Notes. In fact, most of the papers in the present volume survive only in one form. Apart from the correction of obvious spelling and grammatical errors (as noted in the Textual Notes), little is done to alter these texts. Some silent emendation of potentially distracting features is undertaken, as described below under "Regularization".

For the remaining papers, principles must be employed to guide the choice of copy-text. Russell does not seem to have objected to some house-styling of his work: papers published in America, for instance, follow American conventions for spelling and position of quotation marks. In a collection such as this, however, there is no virtue in retaining in print the peculiarities of house-styling of Russell's various former publishers. Yet some standarization is clearly desirable. Thus, we have introduced our own minimal house-styling. It derives from a careful study of Russell's own practices in manuscript and attempts to approximate Russell's personal system of accidentals, as revealed in his manuscripts. Although most of Russell's systematic preferences in spelling and punctuation seem to have been established early in his career, some evolution of his personal "house-styling" is evident in later manuscripts. Thus, the details of the house-styling which have been imposed here are derived from an examination of manuscripts written within the same time period as the papers contained in this volume. These are exhaustively described below.

By imposing such house-styling we can eliminate a large number of accidental variants in printed texts which are known not to be authorial. Examination of the narrower class of accidentals which remains enables a more rational selection of copy-text to be made. While it is true that Russell let mere house-styling stand, he was anxious that other aspects of his texts should not be changed. Therefore, when accidental variants, other than mere house-styling, are found in a version of a text that he is known to have seen through the press, the plausible inference is that Russell must have sanctioned them.

A strong case can be made, for instance, for taking as copy-text a version of a paper which appears in one of Russell's own collections of his essays, rather than a manuscript of the same paper. But one must exercise caution when dealing with publications in which Russell is not known to have been so directly involved. Holograph accidentals carry authority simply by virtue of being in the author's hand. The burden of proof is clearly on those who wish to adopt the accidentals of any other version of a text. This edition takes a conservative approach towards copy-text, and in general, a manuscript is chosen as copy-text over any published version unless there are good reasons not to do so.

By adopting the accidentals *as a class* from the copy-text a small risk is taken, since there may be a few accidentals in another version which, given a broader knowledge of the publishing circumstances, might be deemed to be part of Russell's final intentions. Nevertheless, a non-copy-text accidental is used only in exceptional cases, where reasons for doing so can be stated (in the Textual Notes).

We have decided to record the accidental variants only when a non-copy-text accidental is preferred. There is one exception to this rule: when an extant manuscript or typescript is not chosen as the copy-text, its accidental variants are listed in the Textual Notes. This is done because of the comparative inaccessibility of these documents, as opposed to journal articles or books.

I. REGULARIZATION

Most of the regularization in this edition amounts to the adoption of Russell's systematic preferences for accidentals—his personal "house style". Every departure from the copy-text is accounted for *either by one of the following regularization rules, or by a textual note.* Since the aim of such regularization is to restore Russell's preferences in accidentals, as determined from his contemporary manuscripts, there is no point in regularizing manuscript copy-texts in this manner. Accordingly, the spelling and forms of punctuation in manuscript copy-texts are kept, unless they are clearly erroneous. Printed copy-texts, however, are regularized in the following respects. (These changes are not recorded in the Textual Notes.)

The order of puncutation and closing quotation marks has been made consistent with Russell's usual style, i.e. terminal punctuation is set before the quotation marks if and only if it is judged to be part of the quoted sentence. In manuscripts of this period he rarely marked for italicization terms such as "a priori", "i.e." and "e.g." and unless there was a clear reason for it, he did not habitually put a comma following "i.e." and "e.g.". These practices have been adopted here. Terminal "-ize" is preferred to "-ise". British spelling, as found in the *Oxford English Dictionary*, is imposed upon American copy-texts. Thus, for example, "centre", "defence", "favour", "labour" and "premiss" are the preferred forms. Diphthongs are not used. During this period Russell seems to have preferred "Leibniz" to "Leibnitz", although manuscripts of earlier years contain both spellings. Copy-texts are regularized to "Leibniz".

II. FURTHER HOUSE-STYLING AND SILENT EMENDATION

In addition to regularization which is intended to restore Russellian accidentals, certain other modifications have been made to various features of all copy-texts. Titles of papers are given a consistent capitalization, and any terminal period is removed. Section headings are centred and sub-section headings italicized. Titles of books are italicized. In salutations of letters a comma with a dash is used after "Sir". Where Russell's address or a date is provided in a letter, it is put at the end. Periods are removed after names like "Gregory XVI." Three dots are used in ellipses (four, when one of them functions as a period). In non-mathematical contexts, numbers below 100 are given in words. Footnote indicators have been replaced by a continuous numeration through each paper. Foreign words and phrases are italicized, unless they are enclosed in quotation marks in the copy-text. Accents are also silently corrected.

Abbreviations are normally expanded, except for those of names of people, places and organizations. Abbreviations are not, however, expanded in manuscript outlines, unless a particular short form might be distracting. Short forms in such outlines are preserved as much as is reasonable in order to maintain the character of these documents.

Wherever possible, single quotation marks are changed to double. In manuscripts and typescripts containing authorial alterations, capitals are changed to lower case for words that originally began a sentence, but were moved to a later position by an insertion or transposition. In Russell's review articles, bibliographical details of the books under discussion, which appear as footnotes in the copy-texts, are moved to the beginning. Since such references are often supplied by the publisher, they are not regarded as part of the copy-text and hence are regularized in content, as well as position, as part of our house style. Subheadings are removed from newspaper articles because they are certain to have been supplied editorially.

III. COPY-TEXT DECISIONS IN VOLUME 8

Only seven papers in this volume required selection of the copy-text from one of a number of alternate versions. The versions of Papers **1, 2, 4** and **5** which appear in *Mysticism and Logic, and Other Essays* (1918) are selected as copy-texts, since in that collection of his own essays Russell must certainly have had the opportunity to express his preferences in accidentals.

The typescript which was the printer's copy for "Professor Dewey's *Essays in Experimental Logic*", Paper **16**, is taken as copy-text, since it bears corrections in Russell's hand and is the best documentary evidence of his final intentions regarding accidentals.

The version of "The Philosophy of Logical Atomism", Paper **18**, which was published in *The Monist* is taken as copy-text, since the other versions of the paper were published decades later by others and were intended to be faithful reproductions of the former. However, both the Minnesota edition and Marsh's book introduce important substantive corrections to the text.

"On Bad Passions", Paper **19**, is based on a manuscript entitled "Morality and Oppressive Impulses" (RA 220.011910). However, given the incompleteness of the manuscript, the copy-text is *The Cambridge Magazine*, 8 (1 Feb. 1919): 359.

Guide to the Textual Notes

THE PRINCIPAL PURPOSE of the Textual Notes is to provide a record of all substantive variants and of such accidental variants as require recording. They also are intended to present all the known evidence of the progression of Russell's expression of his thought by recording authorial alterations in manuscripts, as well as subsequent revision in typescripts, proofs and later printings. The Textual Notes permit the recovery of the various versions of a text by providing the materials needed for their reconstruction. The notes also record editorial emendations of the text. The integration of the list of editorial emendations with the list of authorial alterations and variants allows the reader to find in one place all of the textual material bearing on a given passage.

Format

A brief physical description of the copy-text and other pertinent textual documents is supplied for each paper. Unless otherwise identified, the archival location of these documents is McMaster. The description of holograph or typed documents provides an exact statement of their foliation (the numbering of the leaves), the paper size, and whether they are written in pencil or ink, typed or mimeographed. Italic numbers in the foliation refer to unnumbered leaves. Also included in the description is an identification of the symbols used in the textual notes to denote the various texts of the paper at hand. The most common symbol is "CT", the abbreviation for "copy-text".

Record of Authorial Alterations

For manuscript and typescript copy-texts the most frequent kind of note concerns authorial alterations. A precise vocabulary is used to cover insertions, deletions, and words written over other words. Insertions are normally indicated by the single word *"inserted"*, written to the right of the square bracket following the reading from the text. More precise information is supplied, as in *"inserted in margin"*, when the nature of the insertion requires further explanation. The expressions *"above deleted"*, *"before deleted"* and *"after deleted"* are used to indicate that the accepted reading (on the left of the square bracket) is found, respectively, *above, before* or *after* the reading which is given at the end of the note. The expression *"transposed from"* indicates that the word order has been changed. The expression *"written over"* is self-explanatory. The term *"replaced"* is employed when the nature of the altera-

367

tion would be obscured by the use of the other terms. For example, at 6: 4 "We have therefore" is said to have *replaced* "Thus we have" in the manuscript. The original reading "Thus we have" was altered by deleting the first word, writing a capital "W" over the second and inserting the word "therefore". While these changes might have been recorded in three separate textual notes employing the other terminology, it is clear that they are dependent upon one another and should be combined. The presence of cancelled illegible words is rarely recorded. False starts, letters written over the same letters, words written over the same words, and incomplete words are also not recorded (except when they are part of a larger alteration or are otherwise thought to be of interest).

Each note is comprised of a number of distinct components, as in the following example:

254: 13 the stuff of the world CT] *above deleted* everything

In "254: 13 the stuff of the world", the page/line reference to the present volume is followed by the reading at that location in the text. "CT" indicates that this reading coincides with the final reading in the copy-text. A right-hand square bracket completes this component of the note. The next component is a phrase describing the nature and location of the alteration in the copy-text. Editorial comments, which are found always to the right of the square bracket, are in italic. The final component is the prior reading. The complete note is to be understood as follows: At page 254, line 13, the reading "the stuff of the world" is from the copy-text where it appears immediately above the deleted word "everything".

Record of Variants

Another kind of note records a variant reading from another version of a paper. Where the variant reading is adopted in this text, the variants are recorded thus:

81: 26 in which 15] which in CT

This note indicates that the copy-text reading is erroneous, and that the former reading from *The Monist*, indicated here by "15", has been restored. Where several versions are collated, the variants are presented as follows:

174: 3 words 56, MIN] the words CT

The text printed in *Logic and Knowledge* (1956), edited by R. C. Marsh, is indicated by "56". In this case, it is in agreement with the text in the Minnesota edition of "The Philosophy of Logical Atomism", indicated by "MIN". The note records that this reading has been substituted for that of the copy-text. When a collated version has the same reading as CT, its symbol is not provided in the textual note.

Compound Textual Notes

Occasionally, more than two variant readings must be reported for a given passage. An additional square bracket is often used to distinguish the three (or more) readings. In the following example, the reader is provided with the English and French variants. The note indicates that the copy-text reading has been retained:

13: 7 possibly CT] probably COL, 14] probablement 14a

Deleted passages in manuscript or typescript copy-texts sometimes contain other levels of authorial alteration which ought to be recorded. However, since the passages in which these changes occur are no longer a part of the text, there is no reading in the text to which they can be keyed. Thus, another method is introduced to record these alterations. The comments in angle brackets in the note for 273: 1, for instance, indicate the nature of the changes at precisely the place where they occur in the deleted passage.

Editorial Emendations

Sometimes the text is emended editorially. Thus, for example, the following textual note records the fact that the page reference "p. 124–6" replaces the one given in the copy-text:

58: 40 p. 124–6] p. 124 CT

That no text is cited as the source of the preferred reading indicates that the text was editorially altered.

1 The Relation of Sense-Data to Physics

The copy-text (CT) is *Mysticism and Logic, and Other Essays* (1918), 145–79. There are a number of other versions of the paper with which it has been collated. The first is the manuscript fragment (MS) (RA 220.011400) "The Relation of sense-data to physics" (formerly titled "Can Physics be made verifiable?"). Only "I. *The Problem stated.*" of this is extant. Its two leaves are foliated 1–2; measure 221 × 286 mm.; and are written in ink. A mimeographed version of the paper (COL) was distributed to members of the Philosophical Club of Columbia. (A photocopy of COL is in the Russell Archives [RA REC. ACQ. 232(b)].) And finally there are the English and French versions (14 and 14a) in *Scientia*, 16 (July 1914): 1–27 and supp. 3–34, where the paper was first published.

5: 4 verifiable CT] *verifiable* MS
5: 7 , so far as physics is concerned, CT] *inserted in MS*
5: 8–9 etc., with certain spatio-temporal relations. CT] etc. MS, COL
5: 10 contents CT] *after deleted* phe *in MS*
5: 11 molecules CT] *above deleted* atoms *in MS*
5: 15 this MS] their CT
5: 18 namely MS] namely, CT
5: 19 the other term CT] the other MS
5: 19 essentially incapable CT] incapable COL
5: 20–1 objects of sense CT] les objets de la physique 14a
5: 24 some principle CT] *inserted in MS*
5: 25 e.g. CT] *inserted in MS*
5: 33 what can be experienced CT] *above deleted* sense-data *in MS*

6: 3 physical objects CT] les choses physiques 14a
6: 4 We have therefore CT] *replaced* Thus we have *in MS*
6: 14 patch CT] nuance 14a *twice*
6: 18 sense: *sense* CT] la donné sensorielle: la *sensation* 14a
6: 23 acquaintance with a particular CT] la notion d'une particularité 14a
6: 29 there CT] these COL
6: 35 primitively CT] immédiatement 14a
7: 9 *sensibilia* CT] "sensibilia" [objets sensibles] 14a
7: 34 these CT] ces organes, nerfs et cerveau 14a
8: 4 mind CT] human mind COL
8: 18 controversies CT] questions 14a *Also at 8: 20.*
8: 30 new realists CT] nouveaux réalists de l'Amérique 14a
8: 34 discussions CT] discussion COL
8: 36 In COL] in CT] En 14a
9: 14 *B* is part of *A.* CT] *B* is part of *A.* (Thus, for example, the existence of a plum-pudding is logically dependent upon that of the plums.) COL
9: 28 physiological not psychical CT] comme physiologique et non comme physique 14a
10: 4 Nunn CT] Munn 14a
10: 12 an undeserved advantage CT] un avantage 14a
10: 39 others; COL] others: CT] autres; 14a
11: 39 method, as I have shown elsewhere, CT] method 14a
12: 15–16 the stimulus for its application CT] l'idée 14a
12: 19 physics. CT] la physique[1] ⟨*Footnote:* [1] Ses résultats paraîtront dans les quatrième volume des "Principia Mathematica".⟩ 14a

12: 26 The inferences which are unavoidable CT] Les inférences qui doivent être évitées 14a

12: 43 solipsism CT] le point de vue "solipsistique" 14a

13: 7 possibly CT] probably COL, 14] probablement 14a

13: 9 an illustrative hypothesis CT] ⟨an *erased*⟩ illustrative hypotheses COL

13: 9–10 a dogmatic CT] an ultimate COL, 14] ultime 14a

13: 16 less smooth and tidy CT] moins simple et moins régulière 14a

13: 36 of combining CT] de savoir comment combiner 14a

14: 37–40 a plane (though in this case there will be many different perspectives in which the penny is of the same size; when one arrangement is completed these will form a circle concentric with the penny) CT] a straight line COL, 14] une ligne droit 14a

15: 3 perspectives CT] proportions 14a

15: 15 constructed CT] constant 14a

16: 12–13 there is a good meaning for the statement CT] on peut proposer l'affirmation 14a

16: 20–1 the subjectivity of sense-data CT] la subjectivité 14a

16: 31 still remain COL] will remain CT] resteront 14a

17: 6 the information CT] les notions 14a

17: 8 Jones CT] Jean 14a *Also at 17: 9, 17: 10.*

17: 14–15 The *matter* ... diminishes. CT] *in quotation marks in 14a*

17: 16 probable CT] admissible 14a

17: 16 there is something in this definition CT] cette définition donne une première approximation de la verité 14a

17: 42 an indefinite number CT] un nombre infini 14a

18: 2–4 This is in some sense an empirical fact, but it would be hard to state it precisely, because "causal efficacy" is difficult to define. CT] This is an empirical fact. COL, 14] C'est un fait empirique. 14a

18: 27–8 earlier or later than, or simultaneous with CT] earlier or later than COL] antérieur et postérieur 14a

18: 36 convenient CT] admissible 14a

18: 38 compare CT] compare a forthcoming work called: COL, 14] comparez un travail à paraître bientôt, intitulé: 14a

18: 41 theory CT] views COL

19: 2 exactly simultaneous CT] simultaneous COL *Also at 19: 3, 19: 17, 19: 18.*

19: 16 Its motive CT] Sa raison d'être 14a

19: 29 perspectives CT] perspections COL

19: 35–6 the one thing simultaneously seen by many people CT] one thing seen by many people simultaneously COL

20: 42 such CT] much COL

20: 43 point CT] question 14a *Also at 22: 1.*

20: 43 such "sensibilia" as 14] such "sensibilia", as CT

21: 33 the empirical success of physics CT] les résultats de la physique 14a

21: 36 is CT] are COL, 14] est 14a

22: 17 a bare CT] bare COL

22: 20 First, COL, 14] First CT

22: 21 a nothing CT] l'inexistant 14a

22: 26 the sense-datum CT] sense-datum COL

23: 41 *14 CT] 14 COL

23: 42 *14.02 CT] 14.02 COL

24: 35 the single CT] single COL

24: 37–8 moment of dreaming CT] moment COL, 14] moment 14a

24: 38 suspicion CT] our suspicion COL

24: 42 p. 305 CT] p. 30 14a

25: 10–11 This might ... dreams. COL] This might be used to condemn the "things" inferred from the data of dreams. CT] On peut se servir de cette constatation pour condamner les lois de la physique; mais il est plus simple de s'en servir pour condamner les "choses" inférées des donnés des rêves. 14a

25: 13–16 supposes. I have no wish to combat psychological theories of dreams, such as those of the psycho-analysts. But there certainly are cases where (whatever psychological causes may contribute) the presence of physical causes also is very evident. CT] supposes. COL, 14] suppose. 14a

25: 25 except through the discovery of CT] but only by COL, 14] mais seulement grâce aux 14a

25: 26 experiences CT] experience COL

2 Mysticism and Logic

The copy-text (CT) is *Mysticism and Logic, and Other Essays* (1918), 1–32. The first publication of this paper is 14, *The Hibbert Journal*, 12 (July 1914): 780–803. As Russell says (in footnote 3), several passages from this paper also appear in *Our Knowledge of the External World* (14a). The following table identifies the parallel passages:

CT	14a
30: 1–3	19
34: 12–22	166
36: 30–40: 18	20–6
40: 34–9	166
40: 40–41: 3	19
41: 4–6	45–6
41: 7–9	19–20
41: 9–15	46
41: 15–21	45
41: 22–42: 2	46–7
42: 16–28	166–7
43: 16–44: 11	11–12
44: 12–32	14–15
44: 33–45: 6	16–17
47: 9–48: 15	26–8

The textual notes provide a collation of CT, 14 and 14a.

30: 1–3 Metaphysics, or the attempt … impulses, CT] Metaphysics, from the first, has been developed by the union or the conflict of these two attitudes. 14a
30: 10–11 always must CT] must always 14
31: 17 of soul CT] of the soul 14
31: 22 flame in CT] flame of 14
31: 22 depths CT] depth 14
31: 29 cave CT] cave[2] ⟨*Footnote:* [2] *Republic,* 517.⟩ 14 *See T33: 41.*
31: 30–33: 19 senses: ¶Imagine … eyes.[2] ¶But] senses: ¶Imagine[2] … eyes. ¶But CT] senses. But 14
31: 40 *Philosophy* CT] *Philosophers* 14
33: 26 truth, 14] truth CT
33: 34–35 Parmenides. ¶After CT] Parmenides.[1] ⟨*Footnote:* [1] *Parmenides,* 130.⟩ After 14
33: 41 *Republic … Vaughan.* CT] *No footnote in 14.*

33: 41 514–17] 514 CT
34: 12 he CT] she 14a
34: 16 Hegel: CT] Hegel:[1] ⟨*Footnote:* [1]"With Parmenides," Hegel says, "philosophising proper began." *Werke* (edition of 1840), vol. xiii. p. 274.⟩ 14a
35: 5 subjective CT] equal subjective 14
36: 35–8 have been printed … written. CT] are from a course of Lowell lectures "On Scientific Method in Philosophy," shortly to be published by the Open Court Publishing Company. 14
37: 16 realm CT] realms 14, 14a
37: 27 are sometimes CT] may be 14a
37: 29 strong CT] stong 14
38: 3 *intellectual* CT] intellectual 14, 14a
38: 3 *sympathy* CT] sympathy 14
38: 16 to secure CT] designed to secure 14, 14a
38: 25 him CT] M. Bergson 14a
38: 29 capacity 14, 14a] capacity, CT
38: 41 It is greater, as a rule, CT] Speaking broadly, it is greater 14a
39: 2 see CT] find 14a
39: 35 intuition which seems CT] intuitions which seem 14, 14a
40: 14 habits 14, 14a] habit CT
40: 18–26 acceptance. ¶In advocating … thought. CT] acceptance. 14, 14a
40: 34–9 The conception … idea. CT] The great conception of a reality behind the passing illusions of sense, a reality one, indivisible, and unchanging, was thus introduced into Western philosophy by Parmenides, not, it would seem, for mystical or religious reasons, but on the basis of a logical argument as to the impossibility of not-being. All the great metaphysical systems—notably those of Plato, Spinoza, and Hegel—are the outcome of this fundamental idea. 14a
40: 40–41: 3 The logic … arisen. CT] The logic used in defence of mysticism seems to me faulty as logic, and in a later lecture I shall criticise it on this ground. 14a
40: 40 me 14, 14a] be CT
41: 4–6 Belief … metaphysics. CT] Belief in the unreality of the world of sense arises with irresistible force in certain moods—moods which, I imagine, have some simple physiological basis, but are

none the less powerfully persuasive. The conviction born of these moods is the source of most mysticism and of most metaphysics. 14a

41: 7–9 the more ... West. CT] But the more thorough-going mystics do not employ logic, which they despise: they appeal instead directly to the immediate deliverance of their insight. Now, although fully developed mysticism is rare in the West, some tincture of it colours the thoughts of many people, particularly as regards matters on which they have strong convictions not based on evidence. 14a

41: 10 intensity of emotional conviction CT] emotional intensity of such a mood 14a

41: 11 grounds CT] reasons 14a

41: 13 ground CT] reason 14a

41: 15–16 The resulting logic CT] The belief or unconscious conviction that all propositions are of the subject–predicate form—in other words, that every fact consists in some thing having some quality—14a

41: 17 anxious CT] honestly anxious 14a

41: 18–19 the errors of their logic CT] their error very quickly 14a

41: 23 mystics CT] mystics—notably Plato, Spinoza, and Hegel 14a

41: 34–5 The impulse ... fades, CT] While the mystic mood is dominant, the need of logic is not felt; as the mood fades, the impulse to logic reasserts itself, 14a

42: 7–15 insight. As a Persian ... mass. CT] insight. 14

42: 16–17 The arguments for the contention CT] The contention 14a

42: 18 fallacious CT] based upon fallacious reasoning 14a

42: 27 feeling, even though time be real, CT] feeling, 14a

42: 31 for CT] of 14

42: 32 past—14] past, CT

43: 7 time CT] the time 14

43: 17 required for CT] important and vital to 14a

43: 18–19 Something of Hellenism, something, too, of Oriental resignation, CT]

Something of Hellenism 14a

43: 19 its hurrying Western self-assertion CT] the new spirit 14a

43: 20 mature wisdom CT] wisdom 14a

43: 21 In spite of its appeals to science, CT] And it is time to remember that biology is neither the only science, nor yet the model to which all other sciences must adapt themselves. Evolutionism, as I shall try to show, is not a truly scientific philosophy, either in its method or in the problems which it considers 14a

43: 21 philosophy, I think, CT] philosophy 14a

43: 33–9 family. The sun ... ended. ¶But CT] family. But 14

43: 33 the planets CT] planets 14a

44: 3 ideal 14, 14a] idea CT

44: 8 aspiration CT] aspirations 14a

44: 11–27 process. ¶Life ... distance. CT] process. 14

44: 12 this CT] his 14a

44: 22 which CT] who 14a

44: 24 an 14a] no CT

44: 26 we reach 14a] it reaches CT

44: 28 I CT] Now I 14a

44: 28 propose CT] propose at present 14a

44: 29 I wish only to maintain CT] At present I wish to make only two criticisms of it—first, that its truth does not follow from what science has rendered probable concerning the facts of evolution, and secondly, 14a

44: 31 touching CT] really touching 14a

44: 37 can CT] really can 14, 14a

44: 38 attain truth, CT] become scientific—and it is our object to discover how this can be achieved—14a

44: 40–45: 6 science. Knowledge ... disprove. CT] science. 14

45: 7 change CT] a change 14

45: 39 *Ibid.* 14] *Ethics* CT

47: 11 a scientific philosophy CT] philosophy 14a

48: 2 psychology CT] science of psychology 14a

48: 42 contact 14] constant CT

3 Preface to Poincaré,
Science and Method

The copy-text (CT) is *Science and Method* (1914), 5–8.

No textual notes.

4 On Scientific Method
in Philosophy

The copy-text (CT) is *Mysticism and Logic, and Other Essays* (1918), 97–124. CT has been collated with the pamphlet version (14).

58: 1 astronomy; 14] astronomy: CT
58: 40 p. 124–6] p. 124 CT
59: 3 'substance', 14] 'substance' CT
59: 16 being merely 14] merely being CT
59: 17 that] what CT
59: 25 clearly CT] obviously 14
60: 35 Evolution CT] phenomena 14 *The variants in the quotation as it is given in 14 result from the fact that in 14 the second edition of Spencer was used.*
60: 38–40 assign the *causes* ... due, CT] ascertain the laws to which manifestations in general and in detail conform, would be absurd if the agency to which they are due 14
60: 41 *First Principles* (1862), Part II, beginning of Chap. viii. CT] *First Principles*, Part II, beginning of chap. vi. 14
61: 2 deductive Science impossible CT] Science, equally with Philosophy, would be impossible 14
61: 14 apply CT] applied 14
61: 31–2 generally CT] very generally 14
62: 14 that this CT] that the 14
65: 20 characteristic 14] charateristic CT
65: 24 Special CT] Such special 14
65: 25 facts of this kind CT] facts 14
66: 9 the right logical CT] the logical 14
66: 24 anything definite CT] anything 14
67: 9 theory of knowledge CT] epistemology 14
67: 18 coherence CT] coherency 14
68: 13 evident. 14] evident CT
69: 3 point CT] points 14
70: 1 wholly CT] purely 14
70: 10 at any rate so far as geometry is concerned, "It is not possible", CT] "It is not possible," at any rate 14
71: 38 causal 14] casual CT

5 The Ultimate Constituents
of Matter

The copy-text (CT) is *Mysticism and Logic, and Other Essays* (1918), 125–44. CT has been collated with 15, *The Monist*, 25 (July 1915): 399–417.

75: 1 article[1]] *The footnote follows the title in CT.*
75: 40 February, 1915.] February, 1915. Reprinted from *The Monist*, July, 1915. CT
75: 42–3 pp. 191–218. CT] pp. 151–218. 15
76: 29–30 (in one of several possible senses) outside CT] outside 15
78: 40 if (in a sense) CT] if 15
79: 42 (Fraser's edition 1901), I, p. 384. CT] (Fraser's edition), I, p. 266; *Three Dialogues* (published by Open Court Pub. Co.), p. 15. 15
81: 26 in which 15] which in CT
82: 14 we must regard CT] we must, instead, regard 15
83: 20 suitably CT] suitable 15
83: 42 particulars CT] present particulars 15
83: 43 the sun of eight minutes ago CT] the sun 15
84: 1 the sun of eight minutes ago CT] the sun at the present time 15
85: 22 partly 15] party CT

6 Letter on Sense-Data

The copy-text (CT) is *The Journal of Philosophy, Psychology, and Scientific Methods*, 12 (8 July 1915): 391–2.

87: *title* Letter on Sense-Data] Letter from Bertrand Russell CT
88: 12 causally] casually CT

7 Note on C. D. Broad's Article
in the July *Mind*

The copy-text (CT) is *Mind*, n.s. 28 (Jan. 1919): 124.

No textual notes.

8 Competitive Logic

The copy-text (CT) is *The Nation*, 14 (31 Jan. 1914): 771–2.

95: 25 manuscripts] MSS. CT

9 Review of Ruge *et al.*, *Encyclopedia of the Philosophical Sciences*

The copy-text (CT) is *The Cambridge Review*, 35 (27 Nov. 1913): 161.

No textual notes.

10 Mr. Balfour's Natural Theology

The copy-text (CT) is *The Cambridge Review*, 35 (4 March 1914): 338–9.

No textual notes.

11 Idealism on the Defensive

The copy-text (CT) is *The Nation*, 21 (8 Sept. 1917): 588, 590.

106: 9 Thorndike] Thorndyke CT

12 Metaphysics

The copy-text (CT) is *The English Review*, 25 (Oct. 1917): 381–4.

112: 17 McDougall] MacDougall CT
113: 23 looking for,] looking, for CT
113: 41 solely] sole CT

13 A Metaphysical Defence of the Soul

The copy-text (CT) is *The Nation*, 22 (10 Nov. 1917): 210, 212.

No textual notes.

14 Pure Reason at Königsberg

The copy-text (CT) is *The Nation*, 23 (20 July

1918): 426, 428.

119: *title* Königsberg] Koenigsberg CT
120: 6 Leibniz] Leibnitz CT *Also at 120: 27, 120: 40, 120: 41.*
120: 14 *Critique of Pure Reason,*] "Critique of Pure Reason," CT
120: 39–121: 1 *Studies in the Cartesian Philosophy*] "Studies in the Cartesian Philosophy" CT
121: 5 *Reflexionen*] "Reflexionen" CT
121: 5 *Lose Blätter*] "Lose Blätter" CT
121: 8 *Critique*] "Critique" CT *Also at 121: 13, 121: 31, 121: 38.*

15 Review of Broad, *Perception, Physics, and Reality*

The copy-text (CT) is *Mind*, n.s. 27 (Oct. 1918): 492–8.

125: 9 "Refutation of Idealism"] *Refutation of Idealism* CT
126: 29 On causation] On Causation CT
127: 4 compels] compe!s CT
128: 4 acceptable] acceptible CT

16 Professor Dewey's *Essays in Experimental Logic*

The copy-text (CT) is the typescript which was the printer's copy (RA REC. ACQ. 411). Its forty-one leaves are foliated *1*, 2–5, 7–42 and measure 205 × 258 mm. CT has been collated with 19, *The Journal of Philosophy, Psychology, and Scientific Methods*, 16 (2 Jan. 1919): 5–26. A carbon copy of CT (RA 220.011920) is also extant. An invoice dated 12 October 1918 (RA 710.051887) indicates that two carbons were made. 1 July 1918 is given as the date for typing this essay.

CT is extensively marked up in pencil for the printer. It also bears occasional ink corrections, in two different hands, one being Russell's. Only his corrections are adopted and recorded. Russell's ink correction at 135: 34 is present also on the carbon.

The typist, Eva Kyle, wrote a few notes in the margins of both the CT and the carbon: At 140: 26 "motived" is underlined in pencil and beside this line in pencil is a question mark. Her inability to read Russell's manuscript at one point, no doubt, resulted in the comment in pencil on both the CT and the carbon at 142: 19: "See MSS p17". Another note in pencil on fol. 20 of CT (see 143: 33) reads: "? wouldn't it be better without 'journey'. MSS. p. 20."

The first leaf of the typescript has in faint pencil in Russell's hand at the top: "See pp 26–30, beginning 'Prof. Dewey, in an admirable passage'". This is a note to Lady Constance Malleson, to whom he gave the typescript. The left margin of the first leaf has been stamped: "THE JOURNAL OF PHILOSOPHY | PSYCHOLOGY AND SCIENTIFIC METHODS | SUB-STATION 84 | NEW YORK CITY ". Next to it is the inscription: "Return with proof to, | Mr. Bertrand Russell | Care H. Wildon Carr | 107 Church Street, | Chelsea, s.w. 3, London, England".

132: *title* Professor Dewey's *Essays in Experimental Logic*] Professor Dewey's "ESSAYS IN EXPERIMENTAL LOGIC" CT
134: 8 outlook 19] mind CT
134: 10 is to my mind 19] seems to me CT
135: 8 judgment 19] judgments CT
135: 34 [the realists] CT] *square brackets inserted by hand in CT*
136: 2 method CT] methods 19
136: 33 a datum CT] datum 19
138: 3 just and such 19] just such ⟨such *inserted in pencil*⟩ and such CT
138: 28 Hertz's *Prinzipien der Mechanik*] Herz's "Principien der Mechanik" CT
139: 5 view. CT] *before deleted* Professor Dewey is on the side of civilization; he does not wish to stir up men's barbarous impulses and destroy their sense of truth in order to bolster up some ancient evil.
140: 6 known.) 19] known). CT
140: 20 casual CT] causal 19
140: 22 inference, but 19] inference. But CT
140: 29 near-to 19] near to CT
141: 25 very vague 19] the vaguest CT
141: 35 Z, say 19] Z say CT
141: 37 theory: 19] theory, CT
142: 2 at any moment CT] any moment 19
142: 18 Means by Practical" 19] means by

practical" CT
142: 19 common CT] *inserted in ink over the same word written in pencil in space left blank by typist*
142: 22 the idea 19] an idea CT
142: 25 behaviorist CT] *corrected in pencil from* behaviourist
143: 40 be 19] me CT
144: 34 learnt CT] learned 19 *Also at 150: 21.*
146: 8 begins only 19] only begins CT
146: 23 strong 19] a strong CT
146: 35 insincerity 19] insincerity, CT
146: 40 *it* is 19] it *is* CT
146: 42 326–7 19] 327 CT
147: 9 *External World* 19] "External World" CT
147: 11–12 monads, or parts of monads. 19] monads (or parts of monads). CT
147: 28 and, 19] and CT
148: 5 import. (P. 72–3)] import … " (pp. 72–3). 19] import" (p. 73) … " CT
148: 20 *Psychology* 19] Psychology CT
149: 4 Existence of the World as a Logical Problem 19] existence of the world as a logical problem CT
149: 17 then 19] there CT
149: 36 common sense.] common-sense. CT
151: 22 *Monist* 19] "Monist" CT
151: 23 thing 19] theory CT
151: 41 *Proc. Arist. Soc.*, 19] Proc. Arist. Soc. CT
152: 4 think he has not shown 19] do not at present know CT
152: 26 so called 19] so-called CT
152: 26 this 19] the CT
153: 19 theory.)] theory). CT
154: 21–2 many people in the newer countries CT] *inserted in ink above ink deletion* the United States

17 The Philosophy of Logical Atomism

The copy-text (CT) is *The Monist*, 28 (Oct. 1918): 495–527; 29 (Jan. 1919): 32–63; 29 (April 1919): 190–222; 29 (July 1919): 345–80. The textual notes provide a collation of CT with 56, *Logic and Knowledge* (1956), edited by R. C. Marsh, and with MIN, Russell's personal copy of the stencil version prepared at the University of Minnesota.

160: 1 (The following articles are the first two lectures CT] The following [is the text] 56

160: 2 London CT] [Gordon Square] London, 56

160: 2 and CT] [which] 56

160: 6 dead CT] dead* ⟨*Footnote*: *[This was written in 1918 as a preface to publication in three consecutive issues of *The Monist*. I have made four trivial editorial changes for the present reprinting in an entirely different format.—R.C.M.] 56

160: 8–9 them. The six other lectures ... B.R.) CT] them. 56

160: 26 kind of CT] kind MIN

161: 7 that that CT] that MIN

161: 20 "particulars"—] "particulars",— CT

164: 32–3 what we say false, and it is an objective fact which makes what we say true MIN, 56] what we say true CT

165: 10 fact—] fact,— CT

165: 40 alive",] alive," CT

168: 2 round CT] around MIN, 56

168: 28 *Q.*:] .... CT *Also at 168: 39, 169: 9, 180: 30, 180: 37, 190: 12, 190: 17, 190: 20, 190: 27, 190: 30, 190: 36, 191: 1, 211: 20, 233: 1, 233: 13.*

168: 41 or do you CT] or do you never come back to prove it, or do you MIN

170: 14–16 entities. All the kinds ... entities: CT] entities: MIN

170: 16 *Twelfth Night*] Twelfth Night CT *Also at 171: 8.*

172: 8 propositions, but only with 56, MIN] facts but only to CT *In MIN at the end of the sentence there is the following footnote*: *The Monist* reads (vol. 28, pp. 513–14) "—which they do not have in common with all facts but only to those which are about Socrates or mortality." Something may have been omitted from *The Monist*. The above emendation seems to preserve the sense.

173: 20 does not CT] doesn't 56, MIN

173: 23 "the] "The CT

174: 3 words 56, MIN] the words CT

174: 30 London;] London: CT

175: 18–19 procedure CT] precedure MIN

176: 25 the names CT] names MIN

177: 5 facts—] facts—, CT

177: 16 or dyadic CT] of dyadic MIN *Russell made this correction in his copy of MIN*.

178: 8 Names CT] Name MIN

178: 13 you CT] we MIN

180: 7 but that facts CT] *These words are omitted by Marsh. His letter of 24 May 1956 to Russell reads*: Dear Lord Russell, ¶Unwin had an extra copy of the proof of your Hibbert Journal article, and I have enjoyed reading it very much indeed. It seems to be exactly the sort of statement needed to waken British philosophers from their dogmatic slumbering.* ⟨*Footnote*: *But let us hope without Kantian consequences.*⟩ ¶On Galley six toward the bottom (immediately below the rule) you quote the Minnesota edition of the lectures on logical atomism and repeat a corruption which Feigl allowed to creep into the text. The text we are issuing in the book reads: 'I do myself think that complexes—I do not like to talk of complexes—are composed of simples, but ...' ¶You saw this in the proof and give it your blessing, and I am sure you will admit that the phrase 'but that facts' inserted there by someone confuses the issue, quite apart from the point that (if the *Monist* is to be relied upon) you never said it. *Since Russell's response to Marsh's comments is unknown and since the passage does in fact occur in* The Monist, *it is not regarded here as a corruption.*

182: 29–30 "red" in inverted commas ... "red". CT] "red." MIN

183: 7 dyadic, or of dyadic CT] dyadic MIN

183: 9 reduction 56, MIN] deduction CT

183: 38 example 56, MIN] an example CT

184: 3 possible 56, MIN] impossible CT

184: 23 bring CT] being MIN

185: 7 Fact 56] Fact. CT *Also at 185: 8.*

187: 25 Harvard CT] Harvard* ⟨*Footnote*: *[in 1914—R.C.M.]⟩ 56

188: 19 bald", then, if] bald." If CT

192: 7 belief?] belief. CT

192: 18 of opinion CT] of the opinion MIN, 56

195: 41 *The Monist* CT] *The Monist*,* ⟨*Foot-

note: *[The three parts of this essay are the fifth paper in this collection.—R.C.M.]⟩ 56

197: 9 ⟨which puts it⟩] *editorial insertion*

197: 16 analysis CT] analyses 56

199: 40 4. MIN] 4 CT

204: 6–7 complex MIN] complete CT *Russell made this correction in his copy of MIN.*

205: 12–13 propositional function MIN] proposition CT *Russell made this correction in his copy of MIN.*

205: 38–9 an *x* CT] a *x* MIN, 56

211: 6 then all *a*'s are *c*'s." 56, MIN] then all *a*'s are *c*'s. CT

214: 20 and "the CT] and the "the MIN

219: 8 "primary occurrence" 56, MIN] "primary occurrence CT

219: 34 for] of CT

220: 36 propositional CT] prepositional 56

222: 27 tomorrow"—] tomorrow,"— CT

226: 18 things CT] thing MIN

226: 21 all things 56, MIN] all the things CT

228: 5 think CT] thing MIN

229: 7 propositions CT] proposition 56

230: 1 30,001st 56] 30,001th CT

230: 8 members 56, MIN] numbers CT

230: 15–16 classes of classes of particulars MIN, 56] classes of classes or particulars CT

231: 2 it is CT] is it 56] is is MIN

232: 30 *20] p. 20 CT] page 20 56

232: 31 Chapter 56] Chapt. CT

232: 42 [These lectures ... Ed.] CT] [These lectures were given 'in Dr. Williams's library in Gordon Square,' Russell informs me, on eight consecutive Tuesdays. Although University College London, stands nearby, this was probably the only lecture audience in Gordon Square proper.—R.C.M.] 56

233: 10 meanings 56, MIN] meaning CT

233: 18 travelled 56] traveled CT

233: 30 from 56, MIN] to CT

234: 6 dwelt CT] dealt 56

236: 22 given—] given,— CT

237: 41–2 Chapters III and IV (Open Court Publishing Co., 1914). CT] Chapters III and IV. 56

243: 42 dullness] dulness CT

18 Manuscript Notes

18a On Sensations and Ideas

The copy-text (CT) is the manuscript. Its six leaves are foliated *1*, 2–6; measure 202 × 250 mm.; and are written in ink.

252: 1 Sensations and CT] *inserted*

252: 24 him CT] *after deleted* the

252: 29–253: 2 Every psychical ... themselves. CT] *Quotation editorially supplied.*

253: 30 them] them" CT

253: 32 *ibid.*] ib. CT

253: 38 *Standpunkte* (1874), pp. 115–16.] *Standpunkte*, (1874) p. 115. CT

254: 11 E. B. Holt] E. V. Holt CT

254: 13 the stuff of the world CT] *above deleted* everything

254: 15 and CT] *inserted*

254: 16 causal CT] *inserted*

254: 25–6 of the above kind CT] *inserted*

254: 29 it CT] *inserted*

254: 30 In this paper CT] *inserted*

254: 30 respects CT] *before deleted* in this paper

254: 34 shall CT] *above deleted* propose to

254: 36 kind of event CT] *above deleted* phenomenon

255: 4 a single CT] *above deleted* one

255: 7 the CT] *written over* our *on second occurrence*

255: 13 according CT] *after deleted* of

255: 33–4 an exclusively mental CT] *replaced* a mental

255: 38 from him CT] *inserted*

18b Behaviourism and Knowledge

The copy-text (CT) is the manuscript. Its four leaves are foliated 1–4; measure 205 × 263 mm.; and are written in ink. "[Impt. MS]" is written in the upper right corner of fol. 1. "*B & Kn*" is written in the upper left corner of fos. 2–4.

256: 2 knowledge CT] *written over* beha

256: 34 theoretically CT] *inserted*

257: 11 end CT] *above deleted* purpose

18c Introspection as a Source of Knowledge

The copy-text (CT) is the manuscript. Its eight leaves are foliated 1–8; measure 150 × 219 mm.; and are written in ink. "*In.*" is written in the upper left corner of fol. 2.

257: 35 Introspection as a Source of Knowledge] Introspection as a source of knowledge CT

257: 38 smells, etc.] smells etc. CT

258: 17 Can CT] *after deleted* (1)

258: 18 Introspection? We CT] *replaced* Introspection? and ¶(2) Can we include anything except beliefs under Introspection? ¶As to (1), we

258: 19 anything. CT] *before deleted* As to (2), we cannot include anything except beliefs.

259: 19 visceral CT] *above deleted* visual

260: 12–13 Knight Dunlap, *Psychological Review*, 1912, pp. 404–413, "The Case Against Introspection"] *Knight Dunlap*, Psychal. Review 1912, pp. 404–413, "The case against introspection" CT

260: 16 "The Nature of Perceived Relations"] "The nature of perceived relations" CT

260: 21 John B. Watson, *ibid.*, 1913, "Psychology as the Behaviorist Views It"] *John B. Watson*, ib. 1913, "Psychology as the Behaviourist views it" CT

260: 25–6 Eliott Park Frost, *ibid.*, 1914, pp. 204–211, "Cannot Psychology Dispense with Consciousness?"] *Eliott Park Frost*, ib 1914 pp 204–211 "Cannot Psychology dispense with consciousness?" CT

260: 28 Knight Dunlap, 1916, pp. 49–70] *Knight Dunlap* 1916, pp 49–70 CT

18d Three Notes on Memory

The copy-text (CT) is the manuscript. Its four leaves are foliated [1], 1–2, [1]; measure 200 × 250 mm.; and are written in ink.

"*Memory 1*" is written in the upper right corner of the first leaf. Fol. 1 is entitled "*Problems of Memory.*" Fol. 2 has "*Problems of Memory* (continued)" at the top. The last leaf is untitled.

261: 1 Three Notes on Memory] *The title is editorially supplied. The three notes are not numbered in CT.*

261: 3 "Subject".] "Subject" CT

261: 4 sensation.] sensation CT

261: 9 past.] past CT

261: 13 case.] case CT

262: 24 G. and G.,] G and G CT

18e Views as to Judgment, Discarding the Subject

The copy-text (CT) is the manuscript. Its six leaves are foliated 1–6; measure 149 × 220 mm.; and are written in ink.

263: 3 Views as to Judgment, Discarding the Subject] Views as to Judgment, discarding the Subject. CT

263: 8 (c) CT] *written over* (b)

263: 17 (α) CT] *inserted*

264: 10 two] 2 CT *Also at 264: 17.*

264: 12 plus] + CT *Also at 264: 16.*

264: 18 one] 1 CT

18f Belief and Judgment

The copy-text (CT) is the manuscript. Its two leaves are foliated *1–2*; measure 149 × 219 mm.; and are written in ink.

265: 20 II,] II CT

265: 34 than CT] *written over* that *Also at 265: 35.*

18g Three Subjects

The copy-text (CT) is the manuscript. Its six leaves are foliated 1–5, *1*; and are written in ink. The first five leaves measure 199 × 248 mm. and the final leaf measures 220 × 250 mm. "*C. H.*" is written in the upper left corner of the first fol.

266: 5 Three Subjects] *The title is editorially supplied.*

266: 8 true judgments CT] *after deleted* Propositions

266: 15 *in rerum natura*] in rerum natura CT

267: 24 What makes a symbol symbolize? CT] *This sentence is written twice: once at the bottom of fol. 4 and once at the top of fol.*

5. The repetition is deleted here editorially.

267: 31 "means". CT] *before deleted* ¶There

267: 31 "means". CT] *An unnumbered folio of notes on belief and causal efficacy is filed with CT. These notes have not been included here.*

18h Propositions

The copy-text (CT) is the manuscript. Its two leaves are paginated 1, 2 (verso of 1), 3; measure 198 × 252 mm.; and are written in ink. "tB" is written in the upper left corner of fol. 1. "July 31.18" is written in the upper right corner of fos. 1 and 3. "Miss Wrinch, or Demos" is written in pencil on the verso of page 3.

268: 5 I did not think this could CT] *replaced* I do not think this can

268: 9–10 ; but perhaps a purely formal dualism can be constructed to meet the case (see ⟨p. 269⟩) CT] *inserted The editorial emendation to "⟨p. 269⟩" replaces an internal reference to p. 3 of the manuscript.*

268: 18 *fact* CT] *replaced facts*

268: 24 wishes, etc.] wishes etc. CT

268: 31 desire, etc.] desire etc. CT

268: 34 doubting, etc.] doubting etc. CT

269: 1 ⟨In what follows⟩] On p. 3 CT

269: 8 complex CT] *inserted*

269: 20 "$z \doteq Rw$" CT] *written over* "$x \doteq Ry$"

269: 20 itself a positive fact, CT] *inserted*

18i Thoughts on Language, Leading to Language on Thought

The copy-text (CT) is the manuscript. Its four leaves are foliated 1–4; measure 198 × 252 mm.; and are written in ink. "tB" is written in the upper left corner of fol. 1. "Aug. 10.18" is written in the upper right corners of fos. 1–4.

269: 28–9 Thoughts on Language, Leading to Language on Thought] Thoughts on Language, leading to Language on Thought. CT

269: 33 things CT] *written over* θs

270: 18 *Facts and Propositions*] *facts and propositions* CT

271: 18 so] say CT

271: 34 As a first approximation, CT] *inserted*

271: 40 fundamental. CT] *At the end of CT is the following note which has been editorially deleted:* Paper for Aristotelian (Carr: *not* Introspection, but) *Propositions: What they are and how they mean.*

19 On "Bad Passions"

The copy-text (CT) is *The Cambridge Magazine*, 8 (1 Feb. 1919): 359. It has been collated with a manuscript (RA 220.011910) entitled "Morality and Oppressive Impulses" (18). The two leaves of the manuscript are paginated 1, 2 (verso of 1), 3, 4 (verso of 3); measure 202 × 250 mm. and are written in ink. Deleted in the upper right corner of page 1 is "Aug. 29.18."

273: 1 One CT] *In the manuscript (18), before the text itself begins, the following notes appear:* In the American Journal of Philosophy for ⟨for *above deleted* ,⟩ 1915, there is an article by G. Stanley Hall, on ⟨on *inserted*⟩ "The Freudian methods applied to anger" (pp 438–443), some extracts from which may serve to introduce our subject. ¶p. 439. "The German criminalist, Friedrich, says that probably every man might be caused to commit murder if provocation were sufficient, and that those of us who have never committed this crime owe it to circumstances and not to superior power of inhibition." ¶p. 440. "Some temperaments seem to crave, if not need, outbreaks of it [rage] ⟨[rage] *inserted*⟩ at certain intervals, like a certain well-poised lady, so sweet-tempered that every one imposed on her, till one day at the age of 23 she had her first ebullition of temper and went about to her college mates telling them plainly what she thought of them. She went home rested and happy, full of the peace that passeth understanding. Otto Heinze, and by implication Pfister, think nations that have too long or too assiduously cultivated peace must inevitably, sooner or later, relapse to the barbarisms of war, to vent their instincts for combat." ¶p. 443. "Richardson has collected 882 cases of mild anger,... and finds ... that very much of the impulsion that makes us work and strive, attack and solve problems has an element of anger at its root."

273: 1 One of the most difficult problems CT] *replaced* The problem *in 18*

273: 3 cruelty, CT] cruelty, jealosy 18

273: 7 to be CT] *inserted in 18*

273: 7 Moreover, CT] Moreover 18

273: 10–27 Professor Stanley Hall ... otherwise. CT] *not present in 18, but see T273: 1*

273: 10–11 "The Freudian Methods Applied to Anger"] "The Fiendian methods applied to anger" CT

273: 11 *American Journal of Psychology*] American Journal of Philosophy CT

273: 29 Rewards CT] rewards 18

273: 29 punishments; CT] punishments, 18

273: 29 Sublimation, CT] sublimation 18

273: 30 outlets; CT] outlets, 18

273: 30 Physiological CT] physiological 18

273: 32 (1).] (1) CT

273: 32 Rewards CT] Reward 18

273: 36 them; CT] them: 18

273: 37 of, CT] of 18

273: 38 murdered CT] *replaced* would murder *in 18*

273: 39 came CT] *written over* come *in 18*

274: 7 (2). 18] (2) CT

274: 7 have CT] has 18

274: 8 religion 18] reiigion CT

274: 9 belief CT] beliefs 18

274: 10 primarily CT] *above deleted* in the main *in 18*

274: 11 , I am told, CT] *inserted in 18*

274: 16 above, CT] above 18

274: 16 cases CT] *above deleted* instances *in 18*

274: 17 , in the first instance CT] *inserted in 18*

274: 19 true 18] truer CT

274: 21 rage, CT] rage: 18

274: 21 tigerish CT] tigreish 18

274: 22 outlet CT] outlet, 18

274: 39 had had CT] had 18

275: 1 now, CT] now; 18

275: 2 pressing.] depressing. CT] pressing. Like all such problems, it will have to be solved by compromise. 18

275: 10 altogether CT] *after deleted* utterly tran *in 18*

275: 10–11 Such books ... direction. CT] *missing in 18*

275: 12–13 is to be sought in facts of this kind. CT] lies in this fact. 18

275: 15 distinguishing features CT] *above deleted* characteristics *in 18*

20 On Propositions: What They Are and How They Mean

The copy-text (CT) is *Aristotelian Society, Supplementary Volume: Problems of Science and Philosophy*, 2 (1919): 1–43. The textual notes provide a collation of CT and passages of major verbal similarity in 21, *The Analysis of Mind* (1921). The passages which have been collated with 21 are identified in the table below; variants between the corresponding passages are recorded in the textual notes.

CT	21
283: 24–284: 5	203–4
284: 37–285: 2	153–4
285: 39–286: 10	120–1
286: 12–18	118
286: 38–41	120n.
290: 15–22	197
290: 24–291: 18	198–200
291: 19–292: 25	200–3
297: 38–298: 2	252
298: 38–299: 1	250
299: 14–21	251
299: 22–301: 9	247–50

The textual notes also provide a collation of CT and 56, *Logic and Knowledge* (1956), edited by R. C. Marsh.

278: 36–41 In what follows ... construction CT] *In CT the footnote is to the title of the paper.*

280: 41–2 No. 102 (April, 1917), pp. 188–196. 56] No. 102, pp. 188–196 (April, 1917). CT

281: 5 reply:] reply; CT

282: 42–3 (New York, 1914), by John B. Watson ... University. 56] , by John B.

Watson ... University, New York, 1914.
CT
283: 24–284: 5 The stimulus ... habit. (Pp.
329–330) CT] *Quoted on pp. 203–4 in 21.*
284: 37 an ordinary CT] any 21
284: 40 experiment.) CT] experiment.)
Galton, as every one knows, investigated
visual imagery, and found that education
tends to kill it: the Fellows of the Royal
Society turned out to have much less of it
than their wives. 21
284: 41–2 whatever to reject the conclusion
originally suggested by Galton's investigations, namely, CT] to doubt his conclusion 21
285: 1 the power CT] power 21
285: 39 This brings us CT] We come now 21
285: 41–286: 1 the objection ... data. CT] an
objection which is really more strongly felt
than the objection of privacy. And we obtain a definition of introspection more in
harmony with usage if we define it as observation of data not subject to physical
laws than if we define it by means of privacy. No one would regard a man as introspective because he was conscious of having a stomach-ache. Opponents of introspection do not mean to deny the obvious
fact that we can observe bodily sensations
which others cannot observe. 21
286: 1–2 Knight Dunlap, a vigorous opponent of introspection, CT] Knight Dunlap
21
286: 5 is concerned with *localization* CT] , in
the sense which now concerns us, has to
do with *localization* 21
286: 6 localized in CT] localized, like visual
images, in 21
286: 8–10 In either case ... reject them. CT]
If you have a visual image of your friend
sitting in a chair which in fact is empty,
you cannot locate the image in your body,
because it is visual, nor (as a physical
phenomenon) in the chair because the
chair, as a physical object, is empty. Thus
it seems to follow that the physical world
does not include all that we are aware of,
and that images, which are introspective
data, have to be regarded, for the present,

as not obeying the laws of physics; this is,
I think, one of the chief reasons why an
attempt is made to reject them. 21
286: 12–18 We may distinguish ... surprised. CT] Confining ourselves, for the
moment, to sensations, we find that there
are different degrees of publicity attaching
to different sorts of sensations. If you feel
a toothache when the other people in the
room do not, you are in no way surprised;
but if you hear a clap of thunder when
they do not, you begin to be alarmed as to
your mental condition. Sight and hearing
are the most public of the senses; smell
only a trifle less so; touch, again, a trifle
less, since two people can only touch the
same spot successively, not simultaneously. 21
286: 38–41 See also his articles ... "that 'introspection,' CT] See also *ib.*, 1912, "The
Nature of Perceived Relations," where he
says: " 'Introspection,' 21
287: 39 to regard 56] so regard CT
290: 15 A person "understands" CT] We
may say that a person understands 21
290: 19 understanding. CT] understanding,
since they cannot use words. 21
290: 20 to "understanding" a word that a
person CT] in order that a man should
"understand" a word, that he 21
290: 24 is, in fact, CT] is 21
290: 25 causal law, and there CT] causal law
governing our use of the word and our
actions when we hear it used. There 21
290: 25–7 using a word ... Kepler's laws.
CT] who uses a word correctly should be
able to tell what it means than there is why
a planet which is moving correctly should
know Kepler's laws. 21
290: 28–9 let us suppose that CT] let us take
instances of various situations. ¶Suppose
21
290: 29–30 friend. You say "look out CT]
friend, and while crossing a street you say,
"Look out 21
290: 34 regarded as belonging CT] taken to
belong 21
290: 41–291: 1 actually incipiently CT] incipiently 21

291: 1 imagined CT] imaged 21

291: 2 need not detain us at present CT] is not important in the present connection 21

291: 15 associate CT] may associate 21

291: 16 "means"; thus the word acquires CT] "means," or a representative of various objects that it "means." ¶In the fourth case, the word acquires, through association, 21

291: 19 So far, everything can be accounted for by behaviour. But CT] So far, all the uses of words that we have considered can be accounted for on the lines of behaviourism. ¶But 21

291: 21 a feature CT] some feature 21

291: 21–2 environment; we ... take 56] environment, we have not considered what we may call its "narrative" use, of which we may take CT] environment. This is only one of the ways in which language may be used. There are also its narrative and imaginative uses, as in history and novels. Let us take 21

291: 24–5 Let us ... time. On some CT] We spoke a moment ago of a child who hears the word "motor" for the first time when crossing a street along which a motor-car is approaching. On a 21

291: 32 lines—indeed, it does not call for any particular behaviour. CT] lines. 21

292: 2 "meaning" CT] narrative "meaning" 21

292: 4–5 We may say that, while words CT] ¶Yet this might perhaps be regarded as something of an over-statement. The words alone, without the use of images, may cause appropriate emotions and appropriate behaviour. The words have been used in an environment which produced certain emotions; by a telescoped process, the words alone are now capable of producing similar emotions. On these lines it might be sought to show that images are unnecessary. I do not believe, however, that we could account on these lines for the entirely different response produced by a narrative and by a description of present facts. Images, as contrasted with sensations, are the response expected

during a narrative; it is understood that present action is not called for. Thus it seems that we must maintain our distinction: words 21

292: 5 cause sensations, CT] lead to sensations, while 21

292: 6 intended to cause CT] only intended to lead to 21

292: 7–8 thus two other ways in which words can mean (perhaps not fundamentally distinct), CT] thus, in addition to our four previous ways in which words can mean, two new ways, 21

292: 11 where CT] when 21

292: 15 of CT] for 21

292: 17 has occurred CT] occurred 21

292: 18 words CT] words, including their occurrence in inner speech, 21

292: 19–20 This way of using words, since it depends upon images, CT] If we are right, the use of words in thinking depends, at least in its origin, upon images, and 21

292: 21 words: that, primarily 56] words: that, primarily, CT] words, namely that, originally 21

292: 24 reduced to CT] brought into connection with 21

292: 30 common sense 56] common-sense CT

293: 12 calligraphy 56] caligraphy CT

293: 23 imagination-image 56] imagination image CT

295: 39 my *Knowledge of the External World.*] my "Knowledge of the External World." CT] my *Our Knowledge of the External World.* 56

297: 38 "Everyone", says William James, "knows CT] Thus James says: "Everyone knows 21

298: 38–9 various feelings that may attach to a proposition, any one of which constitutes belief. Of these I would instance CT] at least three kinds of belief, namely 21

298: 40 Vol. II, Chap. XXI 56] Chap. XXI, vol. ii CT] vol. ii 21

299: 1 non-temporal assent CT] assent 21

299: 14–16 When a belief ... follows: CT] We may sum up our analysis, in the case of bare assent to a proposition not expressed in words, as follows: 21

299: 17 assent; CT] assent, which is presumably a complex sensation demanding analysis; 21

299: 18 feeling of assent CT] assent 21

299: 19–21 that that ... assent. CT] that the proposition in question is what is assented to. For other forms of belief-feeling or of content, we have only to make the necessary substitutions in this analysis. 21

299: 22–35 It might be urged, as against the above theory, that ... Spinoza: CT] In this view belief is not a positive phenomenon, though doubt and disbelief are so. What we call belief, according to this hypothesis, involves only the appropriate content, which will have the effects characteristic of belief unless something else operating simultaneously inhibits them. James (*Psychology*, vol. ii, p. 288) quotes with approval, though inaccurately, a passage from Spinoza embodying this view: 21

299: 38 James's 21, 56] James' CT

300: 10 Now if CT] If 21

300: 10 would seem to follow CT] follows 21

300: 11 this CT] the 21

300: 11 feeling of belief CT] feeling called "belief" 21

300: 24 What most recommends the above view, to my mind, is CT] There is a great deal to be said in favour of this view, and I have some hesitation in regarding it as inadequate. It fits admirably with the phenomena of dreams and hallucinatory images, and it is recommended by 21

300: 27 seems to be CT] may be regarded, in this view, as 21

300: 32 given. (When we speak ... action. CT] given. 21

300: 38 may CT] must 21

301: 1 does not account for any but CT] accounts only for some of 21

301: 2–5 either memory ... event CT] memory 21

301: 5 the beliefs CT] beliefs 21

301: 7 there are CT] there must be 21

301: 7 doubt or desire CT] doubt 21

Bibliographical Index

THE WORKS REFERRED to by Russell and by the editor are cited here in full. The year in italics following the author's name is that of the edition described, or else that of first publication. Full bibliographical data are not provided for pre-1800 titles. Where relevant, an index of the pages on which the work is mentioned follows the citation. Page numbers in roman type indicate Russell's text and textual matter in the Appendixes; page numbers in italics indicate editorial matter.

The bulk of Russell's working library is housed in the Russell Archives at McMaster University. The phrase "(Russell's library.)" indicates relevant volumes in that library.

The Bibliographical Index excludes unpublished correspondence referred to in the editorial matter, papers by Russell printed in this volume, the copy-text information found in each Headnote, and the list of readings printed in Appendix III.

ABEL, REUBEN, *1955*. *The Pragmatic Humanism of F. C. S. Schiller*. New York: King's Crown Press, Columbia University.
Referred to: *348*.

ALEXANDER, S., *1889*. *Moral Order and Progress: An Analysis of Ethical Conceptions*. London: Trübner.
Referred to: *336*.

—— *1914*. "The Basis of Realism". *Proceedings of the British Academy*, 6: 279–314.
Referred to: 75n.

—— *1920*. *Space, Time and Deity: The Gifford Lectures at Glasgow, 1916–1918*. 2 vols. London: Macmillan.
Referred to: *338*.

BAIN, ALEXANDER, *1859*. *The Emotions and the Will*. London: John W. Parker and Son.
Referred to: 298n.

BALFOUR, ARTHUR JAMES, 1st EARL, *1879*. *A Defence of Philosophic Doubt: Being an Essay on the Foundations of Belief*. London: Macmillan.
Referred to: 99.

—— *1895*. *The Foundations of Belief: Being Notes Introductory to the Study of Theology*. London: Longmans, Green.
Referred to: 99.

—— *1914*. The Gifford Lectures. In *The Times* (London).

[1]. "Mr. Balfour on Theism. The Plain Man's Picture of Philosophy. Opening Gifford Lecture". 13 Jan.: 8.

[2]. "Mr. Balfour on Design. Our Logical Series of Beliefs. Second Gifford Lecture". 15 Jan.: 4.

[3]. "Emotions and Belief. Mr. Balfour on Aesthetic Values. Third Gifford Lecture". 17 Jan.: 5.

[4]. "Mr. Balfour on Ethics. Limitations of Natural Selection. Need of a Theistic Setting". 20 Jan.: 10.

[5]. "Mr. Balfour on Belief. The Basis of Knowledge Analysed. Need of a Theistic Setting". 22 Jan.: 10.

[6]. "The External World. Mr. Balfour on the Tangle of Science. Causal and Cognitive Series". 24 Jan.: 5.

[7]. "Mr. Balfour on Chance. Probability in Theory and Practice. The Mathematical Calculus". 27 Jan.: 10.

[8]. "Mr. Balfour on Mill. The Law of Causation Criticized. Our Hope of Progress". 29 Jan.: 10.

[9]. "Mr. Balfour on Guiding Beliefs. Favouritism in Science. The Vital Impulse of Progress". 5 Feb.: 6.

[10]. "Mr. Balfour on Theism. A Summary of the Lectures and an Appeal. Beliefs as Natural Products". 7 Feb.: 4.

Reprinted in his *1915*.

Referred to: *341*.

—— *1915*. *Theism and Humanism, Being the Gifford Lectures Delivered at the University of Glasgow, 1914*. London, New York and Toronto: Hodder and Stoughton.

Referred to: *99, 341, 342*.

—— *1923*. *Theism and Thought: A Study in Familiar Beliefs, Being the Second Course of Gifford Lectures Delivered at the University of Glasgow 1922–23*. London: Hodder and Stoughton.

Referred to: *99*.

BERGSON, HENRI, *1896*. *Matière et mémoire: Essai sur la relation du corps à l'esprit*. Paris: Félix Alcan. (Russell's library: 1910 [i.e. 16th] impression.) Translated into English as his *1911a*.

Referred to: *355, 360*.

—— *1903*. "Introduction à la métaphysique". *Revue de métaphysique et de morale*, 11: 1–36. Translated into English as his *1912*.

Referred to: *336*.

—— *1907*. *L'Évolution créatrice*. Paris: Félix Alcan. (Russell's library: 1911 [i.e. 17th] impression.) Translated into English as his *1911*.

Referred to: *338*.

—— *1911*. *Creative Evolution*. Translated by Arthur Mitchell. London: Macmillan. Translation of his *1907*.

Referred to: *338*.

—— *1911a. Matter and Memory*. Translated by Nancy Margaret Paul and W. Scott Palmer. London: Swan Sonnenschein; New York: Macmillan. (Russell's library.) Translation of his *1896*.

Referred to: *360*.

—— *1912. An Introduction to Metaphysics*. Translated by T. E. Hulme. New York and London: G. P. Putnam's Sons. Translation of his *1903*.

Referred to: 38n., *336*.

BERKELEY, GEORGE, *1710. A Treatise concerning the Principles of Human Knowledge*.

Referred to: *350*.

—— *1901. Three Dialogues between Hylas and Philonous*. In Vol. 1 of *The Works of George Berkeley, D. D.* Edited by Alexander Campbell Fraser. 4 vols. Oxford: at the Clarendon Press. (Russell's library: 1871 [i.e. 1st Fraser ed.].) 1st ed., 1713.

Referred to: 79n.

Bible.

Referred to: *336, 353*.

BLACKWELL, KENNETH, *1973*. "Our Knowledge of *Our Knowledge*". *Russell: The Journal of the Bertrand Russell Archives*, no. 12: 11–13.

Referred to: *4*.

—— *1981*. "The Early Wittgenstein and the Middle Russell". In *Perspectives on the Philosophy of Wittgenstein*. Edited by Irving Block. Oxford: Basil Blackwell.

Referred to: *351*.

BOOLE, GEORGE, *1847. The Mathematical Analysis of Logic, Being an Essay towards a Calculus of Deductive Reasoning*. Cambridge: Macmillan, Barclay & Macmillan; London: George Bell. Reprinted in Vol. 1 of his *Studies in Logic and Probability*. La Salle, Ill.: Open Court, 1952.

Referred to: *352*.

—— *1854. An Investigation of the Laws of Thought, on which Are Founded the Mathematical Theories of Logic and Probabilities*. London: Walton and Maberly; Cambridge: Macmillan. Reprinted in Vol. 2 of his *Collected Logical Works*. Chicago and London: Open Court, 1916.

Referred to: *352*.

BOSANQUET, BERNARD, *1888. Logic, or the Morphology of Knowledge*. 2 vols. Oxford: At the Clarendon Press. (Russell's library.)

Referred to: 58n., *337, 349, 355, 358*.

—— *1911. Logic, or the Morphology of Knowledge*. 2nd ed. 2 vols. Oxford: At the Clarendon Press.

Referred to: *349, 355, 358*.

BRADLEY, F. H., *1883. The Principles of Logic*. London: Kegan Paul, Trench.

Referred to: 208, *348, 349, 352, 358*.

—— *1914. Essays on Truth and Reality.* Oxford: At the Clarendon Press. (Russell's library.)
Referred to: *349.*

—— *1922. The Principles of Logic.* 2nd ed., revised. 2 vols. London: Oxford University Press. (Russell's library.)
Referred to: *352, 358.*

BRENTANO, FRANZ, *1874. Psychologie vom empirischen Standpunkte.* 2 vols. Leipzig: Duncker & Humblot. Translated into English as his *1973.*
Referred to: 253n., 298n., *354.*

—— *1973. Psychology from an Empirical Standpoint.* Translated by A.C. Rancurello, D.B. Terrell and Linda L. McAlister. London: Routledge & Kegan Paul. Translation of his *1874.*
Referred to: *360.*

BROAD, C.D., *1914. Perception, Physics, and Reality; an Enquiry into the Information that Physical Science Can Supply about the Real.* Cambridge: At the University Press. (Russell's library.)
Referred to: 125, *345, 346.*

—— *1915.* "Phenomenalism". *Proceedings of the Aristotelian Society,* n.s. 15: 227–51.
Referred to: *87.*

—— *1918.* "A General Notation for the Logic of Relations". *Mind,* n.s. 27: 284–303.
Referred to: *89,* 90.

—— *1923. Scientific Thought.* (International Library of Psychology, Philosophy and Scientific Method.) London: Kegan Paul, Trench, Trubner; New York: Harcourt, Brace.
Referred to: *124.*

—— *1925. The Mind and Its Place in Nature.* (International Library of Psychology, Philosophy and Scientific Method.) London: Kegan Paul, Trench, Trubner; New York: Harcourt, Brace.
Referred to: *124.*

BURNET, JOHN, *1908. Early Greek Philosophy.* 2nd ed. London: Adam and Charles Black. (Russell's library.) 1st ed., 1892.
Referred to: 31n., *335.*

BUTLER, SAMUEL, *1878. Life and Habit.* London: Trübner.
Referred to: *342.*

—— *1879. Evolution, Old and New; or, the Theories of Buffon, Dr. Erasmus Darwin, and Lamarck, as Compared with that of Mr. Charles Darwin.* London: Hardwicke and Bogue.
Referred to: *342.*

—— *1880. Unconscious Memory: A Comparison between the Theory of Dr. Ewald Hering, Professor of Physiology at the University of Prague, and the "Philosophy of the Unconscious" of Dr. Edward von Hartmann* [...]. London: David Bogue.
Referred to: *342.*

—— *1887. Luck, or Cunning, as the Main Means of Organic Modification? An Attempt to Throw Additional Light upon the Late Mr. Charles Darwin's Theory of Natural Selection.* London: Trübner.

Referred to: *342.*

—— *1903. The Way of All Flesh.* London: Grant Richards. (Russell's library: Jacket Library ed., [n.d.].)

Referred to: 112.

—— *1909. God the Known and God the Unknown.* London: A. C. Fifield.

Referred to: *342.*

CAIRD, EDWARD, *1877. A Critical Account of the Philosophy of Kant, with an Historical Introduction.* Glasgow: James Maclehose.

Referred to: *345.*

—— *1889. The Critical Philosophy of Immanuel Kant.* 2 vols. Glasgow: James Maclehose & Sons.

Referred to: *345.*

The Cambridge Magazine. "Calendar". 1 (28 Feb. 1914): 396.

Referred to: *28.*

CANNON, WALTER B., *1915. Bodily Changes in Pain, Hunger, Fear and Rage: An Account of Recent Researches into the Function of Emotional Excitement.* New York and London: D. Appleton. (Russell's library: 1916 ed.)

Referred to: 275, *358.*

CANTOR, GEORG, *1915. Contributions to the Founding of the Theory of Transfinite Numbers.* Translated by Philip E. B. Jourdain. Chicago and London: Open Court.

Referred to: *353.*

[CELÂLEDDIN, RÛMÎ, MEVLÂNÂ], *1887. Masnavi i Ma'navi: The Spiritual Couplets of Maulána Jalálu-'d-Dín Muhammad i Rúmí.* Translated by E. H. Whinfield. London: Trübner.

Referred to: 42n.

CELLINI, BENVENUTO, *1908. The Life of Benvenuto Cellini.* Translated by John Addington Symonds. 5th ed. London: Macmillan. 1st ed. of this translation, 1887.

Referred to: *357.*

CHUANG TZU, *1889. Chuang Tzu: Mystic, Moralist, and Social Reformer.* Translated by Herbert A. Giles. London: Bernard Quaritch.

Referred to: *337, 353.*

CLARK, RONALD W., *1975. The Life of Bertrand Russell.* London: Jonathan Cape and Weidenfeld & Nicolson.

Referred to: *333.*

COUTURAT, LOUIS, *1901. La Logique de Leibniz: d'après des documents inédits.* Paris: Félix Alcan. (Russell's library.)

Referred to: 120n., 202n., *352.*

—— *1903. Opuscules et fragments inédits de Leibniz.* 1 vol. in 4. Paris: Félix Alcan.

Referred to: *340.*

DARWIN, CHARLES, *1899. The Origin of Species by Means of Natural Selection, or the Preservation of Favoured Races in the Struggle for Life.* London: John Murray. (Russell's library.) 1st ed. 1859.
Referred to: 43.

DAUBEN, JOSEPH WARREN, *1979. Georg Cantor: His Mathematics and Philosophy of the Infinite.* Cambridge, Mass.: Harvard University Press.
Referred to: 353.

DEMOS, RAPHAEL, *1917.* "A Discussion of a Certain Type of Negative Proposition". *Mind*, n.s. 26: 188–96.
Referred to: 187, 280n., 350, 358.

DESCARTES, RENÉ, *1637. Discourse on the Method of Rightly Conducting the Reason.* Reprinted in Vol. 1 of his *1911–12.*
Referred to: 344.

—— *1641. Meditations on First Philosophy.* Reprinted in Vol. 1 of his *1911–12.*
Referred to: 349.

—— *1641a.* "Reply to the Second Set of Objections". First published with his *1641.* Reprinted in Vol. 2 of his *1911–12.*
Referred to: 345.

—— *1911–12. The Philosophical Works of Descartes.* Translated by Elizabeth S. Haldane and G. R. T. Ross. 2 vols. Cambridge: At the University Press.
Referred to: 345.

—— *1970. Philosophical Letters.* Translated and edited by Anthony Kenny. Oxford: Clarendon Press.
Referred to: 344.

DEWEY, JOHN, *1905.* "Beliefs and Existences". *Philosophical Review,* 15: 113–19. Reprinted in Vol. 3 of his *1976–83.*
Referred to: 351.

—— *1916. Essays in Experimental Logic.* Chicago: University of Chicago Press. (Russell's library.)
Referred to: *132,* 134ff., 193, 253n., *346, 347, 348, 353.*

—— *1967–72. The Early Works, 1882–1898.* Edited by George E. Axtelle *et al.* 5 vols. Carbondale and Edwardsville: Southern Illinois University Press; London and Amsterdam: Feffer & Simons.
Referred to: 348.

—— *1976–83. The Middle Works, 1899–1924.* Edited by Jo Ann Boydston. 13 vols. Carbondale and Edwardsville: Southern Illinois University Press; London and Amsterdam: Feffer & Simons.
Referred to: 348.

DUNLAP, KNIGHT, *1912.* "Discussion: The Case against Introspection". *The Psychological Review,* 19: 404–12.
Referred to: 250, 260, 286n.

—— *1912a.* "The Nature of Perceived Relations". *The Psychological Review,* 19: 415–46.

Referred to: 260, 286n.

—— *1916*. "Thought-Content and Feeling". *Psychological Review*, 23: 49–70.
Referred to: 260, 286n.

Encyklopädie der mathematischen Wissenschaften mit Einschluss ihrer Anwendung. 6
vols. in 23. Leipzig: B. G. Teubner, 1898–1904.
Referred to: 94, *339*.

The English Catalogue of Books.
Referred to: *50*.

FRYE, NORTHROP, *1967*. "Blake, William". In Vol. 1 of *The Encyclopedia of
Philosophy*. Edited by Paul Edwards. 8 vols. in 4. New York: Macmillan;
London: Collier-Macmillan.
Referred to: *335*.

GALTON, FRANCIS, *1883*. *Inquiries into Human Faculty and Its Development*. New
York: Macmillan.
Referred to: *359*.

GRATTAN-GUINNESS, I., *1977*. *Dear Russell–Dear Jourdain: A Commentary on Rus-
sell's Logic, Based on His Correspondence with Philip Jourdain*. London:
Duckworth.
Referred to: *xxx*, *158*.

GRIFFIN, NICHOLAS, *1977*. "Russell's 'Horrible Travesty' of Meinong". *Russell:
The Journal of the Bertrand Russell Archives*, nos. 25–8: 39–51.
Referred to: *351*.

HALL, G. STANLEY, *1915*. "The Freudian Methods Applied to Anger". *The
American Journal of Psychology*, 26: 438–43.
Referred to: *272, 273, 274, 275, 381*.

HANNEQUIN, ARTHUR, *1895*. *Essai critique sur l'hypothèse des atomes dans la science
contemporaine*. Paris: G. Masson.
Referred to: *xxx*.

HEGEL, G. W. F., *1817*. *Encyklopädie der philosophischen Wissenschaften im Grund-
risse*. Heidelberg: A. Oswald.
Referred to: *339*.

—— *1874*. *The Logic of Hegel*. Translated by William Wallace. Oxford: At the
Clarendon Press. 1st German ed., 1817.
Referred to: *352, 358*.

—— *1892*. *The Logic of Hegel*. Translated by William Wallace. 2nd ed., revised.
Oxford: At the Clarendon Press.
Referred to: *352, 358*.

—— *1931*. *The Phenomenology of Mind*. Translated by J. B. Baillie. 2nd ed., revised. London: George Allen & Unwin; New York: Macmillan. 1st ed.,
1910. 1st German ed., 1807.
Referred to: *335*.

HEINE, HEINRICH, *1907*. "The Return Home". In *Heine's Book of Songs*. Translated by John Todhunter. Oxford: At the Clarendon Press. In German as
"Die Heimkehr". In Vol. 1 of his *Sämmtliche Werke*. Hamburg: Hoffman

and Campe, 1885. (Russell's library.)
Referred to: *338*.

HERTZ, HEINRICH, *1894*. *Die Prinzipien der Mechanik, in neuem Zusammenhange dargestellt*. (Gesammelte Werke von Heinrich Hertz, Vol. 3.) Leipzig: Johann Ambrosius Barth. (Russell's library.) Translated into English as his *1899*.
Referred to: 138.

—— *1899*. *The Principles of Mechanics Presented in a New Form*. Translated by D. E. Jones and J. T. Walley. London and New York: Macmillan. Translation of his *1894*.
Referred to: *347*.

HOLT, EDWIN B., *1912*. "The Place of Illusory Experience in a Realistic World". In Holt *et al.*, *1912*.
Referred to: 24n., *338*.

—— *1914*. *The Concept of Consciousness*. London: George Allen.
Referred to: *354*.

—— WALTER T. MARVIN, WILLIAM PEPPERRELL MONTAGUE, RALPH BARTON PERRY, WALTER B. PITKIN AND EDWARD GLEASON SPAULDING, *1912*. *The New Realism; Coöperative Studies in Philosophy*. New York: Macmillan.
Referred to: *333, 338, 343, 353*.

HUME, DAVID, *1739–40*. *A Treatise of Human Nature*.
Referred to: 262, *350, 359*.

—— *1748*. *An Enquiry concerning the Human Understanding*.
Referred to: *334, 359*.

—— *1890*. *A Treatise of Human Nature, Being an Attempt to Introduce the Experimental Method of Reasoning into Moral Subjects, and Dialogues concerning Natural Religion*. Edited by T. H. Green and T. H. Grose. New ed. 2 vols. London and New York: Longmans, Green. (Russell's library.)
Referred to: 262, *355*.

JAMES, WILLIAM, *1890*. *The Principles of Psychology*. 2 vols. London: Macmillan. (Russell's library: 1891 [i.e. 4th] impression.) Reprinted as his *1981*.
Referred to: 148, 298n., 299, 300, *348, 355, 356*.

—— *1904*. "Does 'Consciousness' Exist?" *The Journal of Philosophy, Psychology and Scientific Methods*, 1: 477–91. Reprinted in his *1912* and *1976*.
Referred to: 116, *347, 353*.

—— *1907*. *Pragmatism, a New Name for Some Old Ways of Thinking: Popular Lectures on Philosophy*. New York, London and Bombay: Longmans, Green. (Russell's library.) Reprinted as his *1975*.
Referred to: *344, 358*.

—— *1911*. *Some Problems of Philosophy: A Beginning of an Introduction to Philosophy*. London, New York and Bombay: Longmans, Green. (Russell's library.)
Referred to: 58n.

—— *1912*. *Essays in Radical Empiricism*. London, New York and Bombay:

Longmans, Green. (Russell's library.) Reprinted as his *1976*.
Referred to: *xxi*, 193, 289, *333*, *351*, *359*.

—— *1920*. "Philosophical Conceptions and Practical Results". In his *Collected Essays and Reviews*. New York, London and Bombay: Longmans, Green. Reprinted as "The Pragmatic Method" in his *1978*. 1st ed., 1898.
Referred to: *355*.

—— *1975*. *Pragmatism*. (The Works of William James.) Cambridge, Mass. and London: Harvard University Press.
Referred to: *358*.

—— *1976*. *Essays in Radical Empiricism*. (The Works of William James.) Cambridge, Mass. and London: Harvard University Press.
Referred to: *359*.

—— *1978*. *Essays in Philosophy*. (The Works of William James.) Cambridge, Mass. and London: Harvard University Press.
Referred to: *355*.

—— *1981*. *The Principles of Psychology*. 3 vols. (The Works of William James.) Cambridge, Mass. and London: Harvard University Press.
Referred to: *348*, *355*.

JOACHIM, HAROLD H., *1906*. *The Nature of Truth*. Oxford: At the Clarendon Press.
Referred to: *360*.

The Journal of Philosophy, Psychology and Scientific Methods. "Notes and News". 12 (1915): 307–8.
Referred to: 88n.

KANT, IMMANUEL, *1781*. *The Critique of Pure Reason*. Translated as his *1929*.
Referred to: 66, 69, 120, 121, *333*, *334*, *337*.

—— *1783*. *Prolegomena to Any Future Metaphysics*.
Referred to: *345*, *352*.

—— *1882–84*. *Reflexionen Kants zur kritischen Philosophie. Aus Kants handschriftlichen Aufzeichnungen*. Edited by Benno Erdmann. 2 vols. Leipzig: Fues (R. Reisland).
Referred to: 121.

—— *1889*. *Lose Blätter aus Kants Nachlass*. Edited by Rudolf Reicke. Königsberg in Pr.: Ferd. Beyer.
Referred to: 121.

—— *1929*. *Critique of Pure Reason*. Translated by Norman Kemp Smith. London: Macmillan.
Referred to: *119*.

LAIRD, JOHN, *1917*. *Problems of the Self: An Essay on the Shaw Lectures Given in the University of Edinburgh, March 1914*. London: Macmillan.
Referred to: 116–18, *344*, *345*.

—— *1936*. *Recent Philosophy*. (Home University Library of Modern Knowledge, No. 135.) London: Thornton Butterworth.
Referred to: *115*.

LOCKE, JOHN, *1690*. *An Essay concerning Human Understanding*.
Referred to: *334*.

LOSSKY, N. O., *1919*. *The Intuitive Basis of Knowledge: An Epistemological Inquiry*.
Translated by Nathalie A. Duddington. London: Macmillan.
Referred to: *329*.

—— See also Ruge *et al*. *1913*.

LUKASIEWICZ, JAN, *1920*. "O Logice trójwartościowej". *Ruch Filozoficzny*, 5:
170–1. Reprinted as "Three-Valued Logic" in his *Selected Works*. Edited by
L. Borkowski. (Studies in Logic and the Foundations of Mathematics.)
Amsterdam and London: North Holland Publishing Company; Warsaw:
Polish Scientific Publishers, 1970.
Referred to: *350*.

MACH, ERNST, *1897*. *Contributions to the Analysis of the Sensations*. Translated by
C. M. Williams. Chicago and London: Open Court. 1st German ed., 1866.
Referred to: *333*.

Masnavi: *see* Celâleddin *1887*.

McDOUGALL, WILLIAM, *1911*. *Body and Mind: A History and a Defense of Animism*.
London: Methuen.
Referred to: *343*.

MEACHAM, STANDISH, *1970*. *Lord Bishop: The Life of Samuel Wilberforce, 1805–
1873*. Cambridge, Mass.: Harvard University Press.
Referred to: *341–2*.

MEINONG, ALEXIUS, *1899*. "Über Gegenstände höherer Ordnung und deren Ver-
hältniss zur inneren Wahrnehmung". *Zeitschrift für Psychologie und
Physiologie des Sinnesorgane*, 21: 182–272. Reprinted in Vol. 2 of his *1968–78*.
Referred to: *353*.

—— *1906*. *Über die Erfahrungsgrundlagen unseres Wissens*. (Abhandlungen zur Di-
daktik und Philosophie der Naturwissenschaft, Band 1, Heft 6; Sonderhefte
der *Zeitschrift für den physikalischen und chemischen Unterricht*.) Berlin: Julius
Springer. Reprinted in Vol. 5 of his *1968–78*.
Referred to: 22n.

—— *1910*. *Über Annahmen*. 2nd ed., revised. Leipzig: Johann Ambrosius Barth.
1st ed., 1902. Translated into English as his *1983*.
Referred to: *353*.

—— *1968–78 Gesamtausgabe*. Edited by Rudolf Haller, Rudolf Kindinger and
Roderick M. Chisholm. 8 vols. Graz: Akademische Druck.

—— *1983*. *On Assumptions*. Edited and translated by James Heanue. Berkeley,
Los Angeles and London: University of California Press. Translation of his
1910.
Referred to: *353*.

MOORE, G. E., *1903*. "Refutation of Idealism". *Mind*, n.s. 12: 433–53. Reprinted
in his *1922*.
Referred to: *125*, *345*, *346*, *354*, *359*.

—— *1922. Philosophical Studies.* (International Library of Psychology, Philosophy and Scientific Method.) London: Kegan Paul, Trench, Trubner. (Russell's library.)

Referred to: *359*.

MORGENBESSER, SIDNEY, ed., *1977. Dewey and His Critics: Essays from the Journal of Philosophy.* New York: The Journal of Philosophy.

Referred to: *132*.

The Nation.

Referred to: 107.

NICOD, J. G. P., *1916.* "A Reduction in the Number of Primitive Propositions of Logic". *Proceedings of the Cambridge Philosophical Society,* 19: 32–41.

Referred to: *350*.

NUNN, T. PERCY, *1909–10.* "Are Secondary Qualities Independent of Perception? I". *Proceedings of the Aristotelian Society,* n.s. 10: 191–218.

Referred to: 10, 75n., 82n.

PERRY, RALPH BARTON, *1912. Present Philosophical Tendencies: A Critical Survey of Naturalism, Idealism, Pragmatism and Realism together with a Synopsis of the Philosophy of William James.* London, Bombay and Calcutta: Longmans, Green.

Referred to: *333, 339.*

PLATO. *Meno.*

Referred to: *348*.

—— *Timaeus.*

Referred to: 47.

—— *1852. The Republic of Plato.* Translated by John Llewelyn Davies and David James Vaughan. Cambridge: Macmillan.

Referred to: 33n., *335*.

—— *1875. Parmenides.* In Vol. 4 of *The Dialogues of Plato.* Translated by B. Jowett. 5 vols. 2nd. ed. Oxford: at the Clarendon Press. (Russell's library.) 1st ed., 1871.

Referred to: *335*.

POINCARÉ, HENRI, *1902. La Science et l'hypothèse.* Paris: Ernest Flammarion. Translated into English as his *1905, 1905a.*

Referred to: *336, 342.*

—— *1904. La Valeur de la science.* Paris: Ernest Flammarion.

Referred to: *336*.

—— *1905. Science and Hypothesis.* [Translated by William John Greenstreet.] London and Newcastle-on-Tyne: Walter Scott. Translation of his *1902.*

Referred to: *337, 342.*

—— *1905a. Science and Hypothesis.* Translated by George Bruce Halstead. New York: The Science Press. Translation of his *1902.*

Referred to: *342*.

—— *1905b.* "Les Mathématiques et la logique". *Revue de métaphysique et de*

morale, 13: 815–35. Reprinted as Pt. 2, Chap. 3 of his *1908*.
Referred to: *337*.

—— *1906*. "Les Mathématiques et la logique". *Revue de métaphysique et de morale*, 14: 17–34; 294–317. Reprinted as Pt. 2, Chaps. 4–5 of his *1908*.
Referred to: *337*.

—— *1908*. *Science et méthode*. Paris: Ernest Flammarion. Translated into English as his *1914*.
Referred to: *50, 336*.

—— *1910*. *Savants et écrivains*. Paris: Ernest Flammarion.
Referred to: *337*.

—— *1913*. *Dernières Pensées*. Paris: Ernest Flammarion.
Referred to: *336*.

—— *1914*. *Science and Method*. Preface by Bertrand Russell. Translated by Francis Maitland. London, Edinburgh and New York: Thomas Nelson and Sons, [n.d.]. Translation of his *1908*.
Referred to: *50*.

POST, E. L., *1921*. "Introduction to a General Theory of Elementary Propositions". *American Journal of Mathematics*, 43: 163–85.
Referred to: *350*.

Revue de métaphysique et de morale. Vol. 21, no. 5 (Sept. 1913).
Referred to: *50, 52*.

RITCHIE, DAVID G., *1893*. *Darwin and Hegel, with Other Philosophical Studies*. London: Swan Sonnenschein; New York: Macmillan.
Referred to: *336*.

ROBB, ALFRED A., *1913*. *A Theory of Time and Space*. Cambridge: W. Heffer and Sons; London: Simpkin Marshall.
Referred to: *18n*.

—— *1914*. *A Theory of Time and Space*. Cambridge: At the University Press.
Referred to: *18n*.

ROYCE, JOSIAH, *1905*. "The Relation of the Principles of Logic to the Foundations of Geometry". *Transactions of the American Mathematical Society*, 24: 353–415. Reprinted in his *1951*.
Referred to: *350*.

—— *1951*. *Royce's Logical Essays: Collected Logical Essays of Josiah Royce*. Edited by Daniel S. Robinson. Dubuque, Iowa: Wm. C. Brown.
Referred to: *349, 350*.

RUGE, ARNOLD, WILHELM WINDELBAND, JOSIAH ROYCE, LOUIS COUTURAT, BENEDETTO CROCE, FEDERIGO ENRIQUES AND NICHOLAJ LOSSKIJ., *1913*. *Logic*. Translated by Ethel Meyer. (*Encyclopaedia of the Philosophical Sciences*, Vol. 1.) London: Macmillan.
Referred to: *93, 94, 340, 341, 349*.

RUSSELL, BERTRAND ARTHUR WILLIAM, 3RD EARL, *1897*. *An Essay on the Foundations of Geometry*. Cambridge: At the University Press.

Referred to: *xi.*

—— *1900. A Critical Exposition of the Philosophy of Leibniz, with an Appendix of Leading Passages.* Cambridge: At the University Press. 2nd ed., 1937.
Referred to: *338, 340, 345, 350.*

—— *1901.* "Sur la Logique des relations avec des applications à la théorie des séries. *Revue de mathématiques (Rivista di matematica),* 7: 115–48. Translated as "The Logic of Relations" in his *1956.*
Referred to: *90, 339.*

—— *1902.* "Théorie générale des séries bien-ordonnés". *Revue de mathématiques (Rivista di matematica),* 8: 12–43.
Referred to: *90, 339.*

—— *1903. The Principles of Mathematics.* Cambridge: Cambridge University Press. 2nd ed., 1937.
Referred to: *xii, xiv, 105,* 108, *111,* 160, *343, 345, 346, 349, 351, 353.*

—— *1904.* "Meinong's Theory of Complexes and Assumptions". *Mind,* n.s. 13: 204–19, 336–54, 509–24. Reprinted in his *1973.*
Referred to: *353, 360.*

—— *1905.* "On Denoting". *Mind,* 14: 479–93. Reprinted in his *1956* and *1973.*
Referred to: *350, 353.*

—— *1906.* "Les Paradoxes de la logique". *Revue de métaphysique et de morale,* 14: 627–50. Reply to Poincaré *1906.*
Referred to: *337.*

—— *1907.* "On the Nature of Truth". *Proceedings of the Aristotelian Society,* n.s. 7: 28–49. Sections I and II reprinted as "The Monistic Theory of Truth" in his *1910.*
Referred to: 301n., *351.*

—— *1910. Philosophical Essays.* London, New York and Bombay: Longmans, Green. New ed., London: George Allen & Unwin, 1966.
Referred to: 301n., *336, 342, 351.*

—— *1910–13. See* Whitehead and Russell *1910–13.*

—— *1911.* "Knowledge by Acquaintance and Knowledge by Description". *Proceedings of the Aristotelian Society,* n.s. 11: 108–28. Reprinted in his *1918.*
Referred to: *353.*

—— *1912. The Problems of Philosophy.* (Home University Library of Modern Knowledge, No. 35.) London: Williams and Norgate, [n.d.].
Referred to: *xvii, xxii, xxvii, 28, 351, 353, 354, 359, 360.*

—— *1912a.* "On the Relations of Universals and Particulars". *Proceedings of the Aristotelian Society,* n.s. 12: 1–24. Reprinted in his *1956.*
Referred to: *xxiii,* 151n.

—— *1912b.* "The Philosophy of Bergson". *The Monist,* 22: 321–47. Reprinted as "Bergson" in his *A History of Western Philosophy.* New York: Simon and Schuster, 1945.
Referred to: *xxx, 337.*

Referred to: *xix, xxxviii, xxxix, 157, 158, 248, 277, 315, 333, 347, 352*.

—— *1919a*. "Democracy and Direct Action". *The Dial*, 66: 445–8. Also in *English Review*, 28 (1919): 396–403.

Referred to: *277*.

—— *1921*. *The Analysis of Mind*. London: George Allen & Unwin.

Referred to: *xxii, xxiii, 158, 247, 248, 250, 251, 277, 313, 351, 353, 354, 355, 356, 357, 358, 382*.

—— *1921a*. "Sensations". Unpublished manuscript. RA 210.006598.

Referred to: *354*.

—— *1922*. "Philosophic Idealism at Bay". Review of Sinclair *1922*. *The Nation & the Athenaeum*, 31: 625–6. Reprinted in Vol. 9 of *The Collected Papers of Bertrand Russell*. Edited by John G. Slater. London: George Allen & Unwin, forthcoming.

Referred to: *105*.

—— *1923*. "Vagueness". *Australasian Journal of Psychology and Philosophy*, 1: 84–92.

Referred to: *349*.

—— *1923a*. Review of Broad *1923*. *Mathematical Gazette*, 11: 395–9.

Referred to: *124*.

—— *1925*. *The ABC of Relativity*. London: Kegan Paul, Trench, Trubner; New York: Harper & Brothers.

Referred to: *334, 338*.

—— *1925a*. "Mind and Matter". Review of Broad *1925*. *The Nation & the Athenaeum*, 38: 323.

Referred to: *124*.

—— *1926*. *Our Knowledge of the External World as a Field for Scientific Method in Philosophy*. Rev. ed. London: George Allen & Unwin. *See also his 1914, 1929*.

Referred to: *xv, 333, 347, 360*.

—— *1926a*. Review of Broad *1925*. *Mind*, 35: 72–80.

Referred to: *124*.

—— *1927*. *The Analysis of Matter*. London: Kegan Paul, Trench, Trubner; New York: Harcourt, Brace.

Referred to: *338*.

—— *1929*. *Our Knowledge of the External World as a Field for Scientific Method in Philosophy*. 2nd. ed. New York: W. W. Norton. *See also his 1914, 1926*.

Referred to: *xv, 333, 347, 360*.

—— *1936*. "Philosophy in the Twentieth Century". Review of Laird *1936*. *The Listener*, 16: supp. iii.

Referred to: *115*.

—— *1940*. *An Inquiry into Meaning and Truth*. London: George Allen and Unwin.

Referred to: *351*.

—— *1948*. "Whitehead and *Principia Mathematica*". *Mind*, 57: 137–8.

Referred to: *89*.

—— *1956*. *Logic and Knowledge: Essays, 1901–1950*. Edited by Robert Charles Marsh. London: George Allen & Unwin.

Referred to: *159, 276, 339, 377*.

—— *1959*. *My Philosophical Development*. London: George Allen & Unwin.

Referred to: *4, 89, 333, 338*.

—— *1967*. *The Autobiography of Bertrand Russell*. Vol. 1: *1872–1914*. London: George Allen and Unwin.

Referred to: *105*.

—— *1968*. *The Autobiography of Bertrand Russell*. Vol. II: *1914–1944*. London: George Allen and Unwin.

Referred to: *99*.

—— *1969*. *The Autobiography of Bertrand Russell*. Vol. 3: *1944–1967*. London: George Allen and Unwin.

Referred to: *353*.

—— *1972*. *Russell's Logical Atomism*. Edited by David Pears. London: Fontana.

Referred to: *159*.

—— *1973*. *Essays in Analysis*. Edited by Douglas Lackey. London: George Allen & Unwin.

Referred to: *360*.

—— *1984*. *Theory of Knowledge: The 1913 Manuscript*. Edited by Elizabeth Ramsden Eames in collaboration with Kenneth Blackwell. (The Collected Papers of Bertrand Russell, Vol. 7.) London: George Allen & Unwin.

Referred to: *xiv, xvi, xvii, xix, xxi, 333, 349, 351*.

—— P. W. BRIDGMAN, ALBERT EINSTEIN, L. INFELD, J. F. JOLIOT-CURIE, H. J. MULLER, C. F. POWELL, J. ROTBLAT AND HIDEKI YUKAWA, *1955*. "Texts of Scientists' Appeal for Abolition of War". *The New York Times*, 10 July 1955, p. 25. Reprinted as "The Russell–Einstein Manifesto" in J. Rotblat. *Pugwash—the First Ten Years*. London: Heinemann, 1967. Max Born and Linus Pauling were later signatories.

Referred to: *329*.

The Russell–Einstein Manifesto: see Russell *et al.*, *1955*.

SANTAYANA, GEORGE, *1906*. *The Life of Reason, or the Phases of Human Progress: Reason in Science*. New York: Charles Scribner's Sons. Reprinted as his *1936*.

Referred to: *336*.

—— *1936*. *The Life of Reason: Reason in Science*. (The Works of George Santayana, Vol. 5.) New York: Charles Scribner's Sons.

Referred to: *336*.

SCHMID, ANNE-FRANÇOISE, *1978*. *Une Philosophie de savant: Henri Poincaré et la logique mathématique*. Paris: François Maspero.

Referred to: *337*.

SHEFFER, HENRY MAURICE, *1913*. "A Set of Five Independent Postulates for Boolean Algebras, with Application to Logical Constants". *Transactions of the American Mathematical Society*, 14: 481–8.
Referred to: *350*.

SIGWART, CHRISTOPH, *1895*. *Logic*. Translated by Helen Dendy. 2 vols. (Library of Philosophy.) London: Swan Sonnenschein; New York: Macmillan. 1st German ed., 1873.
Referred to: *339*.

SINCLAIR, MAY, *1917*. *A Defence of Idealism: Some Questions & Conclusions*. London: Macmillan.
Referred to: *105*, 106–10, 112–14, *342, 343, 344*.

—— *1917a*. *A Defence of Idealism: Some Questions and Conclusions*. New York: Macmillan.
Referred to: 105, *342, 343, 344*.

—— *1922*. *The New Idealism*. London: Macmillan.
Referred to: *105*.

SLEIGH, ROBERT, *1982*. "Truth and Sufficient Reason in the Philosophy of Leibniz". In *Leibniz: Critical and Interpretive Essays*. Edited by Michael Hooker. Minneapolis: University of Minnesota Press.
Referred to: *352*.

SMITH, NORMAN KEMP, *1902*. *Studies in the Cartesian Philosophy*. London and New York: Macmillan.
Referred to: 120–1.

—— *1918*. *A Commentary to Kant's 'Critique of Pure Reason'*. London: Macmillan.
Referred to: 120–2, *345, 352*.

SPENCER, HERBERT, *1862*. *First Principles*. London: Williams and Norgate.
Referred to: 60n., *337, 347*.

SPINOZA, BENEDICTUS DE, *1677*. *Ethics*.
Referred to: 45n., 299–300, *360*.

—— *1910*. *Ethics and De Intellectus Emendatione*. Translated by A. Boyle. (Everyman's library.) London: J. M. Dent & Sons; New York: E. P. Dutton.
Referred to: *336, 351*.

STIRLING, JAMES HUTCHISON, *1881*. *Text-Book to Kant*. Edinburgh: Oliver and Boyd; London: Simpkin, Marshall.
Referred to: *345*.

TENNYSON, ALFRED, LORD, *1974*. "Flower in the Crannied Wall". In *The Poetical Works of Tennyson*. Edited by G. Robert Stange. Boston: Houghton Mifflin. 1st published 1869.
Referred to: *350*.

WATSON, JOHN B., *1913*. "Psychology as the Behaviorist Views It". *The Psychological Review*, 20: 158–77.

Referred to: 260, 285, *359*.

—— *1914*. *Behavior: An Introduction to Comparative Psychology*. New York: Henry Holt. (Russell's library.)
Referred to: 282n., 283, 284, 285, *358, 359*.

—— *1916*. "The Psychology of Wish Fulfillment". *The Scientific Monthly*, 3: 479–87.
Referred to: 288n.

WHITEHEAD, ALFRED NORTH, *1919*. *An Enquiry concerning the Principles of Natural Knowledge*. Cambridge: At the University Press. (Russell's library.)
Referred to: *338*.

—— AND BERTRAND RUSSELL, *1910–13*. *Principia Mathematica*. 3 vols. Cambridge: At the University Press.
Referred to: *xi, xii, xiii, xiv, xvi, xxv, xxvi, xxxi*, 23n., *89*, 90, *105*, 108, *111*, 176, 179, 187, 232, *248*, *333, 339, 343, 349, 351, 352, 353, 357*.

—— *1925–27*. *Principia Mathematica*. 2nd ed. 3 vols. Cambridge: At the University Press.
Referred to: *349, 350, 353*.

WINDEBAND, W., *1893*. *A History of Philosophy, with Especial Reference to the Formation and Development of Its Problems and Conceptions*. Translated by James H. Tufts. New York and London: Macmillan. 1st German ed., 1892.
Referred to: *339*.

WITTGENSTEIN, LUDWIG, *1913*. "Notes on Logic, September 1913". Translated [as version 1] and rearranged [as version 2] by Bertrand Russell. Manuscript and typescript of version 1 in RA; published in App. 1 of 2nd ed. of his *1961*. Version 2 1st published in *The Journal of Philosophy*, 54 (1957): 231–45; reprinted in App. 1 of his *1961*.
Referred to: *xix, xx, xxxv*.

—— *1921*. "Logisch–Philosophische Abhandlung". Introduction by Bertrand Russell. *Annalen der Naturphilosophie*, 14: 185–262. Translated into English as his *1922*.
Referred to: *350*.

—— *1922*. *Tractatus Logico-Philosophicus*. Translated by C. K. Ogden. Introduction by Bertrand Russell. (International Library of Psychology, Philosophy and Scientific Method.) London: Kegan Paul, Trench, Trubner. (Russell's library.)
Referred to: *350*.

—— *1961*. *Notebooks 1914–1916*. Edited by G. H. von Wright and G. E. M. Anscombe. Translated by G. E. M. Anscombe. Oxford: Basil Blackwell. 2nd ed., 1979.
Referred to: *349*.

WOLF, A., *1908–09*. "Natural Realism and Present Tendencies in Philosophy". *Proceedings of the Aristotelian Society*, n.s. 9: 141–82.
Referred to: 22.

WOOLF, VIRGINIA, *1940*. *Roger Fry: A Biography*. London: The Hogarth Press.
Referred to: *340*.

WORDSWORTH, WILLIAM, *1807*. "Ode: Intimations of Immortality from Recollections of Early Childhood". In *The Poetical Works of Wordsworth*. London: Frederick Warne, 1890. (Russell's library.)
Referred to: *336*.

General Index

PAGE NUMBERS IN roman type refer to Russell's text and textual matter in the Appendixes; page numbers in italics refer to editorial matter. The Textual Notes are indexed only for major authorial alterations and variants.

For Russell's many definitions of terms and things, see the index entry "definition(s)". For additional subjects, see both the main table of contents and the table of contents for Paper **17**. For authors, see also the Bibliographical Index.

A

Abel, Reuben *348*
Aberdeen University *115*
Absolute (Hegelian) 184, *336*
absolute pluralism 65
absolute pragmatism *341*
absolute space 70
abstract ideas: Berkeley and Hume on 183
abstract thought: its ill effects *xxvi*
acquaintance
  and analysis 173
  and intuition 39
  James on 252
  and names 178–9
  with particulars 6, 181, 182
  with sensibilia 7
action 46, 148, 287
Adickes, Erich *121*
aesthetics 100
Alexander, Samuel *56, 74, 343*
Allen, Clifford *276*
ambiguity: of language 174
American New Realists *xxii*, 193, *252, 254, 294, 338, 343, 344, 346*
  see also neutral monism; pragmatism
analysis
  Bradley on *348–9*
  in British philosophy 53
  and complexity 173, 180
  contrasted to intuition 138–9
  contrasted with definition 173, 174
  and logic 65
  paradox of 150
  as philosophical method 66, 70, 160–3, 169, 172, 234

analytic realists 134, *346*
anger: Hall on 273
appearance 9–11, 17–20, 35–40
  see also sense-data; sensibilia
a priori *xii*, 65
Aristotelian Society *xxiii*, 87, 276, 301, *309, 329, 333, 349, 353*
Aristotelian tradition *43*
Aristotle 57, 93, 202
arithmetic *xiv*, 234
Asquith, H. H. *272*
astrology 47
astronomy 47, 58, 130
Athens *163*
atomic facts 177, 270
atomic propositions 177, 178
atomistic realism 107–8, 112, *343*
attention 6
aversion 257
awareness 252–5
  see also acquaintance
axiom
  of arithmetic *xiv*
  of infinity 210
  multiplicative 210, *333*
  of physics *xiii, xiv, xvi*

B

Balfour, Arthur James, 1st Earl *99*, 100–4, *341, 342*
Beethoven, Ludwig van 274, 275
behaviour: Dewey on 143
behaviourism
  BR's attitude towards 147, *247–8, 250, 251, 276*